THE

FOREIGN BIBLICAL LIBRARY.

EDITED BY THE

REV. W. ROBERTSON NICOLL, M.A,

Editor of the " Expositor.'

KURTZ'S CHURCH HISTORY

FUNK & WAGNALLS COMPANY,

NEW YORK AND LONDON.

CHURCH HISTORY.

BY

PROFESSOR KURTZ.

AUTHORIZED TRANSLATION BY THE
REV. JOHN MACPHERSON, M.A.

IN THREE VOLUMES. VOL III.

FUNK & WAGNALLS COMPANY,
NEW YORK AND LONDON.

CONTENTS.

THIRD DIVISION.—*SECOND SECTION.*

CHURCH HISTORY OF THE SEVENTEENTH CENTURY.

I. RELATIONS BETWEEN THE DIFFERENT CHURCHES.

THIRD SECTION.

CHURCH HISTORY IN THE EIGHTEENTH CENTURY.

I. THE CATHOLIC CHURCH IN EAST AND WEST.

FOURTH SECTION.

CHURCH HISTORY OF THE NINETEENTH CENTURY.

I. GENERAL AND INTRODUCTORY.

CONTENTS.

SECOND SECTION.

CHURCH HISTORY OF THE SEVENTEENTH CENTURY.

I.—Relations between the Different Churches.

§ 152. EAST AND WEST.

THE papacy formed new plans for conquest in the domain of the Eastern church, but with at most only transient success. Still more illusory were the hopes entertained for a while in Geneva and London in regard to the Calvinizing of the Greek church.

1. **Roman Catholic Hopes.**—The Jesuit missions among the Turks and schismatic Greeks failed, but among the Abyssinians some progress was made. By promising Spanish aid, the Jesuit Paez succeeded, in A.D. 1621, in inducing the Sultan Segued tc abjure the Jacobite heresy. Mendez was made Abyssinian patriarch by Urban VIII. in A.D. 1626, but the clergy and people repeatedly rebelled against sultan and patriarch. In A.D. 1642 the next sultan drove the Jesuits out of his kingdom, and in it henceforth no traces of Catholicism were to be found.—In Russia the false Demetrius, in A.D. 1605, working in Polish Catholic interests, sought to catholicize the empire; but this only convinced the Russians that he was no true czar's son. When his Catholic Polish bride entered Moscow with 200 Poles, a riot ensued, in which Demetrius lost his life.[1]

2. **Calvinistic Hopes.**—Cyril Lucar, a native of Crete, then under Venetian rule, by long residence in Geneva had come to entertain a strong liking to the Reformed church. Expelled from his situation

---

[1] Merimée, "The Russian Impostors: the False Demetrius." London, 1852.

as rector of a Greek seminary at Ostrog by Jesuit machinations, he
was made Patriarch of Alexandria in A.D. 1602 and of Constantinople
in A.D. 1621.   He maintained a regular correspondence with Reformed
divines in Holland, Switzerland, and England.   In A.D. 1628 he sent
the famous Codex Alexandrinus as a present to James I.   He wrought
expressly for a union of the Greek and Reformed churches, and for
this end sent, in A.D. 1629, to Geneva an almost purely Calvinistic
confession.   But the other Greek bishops opposed his union schemes,
and influential Jesuits in Constantinople accused him of political
faults.   Four times the sultan deposed and banished him, and at
last, in A.D. 1638, he was strangled as a traitor and cast into the sea.—
One of his Alexandrian clergy, Metrophanes Critopulus, whom in
A.D. 1616 he had sent for his education to England, studied several
years at Oxford, then at German Protestant universities, ending with
Helmstadt, where, in A.D. 1625, he composed in Greek a confession of
the faith of the Greek Orthodox Church.   It was pointedly antagonistic to the Romish doctrine, conciliatory toward Protestantism,
while abandoning nothing essential in the Greek Orthodox creed,
and showing signs of the possession of independent speculative power.
Afterwards Metrophanes became Patriarch of Alexandria, and in the
synod, presided over by Lucar's successor, Cyril of Berrhoë, at Constantinople in A.D. 1638, gave his vote for the formal condemnation
of the man who had been already executed.[1]

3. Orthodox Constancy.—The Russian Orthodox church, after its
emancipation from Constantinople and the erection of an independent
patriarchate at Moscow in A.D. 1589 (§ 73, 4), had decidedly the pre-
eminence over the Greek Orthodox church, and the Russian czar
took the place formerly occupied by the East Roman emperor as
protector of the whole Orthodox church.   The dangers to the Orthodox
faith threatened by schemes of union with Catholics and Protestants
induced the learned metropolitan, Peter Mogilas of Kiev, to compose
a new confession in catechetical form, which, in A.D. 1643, was formally authorized by the Orthodox patriarchs as Ὀρθόδοξος ὁμολογία τῆς
καθολικῆς καὶ ἀποστολικῆς ἐκκλησίας τῆς ἀνατολικῆς.—Thirty years later a
controversy on the eucharist broke out between the Jansenists Nicole
and Arnauld, on the one side, and the Calvinists Claude and Jurieu, on
the other (§ 157, 1), in which both claimed to be in agreement with
the Greek church.   A synod was convened under Dositheus of Jerusalem in A.D. 1672, at the instigation of French diplomatists, where
the questions raised by Cyril were again taken into consideration.

---

[1] Neale, "History of the Holy Eastern Church," vol. ii., p. 356 ff.
Cyrillus Lucaris, "Confessio Christianæ Fidei." Geneva, 1633. Smith
"Collectanea de Cyrillo Lucario." London, 1707.

Maintaining a friendly attitude toward the Romish church, it directed a violent polemic against Calvinism. In order to save the character of the Constantinopolitan chair for constant Orthodoxy, Cyril's confession of A.D. 1629 was pronounced a spurious, heretical invention, and a confession composed by Dositheus, in which Cyril's Calvinistic heresies were repudiated, was incorporated with the synod's acts.

§ 153. CATHOLICISM AND PROTESTANTISM.

The Jesuit counter-reformation (§ 151) was eminently successful during the first decades of the century in Bohemia. The Westphalian Peace restrained its violence, but did not prevent secret machinations and the open exercise of all conceivable arts of seduction. Next to the conversion of Bohemia, the greatest triumph of the restoration was won in France in the Revocation of the Edict of Nantes. Besides such victories the Catholics were able to glory in the conversion of several Protestant princes. New endeavours at union were repeatedly made, but these in every case proved as fruitless as former attempts had done.

1. Conversions of Protestant Princes.—The first reigning prince who became a convert to Romanism was the Margrave James III. of Baden. He went over in A.D. 1590 (§ 144, 4), but as his death occurred soon after, his conduct had little influence upon his people. Of greater consequence was the conversion, in A.D. 1614, of the Count-palatine Wolfgang William of Neuburg, as it prepared the way for the catholicizing of the whole Palatinate, which followed in A.D. 1685. Much was made of the passing over to the Catholic church of Christina of Sweden, the highly gifted but eccentric daughter of Gustavus Adolphus. As she had resigned the crown, the pope gained no political advantage from his new member, and Alexander VII. had even to contribute to her support. The Elector of Saxony, Frederick Augustus II., passed over to the Roman Catholic church in A.D. 1697, in order to qualify himself for the Polish crown; but the rights of his Protestant subjects were carefully guarded. An awkwardness arose from the fact that the prince was pledged by the directory of the Regensburg Diet of A.D. 1653 to care for the interests of the evangelical church. Now that he had become a Catholic, he still formally promised to do so, but had his duties discharged by a commissioner. Subsequently this officer

was ordered to take his directions from the evangelical council of Dresden.

2. The Restoration in Germany and the Neighbouring States (§ 151, 1).— Matthias having, in violation of the royal letter of his predecessor Rudolph II. (§ 189, 19), refused to allow the Protestants of Bohemia to build churches, was driven out; the Jesuits also were expelled, and the Calvinistic Elector-palatine Frederick V. was chosen as prince in A.D. 1619. Ferdinand II. (A.D. 1619–1637) defeated him, tore up the royal letter, restored the Jesuits, and expelled the Protestant pastors. Efforts were made by Christian IV. of Denmark and other Protestant princes to save Protestantism, but without success. Ferdinand now issued his Restitution Edict of A.D. 1629, which deprived Protestants of their privileges, and gave to Catholic nobles unrestricted liberty to suppress the evangelical faith in their dominions. It was then that Gustavus Adolphus of Sweden, in religious not less than political interests, made his appearance as the saviour of Protestantism.[1] The unhappy war was brought to an end in A.D. 1648 by the publication at Münster and Osnabrück of the Peace of Westphalia, which Innocent X. in his bull "*Zelo Domus Dei*" of A.D. 1651 pronounced "null and void, without influence on past, present, and future." Germany lost several noble provinces, but its intellectual and religious freedom was saved. Under Swedish and French guarantee the Augsburg Religious Peace was confirmed and even extended to the Reformed, as related to the Augsburg Confession. The church property was to be restored on January 1st, A.D. 1624. The political equality of Protestants and Catholics throughout Germany was distinctly secured. In Bohemia, however, Protestantism was thoroughly extirpated, and in the other Austrian states the oppression continued down to the time of Joseph II. In Silesia, from the passing of the Restitution Edict, over a thousand churches had been violently taken from the evangelicals. No compensation was now thought of, but rather the persecution continued throughout the whole century (§ 165, 4), and many thousands were compelled to migrate, for the most part to Upper Lusatia.

3. Also in Livonia, from A.D. 1561 under Polish rule, the Jesuits gained a footing and began the restoration, but under Gustavus Adolphus from A.D. 1621 their machinations were brought to an end. —The ruthless Valteline Massacre of A.D. 1620 may be described as a Swiss St. Bartholomew on a small scale. All Protestants were murdered in one day. The conspirators at a signal from the clock tower

[1] Stevens, "Life and Times of Gustavus Adolphus." New York, 1884. Trench, "Gustavus Adolphus in Germany, and other Lectures on the Thirty Years' War." London. Gardiner, "The Thirty Years' War" in "Epochs of Modern History." London, 1881.

in the early morning broke into the houses of heretics, and put all to death, down to the very babe in the cradle. Between four and five hundred were slaughtered.—In Hungary, at the close of the preceding century only three noble families remained Catholic, and the Protestant churches numbered 2,000; but the Jesuits, who had settled there under the protection of Rudolph II. in 1579, resumed their intrigues, and the Archbishop of Gran, Pazmany, wrought hard for the restoration of Catholicism. Rakoczy of Transylvania, in the Treaty of Linz of A.D. 1645, concluded a league offensive and defensive with Sweden and France, which secured political and religious liberty for Hungary; but of the 400 churches of which the Protestants had been robbed only ninety were given back. The bigoted Leopold I., from A.D. 1655 king of Hungary, inaugurated a yet more severe persecution, which continued until the publication of the Toleration Edict of Joseph II. in A.D. 1781. The 2,000 Protestant congregations were by this time reduced to 105.

4. The Huguenots in France (§ 139, 17).—Henry IV. faithfully fulfilled the promises which he made in the Edict of Nantes; but under Louis XIII., A.D. 1610–1643, the oppressions of the Huguenots were renewed, and led to fresh outbreaks. Richelieu withdrew their political privileges, but granted them religious toleration in the Edict of Nismes, A.D. 1629. Louis XIV., A.D. 1643–1715, at the instigation of his confessors, sought to atone for his sins by purging his land of heretics. When bribery and court favour had done all that they could do in the way of conversions, the fearful dragonnades began, A.D. 1681. The formal Revocation of the Edict of Nantes followed in A.D. 1685, and persecution raged with the utmost violence. Thousands of churches were torn down, vast numbers of confessors were tortured, burnt, or sent to the galleys. In spite of the terrible penal laws against emigrating, in spite of the watch kept over the frontiers, hundreds of thousands escaped, and were received with open arms as *refugees* in Brandenburg, Holland, England, Denmark, and Switzerland. Many fled into the wilds of the Cevennes, where under the name of Camisards they maintained a heroic conflict for years, until at last exterminated by an army at least ten times their strength. The struggle reached the utmost intensity of bitterness on both sides in A.D. 1702, when the fanatical and inhumanly cruel inquisitor, the Abbé du Chaila, was slain. At the head of the Camisard army was a young peasant, Jean Cavalier, who by his energetic and skilful conduct of the campaign astonished the world. At last the famous Marshal Villars, by promising a general amnesty, release of all prisoners, permission to emigrate with possessions, and religious toleration to those who remained, succeeded in persuading Cavalier to lay down his arms. The king ratified this bargain, only refusing the right of

religious freedom. Many, however, submitted; while others emigrated, mostly to England. Cavalier entered the king's service as colonel; but distrusting the arrangements fled to Holland, and afterwards to England, where in A.D. 1740 he died as governor of Jersey. In A.D. 1707 a new outbreak took place, accompanied by prophetic fanaticism, in consequence of repeated dragonnades, but it was put down by the stake, the gallows, the axe, and the wheel. France had lost half a million of her most pious, industrious, and capable inhabitants, and yet two millions of Huguenots deprived of all their rights remained in the land.[1]

5. The Waldensians in Piedmont (§ 139, 25).—Although in A.D. 1654 the Duke of Savoy confirmed to the Waldensians their privileges, by Easter of the following year a bloody persecution broke out, in which a Piedmontese army, together with a horde of released prisoners and Irish refugees, driven from their native land by Cromwell's severities, to whom the duke had given shelter in the valleys, perpetrated the most horrible cruelties. Yet in the desperate conflict the Waldensians held their ground. The intervention of the Protestant Swiss cantons won for them again a measure of toleration, and liberal gifts from abroad compensated them for their loss of property. Cromwell too sent to the relief of the sufferers the celebrated Lord Morland in A.D. 1658. While in the valleys he got possession of a number of MSS. (§ 108, 11), which he took home with him and deposited in the Cambridge Library. In A.D. 1685 the persecution and civil war were again renewed at the instigation of Louis XIV. The soldiers besieged the valleys, and more than 14,000 captives were consigned to fortresses and prisons. But the rest of the Waldensians plucked up courage, inflicted many defeats upon their enemy, and so moved the government in A.D. 1686 to release the prisoners and send them out of the country. Some found their way to Germany, others fled to Switzerland. These last, aided by Swiss troops, and led by their own pastor, Henry Arnaud, made an attack upon Piedmont in A.D. 1689, and conquered again their own country. They continued in possession, notwithstanding all attempts to dislodge them.

6. The Catholics in England and Ireland.—When James I., A.D. 1603–1625, the son of Mary Stuart, ascended the English throne (§ 139, 11), the Catholics expected from him nothing short of the complete restoration of the old religion. But great as James' inclination towards

---

[1] Bray, "Revolt of the Protestants of the Cevennes." London, 1870. Poole, "History of the Huguenots of the Dispersion." London, 1880. Agnew, "Protestant Exiles from France in the Reign of Louis XIV." 8 vols. London, 1871. Weiss, "History of French Protestant Refugees." London, 1854

Catholicism may have been, his love of despotic authority was still greater. He therefore rigorously suppressed the Jesuits, who disputed the royal supremacy over the church; and the bitterness of the Catholics now reached its height. They organized the so-called Gunpowder Plot, with the intention of blowing up the royal family and the whole Parliament at the first meeting of the house. At the head of the conspiracy stood Rob. Catesby, Thomas Percy of Northumberland, and Guy Fawkes, an English officer in the Spanish service. The plan was discovered shortly before the day appointed for its execution. On November 5th, A.D. 1605, Fawkes, with lantern and matches, was seized in the cellar. The rest of the conspirators fled, but, after a desperate struggle, in which Catesby and Percy fell, were arrested, and, together with two Jesuit accomplices, executed as traitors. Great severities were then exercised toward the Catholics, not only in England, but also in Ireland, where the bulk of the population was attached to the Romish faith. James I. completed the transference of ecclesiastical property to the Anglican church, and robbed the Irish nobles of almost all their estates, and gifted them over to Scottish and English favourites. All Catholics, because they refused to take the oath of supremacy, i.e. to recognise the king as head of the church, were declared ineligible for any civil office. These oppressions at last led to the fearful Irish massacre. In October, A.D. 1641, a desperate outbreak of the Catholics took place throughout the country. It aimed at the destruction of all Protestants in Ireland. The conspirators rushed from all sides into the houses of the Protestants, murdered the inhabitants, and drove them naked and helpless from their homes. Many thousands died on the roadside of hunger and cold. In other places they were driven in crowds into the rivers and drowned, or into empty houses, which were burnt over them. The number of those who suffered is variously estimated from 40,000 to 400,000. Charles I., A.D. 1625–1649, was suspected as instigator of this terrible deed, and it may be regarded as his first step toward the scaffold (§ 155, 1). After the execution of Charles, Oliver Cromwell, in A.D 1649, at the call of Parliament, took fearful revenge for the Irish crime. In the two cities which he took by storm he had all the citizens cut down without distinction. Panic-stricken, the inhabitants of the other cities fled to the bogs. Within nine months the whole island was reconquered. Hundreds of thousands, driven from their native soil, wandered as homeless fugitives, and their lands were divided among English soldiers and settlers. During the time of the English Commonwealth, A.D. 1649–1660, all moderate men, even those who had formerly demanded religious toleration, not only for all Christian sects, but also for Jews and Mohammadans, and even atheists, were now at one in excluding Catholics from its benefit, because they all saw in the Catholics a party ready at any moment to prove traitors to their country at the bidding of a foreign sovereign. —The Restoration under Charles II. could not greatly ameliorate the calamities of the Irish. Religious persecution indeed ceased, but the property taken from the Catholic church and native owners still remained in the hands of the Anglican church and the Protestant occupiers. To counterbalance the Catholic proclivities of Charles II. (§ 155, 3), the English Parliament of A.D. 1673 passed the Test Act, which required every civil and military officer to take the test oaths, condemning transubstantiation and the worship of the saints, and to receive the communion according to the Anglican rite as members of the State church. The statements of a certain Titus Oates, that the Jesuits had organized a plot for murdering the king and restoring the papacy, led to fearful riots in A.D. 1678 and many executions. But the reports were seemingly unfounded, and were probably the fruit of an intrigue to deprive the king's Catholic brother, James II., of the right of succession. When James ascended the throne, in A.D. 1685, he immediately entered into negotiations with Rome, and filled almost all offices with Catholics. At the invitation of the Protestants, the king's son-in-law, William III. of Orange, landed in England in A.D. 1688, and on James' flight was declared king by the Parliament. The Act of Toleration, issued by him in A.D. 1689, still withheld from Papists the privileges now extended to Protestant dissenters (§ 155, 3).[1]

7. Union Efforts.—(1) Although Hugo Grotius distinctly took the side of the Remonstrants (§ 160, 2), his whole disposition was essentially irenical. He attempted, but in vain, not only the reconciliation of the Arminians and Calvinists, but also the union of all Protestant sects on a common basis. Toward Catholicism he long maintained a decidedly hostile attitude. But through intimate intercourse with distinguished Catholics, especially during his exile in France, his feelings were completely changed. He now invariably expressed himself more favourably in regard to the faith and the institutions of the Catholic church. Its semi-Pelagianism was acceptable to him as a decided Arminian. In his "Votum pro Pace" he recommended as the only possible way to restore ecclesiastical union, a return to Catholicism, on the understanding that a thorough reform should be made. But that he was himself ready to pass over, and was hindered only by his sudden death in A.D. 1645, is merely an illusion of

[1] Macaulay, "History of England from the Accession of James II." London, 1846. Hassencamp, "History of Ireland from the Reformation to the Union." London, 1888. Adair, "Rise and Progress of the Presbyterian Church of Ireland from 1623 to 1670." Belfast, 1866. Hamilton, "History of Presbyterian Church in Ireland." Edin., 1887

Romish imagination.[1]—(2) King Wladislaus IV. of Poland thought
a union of Protestants and Catholics in his dominions not impossible,
and with this end in view arranged the Religious Conference of Thorn
in A.D. 1645. Prussia and Brandenburg were also invited to take
part in it. The elector sent his court preacher, John Berg, and
asked from the Duke of Brunswick the assistance of the Helmstadt
theologian, George Calixt. The chief representatives of the Lutheran
side were Abraham Calov, of Danzig, and John Hülsemann, of Wittenberg. That Calixt, a Lutheran, took the part of the Reformed,
intensified the bitterness of the Lutherans at the outset. The result
was to increase the split on all sides. The Reformed set forth their
opinions in the "*Declaratio Thorunensis,*" which in Brandenburg obtained symbolical rank.—(3) J. B. Bossuet, who died in A.D. 1704, Bishop
of Meaux, used all his eloquence to prepare a way for the return of
Protestants to the church in which alone is salvation. In several
treatises he gave an idealized exposition of the Catholic doctrine,
glossed over what was most offensive to Protestants, and sought by
subtlety and sophistry to represent the Protestant system as contradictory and untenable.[2] During the same period the Spaniard Spinola,
Bishop of Neustadt, who had come into the country as father confessor
of the empress, proposed a scheme of union at the imperial court.
The controverted points were to be decided at a free council, but the
primacy of the pope and the hierarchical system, as founded *jure
humano*, were to be retained. In prosecuting his scheme, with the
secret support of Leopold I., Spinola, between A.D. 1676 and 1691,
travelled through all Protestant Germany. He found most success,
out of respect for the emperor, in Hanover, where the Abbot of Loccum,
Molanus, zealously advocated the proposed union, in which on the
Catholic side Bossuet, on the Protestant side the great philosopher
Leibnitz, took part. But the negotiations ended in no practical result.
That Leibnitz had himself been already secretly inclined to Catholicism,
some think to have proved by a manuscript, found after his death,
entitled in another's hand, "*Systema Theologicum Leibnitii.*" Favourably disposed as Leibnitz was to investigate and recognise what was
profound and true even in Catholicism, so that he reached the conviction
that neither of the two churches had given perfect and adequate expression to Christian truth, he has apparently sought in this work to make

[1] Butler, "Life of Hugo Grotius." London, 1826. Motley, "John
of Barneveld," vol. ii. New York, 1874.
[2] "An Exposition of the Doctrine of the Catholic Church in Matters
of Controversy." London, 1685. "Variations of Protestantism." 2
vols. Dublin, 1836. Butler, "Some Account of the Life and Writings
of Bishop Bossuet." London, 1812.

clear to himself what and how much of specifically Catholic doctrines were justifiable, and to sketch out a system of doctrine occupying a place superior to both confessions. In this treatise many doctrines are expressed in a manner quite divergent from that of the Tridentine creed, while several expressions show how clearly he perceived the contradiction between his own Protestant faith and the Romish system, amid all his attempts to effect a reconciliation.

8. The Lehnin Prophecy.—The hope entertained, about the end of the seventeenth century, by Catholics throughout Germany of the speedy restoration of the mother church was expressed in the so called Vaticinium Lehninense. Professedly composed in the thirteenth century by a monk called Hermann, of the cloister of Lehnin in Brandenburg, it characterized with historical accuracy in 100 Leonine verses the Brandenburg princes down to Frederick III., of whose coronation in A.D. 1701 it is ignorant, and after this proceeds in a purely fanciful and arbitrary manner. From Joachim II., who openly joined the Reformation, it enumerates eleven members, so that the history is just brought down to Frederick William III. With the eleventh the Hohenzollern dynasty ends, Germany is united, the Catholic church restored, and Lehnin raised again to its ancient glory. Under Frederick William IV., the Catholics diligently sought to prove the genuineness of the prophecy, and by arbitrary methods to extend it so as to include this prince. Lately " the deadly sin of Israel " spoken of in it has been pointed to as a prophecy of the *Kultur-kampf* of our own day (§ 197). The first certain trace of the poem is in A.D. 1693. Hilgenfeld thinks that its author was a fanatical pervert, Andr. Fromm, who was previously a Protestant pastor in Berlin, and died in A.D. 1685 as canon of Leitmeritz, in Bohemia.

§ 154. LUTHERANISM AND CALVINISM.

The Reformed church made its way into the heart of Lutheran Germany (§ 144) by the Calvinizing of Hesse-Cassel and Lippe, and by the adherence of the electoral house of Brandenburg. Renewed attempts to unite the two churches were equally fruitless with the endeavours after a Catholic-Protestant union.

1. Calvinizing of Hesse-Cassel, A.D. 1605-1646.—Philip the Magnanimous, died 1567, left to his eldest son, William IV., one half of his territories, comprising Lower Hesse and Schmalcald, with residence at Cassel; to Louis IV. a fourth part, *viz.* Upper Hesse, with residence at Marburg; while his two youngest sons, Philip and George, were

made counts, with their residence at Darmstadt. Philip died in 1583 and Louis in 1604, both childless; in consequence of which the greater part of Philip's territory and the northern half of Upper Hesse with Marburg fell to Hesse-Cassel, and the southern half with Giessen to Hesse-Darmstadt.—Landgrave William IV. of Hesse-Cassel sympathised with his father's union and levelling tendencies, and by means of general synods wrought eagerly to secure acceptance for them throughout Hesse by setting aside the *ubiquitous* Christology (§ 142, 9) and the Formula of Concord, while firmly maintaining the *Corpus Doctrinæ Philippicum* (§ 142, 10). The fourth and last of those general synods was held in 1582. Further procedure was meanwhile rendered impossible by the increase of opposition. For, on the one hand, Louis IV., under the influence of the acute and learned but contentious Ægidius Hunnius, professor of theology at Marburg, 1576–1592, became more and more decidedly a representative of exclusive Lutheranism; and, on the other hand, William's Calvinizing schemes became from day to day more reckless. His son and successor Maurice went forward more energetically along the same lines as his father, especially after the death of his uncle Louis in 1604, who bequeathed to him the Marburg part of his territories. These had been given him on condition that he should hold by the confession and its apology as guaranteed by Charles V. in 1530. But in 1605 he forbad the Marburg theologians to set forth the ubiquity theology; and when they protested, issued a formal prohibition of the dogma with its presuppositions and consequences, and insisted on the introduction of the Reformed numbering of the commandments of the decalogue, and the breaking of bread at the communion, and the removal of the remaining images from the churches (§ 144, 2). The theologians again protested, and were deprived of their offices. The result was the outbreak of a popular tumult at Marburg, which Maurice suppressed by calling in the military. When in several places in Upper and even in Lower Hesse opposition was persisted in, and the resisting clergy could not be won over either by persuasion and threatening or by persecution, Maurice in 1607 convened consultative diocesan synods at Cassel, Eschwege, Marburg, St. Goar, and soon after a general synod at Cassel, which, giving expression on all points to the will of the landgrave, drew up, besides a new hymnbook and catechism, a new "Christian and correct confession of faith," by which they openly and decidedly declared their attachment to the Reformed church. Soon Hesse accepted these conclusions, but not the rest of the state, where the opposition of the nobles, clergy, and people, in spite of all attempts to enforce this acceptance by military power, imprisonment, and deposition, could not be altogether overcome.—Meanwhile George's son and successor Louis V., 1596–1626, had been eagerly seeking to make capital of those troubles in his cousin's domains in favour of the Darmstadt dynasty. He gave his protection to the professors expelled from Marburg in 1605, founded in 1607 a Lutheran university at Giessen, and made accusations against his cousin before the imperial supreme court, which in 1623, on the basis of the will of Louis IV. and the Religious Peace of Augsburg (§ 137, 5), declared the inheritance forfeited, and entrusted the electors of Cologne and Saxony with the execution of the sentence. These in conjunction with the troops of the league under Tilly attacked Upper and Lower Hesse; the Lutheran University of Giessen was transferred to Marburg, and Upper Hesse, after the banishment of the Reformed pastors, went over wholly to the Lutheran confession. Maurice, completely broken down, resigned in favour of his son William V., who was obliged to make an agreement, according to which he made over Upper Hesse, Schmalcald, and Katzenelnbogen to George II. of Hesse-Darmstadt, the successor of Louis V. In consequence of his attachment to Gustavus Adolphus in the Thirty Years' War the ban of the empire was pronounced upon William. He died in 1637. His widow, Amalie Elizabeth, undertook the government on behalf of her young son William VI., and in 1646, after repeated victories over George's troops, made a new agreement with him, by which the territories taken away in 1627 were restored to Hesse-Cassel, under a guarantee, however, that the *status quo* in matters of religion should be preserved, and that they should continue predominantly Lutheran. The university property was divided; Giessen obtained a Lutheran, Marburg a Reformed institution, and Lower Hesse received a moderately but yet essentially Reformed ecclesiastical constitution.

2. Calvinizing of Lippe, A.D. 1602.—Count Simon VI. of Lippe, in his eventful life, was brought into close relations with the Reformed Netherlands and with Maurice of Hesse. His dominions were thoroughly Lutheran, but from A.D. 1602 Calvinism was gradually introduced under the patronage of the prince. The chief promoter of this innovation was Dreckmeyer, chosen general superintendent in A.D. 1599. At a visitation of churches in A.D. 1602, the festivals of Mary and the apostles, exorcism, the sign of the cross, the host burning candles, and Luther's catechism were rejected. Opposing pastors were deposed, and Calvinists put in their place. The city Lemgo stood out longest, and persevered in its adherence to the Lutheran confession during an eleven years' struggle with its prince, from A.D. 1606 to 1617. After the death of Simon VI., his successor, Simon VII., allowed the city the free exercise of its Lutheran religion.

3. The Elector of Brandenburg becomes Calvinist, A.D. 1613.—John Sigismund, A.D. 1608–1619, had promised his grandfather, John George, to maintain his connexion with the Lutheran church. But his own incli

nation, which was strengthened by his son's marriage with a princess
of the Palatinate, and his connexion with the Netherlands, made him
forget his promise. Also his court preacher, the crypto-Calvinist
Solomon Fink, contributed to the same result. On Christmas Day, A.D.
1613, he went over to the Reformed church. In order to share in the
Augsburg Peace, he still retained the Augsburg Confession, naturally
in the form known as the *Variata*. In A.D. 1624, he issued a Calvinist
confession of his own, the *Confessio Sigismundi* or *Marchica*, which
sought to reconcile the universality of grace with the particularity of
election (§ 168, 1). His people, however, did not follow the prince, not
even his consort, Anne of Prussia. The court preacher, Gedicke, who
would not retract his invectives against the prince and the Reformed
confession, was obliged to flee from Berlin, as also another preacher,
Mart. Willich. But when altars, images, and baptismal fonts were
thrown out of the Berlin churches, a tumult arose, in A.D. 1615, which
was not suppressed without bloodshed. In the following year the
elector forbade the teaching of the *communicatio idiomatum* and the
ubiquitas corporis (§ 141, 9) at the University of Frankfort-on-the-
Oder. In A.D. 1614, owing to the publication of a keen controversial
treatise of Hutter (§ 158, 5) he forbade any of his subjects going to
the University of Wittenberg, and soon afterwards struck out the
Formula of Concord from the collection of the symbolical books of the
Lutheran church of his realm.—Continuation, § 169, 1.

4. **Union Attempts.**—Hoë von Hoënegg, of an old Austrian family,
was from A.D. 1612 chief court preacher at Dresden, and as spiritual
adviser of the elector, John George, on the outbreak of the Thirty
Years' War, got Lutheran Saxony to take the side of the Catholic
emperor against the Calvinist Frederick V. of the Palatinate, elected
king of Bohemia. In A.D. 1621, he had proved that "on ninety-nine
points the Calvinists were in accord with the Arians and the Turks."
At the Religious Conference of Leipzig of A.D. 1631 a compromise was
accepted on both sides; but no practical result was secured. The
Religious Conference of Cassel, in A.D. 1661, was a well meant endeavour
by some Marburg Reformed theologians and Lutherans of the school
of Calixt (§ 158, 2); but owing to the agitation caused by the Synergist
controversy, no important advance toward union could be accomplished. The union efforts of Duke William of Brandenburg, A.D. 1640-
1688, were opposed by Paul Gerhardt, preacher in the church of St.
Nicholas in Berlin. On refusing to abstain from attacks on the
Reformed doctrine he was deposed from his office. He was soon appointed pastor at Lübben in Lusatia, where he died in A.D. 1676.—The
most zealous apostle of universal Protestant union, embracing even
the Anglican church, was the Scottish Presbyterian John Durie. From
A.D. 1628 when he officiated as pastor of an English colony at Elbing,

till his death at Cassel in A.D. 1640, he devoted his energies unweariedly to this one task. He repeatedly travelled through Germany,
Sweden, Denmark, England, and the Netherlands, formed acquaintance with clerical and civil authorities, had intercourse with them
by word and letter, published a multitude of tracts on this subject;
but at last could only look back with bitter complaints over the lost
labours of a lifetime.[1]—Continuation, § 169, 1.

§ 155. ANGLICANISM AND PURITANISM.[2]

On the outbreak of the English Revolution, occasioned by
the despotism of the first two Stuarts, crowds of Puritan exiles
returned from Holland and North America to their old home.
They powerfully strengthened their secret sympathisers in
their successful struggle against the episcopacy of the State
church (§ 131, 6); but, breaking up into rival parties, as
Presbyterians and Independents (§ 143, 3, 4), gave way to
fanatical extravagances. The victorious party of Independents also split into two divisions: the one, after the old
Dutch style, simple and strict believers in Scripture; the
other, first in Cromwell's army, fanatical enthusiasts and
visionary saints (§ 161, 1). The Restoration, under the last
two Stuarts, sought to re-introduce Catholicism. It was
William of Orange, by his Act of Toleration of A.D. 1689,
who first brought to a close the Reformation struggles
within the Anglican church. It guaranteed, indeed, all the

---

[1] "The Work of John Durie in behalf of Christian Union in the
Seventeenth Century," by Dr. Briggs in *Presbyterian Review*, vol.
viii., 1887, pp. 297-300. To which is attached an account by Durie
himself, never before published, of his own union efforts from July,
1631, till September, 1633. See pp. 301-309.

[2] Clarendon, "History of the Rebellion in England, 1649-1666." 8
vols. Oxford, 1667. Burnet, "History of his Own Time, 1660-1713."
2 vols. London, 1724. Guizot, "History of English Revolution of
1640." London, 1856. Gardiner, "History of England, 1603-1642."
10 vols. London, 1885. Marsden, "History of Early and Later Puritans, down to the Ejection of the Nonconformists in 1662." 2 vols.
London, 1853. Masson, "Life of Milton." 4 vols. London, 1859 ff.

pre-eminent privileges of an establishment to the Anglican and Episcopal church, but also granted toleration to dissenters, while refusing it to Catholics.

1. The First Two Stuarts.—James I., dominated by the idea of the royal supremacy, and so estranged from the Presbyterianism in which he was brought up (§ 139, 11), as king of England, A.D. 1603–1625, attached himself to the national Episcopal church, persecuted the English Puritans, so that many of them again fled to Holland (§ 143, 4), and forced Episcopacy upon the Scotch. Charles I., A.D. 1625–1649, went beyond his father in theory and practice, and thus incurred the hatred of his Protestant subjects. William Laud, from A.D. 1633 Archbishop of Canterbury, was the recklessly zealous promoter of his despotic ideas, representing the Episcopacy, by reason of its Divine institution and apostolic succession, as the foundation of the church and the pillar of an absolute monarchy. Laud used his position as primate to secure the introduction of his own theory into the public church services, among other things making the communion office an imitation as near as possible of the Romish mass. But when he attempted to force upon the Scotch such "Baal-worship" by the command of the king, they formed a league in A.D. 1638 for the defence of Presbyterianism, the so called Great Covenant, and emphasised their demand by sending an army into England. The king, who had ruled for eleven years without a Parliament, was obliged now to call together the representatives of the people. Scarcely had the Long Parliament, A.D. 1640–1653, in which the Puritan element was supreme, pacified the Scotch, than oil was anew poured on the flames by the Irish massacre of A.D. 1641 (§ 153, 6). The Lower House, in spite of the persistent opposition of the court, resolved on excluding the bishops from the Upper House and formally abolishing Episcopacy; and in A.D. 1643, summoned the Westminster Assembly to remodel the organization of the English church, at which Scotch representatives were to have a seat. After long and violent debates with an Independent minority, till A.D. 1648, the Assembly drew up a Presbyterian constitution with a Puritan service, and in the Westminster Confession a strictly Calvinistic creed. But only in Scotland were these decisions heartily accepted. In England, notwithstanding their confirmation by the Parliament, they received only partial and occasional acceptance, owing to the prevalence of Independent opinions among the people.—Since A.D. 1642, the tension between court and Parliament had brought about the Civil War between Cavaliers and Roundheads. In A.D. 1645, the royal troops were cut to pieces at Naseby by the parliamentary army under Fairfax and Cromwell. The king fled to

the Scotch, by whom he was surrendered to the English Parliament in A.D. 1647. But when now the fanatical Independents, who formed a majority in the army, began to terrorise the Parliament, it opened negotiations for peace with the king. He was now ready to make almost any sacrifice, only on religious and conscientious grounds he could not agree to the unconditional abandonment of Episcopacy. Even the Scotch, whose Presbyterianism was now threatened by the Independents, as before it had been by the Episcopalians, longed for the restoration of royalty, and to aid in this sent an army into England in A.D. 1648. But they were defeated by Cromwell, who then dismissed the Parliament and had all its Presbyterian members either imprisoned or driven into retirement. The Independent remnant, known as the Rump Parliament, A.D. 1648–1653, tried the king for high treason and sentenced him to death. On January 30th, A.D. 1649, he mounted the scaffold, on which Archbishop Laud had preceded him in A.D. 1645, and fell under the executioner's axe.[1]

2. The Commonwealth and the Protector.—Ireland had never yet atoned for its crime of A.D. 1641 (§ 153, 6), and as it refused to acknowledge the Commonwealth, Cromwell took terrible revenge in A.D. 1649. In A.D. 1650 at Dunbar, and in A.D. 1651 at Worcester, he completely destroyed the army of the Scots, who had crowned Charles II., son of the executed king, drove out, in April A.D. 1653, the Rump of the Long Parliament, which had come to regard itself as a permanent institution, and in July opened, with a powerful speech, two hours in length, on God's ways and judgments, the Short or Barebones' Parliament, composed of " pious and God-fearing men " selected by himself. In this new Parliament which, with prayer and psalm-singing, wrought hard at the re-organization of the executive, the bench, and the church, the two parties of Independents were represented, the fanatical enthusiasts indeed predominating, and so victorious in all matters of debate. To this party Cromwell himself belonged. His attachment to it, however, was considerably cooled in consequence of the excesses of the Levellers (§ 161, 2), and the fantastic policy of the parliamentarian Saints disgusted him more and more. When therefore, on December 12th, A.D. 1653, after five months' fruitless opposition to the radical demands of the extravagant majority, all the most moderate members of the Parliament had resigned their seats and returned their mandates into Cromwell's hands, he burst in upon

---

[1] Mitchell, " The Westminster Assembly." London, 1882. Mitchell and Struthers, " Minutes of Westminster Assembly." Edinburgh, 1874. Macpherson, " Handbook to Westminster Confession." 2nd ed. Edinburgh, 1882. Hetherington, " History of Westminster Assembly." 4th ed. Edinburgh, 1878.

the psalm-singing remnant with his soldiers, and entered upon his
life-long office of the Protector of the Commonwealth with a new constitution. He proclaimed toleration of all religious sects, Catholics
only being excepted on political grounds (§ 153, 6), giving equal rights
to Presbyterians, and offering no hindrance to the revival of Episcopacy.
He yet remained firmly attached to his early convictions. He believed
in a kingdom of the saints embracing the whole earth, and looked on
England as destined for the protection and spread of Protestantism.
Zürich greeted him as the great Protestant champion, and he showed
himself in this *rôle* in the valleys of Piedmont (§ 153, 5), in France, in
Poland, and in Silesia. He joined with all Protestant governments into
a league, offensive and defensive, against fanatical attempts of Papists
to recover their lost ground. When Spain and France sued for his
alliance, he made it a condition with the former that, besides allowing
free trade with the West Indies, it should abolish the Inquisition,
and of France he required an assurance that the rights of Huguenots
should be respected. And when in Germany a new election of
emperor was to take place, he urged the great electors that they
should by no means allow the imperial throne to continue with the
Catholic house of Austria. Meanwhile his path at home was a thorny
one. He was obliged to suppress fifteen open rebellions during five
years of his reign, countless secret plots threatened his life every day,
and his bitterest foes were his former comrades in the camp of the
the saints. After refusing the crown offered him in A.D. 1657, without
being able thereby to quell the discontents of parties, he died on
September 3rd, A.D. 1658, the anniversary of his glorious victories of
Dunbar and Worcester.[1]

8. The Restoration and the Act of Toleration.—The Restoration of
royalty under Charles II., A.D. 1660–1685, began with the reinstating
of the Episcopal church in all the privileges granted to it under
Elizabeth. The Corporation Act of December, A.D. 1661, was the first
of a series of enactments for this purpose. It required of all magistrates and civil officers that they should take an oath acknowledging
the royal supremacy and communicate in the Episcopal church. The
Act of Uniformity of May, A.D. 1662, was still more oppressive. It
prohibited any clergyman entering the English pulpit or discharging
any ministerial function, unless he had been ordained by a bishop,
had signed the Thirty-nine Articles, and undertook to conduct worship

---

[1] Carlyle, "Cromwell's Letters and Speeches." 2 vols. London, 1845.
Guizot, "Life of Cromwell." London, 1877. Paxton Hood, "Oliver
Cromwell." London, 1882. Picton, "Oliver Cromwell." London, 1878.
Harrison, "Oliver Cromwell." London, 1888. Barclay, "The Inner
Life of the Religious Societies of the Commonwealth." London, 1877

exactly in accordance with the newly revised Book of Common Prayer More than 2,000 Puritan ministers, who could not conscientiously sub-mit to those terms, were driven out of their churches. Then in June, A.D. 1664, the Conventicle Act was renewed, enforcing attendance at the Episcopal church, and threatening with imprisonment or exile all found in any private religious meeting of more than five persons. In the following year the Five Mile Act inflicted heavy fines on all nonconformist ministers who should approach within five miles of their former congregation or indeed of any city. All these laws, although primarily directed against all Protestant dissenters, told equally against the Catholics, whom the king's Catholic sympathies would willingly have spared. When now his league with Catholic France against the Protestant Netherlands made it necessary for him to appease his Protestant subjects, he hoped to accomplish this and save the Catholics by his "Declaration of Indulgence" of A.D. 1672, issued with the consent of Parliament, which suspended all penal laws hitherto in force against dissenters. But the Protestant non-conformists saw through this scheme, and the Parliament of A.D. 1678 passed the anti-Catholic Test Act (§ 153, 6). Equally vain were all later attempts to secure greater liberties and privileges to the Catho-lics. They only served to develop the powers of Parliament and to bring the Episcopalians and nonconformists more closely together. After spending his whole life oscillating between frivolous unbelief and Catholic superstition, Charles II., on his death-bed, formally went over to the Romish church, and had the communion and extreme unction administered by a Catholic priest. His brother and successor James II., A.D. 1685–1688, who was from A.D. 1672 an avowed Catholic, sent a decla-ration of obedience to Rome, received a papal nuncio in London, and in the exercise of despotic power issued, in A.D. 1687, a "Declaration of Freedom of Conscience," which, under the fair colour of universal toleration and by the setting aside of the test oath, enabled him to fill all civil and military offices with Catholics. This act proved equally oppressive to the Episcopalians and to Protestant dissenters. This intrigue cost him his throne. He had, as he himself said, staked three kingdoms on a mass, and lost all the three. William III. of Orange, A.D. 1689–1702, grandson of Charles I. and son-in-law of James II., gave a final decision to the rights of the national Episcopal church and the position of dissenters in the Act of Toleration of A.D. 1689, which he passed with consent of the Parliament. All penal laws against the latter were abrogated, and religious liberty was extended to all with the exception of Catholics and Socinians. The retention of the Corporation and Test Acts, however, still excluded them from the exercise of all political rights. They were also still obliged to pay tithes and other church dues to the Episcopal clergy of their dioceses, and their marriages and baptisms had to be administered in the parish churches. Their ministers were also obliged to subscribe the Thirty-nine Articles, with reservation of those points opposed to their principles. The Act of Union of A.D. 1707, passed under Queen Anne, a daughter of James II., which united England and Scotland into the one kingdom of Great Britain, gave legitimate sanction to a separate ecclesiastical establishment for each country. In Scotland the Presbyterian churches continued the established church, while the Episcopal was tolerated as a dissenting body. Congregationalism, however, has been practically limited to England and North America.[1]— Continuation, § 202, 5.

II.—The Roman Catholic Church.

§ 156. THE PAPACY, MONKERY, AND FOREIGN MISSIONS.

Notwithstanding the regeneration of papal Catholicism since the middle of the sixteenth century, Hildebrand's politico-theocratic ideal was not realized. Even Catholic princes would not be dictated to on political matters by the vicar of Christ. The most powerful of them, France, Austria, and Spain, during the sixteenth century, and subsequently also Portugal, had succeeded in the claim to the right of excluding objectionable candidates in papal elections. Ban and interdict had lost their power. The popes, however, still clung to the idea after they had been obliged to surrender the reality, and issued from time to time powerless protestations against disagreeable facts of history. Several new monkish orders were instituted during this century, mostly for teaching the young and tending the sick, but some also expressly for the promoting of theological science. Of all the orders, new and old, the Jesuits were by far the most powerful. They were regarded with jealousy and suspicion by the other orders. In respect of doctrine the Dominicans

---

[1] Guizot, "Richard Cromwell and the Restoration of Charles II." 2 vols. London, 1856. Macpherson, "History of Great Britain from the Restoration." London, 1875.

were as far removed from them as possible within the limits
of the Tridentine Creed. But notwithstanding any such
mutual jealousies, they were all animated by one yearning
desire to oppose, restrict, and, where that was possible, to
uproot Protestantism. With similar zeal they devoted themselves with wonderful success to the work of foreign missions.

1. The Papacy.—Paul V., A.D. 1605–1621, equally energetic in his
civil and in his ecclesiastical policy, in a struggle with Venice, was
obliged to behold the powerlessness of the papal interdict. His successor, Gregory XV., A.D. 1621–1623, founded the Propaganda, prescribed
a secret scrutiny in papal elections, and canonized Loyola, Xavier, and
Neri. He enriched the Vatican Library by the addition of the valuable treasures of the Heidelberg Library, which Maximilian I. of
Bavaria sent him on his conquest of the Palatinate. Urban VIII., A.D.
1623–1644, increased the Propaganda, improved the Roman "Breviary"
(§ 56, 2), condemned Jansen's *Augustinus* (§ 156, 5), and compelled
Galileo to recant. But on the other hand, through his onesided
ecclesiastical policy he was led into sacrificing the interests of the
imperial house of Austria. Not only did he fail to give support to
the emperor, but quite openly hailed Gustavus Adolphus, the saviour
of German Protestantism, as the God-sent saviour from the Spanish-
Austrian tyranny. For this he was pronounced a heretic at the
imperial court, and threatened with a second edition of the sack of
Rome (§ 132, 2). At the same time his soul was so filled with fanati-.
cal hatred against Protestantism, that in a letter of 1631 he congratu-
lated the Emperor Ferdinand II. on the destruction of Magdeburg as
an act most pleasing to heaven and reflecting the highest credit upon
Germany, and expressed the hope that the glory of so great a victory
should not be restricted to the ruins of a single city. On receiving
the news of the death of Gustavus Adolphus in 1632 he broke out into
loud jubilation, saying that now "the serpent was slain which with
its poison had sought to destroy the whole world." His successor,
Innocent X., A.D. 1644–1655, though vigorously protesting against the
Peace of Westphalia (§ 153, 2), was, owing to his abject subserviency
to a woman, his own sister-in-law, reproached with the title of a new
Johanna Papissa. Alexander VII., A.D. 1655–1667, had the expensive
guardianship of his godchild Christina of Sweden (§ 153, 1), and fanned
into a flame the spark kindled by his predecessor in the Jansenist controversy (§ 156, 5), so that his successor, Clement IX., A.D. 1667–1670,
could only gradually extinguish it. Clement X., A.D. 1670–1676, by
his preference for Spain roused the French king Louis XIV., who
avenged himself by various encroachments on the ecclesiastical ad-

ministration in his dominions. Innocent XI., A.D. 1676–1689, was a powerful pope, zealously promoting the weal of the church and the Papal States by introducing discipline among the clergy and attacking the immorality that prevailed among all classes of society. He unhesitatingly condemned sixty-five propositions from the lax Jesuit code of morals. Against the arrogant ambassador of Louis XIV. he energetically maintained his sovereign rights in his own domains, while he unreservedly refused the claims of the French clergy, urged by the king on the ground of the exceptional constitution of the Gallican church. Alexander VIII., A.D. 1689–1691, continued the fight against Gallicanism, and condemned the Jesuit distinction between theological and philosophical sin (§ 149, 10). Innocent XII., A.D. 1691–1700, could boast of having secured the complete subjugation of the Gallican clergy after a hard struggle. He too wrought earnestly for the reform of abuses in the curia. Specially creditable to him is the stringent bull "*Romanum decet pontificem*" against nepotism, which extirpated the evil disease, so that it was never again openly practised as an acknowledged right.—Continuation, § 165, 1.

2. The Jesuits and the Republic of Venice.—Venice was one of the first of the Italian cities to receive the Jesuits with open arms, A.D. 1530. But the influence obtained by them over public affairs through school and confessional, and their vast wealth accumulated from bequests and donations, led the government, in A.D. 1605, to forbid their receiving legacies or erecting new cloisters. In vain did Paul V. remonstrate. He then put Venice under an interdict. The Jesuits sought to excite the people against the government, and for this were banished in A.D. 1606. The pious and learned historian of the Council of Trent and adviser of the State, Paul Sarpi, proved a vigorous supporter of civil rights against the assumptions of the curia and the Jesuits. When in A.D. 1607 he refused a citation of Inquisition, he was dangerously wounded by three dagger stabs, inflicted by hired bandits, in whose stilettos he recognised the *stilum curiæ*. He died in A.D. 1623. After a ten months' vain endeavour to enforce the interdict, the pope at last, through French mediation, concluded a peace with the republic, without, however, being able to obtain either the abolition of the objectionable ecclesiastico-political laws or permission for the return of the Jesuits. Only after the republic had been weakened through the unfortunate Turkish war of A.D. 1645 was it found willing to submit. Even in A.D. 1653 it refused the offer of 150,000 ducats from the Jesuit general for the Turkish campaign; but when Alexander VII. suppressed several rich cloisters, their revenues were thankfully accepted for this purpose. In A.D. 1657, on the pope's promise of further pecuniary aid, the decree of banishment was withdrawn. The Jesuit fathers now returned in crowds, and soon regained

much of their former influence and wealth. No pope has ever since issued an interdict against any country.[1]

3. The Gallican Liberties.—Although Louis XIV. of France, A.D. 1643–1715, as a good Catholic king, powerfully supported the claims of papal dogmatics against the Jansenists (§§ 156, 5; 164, 7), he was by no means unfaithful to the traditional ecclesiastical polity of his house (§§ 96, 21; 110, 1, 9, 13, 14), and was often irritated to the utmost pitch by the pope's opposition to his political interests. He rigorously insisted upon the old customary right of the Crown to the income of certain vacant ecclesiastical offices, the *jus regaliæ*, and extended it to all bishoprics, burdened church revenues with military pensions, confiscated ecclesiastical property, etc. Innocent XI. energetically protested against such exactions. The king then had an assembly of the French called together in Paris on March 19th, A.D. 1682, which issued the famous Four Propositions of the Gallican Clergy, drawn up by Bishop Bossuet of Meaux. These set forth the fundamental rights of the French church: (1) In secular affairs the pope has no jurisdiction over princes and kings, and cannot release their subjects from their allegiance; (2) The spiritual power of the pope is subject to the higher authority of the general councils; (3) For France it is further limited by the old French ecclesiastical laws; and, (4) Even in matters of faith the judgment of the pope without the approval of a general assembly of the church is not unalterable. Innocent consequently refused to institute any of the newly appointed bishops. He was not even appeased by the Revocation of the Edict of Nantes in A.D. 1685. He was pleased indeed, and praised the deed, and celebrated it by a *Te Deum*, but objected to the violent measures for the conversion of Protestants as contrary to the teaching of Christ. Then also there arose a keen struggle against the mischievous extension of the right of asylum on the part of foreign embassies at Rome. On the pope's representation all the powers but France agreed to a restriction of the custom. The pope tolerated the nuisance till the death of the French ambassador in A.D. 1687, but then insisted on its abolition under pain of the ban. In consequence of this Louis sent his new ambassador into Rome with two companies of cavaliers, threw the papal nuntio in France into prison, and laid siege to the papal state of Avignon (§ 110, 4). But Innocent was not thus to be terrorized, and the French ambassador was obliged, after eighteen months' vain demonstrations, to quit Rome. Alexander VIII. repeated the condemnation of the Four Propositions, and Innocent XIII. also stood firm. The French episcopate, on the pope's persistent refusal to install bishops

---

[1] Bargraves, "Alexander VII. and His Cardinals." Ed. by Robertson. London, 1866.

rominated by the king, was at last constrained to submit. "Lying at the feet of his holiness," the bishops declared that everything concluded in that assembly was null and void; and even Louis XIV., under the influence of Madame de Maintenon (§ 157, 3), wrote to the pope in A.D. 1693, saying that he recalled the order that the Four Propositions should be taught in all the schools. There still, however, survived among the French clergy a firm conviction of the Gallican Liberties, and the *droit de régale* continued to have the force of law.[1] —Continuation, § 197, 1.

4. Galileo and the Inquisition.—Galileo Galilei, professor of mathematics at Pisa and Padua, who died in A.D. 1642, among his many distinguished services to the physical, mathematical, and astronomical sciences, has the honour of being the pioneer champion of the Copernican system. On this account he was charged by the monks with contradicting Scripture. In A.D. 1616 Paul V., through Cardinal Bellarmine, threatened him with the Inquisition and prison unless he agreed to cease from vindicating and lecturing upon his heretical doctrine. He gave the required promise. But in A.D. 1632 he published a dialogue, in which three friends discussed the Ptolemaic and Copernican systems, without any formal conclusion, but giving overwhelming reasons in favour of the latter. Urban VIII., in A.D. 1636, called upon the Inquisition to institute a process against him. He was forced to recant, was condemned to prison for an indefinite period, but was soon liberated through powerful influence. How far the old man of seventy-two years of age was compelled by torture to retract is still a matter of controversy. It is, however, quite evident that it was forced from him by threats. But that Galileo went out after his recantation, gnashing his teeth and stamping his feet, muttering, "Nevertheless it moves!" is a legend of a romancing age. This, however, is the fact, that the Congregation of the Index declared the Copernican theory to be false, irrational, and directly contrary to Scripture; and that even in A.D. 1660 Alexander VII., with apostolic authority, formally confirmed this decree and pronounced it *ex cathedrâ* (§ 149, 4) irrevocable. It was only in A.D. 1822 that the curia set it aside, and in a new edition of the Index (§ 149, 14) in A.D. 1835 omitted the works of Galileo as well as those of Copernicus.[2]

5. The Controversy on the Immaculate Conception (§ 112, 4) received

---

[1] Cunningham, "Discussions on Church Principles." Edin., 1863. Chap. v.: "The Liberties of the Gallican Church," pp. 133–163.

[2] Von Gebler, "Galileo Galilei and the Roman Curia," transl. by Sturge. London, 1879. Madden, "Galileo and the Inquisition." London, 1863. Brewster, "Martyrs of Science." Edin., 1841. Von Gebler denies that any condemnation *ex cathedra* was given.

a new impulse from the nun Mary of Jesus, died 1665, of Agreda, in Old Castile, superior of the cloister there of the Immaculate Conception, writer of the "Mystical City of God." This book professed to give an inspired account of the life of the Virgin, full of the strangest absurdities about the immaculate conception. The Sorbonne pronounced it offensive and silly; the Inquisition in Spain, Portugal, and Rome forbad the reading of it; but the Franciscans defended it as a divine revelation. A violent controversy ensued, which Alexander VII. silenced in A.D. 1661 by expressing approval of the doctrine of the immaculate conception set forth in the book.—Continuation, § 185, 2.

6. The Devotion of the Sacred Heart of Jesus.— The nun Margaret Alacoque, in the Burgundian cloister of *Paray le Monial*, born A.D. 1647, recovering from a painful illness when but three years old, vowed to the mother of God, who frequently appeared to her, perpetual chastity, and in gratitude for her recovery adopted the name of Mary, and when grown up resisted temptations by inflicting on herself the severest discipline, such as long fasts, sharp flagellations, lying on thorns, etc. Visions of the Virgin no longer satisfied her. She longed to lavish her affections on the Redeemer himself, which she expressed in the most extravagant terms. She took the Jesuit La Colombière as her spiritual adviser in A.D. 1675. In a new vision she beheld the side of her Beloved opened, and saw his heart glowing like a sun, into which her own was absorbed. Down to her death in A.D. 1690 she felt the most violent burning pains in her side. In a second vision she saw her Beloved's heart burning like a furnace, into which were taken her own heart and that of her spiritual adviser. In a third vision he enjoined the observance of a special "Devotion of the Sacred Heart" by all Christendom on the Friday after the octave of the *Corpus Christi* festival and on the first Friday of every month. La Colombière, being made director, put forth every effort to get this celebration introduced throughout the church, and on his death the idea was taken up by the whole Jesuit order. Their efforts, however, for fully a century proved unavailing. At this point, too, their most bitter opponents were the Dominicans. But even without papal authority the Jesuits so far succeeded in introducing the absurdities of this cult, and giving expression to it in word and by images, that by the beginning of the eighteenth century there were more than 300 male and female societies engaged in this devotion, and at last, in A.D. 1765, Clement XIII., the great friend of the Jesuits, gave formal sanction to this special celebration.—Continuation, § 188, 12.

7. New Congregations and Orders.—(1) At the head of the new orders of this century stands the Benedictine Congregation of St. Banne at Verdun, founded by Didier de la Cour. Elected Abbot of St. Banne in A.D. 1596, he gave his whole strength to the reforming of this

cloister, which had fallen into luxurious and immoral habits. By a
papal bull of A.D. 1604 all cloisters combining with St. Banne into a
congregation were endowed with rich privileges. Gradually all the
Benedictine monasteries of Lorraine and Alsace joined the union.
Didier's reforms were mostly in the direction of moral discipline and
asceticism; but in the new congregation scholarship was represented
by Calmet, Ceillier, etc., and many gave themselves to work as
teachers in the schools.—(2) Much more important for the promotion
of theological science, especially for patristics and church history,
was another Benedictine congregation founded in France in A.D. 1618
by Laurence Bernard, that of St. Maur, named after a disciple of St.
Benedict. The members of this order devoted themselves exclusively
to science and literary pursuits. To them belonged the distinguished
names, Mabillon, Montfaucon, Reinart, Martène, D'Achery, Le Nourry,
Durand, Surius, etc. They showed unwearied diligence in research
and a noble liberality of judgment. The editions of the most celebrated Fathers issued by them are the best of the kind, and this may
also be said of the great historical collections which we owe to their
diligence.—(3) The Fathers of the Oratory of Jesus are an imitation of
the Priests of the Oratory founded by Philip Neri (§ 149, 7). Peter
of Barylla, son of a member of parliament, founded it in A.D. 1611
by building an oratory at Paris. He was more of a mystic than of
a scholar, but his order sent out many distinguished and brilliant
theologians ; e.g. Malebranche, Morinus, Thomassinus, Rich. Simon,
Houbigant.—(4) The Piarists, *Patres scholarum piarum*, were founded
in Rome in A.D. 1607 by the Spaniard Joseph Calasanza. The order
adopted as a fourth vow the obligation of gratuitous tuition. They
were hated by the Obscurantist Jesuits for their successful labours
for the improvement of Catholic education, especially in Poland and
Austria, and also because they objected to all participation in political
schemes.—(5) The Order of the Visitation of Mary, or *Salesian Nuns*, instituted in A.D. 1610 by the mystic Francis de Sales and Francisca
Chantal (§ 157, 1). They visited the poor and sick in imitation of
Elizabeth's visit to the Virgin (Luke i. 39) ; but the papal rescript of
A.D. 1618 gave prominence to the education of children.

8.—(6) The Priests of the Missions and Sisters of Charity were both
founded by Vincent de Paul. Born of poor parents, he was, after
completing his education, captured by pirates, and as a slave converted his renegade master to Christianity. As domestic chaplain to
the noble family of Gondy he was characterized in a remarkable degree
for unassuming humility, and he wrought earnestly and successfully
as a home missionary. In A.D. 1618 he founded the order of Sisters of
Mercy, who became devoted nurses of the sick throughout all France,
and in A.D. 1627 that of the Priests of the Missions, or Lazarists, who

travelled the country attending to the spiritual and bodily wants of men. After the death of the Countess Gondy in A.D. 1625, he placed at the head of the Sisters of Mercy the widow Louise le Gras, distinguished equally for qualities of head and heart. Vincent died in A.D. 1660, and was subsequently canonized.[1] — (7) The Trappists, founded by De Rancé, a distinguished canon, who in A.D. 1664 passed from the extreme of worldliness to the extreme of fanatical asceticism. The order got its name from the Cistercian abbey La Trappe in Normandy, of which Rancé was commendatory abbot. Amid many difficulties he succeeded, in A.D. 1665, in thoroughly reforming the wild monks, who were called "the bandits of La Trappe.' His rule enjoined on the monks perpetual silence, only broken in public prayer and singing and in uttering the greeting as they met, *Memento mori.* Their bed was a hard board with some straw; their only food was bread and water, roots, herbs, some fruit and vegetables, without butter, fat, or oil. Study was forbidden, and they occupied themselves with hard field labour. Their clothing was a dark-brown cloak worn on the naked body, with wooden shoes. Very few cloisters besides La Trappe submitted to such severities (§ 185, 2).—(8) The English Nuns, founded at St. Omer, in France, by Mary Ward, the daughter of an English Catholic nobleman, for the education of girls. Originally composed of English maidens, it was afterwards enlarged by receiving those of other nationalities, with establishments in Germany, Italy, and the Netherlands. It did not obtain papal confirmation, and in A.D. 1630 Urban VIII., giving heed to the calumnies of enemies, formally dissolved it on account of arrogance, insubordination, and heresy. All its institutions and schools were then closed, while Mary herself was imprisoned and given over to the Inquisition in Rome. Urban was soon convinced of her innocence and set her free. Her scattered nuns were now collected again, but succeeded only in A.D. 1703 in obtaining confirmation from Clement XI. Their chief tasks were the education of youth and care of the sick. They were arranged in three classes, according to their rank in life, and were bound by their vows for a year or at the most three years, after which they might return to the world and marry. Their chief centre was Bavaria with the mother cloister in Munich.—Continuation, § 165, 2.

9. **The Propaganda.**—Gregory XV. gave unity and strength to the efforts for conversion of heretics and heathens by instituting, in A.D, 1662, the *Congregatio de Propaganda Fide.* Urban VIII. in A.D. 1627 attached to it a missionary training school, recruited as far as possible from natives of the respective countries, like Loyola's *Collegium Germanicum* founded in A.D. 1552 (§ 151, 1). He was thus able every

---

[1] Wilson, "Life of Vincent de Paul." London, 1874.

Epiphany to astonish Romans and foreigners by what seemed a repetition of the pentecostal miracle of tongues. At this institute training in all languages was given, and breviaries, mass and devotional books, and handbooks were printed for the use of the missions. It was also the centre from which all missionary enterprises originated.—Continuation, § 204, 2.

10. Foreign Missions.—Even during this century the Jesuits excelled all others in missionary zeal. In A.D. 1608 they sent out from Madrid mission colonies among the wandering Indians of South America, and no Spaniard could settle there without their permission. The most thoroughly organized of these was that of Paraguay, in which, according to their own reports, over 100,000 converted savages lived happily and contented under the mild, patriarchal rule of the Jesuits for 140 years, A.D. 1610–1750; but according to another well informed, though perhaps not altogether impartial, account, that of Ibagnez, a member of the mission, expelled for advising submission to the decree depriving it of political independence, the paternal government was flavoured by a liberal dose of slave-driver despotism. It was at least an undoubted fact, notwithstanding the boasted patriarchal idyllic character of the Jesuit state, that the order amassed great wealth from the proceeds of the industry of their *protégés*.—Continuation, § 165, 3.

11. In the East Indies (§ 150, 1) the Jesuits had uninterrupted success. In A.D. 1606, in order to make way among the Brahmans, the Jesuit Rob. Nobili assumed their dress, avoided all contact with even the converts of low caste, giving them the communion elements not directly, but by an instrument, or laying them down for them outside the door, and as a Christian Brahman made a considerable impression upon the most exclusive classes.—In Japan the mission prospects were dark (§ 150, 2). Mendicants ard Jesuits opposed and mutually excommunicated one another. The Catholic Spaniards and Portuguese were at feud among themselves, and only agreed in intriguing against Dutch and English Protestants. When the land was opened to foreign trade, it became the gathering point of the moral scum of all European countries, and the traffic in Japanese slaves, especially by the Portuguese, brought discredit on the Christian cause. The idea gained ground that the efforts at Christianization were but a prelude to conquest by the Spaniards and Portuguese. In the new organization of the country by the *shiogun* Ijejasu all governors were to vow hostility to Christians and foreigners. In A.D. 1606 he forbad the observance of the Christian religion anywhere in the land. When the conspiracy of a Christian daimio was discovered, he caused, in A.D. 1614, whole shiploads of Jesuits, mendicants, and native priests to be sent out of the country. But as many of the banished returned, death was threatend against all who might be found, and in A.D. 1624 all foreigners, w th the ex-

ception of Chinese and Dutch, were rigorously driven out. And now a bloody persecution of native Christians began. Many thousands fled to China and the neighbouring islands; crowds of those remaining were buried alive or burnt on piles made up of the wood of Christian crosses. The victims displayed a martyr spirit like those of the early days. Those who escaped organized in A.D. 1637 an armed resistance, and held the fortress of Arima in face of the *shiogun's* army sent against them. After a three months' siege the fortress was conquered by the help of Dutch cannon; 37,000 were massacred in the fort, and the rest were hurled down from high rocks. . The most severe enactments were passed against Christians, and the edicts filled with fearful curses against "the wicked sect" and "the vile God" of the Christians were posted on all the bridges, street corners, and squares. Christianity now seemed to be completely stamped out. The recollection of this work, however, was still retained down to the nineteenth century. For when French missionaries went in A.D. 1860 to Nagasaki, they found to their surprise in the villages around thousands (?) who greeted them joyfully as the successors of the first Christian missionaries.

12. In China, after Ricci's death (§ 150, 1), the success of the mission continued uninterrupted. In A.D. 1628 a German Jesuit, Adam Schell, went out from Cologne, who gained great fame at court for his mathematical skill. Louis XIV. founded at Paris a missionary college, which sent out Jesuits thoroughly trained in mathematics. But Dominicans and Franciscans over and over again complained to Rome of the Jesuits. They never allowed missionaries of other orders to come near their own establishments, and actually drove them away from places where they had begun to work. They even opposed priests, bishops, and vicars-apostolic sent by the Propaganda, declared their papal briefs forgeries, forbad their congregations to have any intercourse with those "heretics," and under suspicion of Jansenism brought them before the Inquisition of Goa. Clement X. issued a firm-toned bull against such proceedings; but the Jesuits gave no heed to it, and attended only to their own general. The papal condemnation a century later of the Jesuits' accommodation scheme, and their permission of heathen rites and beliefs to the new converts, complained against by the Dominicans, was equally fruitless. In A.D. 1645 Innocent X. forbad this practice on pain of excommunication; but still they continued it till the decree was modified by Alexander VII. in A.D. 1656. After persistent complaints by the Dominicans, Innocent XII. appointed a new congregation in Rome to investigate the question, but their deliberations yielded no result for ten years. At last Clement XI. confirmed the first decree of Innocent X., condemned anew the so called Chinese rites, and sent the legate Thomas of Tournon in A.D. 1703 to enforce his decision. Tournon, received at first by the emperor

at Pekin with great consideration, fell into disfavour through Jesuit intrigues, was banished from the capital, and returned to Nankin. But as he continued his efforts from this point, and an attempt to poison him failed in A.D. 1707, he went to Macao, where he was put in prison by the Portuguese, in which he died in A.D. 1710. Clement XI., in A.D. 1715, issued his decree against the Chinese rites in a yet severer form; but the Franciscan who proclaimed the papal bull was put in prison as an offender against the laws of the country, and, after being maltreated for seventeen months, was banished. So proudly confident had the Jesuits become, that in A.D. 1720 they treated with scorn and contempt the papal legate Mezzabarba, Patri- arch of Alexandria, who tried by certain concessions to move them to submit. A more severe decree of Clement XII. of A.D. 1735 was scoffed at by being proclaimed only in the Latin original. Benedict XIV. succeeded for the first time, in A.D. 1742, in breaking down their oppo- sition, after the charges had been renewed by the Capuchin Norbert. All the Jesuit missionaries were now obliged by oath to exclude all pagan customs and rites; but with this all the glory and wonderful success of their Asiatic missions came to an end.—Continuation, § 165, 8.

13. Trade and Industry of the Jesuits.—As Christian missions gene- rally deserve credit, not only for introducing civilization and culture along with the preaching of the gospel into far distant heathen lands, but also for having greatly promoted the knowledge of countries, peoples, and languages among their fellow countrymen at home, open- ing up new fields for colonization and trade, these ends were also served by the world-wide missionary enterprises of the Jesuits, and were in perfect accordance with the character and intention of this order, which aimed at universal dominion. In carrying out these schemes the Jesuits abandoned the ascetical principles of their founder and their vow of poverty, amassing enormous wealth by securing in many parts a practical monopoly of trade. Their fifth general, Aquaviva (§ 149, 8), secured from Gregory XIII., avowedly in favour of the mission, exclusive right to trade with both Indies. They soon erected great factories in all parts of the world, and had ships laden with valuable merchandise on all seas. They had mines, farms, sugar plantations, apothecary shops, bakeries, etc., founded barks, sold relics, miracle-working amulets, rosaries, healing Ignatius- and Xavier-water (§ 149, 11), etc., and in successful legacy-hunting excelled all other orders. Urban VIII. and Clement XI. issued severe bulls against such abuses, but only succeeded in restricting them to some extent.—Continuation, § 165, 9.

14. An Apostate to Judaism.—Gabriel, or as he was called after circum- cision, Uriel Acosta, was sprung from a noble Portuguese family, origi-

nally Jewish. Doubting Christianity in consequence of the traffic in
indulgences, he at last repudiated the New Testament in favour of the
Old. He refused rich ecclesiastical appointments, fled to Amsterdam,
and there formally went over to Judaism. Instead of the biblical
Mosaism, however, he was disappointed to find only Pharisaic pride
and Talmudic traditionalism, against which he wrote a treatise in
A.D. 1623. The Jews now denounced him to the civil authorities as a
denier of God and immortality. The whole issue of his book was burnt.
Twice the synagogue thundered its ban against him. The first was
withdrawn on his recantation, and the second, seven years after, upon
his submitting to a severe flagellation. In spite of all he held to his
Sadducean standpoint to his end in A.D. 1647, when he died by his own
hand from a pistol shot, driven to despair by the unceasing persecution of the Jews.

§ 157. QUIETISM AND JANSENISM.

Down to the last quarter of the seventeenth century the
Spanish Mystics (§ 149, 16), and especially those attached to
Francis de Sales, were recognised as thoroughly orthodox.
But now the Jesuits appeared as the determined opponents
of all mysticism that savoured of enthusiasm. By means of
vile intrigues they succeeded in getting Molinos, Guyon, and
Fénelon condemned, as "Quietist" heretics, although the
founder of their party had been canonized and his doctrine
solemnly sanctioned by the pope. Yet more objectionable
to the Jesuits was that reaction toward Augustinianism
which, hitherto limited to the Dominicans (§ 149, 13), and
treated by them as a theological theory, was now spreading among other orders in the form of French Jansenism,
accompanied by deep moral earnestness and a revival of the
whole Christian life.

1. Francis de Sales and Madame Chantal.—Francis Count de Sales,
from A.D. 1602 Bishop of Geneva, i.e. *in partibus*, with Annecy as his
residence, had shown himself a good Catholic by his zeal in rooting
out Protestantism in Chablais, on the south of the Genevan lake. In
A.D. 1604 meeting the young widowed Baroness de Chantal, along with
whom at a later period he founded the Order of the Visitation of Mary
(§ 156, 7), he proved a good physician to her amid her sorrow, doubts,

and temptations. He sought to qualify himself for this task by reading the writings of St. Theresa. Teacher and scholar so profited by
their mystical studies, that in A.D. 1665 Alexander VII. deemed the one
worthy of canonization and the other of beatification. In A.D. 1877
Pius IX. raised Francis to the dignity of *doctor ecclesiæ*. His "Introduction to the Devout Life" affords a guide to laymen to the life of
the soul, amid all the disturbances of the world resting in calm contemplation and unselfish love of God. In the Catholic Church, next
to À Kempis' "Imitation of Christ," it is the most appreciated and
most widely used book of devotion. In his "*Theotime*" he leads the
reader deeper into the yearnings of the soul after fellowship with God,
and describes the perfect peace which the soul reaches in God.[1]

2. Michael Molinos.—After Francis de Sales a great multitude of
male and female apostles of the new mystical gospel sprang up, and
were favourably received by all the more moderate church leaders.
The reactionaries, headed by the Jesuits, sought therefore all the more
eagerly to deal severely with the Spaniard Michael Molinos. Having
settled in Rome in A.D. 1669, he soon became the most popular of father
confessors. His "Spiritual Guide" in A.D. 1675 received the approval
of the Holy Office, and was introduced into Protestant Germany through
a Latin translation by Francke in A.D. 1687, and a German translation in
A.D. 1699 by Arnold. In it he taught those who came to the confessional
that the way to the perfection of the Christian life, which consists in
peaceful rest in the most intimate communion with God, is to be found
in spiritual conference, secret prayer, active and passive contemplation, in rigorous destruction of all self-will, and in disinterested love
of God, fortified, wherever that is possible, by daily communion. The
success of the book was astonishing. It promptly influenced all ranks
and classes, both men and women, lay and clerical, not only in Italy,
but also by means of translations in France and Spain. But soon a
reaction set in. As early as A.D. 1681 the famous Jesuit Segneri issued a
treatise, in which he charged Molinos' contemplative mysticism with
onesidedness and exaggeration. He was answered by the pious and
learned Oratorian Petrucci. A commission, appointed by the Inquisition to examine the writings of both parties, pronounced the views of
Molinos and Petrucci to be in accordance with church doctrine and
Segneri's objections to be unfounded. All that Jesuitism reckoned
as foundation, means, and end of piety was characterized as purely
elementary. No hope could be entertained of winning over Innocent
XI., the bitter enemy of the Jesuits. But Louis XIV. of France,
at the instigation of his Jesuit father confessor, Lachaise, expressed

---

[1] Marsolier, "Life of Francis de Sales," translated by Coombes,
London, 1812.

through his ambassador his surprise that his holiness should, not
only tolerate, but even encourage and support so dangerous a heretic,
who taught all Christendom to undervalue the public services of the
Church.   In A.D. 1685 Innocent referred the matter to the tribunal
of the Inquisition.   Throughout the two years during which the
investigation proceeded all arts were used to secure condemnation.
Extreme statements of fanatical adherents of Molinos were not rarely
met with, depreciating the public ordinances and ceremonies, confession,
hearing of mass, church prayers, rosaries, etc.   The pope, facile with
age, amid groans and lamentations, allowed things to take their course,
and at last confirmed the decree of the Inquisition of August 28th,
A.D. 1687, by which Molinos was found guilty of spreading godless
doctrine, and sixty-eight propositions, partly from his own writings,
partly from the utterances of his adherents, were condemned as heretical
and blasphemous.   The heretic was to abjure his heresies publicly, clad
in penitential garments, and was then consigned to lifelong solitary
confinement in a Dominican cloister, where he died in A.D. 1697.[1]

8. Madame Guyon and Fénelon.—After her husband's death, Madame
Guyon, in company with her father confessor, the Barnabite Lacombe,
who had been initiated during a long residence at Rome into the
mysteries of Molinist mysticism, spent five years travelling through
France, Switzerland, Savoy, and Piedmont.   Though already much suspected, she won the hearts of many men and women among the clergy
and laity, and enkindled in them by personal conference, correspondence, and her literary work, the ardour of mystical love.   Her brilliant
writings are indeed disfigured by traces of foolish exaggeration, fanaticism and spiritual pride.   She calls herself the woman of Revelation
xii. 1, and the *mère de la grace* of her adherents.   The following
are the main distinguishing characteristics of her mysticism : The
necessity of turning away from everything creaturely, rejecting all
earthly pleasure and destroying every selfish interest, as well as of
turning to God in passive contemplation, silent devotion, naked faith,
which dispensed with all intellectual evidence, and pure disinterested
love, which loves God for Himself alone, not for the eternal salvation
obtained through Him.   On her return to Paris with Lacombe in
A.D. 1686 the proper martyrdom of her life began.   Her chief persecutor was her step-brother, the Parisian superior of the Barnabites,
La Mothe, who spread the most scandalous reports about his half-sister
and Lacombe, and had them both imprisoned by a royal decree in
A.D. 1688.   Lacombe never regained his liberty.   Taken from one
prison to another, he lost his reason, and died in an asylum in A.D.

---

[1] "Golden Thoughts from the 'Spiritual Guide' of Molinos." With
preface by J. H. Shorthouse.   London, 1883.

1699. Madame Guyon, however, by the influence of Madame de Maintenon, was released after ten months' confinement. The favour of this
royal dame was not of long continuance. Warned on all sides of the
dangerous heretic, she broke off all intercourse with her in A.D. 1693,
and persuaded the king to appoint a new commission, in A.D. 1694, with
Bishop Bossuet of Meaux at its head, to examine her suspected writings.
This commission meeting at Issy, had already, in February, A.D. 1695,
drawn up thirty test articles, when Fénelon, tutor of the king's grandson,
and now nominated to the archbishopric of Cambray, was ordered by
the king to take part in the proceedings. He signed the articles,
though he objected to much in them, and had four articles of his own
added. Madame Guyon also did so, and Bossuet at last testified for
her that he had found her moral character stainless and her doctrine
free from Molinist heresy. But the bigot Maintenon was not satisfied
with this. Bossuet demanded the surrender of this certificate that he
might draw up another; and when Madame Guyon refused, on the
basis of a statement by the crazed Lacombe, she was sent to the Bastile
in A.D. 1696. In A.D. 1697 Fénelon had written in her defence his
"*Explication des Maximes des Saintes sur la Vie Intérieur*," showing
that the condemned doctrines of passive contemplation, secret prayer,
naked faith, and disinterested love, had all been previously taught by
St. Theresa, John of the Cross, Francis de Sales, and other saints. He
sent this treatise for an opinion to Rome. A violent controversy then
arose between Bossuet and Fénelon. The pious, well-meaning pope,
Innocent XII., endeavoured vainly to bring about a good understanding.
Bossuet and the all-powerful Maintenon wished no reconciliation, but
condemnation, and gave the king and pope no rest till very reluctantly
he prohibited the objectionable book by a brief in A.D. 1699, and
condemned twenty-three propositions from it as heretical. Fénelon,
strongly attached to the church, and a bitter persecutor of Protestants,
made an unconditional surrender, as guilty of a defective exposition
of the truth. But Madame Guyon continued in the Bastile till A.D.
1701, when she retired to Blois, where she died in A.D. 1717. Bossuet
had died in A.D. 1704, and Fénelon in A.D. 1715. She published only
two of her writings: "An Exposition of the Song," and the "*Moyen
Court et très Facile de faire Oraison*." Many others, including her translation and expositions of the Bible, were during her lifetime edited in
twenty volumes by her friend, the Reformed preacher of the Palatinate,
Peter Poiret.[1]

---

[1] Upham, "Life, Religious Opinions, and Experience of Madame de
la Mothe Guyon, with an account of Fénelon." London, 1854. Brooke,
"Exemplary Life of the Pious Lady Guion." Bristol, 1806. Butler,
"Life of Fénelon." London, 1810.

4. Mysticism Tinged with Theosophy and Pantheism. — Antoinette Bourignon, the daughter of a rich merchant of Lille, in France, while matron of a hospital in her native city, had in A.D. 1662 gathered around her a party of believers in her theosophic and fantastic revelations. She was obliged to flee to the Netherlands, and there, by the force of her eloquence in speech and writing, spread her views among the Protestants. Among them she attracted the great scientist Swammerdam. But when she introduced politics, she escaped imprisonment only by flight. Down to her death in A.D. 1680 she earnestly and successfully prosecuted her mission in north-west Germany. Peter Poiret collected her writings and published them in twenty-one volumes at Amsterdam, in A.D. 1679.—Quite of another sort was the pantheistic mysticism of Angelus Silesius. Originally a Protestant physician at Breslau, he went over to the Romish church in A.D. 1653, and in consequence received from Vienna the honorary title of physician to the emperor. He was made priest in A.D. 1661, and till his death in A.D. 1677 maintained a keen polemic against the Protestant church with all a pervert's zeal. Most of his hymns belong to his Protestant period. As a Catholic he wrote his "*Cherubinischer Wandersmann*," a collection of rhymes in which, with childish *naïveté* and hearty, gushing ardour, he merges self into the abyss of the universal Deity, and develops a system of the most pronounced pantheism.

5. Jansenism in its first Stage.—Bishop Cornelius Jansen, of Ypres, who died in A.D. 1638, gave the fruits of his lifelong studies of Augustine in his learned work, "*Augustinus s. doctr. Aug. de humanæ Naturæ Sanitate, Ægritudine, et Medicina adv. Pelagianos et Massilienses*," which was published after his death in three volumes, Louvain, 1640 The Jesuits induced Urban VIII., in A.D. 1642, to prohibit it in his bull *In eminenti.* Augustine's numerous followers in France felt themselves hit by this decree. Jansen's pupil at Port Royal from A.D. 1635, Duvergier de Hauranne, usually called St. Cyran, from the Benedictine monastery of which he was abbot, was the bitter foe of the Jesuits and Richelieu, who had him cast into prison in A.D. 1638, from which he was liberated after the death of the cardinal in A.D. 1643, and shortly before his own. Another distinguished member of the party was Antoine Arnauld, doctor of the Sorbonne, who died in A.D. 1694, the youngest of twenty children of a parliamentary advocate, whose powerful defence of the University of Paris against the Jesuits called forth their hatred and lifelong persecution. His mantle, as a vigorous polemist, had fallen upon his youngest son. Very important too was the influence of his much older sister, Angelica Arnauld, Abbess of the Cistercian cloister of Port Royal des Champs, six miles from Paris, which under her became the centre of religious life and effort for all

France. Around her gathered some of the noblest, most pious, and talented men of the time: the poet Racine, the mathematician and apologist Pascal, the Bible translator De Sacy, the church historian Tillemont, all ardent admirers of Augustine and determined opponents of the lax morality of the Jesuits. Arnauld's book, "*De la fréquente Communion*," was approved by the Sorbonne, the Parliament, and the most distinguished of the French clergy; but in A.D. 1653 Innocent X. condemned five Jansenist propositions in it as heretical. The Augustinians now maintained that these doctrines were not taught in the sense attributed to them by the pope. Arnauld distinguished the *question du fait* from the *question du droit*, maintaining that the latter only were subject to the judgment of the Holy See. The Sorbonne, now greatly changed in composition and character, expelled him on account of this position from its corporation in A.D. 1656. About this time, at Arnauld's instigation, Pascal, the profound and brilliant author of "*Pensées sur la Religion*," began, under the name of Louis de Montalte to publish his famous "Provincial Letters," which in an admirable style exposed and lashed with deep earnestness and biting wit the base moral principles of Jesuit casuistry. The truly annihilating effect of these letters upon the reputation of the powerful order could not be checked by their being burnt by order of Parliament by the hangman at Aix in A.D. 1657, and at Paris in A.D. 1660. But meanwhile the specifically Jansenist movement entered upon a new phase of its development. Alexander VII. had issued in A.D. 1656 a bull which denounced the application of the distinction *du fait* and *du droit* to the papal decrees as derogatory to the holy see, and affirmed that Jansen taught the five propositions in the sense they had been condemned. In order to enforce the sentence, Annal, the Jesuit father confessor of Louis XIV., obtained in 1661 a royal decree requiring all French clergy, monks, nuns, and teachers to sign a formula unconditionally accepting this bull. Those who refused were banished, and fled mostly to the Netherlands. The sorely oppressed nuns of Port Royal at last reluctantly agreed to sign it; but they were still persecuted, and in A.D. 1664 the new archbishop, Perefixe, inaugurated a more severe persecution, placed this cloister under the interdict, and removed some of the nuns to other convents. In A.D. 1669, Alexander's successor, Clement IX., secured the submission of Arnauld, De Sacy, Nicole, and many of the nuns by a policy of mild connivance. But the hatred of the Jesuits was still directed against their cloister. In A.D. 1705 Clement XI. again demanded full and unconditioned acceptance of the decree of Alexander VII., and when the nuns refused, the pope, in A.D. 1708, declared this convent an irredeemable nest of heresy, and ordered its suppression, which was carried out in A.D. 1709. In A.D. 1710 cloister and church were levelled to the ground, and the very corpses taken out of their graves.[1]—Continuation, § 165, 7.

§ 158. Science and Art in the Catholic Church.

Catholic theology flourished during the seventeenth century as it had never done since the twelfth and thirteenth. Especially in the liberal Gallican church there was a vigorous scientific life. The Parisian Sorbonne and the orders of the Jesuits, St. Maur, and the Oratorians, excelled in theological, particularly in patristic and historical, learning, and the contemporary brilliancy of Reformed theology in France afforded a powerful stimulus. But the best days of art, especially Italian painting, were now past. Sacred music was diligently cultivated, though in a secularized style, and many gifted hymn-writers made their appearance in Spain and Germany.

1. Theological Science (§ 149, 14).—The parliamentary advocate, Mich. le Jay, published at his own expense the Parisian Polyglott in ten folio vols., A.D. 1629–1645, which, besides complete Syriac and Arabic translations, included also the Samaritan. The chief contributor was the Oratorian Morinus, who edited the LXX. and the Samaritan texts, which he regarded as incomparably superior to the Masoretic text corrupted by the Jews. The Jansenists produced a French translation of the Bible with practical notes, condemned by the pope, but much read by the people. It was mainly the work of the brothers De Sacy. The New Testament was issued in A.D. 1667 and the Old Testament somewhat later, called the Bible of Mons from the fictitious name of the place of publication. Richard Simon, the Oratorian, who died in A.D. 1712, treated Scripture with a boldness of criticism never before heard of within the church. While opposed by many on the Catholic side, the curia favoured his work as undermining the Protestant doctrine of Scripture. Cornelius à Lapide, who died A.D. 1637, expounded Scripture according to the fourfold sense.—In systematic theology the old scholastic method still held sway. Moral theology was wrought out in the form

---

[1] Beard, "Port Royal." 2 vols. London, 1861. St. Amour, 'Journal in France and Rome, containing Account of Five Points of Controversy between Jansenists and Molinists." London, 1664. Schimmelpenninck, "Select Memoirs of Port Royal." Fourth edition 2 vols. London, 1835.

of casuistry with unexampled lasciviousness, especially by the Jesuits (§ 149, 10). The work of the Spaniard Escobar, who died in A.D. 1669, ran through fifty editions, and that of Busembaum, professor in Cologne and afterwards rector of Münster, who died A.D. 1668, went through seventy editions. On account of the attempted assassination of Louis XV. by Damiens in A.D. 1757, with which the Jesuits and their doctrine of tyrannicide were charged, the Parliament of Toulouse in A.D. 1757, and of Paris in A.D. 1761, had Busembaum's book publicly burnt, and several popes, Alexander VII., VIII., and Innocent XI., condemned a number of propositions from the moral writings of these and other Jesuits. Among polemical writers the most distinguished were Becanus, who died in A.D. 1624, and Bossuet (§ 153, 7). Among the Jansenists the most prominent controversialists were Nicole and Arnauld, who, in order to escape the reproach of Calvinism, sought to prove the Catholic doctrine of the supper to be the same as that of the apostles, and were answered by the Reformed theologians Claude and Jurieu. In apologetics the leading place is occupied by Pascal with his brilliant "Pensées." Huetius, a French bishop and editor of Origen, who died in A.D. 1721, replied to Spinoza's attacks on the Pentateuch, and applying to reason itself the Cartesian principle, that philosophy must begin with doubt, pointed the doubter to the supernatural revealed truths in the Catholic church as the only anchor of salvation. The learned Jesuit Dionysius Petavius, who died in A.D. 1652, edited Epiphanius and wrote gigantic chronological works and numerous violent polemics against Calvinists and Jansenists. His chief work is the unfinished patristic-dogmatic treatise in five vols. folio, A.D. 1680, "De theologicis Dogmatibus." The Oratorian Thomassinus wrote an able archæological work: "Vetus et Nova Eccl. Disciplina circa Beneficia et Beneficiarios."

2. In church history, besides those named in § 5, 2, we may mention Pagi, the keen critic and corrector of Baronius. The study of sources was vigorously pursued. We have collections of mediæval writings and documents by Sirmond, D'Achery, Mabillon, Martène, Baluzius; of acts of councils by Labbé and Cossart, those of France by Jac. Sirmond, and of Spain by Aguirre; acts of the martyrs by Ruinart; monastic rules by Holstenius, a pervert, who became Vatican librarian, and died at Rome A.D. 1661. Dufresne Ducange, an advocate, who died in A.D. 1688, wrote glossaries of the mediæval and barbarous Latin and Greek, indispensable for the study of documents belonging to those times. The greatest prodigy of learning was Mabillon, who died in A.D. 1707, a Benedictine of St. Maur, and historian of his order. Pet. de Marca, who died Archbishop of Paris A.D. 1662, wrote the famous work on the Gallican liberties "De Concordia Sacerdotii et Imperii." The Jansenist doctor of the Sorbonne, Elias du Pin, who died A.D. 1719, wrote

"*Nouvelle Bibliothèque des Auteurs Eccles.*" in forty-seven vols. The Jesuit Maimbourg, died A.D. 1686, compiled several party histories of Wiclifism, Lutheranism, and Calvinism; but as a Gallican was deprived of office by the pope, and afterwards supported by a royal pension. The Antwerp Jesuits Bolland, Henschen, Papebroch started, in A.D. 1643, the gigantic work "*Acta Sanctorum,*" carried on by the learned members of their order in Belgium, known as Bollandists. It was stopped by the French invasion of A.D. 1794, when it had reached October 15th with the fifty-third folio vol. The Belgian Jesuits continued the work from A.D. 1845-1867, reaching in six vols. the end of October, but not displaying the ability and liberality of their predecessors. In Venice Paul Sarpi (§ 155, 2) wrote a history of the Tridentine Council, one of the most brilliant historical works of any period. Leo Allatius, a Greek convert at Rome, who died in A.D. 1669, wrote a work to show the agreement of the Eastern and Western churches. Cardinal Bona distinguished himself as a liturgical writer.—In France pulpit eloquence reached the highest pitch in such men as Flechier, Bossuet, Bourdaloue, Fénelon, Massillon, and Bridaine. In Vienna Abraham à St. Clara inveighed in a humorous, grotesque way against the corruption of manners, with an undercurrent of deep moral earnestness. Similar in style and spirit, but much more deeply sunk in Catholic superstition, was his contemporary the Capuchin Martin of Cochem, who missionarized the Rhine Provinces and western Germany for forty years, and issued a large number of popular religious tracts.—Continuation, § 165, 14.

3. Art and Poetry (§ 149, 15).—The greatest master of the musical school founded by Palestrina was *Allêgri*, whose *Miserere* is performed yearly on the Wednesday afternoon of Passion Week in the Sistine Chapel in Rome. The oratorio originated from the application of the lofty music of this school to dramatic scenes drawn from the Bible, for purely musical and not theatrical performance. Philip Neri patronized this music freely in his oratory, from which it took the name. This new church music became gradually more and more secularized and approximated to the ordinary opera style.—In ecclesiastical architecture the Renaissance style still prevailed, but debased with senseless, tasteless ornamentation.—In the Italian school of painting the decline, both in creative power and imitative skill, was very marked from the end of the sixteenth century. In Spain during the seventeenth century religious painting reached a high point of excellence in Murillo of Seville, who died in A.D. 1682, a master in representing calm meditation and entranced felicity.—The two greatest poets of Spain, the creators of the Spanish drama, Lope de Vega (died A.D. 1635) and Pedro Calderon (died A.D. 1681), both at first soldiers and afterwards priests, flourished during this century. The elder excelled the younger, not only in

fruitfulness and versatility (1,500 comedies, 320 autos, § 115, 12, etc.), but also in poetic genius and patriotism. Calderon, with his 122 dramas, 73 festival plays, 200 preludes, etc., excelled De Vega in artistic expression and beauty of imagery. Both alike glorify the Inquisition, but occasionally subordinate Mary and the saints to the great redemption of the cross.—Specially deserving of notice is the noble German Jesuit Friedr. von Spee, died A.D. 1635. His spiritual songs show deep love to the Saviour and a profound feeling for nature, approaching in some respects the style of the evangelical hymn-writers. Spee was a keen but unsuccessful opponent of witch prosecution. Another eminent poetic genius of the age was the Jesuit Jac. Balde of Munich, who died in A.D. 1688. He is at his best in lyrical poetry. A deep religious vein runs through all his Latin odes, in which he enthusiastically appeals to the Virgin to raise him above all earthly passions. To Herder belongs the merit of rescuing him from oblivion.

III.—The Lutheran Church.

§ 159. ORTHODOXY AND ITS BATTLES.[1]

The Formula of Concord commended itself to the hearts and intelligences of Lutherans, and secured a hundred years' supremacy of orthodoxy, notwithstanding two Christological controversies. Gradually, however, a new dogmatic scholasticism arose, which had the defects as well as the excellences of the mediæval system. The orthodoxy of this school deteriorated, on the one hand, into violent polemic on confessional differences, and, on the other, into undue depreciation of outward forms in favour of a spiritual life and personal piety. These tendencies are represented by the Syncretist and Pietist controversies.

1. Christological Controversies.—(1) The Cryptist and Kenotist Controversy between the Giessen and Tübingen theologians, in A.D. 1619, about Christ's state of humiliation, led to the publication of many violent treatises down to A.D. 1626. The Kenotists of Giessen, with Mentzer and Feuerborn at their head, assigned the humiliation only to the human nature, and explained it as an actual κένωσις, i.e. a complete but voluntary resigning of the omnipresence and omnipotence im-

---

[1] Dorner, "History of Protestant Theology," vol. ii., pp. 98–251.

manent in His divinity (κτῆσις, but not χρῆσις), yet so that He could have them at His command at any moment, *e.g.* in His miracles. The Cryptists of Tübingen, with Luc. Osiander and Thumm at their head, ascribed humiliation to both natures, and taught that all the while Christ, even *secundum carnem*, was omnipresent and ruled both in heaven and earth, but in a hidden way; the humiliation is no κένωσις, but only a κρύψις. After repeated unsuccessful attempts to bring about a reconciliation, John George, Elector of Saxony, in A.D. 1623, accepted the Kenotic doctrine. But the two parties still continued their strife.[1]— 2. The Lütkemann Controversy on the humanity of Christ in death was of far less importance. Lütkemann, a professor of philosophy at Rostock, affirmed that in death, because the unity of soul and body was broken, Christ was not true man, and that to deny this was to destroy the reality and the saving power of his death. He held that the incarnation of Christ lasted through death, because the divine nature was connected, not only with the soul, but also with the body Lütkemann was obliged to quit Rostock, but got an honourable call to Brunswick as superintendent and court preacher, and there died in A.D. 1655. Later Lutherans treated the controversy as a useless logomachy.

2. The Syncretist Controversy.—Since the Hofmann controversy (§ 141, 15) the University of Helmstadt had shown a decided humanistic tendency, and gave even greater freedom in the treatment of doctrines than the Formula of Concord, which it declined to adopt. To this school belonged George Calixt, and from A.D. 1614 for forty years he laboured in promoting its interests. He was a man of wide culture and experience, who had obtained a thorough knowledge of church history, and acquaintance with the most distinguished theologians of all churches, during his extensive foreign travels, and therewith a geniality and breadth of view not by any means common in those days. He did not indeed desire any formal union between the different churches, but rather a mutual recognition, love, and tolerance. For this purpose he set, as a secondary principle of Christian theology, besides Scripture, as the primary principle, the consensus of the first five centuries as the common basis of all churches, and sought to represent later ecclesiastical differences as unessential or of less consequence. This was denounced by strict Lutherans as Syncretism and Cryptocatholicism. In A.D. 1639 the Hanoverian preacher Buscher charged him with being a secret Papist. After the Thorn Conference of A.D. 1645, a violent controversy arose, which divided Lutherans into two camps. On the one side were the universities of Helmstadt and Königsberg; on the other hand, the theologians of the electorate of

---

[1] Bruce. "Humiliation of Christ." p. 131. Edin., 1876.

Saxony, Hülsemann of Leipzig, Waller of Dresden, and Abr. Calov, who died professor in Wittenberg in A.D. 1686. Calov wrote twenty-six controversial treatises on this subject. Jena vainly sought to mediate between the parties. In the *Theologorum Sax. Consensus repetitus Fidei vera Lutheranæ* of A.D. 1655, for which the Wittenberg divines failed to secure symbolical authority, the following sentiments were branded as Syncretist errors: That in the Apostles' Creed everything is taught that is necessary to salvation; that the Catholic and Reformed systems retain hold of fundamental truths; that original sin is of a merely privative nature; that God *indirecte, improprie, et per accidens* is the cause of sin; that the doctrine of the Trinity was first clearly revealed in the New Testament, etc. Calixt died A.D. 1656 in the midst of most violent controversies. His son Ulrich continued these, but had neither the ability nor moderation of his father. Even the peaceably disposed Conference of Cassel of A.D. 1661 (§ 154, 4) only poured oil on the flames. The strife lost itself at last in actions for damages between the younger Calixt and his bitter opponent Strauch of Wittenberg. Wearied of these fruitless discussions, theologians now turned their attention to the rising movement of Pietism.[1]

3. The Pietist Controversy in its First Stage.—Philip Jacob Spener born in Alsace in A.D. 1635, was in his thirty-first year, on account of his spirituality, distinguished gifts, and singularly wide scholarship, made president of a clerical seminary at Frankfort-on-Main. In A.D. 1686 he became chief court preacher at Dresden, and provost of Berlin in A.D. 1691, when, on account of his intense earnestness in pastoral work, he had been expelled from Dresden. He died in Berlin in A.D. 1705. His year's attendance at Geneva after the completion of his curriculum at Strassburg had an important influence on his whole future career. He there learned to value discipline for securing purity of life as well as of doctrine, and was also powerfully impressed by the practical lectures of Labadie (§ 163, 7) and the reading of the "Practice of Piety" and other ascetical writings of the English Puritans (§ 162, 3). Though strongly attached to the Lutheran church, he believed that in the restoration of evangelical doctrine by the Wittenberg Reformation, "not by any means had all been accomplished that needed to be done," and that Lutheranism in the form of the orthodoxy of the age had lost the living power of the reformers, and was in danger of burying its talent in dead and barren service of the letter. There was therefore a pressing need of a new and wider reformation. In the Lutheran church, as the depository of sound doctrine, he recognised the fittest field for the development of a

---

[1] Dowding, "German Theology during the Thirty Years' War: Life and Correspondence of G. Calixt." 2 vols. Oxford, 1863.

genuinely Christian life ; but he heartily appreciated any true spiritual movement in whatsoever church it arose. He went back from
scholastic dogmatics to Holy Scripture as the living source of saving
knowledge, substituted for the external orthodox theology the theology
of the heart, demanded evidence of this in a pious Christian walk :
these were the means by which he sought to promote his reformation.
A whole series of Lutheran theologians of the seventeenth century
(§ 159) had indeed contributed to this same end by their devotional
works, hymns, and sermons. What was new in Spener was the conviction of the insufficiency of the hitherto used means and the undue
prominence given to doctrine, and his consequent effort vigorously
made to raise the tone of the Christian life. In his childlike, pious
humility he regarded himself as by no means called to carry out
this work, but felt it his duty to insist upon the necessity of it, and
indicate the means that should be used to realize it. This he did in
his work of A.D. 1675, "*Pia Desideria.*" As it was his aim to recom-
mend biblical practical Christianity to the heart of the individual
Christian, he revived the almost forgotten doctrine "Of Spiritual
Priesthood" in a separate treatise. In A.D. 1670 he began to have
meetings in his own house for encouraging Christian piety in the
community, which soon were imitated in other places. Spener's influence on the Lutheran church became greater and wider through his
position at Dresden. Stirred up by his spirit, three young graduates
of Leipzig, A. H. Francke, Paul Anton, and J. K. Schade, formed in
A.D. 1686 a private *Collegia Philobiblica* for practical exposition of
Scripture and the delivery of public exegetical lectures at the university in the German language. But the Leipzig theological faculty,
with J. B. Carpzov II. at its head, charged them with despising the
public ordinances as well as theological science, and with favouring
the views of separatists. The *Collegia Philobiblica* was suppressed, and
the three friends obliged to leave Leipzig in A.D. 1690. This marked
the beginning of the Pietist controversies. Soon afterwards Spener
was expelled from Dresden ; but in his new position at Berlin he secured
great influence in the appointments to the theological faculty of the
new university founded at Halle by the peace-loving elector Frederick
III. of Brandenburg, in opposition to the contentious universities of
Wittenberg and Leipzig. Francke, Anton, and Breithaupt were made
professors of theology. Halle now won the position which Wittenberg
and Geneva had held during the Reformation period, and the Pietist
controversy thus entered upon a second, more general, and more critical
epoch of its history.[1]—Continuation, § 166, 1.

---

[1] Wildenhahn, " Life of Spener," translated by Wenzel. Philadelphia, 1881. Guericke, " Life of A. H. Francke." London, 1847.

4. Theological Literature (§ 142, 6).—The "*Philologia Sacra*" of Sol. Glassius of Jena, published in A.D. 1623, has ranked as a classical work for almost two centuries. From A.D. 1620 till the end of the century, a lively controversy was carried on about the Greek style of the New Testament, in which Lutherans, and especially the Reformed, took part. The purists maintained that the New Testament idiom was pure and classical, thinking that its inspiration would otherwise be endangered. The first historico-critical introduction to the Scriptures was the "*Officina Biblica*" of Walther in A.D. 1636. Pfeiffer of Leipzig gained distinction in biblical criticism and hermeneutics by his "*Critica Sacra*" of A.D. 1680 and "*Hermeneutica*" of A.D. 1684. Exegesis now made progress, notwithstanding its dependence on traditional interpretations of doctrinal proof passages and its mechanical theory of inspiration. The most distinguished exegetes were Erasmus Schmidt of Wittenberg, who died in A.D. 1637: he wrote a Latin translation of New Testament with admirable notes, and a very useful concordance of the Greek New Testament, under the title Ταμεῖον, which has been revised and improved by Bruder; Seb. Schmidt of Strassburg, who wrote commentaries on several Old Testament books and on the Pauline epistles; and Abr. Calov of Wittenberg, who died in A.D. 1686, in his 74th year, whose "*Biblia Illustrata*," in four vols., is a work of amazing research and learning, but composed wholly in the interests of dogmatics.—Little was done in the department of church history. Calixt awakened a new enthusiasm for historical studies, and Gottfried Arnold (§ 159, 2), pietist, chiliast, and theosophist, bitterly opposed to every form of orthodoxy, and finding true Christianity only in sects, separatists, and heretics, set the whole theological world astir by his "*Unparteiische Kirchen- und Ketzer-historie*," in A.D. 1699 (§ 5, 3).

5. The orthodox school applied itself most diligently to dogmatics in a strictly scholastic form. Hutter of Wittenberg, who died in A.D. 1616, wrote "*Loci communes theologici*" and "*Compendium Loc. Theol.*" John Gerhard of Jena, who died in A.D. 1637, published in A.D. 1610 his "*Loc. Theologici*" in nine folio vols., the standard of Lutheran orthodoxy. J. Andr. Quenstedt of Wittenberg, who died A.D. 1688, exhibited the best and worst of Lutheran scholasticism in his "*Theol. didactico-polemica.*" The most important dogmatist of the Calixtine school was Conrad Horneius. Calixt himself is known as a dogmatist only by his lectures; but to him we owe the generally adopted distinction between morals and dogmatics as set forth in his "*Epitome theol. Moralis.*"—Polemics were carried on vigorously. Hoë von Hoënegg of Dresden (§ 154, 3, 4) and Hutter of Wittenberg were bitter opponents of Calvinism and Romanism. Hutter was styled by his friends *Malleus Calvinistorum* and *Redonatus Lutherus*. The ablest and most dignified polemic against Romanism was that of John Gerhard in his "*Confessio Catholica.*"

Nich. Hunnius, son of Ægid. Hunnius, and Hutter's successor at Wittenberg, from A.D. 1623 superintendent at Lübeck, distinguished himself as an able controversialist against the papacy by his "*Demonstratio
Ministerii Lutherani Divini atque Legitimi.*" Against the Socinians he
wrote his "*Examen Errorum Photinianorum*," and against the fanatics
a "Chr. Examination of the new Paracelsist and Weigelian Theology."
His principal work is his "Διάσκεψις de *Fundamentali Dissensu Doctrinæ Luth. et Calvin.*" His "*Epitome Credendorum*" went through
nineteen editions. The most incessant controversialist was Abr. Calov,
who wrote against Syncretists, Papists, Socinians, Arminians, etc.—
Continuation, § 167, 4.

§ 160. THE RELIGIOUS LIFE.

The attachment of the Lutheran church of this age to pure
doctrine led to a one-sided over-estimation of it, often ending
in dead orthodoxy. But a succession of able and learned
theologians, who recognised the importance of heart theology
as well as sound doctrine, corrected this evil tendency by
Scripture study, preaching, and faithful pastoral work. A
noble and moderate mysticism, which was thoroughly orthodox in its beliefs, and opposing orthodoxy only where that
had become external and mechanical, had many influential
representatives throughout the whole country, especially
during the first half of it. But also separatists, mystics, and
theosophists made their appearance, who were decidedly
hostile to the church. Sacred song flourished afresh amid
the troubles of the Thirty Years' War; but gradually lost its
sublime objective church character, which was poorly compensated by a more flowing versification, polished language,
and elegant form. A corresponding advance was also made
in church music.

1. **Mysticism and Asceticism.**—At the head of the orthodox mystics stands John Arndt. His "True Christianity" and his "*Paradies-
gärtlein*" are the most widely read Lutheran devotional books, but
called forth the bitter hostility of those devoted to the maintenance
of a barren orthodoxy. He died in A.D. 1621, as general superintendent at Celle. He had been expelled from Anhalt because he would

not condemn exorcism as godless superstition, and was afterwards
in Brunswick publicly charged by his colleague Denecke and other
Lutheran zealots with Papacy, Calvinism, Osiandrianism, Flacianism,
Schwenckfeldism, Paracelsism, Alchemism, etc. As men of a similar
spirit, anticipators of the school of Spener, may be named John Gerhard
of Jena, with his "*Meditationes Sacræ*" and "*Schola pietatis*," and
Christian Scriver, whose "Gotthold's Emblems" is well known to
English readers. Rahtmann of Danzig maintained that the word
of God in Scripture has not in itself the power to enlighten and
convert men except through the gracious influence of God's Spirit.
He was supported, after a long delay, in A.D. 1626 by the University
of Rostock, but opposed by Königsberg, Jena, and Wittenberg. In
A.D. 1628, the Elector of Saxony obtained the opinion of the most famous
theologians of his realm against Rahtmann; but his death, which
soon followed, brought the controversy to a close.—The Württemberg
theologian, John Valentine Andreä, grandson of one of the authors of
the Formula of Concord, was a man of striking originality, famous
for his satires on the corruptions of the age. His "Order of Rosicrucians," published at Cassel in A.D. 1614, ridiculed the absurdities
of astrology and alchemy in the form of a satirical romance. His
influence on the church of his times was great and wholesome, so that
even Spener exclaimed: "Had I the power to call any one from the
dead for the good of the church, it would be J. V. Andreä." His
later devotional work was almost completely forgotten until attention
was called to it by Herder.[1]

2. Mysticism and Theosophy.— A mystico-theosophical tendency,
partly in outward connexion with the church, partly without and
in open opposition to it, was fostered by the alchemist writings of
Agrippa and Paracelsus, the theosophical works of Weigel (§ 146, 2)
and by the profound revelations of the inspired shoemaker of Görlitz, Jacob Boehme, *philosophus teutonicus*, the most talented of all the
theosophists. In a remarkable degree he combined a genius for
speculation with the most unfeigned piety that held firmly by the old
Lutheran faith. Even when an itinerant tradesman, he felt himself
for a period of seven days in calm repose, surrounded by the divine
light. But he dates his profound theosophical enlightenment from
a moment in A.D. 1594, when as a young journeyman and married,
thrown into an ecstasy, he obtained a knowledge of the divine mysteries down to the ultimate principles of all things and their inmost
quality. His theosophy, too, like that of the ancient gnostics, springs
out of the question about the origin of evil. He solves it by assuming

[1] Jennings, "The Rosicrucians: their Rites and Mysteries." London, 1887.

an emanation of all things from God, in whom fire and light, bitter and sweet qualities, are thoroughly tempered and perfectly combined, while in the creature derived by emanation from him they are in disharmony, but are reconciled and reduced to godlike harmony through regeneration in Christ. Though opposed by Calov, he was befriended by the Dresden consistory. Boehme died in A.D. 1624, in retirement at Görlitz, in the arms of his family.[1]—In close connexion with Boehmists, separatists, and Pietists, yet differing from them all, Gottfried Arnold abused orthodoxy and canonized the heretics of all ages. In A.D. 1700 he wrote "The Mystery of the Divine Sophia." When Adam, originally man and woman, fell, his female nature, the heavenly Sophia, was taken from him, and in his place a woman of flesh was made for him out of a rib; in order again to restore the paradisiacal perfection Christ brought again the male part into a virgin's womb, so that the new creature, the regenerate, stands before God as a "male-virgin"; but carnal love destroys again the connexion thus secured with the heavenly Sophia. But the very next year he reached a turning-point in his life. He not only married, but in consequence accepted several appointments in the Lutheran church, without, however, signing the Formula of Concord, and applied his literary skill to the production of devotional tracts.

3. Sacred Song (§ 142, 3).—The first epoch of the development of sacred song in this century corresponds to the period of the Thirty Years' War, A.D. 1618-1648. The Psalms of David were the model and pattern of the sacred poets, and the profoundest songs of the cross and consolation bear the evident impress of the times, and so individual feeling comes more into prominence. The influence of Opitz was also felt in the church song, in the greater attention given to correctness and purity of language and to the careful construction of verse and rhyme. Instead of the rugged terseness and vigour of earlier days, we now find often diffuse and overflowing utterances of the heart. John Hermann of Glogau, who died in A.D. 1647, composed 400 songs, embracing these: "Alas! dear Lord, what evil hast Thou done?' "O Christ, our true and only Light"; "Ere yet the dawn hath filled the skies"; "O God, thou faithful God." Paul Flemming, a physician in Holstein, who died in A.D. 1640, wrote on his journey to Persia, "Where'er I go, whate'er my task." Matthew Meyffart, professor and pastor at Erfurt, who died in A.D. 1642, wrote "Jerusalem, thou city fair and high." Martin Rinkart, pastor at Eilenburg in Saxony, who died A.D. 1648, wrote, "Now thank we all our God." Appelles von Löwenstern, who died A.D. 1648, composed, "When anguished and perplexed, with many a sigh and

---

[1] Martensen. "Life and Works of Jacob Boehme." London, 1886.

tear." Joshua Stegmann, superintendent in Rinteln, who died A.D. 1632, wrote, "Abide among us with thy grace." Joshua Wegelin, pastor in Augsburg and Pressburg, wrote, "Since Christ is gone to heaven, his home." Justus Gesenius, superintendent in Hanover, who died in A.D. 1673, wrote, " When sorrow and remorse." Tob. Clausnitzer, pastor in the Palatinate, who died A.D. 1648, wrote, "Blessed Jesus, at thy word." The poets named mostly belong to the first Silesian school gathered round Opitz. A more independent position, though not uninfluenced by Opitz, is taken up by John Rist, who died in A.D. 1667. He composed 658 sacred songs, of which many are remarkable for their vigour, solemnity, and elevation ; e.g. " Arise, the kingdom is at hand "; " Sink not yet, my soul, to slumber"; "O living Bread from heaven "; " Praise and thanks to Thee be sung." At the head of the Königsberg school of the same age stood Simon Dach, professor of poetry at Königsberg, who died in A.D. 1659. He composed 150 spiritual songs, among which the best known are, " O how blessed, faithful souls, are ye!" "Wouldest thou inherit life with Christ on high ?" The most distinguished members of this school are: Henry Alberti, organist at Königsberg, author of "God who madest earth and heaven "; and George Weissel, pastor in Königsberg, who died in A.D. 1655, author of " Lift up your heads, ye mighty gates."

4. From the middle of the seventeenth century sacred song became more subjective, and so tended to fall into a diversity of groups. No longer does the church sing through its poets, but the poets give direct expression to their individual feelings. Confessional songs are less frequent, and their place is taken by hymns of edification with reference to various conditions of life ; songs of death, the cross and consolation, and hymns for the family become more numerous. With objectivity special features of the church song disappear in the hymns of the period ; but some of its essential characteristics remain, especially the popular form and contents, the freshness, liveliness, and simplicity of diction, the truths of personal experience, the fulness of faith, etc. We distinguish three groups: (1) The Transition Group, passing from objectivity to subjectivity. Its greatest masters, indeed after Luther the greatest sacred poet of the evangelical church, is undoubtedly Paul Gerhardt, who died A.D. 1676, the faith witness of the Lutheran faith under the wars and in persecution (§ 154, 4). In him we find the new subjective tendency in its noblest form ; but there is also present the old objective style, giving immediate expression to the consciousness of the church, adhering tenaciously to the confession, and a grand popular ring that reminds us of the fulness and power of Luther. His 131 songs, if not all church songs in the narrower sense, are almost all genuine poems: e.g. " All my heart this night rejoices "; " Cometh sunshine after rain "; " Go forth, my heart, and

seek delight"; "Be thou content: be still before"; "O world, behold upon the tree "; " Now all the woods are sleeping "; and " Ah, wounded head, must thou?" based on Bernard's *Salve, caput cruentatum.* To this school also belongs George Neumark, librarian at Weimar, who died in A.D. 1681, author of "Leave God to order all thy ways." Also John Franck, burgomaster at Guben in Lusatia, who died A.D. 1677 next to Gerhardt the greatest poet of his age. His 110 songs are less popular and hearty, but more melodious than Gerhardt's; *e.g.* " Redeemer of the nations, come "; " Ye heavens, oh haste your dews to shed "; "Deck thyself, my soul, with gladness." George Albinus, pastor at Naumburg, died A.D. 1679, wrote: "Not in anger smite us, Lord " ; " World, farewell! Of thee I'm tired."—(2) The next stage of the sacred song took the Canticles instead of the Psalter as its model The spiritual marriage of the soul is its main theme. Feeling and fancy are predominant, and often degenerate into sentimentality and trifling. It obtained a new impulse from the addition of a mystical element. Angelus Silesius (§ 156, 4) was the most distinguished representative of this school, and while Protestant he composed several beautiful songs; *e.g.* "O Love, who formedst me to wear "; "Thou holiest Love, whom most I love "; "Loving Shepherd, kind and true." Christian Knorr v. Rosenroth, who died at Sulzbach A.D. 1689, wrote "Dayspring of eternity." Ludämilie Elizabeth, Countess of Schwarzburg-Rudolstadt, who died in A.D. 1672, wrote 215 "Songs of Jesus." Caspar Neumann, professor and pastor at Breslau, died A.D. 1715, wrote, "Lord, on earth I dwell in pain."—(3) Those of Spener's Time and Spirit, men who longed for the regeneration of the church by practical Christianity. Their hymns are for the most part characterized by healthy piety and deep godliness. Spener's own poems are of slight importance. J. Jac. Schütz, Spener's friend, a lawyer in Frankfort, who died A.D. 1690, composed only one, but that a very beautiful hymn: " All praise and thanks to God most high." Samuel Rodigast, rector in Berlin, died A.D. 1708, wrote, "Whate'er my God ordains is right." Laurentius Laurentii, musical director at Bremen, died A.D. 1722, wrote, "Is my heart athirst to know?" "O thou essential Word."—Gottfried Arnold, died A.D. 1714, wrote, "Thou who breakest every chain"; "How blest to all thy followers, Lord, the road!"— In Denmark, where previously translations of German hymns were used, Thomas Kingo, from A.D. 1677 Bishop of Fünen, died A.D. 1703, was the much-honoured founder of Danish national hymnology.[1]—Continuation, § 166, 6.

---

[1] All the translations of hymns referred to in this and the preceding section are from Miss Winkworth's " *Lyra Germanica.*" London, 1885.

5. Sacred Music (§ 142, 5).—The church music in the beginning of the seventeenth century was affected by the Italian school, just as church song was by the influence of Opitz. The greatest master during the transition stage was John Crüger, precentor in the church of St. Nicholas in Berlin, died A.D. 1662. He was to the chorale what Gerhardt was to the church song. We have seventy-one new melodies of his, admirably adapted to Gerhardt's, Hunnius's, Franck's, Dach's, and Rinkart's songs, and used in the church till the present time. With the second half of the century we enter on a new period, in which expression and musical declamation perish. Choir singing now, to a great extent, supersedes congregational singing. Henry Schütz, organist to the Elector of Saxony, died A.D. 1672, is the great master of this Italian sacred concert style. He introduced musical compositions on passages selected from the Psalms, Canticles, and prophets, in his "*Symphoniœ Sacrœ*" of A.D. 1629. After a short time a radical reform was made by John Rosenmüller, organist of Wolfenbüttel, died A.D. 1686. A reaction against the exclusive adoption of the Italian style was made by Andr. Hammerschmidt, organist at Zittau, died A.D. 1675, one of the noblest and most pious of German musicians. By working up the old church melodies in the modern style, he brought the old hymns again into favour, and set hymns of contemporary poets to bright airs suited to modern standards of taste. The accomplished musician Rud. Ahle, organist and burgomaster at Mühlhausen, died A.D. 1673, introduced his own beautiful airs into the church music for Sundays and festivals. His sacred airs are distinguished for youthful freshness and power, penetrated by a holy earnestness, and quite free from that secularity and frivolousness which soon became unpleasantly conspicuous in such music.—Continuation, § 167, 7.

6. The Christian Life of the People.—The rich development of sacred poetry proves the wonderful fulness and spirituality of the religious life of this age, notwithstanding the many chilling separatistic controversies that prevailed during the terrible upheaval of the Thirty Years' War. The abundance of devotional literature of permanent worth witnesses to the diligence and piety of the Lutheran pastors. Ernest the Pious of Saxe-Gotha, who died A.D. 1675, stands forth as the ideal of a Christian prince. For the Christian instruction of his people he issued, in the midst of the confusion and horrors of the war, the famous Weimar or Ernestine exposition of the Bible, upon which John Gerhard wrought diligently, along with other distinguished Jena theologians. It appeared first in A.D. 1641, and by A.D. 1768 had gone through fourteen large editions. A like service was done for South Germany by the "Württemberg Summaries," composed by three Württemberg theologians at the request of Duke Eberhard III., a concise, practical exposition of all the books of Scripture, which for a century and a half formed the basis of the weekly services (*Bibelstunden*) at Württemberg.—Continuation, § 167, 8.

7. **Missions.**—In the Lutheran church, missionary enterprise had rather fallen behind (§ 142, 8). Gustavus Adolphus of Sweden carried on the Lapp mission with new zeal, and Denmark, too, gave ready assistance. A Norwegian pastor, Thomas Westen, deserves special mention as the apostle of the mission. A German, Peter Heyling of Lübeck, went on his own account as a missionary to Abyssinia in A.D. 1635, while several of his friends at the same time went to other eastern lands. Of these others no trace whatever has been found. An Abyssinian abbot who came to Europe brought news of Heyling. At first he was hindered by the machinations of the Jesuits; but when these were expelled, he found favour at court, became minister to the king, and married one of the royal family. What finally came of him and his work is unknown. Toward the end of the century two great men, the philosopher Leibnitz and the founder of the Halle Orphanage, A. H. Francke, warmly espoused the cause of foreign missions. The ambitious and pretentious schemes of the philosopher ended in nothing, but Francke made his orphanages, training colleges and centres from which the German Lutheran missions to the heathens were vigorously organized and successfully wrought.—Continuation, § 167, 9.

IV.—The Reformed Church.

§ 161. THEOLOGY AND ITS BATTLES.

The Reformed scholars of France vied with those of St. Maur and the Oratory, and the Reformed theologians of the Netherlands, England, and Switzerland were not a whit behind. But an attempt made at a general synod at Dort to unite all the Reformed national churches under one confession failed. Opposition to Calvin's extreme theory of predestination introduced a Pelagianizing current into the Reformed church, which was by no means confined to professed Arminians. In the Anglican church this tendency appeared in the forms of latitudinarianism and deism (§ 164, 3); while in France it took a more moderate course, and approximated rather to the Lutheran doctrine. It was a reaction of latent Zwinglianism against the dominant Calvinism. The Voetian school successfully opposed the introduction of the Cartesian philosophy, and secured supremacy to a scholasticism which held its own alongside of that of the Lutherans. In opposition to it, the Cocceian federal school undertook to produce a purely biblical system of theology in all its departments.

1. **Preliminaries of the Arminian Controversy.**—In the *Confessio Belgica* of A.D. 1562 the Protestant Netherlands had already a strictly Calvinistic symbol, but Calvinism had not thoroughly permeated the church doctrine and constitution. There were more opponents than supporters of the doctrine of predestination, and a Melanchthonian-synergistic (§ 141, 7), or even an Erasmian-semipelagian, (§ 125, 3) doctrine, of the freedom of the will and the efficacy of grace, was more frequently taught and preached than the Augustinian-Calvinistic doctrine. So also Zwingli's view of the relation of church and state was in much greater favour than the Calvinistic Presbyterial church government with its terrorist discipline. But the return of the exiles in A.D. 1572, who had adopted strict Calvinistic views in East Friesland and on the Lower German Rhine, led to the adoption of a purely Calvinistic creed and constitution. The keenest opponent of this movement was Coornhert, notary and secretary for the city of Haarlem, who combated Calvinism in numerous writings, and depreciated doctrine generally in the interests of practical living Christianity. Political as well as religious sympathies were enlisted in favour of this freer ecclesiastical tendency. The Dutch War of Independence was a struggle for religious freedom against Spanish Catholic fanaticism. The young republic therefore became the first home of religious toleration, which was scarcely reconcilable with a strict and exclusive Calvinism.—Meanwhile within the Calvinistic church a controversy arose, which divided its adherents in the Netherlands into two parties. In opposition to the strict Calvinists, who as supralapsarians held that the fall itself was included in the eternal counsels of God, there arose the milder infralapsarians, who made predestination come in after the fall, which was not predestinated but only foreseen by God.

2. **The Arminian Controversy.**—In A.D. 1588, James Arminius (born A.D. 1560), a pupil of Beza, but a declared adherent of the Ramist philosophy (§ 143, 6), was appointed pastor in Amsterdam, and ordered by the magistrates to controvert Coornhert's universalism and the infralapsarianism of the ministers of Delft. He therefore studied Coornhert's writings, and by them was shaken in his earlier beliefs. This was shown first in certain sermons on passages from Romans, which made him suspected of Pelagianism. In A.D. 1603 he

was made theological professor of Leyden, where he found a bitter opponent in his supralapsarian colleague, Francis Gomarus. From the class-rooms the controversy spread to the pulpits, and even into domestic circles. A public disputation in A.D. 1608, led to no pacific result, and Arminius continued involved in controversies till his death in A.D. 1609. Although decidedly inclined toward universalism, he had directed his polemic mainly against supralapsarianism, as making God himself the author of sin. But his followers went beyond these limits. When denounced by the Gomarists as Pelagians, they addressed to the provincial parliament of Holland and West Friesland, in A.D. 1610, a remonstrance, which in five articles repudiates supralapsarianism and infralapsariansm, and the doctrines of the irresistibility of grace, and of the impossibility of the elect finally falling away from it, and boldly asserts the universality of grace. They were hence called Remonstrants and their opponents Contraremonstrants. Parliament, favourably inclined toward the Arminians, pronounced the difference non-fundamental, and enjoined peace. When Vorstius, who was practically a Socinian, was appointed successor to Arminius, Gomarus charged the Remonstrants with Socinianism. Their ablest theological representative was Simon Episcopius, who succeeded Gomarus at Leyden in A.D. 1612, supported by the distinguished statesman, Oldenbarneveldt, and the great jurist, humanist, and theologian, Hugo Grotius of Rotterdam. Maurice of Orange, too, for a long time sided with them, but in A.D. 1617 formally went over to the other party, whose well-knit unity, strict discipline, and rigorous energy commended them to him as the fittest associates in his struggle for absolute monarchy. The republican-Arminian party was conquered, Oldenbarneveldt being executed in 1619, Grotius escaping by his wife's strategem. The Synod of Dort was convened for the purpose of settling doctrinal disputes. It held 154 sessions, from Nov. 13th, 1618, to May 9th, 1619. Invitations were accepted by twenty-eight theologians from England, Scotland, Germany, and Switzerland. Brandenburg took no part in it (§ 154, 3), and French theologians were refused permission to go. Episcopius presented a clear and comprehensive apology for the Remonstrants, and bravely defended their cause before the synod. Refusing to submit to the decisions of the synod, they were at the fifty-seventh session expelled, and then excommunicated and deprived of all ecclesiastical offices. The Heidelberg Catechism and the Belgic Confession were unanimously adopted as the creed and manual of orthodox teaching. In the discussion of the five controverted points, the opposition of the Anglican and German delegates prevented any open and manifest insertion of supralapsarian theses, so that the synodal canons set forth only an essentially infralapsarian theory of predestination.—

Remonstrant teachers were now expelled from most of the states of the union. Only after Maurice's death in A.D. 1625 did they venture to return, and in A.D. 1630 they were allowed by statute to erect churches and schools in all the states. A theological seminary at Amsterdam, presided over by Episcopius till his death, in A.D. 1643, rose to be a famous seat of learning and nursery of liberal studies. The number of congregations, however, remained small, and their importance in church history consists rather in the development of an independent church life than in the revival of a semipelagian and rationalistic type of doctrine.[1]

8. Consequences of the Arminian Controversy.—The Dort decrees were not accepted in Brandenburg, Hesse, and Bremen, where a moderate Calvinism continued to prevail. In England and Scotland the Presbyterians enthusiastically approved of the decrees, whereas the Episcopalians repudiated them, and, rushing to the other extreme of latitudinarianism, often showed lukewarm indifferentism in the way in which they distinguished articles of faith as essential and non-essential. The worthiest of the latitudinarians of this age was Chillingworth, who sought an escape from the contentions of theologians in the Catholic church, but soon returned to Protestantism. seeking and finding peace in God's word alone. Archbishop Tillotson was a famous pulpit orator, and Gilbert Burnet, who died A.D. 1715, was author of a "History of the English Reformation." In the French Reformed church, where generally strict Calvinism prevailed, Amyrault of Saumur, who died A.D. 1664, taught a *universalismus hypotheticus*, according to which God by a *decretum universale et hypotheticum* destined all men to salvation through Jesus Christ, even the heathen, on the ground of a *fides implicita*. The only condition is that they believe, and for this all the means are afforded in *gratia resistibilis*, while by a *decretum absolutum et speciale* only to elect persons is granted the *gratia irresistibilis*. The synods of Alençon, A.D. 1637, and Charenton, A.D. 1644, supported by Blondel, Daillé, and Claude, declared these doctrines allowable; but Du Moulin of Sedan, Rivetus and Spanheim of Leyden, Maresius of Groningen, and others, offered violent opposition. Amyrault's colleague, De la Place, or

---

[1] The "Works of Arminius," transl. by Nicholls, to which are added Brandt's "Life of Arminius," etc. 8 vols. London, 1825. Scott, "Translation of Articles of Synod of Dort." London, 1818. Hales, "Letters from the Synod of Dort." Glasgow, 1765. Calder, "Life of Simon Episcopius." New York, 1837. Cunningham, "Reformation and Theology of Reformation": Essay VIII., "Calvinism and Arminianism," pp. 412–470. Motley, "John of Barneveldt." 2 vols. London, 1874.

Placæus, who died A.D. 1655, went still further, repudiating the **un-conditional** imputation of Adam's sin, and representing original **sin** simply as an evil which becomes guilt only as our own actual transgression. The synods just named condemned this doctrine. Somewhat later Claude Pajon of Saumur, who died A.D. 1685, roused a bitter discussion about the universality of grace, by maintaining that in conversion divine providence wrought only through the circumstances of the life, and the Holy Spirit through the word of God. Several French synods condemned this doctrine, and affirmed an immediate as well as a mediate operation of the Spirit and providence.—Genuine Calvinism was best represented in Switzerland, as finally expressed in the Formula Consensus *Helvetica* of Heidegger of Zürich, adopted in A.D. 1675 by most of the cantons. It was, like the *Formula Concordiæ*, a manual of doctrine rather than a confession. In opposition to Amyrault and De la Place, it set forth a strict theory of predestination and original sin, and maintained with the Buxtorfs, against Cappellus of Saumur, the inspiration of the Hebrew vowel points.

4. **The Cocceian and Cartesian Controversies.**—If not the founder, certainly the most distinguished representative in the Netherlands of that scholasticism which sought to expound and defend orthodoxy, was Voetius, who died A.D. 1676, from A.D. 1607 pastor in various places, and from A.D. 1634 professor at Utrecht. A completely different course was pursued by Cocceius of Bremen, who died A.D. 1669, professor at Franeker in A.D. 1636, and at Leyden in A.D. 1650. The famous Zürich theologian, Bullinger (§ 138, 7), had in his " *Compend. Rel. Chr.*" of A.D. 1556, viewed the whole doctrine of saving truth from the point of view of a covenant of grace between God and man ; and this idea was afterwards carried out by Olevianus of Heidelberg (§ 144, 1) in his " *De Substantia Fœderis*," of A.D. 1585. This became the favourite method of distribution of doctrine in the whole German Reformed church. In the Dutch church it was regarded as quite unobjectionable. In England it was adopted in the Westminster Confession of A.D. 1648 (§ 155, 1), and in Switzerland in A.D. 1675, in the *Formula Consensus*. Cocceius is therefore not the founder of the federal theology. He simply gave it a new and independent development, and freed it from the trammels of scholastic dogmatics. He distinguished a twofold covenant of God with man : the *fœdus operum s. naturæ* before, and the *fœdus gratiæ* after the fall. He then subdivided the covenant of grace into three economies : before the law until Moses; under the law until Christ; and after the law in the Christian church. The history of the kingdom of God in the Christian era was arranged in seven periods, corresponding to the seven apocalyptic epistles, trumpets, and seals. In his treatment of

his theme, he repudiated philosophy, scholasticism, and tradition, and held simply by Scripture. He is thus the founder of a purely biblical theology. He attached himself as closely as possible to the prevailing predestinationist orthodoxy, but only externally. In his view the sacred history in its various epochs adjusted itself to the needs of human personality, and to the growing capacity for appropriating it. Hence it was not the idea of election, but that of grace, that prevailed in his system. Christ is the centre of all history, spiritual, ecclesiastical, and civil; and so everything in Scripture, history, doctrine, and prophecy, necessarily and immediately stands related to him. The O.T. prophecies and types point to the Christ that was to come in the flesh, and all history after Christ points to his second coming; and O. and N.T. give an outline of ecclesiastical and civil history down to the end of time. Thus typology formed the basis of the Cocceian theology. In exegesis, however, Cocceius avoided all arbitrary allegorizing. It was with him an axiom in hermeneutics, *Id significan verba, quod significare possunt in integra oratione, sic ut omnino inter se conveniant.* Yet his typology led him, and still more many of his adherents, into fantastic exegetical errors in the prophetic treatment of the seven apocalyptic periods.

5. A controversy, occasioned by Cocceius' statement, in his commentary on Hebrews in A.D. 1658, that the Sabbath, as enjoined by the O.T. ceremonial law, was no longer binding, was stopped in A.D. 1659 by a State prohibition. Voetius had not taken part in it. But when Cocceius, in A.D. 1665, taught from Romans iii. 25, that believers under the law had not full "ἄφεσις," only a "πάρεσις," he felt obliged to enter the lists against this "Socinian" heresy. The controversy soon spread to other doctrines of Cocceius and his followers, and soon the whole populace seemed divided into Voetians and Cocceians (§ 162, 5). The one hurled offensive epithets at the other. The Orange political party sought and obtained the favour of the Voetians, as before they had that of the Gomarists; while the liberal republican party coalesced with the Cocceians. Philosophical questions next came to be mixed up in the discussion. The philosophy of the French Catholic Descartes (§ 164, 1), settled in A.D. 1629 in Amsterdam, had gained ground in the Netherlands. It had indeed no connexion with Christianity or church, and its theological friends wished only to have it recognised as a formal branch of study. But its fundamental principle, that all true knowledge starts from doubt, appeared to the representatives of orthodoxy as threatening the church with serious danger. Even in A.D. 1643 Voetius opposed it, and mainly in consequence of his polemic, the States General, in A.D. 1656, forbad it being taught in the universities. Their common opposition to scholasticism, however, brought Cocceians and Cartesians more closely to one

another. Theology now became influenced by Cartesianism. Roëll,
professor at Franeker and Utrecht, who died A.D. 1718, taught that
the divinity of the Scriptures must be proved to the reason, since the
testimonium Spir. s. internum is limited to those who already believe,
rejected the doctrine of the imputation of original sin, the doctrine
that death is for believers the punishment of sin, and the application
of the idea of eternal "generation" to the Logos, to whom the predi-
cate of sonship belongs only in regard to the decree of redemption and
incarnation. Another zealous Cartesian, Balth. Bekker, not only
repudiated the superstitions of the age about witchcraft (§ 117, 4),
but also denied the existence of the devil and demons. The Cocceians
were in no way responsible for such extravagances, but their opponents sought to make them chargeable for these. The stadtholder,
William III., at last issued an order, in A.D. 1694, which checked for a
time the violence of the strife.

6. **Theological Literature.**—Biblical oriental philology flourished in
the Reformed church of this age. Drusius of Franeker, who died A.D.
1616, was the greatest Old Testament exegete of his day. The two
Buxtorfs of Basel, the father died A.D. 1629, the son A.D. 1664, the
greatest Christian rabbinical scholars, wrote Hebrew and Chaldee
grammars, lexicons, and concordances, and maintained the antiquity
and even inspiration of the Hebrew vowel points against Cappellus of
Saumur. Hottinger of Zürich, who died A.D. 1667, vied with both in
his knowledge of oriental literature and languages, and wrote extensively on biblical philology, and besides found time to write a comprehensive and learned church history. Cocceius, too, occupies a
respectable place among Hebrew lexicographers. In England, both
before and after the Restoration, scholarship was found, not among
the controversial Puritans, but among the Episcopal clergy. Brian
Walton, who died A.D. 1661, aided by the English scholars, issued an
edition of the "London Polyglott" in six vols., in A.D. 1657, which, in
completeness of material and apparatus, as well as in careful textual
criticism, leaves earlier editions far behind. Edm. Castellus of Cambridge in A.D. 1669 published his celebrated "*Lexicon Heptaglottum.*"
The Elzevir printing-house at Amsterdam and Leyden, boldly assuming the prerogatives of the whole body of theological scholars, issued a
textus receptus of the N.T. in A.D. 1624. The best established exegetical
results of earlier times were collected by Pearson in his great compendium, the "*Critici Sacri,*" nine vols. fol., London, 1660; and Matthew
Pœl in his "*Synopsis Criticorum,*" five vols. fol., London, 1669. Among
the exegetes of this time the brothers, J. Cappellus of Sedan, who died
A.D. 1624, and Louis Cappellus II. of Saumur, who died A.D. 1658, were
distinguished for their linguistic knowledge and liberal criticism.
Pococke of Oxford and Lightfoot of Cambridge were specially eminent

orientalists. Cocceius wrote commentaries on almost all the books of Scripture, and his scholar Vitringa of Franeker, who died A.D. 1716, gained great reputation by his expositions of Isaiah and the Apocalypse. Among the Arminians the famous statesman Grotius, who died A.D. 1645, was the greatest master of grammatico-historical exposition in the century, and illustrated Scripture from classical literature and philology. The Reformed church too gave brilliant contributions to biblical archæology and history. John Selden wrote "*De Syndriis Vett. Heb.,*" "*De diis Syris,*" etc. Goodwin wrote "Moses and Aaron." Ussher wrote "*Annales V. et N.T.*" Spencer wrote "*De Legibus Heb.*" The Frenchman Bochart, in his "*Hierozoicon*" and "*Phaleg,*" made admirable contributions to the natural history and geography of the Bible.

7. Dogmatic theology was cultivated mainly in the Netherlands. Maccovius, a Pole, who died A.D. 1644, a professor at Franeker, introduced the scholastic method into Reformed dogmatics. The Synod of Dort cleared him of the charge of heresy made against him by Amesius, but condemned his method. Yet it soon came into very general use. Its chief representatives were Maresius of Groningen, Voetius and Mastricht of Utrecht, Hoornbeck of Leyden, and the German Wendelin, rector of Zerbst. Among the Cocceians the most distinguished were Heidanus of Leyden, Alting of Groningen, and, above all, Hermann Witsius of Franeker, whose "Economy of the Covenants" is written in a conciliatory spirit. The most distinguished Arminian dogmatist after Episcopius was Phil. Limborch of Amsterdam, who died A.D. 1712, in high repute also as an apologist, exegete, and historian. The greatest dogmatist of the Anglican church was Pearson, who died A.D. 1686, author of "An Exposition of the Creed." The Frenchman Peyrerius obtained great notoriety from his statement, founded on Romans v. 12, that Adam was merely the ancestor of the Jews (Gen. ii. 7), while the Gentiles were of pre-Adamite origin (Gen. i. 26), and also by maintaining that the flood had been only partial. He gained release from prison by joining the Catholic church and recanted, but stil' held by his earlier views.—Ethics, consisting hitherto of little more than an exposition of the decalogue, was raised by Amyrault into an independent science. Amesius dealt with cases of conscience. Grotius, in his "*De Veritate Relig. Chr.*" and Abbadie, French pastor at Berlin, and afterwards in London, who died A.D. 1727, in his "*Vérité de la Rel. Chrét.,*" distinguished themselves as apologists. Claude and Jurieu gained high reputation as controversialists against Catholicism and its persecution of the Huguenots.—The Reformed church also in the interests of polemics pursued historical studies. Hottinger of Zürich, Spanheim of Leyden, Sam. Basnage of Zütpfen, and Jac. Basnage of the Hague, produced general church histories. Among the

numerous historical monographs the most important are **Hospinian's**
"*De Templis*," "*De Monachis*," "*De Festis*," "*Hist. Sacramentaria*,"
"*Historia Jesuitica*"; Blondel's "*Ps.-Isidorus*," "*De la Primauté de
l'Egl.*," "*Question si une Femme a été Assisse au Siège Papal*" (§ 82, 6),
"*Apologia sent. Hieron. de Presbyt.*" Also Daillé of Saumur on the non-
genuineness of the "Apostolic Constitutions" and the Ps.-Dionysian
writings, and his "*De Usu Patrum*" in opposition to Cave's Catholicizing over-estimation of the Fathers.   We have also the English
scholar Ussher, who died A.D. 1656, "*Brit. Ecclesiarum Antiquitates*";
H. Dodwell, who died A.D. 1711, "*Diss. Cyprianicæ*," etc.; Wm. Cave,
who died A.D. 1713, "Hist. of App. and Fathers," "*Scriptorum Ecclst.
Hist. Literaria*," etc.—Special mention should be made of Eisenmenger,
professor of oriental languages at Heidelberg.   In his "*Entdecktes
Judenthum*," two vols. quarto, moved by the over-bearing arrogance of
the Jews of his day, he made an immense collection of absurdities and
blasphemies of rabbinical theology from Jewish writings.   At his own
expense he printed 2,000 copies; for these the Jews offered him 12,000
florins, but he demanded 30,000.   They now persuaded the court at
Venice to confiscate them before a single copy was sold.   Eisenmenger
died in A.D. 1704, and his heirs vainly sought to have the copies of his
work given up to them.   Even the appeal of Frederick I. of Prussia
was refused.   Only when the king had resolved, in A.D. 1711, at his
own expense to publish an edition from one copy that had escaped confiscation, was the Frankfort edition at last given back.

8. The Apocrypha Controversy (§ 136, 4).—In A.D. 1520 Carlstadt raised
the question of the books found only in the LXX., and answered it in
the style of Jerome (§ 59, 1).   Luther gave them in his translation as
an appendix to the O.T. with the title "Apocrypha, *i.e.* Books, not
indeed of Holy Scripture, but useful and worthy to be read."   Reformed
confessions took up the same position.   The Belgic Confession agreed
indeed that these books should be read in church, and proof passages
taken from them, in so far as they were in accord with the canonical
Scriptures.   The Anglican Book of Common Prayer gives readings
from these books.   On the other hand, although at the Synod of Dort
the proposal to remove at least the apocryphal books of Ezra or Esdras,
Tobit, Judith, Bel and the Dragon, was indeed rejected, it was ordered
that in future all apocryphal books should be printed in smaller type
than the canonical books, should be separately paged, with a special
title, and with a preface and marginal notes where necessary.   Their
exclusion from all editions of the Bible was first insisted on by English
and Scotch Puritans.   This example was followed by the French,
but not by the German, Swiss, and Dutch Reformed churches.—Continuation, § 184, 4.

§ 162. THE RELIGIOUS LIFE.[1]

The religious life in the Reformed church is characterized generally by harsh legalism, rigorous renunciation of the world, and a thorough earnestness, coupled with decision and energy of will, which nothing in the world can break or bend. It is the spirit of Calvin which impresses on it this character, and determines its doctrine. Only where Calvin's influence was less potent, *e.g.* in the Lutheranized German Reformed, the catholicized Anglican Episcopal Church, and among the Cocceians, is this tendency less apparent or altogether wanting. On the other hand, often carried to the utmost extreme, it appears among the English Puritans (§§ 143, 3; 155, 1) and the French Huguenots (§ 153, 4), where it was fostered by persecution and oppression.

1. **England and Scotland.**—During the period of the English Revolution (§ 155, 1, 2), after the overthrow of Episcopacy, Puritanism became dominant; and the incongruous and contradictory elements already existing within it assumed exaggerated proportions (§ 143, 3, 4), until at last the opposing parties broke out into violent contentions with one another. The ideal of Scottish and English Presbyterianism was the setting up of the kingdom of Christ as a theocracy, in which church and state were blended after the O.T. pattern. Hence all the institutions of church and state were to be founded on Scripture models, while all later developments were set aside as deteriorations from that standard. The ecclesiastical side of this ideal was to be realized by the establishment of a spiritual aristocracy represented in presbyteries and synods, which, ruling the presbyteries through the synods, and the congregations through the presbyteries, regarded itself as called and under obligation to inspect and supervise all the details of the private as well as public life of church members, and all this too by Divine right. Regarding their system as alone having divine institution, Presbyterians could not recognise any other religious or ecclesiastical party, and must demand uniformity, not only in regard to doctrine and creed, but also in regard to constitution, discipline,

---

[1] Barclay, "The Inner Life of the Religious Societies of the Commonwealth." Second ed. London, 1877. Dr. Stoughton's "History of Religion in England from Opening of Long Parliament to End of Eighteenth Century." London.

and worship.[1]—On the other hand, Independent Congregationalism, inasmuch as it made prominent the N.T. ideas of the priesthood of all believers and spiritual freedom, demanded unlimited liberty to each separate congregation, and unconditional equality for all individual church members. It thus rejected the theocratic ideal of Presbyterianism, strove after a purely democratic constitution, and recognised toleration of all religious views as a fundamental principle of Christianity. Every attempt to secure uniformity and stability of forms of worship was regarded as a repressing of the Spirit of God operating in the church, and so alongside of the public services private conventicles abounded, in which believers sought to promote mutual edification. But soon amid the upheavals of this agitated period a fanatical spirit spread among the various sects of the Independents. The persecutions under Elizabeth and the Stuarts had awakened a longing for the return of the Lord, and the irresistible advance of Cromwell's army, composed mostly of Independents, made it appear as if the millennium was close at hand. Thus chiliasm came to be a fundamental principle of Independency, and soon too prophecy made its appearance to interpret and prepare the way for that which was coming. From the *Believers* of the old Dutch times we now come to the Saints of the early Cromwell period. These regarded themselves as called, in consequence of their being inspired by God's Spirit, to form the "kingdom of the saints" on earth promised in the last days, and hence also, from Daniel ii. and vii., they were called Fifth Monarchy Men. The so called Short Parliament of A.D. 1653, in which these Saints were in a majority, had already laid the first stones of this structure by introducing civil marriage, with the strict enforcement, however, of Matthew v. 32, as well as by the abolition of all rights of patronage and all sorts of ecclesiastical taxes, when Cromwell dissolved it. The Saints had not and would not have any fixed, formulated theological system. They had, however, a most lively interest in doctrine, and produced a great diversity of Scripture expositions and dogmatic views, so that their deadly foes, the Presbyterians, could hurl against them old and new heretical designations by the hundred. The fundamental doctrine of predestination, common to all Puritans, was, even with them, for the most part, a presupposition of all theological speculation.

2. At the same time with the *Saints* there appeared among the Independents the Levellers, political and social revolutionists, rather than an ecclesiastical and religious sect. They were unjustly charged

---

[1] See Macpherson, "Presbyterianism" (Edin., 1883), pp. 8-10, where charges of intolerance such as those made against Presbyterianism in the text are repudiated.

with claiming an equal distribution of goods. **Over against the** absolutist theories of the Stuarts, all the Independents maintained that the king, like all other civil magistrates, is answerable at all times and in all circumstances to the people, to whom all sovereignty originally and inalienably belongs. This principle was taken by the Levellers as the starting-point of their reforms. As their first regulative principle in reconstructing the commonwealth and determining the position of the church therein they did not take the theocratic constitution of the O.T., as the Presbyterians did, nor the biblical revelation of the N.T., as the moderate Independents did, nor even the modern professed prophecy of the "Saints," but the law of nature as the basis of all revelation, and already grounded in creation, with the sovereignty of the people as its ultimate foundation. While the rest of the Independents held by the idea of a Christian state, and only claimed that all Christian denominations, with the exception of the Catholics (§ 153, 6), should enjoy all political rights, the Levellers demanded complete separation of church and state. This therefore implied, on the one hand, the non-religiousness of the state, and, on the other, again with the exception of Catholics, the absolute freedom. independence, and equality of all religious parties, even non-Christian sects and atheists. Yet all the while the Levellers themselves were earnestly and warmly attached to Christian truth as held by the other Independents.—Roger Williams (§ 163, 8), a Baptist minister, in A.D. 1631 transplanted the first seeds of Levellerism from England to North America, and by his writings helped again to spread those views in England. When he returned home in A.D. 1651 he found the sect already flourishing. The ablest leader of the English Levellers was John Lilburn. In A.D. 1638, when scarcely twenty years old, he was flogged and sentenced to imprisonment for life, because he had printed Puritan writings in Holland and had them circulated in England. Released on the outbreak of the Revolution, he joined the Parliamentary army, was taken prisoner by the Royalists and sentenced to death, but escaped by flight. He was again imprisoned for writing libels on the House of Lords. Set free by the Rump Parliament, he became colonel in Cromwell's army, but was banished the country when it was found that the spread of radicalism endangered discipline. Till the dissolution of the Short Parliament his followers were in thorough sympathy with the Saints. Afterwards their ways went more and more apart; the Saints drifted into Quakerism (§ 163, 4), while the Levellers degenerated into deism (§ 164, 8).

3. Out of the religious commotion prevailing in England before, during, and after the Revolution there sprang up a voluminous devotional literature, intended to give guidance and directions for holy

living. Its influence was felt in foreign lands, especially in the Reformed churches of the continent, and even German Lutheran Pietism was not unaffected by it (§ 159, 3). That this movement was not confined to the Puritans, among whom it had its origin, is seen from the fact that during the seventeenth century many such treatises were issued from the University Press of Cambridge. Lewis Bayly, Bishop of Bangor A.D. 1616–1632, wrote one of the most popular books of this kind, "The Practice of Piety," which was in A.D. 1635 in its thirty-second and in A.D. 1741 in its fifty-first edition, and was also widely circulated in Dutch, French, German, Hungarian, and Polish translations.—Out of the vast number of important personages of the Revolution period we name the following three: (1) In John Milton, the highly gifted poet as well as eloquent and powerful politician, born A.D. 1608, died A.D. 1674, we find, on the basis of a liberal classical training received in youth, all the motive powers of Independency, from the original Puritan zeal for the faith and Reformation to the politico-social radicalism of the Levellers, combined in full and vigorous operation. From Italy, the beloved land of classical science and artistic culture, he was called back to England in A.D. 1640 at the first outburst of freedom-loving enthusiasm (§ 155, 1), and made the thunder of his controversial treatises ring over the battlefield of parties. He fought against the narrowness of Presbyterian control of conscience not less energetically than against the hierarchism of the Episcopal church; vindicates the permissibility of divorce (in view, no doubt, of his own first unhappy marriage); advanced in his "*Areopagitica*" of A.D. 1644 a plea for the unrestricted liberty of the press; pulverized in his "*Iconoclastes*" of A.D. 1649 the Εἰκὼν βασιλική, ascribed to Charles I.; in several tracts, "*Defensio pro Populo Anglicano*," etc., justified the execution of the king against Salmasius's "*Defensio Regia pro Carolo I.*"; and, even after he had in A.D. 1652 become incurably blind, he continued unweariedly his polemics till silenced by the Restoration. The "*Iconoclastes*" and "*Defensio*" were burned by the hangman, but he himself was left unmolested. He now devoted himself to poetry. "Paradise Lost" appeared in A.D. 1665, and "Paradise Regained" in A.D. 1671. To this period, when he had probably turned his back on all existing religious parties, belongs the composition of his "*De doctrina Christiana*," a first attempt at a purely biblical theology, Arian in its Christology and Arminian in its soteriology.[1]—(2) Richard Baxter, born A.D. 1615, died A.D. 1691, was quite a different sort of man, and showed throughout a decidedly irenical tendency. At once attracted and repelled by the Independent movement in

---

[1] Masson, "Life of John Milton." 4 vols. London, 1859. Pattison, "Milton" in "English Men of Letters" series. London, 1880.

Cromwell's army, he joined the force in A.D. 1645 as military chaplain, hoping to moderate, if not to check, their extravagances. A severe illness obliged him to withdraw in A.D. 1647. After his recovery he returned to his former post as assistant-minister at Kidderminster in Worcestershire, and there remained till driven out by the Act of Uniformity of A.D. 1662 (§ 155, 3). Those fourteen years formed the period of his most successful labours. He then composed most of his numerous devotional works, three of which, " The Saint's Everlasting Rest," "The Reformed Pastor," " A Call to the Unconverted," are still widely read in the original and in translations. At first he hoped much from the Restoration ; but when, on conscientious grounds, he refused a bishopric, he met only with persecution, ill treatment and imprisonment. Through William's Act of Toleration of A.D. 1689, he was allowed to pass the last year of his life in London. On the doctrine of predestination he took the moderate position of Amyrault (§ 161, 3). His ideal church constitution was a blending of Presbyterianism and Episcopacy, by restoring the original episcopal constitution of the second century, when even the smaller churches had each its own bishop with a presbytery by his side.[1]—(3) John Bunyan, born A.D. 1628, died A.D. 1688, was in his youth a tinker or brazier, and as such seems to have led a rough, wild life. On the outbreak of the Civil War in A.D. 1642, he was drafted into the Parliamentary army.[2] At the close of the war he married a poor girl from a Puritan family, whose only marriage portion consisted in two Puritan books of devotion. It was now that the birthday of a new spiritual life began to dawn in him. He joined the Baptist Independents, the most zealous of the Saints of that time, was baptized by them in A.D. 1655, and travelled the country as a preacher, attracting thousands around him everywhere by his glorious eloquence. In A.D. 1660 he was thrown into prison, from which he was released by the Indulgence of A.D. 1672 (§ 155, 3). He now settled in Bedford, and from this time till his death, amid persecution and oppression, continued his itinerant preaching with ever-increasing zeal and success. " The Pilgrim's Progress " was written by him in

---

[1] " *Reliquiæ Baxterianæ :* Baxter's Narrative of most Memorable Passages in his own Life." London, 1696. Orme, " Life and Times of Richard Baxter, with Critical Examination of his Writings." London, 1830. Stalker, " Baxter " in " Evangelical Succession Lectures." Second series. Edinburgh, 1883.

[2] Froude disputes this, and says, p. 12, that probably he was on the side of the Royalists. Brown has shown it to be almost certain that in 1644, not 1642, Bunyan, then in his sixteenth year, joined the Parliamentary forces. See Brown's " Life," pp. 42–52.

prison. It is an allegory of the freshest and most lively form, worthy to rank alongside the "Imitation of Christ" (§ 114, 7). In it the fanatical endeavour of the Saints to rear a millennial kingdom on earth is transfigured into a struggle overcoming all hindrances to secure an entrance into the heavenly Zion above. It has passed through numberless editions, and has been translated into almost all known languages.[1]

4. The Netherlands.—From England the Reformed Pietism was transplanted to the Netherlands, where William Teellinck may be regarded as its founder. After finishing his legal studies he resided for a while in England, where he made the acquaintance of the Puritans and their writings, and was deeply impressed with their earnest and pious family life. He then went to Leyden to study theology, and in A.D. 1606 began a ministry that soon bore fruit. He was specially blessed at Middelburg in Zealand, where he died A.D. 1629. His writings, larger and smaller, more than a hundred in number, in which a peculiar sweetness of mystical love for the Redeemer is combined with stern Calvinistic views, after the style of St. Bernard, were circulated widely in numerous editions, eagerly read in many lands, and for fully a century exerted a powerful influence throughout the whole Reformed church. Teellinck in no particular departed from the prevailing orthodoxy, but unwittingly toned down its harshness in his tracts, and with the gentleness characteristic of him counselled brotherly forbearance amid the bitterness of the Arminian controversy. In spite of much hostility, which his best efforts could not prevent, many university theologians stood by his side as warm admirers of his writings. It will not be wondered at that among these was the pious Amesius of Franeker (§ 161, 7), the scholar of the able Perkins (§ 143, 5); but it is more surprising to find here the powerful champion of scholastic orthodoxy, Voetius of Utrecht, and his vigorous partisan, Hoornbeeck of Leyden. Voetius especially, who even in his preacademic career as a pastor had pursued a peculiarly exemplary and godly life, styled Teellinck the Reformed Thomas à Kempis, and owned his deep indebtedness to his devout writings. He opened his academic course in A.D. 1634 with an introductory discourse, " *De Pietate cum Scientia conjungenda*," and year after year gave lectures on ascetical theology, out of which

---

[1] Brown, "Life of Bunyan." London, 1885. Autobiography in "Grace Abounding," 1622. Southey, "Life of John Bunyan." London, 1830. Macaulay, "Essay on Bunyan," in *Edinburgh Review*, 1830. Froude, "Bunyan," in "English Men of Letters." London, 1880. Nicoll, "Bunyan," in " Evangelical Succession Lectures." Third series. Edinburgh, 1883.

grew his treatise published in A.D. 1664, "Τὰ 'Ασκητικὰ s. Exercita Pietatis in usum Juventutis Acad.," which is a complete exposition of evangelical practical divinity in a thoroughly scholastic form.

5. During the controversy in the Dutch Reformed Church between Voetians and Cocceians, beginning in A.D. 1658, the former favoured the pietistic movement. In the German Pietist controversy the Cocceians were with the Pietists in their biblical orthodoxy joined with confessional indifferentism, but with the orthodox in their liberality and breadth on matters of life and conduct. The earnest, practical piety of the Voetians, again, made them sympathise with the Lutheran Pietists, and their zeal for pure doctrine and the Church confession brought them into relation with the orthodox Lutherans. As discord between the theologians arose over the obligation of the Sabbath law, so the difference among the people arose out of the question of Sabbath observance. The Voetians maintained that the decalogue prohibition of any form of work on Sabbath was still fully binding, while the Cocceians, on the ground of Mark ii. 27, Galatians iv. 9, Colossians ii. 16, etc., denied its continued obligation, their wives often, to the annoyance of the Voetians, sitting in the windows after Divine service with their knitting or sewing. But the opposition did not stop there; it spread into all departments of life. The Voetians set great value upon fasting and private meditation, avoided all public games and plays, dressed plainly, and observed a simple, pious mode of life; their pastors wore a clerical costume, etc. The Cocceians, again, fell in with the customs of the time, mingled freely in the mirth and pastimes of the people, went to public festivals and entertainments, their women dressed in elegant, stylish attire, their pastors were not bound by hard and fast symbols, but had full Scripture freedom, etc.—Continuation, § 169, 2.

6. France, Germany, and Switzerland.—The Reformed church of France has gained imperishable renown as a martyr-church. Fanatical excesses, however, appeared among the prophets of the Cevennes (§ 158, 4), the fruits of which continued down into the eighteenth century, and appeared now and again in England, Holland, and Germany (§ 160, 2, 7).—In Germany the Reformed church, standing side by side with the numerically far larger Lutheran church, had much of the sternness and severity that characterized the Romanic-Calvinistic party in doctrine, worship, and life greatly modified; but where the Reformed element was predominant, as in the Lower Rhine, it was correspondingly affected by a contrary influence. The Reformed church in Germany in its service of praise kept to the psalms of Marot and Lobwasser (§ 143, 2). Maurice of Hesse published Lobwasser's in A.D. 1612, accompanied by some new bright melodies, for the use of the churches in the land. Lutheran hymns, however, gradually

found their way into the Reformed church, which also produced two gifted poets of its own. Louisa Henrietta, Princess of Orange, wife of the great elector, and Paul Gerhardt's sovereign, wrote "Jesus my Redeemer lives"; and Joachim Neander, pastor in Bremen, wrote, "Thou most Highest! Guardian of mankind," "To heaven and earth and sea and air," "Here behold me, as I cast me."—In German Switzerland the noble Breitinger of Zürich, who died A.D. 1645, the greatest successor of Zwingli and Bullinger, wrought successfully during a forty years' ministry, and did much to revive and quicken the church life. That the spirit of Calvin and Beza still breathed in the church of Geneva is proved by the reception given there to such men as Andreä (§ 160, 1), Labadie (§ 163, 7), and Spener (§ 159, 3).

7. Foreign Missions.—From two sides the Reformed church had outlets for its Christian love in the work of foreign missions; on the one side by the cession of the Portuguese East Indian colonies to the Netherlands in the beginning of the seventeenth century, and on the other side by the continuous formation of English colonies in North America throughout the whole century. In regard to missionary effort, the Dutch government followed in the footsteps of her Portuguese predecessors. She insisted that all natives, before getting a situation, should be baptized and have signed the Belgic Confession, and many who fulfilled these conditions remained as they had been before. But the English Puritans settled in America showed a zeal for the conversion of the Indians more worthy of the Protestant name. John Eliot, who is rightly styled the apostle of the Indians, devoted himself with unwearied and self-denying love for half a century to this task. He translated the Bible into their language, and founded seventeen Indian stations, of which during his lifetime ten were destroyed in a bloody war. Eliot's work was taken up by the Mayhew family, who for five generations wrought among the Indians. The last of the noble band, Zacharias Mayhew, died on the mission field in A.D. 1808, in his 87th year.[1]—Continuation, § 172, 5.

V.—Anti- and Extra-Ecclesiastical Parties.

§ 163.   SECTS AND FANATICS.

Socinianism during the first decades of the century made extraordinary progress in Poland, but then collapsed under the persecution of the Jesuits. Related to the continental

---

[1] "Life of John Eliot, Apostle of the Indians." By John Wilson, afterwards of Bombay. Edin., 1828.

Anabaptists were the English Baptists, who rejected infant baptism ; while the Quakers, who adopted the old fanatical theory of an inner light, set baptism and the Lord's supper entirely aside.   In the sect of the Labadists we find a blending of Catholic quietist mysticism and Calvinistic Augustinianism.   Besides those regular sects, there were various individual enthusiasts and separatists.   These were most rife in the Netherlands, where the free civil constitution afforded a place of refuge for all exiles on account of their faith.   Here only was the press free enough to serve as a thoroughgoing propaganda of mysticism and theosophy. Finally the Russian sects, hitherto little studied, call for special attention.

1. The Socinians (§ 148, 4).—The most important of the Socinian congregations in Poland, for the most part small and composed almost exclusively of the nobility, was that at Racau in the Sendomir Palatinate.   Founded in 1569, this city, since 1600 under James Sieninski, son of the founder, recognised Socinianism as the established religion; and an academy was formed there which soon occupied a distinguished position, and gave such reputation to the place that it could be spoken of as "the Sarmatian Athens."   But the congregation at Lublin, next in importance to that of Racau, was destroyed as early as 1627 by the mob under fanatical excitement caused by the Jesuits. The same disaster befell Racau itself eleven years later.   A couple of idle schoolboys had thrown stones at a wooden crucifix standing before the city gate, and had been for this severely punished by their parents, and turned out of school.   The Catholics, however, made a complaint before the senate, where the Jesuits secured a sentence that the school should be destroyed, the church taken from "the Arians," the printing press closed, but the ministers and teachers outlawed and branded with infamy.   And the Jesuits did not rest until the Reichstag at Warsaw in 1658 issued decrees of banishment against "all Arians," and forbad the profession of "Arianism" under pain of death.—The Davidist non-adoration party of Transylvanian Unitarians (§ 148, 3) was finally overcome, and the endeavours after conformity with the Polish Socinians prevailed at the Diet of Deesch in 1638, where all Unitarian communities engaged to offer worship to Christ, and to accept the baptismal formula of Matthew xxviii. 19. And under the standard of this so called *Complanatio Deesiana* 106 Unitarian congregations, with a membership of 60,000 souls, exist in

Transylvania to this day.—In Germany Socinianism had, even in the beginning of the century, a secret nursery in the University of Altdorf, belonging to the territory of the imperial city of Nuremberg. Soner, professor of medicine, had been won over to this creed by Socinians residing at Leyden, where he had studied in 1597, 1598, and now used his official position at Altdorf for, not only instilling his Unitarian doctrines by means of private philosophical conversations into the minds of his numerous students, who flocked to him from Poland, Transylvania, and Hungary, but also for securing the adhesion of several German students. Only after his death in 1612 did the Nuremberg council come to know about this propaganda. A strict investigation was then made, all Poles were expelled, and all the Socinian writings that could be discovered were burned.—The later Polish Exultants sought and found refuge in Germany, especially in Silesia, Prussia, and Brandenburg, as well as in the Reformed Palatinate, and also founded some small Unitarian congregations, which, however, after maintaining for a while a miserable existence, gradually passed out of view. They had greater success and spread more widely in the Netherlands, till the states-general of 1653, in consequence of repeated synodal protests, and on the ground of an opinion given by the University of Leyden, issued a strict edict against the Unitarians, who now gradually passed over to the ranks of the Remonstrants (§ 161, 2) and the Collegiants. Also in England, since the time of Henry VIII., antitrinitarian confessors and martyrs were to be found. Even in 1611, under James I., three of them had been consigned to the flames. The Polish Socinians took occasion from this to send the king a Racovian Catechism; but in 1614 it was, by order of parliament, burned by the hands of the hangman. The Socinians were also excluded from the benefit of the Act of Toleration of 1689, which was granted to all other dissenters (§ 155, 3). The progress of deism, however, among the upper classes (§§ 164, 3; 171, 1) did much to prevent the extreme penal laws being carried into execution.—The following are the most distinguished among the numerous learned theologians of the Augustan age of Socinian scholarship, who contributed to the extending, establishing, and vindicating of the system of their church by exegetical, dogmatic, and polemical writings: John Crell, died 1631; Jonas Schlichting, died 1661; Von Wolzogen, died 1661; and Andr. Wissowatius, a grandson of Faustus Socinus, died 1678; and with these must also be ranked the historian of Polish Socinianism, Stanislaus Lubienicki, died 1675, whose "*Hist. Reformat. Polonicæ*," etc., was published at Amsterdam in 1685.

2. The Baptists of the Continent.—(1) The Dutch Baptists (§ 147, 2). Even during Menno's lifetime the Mennonites had split into the *Coarse* and the *Fine*. The *Coarse*, who had abandoned much of the primitive

severity of the sect, and were by far the most numerous, were again divided during the Arminian controversy into Remonstrants and Predestinationists. The former, from their leader, were called Galenists, and from having a lamb as the symbol of their Church, Lambists. The latter were called Apostoolers from their leader, and Sunists because their churches had the figure of the sun as a symbol. The Lambists, who acknowledged no confession of faith, were most numerous. In A.D. 1800, however, a union of the two parties was effected, the Sunists adopting the doctrinal position of the Lambists.—During the time when Arminian pastors were banished from the Netherlands, three brothers Van der Kodde founded a sect of Collegiants, which repudiated the clerical office, assigned preaching and dispensation of sacraments to laymen, and baptized only adults by immersion. Their place of baptism was Rhynsburg on the Rhine, and hence they were called Rhynsburgers. Their other name was given them from their assemblies, which they styled *collegia*.—(2) The Moravian Baptists (§ 147, 8). The Thirty Years' War ruined the flourishing Baptist congregations in Moravia, and the reaction against all non-Catholics that followed the battle of the White Mountain near Prague, in A.D. 1620, told sorely against them. In A.D. 1622 a decree for their banishment was issued, and these quiet, inoffensive men were again homeless fugitives. Remnants of them fled into Hungary and Transylvania, only to meet new persecutions there. A letter of protection from Leopold I., A.D. 1659, secured them the right of settling in three counties around Pressburg. But soon these rigorous persecutions broke out afresh; they were beset by Jesuits seeking to convert them, and when this failed they were driven out or annihilated. At last, by A.D. 1757–1762, they were completely broken up, and most of them had joined the Roman Catholic church. A few families preserved their faith by flight into South Russia, where they settled in Wirschenka. When the Toleration Edict of Joseph II., of A.D. 1781, secured religious freedom to Protestants in Austria, several returned again to the faith of their fathers, in the hope that the toleration would be extended to them; but they were bitterly disappointed. They now betook themselves to Russia, and together with their brethren already there, settled in the Crimea, where they still constitute the colony of Hutersthal.

8. The English Baptists.—The notion that infant baptism is objectionable also found favour among the English Independents. Owing to the slight importance attached to the sacraments generally, and more particularly to baptism, in the Reformed church, especially among the Independents, the supporters of the practice of the church in regard to baptism to a large extent occupied common ground with its opponents. The separation took place only after the

rise of the fanatical prophetic sects (§ 161, 1). We must, however, distinguish from the continental Anabaptists the English Baptists, who enjoyed the benefit of the Toleration Act of William III., of A.D 1689, along with the other dissenters, by maintaining their Independent-Congregationalist constitution (§ 155, 3). In A.D. 1691, over the Arminian question, they split up into Particular and General, or Regular and Free Will, Baptists. The former, by far the more numerous, held by the Calvinistic doctrine of *gratia particularis*, while the latter rejected it. The Seventh-Day Baptists, who observed the seventh instead of the first day of the week, were founded by Bampfield in A.D. 1665.[1]—From England the Baptists spread to North America, in A.D. 1630, where Roger Williams (§ 162, 2), one of their first leaders, founded the little state of Rhode Island, and organized it on thoroughly Baptist-Independent principles.[2]—Continuation, § 170, 6.

4. The Quakers.—George Fox, born A.D. 1624, died A.D. 1691, was son of a poor Presbyterian weaver in Drayton, Leicestershire. After scant schooling he went to learn shoemaking at Nottingham, but in A.D. 1643 abandoned the trade. Harassed by spiritual conflicts, he wandered about seeking peace for his soul. Upon hearing an Independent preach on 2 Peter i. 19, he was moved loudly to contradict the preacher. "What we have to do with," he said, "is not the word, but the Spirit by which those men of God spake and wrote." He was seized as a disturber of public worship, but was soon after released. In A.D. 1649 he travelled the country preaching and teaching, addressing every man as "thou," raising his hat to none, greeting none, attracting thousands by his preaching, often imprisoned, flogged, tortured, hunted like a wild beast. The core of his preaching was, not Scripture, but the Spirit, not Christ without but Christ within, not outward worship, not churches, "steeple-houses," and bells, not doctrines and sacraments, but only the inner light, which is kindled by God in the conscience of every man, renewed and quickened by the Spirit of Christ, which suddenly lays hold upon it. The number of his followers increased from day to day. In A.D. 1652 he found, along with his friends, a kindly shelter in the house of Thomas Fell, of Smarthmore near Preston, and in his wife Margaret a motherly

---

[1] Crosby, "History of the English Baptists." 4 vols. London, 1738. Ivimey, "History of the English Baptists from 1688-1760." 2 vols. London, 1830. Cramp, "History of the Baptists to end of 18th Century." 3 vols. London, 1872.

[2] Backus, "History of the English-American Baptists." 2 vols. Boston, 1777. Cox and Hoby, "The Baptists in America." New York, 1836. Hague, "The Baptists Transplanted," etc. New York, 1846.

counsellor, who devoted her whole life to the cause. They called
themselves "The Society of Friends." The name Quaker was given
as a term of reproach by a violent judge, whom Fox bad "quake
before the word of God." After the overthrow of the hopes of the
Saints through the dissolution of the Short Parliament and Cromwell's apostasy (§ 155, 2), many of them joined the Quakers, and led
them into revolutionary and fanatical excesses. Confined hitherto to
the northern counties, they now spread in London and Bristol, and
over all the south of England. In January, A.D. 1655, they held a fort-
night's general meeting at Swannington, in Leicestershire. Crowds
of apostles went over into Ireland, to North America and the West
Indies, to Holland, Germany, France, and Italy, and even to Constantinople. They did not meet with great success. In Italy they
encountered the Inquisition, and in North America the severest penal
laws were passed against them. In A.D. 1656 James Naylor, one of
their most famous leaders, celebrated at Bristol the second coming of
Christ "in the Spirit," by enacting the scene of Christ's triumphal
entry into Jerusalem. But the king of the new Israel was scourged,
branded on the forehead with the letter B as a blasphemer, had his
tongue pierced with a redhot iron, and was then cast into prison.
Many absurd extravagances of this kind, which drew down upon
them frequent persecutions, as well as the failure of their foreign
missionary enterprises, brought most of the Quakers to adopt more
sober views. The great mother Quakeress, Margaret Fell, exercised a
powerful influence in this direction. George Fox, too, out of whose
hands the movement had for a long time gone, now lent his aid.
Naylor himself, in A.D. 1659, issued a recantation, addressed "to all the
people of the Lord," in which he made the confession, "My judgment
was turned away, and I was a captive under the power of darkness."

5. The movement of Quakerism in the direction of sobriety and
common sense was carried out to its fullest extent during the Stuart
Restoration, A.D. 1660–1688. Abandoning their revolutionary tendencies through dislike to Cromwell's violence, and giving up most of their
fanatical extravagances, the Quakers became models of quiet, orderly
living. Robert Barclay, by his "Catechesis et Fidei Confessio," of A.D.
1673, gave a sort of symbolic expression to their belief, and vindicated
his doctrinal positions in his "Theologiæ vere Christianæ Apologia" of
A.D. 1676. During this period many of them laid down their lives for
their faith. On the other side of the sea they formed powerful settlements, distinguished for religious toleration and brotherly love. The
chief promoter of this new departure was William Penn, A.D. 1644–
1718, son of an English admiral, who, while a student at Oxford,
was impressed by a Quaker's preaching, and led to attend the prayer
and fellowship meetings of the Friends. In order to break his con-

nexion with this party, his father sent him, in A.D. 1661, to travel in France and Italy. The frivolity of the French court failed to attract him, but for a long time he was spellbound by Amyrault's theological lectures at Saumur. On his return home, in A.D. 1664, he seemed to have completely come back to a worldly life, when once again he was arrested by a Quaker's preaching. In A.D. 1668 he formally joined the society. For a controversial tract, *The Sandy Foundation Shaken*, he was sent for six months to the Tower, where he composed the famous tract, *No Cross, no Crown*, and a treatise in his own vindication, "Innocency with her Open Face." His father, who, shortly before his death in A.D. 1670, was reconciled to his son, left him a yearly income of £1,500, with a claim on Government for £16,000. In spite of continued persecution and oppression he continued unweariedly to promote the cause of Quakerism by speech and pen. In A.D. 1677, in company with Fox and Barclay, he made a tour through Holland and Germany. In both countries he formed many friendships, but did not succeed in establishing any societies. His hopes now turned to North America, where Fox had already wrought with success during the times of sorest persecution, A.D. 1671, 1672. In lieu of his father's claim, he obtained from Government a large tract of land on the Delaware, with the right of colonizing and organizing it under English suzerainty. Twice he went out for this purpose himself, in A.D. 1682 and 1699, and formed the Quaker state of Pennsylvania, with Philadelphia as its capital. The first principle of its constitution was universal religious toleration, even to Catholics.[1]

6. The Quaker Constitution, as fixed in Penn's time, was strictly democratic and congregationalist, with complete exclusion of a clerical order. At their services any man or woman, if moved by the Spirit, might pray, teach, or exhort, or if no one felt so impelled they would sit on in silence. Their meeting-houses had not the form or fittings of churches, their devotional services had neither singing nor music. They repudiated water baptism, alike of infants and adults, and recognised only baptism of the Spirit. The Lord's supper, as a symbolical memorial, is no more needed by those who are born again.

---

[1] Of special importance for the early history of the Quakers are, "Letters of Early Friends," edited by Robert Barclay, a descendant of the Quaker apostle. London, 1841. "Fox's Journal; or, Historical Accounts of his Life, Travels, and Sufferings." London, 1694. Penn. "Summary of History, Doctrines, and Discipline of Friends." London, 1692. Tallack, "George Fox; the Quakers and the Early Baptists." London, 1868. Bickley, "George Fox and the Early Quakers." London, 1884. Stoughton, "W. Penn, Founder of Pennsylvania." London, 1883.

Monthly gatherings of all independent members, quarterly meetings
of deputies of a circuit, and a yearly synod of representatives of all
the circuits, administered or drew up the regulations for the several
societies. The Doctrinal Belief of the Quakers is completely dominated
by its central dogma of the "inner light," which is identified with
reason and conscience as the common heritage of mankind. Darkened
and weakened by the fall, it is requickened in us by the Spirit of the
glorified Christ, and possesses us as an inner spiritual Christ, an
inner Word of God. The Bible is recognised as the outer word of
God, but is useful only as a means of arousing the inner word. The
Calvinistic doctrine of election is decidedly rejected, and also that of
vicarious satisfaction. But also the doctrines of the fall, original sin,
justification by faith, as well as that of the Trinity, are very much
set aside in favour of an indefinite subjective theology of feeling.
The operation of the Holy Spirit in man's redemption and salvation
outside of Christendom is frankly admitted. On the other hand, the
ethical-practical element, as shown in works of benevolence, in the
battle for religious freedom, for the abolition of slavery, etc., is
brought to the front. In regard to life and manners, the Quakers
have distinguished themselves in all domestic, civil, industrial, and
mercantile, movements by quiet, peaceful industry, strict integrity,
and simple habits, so that not only did they amass great wealth,
but gained the confidence and respect of those around. They refused
to take oaths or to serve as soldiers, or to engage in sports, or to
indulge in any kind of luxury. In social intercourse they declined
to acknowledge any titles of rank, would not bow or raise the hat to
any, but addressed all by the simple "thou." Their men wore broad-
brimmed hats, a plain, simple coat, without collar or buttons, fastened
by hooks. Their women wore a simple gray silk dress, with like
coloured bonnet, without ribbon, flower, or feathers, and a plain
shawl. Wearing mourning dress was regarded as a heathenish custom.[1]—Continuation, § 211, 3.

7. Labadie and the Labadists.—Jean de Labadie, the scion of an
ancient noble family, born A.D. 1610, was educated in the Jesuit school
at Bordeaux, entered the order, and became a priest, but was released
from office at his own wish in A.D. 1639, on account of delicate health
Even in the Jesuit college the principles that manifested themselves

---

[1] Sewel, "History of the Quakers." 2 vols. London, 1834. Cunningham, "The Quakers, from their Origin in 1624 to the Present
Time." London, 1868. Barclay, "Apology for the True Christian
Divinity: a Vindication of Quakerism." 4th ed. London, 1701. Clark-
son, "A Portraiture of Quakerism." 3 vols. London, 1806. Rowntree, "Quakerism, Past and Present." London, 1839.

in his later life began to take root in him. By Scripture study he
was led to adopt almost Augustinian views of sin and grace, as well
as the conviction of the need of a revival of the church after the
apostolic pattern. This tendency was confirmed and deepened by the
influence of Spanish Quietism, which even the Jesuits had favoured
to some extent. In the interest of these views he wrought laboriously for eleven years as Catholic priest in Amiens, Paris, and other
places, amid the increasing hostility of the Jesuits. Their persecution, together with a growing clearness in his Augustinian convictions, led him formally to go over to the Reformed church in A.D.
1650. He now laboured for seven years as Reformed pastor at
Montauban. In A.D. 1657, owing to political suspicions against him
spread by the Jesuits, he withdrew from Montauban, and, after two
years' labour at Orange, settled at Geneva, where his preaching and
household visitations bore abundant fruit. In A.D. 1666 he accepted a
call to Middelburg, in Zealand. There he was almost as successful
as he had been in Geneva; but there too it began to appear that in
him there burned a fire strange to the Reformed church. The French
Reformed synod took great offence at his refusal to sign the Belgic
Confession. It was found that at many points he was not in sympathy
with the church standards, that he had written in favour of chiliasm
and the Apokatastasis, that in regard to the nature and idea of
the church and its need of a reformation he was not in accord with
the views of the Reformed church. The synod in 1668 suspended
him from office, and, as he did not confess his errors, in the following year deposed him. Labadie then saw that what he regarded
as his lifework, the restoration of the apostolic church, was as little
attainable within the Reformed as within the Catholic church. He
therefore organized his followers into a separate denomination, and
was, together with them, banished by the magistrate. The neighbouring town of Veere received them gladly, but Middelburg now persuaded the Zealand council to issue a decree banishing them from that
town also. The people of Veere were ready to defy this order, but
Labadie thought it better to avoid the risk of a civil war by voluntary
withdrawal; and so he went, in August, A.D. 1669, with about forty
followers, to Amsterdam, where he laid the foundations of an apostolic
church. This new society consisted of a sort of monastic household
consisting only of the regenerate. They hired a commodious house, and
from thence sent out spiritual workers as missionaries, to spread the
principles of the "new church" throughout the land. Within a year
they numbered 60,000 souls. They dispensed the sacrament according
to the Reformed rite, and preached the gospel in conventicles. The
most important gain to the party was the adhesion of Anna Maria
von Schürman, born at Cologne A.D. 1607 of a Reformed family, but

settled from A.D. 1623 with her mother in Utrecht, celebrated for her unexampled attainment in languages, science, and art. When in A.D. 1760, the government, urged by the synod, forbad attendance on the Labadists' preaching, the accomplished and pious Countess-palatine Elizabeth, sister of the elector-palatine, and abbess of the rich cloister of Herford, whose intimate friend Schürman had been for forty years, gave them an asylum in the capital of her little state.

8. In Herford "the Hollanders" met with bitter opposition from the Lutheran clergy, the magistracy, and populace, and were treated by the mob with insult and scorn. They themselves also gave only too good occasion for ridicule. At a sacramental celebration, the aged Labadie and still older Schürman embraced and kissed each other and began to dance for joy. In his sermons and writings Labadie set forth the Quietist doctrines of the limitation of Christ's life and sufferings in the mortification of the flesh, the duty of silent prayer, the sinking of the soul into the depths of the Godhead, the community of goods, etc. Special offence was given by the private marriage of the three leaders, Labadie, Yvon, and Dulignon with young wealthy ladies of society, and their views of marriage among the regenerate as an institution for raising up a pure seed free from original sin and brought forth without pain. The Elector of Brandenburg, hitherto favourable, as guardian of the seminary was obliged, in answer to the complaints of the Herford magistracy, to appoint a commission of inquiry. Labadie wrote a defence, which was published in Latin, Dutch, and German, in which he endeavoured to harmonize his mystical views with the doctrines of the Reformed church. But in A.D. 1671 the magistrates obtained a mandate from the imperial court at Spires, which threatened the abbess with the ban if she continued to harbour the sectaries. In A.D. 1672 Labadie settled in Altona, where he died in A.D. 1674. His followers, numbering 160, remained here undisturbed till the war between Denmark and Sweden broke out in A.D. 1675. They then retired to the castle of Waltha in West Friesland, the property of three sisters belonging to the party. Schürman died in A.D. 1678, Dulignon in A.D. 1679, and Yvon, who now had sole charge, was obliged in A.D. 1688 to abolish the institution of the community of goods, after a trial of eighteen years, being able to pay back much less than he had received. After his death in A.D. 1707 the community gradually fell off, and after the property had gone into other hands on the death of the last of the sisters in A.D. 1725, the society finally broke up.

9. During this age various fanatical sects sprang up. In Thuringia, Stiefel and his nephew Meth caused much trouble to the Lutheran clergy in the beginning of the century by their fanatical enthusiasm,

till convinced, after twenty years, of the errors of their ways. Drabicius, who had left the Bohemian Brethren owing to differences of belief, and then lived in Hungary as a weaver in poor circumstances, boasted in A.D. 1638 of having Divine revelations, prophesied the overthrow of the Austrian dynasty in A.D. 1657, the election of the French king as emperor, the speedy fall of the Papacy, and the final conversion of all heathens; but was put to death at Pressburg in A.D. 1671 as a traitor with cruel tortures. Even Comenius, the noble bishop of the Moravians, took the side of the prophets, and published his own and others' prophecies under the title " *Lux in Tenebris.*"—Jane Leade of Norfolk, influenced by the writings of Böhme, had visions, in which the Divine Wisdom appeared to her as a virgin. She spread her Gnostic revelations in numerous tracts, founded in A.D. 1670 the Philadelphian Society in London, and died in A.D. 1704, at the age of eighty-one. The most important of her followers was John Pordage, preacher and physician, whose theological speculation closely resembles that of Jac. Böhme. To the Reformed church belonged also Peter Poiret of Metz, pastor from A.D. 1664 in Heidelburg, and afterwards of a French congregation in the Palatine-Zweibrücken. Influenced by the writings of Bourignon and Guyon, he resigned his pastorate, and accompanied the former in his wanderings in north-west Germany till his death in 1680. At Amsterdam in A.D. 1687 he wrote his mystical work, "*L'Économie Divine*" in seven vols., which sets forth in the Cocceian method the mysticism and theosophy of Bourignon. He died at Rhynsburg in A.D. 1719.—From the Lutheran church proceeded Giftheil of Württemburg, Breckling of Holstein, and Kuhlmann, who went about denouncing the clergy, proclaiming fanatical views, and calling for impracticable reforms. Of much greater importance was John George Gichtel, an eccentric disciple of Jac. Böhme, who in A.D. 1665 lost his situation as law agent in his native town of Regensburg, his property, and civil rights, and suffered imprisonment and exile from the city for his fanatical ideas. He died in needy circumstances in Amsterdam in A.D. 1710. He had revelations and visions, fought against the doctrine of justification, and denounced marriage as fornication which nullifies the spiritual marriage with the heavenly Sophia consummated in the new birth, etc. His followers called themselves Angelic Brethren, from Matthew xxii. 20, strove after angelic sinlessness by emancipation from all earthly lusts, toils, and care, regarded themselves as a priesthood after the order of Melchizedec for propitiating the Divine wrath.—Continuation, § 170.

10. **Russian Sects.**—A vast number of sects sprang up within the Russian church, which are all included under the general name Raskolniks or apostates. They fall into two great classes in their distinctive character, diametrically opposed the one to the other. (1) The

Starowerzi, or Old Believers. They originated in A.D. 1652, in consequence of the liturgical reform of the learned and powerful patriarch Nikon, which called forth the violent opposition of a large
body of the peasantry, who loved the old forms. Besides stubborn
adhesion to the old liturgy, they rejected all modern customs and
luxuries, held it sinful to cut the beard, to smoke tobacco, to drink tea
and coffee, etc. The Starowerzi, numbering some ten millions, are to
this day distinguished by their pure and simple lives, and are split up
into three parties: (i.) *Jedinowerzi,* who are nearest to the orthodox
church, recognise its priesthood, and are different only in their religious ceremonies and the habits of their social life; (ii.) The Starov-
bradzi, who do not recognise the priesthood of the orthodox church;
and (iii.) the *Bespopowtschini,* who have no priests, but only elders,
and are split up into various smaller sects. Under the peasant Philip
Pustosiwät, a party of Starowerzi, called from their leader Philippins,
fled during the persecution of A.D. 1700 from the government of Olonez,
and settled in Polish Lithuania and East Prussia, where to the number of 1,200 souls they live to this day in villages in the district
of Gumbinnen, engaged in agricultural pursuits, and observing the
rites of the old Russian church.—(2) At the very opposite pole from
the Starowerzi stand the Heretical Sects, which repudiate and condemn everything in the shape of external church organization, and
manifest a tendency in some cases toward fanatical excess, and in
other cases toward rationalistic spiritualism. As the sects showing
the latter tendency did not make their appearance till the eighteenth
century (§ 166, 2), we have here to do only with those of the former
class. The most important of these sects is that of the Men of God, or
Spiritual Christians, who trace their origin from a peasant, Danila
Filipow, of the province of Wladimir. In 1645, say they, the divine
Father, seated on a cloud of flame, surrounded by angels, descended
from heaven on Mount Gorodin in a chariot of fire, in order to restore
true Christianity in its original purity and spirituality. For this
purpose he incarnated himself in Filipow's pure body. He commanded his followers, who in large numbers, mainly drawn from the
peasant class, gathered around him, not to marry, and if already
married to put away their wives, to abstain from all intoxicating
drinks, to be present neither at marriages nor baptisms, but above
all things to believe that there is no other god besides him. After
some years he adopted as his son another peasant, Ivan Suslow, who
was said to have been born of a woman a hundred years old, by communicating to him in his thirtieth year his own divine nature. Ivan,
as a new Christ, sent out twelve apostles to spread his doctrine. The
Czar Alexis put him and forty of his adherents into prison; but
neither the knout nor the rack could wring from them the mysteries

of their faith and worship. At last, on a Friday, the czar caused the
new Christ to be crucified ; but on the following Sunday he appeared
risen again among his disciples. After some years the imprisoning,
crucifying, and resurrection were repeated. Imprisoned a third time
in 1672, he owed his liberation to an edict of grace on the occasion of
the birth of the Prince Peter the Great. He now lived at Moscow
along with the divine father Filipow, who had hitherto consulted his
own safety by living in concealment in the enjoyment of the adoration
of his followers unmolested for thirty years, supported by certain
wealthy merchants. Filipow is said to have ascended up in the presence of many witnesses, in 1700, into the seventh and highest heaven,
where he immediately seated himself on the throne as the " Lord of
Hosts," and the Christ, Suslow, also returned thither in 1716, after
both had reached the hundredth year of the human existence. As
Suslow's successor appeared a new Christ in Prokopi Lupkin, and
after his death, in 1732, arose Andr. Petrow. The last Christ manifestation was revealed in the person of the unfortunate Czar Peter
III., dethroned by his wife Catharine II. in 1762, who, living meanwhile in secret, shall soon return, to the terrible confusion of all
unbelievers. With this the historical tradition of the earlier sect of
the Men of God is brought to a close, and in the Skopsen, or Eunuchs,
who also venerate the Czar Peter III. as the Christ that is to come
again, a new development of the sect has arisen, carrying out its
principles more and more fully (§ 210, 4). Other branches of the
same party, among which, as also among the Skopsen, the fanatical
endeavour to mortify the flesh is carried to the most extravagant
length, are the Morelschiki or Self-Flagellators, the Dumbies, who will
not, even under the severest tortures, utter a sound, etc. The ever-
increasing development of this sect-forming craze, which found its
way into several monasteries and nunneries, led to repeated judicial
investigations, the penitent being sentenced for their fault to confinement in remote convents, and the obdurate being visited with severe
corporal punishments and even with death. The chief sources of
information regarding the history, doctrine, and customs of the " Men
of God " and the Skopsen are their own numerous spiritual songs,
collected by Prof. Ivan Dobrotworski of Kasan, which were sung in
their assemblies for worship with musical accompaniment and solemn
dances. On these occasions their prophets and prophetesses were
wont to prophesy, and a kind of sacramental supper was celebrated
with bread and water. The sacraments of the Lord's supper and
baptism, as administered by the orthodox church, are repudiated and
scorned, the latter as displaced by the only effectual baptism of the
Spirit. They have, indeed, in order to avoid persecution, been
obliged to take part in the services of the orthodox national church,

and to confess to its priests, avoiding, however, all reference to the
sect.[1]

§ 164. PHILOSOPHERS AND FREETHINKERS.[2]

The mediæval scholastic philosophy had outlived itself,
even in the pre-Reformation age ; yet it maintained a linger-
ing existence side by side with those new forms which the
modern spirit in philosophy was preparing for itself.   We
hear an echo of the philosophical ferment of the sixteenth
century in the Italian Dominican Campanella, and in the
Englishman Bacon of Verulam we meet the pioneer of
that modern philosophy which had its proper founder in
Descartes.   Spinoza, Locke, and Leibnitz were in succession
the leaders of this philosophical development.   Alongside of
this philosophy, and deriving its weapons from it for attack
upon theology and the church, a number of freethinkers
also make their appearance.   These, like their more radical
disciples in the following century, regarded Scripture as
delusive, and nature and reason as alone trustworthy sources
of religious knowledge.

1. Philosophy.—Campanella of Stilo in Calabria entered the Dominican
order, but soon lost taste for Aristotelian philosophy and scholastic
theology, and gave himself to the study of Plato, the Cabbala, astrology,
magic, etc. Suspected of republican tendencies, the Spanish government put him in prison in A.D. 1599. Seven times was he put upon
the rack for twenty-four hours, and then confined for twenty-seven
years in close confinement. Finally, in A.D. 1626, Urban VIII. had him
transferred to the prison of the papal Inquisition. He was set free in

---

[1] Heard, "The Russian Church and Russian Dissent." London.
1887. Mackenzie Wallace, "Russia," chaps. xiv., xx. 2 vols. London, 1877. Palmer, "The Patriarch and the Tsar." 6 vols. London.
1871–1876.

[2] Ueberweg, "History of Philosophy," vol. ii., pp. 81–185. Pünjer,
"History of the Christian Philosophy of Religion from the Reformation to Kant." Edin., 1887. Pfleiderer, "Philosophy of Religion,"
vol. i. London, 1887. Erdmann's "History of Philosophy." 8 vols.
London, 1889.

A.D. 1629, and received a papal pension; but further persecutions by the Spaniards obliged him to fly to his protector Richelieu in France, where in A.D. 1639 he died. He composed eighty-two treatises, mostly in prison, the most complete being " *Philosophia Rationalis*," in five vols. In his "*Atheismus Triumphatus*" he appears as an apologist of the Romish system, but so insufficiently, that many said *Atheismus Triumphans* was the more fitting title. His "*Monarchia Messiæ*" too appeared, even to the Catholics, an abortive apology for the Papacy. In his "*Civitas Solis*," an imitation of the "Republic" of Plato, he proceeded upon communistic principles.—**Francis Bacon** of Verulam, long chancellor of England, died A.D. 1626, the great spiritual heir of his mediæval namesake (§ 103, 9), was the first successful reformer of the plan of study followed by the schoolmen. With a prophet's marvellous grasp of mind he organized the whole range of science, and gave a forecast of its future development in his " *De Augmentis* " and " *Novum Organon.*" He rigidly separated the domain of *knowledge,* as that of philosophy and nature, grasped only by experience, from the domain of *faith,* as that of theology and the church, reached only through revelation. Yet he maintained the position : *Philosophia obiter libata a Deo abducit, plene hausta ad Deum reducit.* He is the real author of empiricism in philosophy and the realistic methods of modern times. His public life, however, is clouded by thanklessness, want of character, and the taking of bribes. In A.D. 1621 he was convicted by his peers, deprived of his office, sentenced to imprisonment for life in the Tower, and to pay a fine of £40,000; but was pardoned by the king.[1]—The French Catholic **Descartes** started not from experience, but from self-consciousness, with his " *Cogito ergo, sum* " as the only absolutely certain proposition. Beginning with doubt, he rose by pure thinking to the knowledge of the true and certain in things. The imperfection of the soul thus discovered suggests an absolutely perfect Being, to whose perfection the attribute of being belongs. This is the ontological proof for the being of God.—His philosophy was zealously taken up by French Jansenists and Oratorians and the Reformed theologians of Holland, while it was bitterly opposed by such Catholics as Huetius and such Reformed theologians as Voetius.[2]—**Spinoza,** an apostate Jew in Holland, died A.D. 1677,

---

[1] "Bacon's Works," ed. by Spedding, Ellis, and Heath. 14 vols London, 1870. Spedding, "Letters and Life of Lord Bacon." 2 vols. London, 1862. Macaulay on Bacon in *Edinburgh Review* for 1837. Church, "Bacon" in vol. v. of "Collected Works." London, 1888. Nichol, "Bacon : Life and Pilosophy." 2 vols. Edin., 1888.

[2] " Descartes' Method, Meditations, and Principles of Philosophy." Transl. by Prof. Veitch. Edin., 1850 ff. Fischer, "Descartes and his School." London, 1887.

gained little influence over his own generation by his profound pantheistic philosophy, which has powerfully affected later ages. A violent controversy, however, was occasioned by his " *Tractatus Theologico-politicus*," in which he attacked the Christian doctrine of revelation and the authenticity of the O.T. books, especially the Pentateuch, and advocated absolute freedom of thought.[1] (2) John Locke, died A.D. 1704, with his sensationalism took up a position midway between Bacon's empiricism and Descartes' rationalism, on the one hand, and English deism and French materialism, on the other. His "Essay concerning Human Understanding " denies the existence of innate ideas, and seeks to show that all our notions are only products of outer or inner experience, of sensation or reflection. In this treatise, and still more distinctly in his tract, " The Reasonableness of Christianity," intended as an apology for Christianity, and even for biblical visions and miracles, as well as for the messianic character of Christ, he openly advocated pure Pelagianism that knows nothing of sin and atonement.[2] — Leibnitz, a Hanoverian statesman, who died A.D. 1716, introduced the new German philosophy in its first stage. The philosophy of Leibnitz is opposed at once to the theosophy of Paracelsus and Böhme and to the empiricism of Bacon and Locke, the pantheism of Spinoza, and the scepticism and manichæism of Bayle. It is indeed a Christian philosophy not fully developed. But inasmuch as at the same time it adopted, improved upon, and carried out the rationalism of Descartes, it also paved the way for the later theological rationalism. The foundation of his philosophy is the theory of monads wrought out in his "*Theodicée*" against Bayle and in his " *Nouveaux Essais*," against Locke. In opposition to the atomic theory of the materialists, he regarded all phenomena in the world as eccentricities of so called monads, *i.e.* primary simple and indivisible substances, each of which is a miniature of the whole universe. Out of these monads that radiate out from God, the primary monad, the world is formed into a harmony once for all admired of God: the theory of pre-established harmony. This must be the best of worlds, otherwise it would not have been. In opposition to Bayle, who had argued in a manichæan fashion against God's goodness and wisdom from the existence of evil, Leibnitz seeks to show

---

[1] Willis, "Spinoza : his Ethics, Life, and Influence on Modern Thought." London, 1870. Pollock, "Spinoza : his Life and Philosophy." London, 1880. Martineau, "Spinoza." London, 1882. "Spinoza, Four Essays by Land, Von Floten, Fischer, and Renan." Edited by Prof. Knight. London, 1884.

[2] "Locke's Complete Works." 9 vols. London, 1853. Cousin, "Elements of Psychology : a Critical Examination of Locke's Essay." Edin., 1856. Webb, " Intellectualism of Locke." London, 1858.

that this does not contradict the idea of the best of worlds, nor that of the Divine goodness and wisdom, since finity and imperfection belong to the very notion of creature, a metaphysical evil from which moral evil inevitably follows, yet not so as to destroy the pre-established harmony. Against Locke he maintains the doctrine of innate ideas contests Clarke's theory of indeterminism, maintains the agreement of philosophy with revelation, which indeed is above but not contrary to reason, and hopes to prove his system by mathematical demonstration.[1] —Continuation, § 171, 10.

3. Freethinkers.—The tendency of the age to throw off all positive Christianity first showed openly itself in England as the final outcome of Levellerism (§ 162, 2). This movement has been styled naturalism, because it puts natural in place of revealed religion, and deism, because in place of the redeeming work of the triune God it admits only a general providence of the one God. On philosophic grounds the English deists affirmed the impossibility of revelation, inspiration, prophecy, and miracle, and on critical grounds rejected them from the Bible and history. The simple religious system of deism embraced God, providence, freedom of the will, virtue, and the immortality of the soul. The Christian doctrines of the Trinity, original sin, satisfaction, justification, resurrection, etc., were regarded as absurd and irrational. Deism in England spread almost exclusively among upper-class laymen; the people and clergy stood firmly to their positive beliefs. Theological controversial tracts were numerous, but their polemical force was in great measure lost by the latitudinarianism of their authors. — The principal English deists of the century were (1) Edward Herbert of Cherbury, A.D. 1581–1648, a nobleman and statesman. He reduced all religion to five points: Faith in God, the duty of reverencing Him, especially by leading an upright life, atoning for sin by genuine repentance, recompense in the life eternal.—(2) Thomas Hobbes, A.D. 1588–1679, an acute philosophical and political writer, looked on Christianity as an oriental phantom, and of value only as a support of absolute monarchy and an antidote to revolution. The state of nature is a *bellum omnium contra omnes;* religion is the means of establishing order and civilization. The state should decide what religion is to prevail. Every one may indeed believe what he will, but in regard to churches and worship he must submit to the state as represented by the king. His chief work is "Leviathan; or, The Matter, Form, and Power of a Commonwealth, Ecclesiastical and Civil."—(3) Charles Blount, who died a suicide in A.D. 1693, a rabid opponent of all miracles as mere tricks of priests, wrote "Oracles of

---

[1] Guhrauer, "Leibnitz: a Biography." Transl. by Mackie. Boston, 1845.

Reason," "*Religio Laici*," "Great is Diana of the Ephesians," and translated Philostratus' "Life of Apollonius of Tyana."—(4) Thomas Browne, A.D. 1635–1682, a physician, who in his "*Religio Medici*" sets forth a mystical supernaturalism, took up a purely deistic ground in his "Vulgar Errors," published three years later.—Among the opponents of deism in this age the most notable are Richard Baxter (§ 162, 3) and Ralph Cudworth, A.D. 1617–1688, a latitudinarian and Platonist, who sought to prove the leading Christian doctrines by the theory of innate ideas. He wrote "Intellectual System of the Universe" in A.D. 1678. The pious Irish scientist, Robert Boyle, founded in London, in A.D. 1691, a lectureship of £40 a year for eight discourses against deistic and atheistic unbelief.[1]—Continuation, § 171, 1.

4. A tendency similar to that of the English deists was represented in Germany by Matthias Knutzen, who sought to found a freethinking sect. The Christian "Coran" contains only lies; reason and conscience are the true Bible; there is no God, nor hell nor heaven; priests and magistrates should be driven out of the world, etc. The senate of Jena University on investigation found that his pretension to 700 followers was a vain boast.—In France the brilliant and learned sceptic Peter Bayle, A.D. 1647–1706, was the apostle of a light-hearted unbelief. Though son of a Reformed pastor, the Jesuits got him over to the Romish church, but in a year and a half he apostatised again. He now studied the Cartesian philosophy, as Reformed professor at Sedan, vindicated Protestantism in several controversial tracts, and as refugee in Holland composed his famous "*Dictionnaire Historique et Critique*," in which he avoided indeed open rejection of the facts of revelation, but did much to unsettle by his easy treatment of them.—Continuation, § 171, 8.

---

[1] Leland, "View of Principal Deistical Writers in England." 2nd ed. 2 vols. London, 1755. Halyburton, "Natural Religion Insufficient; or, A Rational Inquiry into the Principles of the Modern Deists." Edin., 1714. Tulloch, "Rational Theology and Christian Philosophy in England in the 17th Century." 2 vols. Edin., 1872. Cairns, "Unbelief in the 18th Century," chap. ii., "Unbelief in the 17th Century." Edin., 1881.

THIRD SECTION.

CHURCH HISTORY OF THE EIGHTEENTH CENTURY.[1]

I.—The Catholic Church in East and West.

§ 165. THE ROMAN CATHOLIC CHURCH.

DURING the first half of the century the Roman hierarchy suffered severely at the hand of Catholic courts, while in the second half storms gathered from all sides, threatening its very existence. Portugal, France, Spain, and Italy rested not till they got the pope himself to strike the deathblow to the Jesuits, who had been his chief supporters indeed, but who had now become his masters. Soon after the German bishops threatened to free themselves and their people from Rome, and what reforms they could not effect by ecclesiastical measures the emperor undertook to effect by civil measures. Scarcely had this danger been overcome when the horrors of the French Revolution broke out, which sought, along with the Papacy, to overthrow Christianity as well. But, on the other hand, during the early decades of

---

[1] Lecky, "History of the Rise and Influence of the Spirit of Rationalism in Europe." 2 vols. London, 1873. Hagenbach, "German Rationalism." Edin., 1865. Hagenbach, "History of Church in 18th and 19th Centuries." 2 vols. London, 1870. Leslie Stephen, "History of English Thought in the 18th Century." 2 vols. London, 1876. Cairns, "Unbelief in the 18th Century." Edin., 1881.

the century Catholicism had gained many victories in another way by the counter-reformation and conversions. Its foreign missions, however, begun with such promise of success, came to a sad end, and even the home missions faded away, in spite of the founding of various new orders. The Jansenist controversy in the beginning of the century entered on a new stage, the Catholic church being driven into open semi-Pelagianism, and Jansenism into fanatical excesses. The church theology sank very low, and the Catholic supporters of "*Illumination*" far exceeded in number those who had fallen away to it from Protestantism.

1. The Popes.—Clement XI., 1700–1721, protested in vain against the Elector Frederick III. of Brandenburg assuming the crown as King Frederick I. of Prussia, on Jan. 18th, A.D. 1701. In the Spanish wars of succession he sought to remain neutral, but force of circumstances led him to take up a position adverse to German interests. The new German emperor, Joseph I., A.D. 1705–1711, scorned to seek confirmation from the pope, and Clement consequently had the usual prayer for the emperor omitted in the church services. The relations became yet more strained, owing to a dispute about the *jus primarum precum*, Joseph claiming the right to revenues of vacancies as the patron. In A.D. 1707, the pope had the joy of seeing the German army driven out, not only of northern Italy, but also of Naples by the French. Again they came into direct conflict over Parma and Piacenza, Clement claiming them as a papal, the emperor claiming them as an imperial, fief. No pope since the time of Louis the Bavarian had issued the ban against a German emperor, and Clement ventured not to do so now. Refusing the invitation of Louis XIV. to go to Avignon, he was obliged either unconditionally to grant the German claims or to try the fortune of war. He chose the latter alternative. The miserable papal troops, however, were easily routed, and Clement was obliged, in A.D. 1708, to acknowledge the emperor's brother, the Grandduke Charles, as king of Spain, and generally to yield to Joseph's very moderate demands. Clement was the author of the constitution *Unigenitus*, which introduced the second stage in the history of Jansenism. After the short and peaceful pontificate of Innocent XIII. A.D. 1721–1724, came Benedict XIII., A.D. 1724–1730, a pious, well-meaning, narrow-minded man, ruled by a worthless favourite, Cardinal Coscia. He wished to canonize Gregory VII., in the fond hope of thereby securing new favour to his hierarchical views, but this was

protested against by almost all the courts. All the greater was the number of monkish saints with which he enriched the heavenly firmament. He promised to all who on their death-bed should say, " Blessed be Jesus Christ," a 2,000 years' shortening of purgatorial pains. His successor Clement XII., A.D. 1730–1740, deprived the wretched Coscia of his offices, made him disgorge his robberies, imposed on him a severe fine and ten years' imprisonment, but afterwards resigned the management of everything to a greedy, grasping nephew. He was the first pope to condemn freemasonry, A.D. 1736. Benedict XIV., A.D. 1740–1758, one of the noblest, most pious, learned, and liberal of the popes, zealous for the faith of his church, and yet patient with those who differed, moderate and wise in his political procedure, mild and just in his government, blameless in life. He had a special dislike of the Jesuits (§ 155, 12), and jestingly he declared, if, as the curialists assert, "all law and all truth" lie concealed in the shrine of his breast, he had not been able to find the key. He wrote largely on theology and canon law, founded seminaries for the training of the clergy, had many French and English works translated into Italian, and was a liberal patron of art. To check popular excesses he tried to reduce the number of festivals, but without success.—Continuation, in Paragraphs 9, 10, 13.

2. Old and New Orders.—Among the old orders that of Ciugny had amassed enormous wealth, and attempts made by its abbots at reformation led only to endless quarrels and divisions. The abbots now squandered the revenues of their cloisters at court, and these institutions were allowed to fall into disorder and decay. When, in A.D. 1790, all cloisters in France were suppressed, the city of Clugny bought the cloister and church for £4,000, and had them both pulled down.— The most important new orders were : (1) The Mechitarist Congregation, originated by Mechitar the Armenian, who, at Constantinople in A.D. 1701, founded a society for the religious and intellectual education of his countrymen ; but when opposed by the rmenian patriarch, fled to the Morea and joined the United Armenians (§ 72, 2). In A.D. 1712 the pope confirmed the congregation, which, during the war with the Turks was transferred to Venice, and in A.D. 1717 settled on the island St. Lazaro. Its members spread Roman Catholic literature in Armenia and Armenian literature in the West. At a later time there was a famous Mechitarist college in Vienna, which did much by writing and publishing for the education of the Catholic youth.—(2) Frères Ignorantins, or Christian Brothers, founded in A.D. 1725 by De la Salle, canon of Rheims, for the instruction of children, wrought in the spirit of the Jesuits through France, Belgium, and North America. After the expulsion of the Jesuits from France in A.D. 1724, they took their place there till themselves driven out by the Revolution in A.D

1790.[1]—(3) The Liguorians or Redemptorists, founded in A.D. 1732 by Liguori, an advocate, who became Bishop of Naples in A.D. 1762. He died in A.D. 1787 in his ninety-first year, was beatified by Pius VII. in A.D. 1816, and canonized by Gregory XVI. in A.D. 1839, and proclaimed *doctor ecclesiæ* by Pius IX. in A.D. 1871 as a zealous defender of the immaculate conception and papal infallibility. His devotional writings, which exalt Mary by superstitious tales of miracles, were extremely popular in all Catholic countries. His new order was to minister to the poor. He declared the pope's will to be God's, and called for unquestioning obedience. Only after the founder's death did it spread beyond Italy.—Continuation, § 186, 1.

3. Foreign Missions.—In the accommodation controversy (§ 156, 12), the Dominicans prevailed in A.D. 1742; but the abolishing of native customs led to a sore persecution in China, from which only a few remnants of the church were saved. The Italian Jesuit Beschi, with linguistic talents of the highest order, sought in India to make use of the native literature for mission purposes and to place alongside of it a Christian literature. Here the Capuchins opposed the Jesuits as successfully as the Dominicans had in China. These strifes and persecutions destroyed the missions.—The Jesuit state of Paraguay (§ 150, 10) was put an end to in A.D. 1750 by a compact between Portugal and Spain. The revolt of the Indians that followed, inspired and directed by the Jesuits, which kept the combined powers at bay for a whole year, was at last quelled, and the Jesuits expelled the country in A.D. 1758.—Continuation § 186, 7.

4. The Counter-Reformation (§ 153, 2).—Charles XII. of Sweden, in A.D. 1707, forced the Emperor Joseph I. to give the Protestants of Silesia the benefits of the Westphalian Peace and to restore their churches. But in Poland in A.D. 1717, the Protestants lost the right of building new churches, and in A.D. 1733 were declared disqualified for civil offices and places in the diet. In the Protestant city of Thorn the insolence of the Jesuits roused a rebellion which led to a fearful massacre in A.D. 1724. The Dissenters sought and obtained protection in Russia from A.D. 1767, and the partition of Poland between Russia, Austria, and Prussia in A.D. 1772 secured for them religious toleration. In Salzburg the archbishop, Count Firmian, attempted in A.D. 1729 a conversion of the evangelicals by force, who had, with intervals of persecution in the seventeenth century, been tolerated for forty years as quiet and inoffensive citizens. But in A.D. 1731 their elders swore on the host and consecrated salt (2 Chron. xiii. 5) to be true to their faith.

---

[1] "Wilson, "The Christian Brothers, their Origin and Work. With a Sketch of the Life of their Founder, the Venerable Jean Baptiste de la Salle." London, 1883.

This "covenant of salt" was interpreted as rebellion, and in spite of the intervention of the Protestant princes, all the evangelicals, in the severe winter of A.D. 1731, 1732, were driven, with inhuman cruelty, from hearth and home. About 20,000 of them found shelter in Prussian Lithuania; others emigrated to America. The pope praised highly "the noble" archbishop, who otherwise distinguished himself only as a huntsman and a drinker, and by maintaining a mistress in princely splendour.

5. In France the persecution of the Huguenots continued (§ 153, 4). The "pastors of the desert" performed their duties at the risk of their lives, and though many fell as martyrs, their places were quickly filled by others equally heroic. The first rank belongs to Anton Court, pastor at Nismes from A.D. 1715; he died at Lausanne A.D. 1760, where he had founded a theological seminary. He laboured unweariedly and successfully in gathering and organizing the scattered members of the Reformed church, and in overcoming fanaticism by imparting sound instruction. Paul Rabaut, his successor at Nismes, was from A.D. 1730 to 1785 the faithful and capable leader of the martyr church. The judicial murder of Jean Calas at Toulouse in A.D. 1762 presents a hideous example of the fanaticism of Catholic France. One of his sons had hanged himself in a fit of passion. When the report spread that it was the act of his father, in order to prevent the contemplated conversion of his son, the Dominicans canonized the suicide as a martyr to the Catholic faith, roused the mob, and got the Toulouse parliament to put the unhappy father to the torture of the wheel. The other sons were forced to abjure their faith, and the daughters were shut up in cloisters. Two years later Voltaire called attention to the atrocity, and so wrought on public opinion that on the revision of the proceedings by the Parisian parliament, the innocence of the ill-used family was clearly proved. Louis XV. paid them a sum of 30,000 livres; but the fanatical accusers, the false witnesses, and the corrupt judges were left unpunished. This incident improved the position of the Protestants, and in A.D. 1787 Louis XVI. issued the Edict of Versailles, by which not only complete religious freedom but even a legal civil existence was secured them, which was confirmed by a law of Napoleon in A.D. 1802.

6. Conversions.—Pecuniary interests and prospect of marriage with a rich heiress led to the conversion, in A.D. 1712, of Charles Alexander while in the Austrian service; but when he became Duke of Württemburg he solemnly undertook to keep things as they were, and to set up no Catholic services in the country save in his own court chapel. Of other converts Winckelmann and Stolberg are the most famous. While Winckelmann, the greatest of art critics, not a religious but an artistic ultramontane, was led in A.D. 1754 through religious indif-

ference into the Romish church, the warm heart of Von Stolberg was
induced, mainly by the Catholic Princess Gallitzin (§ 172, 2) and a
French emigrant, Madame Montague, to escape the chill of rationalism
amid the incense fumes of the Catholic services.—Continuation,
§ 175, 7.

7. The Second Stage of Jansenism (§ 157, 5).—Pasquier Quesnel, priest of
the Oratory at Paris, suspected in 1675 of Gallicanism, because of notes
in his edition of the works of Leo the Great, fled into the Netherlands,
where he continued his notes on the N.T. Used and recommended by
Noailles, Archbishop of Paris, and other French bishops, this "Jansenist" book was hated by the Jesuits and condemned by a brief of
Clement XI. in A.D. 1708. The Jesuit confessor of Louis XIV., Le
Tellier, selected 101 propositions from the book, and induced the king
to urge their express condemnation by the pope. In the Constitution
Unigenitus of A.D. 1713, Clement pronounced these heretical, and the
king required the expulsion from parliament and church of all who
refused to adopt this bull, which caused a division of the French
church into *Acceptants* and *Appellants*. As many of the condemned
propositions were quoted literally by Quesnel from Augustine and
other Fathers, or were in exact agreement with biblical passages,
Noailles and his party called for an explanation. Instead of this the
pope threatened them with excommunication. In A.D. 1715 the king
died, and under the Duke of Orleans' regency in A.D. 1717, four bishops,
with solemn appeal to a general council, renounced the papal constitution as irreconcilable with the Catholic faith. They were soon
joined by the Sorbonne and the universities of Rheims and Nantes,
Archbishop Noailles, and more than twenty bishops, all the congregations of St. Maur and the Oratorians with large numbers of the
secular clergy and the monks, especially of the Lazarists, Dominicans,
Cistercians, and Camaldulensians. The pope, after vainly calling
them to obey, thundered the ban against the Appellants in A.D. 1718.
But the parliament took the matter up, and soon the aspect of affairs
was completely changed. The regent's favourite, Dubois, hoping to
obtain a cardinal's hat, took the side of the Acceptants and carried
the duke with him, who got the parliament in 1720 to acknowledge
the bull, with express reservation, however, of the Gallican liberties,
and began a persecution of the Appellants. Under Louis XV. the
persecution became more severe, although in many ways moderated
by the influence of his former tutor, Cardinal Fleury. Noailles, who
died in 1729, was obliged in 1728 to submit unconditionally, and in
A.D. 1730 the parliament formally ratified the bull. Amid daily
increasing oppression, many of the more faithful Jansenists, mostly
of the orders of St. Maur and the Oratory, fled to the Netherlands,
where they gave way more and more to fanaticism. In 1727 a young

Jansenist priest, Francis of Paris, died with the original text of the appeal in his hands. His adherents honoured him as a saint, and numerous reports of miracles, which had been wrought at his grave in Medardus churchyard at Paris, made this a daily place of pilgrimage to thousands of fanatics. The excited enthusiasts, who fell into convulsions, and uttered prophecies about the overthrow of church and state, grew in numbers and, with that mesmeric power which fanaticism has been found in all ages to possess powerfully influenced many who had been before careless and profane. One of these was the member of parliament De Montgeron, who, from being a frivolous scoffer, suddenly, in 1732, fell into violent convulsions, and in a three-volumed work, " *La Vérité des Miracles Opérés par l'Intercession de François de Paris,*" 1737, came forward as a zealous apologist of the party. The government, indeed, in 1732 ordered the churchyard to be closed, but portions of earth from the grave of the saint continued to effect convulsions and miracles. Thousands of convulsionists throughout France were thrown into prison, and in 1752, Archbishop Beaumont of Paris, with many other bishops, refused the last sacrament to those who could not prove that they had accepted the constitution. The grave of "St. Francis," however, was the grave of Jansenism, for fanatical excess contains the seeds of dissolution and every manifestation of it hastens the catastrophe. Yet remnants of the party lingered on in France till the outbreak of the Revolution, of which they had prophesied.

8. The Old Catholic Church in the Netherlands.—The first Jesuits appeared in Holland in A.D. 1592. The form of piety fostered by superior and inferior clergy in the Catholic church there, a heritage from the times of the Brethren of the Common Life (§ 112, 9), was directed to the deepening of Christian thought and feeling; and this, as well as the liberal attitude of the Archbishop of Utrecht, awakened the bitter opposition of the Jesuits. At the head of the local clergy was Sasbold Vosmeer, vicar-general of the vacant archiepiscopal see of Utrecht. Most energetically he set himself to thwart the Jesuit machinations, which aimed at abolishing the Utrecht see and putting the church of Holland under the jurisdiction of the papal nuncio at Cologne. On the ground of suspicions of secret conspiracy Vosmeer was banished. But his successors refused to be overruled or set aside by the Jesuits. Meanwhile in France the first stage of the Jansenist controversy had been passed through. The Dutch authorities had heartily welcomed the condemned book of their pious and learned countryman; but when the five propositions were denounced, they agreed in repudiating them, without, however, admitting that they had been taught in the sense objected to by Jansen. The Jesuits, therefore, charged them with the Jansenist heresy, and issued in

A.D. 1697 an anonymous pamphlet full of lying insinuations about
the origin and progress of Jansenism in Holland. Its beginning was
traced back to a visit of Arnauld to Holland in A.D. 1681, and
its effects were seen in the circulation of prayer-books, tracts, and
sermons, urging diligent reading of Scripture, in the depreciation of
the worship of Mary, of indulgences, of images of saints and relics,
rosaries and scapularies (§ 188, 20), processions and fraternities, in
the rigoristic strictness of the confessional, the use of the common
language of the country in baptism, marriage, and extreme unction,
etc. The archbishop of that time, Peter Codde, in order to isolate
him, was decoyed to Rome, and there flattered with hypocritical
pretensions of goodwill, while behind his back his deposition was
carried out, and an apostolic vicar nominated for Utrecht in the
person of his deadly foe Theodore de Cock. But the chapter refused
him obedience, and the States of Holland forbad him to exercise
any official function, and under threat of banishment of all Jesuits
demanded the immediate return of the archbishop. Codde was now
sent down with the papal blessing, but a formal decree of deposition
followed him. Meanwhile the government pronounced on his rival
De Cock, who avoided a trial for high treason by flight, a sentence
of perpetual exile. But Codde, though persistently recognised by
his chapter as the rightful archbishop, withheld on conscientious
grounds from discharging official duties down to his death in A.D.
1710. Amid these disputes the Utrecht see remained vacant for
thirteen years. The flock were without a chief shepherd, the inferior
clergy without direction and support, the people were wrought upon
by Jesuit emissaries, and the vacant pastorates were filled by the
nuncio of Cologne. Thus it came about that of the 300,000 Catholics
remaining after the Reformation, only a few thousands continued
faithful to the national party, while the rest became bitter and
extreme ultramontanes, as the Catholic church of Holland still is.
Finally, in A.D. 1723, the Utrecht chapter took courage and chose a
new archbishop in the person of Cornelius Steenowen. Receiving
no answer to their request for papal confirmation, the chapter, after
waiting a year and a half, had him and also his three successors
consecrated by a French missionary bishop, Varlet, who had been
driven away by the Jesuits. But in order to prevent the threatened
loss of legitimate consecration for future bishops after Varlet's death
in A.D. 1742, a bishop elected at Utrecht was in that same year
ordained to the chapter of Haarlem, and in A.D. 1758 the newly
founded bishopric of Deventer was so supplied. All these, like all
subsequent elections, were duly reported to Rome, and a strictly
Catholic confession from electors and elected sent up; but each time,
instead of confirmation, a frightful ban was thundered forth. This,

however, did not deter the Dutch government from formally recognising the elections.—Meanwhile the second and last act of the Jansenist tragedy had been played in France. Many of the persecuted Appellants sought refuge in Holland, and the welcome accorded them seemed to justify the long cherished suspicion of Jansenism against the people of Utrecht. They repelled these charges, however, by condemning the five propositions and the heresies of Quesnel's book; but they expressly refused the bull of Alexander VII. and its doctrine of papal infallibility. This put a stop to all attempts at reconciliation. The church of Utrecht meanwhile prospered. At a council held at Utrecht in A.D. 1765 it styled itself "The Old Roman Catholic Church of the Netherlands," acknowledged the pope, although under his anathema, as the visible head of the Christian church, accepted the Tridentine decrees as their creed, and sent this with all the acts of council to Rome as proof of their orthodoxy. The Jesuits did all in their power to overturn the formidable impression which this at first made there; and they were successful. Clement XIII. declared the council null, and those who took part in it hardened sons of Belial. But their church at this day contains, under one archbishop and two bishops, twenty-six congregations, numbering 6,000 souls.[1]—Continuation, § 200, 3.

9. Suppression of the Order of Jesuits, A.D. 1773.—The Jesuits had striven with growing eagerness and success after worldly power, and instead of absolute devotion to the interests of the papacy, their chief aim was now the erection of an independent political and hierarchical dominion. Their love of rule had sustained its first check in the overthrow of the Jesuit state of Paraguay; but they had secured a great part of the world's trade (§ 156, 13), and strove successfully to control European politics. The Jansenist controversy, however, had called forth against them much popular odium; Pascal had made them ridiculous to all men of culture, the other monkish orders were hostile to them, their success in trade roused the jealousy of other traders, and their interference in politics made enemies on every hand. The Portuguese government took the first decided step. A revolt in Paraguay and an attempt on the king's life were attributed to them, and the minister Pombal, whose reforms they had opposed, had them banished from Portugal in A.D. 1759, and their goods confiscated Clement XIII., A.D. 1758–1769, chosen by the Jesuits and under their influence, protected them by a bull; but Portugal refused to let the bull be proclaimed, led the papal nuncio over the frontier, broke off all relations with Rome, and sent whole shiploads of Jesuits to the

---

[1] Neale, "History of the so called Jansenist Church of Holland." Oxford, 1858.

pope. France followed Portugal's example when the general Ricci
had answered the king's demand for a reform of his orders: *Sint ut
sunt, aut non sint.* For the enormous financial failure of the Jesuit La
Valette, the whole order was made responsible, and at last, in A.D. 1764,
banished from France as dangerous to the state. Spain, Naples, and
Parma, too, soon seized all the Jesuits and transported them beyond
the frontiers. The new papal election on the death of Clement XIII.
was a life and death question with the Jesuits, but courtly influences
and fears of a schism prevailed. The pious and liberal Minorite
Ganganelli mounted the papal throne as Clement XIV., A.D. 1769–
1774. He began with sweeping administrative reforms, forbad the
reading of the bull *In cœna Domini* (§ 117, 3), and, pressed by the
Bourbon court, issued in A.D. 1773 the bull *Dominus ac Redemtor Noster*
suppressing the Jesuit order. The order numbered 22,600 members
and the pope felt, in granting the bull, that he endangered his own
life. Next year he died, not without suspicion of poisoning. All the
Catholic courts, even Austria, put the decree in force. But the heretic
Frederick II. tolerated the order for a long time in Silesia, and
Catherine II. and Paul I. in their Polish provinces.—Pius VI., A.D.
1775–1799, in many respects the antithesis of his predecessor, was
the secret friend of the exiled and imprisoned ex-Jesuits. After
the outbreak of the French Revolution, a proposal was made at
Rome, in A.D. 1792, for the formal restoration of the order, as a means
of saving the seriously imperilled church, but it did not find sufficient
encouragement.

10. Anti-hierarchical Movements in Germany and Italy.—Even before
Joseph II. could carry out his reforms in ecclesiastical polity, the
noble elector Maximilian Joseph III., A.D. 1745–1777, with greater
moderation but complete success, effected a similar reform in the
Jesuit-overrun Bavaria. Himself a strict Catholic, he asserted the
supremacy of the state over a foreign hierarchy, and by reforming
the churches, cloisters, and schools of his country he sought to
improve their position. But under his successor, Charles Theodore,
A.D. 1777–1799, everything was restored to its old condition.—Meanwhile a powerful voice was raised from the midst of the German
prelates that aimed a direct blow at the hierarchical papal system.
Nicholas von Hontheim, the suffragan Bishop of Treves, had under the
name *Justinus Febronius* published, in A.D. 1763, a treatise *De Statu
Ecclesiæ*, in which he maintained the supreme authority of general
councils and the independence of bishops in opposition to the hierarchical pretensions of the popes. It was soon translated into German,
French, Spanish, Portuguese, and Italian. The book made a great impression, and Clement XIII. could do nothing against the bold defender
of the liberties of the church. In A.D. 1778, indeed, Pius VI. had the

poor satisfaction of extorting a recantation from the old man of seventy-seven years, but he lived to see yet more deadly storms burst upon the church. Urged by Charles Theodore, Elector of Bavaria, the pope, in A.D. 1785, had made Munich the residence of a nuncio. The episcopal electors of Mainz, Cologne, and Treves, and the Archbishop of Salzburg, seeing their archiepiscopal rights in danger, met in congress at Ems in A.D. 1786, and there, on the basis of the Febronian proofs, claimed, in the so called **Punctation of Ems**, practical independence of the pope and the restoration of an independent German national Catholic church. But the German bishops found it easier to obey the distant pope than the near archbishops. So they united their opposition with that of the pope, and the undertaking of the archbishops came to nothing.—More threatening still for the existence of the hierarchy was the reign of **Joseph II.** in Austria. German emperor from A.D. 1765, and co-regent with his mother Maria Theresa, he began, immediately on his succession to sole rule in A.D. 1780, a radical reform of the whole ecclesiastical institutions throughout his hereditary possessions. In A.D. 1781 he issued his Edict of Toleration, by which, under various restrictions, the Protestants obtained civil rights and liberty of worship. Protestant places of worship were to have no bells or towers, were to pay stole dues to the Catholic priests, in mixed marriages the Catholic father had the right of educating all his children and the Catholic mother could claim the education at least of her daughters. By stopping all episcopal communications with the papal curia, and putting all papal bulls and ecclesiastical edicts under strict civil control, the Catholic church was emancipated from Roman influences, set under a native clergy, and made serviceable in the moral and religious training of the people, and all her institutions that did not serve this end were abolished. Of the 2,000 cloisters, 606 succumbed before this decree, and those that remained were completely sundered from all connexion with Rome. In vain the bishops and Pius VI. protested. The pope even went to Vienna in A.D. 1782; but though received with great respect, he could make nothing of the emperor. Joseph's procedure had been somewhat hasty and inconsiderate, and a reaction set in, led by interested parties, on the emperor's early death in A.D. 1790.—The Grand-duke Leopold of Tuscany, Joseph's brother, with the aid of the pious Bishop Scipio von Ricci, inclined to Jansenism, sought also in a similar way to reform the church of his land at the Synod of Pistoia, in A.D. 1786. But here too at last the hierarchy prevailed.

11. **Theological Literature.**—The Revocation of the Edict of Nantes, A.D. 1685, gave the deathblow to the French Reformed theology, but it also robbed Catholic theology in France of its spur and incentive. The Huguenot polemic against the papacy, and that of Jansenism against

the semi-pelagianism of the Catholic church, were silenced; but now the most rabid naturalism, atheism, and materialism held the field and the church theology was so lethargic that it could not attempt any serious opposition. Yet even here some names are worthy of being recorded. Above all, Bernard de Montfaucon of St. Maur, the ablest antiquarian of France, besides his classical works, issued admirable editions of Athanasius, Chrysostom, Origen's "*Hexapla*," and the "*Collectio Nova Patrum*." E. Renaudot, a learned expert in the oriental languages, wrote several works in vindication of the "*Perpétuité de la Foi cath.*," a history of the Jacobite patriarchs of Alexandria, etc., and compiled a "*Collectio liturgiarum Oriental,*" in two vols. Of permanent worth is the "*Bibliotheca Sacra*" of the Oratorian Le Long, which forms an admirable literary-historical apparatus for the Bible. The learned Jesuit Hardouin, who pronounced all Greek and Latin classics, with few exceptions, to be monkish products of the thirteenth century, and denied the existence of all pre-Tridentine general councils, edited a careful collection of Acts of Councils in twelve vols. folio in Paris, 1715, and compiled an elaborate chronology of the Old Testament. His pupil, the Jesuit Berruyer, wrote a romancing "*Hist. du Peuple de Dieu,*" which, though much criticised, was widely read. Incomparably more important was the Benedictine Calmet, died A.D. 1757, whose "*Dictionnaire de la Bible*" and "*Commentaire Littéral et Critique*" on the whole Bible are really most creditable for their time. And, finally, the Parisian professor of medicine, Jean Astruc, deserves to be named as the founder of the modern Pentateuch criticism, whose "*Conjectures sur les Mémoires Originaux,*" etc., appeared in Brussels A.D. 1753.—Within the limits of the French Revolution the noble theosophist St. Martin, died A.D. 1805, a warm admirer of Böhme, wrote his brilliant and profound treatises.

12. In Italy the most important contributions were in the department of history. Mansi, in his collection of Acts of Councils in thirty-one vols. folio, A.D. 1759 ff., and Muratori, in his "*Scriptores Rer. Italic.,*" in twenty-eight vols., and "*Antiquitt. Ital. Med. Ævi,*" in six vols., show brilliant learning and admirable impartiality. Ugolino, in a gigantic work, "*Thesaurus Antiquitt. ss.,*" thirty-four folio vols., A.D. 1744 ff., gathers together all that is most important for biblical archæology. The three Assemani, uncle and two nephews, cultured Maronites in Rome, wrought in the hitherto unknown field of Syrian literature and history. The uncle, Joseph Simon, librarian at the Vatican, wrote "*Bibliotheca Orientalis,*" in four vols., A.D. 1719 ff., and edited Ephraem's works in six vols. The elder nephew, Stephen Evodius, edited the "*Acta ss. Martyrum Orient. et Occid.,*" in two vols., and the younger, Joseph Aloysius, a "*Codex Liturgicus Eccles. Univ.,*" in thirteen vols. Among dogmatical works the "*Theologia hist.-dogm.-scholastica,*" in eight vols.

folio, Rome, 1739, of the Augustinian Berti deserves mention. Zaccaria of Venice, in some thirty vols., proved an indefatigable opponent of Febronianism, Josephinism, and such-like movements, and a careful editor of older Catholic works. The Augustinian Florez, died A.D. 1773, did for Spain what Muratori had done for Italy in making collections of ancient writers, which, with the continuations of the brethren of his order, extended to fifty folio volumes.—In Germany the greatest Catholic theologian of the century was Amort. Of his seventy treatises the most comprehensive is the " *Theologia Eclectica, Moralis et Scholastica,*" in four vols. folio, A.D. 1752. He conducted a conciliatory polemic against the Protestants, contested the mysticism of Maria von Agreda (§ 156, 5), and vigorously controverted superstition, miracle-mongering, and all manner of monkish extravagances. To the time of Joseph II. belongs the liberal, latitudinarian supernaturalist Jahn of Vienna, whose "Introduction to the Old Testament," and "Biblical Antiquities" did much to raise the standard of biblical learning. For his anti-clericalism he was deprived of his professorship in A.D. 1805, and died in A.D. 1816 a canon in Vienna. To this century also belongs the greatly blessed literary labours of the accomplished mystic, Sailer, beginning at Ingolstadt in A.D. 1777, and continued at Dillingen from A.D. 1784. Deprived in A.D. 1794 of his professorship on pretence of his favouring the Illuminati, it was not till A.D. 1799 that he was allowed to resume his academic work in Ingolstadt and Landshut. By numerous theological, ascetical, and philosophical tracts, but far more powerfully by his lectures and personal intercourse, he sowed the seeds of rationalism, which bore fruit in the teachings of many Catholic universities, and produced in the hearts of many pupils a warm and deep and at the same time a gentle and conciliatory Catholicism, which heartily greeted, even in pious Protestants, the foundations of a common faith and life. Compare § 187, 1.—Continuation, § 191.

18. The German-Catholic Contribution to the Illumination.—The Catholic church of Germany was also carried away with the current of "the Illumination," which from the middle of the century had overrun Protestant Germany. While the exorcisms and cures of Father Gassner in Regensburg were securing signal triumphs to Catholicism, though these were of so dubious a kind that the bishops, the emperor, and finally even the curia, found it necessary to check the course of the miracle worker, Weishaupt, professor of canon law in Ingolstadt, founded, in A.D. 1776, the secret society of the Illuminati, which spread its deistic ideas of culture and human perfectibility through Catholic South Germany. Though inspired by deadly hatred of the Jesuits, Weishaupt imitated their methods, and so excited the suspicion of the Bavarian government, which, in A.D. 1785, suppressed the order

and imprisoned and banished its leaders.—Catholic theology too was affected by the rationalistic movement. But that the power of the church to curse still survived was proved in the case of the Mainz professor, Laurence Isenbiehl, who applied the passage about Immanuel, in Isaiah vii. 14, not to the mother of Christ, but to the wife of the prophet, for which he was deposed in A.D. 1774, and on account of his defective knowledge of theology was sent back for two years to the seminary. When in A.D. 1778 he published a learned treatise on the same theme, he was put in prison. The pope too condemned his exposition as pestilential, and Isenbiehl "as a good Catholic" retracted. Steinbühler, a young jurist of Salzburg, having been sentenced to death in A.D. 1781 for some contemptuous words about the Catholic ceremonies, was pardoned, but soon after died from the ill-treatment he had received. The rationalistic movement got hold more and more of the Catholic universities. In Mainz, Dr. Blau, professor of dogmatics, promulgated with impunity the doctrine that in the course of centuries the church has often made mistakes. In the Austrian universities, under the protection of the Josephine edict, a whole series of Catholic theologians ventured to make cynically free criticisms, especially in the field of church history. At Bonn University, founded in A.D. 1786 by the Elector-archbishop of Cologne, there were teachers like Hedderich, who sportively described himself on the title page of a dissertation as "*jam quater Romæ damnatus,*" Dereser, previously a Carmelite monk, who followed Eichhorn in his exposition of the biblical miracles, and Eulogius Schneider, who, after having made Bonn too hot for him by his theological and poetical recklessness, threw himself into the French Revolution, for two years marched through Alsace with the guillotine as one of the most dreaded monsters, and finally, in A.D. 1794, was made to lay his own head on the block. —At the Austrian universities, under the protection of the tolerant Josephine legislation, a whole series of Catholic theologians, Royko, Wolff, Dannenmayr, Michl, etc., criticised, often with cynical plainness, the proceedings and condition of the Catholic church. To this class also, in the first stage of his remarkably changeful and eventful career, belongs Ign. Aur. Fessler. From 1773, a Capuchin in various cloisters, last of all in Vienna, he brought down upon himself the bitter hatred of his order by making secret reports to the emperor about the ongoings that prevailed in these convents. He escaped their enmity by his appointment, in 1784, as professor of the oriental languages and the Old Testament at Lemberg, but was in 1787 dismissed from this office on account of various charges against his life, teaching, and poetical writings. In Silesia, in 1791, he went over to the Protestant church, joined the freemasons, held at Berlin the post of a councillor in ecclesiastical and educational affairs for the

newly won Catholic provinces of Poland, and, after losing this position
in consequence of the events of the war of 1806, found employment in
Russia in 1809; first, as professor of oriental languages at St. Petersburg, and afterwards, when opposed and persecuted there also on
suspicion of entertaining atheistical views, as member of a legal
commission in South Russia. Meanwhile having gradually moved
from a deistical to a vague mystical standpoint, he was in 1819 made
superintendent and president of the evangelical consistory at Saratov,
with the title of an evangelical bishop, and after the abolition of that
office in 1833 he became general superintendent at St. Petersburg,
where he died in 1839. His romances and tragedies as well as his
theological and religious writings are now forgotten, but his "Reminiscences of his Seventy Years' Pilgrimage," published in 1824, are
still interesting, and his "History of Hungary," in ten volumes,
begun in 1812, is of permanent value.

14. The French Contribution to the Illumination.—The age of Louis
XIV., with the morals of its Jesuit confessors, the lust, bigotry, and
hypocrisy of its court, its dragonnades and Bastile polemic against
revivals of a living Christianity among Huguenots, mystics, and
Jansenists, its prophets of the Cevennes and Jansenist convulsionists,
etc., called forth a spirit of freethinking to which Catholicism, Jansenism, and Protestantism appeared equally ridiculous and absurd. This
movement was essentially different from English deism. The principle of the English movement was *common sense*, the universal moral
consciousness in man, with the powerful weapon of rational criticism,
maintaining the existence of an ideal and moral element in men, and
holding by the more general principles of religion. French naturalism,
on the other hand, was a philosophy of the *esprit*, that essentially
French lightheartedness which laughed away everything of an ideal
sort with scorn and wit. Yet there was an intimate relationship between
the two. The philosophy of common sense came to France, and was
there travestied into a philosophy *d'esprit*. The organ of this French
philosophy was the " *Encyclopédie* " of Diderot and D'Alembert, and
its most brilliant contributors, Montesquieu, Helvetius, Voltaire, and
Rousseau. Montesquieu, A.D. 1689–1755, whose " *Esprit des Lois* " in two
years passed through twenty-two editions, wrote the " *Lettres Persanes*,"
in which with biting wit he ridiculed the political, social, and ecclesiastical condition of France. Helvetius, A.D. 1715–1771, had his book,
" *De l'Esprit*," burnt in A.D. 1759 by order of parliament, and was
made to retract, but this only increased his influence. Voltaire, A.D.
1694–1778, although treating in his writings of philosophical and
theological matters, gives only a hash of English deism spiced with
frivolous wit, showing the same tendency in his historical and poetical
works, giving a certain eloquence to the commonest and filthiest sub-

jects, as in his "*Pucelle*" and "*Candide*." He obtained, however, an immense influence that extended far past his own days. To the same class belongs Jean Jacques Rousseau, A.D. 1712–1778, belonging to the Roman Catholic church only as a pervert for seventeen years in the middle of his life. Of a nobler nature than Voltaire, he yet often sank into deep immorality, as he tells without reserve, but also without any hearty penitence, in his *Confessions*. His whole life was taken up with the conflict for his ideals of freedom, nature, human rights, and human happiness. In his "*Contrat Social*" of A.D. 1762, he commends a return to the natural condition of the savage as the ideal end of man's endeavour. His "*Emile*" of A.D. 1761 is of epoch-making importance in the history of education, and in it he eloquently sets forth his ideal of a natural education of children, while he sent all his own (natural) children to a foundling hospital.—The physician De la Mettrie, who died at the court of Frederick the Great in A.D. 1751, carried materialism to its most extreme consequences, and the German-Frenchman Baron Holbach, A.D. 1723–1789, wrote the "*Système de la Nature*," which in two years passed through eighteen editions.[1]

15. These seeds bore fruit in the French Revolution. Voltaire's cry "*Écrasez l'infame*," was directed against the church of the Inquisition, the massacre of St. Bartholomew, and the dragonnades, and Diderot had exclaimed that the world's salvation could only come when the last king had been strangled with the entrails of the last priest. The constitutional National Assembly, A.D. 1789–1791, wished to set aside, not the faith of the people, but only the hierarchy, and to save the state from a financial crisis by the goods of the church. All cloisters were suppressed and their property sold. The number of bishops was reduced to one half, all ecclesiastical offices without a pastoral sphere were abolished, the clergy elected by the people paid by the state, and liberty of belief recognised as an inalienable right of man. The legislative National Assembly, A.D. 1791, 1792, made all the clergy take an oath to the constitution on pain of deposition. The pope forbad it under the same threat. Then arose a schism. Some 40,000 priests who refused the oath mostly quitted the country. Avignon (§ 110, 4) had been incorporated in the French territory. The terrorist National Convention, A.D. 1792–1795, which brought the king to the scaffold on January 21st, A.D. 1793, and the queen on October 16th, prohibited all Christian customs, on 5th October abolished the Christian reckoning of time, and on November 7th Christianity itself, laid waste 2,000

---

[1] Cairns, "Unbelief in the Eighteenth Century," chap. iv., "Unbelief in France." Edinburgh, 1881. Morley, "Diderot and the Encyclopedists." 2 vols. London, 1878. Morley, "Voltaire." London, 1872. Lange, "History of Materialism." 3 vols. London, 1877.

churches and converted *Notre Dame* into a *Temple de la Raison*, where a ballet-dancer represented the goddess of reason. Stirred up by the fanatical baron, "Anacharsis" Cloots, "the apostle of human freedom and the personal enemy of Jesus Christ," the Archbishop Gobel, now in his sixtieth year, came forward, proclaiming his whole past life a traud, and owning no other religion than that of freedom. On the other hand, the noble Bishop Gregoire of Blois, the first priest to support the constitution, who voted for the abolition of royalty, but not the execution of the king, was not driven by the terrorism of the convention, of which he was a member, from a bold and open profession of Christianity, appearing in his clerical dress and unweariedly protesting against the vandalism of the Assembly. Robespierre[1] himself said, *"Si Dieu n'existait pas, il faudrait l'inventer,"* passed in A.D. 1794 the resolution, *Le peuple français reconnait l'Être suprême et l'immortalité de l'âme,* and issued an order to celebrate the *fête de l'Être suprême.* The Directory, A.D. 1795–1799, restored indeed Christian worship, but favoured the deistical sect of the Theophilanthropists, whose high-swelling phrases soon called forth public scorn, while in A.D. 1802 the first consul banished their worship from all churches. But meanwhile, in A.D. 1798, in order to nullify the opposition of the pope, French armies had overrun Italy and proclaimed the Church States a Roman Republic. Pius VI. was taken prisoner to France, and died in A.D. 1799 at Valence under the rough treatment of the French, without having in the least compromised himself or his office.[2]

16. The Pseudo-Catholics.—(1) The Abrahamites or Bohemian Deists. When Joseph II. issued his edict of toleration in A.D. 1781, a sect which had hitherto kept itself secret under the mask of Catholicism made its appearance in the Bohemian province of Pardubitz. The Abrahamites were descended from the old Hussites, and professed to follow the faith of Abraham before his circumcision. Their fundamental doctrine was deistic monotheism, and of the Bible they accepted only the ten commandments and the Lord's Prayer. But as they would neither attend the Jewish synagogue nor the churches of any existing Christian sect, the emperor refused them religious toleration, drove them from their homes, and settled them in A.D. 1783 on the eastern frontiers. Many of them, in consequence of persecution, returned to the Catholic church, and even those who remained steadfast did not transmit their faith to their children.

---

[1] This saying is usually attributed to Voltaire. He used the expression in attacking Pierre Bayle.—Erdmann's "Hist. of Phil.," vol. ii., p. 158. Ueberweg, "Hist. of Phil.," vol. ii., p. 125.

[2] Pressensé, "The Church and the Revolution." London, 1869. Jervis, "The Gallican Church and the Revolution." London, 1882.

17. (2) The Frankists.—Jacob Leibowicz, the son of a Jewish rabbi
in Galicia, attached himself in Turkey, where he assumed the name
of Frank, to the Jewish sect of the Sabbatarians, who, repudiating
the Talmud, adopted the cabbalistic book Sohar as the source of their
more profound religious teaching. Afterwards in Podolia, which was
then still Polish, he was esteemed among his numerous adherents as
a Messiah sent of God. Bitterly hated by the rabbinical Jews, and
accused of indulging in vile orgies in their assemblies, many of those
Soharists were thrown into prison at the instigation of Bishop
Dembowski of Kaminetz. But when they turned and accused their
opponents of most serious crimes against Christendom, and, at Frank's
suggestion, pointing out what they alleged to be an identity between
the book Sohar and the Christian doctrine of the Trinity and incarnation, made it known that they were inclined to become converts, they
won the favour of the bishop. He arranged a disputation between the
two parties, pronounced the Talmudists beaten, confiscated all available copies of the Talmud, dragged them through the streets tied to
the tail of a horse, and then burnt them. Dembowski, however, died
soon after in A.D. 1757, and the cathedral chapter expelled the Soharists
from Kaminetz. They appealed to King Augustus III. and to Archbishop Lubienski of Lemberg, renewing their profession of faith in the
Trinity, and promising to be subject to the pope. In a disputation with
the Talmudists lasting three days they sought to prove that the
Talmudists used Christian blood in their services, which afterwards
led to the death of five of the Jews thus accused. By Frank's advice,
who took part neither in this nor in the former disputation, but was
the secret leader of the whole movement, they now formally applied
for admission into the Catholic church, and their leader now entered
Lemberg in great state. They actually submitted to be thus driven
by him, and 1,000 of his adherents were baptized at Lemberg. Frank
was baptized at Warsaw under the name of Joseph, the king himself
acting as sponsor. In all Catholic journals this event was celebrated
as a signal triumph for the Catholic church. But Frank among his
own disciples continued to play the rôle of a miracle-working Messiah.
Hence in A.D. 1760 the Inquisition stepped in. Some of his followers
were imprisoned, others banished, and he himself as a heresiarch condemned to confinement for life with hard labour, from which after
thirteen years he was liberated on the first partition of Poland in A.D.
1772, through the favour of Catherine II., who employed him as secret
political agent. Feeling that his life was insecure in Poland, he went
to Moravia, and at Brünn reorganized his numerous and attached
followers into a well-knit society, by which he was revered as the
incarnation of the Deity, and his beautiful daughter Eva, brought up
by her noble godmother, as "the divine Emuna." How he was per-

mitted, under the protection of the Catholic church, to continue here for sixteen years, playing the *rôle* of a Messiah, and to amass such wealth as enabled him to purchase, in A.D. 1788, from the impoverished prince of Homburg-Birstein his castle at Offenbach, with all the privileges attached to it, is an insoluble mystery. He now called himself Baron von Frank, formed with his followers from Moravia and Poland a brilliant establishment, which outwardly adhered to the Roman Catholic church, although he very seldom attended the Catholic services. Frank died in A.D. 1791, and was buried with great pomp, but without the presence of the Catholic clergy. His daughter Eva was able to maintain the extravagant establishment of her father for twenty-six years, when the debt resting on the castle reached three million florins. At last, in A.D. 1817, the long-threatened catastrophe occurred. Eva died suddenly, and a coffin said to contain her body was actually with all decorum laid in the grave.

§ 166. THE ORIENTAL CHURCHES.

The oppressed condition of the orthodox church in the Ottoman empire continued unchanged. It had a more vigorous development in Russia, where its ascendency was unchallenged. Although the Russian church, from the time of its obtaining an independent patriarchate at Moscow, in A.D. 1589, was constitutionally emancipated from the mother church of Constantinople, it yet continued in close religious affinity with it. This was intensified by the adoption of the common confession, drawn up shortly before by Peter Mogilas (§ 152, 3). The patriarchal constitution in Russia, however, was but short-lived, for Peter I., in 1702, after the death of the Patriarch Hadrian, abolished the patriarchate, arrogated to himself as emperor the highest ecclesiastical office, and in A.D. 1721 constituted " the Holy Synod," to which, under the supervision of a procurator guarding the rights of the state, he assigned the supreme direction of spiritual and ecclesiastical affairs. To these proposals the Patriarch of Constantinople gave his approval. In this reform of the church constitution Theophanes Procopowicz, Metropolitan of Novgorod, was the emperor's right hand.—The monophysite church of Abyssinia was again during this period the scene of Christological controversies.

1. **The Russian State Church.**—From the time of the liturgical reformation of the Patriarch Nikon (§ 163, 10) a new and peculiar service of song took the place of the old unison style that had previously prevailed in the Russian church. Without instrumental accompaniment, it was sustained simply by powerful male voices, and was executed, at least in the chief cities, with musical taste and charming simplicity. Among the theologians, the above-named Procopowicz, who died in A.D. 1736, occupied a prominent position. His "Handbook of Dogmatics," without departing from the doctrines of his church, is characterized by learning, clearness of exposition, and moderation. From the middle of the century, however, especially among the superior clergy, there crept in a Protestant tendency, which indeed held quite firmly by the old theology of the œcumenical synods of the Greek Church, but set aside or laid little stress upon later doctrinal developments. Even the celebrated and widely used catechism, drawn up originally for the use of the Grand-duke Paul Petrovich, by his tutor, the learned Platón, afterwards Metropolitan of Moscow, was not quite free from this tendency. It found yet more decided expression in the dogmatic handbook of Theophylact, archimandrite of Moscow, published in A.D. 1773.—Continuation, § 206, 1.

2. **Russian Sects.**—To the sects of the seventeenth century (§ 163, 10) are to be added spiritualistic gnostics of the eighteenth, in which we find a blending of western ideas with the old oriental mysticism. Among those were the Malakanen, or consumers of milk, because, in spite of the orthodox prohibition, they used milk during the fasts. They rejected all anointings, even chrism and priestly consecration, and acknowledged only spiritual anointing by the doctrine of Christ. They also volatilized the idea of baptism and the Lord's supper into that of a merely spiritual cleansing and nourishing by the word of the gospel. Otherwise they led a quiet and honourable life. More important still in regard to numbers and influence were the Duchoborzen. Although belonging exclusively to the peasant class, they had a richly developed theological system of a speculative character, with a notable blending of theosophy, mysticism, Protestantism, and rationalism. They idealized the doctrine of the sacraments after the style of the Quakers, would have no special places of worship or an ordained clergy, refused to take oaths or engage in military service, and led peaceable and useful lives. They made their first appearance in Moscow in the beginning of the eighteenth century under Peter the Great, and spread through other cities of Old Russia.—Continuation, § 210, 6.

3. **The Abyssinian Church** (§§ 64, 1; 73, 2).—About the middle of

the century a monk appeared, proclaiming that, besides the commonly admitted twofold birth of Christ, the eternal generation of the Father and the temporal birth of the Virgin Mary, there was a third birth through anointing with the Holy Spirit in the baptism in Jordan. He thus convulsed the whole Abyssinian church, which for centuries had been in a state of spiritual lethargy. The *abuna* with the majority of his church held by the old doctrine, but the new also found many adherents. The split thus occasioned has continued till the present time, and has played no unimportant part in the politico-dynastic struggles of the last ten years (§ 184, 9).

II.—The Protestant Churches.

§ 167. THE LUTHERAN CHURCH BEFORE " THE ILLUMINATION."

By means of the founding of the University of Halle in A.D. 1694 a fresh impulse was given to the pietist movement, and too often the whole German Church was embroiled in violent party strifes, in which both sides failed to keep the happy mean, and laid themselves open to the reproach of the adversaries. Spener died in A.D. 1705, Francke in A.D. 1727, and Breithaupt in A.D. 1732. After the loss of these leaders the Halle pietism became more and more gross, narrow, unscientific, regardless of the Church confession, frequently renouncing definite beliefs for hazy pious feeling, and attaching undue importance to pious forms of expression and methodistical modes of life. The conventionalism encouraged by it became a very Pandora's box of sectarianism and fanaticism (§ 170, 1). But it had also set up a ferment in the church and in theology which created a wholesome influence for many years. More than 6,000 theologians from all parts of Germany had down to Francke's death received their theological training in Halle, and carried the leaven of his spirit into as many churches and schools. A whole series of distinguished teachers of theology now rose in almost all the Lutheran churches of the German states, who, avoiding the onesidedness of the pietists and their opponents, taught and preached pure doctrine and a pious life. From Calixt they had learnt to be mild and fair towards the Reformed and Catholic churches, and by Spener they had been roused to a genuine and hearty piety. Gottfried Arnold's protest, onesided as it was, had taught them to discover, even among heretics and sectaries, partial and distorted truths; and from Calov and Löscher they had inherited a zeal for pure doctrine. Most eminent among these were Albert Bengel, of Württemberg, who died in A.D. 1752, and Chr. Aug. Crusius of Leipzig, who died in A.D. 1775. But when the flood of " the Illumination" came rushing in upon the German Lutheran Church about the middle of the century, it overflowed even the fields sown by these noble men.

1. The Pietist Controversies after the Founding of the Halle University (§ 159, 3).—Pietism, condemned by the orthodox universities of Leipzig and Wittenberg, was protected and encouraged in Halle. The crowds of students flocking to this new seminary roused the wrath of the orthodox. The Wittenberg faculty, with Deutschmann at its head, issued a manifesto in A.D. 1695, charging Spener with no less than 264 errors in doctrine. Nor were those of Leipzig silent, Carpzov going so far as to style the mild and peace-loving Spener a *procella ecclesiæ*. Other leading opponents of the pietists were Schelwig of Dantzig, Mayer of Wittenberg, and Fecht of Rostock. When Spener died in A.D. 1705 his opponents gravely discussed whether he could be thought of as in glory. Fecht of Rostock denied that it ould be. Among the later champions of pure doctrine the worthiest and ablest was the learned Löscher, superintendent at Dresden, A.D. 1709–1747, who at least cannot be reproached with dead orthodoxy. His " *Vollständiger Timotheus Verinus*," two vols., 1718, 1721, is by far the most important controversial work against pietism.[1] Francis Buddeus of Jena for a long time sought ineffectually to bring about a reconciliation between Löscher and the pietists of Halle. In A.D. 1710 Francke and Breithaupt obtained a valorous colleague in Joachim Lange; but even he was no match for Löscher in controversy. Mean-

---

[1] Hagenbach, "History of Church in the 18th and 19th Centuries," vol. i., pp. 109, 116. 2 vols. New York, 1869. Dorner, "History of Protestant Theology," vol. ii., p. 208.

while pietism had more and more permeated the life of the people, and occasioned in many places violent popular tumults. In several states conventicles were forbidden; in others, *e.g.* Württemberg and Denmark, they were allowed.

2. The orthodox regarded the pietists as a new sect, with dangerous errors that threatened the pure doctrine of the Lutheran Church; while the pietists maintained that they held by pure Lutheran orthodoxy, and only set aside its barren formalism and dead externalism for biblical practical Christianity. The controversy gathered round the doctrines of the new birth, justification, sanctification, the church, and the millennium. (*a*) The new birth. The orthodox maintained that regeneration takes place in baptism (§ 141, 13), every baptized person is regenerate; but the new birth needs nursing, nourishment, and growth, and, where these are wanting, reawakening. The pietists identified awakening or conversion with regeneration, considered that it was effected in later life through the word of God, mediated by a corporeal and spiritual penitential struggle, and a consequent spiritual experience, and sealed by a sensible assurance of God's favour in the believer's blessed consciousness. This inward sealing marks the beginning, introduction into the condition of babes in Christ. They distinguished a *theologia viatorum*, i.e. the symbolical church doctrine, and a *theologia regenitorum*, which has to do with the soul's inner condition after the new birth. They have consequently been charged with maintaining that a true Christian who has arrived at the stage of spiritual manhood may and must in this life become free from sin.— (*b*) Justification and Sanctification. In opposition to an only too prevalent externalizing of the doctrine of justification, Spener has taught that only living faith justifies, and if genuine must be operative, though not meritorious. Only in faith proved to be living by a pious life and active Christianity, but not in faith in the external and objective promises of God's word, lies the sure guarantee of justification obtained. His opponents therefore accused him of confounding justification and sanctification, and depreciating the former in favour of the latter. And, though not by Spener, yet by many of his followers, justification was put in the background, and in a onesided manner stress was laid upon practical Christianity. Spener and Francke had expressly preached against worldly dissipation and frivolity, and condemned dancing, the theatre, card-playing, as detrimental to the progress of sanctification, and therefore sinful; while the orthodox regarded them as matters of indifference. Besides this, the pietists held the doctrine of a day of grace, assigned to each one within the limit of his earthly life (*terminism*).—(*c*) The Church and the Pastorate. Orthodoxy regarded word and sacrament and the ministry which administered them as the basis and foundation of the church; pietism

held that the individual believers determined the character and existence of the church. In the one case the church was thought to beget,
nurse, and nourish believers; in the other believers, constituted, maintained, and renewed the church, accomplishing this best by conventicles,
in which living Christianity preserved itself and diffused its influence
abroad. The orthodox laid great stress upon clerical ordination and
the grace of office; pietists on the person and his faith. Spener had
taught that only he who has experienced in his own heart the power
of the gospel, *i.e.* he who has been born again, can be a true preacher
and pastor. Löscher maintained that the official acts of an unconverted preacher, if only he be orthodox, may be blessed as well as
those of a converted man, because saving power lies not in the person
of the preacher, but in the word of God which he preaches, in its
purity and simplicity, and in the sacraments which he dispenses in
accordance with their institution. The pietists then went so far as
absolutely to deny that saving results could follow the preaching of
an unconverted man. The proclamation of forgiveness by the church
without the inward sealing had for them no meaning; yea, they
regarded it as dangerous, because it quieted conscience and made
sinners secure. Hence they keenly opposed private confession and
churchly absolution. Of a special grace of office they would know
nothing: the true ordination is the new birth; each regenerate one,
and such a one only, is a true priest. The orthodox insisted above all
on pure doctrine and the church confession; the pietists too regarded
this as necessary, but not as the main thing. Spener decidedly
maintained the duty of accepting the church symbols; but later pietists rejected them as man's work, and so containing errors. Among
the orthodox, again, some went so far as to claim for their symbols
absolute immunity from error. Spener's opposition to the compulsory
use of fixed Scripture portions, prescribed forms of prayer, and the
exorcism formulary occasioned the most violent contentions. On
the other hand, his reintroduction of the confirmation service before
the first communion, which had fallen into general desuetude, was
imitated, and soon widely prevailed, even among the orthodox.—(*d*)
Eschatology. Spener had interpreted the biblical doctrine of the 1,000
years' reign as meaning that, after the overthrow of the papacy and
the conversion of heathens and Jews, a period of the most glorious
and undisturbed tranquillity would dawn for the kingdom of Christ
on earth as prelude to the eternal sabbath. His opponents denounced
this as chiliasm and fanaticism.—(*e*) There was, finally, a controversy
about Divine providence occasioned by the founding of Francke's
orphan house at Halle. The pietists pointed to the establishment and
growth of this institution as an instance of immediate divine providence; while Löscher by indicating the common means employed to

secure success, reduced the whole affair to the domain of general and daily providence, without denying the value of the strong faith in God and the active love that characterized its founder, as well as the importance of the Divine blessing which rested upon the work.[1]

3. Theology (§ 159, 4).—The last two important representatives of the Old Orthodox School were Löscher, who, besides his polemic against pietism, made learned contributions to biblical philology and church history; and his companion in arms, Cyprian of Gotha, who died in A.D. 1745, the ablest combatant of Arnold's "*Ketzerhistorie*," and opponent of union efforts and of the papacy.—The Pietist School, more fruitful in practical than scientific theology, contributed to devotional literature many works that will never be forgotten. The learned and voluminous writer Joachim Lange, who died A.D. 1744, the most skilful controversialist among the Halle pietists, author of the "Halle Latin Grammar," which reached its sixtieth edition in A.D. 1809, published a commentary on the whole Bible in seven folio vols. after the Cocceian method. Of importance as a historian of the Reformation was Salig of Wolfenbüttel, who died in A.D. 1788. Christian Thomasius at first attached himself to the pietists as an opponent of the rigid adherence to the letter of the orthodox, but was repudiated by them as an indifferentist. To him belongs the honour of having turned public opinion against the persecution of witches (§ 117, 4). Out of the contentions of pietists and orthodox there now rose a third school, in which Lutheran theology and learning were united with genuine piety and profound thinking, decided confessionalism with moderation and fairness. Its most distinguished representatives were Hollaz of Pomerania, died 1718 ("*Examen Theologicum Acroamaticum*"); Buddeus of Jena, died 1729 ("*Hist. Ecclst. V.T.*," "*Instit. Theol. Dogma*," "*Isagoge Hist. Theol. Univ.*"); J. Chr. Wolf of Homburg, died 1739 ("*Biblioth. Hebr.*," "*Curæ Philol. et Crit. in N.T.*"): Weismann of Tübingen, died 1747 ("*Hist. Ecclst.*"); Carpzov of Leipzig, died A.D. 1767 as superintendent at Lübeck ("*Critica s. V.T.*," "*Introductio ad Libros cen. V.T.*," "*Apparatus Antiquitt. s. Codicis*"); J. H. Michaelis of Halle, died 1731 ("*Biblia. Hebr. c. Variis Lectionibus et Brev. Annott.*," "*Uberiores Annott. in Hagiograph.*"); assisted in both by his learned nephew Chr. Ben. Michaelis of Halle, died 1764; J. G. Walch of Jena, died 1755 ("*Einl. in die Religionsstreitigkeiten*," "*Biblioth. Theol. Selecta*," "*Biblioth. Patristica*," "*Luther's Werke*"); Chr. Meth. Pfaff of Tübingen, died 1760 ("*K. G., K. Recht, Dogmatik, Moral*"); L. von Mosheim of Helmstädt and Göttingen, died 1755, the father of modern church history ("*Institt. Hist. Ecclst.*," "*Commentarii Rebus Christ. ante Constant. M.*," "*Dissertationes*," etc.); J. Alb. Bengel of

---

[1] Dorner, "History of Protestant Theology," vol. ii., pp. 208-227.

Stuttgart, died 1752 ("*Gnomon N.T.*," a commentary on the N.T. distinguished by pregnancy of expression and profundity of thought; from his interpretation of Revelation he expected the millennium to begin in A.D. 1836); and Chr. A. Crusius of Leipzig, died 1775 ("*Hypomnemata ad Theol. Propheticam.*")—A fourth theological school arose out of the application of the mathematical method of demonstration by the philosopher Chr. von Wolff of Halle, who died A.D. 1754. Wolff attached himself to the philosophical system of Leibnitz, and sought to unite philosophy and Christianity; but under the manipulation of his logico-mathematical method of proof he took all vitality out of the system, and the pre-established harmony of the world became a purely mechanical clockwork. He looked merely to the logical accuracy of Christian truths, without seeking to penetrate their inner meaning, gave formal exercise to the understanding, while the heart was left empty and cold; and thus inevitably revelation and mystery made way for a mere natural theology. Hence the charge brought against the system of tending to fatalism and atheism, not only by narrow pietists like Lange, but by able and liberal theologians like Buddeus and Crusius, was quite justifiable. By a cabinet order of Frederick William I. in A.D. 1723 Wolff was deposed, and ordered within two days, on pain of death, to quit the Prussian states. But so soon as Frederick II. ascended the throne, in A.D. 1740, he recalled the philosopher to Halle from Marburg, where he had meanwhile taught with great success.[1] Sig. Jac. Baumgarten, the pious and learned professor in Halle, who died in A.D. 1757, was the first to introduce Wolff's method into theology. In respect of contents his theology occupies essentially the old orthodox ground. The ablest promoter of the system was John Carpov of Weimar, who died in A.D. 1768 ("*Theol. Revelata Meth. Scientifica Adornata*"). When applied to sermons, the Wolffian method led to the most extreme insipidity and absurdity.

4. Unionist Efforts.—The distinguished theologian Chr. Matt. Pfaff, chancellor of the University of Tübingen, who, without being numbered among the pietists, recognised in pietism a wholesome reaction against the barren worship of the letter which had characterized orthodoxy, regarded a union between the Lutheran and Reformed churches on their common beliefs, which in importance far exceeded the points of difference, as both practicable and desirable; and in A.D. 1720 expressed this opinion in his "*Alloquium Irenicum ad Protestantes,*" in which he answered the challenge of the "*Corpus Evangeli-*

---

[1] Dorner, "History of Protestant Theology," vol. ii., pp. 266–279. Hagenbach, "History of Church in 18th and 19th Centuries," vol. i. pp. 117–127.

corum " at Regensburg (§ 153, 1). His proposal, however, found little favour among Lutheran theologians. Not only Cyprian of Gotha, but even such conciliatory theologians as Weismann of Tübingen and Mosheim of Helmstädt, opposed it. But forty years later a Lutheran theologian, Heumann of Göttingen, demonstrated that " the Reformed doctrine of the supper is true," and proposed, in order to end the schism, that Lutherans should drop their doctrine of the supper and the Reformed their doctrine of predestination. This pamphlet, edited after the author's death by Sack of Berlin, in A.D. 1764, produced a great sensation, and called forth a multitude of replies on the Lutheran side, the best of which were those of Walch of Jena and Ernesti of Leipzig. Even within the Lutheran church, however, it found considerable favour.

5. **Theories of Ecclesiastical Law.**—Of necessity during the first century of the Protestant church its government was placed in the hands of the princes, who, because there were no others to do so, dispensed the *jura episcopalia* as *præcipua membra ecclesiæ*. What was allowed at first in the exigency of these times came gradually to be regarded as a legal right. Orthodox theology and the juristic system associated with it, especially that of Carpzov, justified this assumption in what is called the episcopal system. This theory firmly maintains the mediæval distinction between the spiritual and civil powers as two independent spheres ordained of God; but it installs the prince as *summus episcopus*, combining in his person the highest spiritual with the highest civil authority. In lands, however, where more than one confession held sway, or where a prince belonging to a different section of the church succeeded, the practical difficulties of this theory became very apparent; as, *e.g.*, when a Reformed or Romish prince had to be regarded as *summus episcopus* of a Lutheran church. Driven thus to seek another basis for the claims of royal supremacy, a new theory, that of the territorial system, was devised, according to which the prince possessed highest ecclesiastical authority, not as *præcipuum membrum ecclesiæ*, but as sovereign ruler in the state. The headship of the church was therefore not an independent prerogative over and above that of civil government, but an inherent element in it: *cujus regio, illius et religio*. The historical development of the German Reformation gave support to this theory (§ 126, 6), as seen in the proceedings of the Diet of Spires in A.D. 1526, in the Augsburg and Westphalian Peace. A scientific basis was given it by Puffendorf of Heidelberg, died A.D. 1694, in alliance with Hobbes (§ 163, 3). It was further developed and applied by Christian Thomasius of Halle, died A.D. 1728, and by the famous J. H. Böhmer in his "*Jus Ecclesiasticum Potestantium.*" Thomasius' connexion with the pietists and his indifference to confessions secured for the theory a favourable reception

in that party. Spener himself indeed preferred the Calvinistic presbyterial constitution, because only in it could equality be given to all the three orders, *ministerium ecclesiasticum, magistratus politicus, status œconomicus.* This protest by Spener against the two systems was certainly not without influence upon the construction of a third theory, the collegial system, proposed by Pfaff of Tübingen, died A.D. 1760. According to this scheme there belonged to the sovereign as such only the headship of the church, *jus circa sacra,* while the *jura in sacra,* matters pertaining to doctrine, worship, ecclesiastical law and its administration, installation of clergy, and excommunication, as *jura collegialia,* belonged to the whole body of church members. The normal constitution therefore required the collective vote of all the members through their synods. But outward circumstances during the Reformation age had necessitated the relegating the discharge of these collegial rights to the princes, which in itself was not unallowable, if only the position be maintained that the prince acts *ex commisso,* and is under obligation to render an account to those who have commissioned him. This system, on account of its democratic character, found hearty supporters among the later rationalists. But as a matter of fact nowhere was any of the three systems consistently carried out. The constitution adopted in most of the national churches was a weak vacillation between all the three.[1]

6. Church Song (§ 159, 3) received, during the first half of the century, many valuable contributions. Two main groups of singers may be distinguished : (1) The pietistic school, characterized by a biblical and practical tendency. The spiritual life of believers, the work of grace in conversion, growth in holiness, the varying conditions and experiences of the religious life, were favourite themes. They were fitted, not so much for use in the public services, as for private devotion, and few comparatively have been retained in collections of church hymns. The later productions of this school sank more and more into sentimentalism and allegorical and fanciful play of words. We may distinguish among the Halle pietists an older school, A.D. 1690-1720, and a younger, A.D. 1720-1750. The former, coloured by the fervent piety of Francke, produced simple, hearty, and often profound songs. The most distinguished representatives were Freylinghausen, died A.D. 1739, Francke's son-in-law, and director of the Halle Orphanage, editor in A.D. 1717 of a hymn-book widely used among the pietists, was author of the hymns " Pure Essence, spotless Fount of Light," " The day expires " ; Chr. Fr. Richter, physician to the Orphanage, died A.D. 1711, author of thirty-three beautiful hymns,

[1] Dorner, "History of Protestant Theology," vol. ii., pp. 259-261. Geffcken. "Church and State," 2 vols. Lon., 1887, vol. i., pp. 456-503.

including "God, whom I as Love have known"; Emilia Juliana, Countess of Schwarzburg Rudolstadt, died A.D. 1706, who wrote 586 hymns, including "Who knows how near my end may be?" Schröder, pastor in Magdeburg, died A.D. 1728, wrote "One thing is needful: Let me deem"; Winckler, cathedral preacher of Magdeburg, died A.D. 1722, author of "Strive, when thou art called of God"; Dessler, rector of Nuremburg, died A.D. 1722, composer of "I will not let Thee go, Thou help in time of need," "O Friend of souls, how well is me"; Gotter, died A.D. 1735, who wrote, "O Cross, we hail thy bitter reign"; Cresselius, pastor in Dusseldorf, author of "Awake, O man, and from thee shake." The younger Halle school represents pietism in its period of decay. Its best representatives are J. J. Rambach, professor at Giessen, died A.D. 1735, who wrote "I am baptized into thy name"; Allendorf, court preacher at Cöthen, died A.D. 1773, editor of a collection of poetic renderings from the Canticles.—(2) The poets of the orthodox party, although opposed to the pietists, are all more or less touched by the fervent piety of Spener. Neumeister, pastor at Hamburg, died A.D. 1756, was an orthodox hymn-writer of thoroughly conservative tendencies, zealously opposing the onesidedness of pietism, with a strong, ardent faith in the orthodox creed, but without much significance as a poet. Schmolck, pastor at Schweidnitz, died A.D. 1737, wrote over 1,000 hymns, including "Blessed Jesus, here we stand," "Hosanna to the Son of David! Raise," "Welcome, thou Victor in the strife." Sol. Franck, secretary to the consistory at Weimar, died A.D. 1725, wrote over 300 hymns, including "Rest of the weary, thou thyself art resting now." The mediating party between pietism and orthodoxy, represented by Bengel and Crusius in theology, is represented among hymn-writers by J. Andr. Rothe, died A.D. 1758, and by Mentzer, died A.D. 1734, composer of "Oh, would I had a thousand tongues!" In A.D. 1750 J. Jac. von Moser collected a list of 50,000 spiritual songs printed in the German language.—Continuation, § 171, 1.

7. Sacred Music (§ 159, 5).—Decadence of musical taste accompanied the lowering of the poetic standard, and pietists went even further than the orthodox in their imitation and adaptation of operatic airs. Freylinghausen, not only himself composed many such melodies, but made a collection from various sources in A.D. 1704, retaining some of the more popular of the older tunes.—There now arose, amid all this depravation of taste, a noble musician, who, like the good householder, could bring out of his treasure things new and old. J. Seb. Bach, the most perfect organist who ever lived, was musical director of the School of St. Thomas, Leipzig, and died A.D. 1750. He turned enthusiastically to the old chorale, which no one had ever understood and appreciated as he did. He harmonized the old chorales for the organ, made them the basis for elaborate organ studies, gave expression to his profoundest

feelings in his musical compositions and in his recitatives, duets, and airs, reproduced at the sacred concerts many fine old chorales wedded to most appropriate Scripture passages. He is for all times the un-rivalled master in fugue, harmony, and modulation. In his passion music we have expression given to the profoundest ideas of German Protestantism in the noblest music. After Bach comes a master in oratorio music hitherto unapproached, G. Fr. Handel of Halle, who, from A.D. 1710 till his death in A.D. 1759, lived mostly in England. For twenty-five years he wrought for the opera-house, and only in his later years gave himself to the composing of oratorios. His operas are forgotten, but his oratorios will endure to the end of time. His most perfect work is the "Messiah," which Herder describes as a Christian epic in music. Of his other great compositions, "Samson," "Judas Maccabæus," and "Jephtha" may be mentioned.[1]

8. **The Christian Life and Devotional Literature.**—Pietism led to a powerful revival of religious life among the people, which it sustained by zealous preaching and the publication of devotional works. A similar activity displayed itself among the orthodox. Francke began his charitable labours with seven florins; but with undaunted faith he started his Orphanage, writing over its door the words of Isaiah xl. 31. In faith and benevolence Woltersdorff was a worthy successor of Francke; and Baron von Canstein applied his whole means to the founding of the Bible Institute of Halle. Missions too were now pro-secuted with a zeal and success which witnessed to the new life that had arisen in the Lutheran church.—A remarkable manifestation of the pietistic spirit of this age is seen in The Praying Children in Silesia, A.D. 1707. Children of four years old and upward gathered in open fields for singing and prayer, and called for the restoration of churches taken away by the Catholics. The movement spread over the whole land. In vain was it denounced from the pulpits and forbidden by the authorities. Opposition only excited more and more the zeal of the children. At last the churches were opened for their services. The excitement then gradually subsided. It was, however, long a subject of discussion between the pietists and the orthodox; the latter denouncing it as the work of the devil, the former regard-ing it as a wonderful awakening of God's grace.—Best remembered of the many devotional writers of this period are Bogatsky of Halle, died A.D. 1774, whose "Golden Treasury" is still highly esteemed;[2] and Von Moser, died A.D. 1785, who lived a noble and exemplary life at Stuttgart amid much sore persecution. The great need of simple explanation

---

[1] Burney, "Life of Handel." London, 1784.
[2] Kelly, "Life and Work of Von Bogatsky: a Chapter from the Religious Life of the Eighteenth Century." London, 1889.

of Scripture appears from the great sale of such popular commentaries as those of Pfaff at Tübingen, 1730, Starke at Leipzig, 1741, and the Halle Bible of S. J. Baumgarten, 1748.

9. **Missions to the Heathen.**—The quickening of religious life by pietism bore fruit in new missionary activity. Frederick IV. of Denmark founded in his East Indian possessions the Tranquebar mission in A.D. 1706, under Ziegenbalg and Plutschau. Ziegenbalg, who translated the New Testament into Tamil, died in A.D. 1719. From the Danish possessions this mission carried its work over into the English Indian territories. Able and zealous workers were sent out from the Halle Institute, of whom the greatest was Chr. Fr. Schwartz, who died in A.D. 1798, after nearly fifty years of noble service in the mission field. In the last quarter of the century, however, under the influence of rationalism, zeal for missions declined, the Halle society broke up, and the English were allowed to reap the harvest sown by the Lutherans. The Halle professor Callenberg founded in A.D. 1728 a society for the conversion of the Jews, in the interests of which Stephen Schultz travelled over Europe, Asia, and Africa, preaching the Cross among the Jews. Christianity had been introduced among the Eskimos in Greenland in the eleventh century (§ 93, 5), but the Scandinavian colony there had been forgotten, and no trace of the religion which it had taught any longer remained. This reproach to Christianity lay sore on the heart of Hans Egede, a Norwegian pastor, and he found no rest till, supported by a Danish-Norwegian trading house, he sailed with his family in A.D. 1721 for these frozen and inhospitable shores. Amid almost inconceivable hardships, and with at first but little success, he continued to labour unweariedly, and even after the trading company abandoned the field he remained. In A.D. 1733 he had the unexpected joy of welcoming three Moravian missionaries, Christian David and the brothers Stach. His joy was too soon dashed by the spiritual pride of the new arrivals, who insisted on modelling everything after their own Moravian principles, and separated themselves from the noble Egede, when he refused to yield, as an unspiritual and unconverted man. Egede, on the other hand, though deeply offended at their confounding justification and sanctification, their contempt of pure doctrine, and their unscriptural views and mode of speech, was ready to attribute all this to their defective theological training. He rewarded their unkindness, when they were stricken down in sore sickness, with unwearied, loving care. In A.D. 1736 he returned to Denmark, leaving his son Paul to carry on his work, and continued director of the Greenland Mission Seminary in Copenhagen till his death in A.D. 1758.[1]—Continuation, § 171, 5.

---

[1] Hough, "The History of Christianity in India." 5 vols. London,

§ 168. THE CHURCH OF THE MORAVIAN BRETHREN.[1]

The highly gifted Count Zinzendorf, inspired even as a boy, out of fervent love to the Saviour, with the idea of gathering together the lovers of Jesus, took occasion of the visit of some Moravian Exultants to his estate to realize his cherished project. On the Hutberg he dropped the mustard seed of the dream of his youth into fertile soil, where, under his fervent care, it soon grew into a stately tree, whose branches spread over all European lands, and thence through all parts of the habitable globe. The society which he founded was called "The Society of the United Brethren." The fact that this society was not overwhelmed by the extravagances to which for a time it gave way, that its fraternising with the fanatics, the extravagant talk in which its members indulged about a special covenant with the Saviour, and their not over-modest claims to a peculiar rank in the kingdom of God, did not lead to its utter overthrow in the abyss of fanaticism, and that on the slippery paths of its mystical marriage theory it was able to keep its feet, presents a phenomenon, which stands alone in church history, and more than anything else proves how deeply rooted founder and followers were in the saving truths of the gospel. The count himself laid aside many of his extravagances, and what still remained was abandoned by his sensible and prudent successor Spangenberg, so far as it was not necessarily involved in the fundamental idea of a special covenant with the Saviour. The special service rendered by the society was the protest which it raised against the generally prevailing apostasy. During this period of declension it saved the faith of many

1839. Sherring, "History of Missions in India," edited by Storrow. London, 1888. Pearson, "Memoirs, Life, and Correspondence of Chr. Fr. Schwartz," etc. 2 vols. London, 1834.

[1] Hagenbach, "History of the Christian Church in the 18th and 19th Centuries," New York, 1869; Lectures XVIII. and XIX., pp. 398–445.

pious souls, affording them a welcome refuge, with rich spiritual nourishment and nurture. With the reawakening of the religious life in the nineteenth century, however, its adherents lost ground in Europe more and more, by maintaining their old onesidedness in life and doctrine, their depreciatory estimate of theological science, and the quarrelsome spirit which they generally manifested. But in one province, that of missions to the heathen, their energy and success have never yet been equalled. Their thorough and well-organized system of education also deserves particular mention. At present the Society of the Brethren numbers half a million, distributed among 100 settlements or thereabout.

1. The Founder of the Moravian Brotherhood, Nic. Ludwig Count von Zinzendorf and Pottendorf, was born in Dresden in A.D. 1700. Spener was one of his sponsors at baptism. His father dying early, and his mother marrying a second time, the boy, richly endowed with gifts of head and heart, was brought up by his godly pietistic grandmother, the Baroness von Gersdorf. There in his earliest youth he learned to seek his happiness in the closest personal fellowship with the Lord, and the tendency of his whole future life to yield to the impulses of pious feeling already began to assert itself. In his tenth year he entered the Halle Institute under Francke, where the pietistic idea of the need of the *ecclesiolæ in ecclesia* took firm possession of his heart. Even in his fifteenth year he sought its realization by founding among his fellow students "The Order of the Grain of Mustard Seed" (Matt. xiii. 31). After completing his school course, his uncle and guardian, in order to put an end to his pietistic extravagances, sent him to study law at the orthodox University of Wittenberg. Here he had at first to suffer a sort of martyrdom as a rigid pietist swimming against the orthodox current. His residence at Wittenberg, however, was beneficial to him in freeing him unconsciously of the Halle pietism, which had restrained his spiritual development. He did indeed firmly maintain the fundamental idea of pietism, *ecclesiolæ in ecclesia*, but in his mind it gained a wider significance than pietism had given it. His endeavours to secure a personal conference, and where possible a union, between the Halle and Wittenberg leaders were unsuccessful. In A.D. 1719 he left Wittenberg and travelled for two years, visiting the most distinguished representatives of all confessions and sects. This too fostered his idea of a grand gathering of all who love the Lord Jesus. On his return home,

in A.D. 1721, at the wish of his relatives he entered the service of the Saxon government. But a religious genius like Zinzendorf could find no satisfaction in such employment. And soon an opportunity presented itself for carrying out the plan to which his thoughts and longings were directed.[1]

2. The Founding of the Brotherhood, A.D. 1722–1727. The Schmalcald, and still more the Thirty Years', War, had brought frightful suffering and persecution upon the Bohemian and Moravian Brethren. Many of them sought refuge in Poland and Prussia. One of the refugees was the famous educationist J. Amos Comenius, who died in A.D. 1671, after having been bishop of the Moravians at Lissa in Posen from 1648. Those who remained behind were, even after the Peace of Westphalia, subjected to the cruellest oppression! Only secretly in their houses and at the risk of their lives could they worship God according to the faith of their fathers ; and they were obliged publicly to profess their adherence to the Romish church. Thus gradually the light of the gospel was extinguished in the homes of their descendants, and only a tradition, becoming ever more and more faint, remained as a memory of their ancestral faith. A Moravian carpenter, Christian David, born and reared in the Romish church, but converted by evangelical preaching, succeeded in the beginning of the eighteenth century in fanning into a flame again in some families the light that had been quenched. This little band of believers, under David's leading, went forth in A.D. 1722 and sought refuge on Zinzendorf's estate in Lusatia. The count was then absent, but the steward, with the hearty concurrence of the count's grandmother, gave them the Hutberg at Berthelsdorf as a settlement. With the words of Psalm lxxxiv. 4 on his lips, Christian David struck the axe into the tree for building the first house. Soon the little town of Herrnhut had arisen, as the centre of that Christian society which Zinzendorf now sought with all his heart and strength to develop and promote. Gradually other Moravians dropped in, but a yet greater number from far and near streamed in, of all sorts of religious revivalists pietists, separatists, followers of Schwenckfeld, etc. Zinzendorf had no thought of separation from the Lutheran church. The settlers were therefore put under the pastoral care of Rothe, the worthy pastor of Berthelsdorf (§ 166, 6). To organize such a mixed multitude was no easy task. Only Zinzendorf's glorious enthusiasm for the idea of a congregation of saints, his eminent organizing talents, the wonderful elasticity and tenacity of his will, the extraordinary prudence, circumspection, and wisdom of his management, made it possible to cement the incongruous elements and avoid an open breach.

---

[1] Spangenberg, " Life of Count Zinzendorf." London, 1838.

The Moravians insisted upon restoring their old constitution and discipline, and of the others, each wished to have prominence given to whatever he thought specially important. Only on one point were they all agreed, the duty of refusing to conform to the Lutheran church and its pastor Rothe. The count, therefore, felt obliged to form a new and separatist society. Personally he had no special liking for the old Moravian constitution; but the lot decided in its favour, while the idea of continuing a pre-Reformation martyr church was not without a certain charm. Thus Zinzendorf drew up a constitution with old Moravian forms and names, on the basis of which the colony was established, August 13th, A.D. 1727, under the name of the United Brotherhood.

3. **The Development of the Brotherhood down to Zinzendorf's Death, A.D. 1727-1760.**—With great energy the new society proceeded to found settlements in Germany, Holland, England, Ireland, Denmark, Norway, and North America, as well as among German residents in other lands. In A.D. 1734, Zinzendorf submitted to examination at Tübingen as candidate for license, and in A.D. 1737 received episcopal consecration from the Berlin court preacher, Jablonsky, who was at the same time bishop of the Moravian Brethren, which the same prelate had two years previously granted to Dr. Nitschmann, another member of the society. The efforts of the Brethren to spread their cause now attracted attention. The Saxon government in A.D. 1736 sent to Herrnhut a commission, of which Löscher was a member. But in A.D. 1736, before it submitted its report, which on the whole was favourable, Zinzendorf quitted the country, probably by the elector's command at the instigation of the Austrian government, which objected to the harbouring of so many Bohemian and Moravian emigrants. Like all those at this time persecuted on account of religion he took refuge in Wetterau (§ 170, 2). With his little family of pilgrims he settled at Ronneburg near Büdingen, founded the prosperous churches of Marienborn and Herrnhaag, and travelled extensively in Europe and America. This period of exile was the period when the society was most successful in spreading outwardly, but it was also the period when it suffered most from troubles and dissensions within. It was bitterly attacked by Lutheran theologians, and much more venomously by apostates from its own fold. The Brethren at this time afforded only too much ground for misunderstanding and reproach. To this period belongs the famous fiction of a special covenant, the Pandora-box of all other absurdities; the development of the count's own theological views and peculiar form of expression in his numerous works; the composition and introduction of unsavoury spiritual songs, with their silly conceits and many blasphemous and even obscene pictures and analogies; the market-

crier laudations of their church, the not always pure methods of propaganda, the introduction of a marriage discipline fitted to break down all modest restraints; and, finally, the so-called *Niedlichkeiten*, or boisterous festivals. Even the pietists opposed these antinomian excesses. Tersteegen, too (§ 169, 1), whose mystic tendency inclined him strongly toward pietist views, reproached the Herrnhuters with frivolity. This polemic, disagreable as it was, exercised a wholesome influence upon the society. The count became more guarded in his language, and more prudent in his behaviour, while he set aside the most objectionable excrescences of doctrine and practice that had begun to show themselves in the community. At last, in A.D. 1747, the Saxon government repeated the edict of banishment so far as the person of the founder was concerned, and when, two years later, the society expressly accepted the Augsburg Confession, it was formally recognised in Saxony. In this same year, A.D. 1749, an English act of parliament recognised it as a church with a pure episcopal succession on equal terms with the Anglican episcopal church.—Zinzendorf continued down to his death to direct the affairs of this church, which hung upon him with childlike affection, reflecting his personality, not only in its excellences, but also in all its extravagances. He died in A.D. 1760 in the full enjoyment of that blessedness which his fervent love for the Saviour had brought him.

4. **Zinzendorf's Plan and Work.**—While Zinzendorf received his first impulse from pietism, he soon perceived its onesidedness and narrowness. He would have no conventicle, but one organized community; no ideal invisible, but a real visible church; no narrow methodism, but a rich, free administration of the Christian spirit. He did not, in the first instance, aim at the conversion of the world, nor even at the reformation of the church, but at gathering and preserving those belonging to the Saviour. He hoped, however, to erect a reservoir in which he might collect every little brooklet of living water, from which he might again water the whole world. And when he succeeded in organizing a community, he was quite convinced that it was the Philadelphia of the Apocalypse (iii. 7 ff.), that it introduced " the Philadelphian period " of church history, of which all prophets and apostles had prophesied. His plan had originally reference to all Christendom, and he even took a step toward realizing this universal idea. In order to build a bridge between the Catholic church and his own community, he issued, in A.D. 1727, a Christo-Catholic hymnbook and prayer-book, and had even sketched out a letter to the pope to accompany a copy of his book. He also attempted, by a letter to the patriarchs and then to Elizabeth, empress of Russia, to interest the Greek church in his scheme, dwelling upon the Greek extraction of the church of the Moravian Brethren (§ 79, 2). His gathering of

members, however, was practically limited to the Protestant churches. All confessions and sects afforded him contingents. He was himself heartily attached to the distinctive doctrines of the Lutheran church. But in a society whose distinctive characteristic it was to be the gathering point for the pious of all nationalities, doctrine and confession could not be the uniting bond. It could be only a fellowship of love and not of creed, and the bond a community of loving sentiment and loving deeds. The inmost principle of Lutheranism, reconciliation by the blood of Christ, was saved, indeed was made the characteristic and vital doctrine, the one point of union between Moravians, Lutherans, and Reformed. Over the three parties stood the count himself as *ordinarius;* but this gave an external and not a confessional unity. The subsequent acceptance of the Augsburg Confession, in A.D. 1749, was a political act, so as to receive a civil status, and had otherwise no influence. Instead then of the confession, Zinzendorf made the constitution the bond of union. Its forms were borrowed from the old Moravian church order, but dominated and inspired by Zinzendorf's own spirit. The old Moravian constitution was episcopal and clerical, and proceeded from the idea of the church; while the new constitution of Herrnhut was essentially presbyterial, and proceeded from the idea of the community, and that as a communion of saints. The Herrnhut bishops were only titular bishops; they had no diocese, no jurisdiction, no power of excommunication. All these prerogatives belonged to the united eldership, in which the lay element was distinctly predominant. Herrnhut had no pastors, but only preaching brothers; the pastoral care devolved upon the elders and their assistants. But beside these half-Lutheran and pseudo-Moravian peculiarities, there was also a Donatist element at the basis of the constitution. This lay in the fundamental idea of absolutely true and pure children of God, and reached full expression in the concluding of a special covenant with the Saviour at London on Sept. 16th, A.D. 1741. Leonard Dober for some years administered the office of an elder-general. But at the London synod it was declared that he had not the requisite gifts for that office. Dober now wished to resign. While in confusion as to whom they could appoint, it flashed into the minds of all to appoint the Saviour Himself. "Our feeling and heart conviction was, that He made a special covenant with His little flock, taking us as His peculiar treasure, watching over us in a special way, personally interesting Himself in every member of our community, and doing that for us perfectly which our previous elders could only do imperfectly."

5. Among the numerous extravagances which Zinzendorf countenanced for a time, the following may be mentioned. (1) The notion of the motherhood of the Holy Spirit. Zinzendorf described the holy

Trinity as "man, woman, and child." The Spirit is the mother in three respects: the eternal generation of the Son of God, the conception of the Man Jesus, and the second birth of believers. (2) The notion of the fatherhood of Jesus Christ (Isa. ix. 6). Creation is ascribed solely to the Son, hence Christ is our special, direct Father. The Father of our Lord Jesus Christ is only, "in the language of men, our father-in-law or grandfather." (8) In reference to our Lord's life on earth, Zinzendorf delighted in using terms of contempt, in order to emphasize the depths of His humiliation. (4) In like manner he uses reproachful terms in speaking of the style of the sacred Scriptures, and the inspired community prefers a living Bible. (5) The theory and practice of mystical marriage, according to Ephesians v. 82. The community and each member of it are spiritual brides of Christ, and the marriage relation and begetting of children were set forth and spiritualized in a singularly indelicate manner.

6. Zinzendorf's greatness lay in the fervency of his love of the Saviour, and in the yearning desire to gather under the shadow of the cross all who loved the Lord. His weakness consisted not so much in his manifested extravagances, as in his idea that he had been called to found a society. To the realizing of this idea he gave his life, talents, heart, and means. The advantages of rank and culture he also gave to this one task. He was personally convinced of his Divine call, and as he did not recognise the authority of the written word, but only subjective impressions, it is easily seen how he would drift into absurdities and inconsistencies. The end contemplated seemed to him supremely important, so that to realize it he did not scruple to depart from strict truthfulness.—Zinzendorf's writings, over one hundred in number, are characterized by originality, brilliancy, and peculiar forms of expression. Of his 2,000 hymns, mostly improvised for public services, 700 of the best were revised and published by Knapp. Two are still found in most collections, and are more or less reproduced in our English hymns, "Jesus still lead on," and "Jesus, Thy blood and righteousness."

7. The Brotherhood under Spangenberg's Administration—For its present form the Brotherhood is indebted to its wise and sensible bishop, Aug. Gottl. Spangenberg, who died A.D. 1792. Born in 1704, he became personally acquainted with Zinzendorf in 1727, after he had completed his studies at Jena under Buddæus, and continued ever after on terms of close intimacy with him and his community. Through the good offices of G. A. Francke, son and successor of A. H. Francke, he was called in Sept., 1732, to the office of an assistantship in the theological faculty at Halle, and appointed school inspector of the Orphanage; but very soon offence was taken at the brotherly fellowship which he had not only with the society of Herrnhut, but also

with other separatists. The misunderstanding that thus arose led in April, 1733, to his deprivation under a royal cabinet order, and his expulsion by military power from Halle. He now formally joined the communion of the Brethren. The first half of his signally blessed ministry of sixty years among the Moravians was chiefly devoted to foreign mission work, both in their colonies abroad and in their stations in heathen lands. In Holland in 1734, in England and Denmark in 1735, he obtained official permission for the founding of Moravian colonies in Surinam, in the American state of Georgia, and in Santa Cruz, the forming and management of which he himself undertook, besides directing the mission work in these places. Returning from America in 1762, he won, after Zinzendorf's death, so complete an ascendency in the church in every respect, that he may well be regarded as its second founder. At the Synod of Marienborn, in A.D. 1764, the constitution was revised and perfected. Zinzendorf's monarchical prerogative was surrendered to the eldership, and Spangenberg prudently secured the withdrawal of all excrescences and extravagances. But the central idea of a special covenant was not touched, and Sept. 16th is still held as a grand pentecost festival. In the fifth section of the statutes of the United Brethren at Gnaden, 1819, it distinguishes itself from all the churches as a "society of true children of God; as a family of God, with Jesus as its head." In the fourth section of the "Historical Account of the Constitution of the United Brethren at Gnaden, 1823," the society is described as "a company of living members of the invisible body of Jesus Christ"; and in its litany for Easter morning, it adds as a fourth particular to the article of the creed: "I believe that our brothers *N. N.* and our sisters *N. N.* have joined the church above, and have entered into the joy of the Lord." The synod of A.D. 1848 modified this article, and generally the society's distinctive views are not made so prominent. This liberal tendency had dogmatic expression given to it in Spangenberg's "*Idea Fidei Fratrum.*" Only a few new settlements have been formed since Zinzendorf's death, and none of any importance; while the hitherto flourishing Moravian settlements in Wetterau were destroyed and their members banished, in A.D. 1750, by the reigning prince, Count von Isenburg-Büdingen, on account of their refusing to take the oath of allegiance.—After the first attempt to establish societies among the German emigrants in Livonia and Esthonia in A.D. 1729-1743 had ended in the expulsion of the Herrnhuters, these regions proved in the second half of the century a more fruitful field than any other. They secured there a relation to the national church such as they never attained unto elsewhere. They had in these parts formally organized a church within the church, whose members, mostly peasants, felt convinced that they had been called by the Lord's own voice as His chosen little flock, a proceeding which caused infinite trouble, especially in Livonia, to the faithful pastors, who perceived the deadly mischief that was being wrought, and witnessed against them from God's word. This protest was too powerful and convincing to be disregarded, and now, not only too late, but also in too half-hearted a way, Herrnhut began, in A.D. 1857, to turn back, so as to save its Livonian institute by inward regeneration from certain overthrow.

8. The doctrinal peculiarities of the Brotherhood cannot be quite correctly described as un-Lutheran, or anti-Lutheran. Bengel smartly characterized them in a single phrase: "They plucked up the stock of sound doctrine, stripped off what was most essential and vital, and retained the half of it," which not only then, but even still retains its truth and worth. Salvation is regarded as proceeding purely from the Son, the God-Man, so that the relation of the Father and of the Holy Spirit to redemption is scarcely even nominal; and the redemption of the God-Man again is viewed one-sidedly as consisting only in His sufferings and death, while the other side, that is grounded on His life and resurrection, is either carefully passed over, or its fruit is represented as borrowed from the atoning death. Thus not only justification, but sanctification is derived exclusively from the death of Christ, and this, not so much as a forensic substitutionary satisfaction, although that is not expressly denied, but rather as a Divine love-sacrifice which awakens an answering love in us. The whole of redemption is viewed as issuing from Christ's blood and wounds; and since from this mode of viewing the subject God's grace and love are made prominent rather than His righteousness, we hear almost exclusively of the gospel, and little or nothing of the law. All preaching and teaching were avowedly directed to the awakening of pious feelings of love to God, and thus tended to foster a kind of religious sentimentalism.

9. The peculiarities of worship among the Brethren were also directed to the excitement of pious feeling; their sensuously sweet sacred music, their church hymns, overcharged with emotion, their richly developed liturgies, their restoration of the *agape* with tea, biscuit, and chorale-singing, the fraternal kiss at communion, in their earlier days also washing of the feet, etc. The daily watchword from the O.T. and doctrinal texts from the N.T. were regarded as oracles, and were intended to give a special impress to the religious feelings of the day. As early as A.D. 1727 they had a hymn-book containing 972 hymns. Most of these were compositions of their own, a true reflection of their religious sentiments at that period. It also contained Bohemian and Moravian hymns, translated by Mich. Weiss, and also many old favourites of the evangelical church, often sadly

mutilated. By A.D. 1749 it had received twelve appendices and four supplements. In these appendices, especially in the twelfth, the one-sided tendency to give prominence to feeling was carried to the most absurd lengths of caricature in the use of offensive and silly terms of endearment as applied to the Saviour. Zinzendorf admitted the defects of this production, and had it suppressed in 1751, and in London prepared a new, expurgated edition of the hymn-book. Under Spangenberg's presidency Christian Gregor issued, in A.D. 1778, a hymn-book, containing 542 from Zinzendorf's book and 308 of his own pious rhymes. He also published a chorale book in A.D. 1784. Among their sacred poets Zinzendorf stands easily first. His only son, Christian Renatus, who died A.D. 1752, left behind him a number of sacred songs. Their hymns were usually set to the melodies of the Halle pietists.

10. In regard to the Christian life, the Brotherhood withdrew from politics and society, adopted stereotyped forms of speech and peculiar usages, even in their dress. They sought to live undisturbed by controversy, in personal communion with the Saviour. Their separatism as a covenanted people may be excused in view of the unbelief prevailing in the Protestant church, but it has not been overcome by the reawakening of spiritual life in the Church. As to their ecclesiastical constitution, Christ Himself, as the Chief Elder of the church, should have in it the direct government. The leaders, founding upon Proverbs xvi. 33 and Acts i. 26, held that fit expression was given to this principle by the use of the lot; but soon opposition to this practice arose, and with its abandonment the "special covenant" theory lost all its significance. The lot was used in election of office-bearers, sending of missionaries, admission to membership, etc. But in regard to marriage, it was used only by consent of the candidates for marriage, and an adverse result was not enforced. The administration of the affairs of the society lay with the conference of the united elders. From time to time general synods with legislative power were summoned. The membership was divided into groups of married, widowed, bachelors, maidens, and children, with special duties, separate residences, and also special religious services in addition to those common to all. The church officers were bishops, presbyters, deacons, deaconesses, and acolytes.

11. Missions to the Heathen.—Zinzendorf's meeting with a West Indian negro in Copenhagen awakened in him at an early period the missionary zeal. He laid the matter before the church, and in A.D. 1732 the first Herrnhut missionaries, Dober and Nitschmann, went out to St. Thomas, and in the following year missions were established in Greenland, North America, almost all the West Indian islands, South America, among the Hottentots at the Cape, the East

Indies, among the Eskimos of Labrador, etc. Their missionary enterprise forms the most brilliant and attractive part of the history
of the Moravians. Their procedure was admirably suited to uncultured races, and only for such. In the East Indies, therefore,
they were unsuccessful. They were never wanting in self-denying
missionaries, who resigned all from love to the Saviour. They were
mostly pious, capable artisans, who threw themselves with all their
hearts into their new work, and devoted themselves with affectionate
tenderness to the advancement of the bodily and spiritual interests
of those among whom they laboured. One of the noblest of them all
was the missionary patriarch Zeisberger, who died in A.D. 1808, after
toiling among the North American Indians for sixty-three years.
These missions were conducted at a surprisingly small outlay. The
Brethren also interested themselves in the conversion of the Jews.
In A.D. 1738 Dober wrought among the Jews of Amsterdam; and
with greater success in A.D. 1739, Lieberkühn, who also visited the
Jews in England and Bohemia, and was honoured by them with the
title of "rabbi."[1]

§ 169. THE REFORMED CHURCH BEFORE THE "ILLU-MINATION."

The sharpness of the contest between Calvinism and
Lutheranism was moderated on both sides. The union
efforts prosecuted during the first decades of the century
in Germany and Switzerland were always defeated by
Lutheran opposition. In the Dutch and German Reformed
Churches, even during the eighteenth century, Cocceianism
was still in high repute. After it had modified strict
Calvinism, the opposition between Reformed orthodoxy and
Arminian heterodoxy became less pronounced, and more and
more Arminian tendencies found their way into Reformed
theology. What pietism and Moravianism were for the
Lutheran church of Germany, Methodism was, in a much

---

[1] Spangenberg, "Account of Manner in which the *Unitas Fratrum*
Propagate the Gospel, and Carry on their Missions among the Heathen."
London, 1788. Holmes, "Historical Sketch of the Missions of the
United Brethren for the Propagation of the Gospel among the
Heathen from their Commencement down to 1817." London, 1827.

greater measure, and with a more enduring influence, for
the episcopal church of England.

1. The German Reformed Church.—The Brandenburg dynasty made
unwearied efforts to effect a union between the Lutheran and Reformed
churches throughout their territories (§ 154, 4).   Frederick I. (III.)
instituted for this purpose in A.D. 1703 a *collegium caritativum*, under
the presidency of the Reformed court preacher Ursinus (ranked as
bishop, that he might officiate at the royal coronation), in which also,
on the side of the Reformed, Jablonsky, formerly a Moravian bishop
and, on the part of the Lutherans, the cathedral preacher Winkler
of Magdeburg and Lüttke, provost of Cologne-on-the-Spree, took part
Spener, who wanted not a made union but one which he himself was
making, gave expression to his opinion, and soon passed over. Lüttke
after a few *sederunts* withdrew, and when Winkler in A.D. 1703 published a plan of union, *Arcanum regium*, which the Lutheran church
merely submitted for the approval of the Reformed king, such a storm
of opposition arose against the project, that it had to be abandoned.
In the following year the king took up the matter again in another
way.   Jablonsky engaged in negotiations with England for the
introduction of the Anglican episcopal system into Prussia, in order
by it to build a bridge for the union with Lutheranism.   But even
this plan failed, in consequence of the succession of Frederick William
I. in A.D. 1713, whose shrewd sense strenuously opposed it.—The vacillating statements of the *Confessio Sigismundi* (§ 154, 3) regarding
predestination made it possible for the Brandenburg Reformed theologians to understand it as teaching the doctrine of particular as well
as universal grace, and so to make it correspond with Brandenburg
Reformed orthodoxy.   The rector of the Joachimsthal Gymnasium
in Berlin, Paul Volkmann, in A.D. 1712, interpreted it as teaching
universal grace, and so in his *Theses theologicæ* he constructed a
system of theology, in which the divine foreknowledge of the result,
as the reconciling middle term between the particularism and universalism of the call, was set forth in a manner favourable to the
latter.   The controversy that was aroused over this, in which even
Jablonsky argued for the more liberal view, while on the other side
Barckhausen, Volkmann's colleague, in his *Amica Collatio Doctrinæ de
Gratia, quam vera ref. confitetur Ecclesia, cum Doctr. Volkmanni*, etc.,
came forward under the name of *Pacificus Verinus* as his most determined opponent, was put a stop to in A.D. 1719 by an edict of Frederick
William I., which enjoined silence on both parties, without any result
having been reached.—One of the noblest mystics that ever lived was
Gerhard Tersteegen, died A.D. 1769.   He takes a high rank as a sacred

poet. Anxious souls made pilgrimages to him from far and near for comfort, counsel, and refreshment. Though not exactly a separatist, he had no strong attachment to the church.[1]—The prayer-book of Conrad Mel, pastor and rector at Hersfeld in Hesse, died A.D. 1733, continues to the present day a favourite in pious families of the Reformed communion.

2. The Reformed Church in Switzerland.—The Helvetic Confession, with its strict doctrine of predestination and its peculiar inspiration theory (§ 161, 3), had been indeed accepted, in A.D. 1675, by all the Reformed cantons as the absolute standard of doctrine in church and school; but this obligation was soon felt to be oppressive to the conscience, and so the Archbishop of Canterbury and the kings of England and Prussia repeatedly interceded for its abrogation. In Geneva, though vigorously opposed by a strictly orthodox minority, the *Vénérable Compagnie* succeeded, in A.D. 1706, with the rector of the Academy at its head, J. A. Turretin, whose father had been one of the principal authors of the formula, in modifying the usual terms of subscription, *Sic sentio, sic profiteor, sic docebo, et contrarium non docebo*, into *Sic docebo quoties hoc argumentum tractandum suscipiam, contrarium non docebo, nec ore, nec calamo, nec privatim, nec publice;* and afterwards, in A.D. 1725, it was entirely set aside, and adhesion to the Scriptures of the O. and N.T., and to the catechism of Calvin, made the only obligation. More persistent on both sides was the struggle in Lausanne; yet even there it gradually lost ground, and by the middle of the century it had no longer any authority in Switzerland.—The union efforts made by the Prussian dynasty found zealous but unsuccessful advocates in the chancellor Pfaff of Lutheran Württemberg (§ 167, 4), and in Reformed Switzerland in J. A. Turretin of Geneva.

3. The Dutch Reformed Church.—Toward the end of the seventeenth century, in consequence of threats on the part of the magistrates, the passionate violence of the dispute between Voetians and Cocceians (§ 162, 5) was moderated; but in the beginning of the eighteenth century the flames burst forth anew, reaching a height in 1712, when a marble bust of Cocceius was erected in a Leyden church. An obstinate Voetian, Pastor Fruytier of Rotterdam, was grievously offended at this proceeding, and published a controversial pamphlet full of the most bitter reproaches and accusations against the Cocceians, which, energetically replied to by the accused, was much more hurtful than useful to the interests of the Voetians. At last a favourable hearing was given to a word of peace which a highly respected Voetian, the

---

[1] " Tersteegen : Life and Character, with Extracts from His Letters and Writings." London, 1832. Winkworth, " Christian Singers of Germany." London, 1869.

venerable preacher of eighty years of age, *J. Mor. Mommers*, addressed to the parties engaged in the controversy. He published in A.D. 1738, under the title of "*Eubulus*," a tract in which he proved that neither Cocceius himself nor his most distinguished adherents had in any essential point departed from the faith of the Reformed church, and that from them, therefore, in spite of all differences that had since arisen, the hand of fellowship should not be withheld. In consequence of this, the magistrates of Gröningen first of all decided, that forthwith, in filling up vacant pastorates, a Cocceian and Voetian should be appointed alternately; a principle which gradually became the practice throughout the whole country. At the same time also care was now taken that in the theological faculties both schools should have equal representation. But meanwhile also new departures had been made in each of the two parties. Among the Voetians, after the pattern formerly given them by Teellinck (§ 162, 4), followed up by the Frisian preacher Theod. Brakel, died A.D. 1669, and further developed by Jodocus von Lodenstein of Utrecht, died A.D. 1677, mysticism had made considerable progress; and the Cocceians, in the person of Hermann Witsius, drew more closely toward the pietism of the Voetians and the Lutherans. The most distinguished representative of this conciliatory party was F. A. Lampe of Detmold, afterwards professor in Utrecht, previously and subsequently pastor in Bremen, in high repute in his church as a hymn-writer, but best known by his commentary on John.—These conciliatory measures were frustrated by the publication, in A.D. 1740, of a work by Schortinghuis of Gröningen, which pronounced the Scriptures unintelligible and useless to the natural man, but made fruitful to the regenerate and elect by the immediate enlightenment of the Holy Spirit, evidenced by deep groanings and convulsive writhings. It was condemned by all the orthodox. The author now confined himself to his pastorate, where he was richly blessed. He died in A.D. 1750. His notions spread like an epidemic, till stamped out by the united efforts of the civil and ecclesiastical authorities in A.D. 1752.

4. Methodism.—In the episcopal church of England the living power of the gospel had evaporated into the formalism of scholastic learning and a mechanical ritualism. A reaction was set on foot by John Wesley, born A.D. 1703, a young man of deep religious earnestness and fervent zeal for the salvation of souls. During his course at Oxford, in A.D. 1729, along with some friends, including his brother Charles, he founded a society to promote pious living.[1] Those thus leagued together were scornfully called Methodists. From A.D. 1732, George Whitefield, born in A.D. 1714, a youth burning with zeal for his own

---

[1] For a slightly different account see Tyerman, vol. i., p. 66.

and his fellow men's salvation, wrought enthusiastically along with them. In A.D. 1735 the brothers Wesley went to America to labour for the conversion of the Indians in Georgia. On board ship they met Nitschmann, and in Savannah Spangenberg, who exercised a powerful influence over them. John Wesley accepted a pastorate in Savannah, but encountered so many hindrances, that he decided to return to England in A.D. 1738. Whitefield had just sailed for America, but returned that same year. Meanwhile Wesley visited Marienborn and Herrnhut, and so became personally acquainted with Zinzendorf. He did not feel thoroughly satisfied, and so declined to join the society. On his return he began, along with Whitefield, the great work of his life. In many cities they founded religious societies, preached daily to immense crowds in Anglican churches, and when the churches were refused, in the open air, often to 20,000 or even 30,000 hearers. They sought to arouse careless sinners by all the terrors of the law and the horrors of hell, and by a thorough repentance to bring about immediate conversion. An immense number of hardened sinners, mostly of the lower orders, were thus awakened and brought to repentance amid shrieks and convulsions. Whitefield, who divided his attentions between England and America, delivered in thirty-four years 18,000 sermons; Wesley, who survived his younger companion by twenty-one years, dying in A.D. 1791, and was wont to say the world was his parish, delivered still more. Their association with the Moravians had been broken off in A.D. 1740. To the latter, not only was the Methodists' style of preaching objectionable, but also their doctrine of "Christian perfection," according to which the true, regenerate Christian can and must reach a perfect holiness of life, not indeed free from temptation and error, but from all sins of weakness and sinful lusts. Wesley in turn accused the Herrnhuters of a dangerous tendency toward the errors of the quietists and antinomians. Zinzendorf came himself to London to remove the misunderstanding, but did not succeed. The great Methodist leaders were themselves separated from one another in A.D. 1741. Whitefield's doctrine of grace and election was Calvinistic; Wesley's Arminian.—From A.D. 1748 the Countess of Huntingdon attached herself to the Methodists, and secured an entrance for their preaching into aristocratic circles. With all her humility and self-sacrifice she remained aristocrat enough to insist on being head and organizer. Seeing she could not play this rôle with Wesley, she attached herself closely to Whitefield. He became her domestic chaplain, and with other clergymen accompanied her on her travels. Wherever she went she posed as a "queen of the Methodists," and was allowed to preach and carry on pastoral work. She built sixty-six chapels, and in A.D. 1768 founded a seminary for training preachers at Trevecca in Wales, under the oversight of the able and gentle John Fletcher, reserving supreme control to herself. After Whitefield's death, in A.D. 1770, the opposition between the Calvinistic followers of Whitefield and the Arminian Wesleyans burst out in a much more violent form. Fletcher and his likeminded fellow labourers were charged with teaching the horrible heresy of the universality of grace, and were on that account discharged by the countess from the seminary of Trevecca. They now joined Wesley, around whom the great majority of the Methodists had gathered.

5. The Methodists did not wish to separate from the episcopal church, but to work as a leaven within it. Whitefield was able to maintain this connexion by the aid of his aristocratic countess and her relationship with the higher clergy; but Wesley, spurning such aid, and trusting to his great powers of organization, felt driven more and more to set up an independent society. When the churches were closed against him and his fellow workers, and preaching in the open air was forbidden, he built chapels for himself.[1] The first was opened in Bristol, in A.D. 1739. When his ordained associates were too few for the work, he obtained the assistance of lay preachers. He founded two kinds of religious societies: The *united societies* embraced all, the *band societies* only the tried and proved of his followers. Then he divided the *united societies* again into *classes* of from ten to twenty persons each, and the *class-leaders* were required to give accurate accounts of the spiritual condition and progress of those under their care. Each member of the *united* as well as the *band societies* held a *society ticket*, which had to be renewed quarterly. The outward affairs of the societies were managed by *stewards*, who also took care of the poor. A number of local societies constituted a *circuit* with a superintendent and several itinerant preachers.[2] Wesley superintended all the departments of oversight, administration, and arrangement, supported from A.D. 1744 by an annual conference. Daily preaching and devotional exercises in the chapels, weekly class-meetings, monthly watchnights, quarterly fasts and lovefeasts, an annual service for the renewing of the covenant, and a great multiplication of prayer-meetings, gave a special character to Methodistic piety. Charles Wesley composed hymns for their services. They carefully avoided collision with the services of the state church. The American Methodists, who had been up to this time supplied by Wesley with itinerant missionaries, in A.D. 1784, after the War of Independence, gave vigorous expression to their wish for a more independent ecclesiastical con-

---

[1] Wesley himself continued to preach in the open air till nearly the end of the year 1790.

[2] Further details as to the organization of the societies are given in Tyerman, 1st ed., vol. i.. pp. 444, 445,

stitution, which led Wesley, in opposition to all right order, to ordain for them by his own hand several preachers, and to appoint, in the person of Thomas Coke, a superintendent, who assumed in America the title of bishop. Coke became the founder of the Methodist Episcopal Church of America, which soon outstripped all other denominations in its zeal for the conversion of sinners, and in consequent success. The breach with the mother church was completed by the adoption of a creed in which the Thirty-nine Articles were reduced to twenty-five. At the last conference presided over by Wesley, A.D. 1790, it was announced that they had in Britain 119 circuits, 313 preachers, and in the United States 97 circuits and 198 preachers. After Wesley's death, in A.D. 1791, his autocratic supremacy devolved, in accordance with the Methodist "Magna Charta," the *Deed of Declaration* of A.D. 1784, upon a fixed conference of 100 members, but its hierarchical organization has been the cause of many subsequent splits and divisions.[1]

6. **Theological Literature**—Clericus, of Amsterdam, died A.D. 1736, an Arminian divine, distinguished himself in biblical criticism, hermeneutics, exegesis, and church history. J. J. Wettstein was in A.D. 1730 deposed for heresy, and died in A.D. 1754 as professor at the Remonstrant seminary at Amsterdam. His critical edition of the N.T. of A.D. 1751 had a great reputation. Schultens of Leyden, died A.D. 1750, introduced a new era for O.T. philology by the comparative study of related dialects, especially Arabic. He wrote commentaries on Job and Proverbs. Of the Cocceian exegetes we mention, Lampe of Bremen, died A.D. 1729, "Com. on John," three vols., etc., and J. Marck of Leyden, died A.D. 1731, "Com. on Minor Prophets." In biblical antiquity, Reland of Utrecht, died A.D. 1718, wrote "*Palæstina ex vett.*

---

[1] Southey, "Life of John Wesley." London, 1820. Isaac Taylor, "Wesley and Wesleyanism." London, 1851. Tyerman, "Wesley's Life and Times." 2 vols. 4th ed. London, 1877. Urlin, "Churchman's Life of Wesley." London, 1880. Abbey and Overton, "English Church in 18th Century." 2 vols. London, 1879. Lecky, "History of England in the 18th Century." 2 vols. London, 1878. Stoughton, "History of Religion in England to End of 18th Century." 6 vols. London, 1882.—Jackson, "Life of Charles Wesley." 2 vols. London, 1841.—Tyerman, "Life of Whitefield." 2 vols. London, 1877.—Macdonald, "Fletcher of Madeley." London.—Smith, "History of Methodism." 3 vols. London, 1857. Stevens, "History of Methodism." 3 vols. New York, 1858. Stevens, "History of the Methodist Episcopal Church in the United States." 4 vols. New York, 1864. Bangs, "History of the Methodist Episcopal Church." 4 vols. New York, 1839.

monum. Illustr. Antiquitt. ss."; in ecclesiastical antiquity, Bingham, died A.D. 1723, " Origines Ecclest.; or, Antiquities of the Christian Church," ten vols., 1724, a masterpiece not yet superseded. Of English apologists who wrote against the deists, Leland, died A.D. 1766, " Advantage and Necessity of the Christian Revelation "; Stackhouse, died A.D. 1752, "History of the Bible." Of dogmatists, Stapfer of Bern, died A.D. 1775, and Wyttenbach of Marburg, died A.D. 1779, who followed the Wolffian method. Among church historians, J. A. Turretin of Geneva, died A.D. 1757, and Herm. Venema of Franeker, died A.D. 1787.—The most celebrated of the writers of sacred songs in the English language was the Congregationalist preacher Isaac Watts, died A.D. 1748, whose " Hymns and Spiritual Songs," which first appeared in A.D. 1707, still hold their place in the hymnbooks of all denominations, and have largely contributed to overthrow the Reformed prejudice against using any other than biblical psalms in the public service of praise

§ 170. New Sects and Fanatics.

The pietism of the eighteenth century, like the Reformation of the sixteenth, was followed by the appearance of all sorts of fanatics and extremists. The converted were collected into little companies, which, as *ecclesiolæ in ecclesia*, preserved the living flame amid prevailing darkness, and out of these arose separatists who spoke of the church as Babylon, regarded its ordinances impure, and its preaching a mere jingle of words. They obtained their spiritual nourishment from the mystical and theosophical writings of Böhme, Gichtel, Guyon, Poiret, etc. Their chief centre was Wetterau, where, in the house of Count Casimir von Berleburg, all persecuted pietists, separatists, fanatics, and sectaries found refuge. The count chose from them his court officials and personal servants, although he himself belonged to the national Reformed church. There was scarcely a district in Protestant Germany, Switzerland, and the Netherlands where there were not groups of such separatists; some mere harmless enthusiasts, others circulated pestiferous and immoral doctrines. Quite apart from pietism Swedenborgianism made its appearance, claiming to have a new

revelation. Of the older sects the Baptists and the Quakers
sent off new swarms, and even predestinationism gave rise
to a form of mysticism allied to pantheism.

1. Fanatics and Separatists in Germany.—Juliana von Asseburg, a
young lady highly esteemed in Magdeburg for her piety, declared
that from her seventh year she had visions and revelations, especially
about the millennium. She found a zealous supporter in Dr. J. W.
Petersen, superintendent of Lüneburg. After his marriage with
Eleonóre von Merlau, who had similar revelations, he proclaimed by
word and writing a fantastic chiliasm and the restitution of all
things. He was deposed in A.D. 1692, and died in A.D. 1727.[1] Henry
Horche, professor of theology at Herborn, was the orginator of a similar
movement in the Reformed church. He founded several Philadelphian societies (§ 162, 9) in Hesse, and composed a " mystical and
prophetical bible," the so called " Marburg Bible," A.D. 1712. Of other
fanatical preachers of that period one of the most prominent was
Hochmann, a student of law expelled from Halle for his extravagances
a man of ability and eloquence, and highly esteemed by Tersteegen
Driven from place to place, he at last found refuge at Berleburg, and
died there in A.D. 1721. In Württemberg the pious court chaplain.
Hedinger, of Stuttgart, died A.D. 1703, was the father of pietism and
separatism. The most famous of his followers were Gruber and Rock
who, driven from Württemberg, settled with other separatists at
Wetterau, renouncing the use of the sacraments and public worship.
Of those gathered together in the court of Count Casimir, the most
eminent were Dr. Carl, his physician, the French mystic Marsay, and
J. H. Haug, who had been expelled from Strassburg, a proficient in the
oriental languages. They issued a great number of mystical works,
chief of all the Berleburg Bible, in eight vols., 1726-1742, of which Haug
was the principal author. Its exposition proceeded in accordance
with the threefold sense; it vehemently contended against the church
doctrine of justification, against the confessional writings, the clerical
order, the dead church, etc. It showed occasionally profound insight
and made brilliant remarks, but contained also many trivialities and
absurdities. The mysticism which is prominent in this work lacks
originality, and is compiled from the mystico-theosophical writings of
all ages from Origen down to Madame Guyon.

2. The Inspired Societies in Wetterau.—After the unfortunate issue
of the Camisard War in A.D. 1705 (§ 153, 4) the chief of the prophets

---

[1] Hagenbach, "History of Church in 18th and 19th Centuries,"
vol. i., pp. 159-164.

of the Cevennes fled to England. They were at first well received, but were afterwards excommunicated and cast into prison. In A.D. 1711 several of them went to the Netherlands, and thence made their way into Germany. Three brothers, students at Halle, named Pott, adopted their notion of the gift of inspiration, and introduced it into Wetterau in A.D. 1714. Gruber and Rock, the leaders of the separatists there, were at first opposed to the doctrine, but were overpowered by the Spirit, and soon became its most enthusiastic champions. Prayer-meetings were organized, immense lovefeasts were held, and by itinerant brethren an *ecclesia ambulatoria* was set on foot, by which spiritual nourishment was brought to believers scattered over the land and the children of the prophets were gathered from all countries. The " utterances " given forth in ecstasy were calls to repentance, to prayer, to the imitation of Christ, revelations of the divine will in matters affecting the communities, proclamations of the near approach of the Divine judgment upon a depraved church and world, but without fanatical-sensual chiliasm. Also, except in the contempt of the sacraments, they held by the essentials of the church doctrine. In A.D. 1715 a split occurred between the *true* and the *false* among the inspired. The true maintained a formal constitution, and in A.D. 1716 excluded all who would not submit to that discipline. By A.D. 1719 only Rock claimed the gift of inspiration, and did so till his death in A.D. 1749. Gruber died in A.D. 1728, and with him a pillar of the society fell. Rock was the only remaining prop. A new era of their history begins with their intercourse with the Herrnhuters. Zinzendorf sent them a deputation in A.D. 1730, and paid them a visit in person at Berleberg. Rock's profound Christian personality made a deep impression upon him. But he was offended at their contempt of the sacraments, and at the convulsive character of their utterances. This, however, did not hinder him from expressing his reverence for their able leader, who in return visited Zinzendorf at Herrnhut in A.D. 1732. In the interests of his own society Zinzendorf shrank from identifying himself with those of Wetterau. Rock denounced him as a new Babylon-botcher, and he retaliated by calling Rock a false prophet. When the Herrnhuters were driven from Wetterau in A.D. 1750 (§ 168, 3, 7), the inspired communities entered on their inheritance. But with Rock's death in A.D. 1749 prophecy had ceased among them. They sank more and more into insignificance, until the revival of spiritual life, A.D. 1816–1821, brought them into prominence again. Government interference drove most of them to America.

8. Quite a peculiar importance belongs to J. C. Dippel, theologian, physician, alchemist, discoverer of Prussian blue and *oleum dippelii*, at first an orthodox opponent of pietism, then, through Gottfr. Arnold's influence, an adherent of the pietists, and ultimately of the

separatists. In A.D. 1697, under the name of *Christianus Democritus*, he began to write in a scoffing tone of all orthodox Christianity, with a strange blending of mysticism and rationalism, but without any trace profound Christian experience. Persecuted on every hand, exiled or imprisoned, he went hither and thither through Germany, Holland, Denmark, and Sweden, and found a refuge at last at Berleberg in A.D. 1729. Here he came in contact with the inspired, who did everything in their power to win him over; but he declared that he would rather give himself to the devil than to this Spirit of God. He was long intimate with Zinzendorf, but afterwards poured out upon him the bitterest abuse. He died in the count's castle at Berleberg in A.D. 1734.[1]

4. **Separatists of Immoral Tendency.**—One of the worst was the Buttlar sect, founded by Eva von Buttlar, a native of Hesse, who had married a French refugee, lived gaily for ten years at the court of Eisenach, and then joined the pietists and became a rigid separatist. Separated from her husband, she associated with the licentiate Winter, and founded a Philadelphian society at Allendorf in A.D. 1702, where the foulest immoralities were practised. Eva herself was reverenced as the door of paradise, the new Jerusalem, the mother of all, Sophia come from heaven, the new Eve, and the incarnation of the Spirit. Winter was the incarnation of the Father, and their son Appenfeller the incarnation of the Son. They pronounced marriage sinful; sensual lusts must be slain in spiritual communion, then even carnal association is holy. Eva lived with all the men of the sect in the most shameless adultery. So did also the other women of the community. Expelled from Allendorf after a stay of six weeks, they sought unsuccessfully to gain a footing in various places. At Cologne they went over to the Catholic church. Their immoralities reached their climax at Lüde near Pyrmont. Winter was sentenced to death in A.D. 1706, but was let off with scourging. Eva escaped the same punishment by flight, and continued her evil practices unchecked for another year. She afterwards returned to Altona, where with her followers leading outwardly an honourable life, she attached herself to the Lutheran church, and died, honoured and esteemed, in A.D. 1717.—In a similar way arose in A.D. 1739 the Bordelum sect, founded at Bordelum by the licentiates Borsenius and Bär; and the Brüggeler sect, at Brüggeler in Canton Bern, where in A.D. 1748 the brothers Kohler gave themselves out as the two witnesses (Rev. xi.). Of a like nature too was the sect of Zionites at Ronsdorf in the Duchy of Berg. Elias Eller, a manufacturer at Elberfeld, excited by mys-

---

[1] Hagenbach, "History of the Church in the 18th and 19th Centuries," vol. i., pp. 168–175.

tical writings, married in A.D. 1725 a rich old widow, but soon found more pleasure in a handsome young lady, Anna von Buchel, who by a nervous sympathetic infection was driven into prophetic ecstasy. She proclaimed the speedy arrival of the millennium; Eller identified her with the mother of the man-child (Rev. xii. 1). When his wife had pined away through jealousy and neglect and died, he married Buchel. The first child she bore him was a girl, and the second, a boy, soon died. When a strong opposition arose in Elberfeld against the sect, he, along with his followers, founded Ronsdorf, as a New Zion, in A.D. 1737. The colony obtained civil rights, and Eller was made burgomaster. Anna having died in A.D. 1744, Eller gave his colony a new mother, and practised every manner of deceit and tyranny. After the infatuation had lasted a long time, the eyes of the Reformed pastor Schleiermacher, grandfather of the famous theologian, were at last opened. By flight to the Netherlands he escaped the fate of another revolter, whom Eller persuaded the authorities at Düsseldorf to put to death as a sorcerer. Every complaint against himself was quashed by Eller's bribery of the officials. After his death in A.D. 1750 his stepson continued this Zion game for a long time.

5. Swedenborgianism.—Emanuel von Swedenborg was born at Stockholm, in A.D. 1688, son of the strict Lutheran bishop of West Gothland, Jasper Swedberg. He was appointed assessor of the School of Mines at Stockholm, and soon showed himself to be a man of encyclopædic information and of speculative ability. After long examination of the secrets of nature, in a condition of magnetic ecstasy, in which he thought that he had intercourse with spirits, sometimes in heaven, sometimes in hell, he became convinced, in A.D. 1743, that he was called by these revelations to restore corrupted Christianity by founding a church of the New Jerusalem as the finally perfected church. He published the apocalyptic revelations as a new gospel: "Arcana Cœlestia in Scr. s. Detecta," in seven vols.; " Vera Chr. Rel.," two vols. After his death, in A.D. 1772, his " Vera Christiana Religio" was translated into Swedish, but his views never got much hold in his native country. They spread more widely in England, where John Clowes, rector of St. John's Church, Manchester, translated his writings, and himself wrote largely in their exposition and commendation. Separate congregations with their own ministers, and forms of worship, sprang up through England in A.D. 1788, and soon there were as many as fifty throughout the country. From England the New Church spread to America.—In Germany it was specially throughout Württemberg that it found adherents. There, in A.D. 1765, Oetinger (§ 171, 9) recognised Swedenborg's revelations. and introduced many elements from them into his theosophical system.—Swedenborg's religious

system was speculative mysticism, with a physical basis and rationalizing results. The aim of religion with him is the opening of an intimate correspondence between the spiritual world and man, and giving an insight into the mystery of the connexion between the two. The Bible (excluding the apostolic epistles, as merely expository), pre-eminently the Apocalypse, is recognised by him as God's word ; to be studied, however, not in its literal but in its spiritual or inner sense. Of the church dogmas there is not one which he did not either set aside or rationalistically explain away. He denounces in the strongest terms the church doctrine of the Trinity. God is with him only one Person, who manifests Himself in three different forms: the Father is the principle of the manifesting God ; the Son, the manifested form ; the Spirit, the manifested activity. The purpose of the manifestation of Christ is the uniting of the human and Divine ; redemption is nothing more than the combating and overcoming of the evil spirits. But angels and devils are spirits of dead men glorified and damned He did not believe in a resurrection of the flesh, but maintained that the spiritual form of the body endures after death. The second coming of Christ will not be personal and visible, but spiritual through a revelation of the spiritual sense of Holy Scripture, and is realized by the founding of the church of the New Jerusalem.[1]

6. New Baptist Sects (§ 163, 3).— In Wetterau about A.D. 1708 an anabaptist sect arose called Dippers, because they did not recognise infant baptism and insisted upon the complete immersion of adult believers. They appeared in Pennsylvania in A.D. 1719, and founded settlements in other states. Of the "perfect" they required absolute separation from all worldly practices and enjoyments and a simple, apostolic style of dress. To baptism and the Lord's supper they added washing the feet and the fraternal kiss and anointing the sick. The Seventh-day Baptists observe the seventh instead of the first day of the week, and enjoin on the "perfect" celibacy and the community of goods. New sects from England continued to spread over America. Of these were the Seed or Sucker Baptists, who identified the non-elect with the seed of the serpent, and on account of their doctrine of predestination regarded all instruction and care of children useless. A similar predestinarian exaggeration is seen in the Hard-shell Baptists, who denounce all home and foreign missions as running counter to the Divine sovereignty. Many, sometimes called Campbellites from their founder, reject any party name, claiming to be simply Christians,

---

[1] Tafel, "Documents concerning the Life and Character of Swedenborg." 3 vols. London, 1875. White, "Emanuel Swedenborg his Life and Writings." 2 vols. London. 1867.

and acknowledge only so much in Scripture as is expressly declared to be " the word of the Lord." The Six-Principles-Baptists limit their creed to the six articles of Hebrews vi. 1, 2. The brothers Haldane, about the middle of the eighteenth century, founded in Scotland the Baptist sect of Haldanites, which has with great energy applied itself to the practical cultivation of the Christian life.—Continuation, §§ 208, 1 ; 211, 3.

7. New Quaker Sects. — The Jumpers, who sprang up among the Methodists of Cornwall about A.D. 1760, are in principle closely allied to the early Quakers (§ 163, 4). They leaped and danced after the style of David before the ark and uttered inarticulate howls. They settled in America, where they have adherents still.—The Shakers originated from the prophets of the Cevennes who fled to England in A.D. 1705. They converted a Quaker family at Bolton in Lancashire named Wardley, and the community soon grew. In A.D. 1758 Anna Lee, wife of a farrier Stanley, joined the society, and, as the apocalyptic bride, inaugurated the millennium. She taught that the root of all sin was the relationship of the sexes. Maltreated by the mob, she emigrated to America, along with thirty companions, in A.D. 1774. Though per-secuted here also, the sect increased and formed in the State of New York the *Millennial Church* or *United Society of Believers.* Anna died in A.D. 1784; but her prophets declared that she had merely laid aside the earthly garb and assumed the heavenly, so that only then the veneration of " Mother Anna " came into force. As Christ is the Son of the eternal Wisdom, Anna is the daughter ; as Christ is the second Adam, she is the second Eve, and spiritual mother of believers as Christ is their father. Celibacy, community of goods, common labour (chiefly gardening), as a pleasure, not a burden, common domestic life as brothers and sisters, and constant intercourse with the spirit world, are the main points in her doctrine. By the addition of voluntary proselytes and the adoption of poor helpless children the sect has grown, till now it numbers 3,000 or 4,000 souls in eighteen villages. The capital is New Lebanon in the State of New York. The name Shakers was given them from the quivering motion of body in their solemn dances. In their services they march about singing " On to heaven we will be going," " March heavenward, yea, victorious band," etc. Like the Quakers (§ 163, 6) they have neither a ministry nor sacraments, and their whole manner of life is modelled on that of the Quakers. The purity of the relation of brothers and sisters has always been free from suspicion.[1]

---

[1] Evans, "Shakers: Compendium of Origin, History, Principles, and Doctrines of the United Society of Believers in Christ's Second Coming." New York, 1859. Dixon, " New America." 2 vols. 8th ed.

8. **Predestinarian-Mystical Sects.**—The Hebræans, founded by Ver-
schoor, a licentiate of the Reformed church of Holland deposed under
suspicion of Spinozist views, in the end of the seventeenth century,
held it indispensably necessary to read the word of God in the original.
They were fatalists, and maintained that the elect could commit no sin.
True faith consisted in believing this doctrine of their own sinlessness.
About the same time sprang up the **Hattemists,** followers of *Pontiaan
von Hattem,* a preacher deposed for heresy, with fatalistic views like
the Hebræans, but with a strong vein of pantheistic mysticism. True
piety consisted in the believer resting in God in a purely passive
manner, and letting God alone care for him. The two sects united
under the name of Hattemists, and continued to exist in Holland and
Zealand till about A.D. 1760.

§ 171. RELIGION, THEOLOGY, AND LITERATURE OF THE " ILLUMINATION." [1]

In England during the first half of the century deism had
still several active propagandists, and throughout the whole
century efforts, not altogether unsuccessful, were made to
spread Unitarian views. From the middle of the century,
when the English deistic unbelief had died out, the " Illumination," under the name of rationalism, found an entrance
into Germany. Arminian pelagianism, recommended by
brilliant scholarship, English deism, spread by translations
and refutations, and French naturalism, introduced by a
great and much honoured king, were the outward factors
in securing this result. The freemason lodges, carried

London, 1869. Nordhoff, "The Communistic Societies of the United
States." London, 1874.

[1] Pusey, "Historical Inquiry into the Causes of the Prevalence of
Rationalism in Germany." London, 1828. Rose, "The State of
Protestantism in Germany." Oxford, 1829. Saintes, "A Critical
History of Rationalism in Germany, from its Origin till the Present
Time." London, 1849. Lecky, "History of the Rise and Influence
of the Spirit of Rationalism in Europe." 2 vols. London, 1873.
Farrar, "Critical History of Free Thought in Reference to the
Christian Religion." London, 1863. Hagenbach, "German Rationa-
lism." Edinburgh, 1865. Hurst, "History of Rationalism." New
York, 1865. Gostwick, "German Culture and Christianity, their
Controversy, 1770-1880." New York, 1882.

into Germany from England, a relic of mediævalism, aided
the movement by their endeavour after a universal religion
of a moral and practical kind. The inward factors were
the Wolffian philosophy (§ 167, 3), the popular philosophy,
and the pietism, with its step-father separatism (§ 170), which
immediately prepared the soil for the sowing of rationalism.
Orthodoxy, too, with its formulas that had been outlived,
contributed to the same end. German rationalism is
essentially distinguished from Deism and Naturalism by not
breaking completely with the Bible and the church, but
eviscerating both by its theories of accommodation and by
its exaggerated representations of the limitations of the
age in which the books of Scripture were written and the
doctrines of Christianity were formulated. It thus treats
the Bible as an important document, and the church as a
useful religious institution. Over against rationalism arose
supernaturalism, appealing directly to revelation. It was a
dilution of the old church faith by the addition of more or
less of the water of rationalism. Its reaction was therefore
weak and vacillating. The temporary success of the vulgar
rationalism lay, not in its own inherent strength, but in the
correspondence that existed between it and the prevailing
spirit of the age. The philosophy, however, as well as the
national literature of the Germans, now began a victorious
struggle against these tendencies, and though itself often
indifferent and even hostile to Christianity, it recognised in
Christ a school-master. Pestalozzi performed a similar
service to popular education by his attempts to reform effete
systems.

1. Deism, Arianism, and Unitarianism in the English Church.—(1) The
Deists (§ 164, 3). With Locke's philosophy (§ 164, 2) deism entered
on a new stage of its development. It is henceforth vindicated on
the ground of its reasonableness. The most notable deists of this age
were John Toland, an Irishman, first Catholic, then Arminian, died
A.D. 1722, author of "Christianity not Mysterious," "Nazarenus, or

Jewish, Gentile, and Mohametan Christianity," etc. The Earl of Shaftesbury, died A.D. 1713, wrote "Characteristics of Men," etc. Anthony Collins, J.P. in Essex, died A.D. 1729, author of "Priestcraft in Perfection," "Discourse of Freethinking," etc. Thomas Woolston, fellow of Cambridge, died in prison in A.D. 1733, author of "Discourse on the Miracles of the Saviour." Mandeville of Dort, physician in London, died A.D. 1733, wrote "Free Thoughts on Religion." Matthew Tindal, professor of law in Oxford, died A.D. 1733, wrote "Christianity as Old as the Creation." Thomas Morgan, nonconformist minister, deposed as an Arian, then a physician, died A.D. 1743, wrote "The Moral Philosopher." Thomas Chubb, glover and tallow-chandler in Salisbury, died A.D. 1747, author of popular compilations, "The True Gospel of Jesus Christ." Viscount Bolingbroke, statesman, charged with high treason and pardoned, died A.D. 1751, writings entitled, "Philosophical Works."—Along with the deists as an opponent of positive Christianity may be classed the famous historian and sceptic David Hume, librarian in Edinburgh, died A.D. 1776, author of "Inquiry concerning the Human Understanding," "Natural History of Religion," "Dialogues concerning Natural Religion," etc.[1]—Deism never made way among the people, and no attempt was made to form a sect. Among the numerous opponents of deism these are chief: Samuel Clarke, died A.D. 1729; Thomas Sherlock, Bishop of London, died A.D. 1761; Chandler, Bishop of Durham, died A.D. 1750; Leland, Presbyterian minister in Dublin, died A.D. 1766, wrote "View of Principal Deistic Writers," three vols., 1754; Warburton, Bishop of Gloucester, died A.D. 1779; Nath. Lardner, dissenting minister, died A.D. 1768, wrote "Credibility of the Gospel History," seventeen vols., 1727-1757. With these may be ranked the famous pulpit orator of the Reformed church of France, Saurin, died A.D. 1730, author of *Discours hist., crit., theol., sur les Événements les plus remarkables du V. et N.T.*—(2) The So-called Arians. In the beginning of the century several distinguished theologians of the Anglican church sought to give currency to an Arian doctrine of the Trinity. Most conspicuous was Wm. Whiston, a distinguished mathematician, physicist, and astronomer of the school of Sir Isaac Newton, and his successor in the mathematical chair at Cambridge. Deprived of this office in A.D. 1708 for spreading his heterodox views, he issued in A.D. 1711 a five-volume work, "Primitive Christianity Revived," in which he justified his Arian doctrine of

---

[1] Stephen, "History of English Thought in the 18th Century." 2 vols. London, 1876. Cairns, "Unbelief in the 18th Century." Edinburgh, 1881. Pünjer, "History of Christian Philosophy of Religion from Reformation to Kant," § 5, "The English Deists." Edinburgh, 1887.

the Trinity as primitive and as taught by the ante-Nicene Fathers, and insisted upon augmenting the N.T. canon by the addition of twenty-nine books of the apostolic and other Fathers, including the apostolic "Constitutions" and "Recognitions" which he maintained were genuine works of Clement. Subsequently he adopted Baptist views, and lost himself in fantastic chiliastic speculations. He died A.D. 1752. More sensible and moderate was Samuel Clarke, also distinguished as a mathematician of Newton's school and as a classical philogist. As an opponent of deism in sermons and treatises he had gained a high reputation as a theologian, when his work, "The Scripture Doctrine of the Trinity," in A.D. 1712, led to his being accused of Arianism by convocation; but by conciliatory explanations he succeeded in retaining his office till his death in A.D. 1729. But the excitement caused by the publication of his work continued through several decades, and was everywhere the cause of division. His ablest apologist was Dan. Whitby, and his keenest opponent Dan. Waterland.—(3) The Later Unitarians. The anti-trinitarian movement entered on a new stage in A.D. 1770. After Archdeacon Blackburne of London, in A.D. 1766, had started the idea, at first anonymously, in his "Confessional," he joined in A.D. 1772 with other freethinkers, among whom was his son-in-law Theophilus Lindsey, in presenting to Parliament a petition with 250 signatures, asking to have the clergy of the Anglican church freed from the obligation of subscribing the Thirty-nine Articles and the Liturgy, and to have the requirement limited to assent to the Scriptures. This prayer was rejected in the Lower House by 217 votes against 71. Lindsey now resigned his clerical office, announced his withdrawal from the Anglican church, founded and presided over a Unitarian congregation in London from A.D. 1774, and published a large number of controversial Unitarian tracts. He died in A.D. 1808. The celebrated chemist and physicist Joseph Priestley, A.D. 1733–1806 who had been a dissenting minister in Birmingham from A.D. 1780, joined the Unitarian movement in 1782, giving it a new impetus by his high scientific reputation. He wrote the "History of the Corruptions of Christianity," and the "History of Early Opinions about Jesus Christ," denying that there is any biblical foundation for the orthodox doctrine of the Trinity, and seeking to show that it had been forced upon the church against her will from the Platonic philosophy. These and a whole series of other controversial writings occasioned great excitement, not only among theologians, but also among the English people of all ranks. At last the mob rose against him in A.D. 1791. His house and all his scientific collections and apparatus were burnt. He narrowly escaped with his life, and soon after settled in America, where he wrote a church history in four vols. Of his many English opponents the most eminent was Bishop

Sam. Horsley, a distinguished mathematician and commentator on the works of Sir Isaac Newton.

2. Freemasons. The mediæval institution of freemasons (§ 104, 13) won much favour in England, especially after the Great Fire of London in A.D. 1666. The first step toward the formation of freemason lodges of the modern type was taken about the end of the sixteenth century, when men of distinction in other callings sought admission as honorary members. After the rebuilding of London and the completion of St. Paul's in A.D. 1710, most of the lodges became defunct, and the four that continued to exist united in A.D. 1717 into one grand lodge in London, which, renouncing material masonry, assumed the task of rearing the temple of humanity. In A.D. 1721 the Rev. Mr. Anderson prepared a constitution for this reconstruction of a trade society into a universal brotherhood, according to which all "free masons" faithfully observing the moral law as well as all the claims of humanity and patriotism, came under obligation to profess the religion common to all good men, transcending all confessional differences, without any individual being thereby hindered from holding his own particular views. Although, in imitation of the older institution, all members by reason of their close connexion were bound to observe the strictest secrecy in regard to their masonic signs, rites of initiation and promotion, and forms of greeting, it is not properly a secret society, since the constitution was published in A.D. 1723, and members publicly acknowledge that they are such.—From London the new institute spread over all England and the colonies. Lodges were founded in Paris in A.D. 1725, in Hamburg in A.D. 1737, in Berlin in A.D. 1740. This last was raised in A.D. 1744 into a grand lodge, with Frederick II. as grand master. But soon troubles and disputes arose, which broke up the order about the end of the century. Rosicrucians (§ 160, 1) and alchemists, pretending to hold the secrets of occult science, Jesuits (§ 210, 1), with Catholic hierarchical tendencies, and "Illuminati" (§ 165, 13), with rationalistic and infidel tendencies, as well as adventurers of every sort, had made the lodges centres of quackery, juggling, and plots.[1]

3. The German "Illumination."—(1) Its Precursors. One of the first of these, following in the footsteps of Kuntzen and Dippel, was J. Chr. Edelmann of Weissenfels, who died A.D. 1767. He began in A.D. 1735 the publication of an immense series of writings in a rough but powerful style, filled with bitter scorn for positive Christianity. He went from one sect to another, but never found what he sought. In A.D. 1741 he accepted Zinzendorf's invitation, and stayed with the

---

[1] Halliwell, "The Early History of English Freemasonry." London, 1840.

count for a long time. He next joined the Berleberg separatists, because they despised the sacraments, and contributed to their Bible commentary, though Haug had to alter much of his work before it could be used. This and his contempt for prayer brought the connexion between him and the society to an end. He then led a vagabond life up and down through Germany. Edelmann regarded himself as a helper of providence, and at least a second Luther. Christianity he pronounced the most irrational of all religions; church history a conglomeration of immorality, lies, hypocrisy, and fanaticism; prophets and apostles, bedlamites; and even Christ by no means a perfect pattern and teacher. The world needs only one redemption— redemption from Christianity. Providence, virtue, and immortality are the only elements in religion. No less than 166 separate treatises came from his facile pen.—Laurence Schmidt of Wertheim in Baden, a scholar of Wolff, was author of the notorious "Wertheimer Bible Version," which rendered Scripture language into the dialect of the eighteenth century, and eviscerated it of all positive doctrines of revelation. This book was confiscated by the authorities, and its author cast into prison.

4. (2) **The Age of Frederick the Great.** Hostility to all positive Christianity spread from England and France into Germany. The writings of the English deists were translated and refuted, but mostly in so weak a style that the effect was the opposite of that intended. Whilst English deism with its air of thoroughness made way among the learned, the poison of frivolous French naturalism committed its ravages among the higher circles. The great king of Prussia, Frederick II., A.D. 1740-1786, surrounded by French freethinkers, Voltaire, D'Argens, La Metrie, etc., wished every man in his kingdom to be saved after his own fashion. In this he was quite earnest, although his personal animosity to all ecclesiastical and pietistic religion made him sometimes act harshly and unjustly. Thus, when Francke of Halle (son of the famous A. H. Francke) had exhorted his theological students to avoid the theatre, the king, designating him "hypocrite" Francke, ordered him to attend the theatre himself and have his attendance attested by the manager. His bitter hatred of all "priests" was directed mainly against their actual or supposed intolerance, hypocrisy, and priestly arrogance; and where he met with undoubted integrity, as in Gellert and Seb. Bach, or simple, earnest piety, as in General Ziethen, he was not slow in paying to it the merited tribute of hearty acknowledgment and respect. His own religion was a philosophical deism, from which he could thoroughly refute Holbach's materialistic "*Système de la Nature.*"—Under the name of the German popular philosophy (Moses Mendelssohn, Garve, Eberhard, Platner, Steinbart, etc.), which started from the Wolffian

philosophy, emptied of its Christian contents, there arose a weak, vapoury, and self-satisfied philosophizing on the part of the common human reason. Basedow was the reformer of pedagogy in the sense of the " Illumination," after the style of Rousseau, and crying up his wares in the market made a great noise for a while, although Herder declared that he would not trust calves, far less men, to be educated by such a pedagogue. The " Universal German Library " of the Berlin publisher Nicolai, 106 vols. A.D. 1765-1792, was a literary Inquisition tribunal against all faith in revelation or the church. The "Illumination " in the domain of theology took the name of rationalism. Pietistic Halle cast its skin, and along with Berlin took front rank among the promoters of the "Illumination." In the other universities champions of the new views soon appeared, and rationalistic pastors spread over all Germany, to preach only of moral improvement, or to teach from the pulpit about the laws of health, agriculture, gardening, natural science, etc. The old liturgies were mutilated, hymn-books revised after the barbarous tastes of the age, and songs of mere moral tendency substituted for those that spoke of Christ's atonement. An ecclesiastical councillor, Lang of Regensburg, dispensed the communion with the words : "Eat this bread ! The Spirit of devotion rest on you with His rich blessing! Drink a little wine! The virtue lies not in this wine ; it lies in you, in the divine doctrine, and in God." The Berlin provost, W. Alb. Teller, declared publicly : " The Jews ought on account of their faith in God, virtue, and immortality, to be regarded as genuine Christians." C. Fr. Bahrdt, after he had been deposed for immorality from various clerical and academical offices, and was cast off by the theologians, sought to amuse the people with his wit as a taphouse-keeper in Halle, and died there of an infamous disease in A.D. 1792.

5. (3) The Wöllner Reaction.—In vain did the Prussian government, after the death of Frederick the Great, under Frederick William II., A.D. 1786-1797, endeavour to restore the church to the enjoyment of its old exclusive rights by punishing every departure from its doctrines, and insisting that preaching should be in accordance with the Confession. At the instigation of the Rosicrucians (§ 160, 1) and of the minister Von Wöllner, a country pastor ennobled by the king, the Religious Edict of 1788 was issued, followed by a statement of severe penalties ; then by a *Schema Examinationis Candidatorum ss. Ministerii rite Instituendi ;* and in A.D. 1791, by a commission for examination under the Berlin chief consistory and all the provincial consistories, with full powers, not only over candidates, but also over all settled pastors. But notwithstanding all the energy with which he sought to carry out his edict, the minister could accomplish nothing in the face of public opinion, which favoured the resistance of the chief

consistory. Only one deposition, that of Schulz of Gielsdorf, near Berlin, was effected, in A.D. 1792. Frederick William III., A.D. 1797–1840, dismissed Wöllner in A.D. 1798, and set aside the edict as only fostering hypocrisy and sham piety.

6. The Transition Theology.—Four men, who endeavoured to maintain their own belief in revelation, did more than all others to prepare the way for rationalism : Ernesti of Leipzig, in the department of N.T. exegesis ; Michaelis of Göttingen, in O.T. exegesis ; Semler of Halle, in biblical and historical criticism ; and Töllner of Frankfort-on-the-Oder in dogmatics. J. A. Ernesti, A.D. 1707–1781, from A.D. 1734 rector of St. Thomas' School, from A.D. 1742 professor at Leipzig, colleague to Chr. A. Crusius (§ 167, 3), was specially eminent as a classical scholar, and maintained his reputation in that department, even after becoming professor of theology in A.D. 1758. His *Institutio Interpretis N.T.*, of A.D. 1761, made it an axiom of exegesis that the exposition of Scripture should be conducted precisely as that of any other book. But even in the domain of classical literature there must be an understanding of the author as a whole, and the expositor must have appreciation of the writer's spirit, as well as have acquaintance with his language and the customs of his age. And just from Ernesti's want of this, his treatise on biblical hermeneutics is rationalistic, and he became the father of rationalistic exegesis, though himself intending to hold firmly by the doctrine of inspiration and the creed of the church.— What Ernesti did for the N.T., J. D. Michaelis, A.D. 1717–1791, son of the pious and orthodox Chr. Bened. Michaelis, did for the O.T. He was from A.D. 1750 professor at Göttingen, a man of varied learning and wide influence. He publicly acknowledged that he had never experienced anything of the *testimonium Sp. s. internum*, and rested his proofs of the divinity of the Scriptures wholly on external evidences, *e.g.* miracles, prophecy, authenticity, etc., a spider's web easily blown to pieces by the enemy. No one has ever excelled him in the art of foisting his own notions on the sacred authors and making them utter his favourite ideas. A conspicuous instance of this is his " Laws of Moses," in six vols.—In a far greater measure than either Ernesti or Michaelis did J. Sol. Semler, A.D. 1725–1791, pupil of Baumgarten, and from A.D. 1751 professor at Halle, help on the cause of rationalism. He had grown up under the influence of Halle pietism in the profession of a customary Christianity, which he called his private religion, which contributed to his life a basis of genuine personal piety. But with a rare subtlety of reasoning as a man of science, endowed with rich scholarship, and without any wish to sever himself from Christianity, he undermined almost all the supports of the theology of the church. This he did by casting doubt on the genuineness of the biblical writings, by setting up a theory of inspiration and accommodation

which admitted the presence of error, misunderstanding, and pious
fraud in the Scriptures, by a style of exposition which put aside everything unattractive in the N.T. as "remnants of Judaism," by a critical
treatment of the history of the church and its doctrines, which represented the doctrines of the church as the result of blundering, misconception, and violence, etc. He was a voluminous author, leaving
behind him no less than 171 writings. He sowed the wind, and reaped
the whirlwind, by which he himself was driven along. He firmly
withstood the installation of Bahrdt at Halle opposed Basedow's
endeavours, applied himself eagerly to refute the "Wolfenbüttel Fragments" of Reimarus, edited by Lessing in 1774–1778, which represented
Christianity as founded upon pure deceit and fraud, and defended even
the edict of Wöllner. But the current was not thus to be stemmed,
and Semler died broken-hearted at the sight of the heavy crop from his
own sowing.—J. G. Töllner, A.D. 1724–1774, from A.D. 1756 professor at
Frankfort-on-the-Oder, was in point of learning and influence by no
means equal to those now named; yet he deserves a place alongside
of them, as one who opened the door to rationalism in the department of dogmatics. He himself held fast to the belief in revelation,
miracles, and prophecy, but he also regarded it as proved that God
saves men by the revelation of nature; the revelation of Scripture is
only a more sure and perfect means. He also examined the divine
inspiration of Scripture, and found that the language and thoughts
were the authors' own, and that God was concerned in it in a manner
that could not be more precisely determined. Finally, in treating of
the active obedience of Christ, he gives such a representation of it
as sets aside the doctrine of the church.

7. The Rationalistic Theology.—From the school of these men, especially from that of Semler, went forth crowds of rationalists, who for
seventy years held almost all the professorships and pastorates of Protestant Germany. At their head stands Bahrdt, A.D. 1741–1792, writer
at first of orthodox handbooks, who, sinking deeper and deeper through
vanity, want of character, and immorality, and following in the steps
of Edelmann, wrote 102 vols., mostly of a scurrilous and blasphemous
character. The rationalists, however, were generally of a nobler sort:
Griesbach of Jena, A.D. 1745–1812, distinguished as textual critic of
the N.T.; Teller of Berlin, published a lexicon to the N.T., which
substituted "leading another life" for regeneration, "improvement"
for sanctification, etc.; Koppe of Göttingen, and Rosenmüller of
Leipzig wrote *scholia* on N.T., and Schulze and Bauer on the O.T.
Of far greater value were the performances of J. E. Fichhorn of Göttingen, A.D. 1752–1827, and Bertholdt of Erlangen, A.D. 1774–1822, who
wrote introductions to the O.T. and commentaries. In the department of church history, H. P. C. Henke of Helmstädt and the talented

statesman, Von Spittler of Württemberg, wrote from the rationalistic standpoint. Steinbart and Eberhardt wrote more in the style of the popular philosophy. The subtle-minded J. H. Tieftrunk, A.D. 1760–1837, professor of philosophy at Halle, introduced into theology the Kantian philosophy with its strict categories. Jerusalem, Zollikofer, and others did much to spread rationalistic views by their preaching.[1]

8. **Supernaturalism.**—Abandoning the old orthodoxy without surrendering to rationalism, the supernaturalists sought to maintain their hold of the Scripture revelation. Many of them did so in a very uncertain way: their revelation had scarcely anything to reveal which was not already given by reason. Others, however, eagerly sought to preserve all essentially vital truths. Morus of Leipzig, Ernesti's ablest student, Less of Göttingen, Döderlein of Jena, Seiler of Erlangen, and Nösselt of Halle, were all representatives of this school. More powerful opponents of rationalism appeared in Storr of Tübingen, A.D. 1746–1805, who could break a lance even with the philosopher of Königsberg, Knapp of Halle, and Reinhard of Dresden, the most famous preacher of his age. Reinhard's sermon on the Reformation festival of A.D. 1800 created such enthusiasm in favour of the Lutheran doctrine of justification, that government issued an edict calling the attention of all pastors to it as a model. The most distinguished apologists were the mathematician Euler of St. Petersburg, the physiologist, botanist, geologist, and poet Haller of Zürich and the theologians Lilienthal of Königsberg and Kleuker of Kiel. The most zealous defender of the faith was the much abused Goeze of Hamburg, who fought for the palladium of Lutheran orthodoxy against his rationalistic colleagues, against the theatre, against Barth, Basedow, and such-like, against the "Wolfenbüttel Fragments," against the "Sorrows of Werther," etc. His polemic may have been over-violent, and he certainly was not a match for such an antagonist as Lessing; he was, however, by no means an obscurantist, ignoramus, fanatic, or hypocrite, but a man in solemn earnest in all he did. In the field of church history important services were rendered by Schröckh of Wittenberg and Walch of Göttingen, laborious investigators and compilers, Stäudlin and Planck of Göttingen, and Münter of Copenhagen.—Among English theologians of this tendency toward the end of the century, the most famous was Paley of Cambridge, A.D. 1743–1805, whose "Principles of Moral and Political Philosophy" and "Evidences of Christianity" were obligatory text-books in the uni-

---

[1] Ritschl, "History of Christian Doctr. of Justification and Reconciliation," pp. 347–426. Dorner, "History of Protestant Theology," vol. ii., pp. 277–292. Hagenbach, "History of Church in 18th and 19th Centuries," vol. i., pp. 251–321.

versity. His "*Horæ Paulinæ*" prove the credibility ot the Acts of the Apostles from the epistles, and his "Natural Theology" demonstrates God's being and attributes from nature.

9. Mysticism and Theosophy.—Oetinger of Württemburg, the *Magus* of the South, A.D. 1702–1782, takes rank by himself. He was a pupil of Bengel (§ 167, 3), well grounded in Scripture, but also an admirer of Böhme and sympathising with the spiritualistic visions of Swedenborg But amid all, with his biblical realism and his theosophy, which held corporeity to be the end of the ways of God, he was firmly rooted in the doctrines of Lutheran orthodoxy.—The best mystic of the Reformed church was J. Ph. Dutoit of Lausanne, A.D. 1721–1793, an enthusiastic admirer of Madame Guyon; he added to her quietist mysticism certain theosophical speculations on the original nature of Adam, the creation of woman, the fall, the necessity of the incarnation apart from the fall, the basing of the sinlessness of Christ upon the immaculate conception of his mother, etc. He gathered about him during his lifetime a large number of pious adherents, but after his death his theories were soon forgotten.

10. The German Philosophy.—As Locke accomplished the descent from Bacon to deism and materialism, so Wolff effected the transition from Leibnitz to the popular philosophy. Kant, A.D. 1724–1804, saved philosophy from the baldness and self-sufficiency of Wolffianism, and pointed it to its proper element in the spiritual domain. Kant's own philosophy stood wholly outside of Christianity, on the same platform with rationalistic theology. But by deeper digging in the soil it unearthed many a precious nugget, of whose existence the vulgar rationalism had never dreamed, without any intention of becoming a schoolmaster to lead to Christ. Kant showed the impossibility of a knowledge of the supernatural by means of pure reason, but admitted the ideas of God freedom, and immortality as postulates of the practical reason and as constituting the principle of all religion, whose only content is the moral law. Christianity and the Bible are to remain the basis of popular instruction, but are to be expounded only in an ethical sense. While in sympathy with rationalism, he admits its baldness and self-sufficiency. His keen criticism of the pure reason, the profound knowledge of human weakness and corruption shown in his doctrine of radical evil, his categorical imperative of the moral law, were well fitted to awaken in more earnest minds a deep distrust of themselves, a modest estimate of the boasted excellences of their age, and a feeling that Christianity could alone meet their necessities.—F. H. Jacobi, A.D. 1743–1819, "with the heart a Christian, with the understanding a pagan," as he characterized himself, took religion out of the region of mere reason into the depths of the universal feelings of the soul, and so awakened a positive aspiration.—J. G. Fichte, A.D. 1762–1814, trans-

formed Kantianism, to which he at first adhered, into an idealistic
science of knowledge, in which only the *ego* that posits itself appears
as real, and the *non-ego*, only by its being posited by the *ego;* and
thus the world and nature are only a reflex of the mind. But when,
accused of atheism in A.D. 1798, he was expelled from his position in
Jena, he changed his views, rushing from the verge of atheism into a
mysticism approaching to Christianity. In his " Guide to a Blessed
Life," A.D. 1806, he delivered religion from being a mere servant to
morals, and sought the blessedness of life in the loving surrender of
one's whole being to the universal Spirit, the full expression of which
he found in John's Gospel. Pauline Christianity, on the other hand,
with its doctrine of sin and redemption, seemed to him a deterioration,
and Christ Himself only the most complete representative of the
incarnation of God repeated in all ages and in every pious man.—In
the closing years of the century, Schelling brought forward his theory
of *identity*, which was one of the most powerful instruments in
introducing a new era.[1]

11. **The German National Literature.**—When the powerful strain of
the evangelical church hymn had well-nigh expired in the feeble
lispings of Gellert's sacred poetry, Klopstock began to chant the praises
of the Messiah in a higher strain. But the pathos of his odes met
with no response, and his "Messiah," of which the first three cantos
appeared in A.D. 1748, though received with unexampled enthusiasm,
could do nothing to exorcise the spirit of unbelief, and was more
praised than read. The theological standpoint of Lessing, A.D. 1729–
1781, is set forth in one of his letters to his brother. "I despise the
orthodox even more than you do, only I despise the clergy of the new
style even more. What is the new-fashioned theology of those shallow
pates compared with orthodoxy but as dung-water compared with
dirty water? On this point we are at one, that our old religious
system is false; but I cannot say with you that it is a patchwork of
bunglers and half philosophers. I know nothing in the world upon
which human ingenuity has been more subtly exercised than upon
it. That religious system which is now offered in place of the old
is a patchwork of bunglers and half philosophers." He is offended
at men hanging the concerns of eternity on the spider's thread of
external evidences, and so he was delighted to hurl the Wolfenbüttel
"Fragments" at the heads of theologians and the Hamburg pastor
Goeze, whom he loaded with contumely and scorn. Thoroughly
characteristic too is the saying in the "*Duplik*": That if God hold-

---

[1] Chalybæus, "Historical Development of Speculative Philosophy
from Kant to Hegel." Edin., 1854. Räbiger, "Theological Encyclopædia," vol. i., pp. 73-76.

ing in his right hand all truth, and in his left hand the search after truth, subject to error through all eternity, were to offer him his choice, he would humbly say, "Father the left, for pure truth is indeed for thee alone." In his "*Nathan*" only Judaism and Mohammedanism are represented by truly noble and ideal characters, while the chief representative of Christianity is a gloomy zealot, and the conclusion of the parable is that all three rings are counterfeit. In another work he views revelation as one of the stages in "The Education of the Human Race," which loses its significance as soon as its purpose is served. In familiar conversation with Jacobi he frankly declared his acceptance of the doctrine of Spinoza : Ἐν καὶ πᾶν.[1] Wieland, A.D. 1733–1813, soon turned from his youthful zeal for ecclesiastical orthodoxy to the popular philosophy of the cultured man of the world. Herder, A.D. 1744–1803, with his enthusiastic appreciation of the poetical contents of the Bible, especially of the Old Testament, was not slow to point out the insipidity of its ordinary treatment. Goethe, A.D. 1749–1832, profoundly hated the vandalism of neology, delighted in "The Confessions of a Fair Soul" (§ 172, 2), had in earlier years sympathy with the Herrnhuters, but in the full intellectual vigour of his manhood thought he had no need of Christianity, which offended him by its demand for renunciation of self and the world. Schiller, A.D. 1759–1805, enthusiastically admiring everything noble, beautiful and good, misunderstood Christianity, and introduced into the hearts of the German people Kantian rationalism clothed in rich poetic garb. His lament on the downfall of the gods of Greece, even if not so intended by the poet himself, told not so much against orthodox Christianity as against poverty-stricken deism, which banished the God of Christianity from the world and set in his place the dead forces of nature. And if indeed he really thought that for religion's sake he should confess to no religion, he has certainly in many profoundly Christian utterances given unconscious testimony to Christianity.—The Jacobi philosophy of feeling found poetic interpreters in Jean Paul Richter, A.D. 1763–1825, and Hebel, died A.D. 1826, in whom we find the same combination of pious sentiment which is drawn toward Christianity and the sceptical understanding which allied itself to the revolt against the common orthodoxy. J. H. Voss, a rough, powerful Dutch peasant, who in his "*Luise*" sketched the ideal of a brave rationalistic country parson, and, with the inexorable

---

[1] Stahr, "Lessing: his Life and Works," translated by G. Evans. 2 vols. Boston, 1866. Sime, "Lessing, his Life and Writings." 2 vols. London, 1877. Zimmern, "G. E. Lessing: his Life and Works." London, 1878. Smith, "Lessing as a Theologian," in the *Theologica. Review*, July, 1868.

rigour of an inquisitor, hunted down the night birds of ignorance and oppression. But alongside of those children of the world stood two genuine sons of Luther, Matthias Claudius, A.D. 1740–1815, and J. G. Hamann, A.D. 1730–1788, the "Magus of the North" and the Elijah of his age, of whom Jean Paul said that his commas were planetary systems and his periods solar systems, to whom the philosopher Hemsterhuis erected in the garden of Princess Gallitzin a tablet with the inscription : "To the Jews a stumbling-block, to the Greeks foolishness." With them may also be named two noble sons of the Reformed church, the physiognomist Lavater, A.D. 1741–1801, and the devout dreamer, Jung-Stilling, A.D. 1740–1817. The famous historian, John von Müller, A.D. 1752–1809, well deserves mention here, who more than any previous historian made Christ the centre and summit of all times ; and also the no less famous statesman C. F. von Moser, the most German of the Germans of this century, who, with noble Christian heroism, in numerous political and patriotic tracts, battled against the prevailing social and political vices of his age.

12. The great Swiss educationist Pestalozzi, A.D. 1746–1827, assumed toward the Bible, the church, and Christianity an attitude similar to that of the philosopher of Königsberg. The conviction of the necessity and wholesomeness of a biblical foundation in all popular education was rooted in his heart, and he clearly saw the shallowness of the popular philosophy, whether presented under the eccentric naturalism of Rousseau or the bald utilitarianism of Basedow. His whole life issued from the very sanctuary of true Christianity, as seen in his self-sacrificing efforts to save the lost, to strengthen the weak, and to preach to the poor by word and deed the gospel of the all-merciful God whose will it is that all should be saved. He began his career as an educationist in A.D. 1775 by receiving into his house deserted beggar children, and carried on his experiments in his educational institutions at Burgdorf till A.D. 1798, and at Isserten till A.D. 1804. His writings, which circulated far and wide, gained for his methods recognition and high approval.[1]

§ 172. CHURCH LIFE IN THE PERIOD OF THE "ILLUMINATION."

The ancient faith of the church had even during this age of prevailing unbelief its seven thousand who refused to bow

---

[1] Russell, "A Short Account of the Life and History of Pestalozzi," based on De Guemp's "*L'Histoire de Pestalozzi.*" London, 1888. To be followed by a complete English translation of De Guemp's work

the knee to Baal. The German people were at heart firmly grounded in the Christianity of the Bible and the church, and where the pulpit failed had their spiritual wants supplied by the devout writings of earlier days. Where the modern vandalism of the "Illumination" had mutilated and watered down the books of praise, the old church songs lingered in the memories of fathers and mothers, and were sung with ardour at family worship. For many men of culture, who were more exposed to danger, the Society of the Brethren afforded a welcome refuge. But even among the most accomplished of the nation many stood firmly in the old paths. Lavater and Stilling, Haller and Euler, the two Mosers, father and son, John von Müller and his brother J. G. Müller, are not by any means the only, but merely the best known, of such true sons of the church. In Württemberg and Berg, where religious life was most vigorous, religious sects were formed with new theological views which made a deep impression on the character and habits of the people. Also toward the end of the century an awakened zeal in home and foreign missions was the prelude of the glorious enterprises of our own days.

1. The Hymnbook and Church Music.—Klopstock, followed by Cramer and Schlegel, introduced the vandalism of altering the old church hymns to suit modern tastes and views. But a few, like Herder and Schubert, raised their voices against such philistinism. The "Illuminist" alterations were unutterably prosaic, and the old pathos and poetry of the sixteenth and seventeenth century hymns were ruthlessly sacrificed. The spiritual songs of the noble and pious Gellert are by far the best productions of this period.—Church Music too now reached its lowest ebb. The old chorales were altered into modern forms. A multitude of new, unpopular melodies, difficult of comprehension, with a bald school tone, were introduced; the last trace of the old rhythm disappeared, and a weary monotony began to prevail, in which all force and freshness were lost. As a substitute, secular preludes, interludes, and concluding pieces were brought in. The people often entered the churches during the playing of operatic overtures, and were dismissed amid the noise of a march or waltz.

The church ceased to be the patron and promoter of music; the theatre and concert room took its place. The opera style thoroughly depraved the oratorio. For festival occasions, cantatas in a purely secular, effeminate style were composed. A true ecclesiastical music no longer existed, so that even Winterfeld closed his history of church music with Seb. Bach. It was, if possible, still worse with the mass music of the Roman Catholic church. Palestrina's earnest and capable school was completely lost sight of under the sprightly and frivolous opera style, and with the organ still more mischief was done than in the Protestant church.

2. Religious Characters.—The pastor of Ban de la Roche in Steinthal of Alsace, "the saint of the Protestant church," J. Fr. Oberlin, A.D. 1740–1826, deserves a high place of honour. During a sixty years' pastorate "Father Oberlin" raised his poverty-stricken flock to a position of industrial prosperity, and changed the barren Steinthal into a patriarchal paradise. The same may be said of a noble Christian woman of that age, Sus. Cath. von Klettenberg, Lavater's "Cordata," Goethe's "Fair Soul," whose genuine confessions are wrought into "Wilhelm Meister," the centre of a beautiful Christian circle in Frankfort, where the young Goethe received religious impressions that were never wholly forgotten.—Community of religious yearnings brought together pious Protestants and pious Catholics. The Princess von Gallitzin, her chaplain Overberg, and minister Von Fürstenberg formed a noble group of earnest Catholics, for whom the ardent Lutheran Hamann entertained the warmest affection.

3. Religious Sects.—In Württemberg there arose out of the pietism of Spener, with a dash of the theosophy of Oetinger, the party of the Michelians, so named from a layman, Michael Hahn, whose writings show profound insight into the truths of the gospel. He taught the doctrine of a double fall, in consequence of which he depreciated though he did not forbid marriage; of a restitution of all things; while he subordinated justification to sanctification, the Christ for us to the Christ in us, etc. As a reaction against this extreme arose the Pregizerians, who laid exclusive stress upon baptism and justification, declared assurance and heart-breaking penitence unnecessary, and imparted to their services as much brightness and joy as possible. Both sects spread over Württemberg and still exist, but in their common opposition to the destructive tendencies of modern times, they have drawn more closely together. In their chiliasm and restitutionism they are thoroughly agreed.—The Collenbuschians in Canton Berg propounded a dogmatic system in which Christ empties Himself of His divine attributes, and assumes with sinful flesh the tendencies to sin that had to be fought against, the sufferings of Christ are attributed to the wrath of Satan, and His redemption consists in His overcoming

Satan's wrath for us and imparting His Spirit to enable us to do works of holiness. The most distinguished adherents of Collenbusch were the two Hasencamps and the talented Bremen pastor Menken.

4. **The Rationalistic "Illumination" outside of Germany.**—In Amsterdam, in A.D. 1791, a Restored Lutheran Church or Old Light was organized on the occasion of the intrusion of a rationalistic pastor. It now numbers eight Dutch congregations with 14,000 adherents and 11 pastors. Under the name of **Christo Sacrum** some members of the French Reformed church at Delft, in A.D. 1797, founded a denomination which received adherents of all confessions, holding by the divinity of Christ and His atonement, and treating all confessional differences as non-essential and to be held only as private opinions. In their public services they adopted mainly the forms of the Anglican episcopal church. Though successful at first, it soon became rent by the incongruity of its elements. In England the dissenters and Methodists provided a healthy protest against the lukewarmness of the State church. In William Cowper, A.D. 1731–1800, we have a noble and brilliant poet of high lyrical genius, whose life was blasted by the terrorism of a predestinarian doctrine of despair and the religious melancholy produced by Methodistic agonies of soul.

5. **Missionary Societies and Missionary Enterprise.**—In order to arouse interest in the idea of a grand union for practical Christian purposes, the Augsburg elder, John Urlsperger, travelled through England, Holland, and Germany. The Basel Society for Spreading Christian Truth, founded in A.D. 1780, was the firstfruits of his zeal, and branches were soon established throughout Switzerland and Southern Germany. The Basel Bible Society was founded in A.D. 1804, and the Missionary Society in A.D. 1816.—At a meeting of English Baptist preachers at Kettering, in Northamptonshire, in A.D. 1792, William Carey was the means of starting the Baptist Missionary Society. Carey was himself its first missionary. He sailed for India in A.D. 1793, and founded the Serampore Mission in Bengal. The work of the society has now spread over the East and West Indies, the Malay Archipelago, South Africa, and South America. A popular preacher, Melville Horne, who had been himself in India, published "Letters on Missions," in A.D. 1794, in which he earnestly counselled a union of all true Christians for the conversion of the heathen. In response to this appeal a large number of Christians of all denominations, mostly Independents, founded in A.D. 1795, the London Missionary Society, and in the following year the first missionary ship, *The Duff*, under Captain Wilson, sailed for the South Seas with twenty-nine missionaries on board. Its operations now extend to both Indies, South Africa, and North America; but its chief hold is in the South Seas. In the Society Islands the missionaries wrought for sixteen years without any apparent result, till at last

King Pomare II. of Tahiti sought baptism as the first-fruits of their labours. A victory gained over a pagan reactionary party in A.D. 1815 secured complete ascendency to Christianity. The example of the London Society was followed by the founding of two Scottish societies in A.D. 1796 and a Dutch society in A.D. 1797, and the Church Missionary Society in London in A.D. 1799, for the English possessions in Africa, Asia, etc. The Danish Lutheran (§ 167, 9) and the Herrnhut (§ 168, 11) societies still continued their operations.[1]—Continuation, §§ 183, 184.

---

[1] Marshman, "Life and Times of Marshman, Carey, and Ward." 2 vols. London, 1859. Smith, "Life of William Carey." London, 1886. Wilson, "Missionary Voyage of the Ship *Duff*." London, 1799. Morison, "Fathers and Founders of the London Missionary Society." London, 1844.

FOURTH SECTION.

CHURCH HISTORY OF THE NINETEENTH CENTURY

I.—General and Introductory.

§ 173. SURVEY OF RELIGIOUS MOVEMENTS OF NINETEENTH CENTURY.

A REACTION had set in against the atheistic spirit of the French Revolution, and the victories of A.D. 1813, 1815, encouraged the pious in their Christian confidence. Princes and people were full of gratitude to God. Alexander I., Francis I., and Frederick William III., representing the three principal churches, in A.D. 1815, after the political situation had been determined by the Congress of Vienna, formed "the Holy Alliance," a league of brotherly love for mutual defence and maintenance of peace, to which all the European princes adhered with the exception of the pope, the sultan, and the king of England. Through Metternich's arts it ultimately degenerated into an instrument of repression and tyranny.—Incongruous elements were present everywhere. The restoration of the papacy in A.D. 1814 had given a new impulse to ultramontanism, as did also the Reformation centenary of A.D. 1817 to Protestantism; while supernaturalism and pietism prevailing in the Lutheran and Reformed churches led to renewed attempts at union. Old sects were strengthened and new sects arose. Pantheism, materialism, and atheism, as well as socialism and communism, without concealment attacked Christianity; while pauperism and vagabondage, on the one hand, and the Stock Exchange swindling of capitalists, on the other, spread moral consumption through all classes of society. The ultramontanes, led by the Jesuits, reasserted the most arrogant claims of the papacy. The climax was reached when Pius IX. obtained a decree of council affirming his infallibility, while by the Nemesis of history the royal crown was torn from his head.

§ 174. NINETEENTH CENTURY CULTURE IN RELATION TO CHRISTIANITY AND THE CHURCH.

Down to A.D. 1840, when zeal for it began to abate, philosophy exercised an important influence on the religious development of the age, both in the departments of science and of life. While rationalism was not able to transcend the standpoint of Kant, the other theological tendencies were more or less determined formally, and even materially by the philosophical movements of this period. Alongside of philosophy, literature, itself to a great extent coloured by contemporary philosophy, exerted a powerful influence on the religious opinions of the more cultured among the people. The sciences, too, came into closer relations, partly friendly, partly hostile, to Christianity; and art in some of its masterpieces paid a noble tribute to the church.

1. The German Philosophy (§ 171, 10).—Fries, whose philosophy was Kantian rationalism, modified by elements borrowed from Jacobi, influenced such theologians as De Wette. Schelling, in his "Philosophy of Identity," had advanced from Fichte's idealism to a pantheistic naturalism. From Fichte he had learned that this world is nothing without spirit; but while Fichte recognised this world, the *non-ego*, as reality only in so far as man seizes upon it and penetrates it by his spirit, and so raises it into real being, Schelling regards spirit as nothing else than the life of nature itself. In the lower stages of this nature-life spirit is still slumbering and dreaming, but in man it has attained unto consciousness. The nature-life as a whole, or the world-soul, is God; man is the reflex of God and the world in miniature, a microcosmos. In the world's development God comes into objective being and unfolds his self-consciousness; Christianity is the turning point in the world's history; its fundamental dogmas of revelation, trinity, incarnation, and redemption are suggestive attempts to solve the world's riddle. Schelling's poetic view of the world penetrated all the sciences, and gave to them a new impulse. Though hateful to the old rationalists, this system found ardent admirers among the younger theologians. As Schelling to Fichte, so Hegel was attached to Schelling, and wrought his pantheistic naturalism into a pantheistic spiritualism. Not so much in the life of nature as in the thinking and doing of the human spirit,

the divine revelation is the unfolding of the divine self-consciousness
from non-being into being. Judaism and Christianity are progressive
stages of this process ; Judaism stands far below classic paganism ; but
in Christianity we have the perfect religion, to be developed into
the highest form of philosophy. The Protestant church doctrine
was now again accorded the place of honour. Marheincke developed
Lutheran orthodoxy into a system of speculative theology based on
Hegelian principles; while Göschel infused into it a pietist spirit,
which made many hail the new departure as the long-sought reconciliation of theology and philosophy. But after Hegel's death in
A.D. 1831 the condition of matters suddenly changed. His school
split into an orthodox wing following the master's ecclesiastical
tendencies, and a heterodox wing which deified the human spirit.
Strauss, Bauer, and Feuerbach led this heterodox party in theology,
and Ruge in reference to social, æsthetic, and political questions.
Persecuted by the state in A.D. 1843, the Young Hegelians joined the
rationalists, whom they had before sneered at as "antediluvian
theologians." Schelling, who had been silent for almost thirty years,
took Hegel's chair in Berlin as his decided opponent in A.D. 1841,
and with his dualistic doctrine of potencies, from which he finally
advanced to a Christian gnosticism, obtained a temporary influence
among the younger theologians. He died at the baths of Ragaz in
Switzerland in A.D. 1854. He flashed for a moment like a meteor,
and as suddenly his light was quenched.

2. The domination of the Hegelian philosophy was overthrown by
the split in the school and the radicalism of the adherents of the left
wing, and Schelling in the second stage of his philosophical development had not succeeded in founding any proper school of his own.
A group of younger philosophers, with I. H. Fichte at their head.
starting from the Hegelian dialectic, have striven to free philosophy
from the reproach of pantheism and to develop a speculative theism
in touch with historical Christianity. Other members of this school
are Weisse, Braniss, Chalibæus, Ulrici, Wirth, Romang, etc.—Herbart
renounces all that philosophers from Fichte senior to Fichte junior
had done, and declares the metaphysical end of their systems beyond
the horizon of philosophy, which must limit itself to the province
of experience. His realism is in diametrical opposition to Hegel's
idealism. Toward Christianity his philosophy occupies a position
of indifference. Influenced by Kant's theory of knowledge as well
as by the Fichte-Schelling-Hegel idealism and Herbart's realism,
with an infusion of Leibnitz's monad doctrine, Hermann Lotze of
Göttingen has, since A.D. 1844, set forth a system of "teleological
idealism." He develops his metaphysical principles from what we
have by immediate experience internal and external, and the in-

variability of the causal mechanism in everything that happens in the inner and outer world he explains as the realizing of moral purposes.—Schopenhauer's philosophy, which only in the later years of his life (died A.D. 1860) began to attract attention, is in spirit utterly opposed to the religion and ethics of Christianity. Its task is to describe "The World as Will and Idea"; first at that stage of entering into visibility which is represented in man does will, the thing-in-itself, become joined with idea, and makes its appearance now with it over against the world as a conscious subject. But since idea is regarded as a pure illusion of the will, this leads to a pessimism which takes absolute despair as the only legitimate moral principle. E. von Hartmann went still further in the same direction in his "Philosophy of the Unconscious," published in 1869, of which an English translation in three vols. appeared in 1884. He identifies the will with matter and idea with spirit, demands in addition to the absolute despair of the individual here and hereafter, the complete surrender of the personality to the world-process in order to the attainment of its end, the annihilation of the world. This dissolution of the world consists in the complete withdrawal of the will into the absolute as the only unconscious, so that at last the wrong and misery of being produced by the irrational will are abolished in this withdrawal. From this philosophical standpoint Hartmann attempted in A.D. 1874 to take Christianity to pieces, showing some favour to Vatican Catholicism, but pouring out the vials of his wrath upon Protestantism. His "religion of the future" consists in a yearning for freedom from all the burden and misery of being and share in the world-process by relapsing into the blessedness of non-being.—In France, England, and America much favour has been shown to the atheistic-sensual Positivism of Aug. Comte, which, excluding every form of theology and morals, requires only the so-called exact sciences as the object of philosophy. On his later notions of a "religion of humanity," see § 210, 1. On essentially similar lines proceeds Herbert Spencer, in his "System of Synthetic Philosophy," to whose school also Darwin belonged. His followers are styled agnostics, because they regard all knowledge of God and divine things as absolutely impossible, and evolutionists, because their master endeavours to construct all the sciences on the basis of the evolution theory.

8. The Sciences.—Schelling's profound theories were of all the more significance from their not being restricted to the philosophical strivings of his time, but inspiring the other sciences with the breath of a new life. To the fullest extent the natural sciences exposed themselves to this influence. There was not wanting indeed a certain shadowy mysticism, to which especially the fancies of mesmeric

magnetism largely contributed; but this fog gradually cleared away, and the Christian elements were purified from their pantheistic surroundings. Steffens and Von Schubert taught that the divine book of nature is to be regarded as the reflex and expansion of the divine revelation in Scripture. The Hegelian philosophy, too, seemed at first likely to infuse a Christian spirit into the other sciences. In Göschel, at least, there was a thinker who imparted to jurisprudence a Christian character, and to Christianity a juristic construction. In other respects Hegel's philosophy in its application to the other departments of science gave in many ways a predominance to an abstruse dialectic tendency. Its adherents of the extreme left sought to construct all sciences *a priori* from the pure idea, and at the same time to root out from them the last vestiges of the Christian spirit.

The greatest names in natural science, Copernicus, Kepler, Newton, Haller, Davy, Cuvier, etc., are household words in Christian circles. All these and many more were firmly convinced that there was no conflict between their most brilliant discoveries and Christian truth. In A.D. 1825 the Earl of Bridgwater founded a lectureship, and treatises on the power, wisdom, and goodness of God as manifested in the creation, have been written by Buckland, Chalmers, Whewell, Bell, etc. It was otherwise in Germany. Even Schleiermacher, in his "Letters to Lücke," in A.D. 1829, expressed his fears of the prophesied overthrow of all Christian theories of the world by the incontrovertible results of physical research, and Bretschneider in his "Letters to a Statesman," in A.D. 1830, proclaimed to the world without regret that already what Schleiermacher only feared had actually come to pass. Physicists, awakening from the glamour of the Schelling nature philosophy, pronounced all speculation contraband, and declared pure empiricism, the simple investigation of actual things, the only permissible object of their labour. And although they handed over to theologians and philosophers questions about spirit in and over nature, as not belonging to their province, a younger generation maintained that spirit was non-existent, because it could not be discovered by the microscope and dissecting knife. Carl Vogt defined thought to be a secretion of the brain, and Moleschott regarded life as a mere mode of matter and man's existence after life only as the manuring of the fields. Feuerbach proclaimed that "man is what he eats," and Buchner popularized these views into a gospel for social democrats and nihilists. Oersted, the famous discoverer of electro-magnetism, had sought "the spirit in nature," but the spirit which he found was not that of the Bible and the church. The grandmaster of German scientific research, Alex. von Humboldt, saw in the world a cosmos of noble harmony as a whole and in its parts, but of Christian ideas in God's great book of nature he finds no trace. In A.D. 1859 the great English naturalist Darwin, died A.D. 1882, introduced into the arena the theory of "Natural Selection," by means of which the modification and development of the few primary animal forms through the struggle for existence and the survival of the fittest by sexual selection is supposed, in millions, perhaps milliards, of years, to have brought forth the present variety and manifoldness of animal species. Multitudes of naturalists now accept his theory of the descent of men and apes from a common stem.—In Medicine De Valenti on the Protestant side, with pietistic earnestness, maintains that Christian faith is a vehicle of healing power; while a circle in Munich on the Catholic side make worship of saints and the host a *conditio sine qua non* of all medicine. A more moderate attitude is assumed by the Roman Catholic Dr. Capellmann of Aachen, in his "Pastoral Medicine."

4. Of Christian Jurists we have, on the Protestant side, Stahl, Savigny, Puchta, Jacobson, Richter, Meier, Scheuerl, Hinschius, etc.; and on the Catholic side, Walther, Philipps, etc. Among Historians, the greatest in modern times is Leopold von Ranke, who, with his disciples, occupies a thoroughly Christian standpoint. There has appeared, however, on the part of many Protestant historians, such as Voigt, Leo, Mentzel, Vorreiter, Hurter, Gfroerer, etc., a tendency in the most conspicuous manner to recognise and admire the brilliant phenomena of mediæval Catholicism, even going the length of renouncing the vital principles of Protestantism, and glorifying a Boniface, a Gregory VII., and an Innocent III., and characterizing the Reformation as a revolution. Ultramontanes have been only too ready to turn to their own use all such concessions, but show no inclination to make similar admissions damaging to their side, so that with them history consists rather in the abuse of everything Protestant as vile and perfidious, instead of being a record of independent research. Janssen of Frankfort stands out prominently above the billows of the "*Kulturkampf*" (§ 197), as the greatest master of this ultramontane style of history making.—Geography, first raised to the rank of a science by Carl Ritter, received from its great founder a Christian impress and owes much of its development to the researches of Christian missionaries. Finally, Philology, in the hands of Creuzer, Görres, Sepp, etc., unfolds in a Christian spirit the religion and mythology of classical paganism; and in the hands of Nägelsbach and Lübker expounds the religious life of the ancient world in relation to Christian truth.

5. National Literature (§ 171, 11).—To some extent Goethe, but much more decidedly the romantic school of poets, was attached to Schelling's philosophy of nature. The romancists developed a deep

religiousness of feeling, as shown in Novalis and La Motte Fouqué, and violent opposition to rationalistic theology as shown in Tieck, which in the case of Fr. Schlegel ran to the other extreme of moral frivolity as seen in his "Lucinde." The romantic school as thus represented by Schlegel was joined by the party of Young Germany with its gospel of the rehabilitation of the flesh. Its mouthpiece was the gifted poet Heine. The pantheistic deification of nature by Schelling, and the self-deification of the Hegelian school obtained poetic expression in Leop. Schafer's *Laienbrevier und Weltpriester*, as well as in Sallet's *Laienevangelium;* while the sympathies of the young Hegelians with the revolutionary movements gained utterance in the poems of Herwegh, and in a more serious tone in those of Freiligrath. More recently the views of the *Protestantenverein* (§ 180) have found their poetical representative in Nic. Eichhorn, whose "Jesus of Nazareth," a tragical drama, 1880, deals with the life, works, and sufferings of the "historical Christ," after the style of free Protestant science, with rich psychological analysis of the character in a brilliant imaginative production. Though composed with a view to theatrical representation, it has never yet been put on the stage.

6. The Christian element was present in the noble patriotic songs of E. M. Arndt [1] and Max. von Schenkendorf much more distinctly than in the romantic school. Enthusiasm in the struggle for freedom awakened faith in the living God. Uhland's lovely lyrics, with their enthusiasm for the present interests of the Fatherland, entitle him to rank among patriotic poets, and their brilliant and profound rendering of the old German legends places him in the romantic school, which, however, in clearness and depth he leaves far behind. Without being a distinctively Christian poet, his warm sympathy with the life of the German people gives him a genuine interest in the Christian religion. The same may be said of Rückert's highly finished poems, which transplanted the fragrant flowers of oriental sensuousness and contemplativeness into the garden of German poetry. A more decided Christian consecration of poetic genius is seen in the noble and beautiful lyrics of Emanuel Geibel, died 1884, the greatest and most Christian of the secular poets of the present. Of those ordinarily ranked as sacred poets may be named Knapp, Döring, Spitta, Garve, Vict. Strauss, etc., who for the most part contributed their sacred songs to Knapp's "*Christoterpe*" (1833-1853). A later publication of equal merit, called the "*Neue Christoterpe*," has been edited since 1880 by Kögel, Baur, and Frommel. But with all the Christian depth and spirituality, freshness and warmth, which we meet with in the productions of these Christian poets, none of them

---

[1] Baur, "Religious Life in Germany" London, 1872, pp. 177-196.

has been able to rise to the noble simplicity, power, popular force, and fitting them for church use, objectivity which are present in the old evangelical church hymns. In this respect they all bear too conspicuously the signature of their age, with its subjective tone and the noise and turmoil of present conflicts. Of all modern poets, Rückert alone approaches in his advent hymn the measure and spirit of the old church song.—In the department of novels and romance there has been shown an almost invariable hostility toward Christianity, religion being either entirely avoided or held up to contempt by having as its representatives, simpletons, hypocrites, or knaves.

7. In France, Chateaubriand in his "*Genie du Christianisme*" pronounces an eloquent eulogy on the half-pagan Christianity of the Middle Ages. In another work he makes the representatives of heathenism in 'the age of Constantine act like Homeric heroes, and those of Christianity speak "like theologians of the age of Bossuet." Lamartine may be described as a Christian romancist. Victor Hugo, Balzac, George Sand, Sue, Dumas, etc., influenced by the Revolution, developed an antichristian tendency ; while naked naturalism, photographic realism in depicting the lowest side of Parisian life, especially adultery and prostitution, is represented by Flaubert, Daudet, De Goncourt, Zola, etc.—In Italy, the amiable Manzoni gave noble expression to Christian feeling in his "*Inni Sacri*," and in his masterly romance "*Promessi Sposi*"; and the famous poet Silvio Pellico, in his '*La mia Prigioni*," affords a noble example of the sustaining power of true religion during ten years' rigorous imprisonment in an Austrian dungeon. The most gifted of modern Italian poets, Giacomo Leopardi, sank into despairing pessimism, which expressed itself in the domain of religion in biting satire and savage irony. Among the poets of the present who, with glowing patriotism, not only yearned for the deliverance and unity of Italy, but also lived to see these accomplished, and have since given expression, though from different political and religious standpoints, to the desire for the reconciliation of the free united kingdom with the irreconcilable church, the most distinguished are Aleardi, Carducci, Imbriani, Guercini, Cavalotti.—In Spain, Caecilia Böhl von Faber, although the daughter of a German father, and educated in Germany, introduced, under the name Fernan Caballero, the modern romance in a thoroughly national Spanish style, and in a purely moral and catholic Christian spirit. In the Flemish Provinces, Hendrik Conscience, the able novelist, has described Flemish village life in a spirit fully in sympathy with Christianity.—England had in Lord Byron a poet of the first rank, who more than any other poet had experience in himself of the convulsions and contradictions of his age. In powerful and impressive tones he sets forth the unreconciled disharmonies of nature and of

human life. Incurable pain, despair, weariness of life, and hatred of mankind, without hope, yea without desire for reconciliation, enthusiastic admiration of the ancient world, passionate love of liberty and titanic pride in human might mingle with scenes of grumbling, misery, and profligacy. On the other hand, the rich and mostly solid English novel literature is prevailingly inspired by a Christian spirit.

8. Popular Education.—While the poetic national literature for the most part found entrance only among the cultured and adult circles, this age, almost as fond of writing as of reading, produced an enormous quantity of books for the people and for children. But only a few succeeded in catching the proper tone for the masses and the youth, and still fewer supplied their readers with what was genuinely pious. Pestalozzi's "*Lienhard und Gertrud,*" Hebel's "*Schatzkästlein,*" and Tschokke's "*Goldmacherdorf;*" respected at least the Christian feeling of the people, although they did not strengthen or foster it. But, on the other hand, in recent years a number of writers have appeared, thoroughly popular, and at the same time thoroughly Christian, who, as popular poets and novelists, have become apostles of Christian views, morals, and customs to the people. The most distinguished of these are Jeremiah Gotthelf (Albert Bitzius, died 1854), whose "Kate the Grandmother" was translated in the *Sunday Magazine* for 1865, Von Horn, Carl Stöber, Wildenhahn, Nathusius, Frommel, Weitbrecht, etc. In the Catholic church Albanus Stoltz, died 1883, developed a wonderful power of popular composition. which, however, he subsequently put at the service of a fanatical ultramontanism, and so sacrificed much of its nobility and worth. From the enormous mass of children's books only extremely few attain their aim. In the front rank stands the brilliant patriarch of Christian tale writing, Von Schubert, died 1860. After him are Barth, the author of "Poor Henry," Stober, and the Swiss Spyri, and the Catholic Christian Schmid, author of the "Easter Eggs."—The Public Schools, especially under Dinter (died 1831), member of the consistory and schoolboard of Königsberg, were for a long time nurseries of the tame, flat, and self-satisfied rationalism of the *ancien régime;* but since 1830, and more particularly in consequence of the violent agitations of the seminary director Diesterweg, who died in 1866, put to silence in 1847, but still for his work in connexion with education always highly respected, many of the teachers took a higher flight in the naturalistic-democratic direction. By word and pen Diesterweg carried on a propaganda in favour of a free and liberal education for the people. His disciples, wanting his earnest Christian spirit, carried out recklessly his radical tendencies, and now the Christian faith has no more persistent foes than the teachers of the public schools. In A.D. 1870, a Teachers' Association in Vienna gave a vote of 6,000 in

favour of radicalism. At a Hamburg meeting in A.D. 1872 of 5,100 teachers, progress was shown by individuals raising their voices in defence of Christianity, which, however, were generally drowned in shrieks and hisses. A Teachers' Evangelical Association held its ninth assembly at Hamburg in A.D. 1881 with 1,500 members. Christian opinions are now ably represented in schools, educational journals, and literature. A burning question at present is whether the national school should be preferred to the denominational school. Liberals in church and state say it should; conservatives say it should not; while both parties think their views supported by the experience of the past. The Prussian minister of education, Falk, A.D. 1872–1879, firmly insisted upon the development of the national system, but his successors Von Puttkamer and Von Gossler reverted to the denominational system. The German Evangelical School Congress of Hamburg in October, 1882, demanded that both elementary and secondary schools should have a confessional character.

9. Art.—The intellectual quickening called forth with the opening of the new century imparted new spirit and life to the cultivation of the arts. Winckelmann, died A.D. 1768, had opened the way to an understanding of pagan classical art, and romanticism awakened appreciation of and enthusiasm for mediæval Christian art. The greatest masters of Architecture were Schinckel, Klenze, and Heideloff. The foundation stone of the final part of the Cologne cathedral was laid by a Protestant king, Frederick William IV., in A.D. 1842, and the work was finished by a Protestant builder in A.D. 1880. Statuary had three great masters, who gave expression to profound Christian ideas in bronze and marble, the Italian Canova, the German Dannecker, and greatest of all, the Dane Thorwaldsen, whose Christ and the Apostles and other works form a main attraction to visitors in Copenhagen. Three younger German masters of the art, who have heired their fame, are Rauch, Rietschl, and Drake.—In Painting too a new era now began. A group of gay German artists in Rome, with Overbeck at their head, formed a Society in A.D. 1813, and mostly became perverts to Romanism. Peter Cornelius, the ablest of the school, himself born a Catholic, answered his friends' request to place Luther in a picture of the last judgment, in hell: "Yes, but with the Bible in his hands and the devils trembling before him"; and in a subsequent picture of the judgment, he gave the German reformer his place among the saints in heaven. His pupil, Julius Schnorr von Karolsfeld is well known by his "*Bibel in Bildern.*" Ludwig Richter, the Albert Dürer of the nineteenth century and creator of the modern woodcut, has filled German houses with his artistic and poetic creations, which breathe of God, nature, and the family fireside. The Frenchman, Gustave Doré of Strassburg, has also illustrated the

Bible in a manner worthy of ranking alongside of Schnorr, though a characteristically French striving for effect is everywhere discernible.—Painted Glass (§ 104, 14) for church windows had during the eighteenth century passed almost wholly out of use, but again in the nineteenth came into favour, and was made at Dresden, Nuremberg, and Munich. The most eminent artist in this department was Ainmiller of Munich, specimens of whose workmanship are to be seen in all parts of the world.

10. Music and the Drama.—In Vienna the three great masters of musical composition, Mozart, Haydn, and Beethoven, produced in the department of sacred music some of their noblest works. Mendelssohn, in his St. Paul and Elijah and in his Psalms, sought to reproduce the power and truth of the simple word of God. An early death prevented him giving expression to his ideal of Christ in music. The Hungarian virtuoso Liszt sacrifices sacred calmness and dignity to theatrical effect. His son-in-law, Richard Wagner, inspired by Schopenhauer's philosophy, a richly endowed poet and composer, proclaimed by his followers as the Messiah of the music of the future, going back to mediæval legend, has produced a *quasi*-Christian musical drama, in which the gospel of pessimism takes the place of the gospel of the grace of God.—Quite different is the Passion Play of the Bavarian village Oberammergau, which is a reproduction of the mediæval mysteries (§ 115, 12). It originated in a vow made in 1633 on the occasion of a plague which visited the place, and is repeated every ten years on the Sundays from the end of May to the middle of September. The history of the Saviour's passion is here represented with interludes from Messianic Old Testament passages explained by a chorus like that of the classical tragedy, with appropriate scenery, drapery, and musical accompaniment. In the presence of an immense concourse of strangers for whose accommodation a large amphitheatre had been built, almost all the villagers, men, women, and children, take part in the performance and show rare artistic power. The text of the drama for the most part agrees with the gospel narrative, only occasionally interspersed with legend, and quite free from ultramontane hagiology and mariolatry. The performance of A.D. 1850, and still more that of A.D. 1880, attracted crowds of pilgrims and tourists to the quiet and remote valley. An independent exhibition, falling little behind the original in the artistic character of its composition and production, was given, in 1883, on the Sundays of July and August in the Tyrolese village of Brixlegg, and was visited by similar crowds.

§ 175. Intercourse and Negotiations between the Churches.

Protestants could recognise, as Catholics could not, elements of truth and beauty in the creed of their opponents.
When a peaceful and conciliatory spirit was shown by
individual Catholic clergymen, it was the occasion of
suspicion and persecution on the part of the old Romish
party.   Schemes of union were entertained by the Old
Catholics (§ 190), and negotiations were entered on by the
Greek Orthodox church, on the one hand, and the Roman
Catholic and Anglican churches, on the other, but in both
cases without any practical result.   On the union negotiations between the different Protestant sects, see § 178; and
on the Prusso-Anglican bishopric of Jerusalem, see § 184, 8.
Of the numerous conversions from Protestantism to
Catholicism and from Catholicism to Protestantism, we can
here mention only such as have excited public interest in
some special way.

1. Romanizing Tendencies among Protestants.—Not only in England
where an important high-church party embraced a more than half-
Catholic Puseyism (§ 202, 2), but even in Protestant Germany a
Romanizing current set in on many sides. A taste for the romantic,
artistic, historical (§ 174, 5, 9, 4), as well as feudalist-aristocratic and
hyper-Lutheran ecclesiastical tendencies led the way in this direction
Many sought rest in the bosom of the church "where alone salvation is found," while others, too deeply rooted in evangelical truth,
bewailed the loss of "noble and venerable" institutions in the worship, life, and constitution of the church, but were unable to accept
the various unevangelical accretions which made void the doctrine of
justification by faith alone. This was the position of Löhe of Neuendettelsau, in point of doctrine a strict Lutheran, who published a
selection of Catholic legends as patterns of self-denial for his deaconesses, wished to restore anointing of the sick, etc. Some Protestant
pastors expressed warm sympathy with the pope during his mis-
fortunes in A.D. 1860, and approved of the continuance of the papacy
and the pope's temporal dominion. A conference of Catholics (Count
Stolberg, Dr. Michelis, etc.) and Protestants (Leo, Bindewald, etc.) at
Erfurt in A.D. 1860, on the basis of a common recognition of the moral

advantages of the papacy, sought to bring about a union of the churches. Still more remarkable is the story told by the Old Catholic professor Friedrich. Just before the opening of the Vatican Council, certain evangelical pastors of Saxony wrote letters to Bishop Martin of Paderborn, which Friedrich himself read, urging that at the council permission should be given to priests to marry and to give the cup in the communion to the laity, and promising that in that case they themselves and many like-minded pastors would join the Romish church. That the letters were written and received is unquestionable; but it is doubtful whether folly and imbecility or a wish to hoax and mystify, directed the pen. The writer or writers, as the examination before the consistory of the locality proved, are not to be sought among the pastors whose names are appended. How far the Protestant ultra-conservative reactionary party goes with the ultramontanes and how far it would aid the overthrow and undermining of the Protestant state and evangelical church, is shown by the conduct of the Privy Councillor and Chief Justice Ludwig von Gerlach (§ 176, 1), who, in 1872, in the Prussian House of Representatives, took his place among the ultramontane party of the centre, hostile to the empire and friendly to the Poles, and in his pamphlet " *Kaiser und Papst* " of 1872 described the new German empire as an incarnate antichrist. Also the Lutheran Guelphs of Hanover are zealous supporters of all the demands of the centre in the Prussian parliament and in the German Reichstag.

2. **The Attitude of Catholicism toward Protestantism.**—Every Catholic bishop has still on assuming office to take the oath, *Hæreticos pro posse persequar.* The Jesuits, restored in A.D. 1814, soon pervaded every section with their intolerant spirit. The huge lie that Protestantism is in matters of State as well as of church essentially revolutionary, while Catholicism is the bulwark of the State against revolution and democracy, was affirmed with such audacity that even Protestant statesmen believed it. The Roman Jesuit Perrone (§ 191, 9) taught the Catholic youth in a controversial Italian catechism that " they should feel a creeping horror come over them at the mere mention of the word Protestantism, more even than when a murderous attack was made upon them, for Protestantism and its defenders are in the religious and moral world just the same as the plague and plague-stricken are in the physical world, and in all lands Protestants are the scum of all that is vile and immoral," etc. In a pastoral of A.D. 1855, Von Ketteler, Bishop of Mainz, compared the Germans, who by the Reformation rent the unity of the church, to the Jews who crucified the Messiah. Romish prelates have vied with one another in their abuse of Protestants and Protestantism. In A.D. 1881, Leo XIII. speaking of the spread of Russian nihilism, charged Protestant

missionaries with spreading the dominion of the prince of darkness.
Prof. Hohoff of Paderborn, in his " Hist. Studies on Protestantism and
Socialism," Paderb., 1881, reiterated the accusation : " Yes, it is so,
Protestantism has begotten atheism, materialism, scepticism, nihilism.
The Reformation was the murderer of all science, the greatest foe
of culture and learning, and the falsifier of all history. . .
Melanchthon's *Loci* may be styled the most unscientific production in
the domain of dogmatics. . . . Yes, the Reformation has proved
a prime source of superstition, a step backward in the history of
civilization. . . . The Catholic church has been the champion of
conscience, reason, and freedom. . . . No one is thoroughly capable
of judging historical facts without prejudice as the believing Catholic
Christian."—But while the vast majority of Catholic writers thus abuse
Protestantism, others like Seltmann of Eberswald seek to win over
to the ranks of the Romish church those who can be befooled by fair
speeches. The " Protestant" correspondents in Seltmann's periodical
write under the cloak of anonymity.—In Spain the Reformation was
long attributed to the Augustinians, who were jealous of the Dominicans
as the only dispensers of indulgences, and to Luther's desire to marry ;
but the poet Nuñez de Arca in his " *Vision de Fray Martin*," attributed
it to the corruption of the church and papacy of its time, and regarded
with sympathy the spiritual struggles of the reformer. Though as
a good Catholic he concludes his poem with the ban of the church
against Luther, he yet describes him as a just and well-deserving
man.

3. **Romish Controversy.**—In the beginning of A.D. 1872 the Waldensian Professor Sciarelli published as a challenge the thesis that
the Apostle Peter never set foot in Rome, and Pius IX. with childlike
simplicity gave his consent to a public disputation, which came off at
Rome on 9th and 10th February. Three Protestant champions, with
Sciarelli at their head, were confronted by three Catholics, headed by
Fabiani, before 125 auditors admitted by ticket. Both sides claimed
the victory ; but the shorthand reports were more widely read through
Italy than could be agreeable to the papal court.

4. **Roman Catholic Union Schemes.**—While American Protestant
missionaries strove zealously for the conversion of the schismatical
Eastern Churches, Rome with equal diligence but little success
endeavoured to win over these and the orthodox Greeks to her own
communion. There was great joy over the conversion of the Bulgarians
to Romanism in A.D. 1860. Taking advantage of a national movement for the restoration of a patriarchate independent of Constantinople (§ 207, 3), some French Jesuits succeeded in persuading a small
number of malcontents to agree to a union with Rome. In 1861 the
pope consecrated an old Bulgarian priest, Jos. Sokolski, archbishop

of the united Bulgarian church. Very soon, however, he and almost all his followers returned to their allegiance to the Greek Orthodox church. Leo XIII. in his *encyclical* of A.D. 1880, by giving conspicuous honour to Cyril and Methodius, and uttering kind sentiments about the Christian church in the East, and conferring high rank on dignitaries of the Eastern church, seeks to smooth the way for a union of the two great churches.

5. Greek Orthodox Union Schemes.—In A.D. 1867 the Archbishop of Canterbury addressed a letter to the Patriarch of Constantinople and the whole Eastern church, to open the way to a common understanding and union of the churches, sending a modern Greek translation of the Book of Common Prayer, and asking their assistance at the consecration of an Anglican church at Constantinople. The patriarch Gregorius granted this request, and answered the letter in a friendly manner, passing over the Anglican's warnings against superstitious additions to the doctrine, *e.g.* mariolatry, but characterizing all the contrary doctrines of the Thirty-nine Articles as " very modern." At the same time vigorous measures were being taken with a similar object by members of the Russian and of the Anglican churches. In 1870 Professor Overbeck of Halle undertook to act as intermediary in these negotiations. He had in 1865 published, in answer to the papal encyclical with syllabus of December 8th, 1864 (§ 185, 2), a tract with the motto *Ex oriente lux*, in which he placed the claims of the Orthodox eastern church before the Roman Catholic as well as Protestant. On the opening of the Vatican Council in 1869 he advocated in a pamphlet the breaking up of the papal church and the formation of Catholic national churches. In North America Professor Bjerring, of the Catholic seminary for priests at Baltimore, took the same position. In March, 1871, he went to St. Petersburg, was there ordained as an Orthodox priest, and on his return to New York instituted a Sunday service in the English language according to the Greek rite. Of any further advance in this direction of union nothing is known.

6. Old Catholic Union Schemes.—Döllinger (§ 191, 5) in A.D. 1871 was hopeful of a union not only with the Greek, but also with the Anglican church, and similar hopes were entertained in England and Russia, and distinguished representatives of both communions took part in the Old Catholic congresses (§ 190, 1). On the invitation of Döllinger, as president of the committee commissioned by the Freiburg Congress of A.D. 1874 to treat about union with the Anglican church, forty friends of union from Germany, England, Denmark, France, Russia, Greece, and America met in conference at Bonn. After a lively debate the cleft between East and West was bridged over by a compromise treating the *filioque* as an unnecessary addition to the Nicene symbol, and asserting that, however desirable a mutual under-

standing on doctrinal questions might be, existing differences in constitution, discipline, and worship presented no bar to union. The Catholics presented the Anglicans with fourteen theses essential to union, in which the anti-Protestant doctrines were for the most part toned down, but transubstantiation distinctly asserted. Subsequent conferences never got beyond these preliminaries. It was, however, agreed that, in case of necessity, Anglicans and Old Catholics might dispense the supper to one another.

7. Conversions—The most famous converts of the century were Hurter, the biographer of Innocent III., the Countess Ida von Hahn-Hahn, writer of religious romances, Gfroerer, the church historian, the radical Hegelian Daumer, the historian of ante-tridentine theology Hugo Lämmer, and Dr. Ed. Preuss, who had written against the immaculate conception and for criminal conduct had to flee the country. In A.D. 1844 Carl Haas, a Protestant pastor, went over to the Romish church, but the two new dogmas of Pius IX. led him to study the works of Luther. He now returned to the Lutheran church, vindicating his procedure in a treatise entitled, "To Rome, and from Rome back again to Wittenberg, 1881." Also the Mecklenburg Lutheran pastor, Dr. A. Hager, who, after his conversion, had undertaken the editorship of an ultramontane newspaper in Breslau in 1873, was obliged in a few years to resign the appointment. His return to the evangelical church was being talked about, when he suddenly died in 1883, after having received the last sacrament in the Catholic church. The climax of abuse of Luther and the Lutheran church was reached by the Hanoverian Evers, who had gone over in 1880; in all his scandalous and vituperative writings he describes himself on the title page as "formerly Lutheran pastor." His mud-throwing, however, was carried so far, that even the ultramontane *Köln Volkszeitung* was constrained to advise him to write more decently.

8. The Mortara affair of A.D. 1858 attracted special attention. The eight-year old son of the Jew Mortara of Bologna was violently taken from his parents to Rome because his Christian nurse said that two years before, during a dangerous illness, she had baptized him. The church answered the entreaties of the parents and the universal outcry by saying that the sacrament had an indelible character, and that the pope could not change the law. Again in A.D. 1864, the ten-year old Jewish boy, Joseph Coën, apprentice weaver in Rome, was decoyed by a priest to his cloister and there persuaded to receive baptism. In vain his mother, the Jewish community, and even the French ambassador, urged his restoration; and when, in A.D. 1870, the temporal power of the pope was overthrown, the lad, now sixteen years old, had himself become such a fanatical Catholic that he refused to have anything to do with his mother as an unbeliever.

9. In the Tyrol in A.D. 1830 there were numerous conversions from Catholicism to Protestantism (§ 198, 1). A Catholic priest in Baden, Henhöfer of Mühlhausen, influenced by the writings of Sailer and Boos, went over to the Lutheran church in A.D. 1823, and continued down to his death in A.D. 1862 a vigorous opponent of the prevailing rationalism. Count Leopold von Seldnitzsky, formerly Prince-Bishop of Breslau, felt obliged in 1840, in consequence of the conscientious objections he had to perform his official duties toward church and state during the ecclesiastico-political controversies of 1830 (§ 193, 1), to resign his appointments. He was subsequently led in A.D. 1863, through reading the Scriptures and Luther's works, after a sore struggle, to join the evangelical Church. He devoted all his means to the founding of Protestant educational institutions at Berlin and Breslau. He died in A.D. 1871, in his eighty-fourth year. The proclamation by the Vatican of the dogma of infallibility drove many pious and earnest Catholics out of the Romish communion. Of these Carl von Richthofen, Canon of Breslau, engages our special interest. Son of a pious Lutheran mother, and trained up under Gossner's mild spiritual direction (§ 187, 2), his gentle and deeply religious nature had attached itself to the Roman Catholic church of his father only under the illusion that the Romish doctrine of justification was not wholly irreconcilable with the evangelical doctrine. He at first submitted to but soon renounced the Vatican decree; was excommunicated by Archbishop Förster, voluntarily resigned his emoluments; joined the Old Catholics in A.D. 1873, and the separated Old Lutherans in A.D. 1875. In the following year he died a painful death from the explosion of a petroleum lamp.—Upon the whole Rome has made most converts in America and England; and she has suffered losses more or less severe in France, Belgium, Ireland, Italy, Spain, and Bohemia.

10. The Luther Centenary, A.D. 1883.—The celebration of Luther's birth was carried out with great enthusiasm throughout all Germany, more than a thousand tracts on Luther and the Reformation were published, statues were erected, special services were held in all Lutheran churches, high schools, and universities, and brilliant demonstrations were made at Jena, Worms, Wittenberg, and Eisleben. There were founded at Kiel a Luther-house, at Worms and at the Wartburg Luther libraries, in Leipzig and Berlin Luther churches. At Eisleben a bronze statue of the reformer was solemnly unveiled representing his tearing the papal bull with his right hand and pressing the Bible to his heart with his left. Another noble monument was raised by the munificence of the emperor by the issuing during this year of the first volume of pastor Knaake's critical edition of Luther's works. A "German Luther Institute" aims at assisting children of the poorer clergy and teachers, and a "Reforma-

tion History Society" has undertaken the task of issuing populai tracts on the persons, events and principles of that and the succeeding period based upon original documents. Protestants of all lands, with the exception of the English high-church party, contributed liberally ; the Americans had a copy of the great Luther statue of the Worms monument (§ 178, 1) made and erected in Washington. Even in Italy the liberal press eulogised Luther, while the ultramontanes loaded his memory with unmeasured calumny and reproach. The threatened counter-demonstrations of German ultramontanes fell quite flat and harmless. The Zwingli Centenary of January 1st, A.D. 1884, was celebrated with enthusiasm throughout the Reformed church, especially in Switzerland. On the other hand, the celebration of the five-hundredth anniversary of Wiclif's death on December 31st, 1884, created comparatively little interest.

II.—Protestantism in General.[1]

§ 176. RATIONALISM AND PIETISM.

At the beginning of the century rationalism was generally prevalent, but philosophy and literature soon weakened its foundations, and the war of independence moved the hearts of the people toward the faith of their fathers. Pietism entered the lists against rationalism, and the Halle controversy of A.D. 1830 marked the crisis of the struggle. The rationalists were compelled to make appeal to the people by popular agitators. During A.D. 1840 they managed to found several " free churches," which, however, had for the most part but a short and unprosperous existence. They were more successful in A.D. 1860 with the *Protestantenverein* as the instrument of their propaganda (§ 180).

1. The old Rationalism was attacked by the disciples of Hegel and Schelling, and in A.D. 1834 Röhr of Weimar found Hase of Jena as keen an opponent as any pietist or orthodox controversialist. That recognised leader of the old rationalists had coolly attempted to substitute a new and rational form of doctrine, worship, and constitution for the antiquated formularies of the Reformation, and drew down

---

[1] Kahnis, "Internal History of German Protestantism since the Middle of Last Century." Edin., 1856.

upon himself the rebuke even of those who sympathized with him in his doctrinal views.—In A.D. 1817 Claus Harms of Kiel, on the occasion of the Reformation centenary, opened an attack upon those who had fallen away from the faith of their fathers, by the publication of ninety-five new theses, recalling attention to Luther's almost forgotten doctrines. In A.D. 1827 Aug. Hahn in an academical discussion at Leipzig maintained that the rationalists should be expelled from the church, and Hengstenberg started his *Evangelische Kirchenzeitung*. The jurist Von Gerlach in A.D. 1830 charged Gesenius and Wegscheider of Halle with open contempt of Christian truth, and called for State interference. In all parts of Germany, amid the opposition of scientific theologians and the scorn of philosophers, pietism made way against rationalism, so that even men of culture regarded it as a reproach to be reckoned among the rationalists. Unbelief, however, was widespread among the masses. When Sintenis, preacher in Magdeburg in A.D. 1840, declared the worship of Christ superstitious, and was reprimanded by the consistory, his neighbours, the pastors Uhlich and König, founded the society of the "Friends of Light," whose assembly at Köthen was attended by thousands of clergymen and laymen. In one of these assemblies in A.D. 1844, Wislicenus of Halle, by starting the question, Whether the Scriptures or the reason is to be regarded as the standard of faith? shattered the illusion that rationalism still occupied the platform of the church and Scripture. The left wing of the school of Schleiermacher took offence at the severe measures demanded by Hengstenberg and his party, and in 1846 issued in Berlin a manifesto with eighty-eight signatures against the paper pope of antiquated Reformation confessions and the inquisitorial proceedings of the *Kirchenzeitung* party, as inimical to all liberty of faith and conscience, wishing only to maintain firm hold of the truth that Jesus Christ is yesterday, to-day, and for ever the one and only ground of salvation. The Friends of Light, combining with the German Catholics and the Young Hegelians, founded Free churches at Halle, Königsberg, and many other places. Their services and sermons void of religion, in which the Bible, the living Christ, and latterly even the personal God, had no place, but only the naked worship of humanity, had temporary vitality imparted them by the revolutionary movements of A.D. 1848. This gave the State an excuse, long wished for, to interfere, and soon scarcely a trace of their churches was to be found.

2. Pietism had not been wholly driven out of the evangelical church during the period of ecclesiastical impoverishment, but, purified from many eccentric excesses, and seeking refuge and support for the most part by attaching itself to the community of the Moravian Brethren, it had, even in Württemberg, established itself independently and in

an essentially theosophical-chiliastic spirit. There too a kind of
spiritualism was introduced by the physician and poet Justin Kerner
of Weinsberg, and the philosopher Eschenmayer of Tübingen, with
spirit revelations from above and below. Amid the religious movements of the beginning of the century Pietism gained a decided
advantage. It took the form of a protest against the rationalism
prevailing among the clergy. The earnest and devout sought spiritual
nourishment at conventicles and so-called *Stunden* addressed by
laymen, mostly of the working class, well acquainted with Scripture
and works in practical divinity. Persecuted by the irreligious mob,
the rationalist clergy, and sometimes by the authorities, they by-
and-by secured representatives among the younger clergy and in
the university chairs, and carried on vigorous missions at home
and abroad. This pietism was distinctly evangelical and Protestant.
It did not oppose but endeavoured simply to restore the orthodoxy
of the church confession. Yet it had many of the characteristics
of the earlier pietism: over-estimation of the invisible to the dis-
paragement of the visible church, of sanctification over justification,
a tendency to chiliasm, etc.—Of no less importance in awakening the
religious life throughout Germany, and especially in Switzerland, was
the missionary activity of Madame de Krüdener of Riga. This lady,
after many years of a gay life, forsook the world, and began in A.D.
1814 her travels through Europe, preaching repentance, proclaiming
the gospel message in the prisons, the foolishness of the cross to the
wise of this world, and to kings and princes the majesty of Christ as
King of kings. Wherever she went she made careless sinners tremble,
and drew around her crowds of the anxious and spiritually burdened
of every sort and station. Honoured by some as a saint, prophetess,
and wonder-worker, ridiculed by others as a fool, persecuted as a
dangerous fanatic or deceiver, driven from one country to another, she
died in the Crimea in A.D. 1824.[1]

8. The Königsberg Religious Movement, A.D. 1835-1842.—The pious
theosophist, J. H. Schönherr of Königsberg, starting from the two
primitive substances, fire and water, developed a system of theosophy
in which he solved the riddles of the theogony and cosmogony, of sin
and redemption, and harmonized revelation with the results of natural
science. At first influenced by these views, but from A.D. 1819 expressly dissenting from them, J. W. Ebel, pastor in the same city,
gathered round him a group of earnest Christian men and women,
Counts Kanitz and Finkenstein and their wives, Von Tippelskirch,
afterwards preacher to the embassy at Rome, the theological professor

---

[1] Hagenbach, "History of Church in Eighteenth and Nineteenth
Centuries," vol. ii., pp. 413-416.

H. Olshausen, the pastor Dr. Diestel, and the medical doctor Sachs After some years Olshausen and Tippelskirch withdrew, and dissensions arose which gave opportunity to the ecclesiastical authorities to order an investigation. Ebel was charged with founding a sect in which impure practices were encouraged. He was suspended in A.D. 1835, and at the instigation of the consistory a criminal process was entered upon against him. Dr. Sachs, who had been expelled from the society, was the chief and almost only witness, but vague rumours were rife about mystic rites and midnight orgies. Ebel and Diestel were deposed in A.D. 1839, and pronounced incapable of holding any public office; and as a sect founder Ebel was sentenced to imprisonment in the common jail. On appeal to the court of Berlin, the deposition was confirmed, but all the rest of the sentence was quashed, and the parties were pronounced capable of holding any public offices except those of a spiritual kind. Two reasons were alleged for deposition: (1) That Ebel, though not from the pulpit or in the public instruction of the young, yet in private religious teaching, had inculcated his theosophical views. (2) That both of them as married men had given expression to opinions injurious to the purity of married life. In general they were charged with spreading a doctrine which was in conflict with the principles of Christianity, and making such use of sexual relations as was fitted to awaken evil thoughts in the minds of hearers. Ebel was pronounced guiltless of sectarianism.—Kanitz wrote a book in defence, which represents Ebel and Diestel as martyrs to their pure Christian piety in an age hostile to every pietistic movement; whereas Von Wegnern, followed by Hepworth Dixon, in a romancing and frivolous style, lightly give currency to evil surmisings without offering any solid basis of proof. The whole affair still waits for a patient and unprejudiced investigation.[1]

4. The Bender Controversy.—At the Luther centenary festival of A.D. 1883, Prof. Bender of Bonn declared that in the confessional writings of the Reformation evangelical truth had been obscured by Romish scholasticism, introduced by subtle jurists and sophistical theologians. This called forth vigorous opposition, in which two of his colleagues, 88 theological students, 59 members of the Rhenish synod, took part. General-Superintendent Baur, also, in a new year's address, inveighed against Bender's statements. On the other hand, 170 students of Bonn, 82 of these theological students, gave a grand ovation to the "brave vindicator of academic freedom." The Rhenish and Westphalian synods bewailed the offence given by Bender's address, and protested

[1] Mombert, "Faith Victorious, being an Account of the Life, Labour, and Times of Dr. J. W. Ebel, 1714–1861, compiled from authentic sources." London, 1882. Dixon, "Spiritual Wives." London, 1868.

against its hard and unfounded attacks upon the confessional writings. At the Westphalian synod, Prof. Mangold said that the faculty was as much offended at the address as the church had been, but that its author, when he found how his words had created such feeling, sought in every way to repress the agitation, and had intended only to pass a scientific judgment on ecclesiastical and theological developments.

§ 177. EVANGELICAL UNION AND LUTHERAN SEPARATION.

From A.D. 1817 Prussia favoured and furthered the scheme for union between the two evangelical churches, and over this question a split arose in the camp of pietism. On the one hand were the confessionalists, determined to maintain what was distinctive in their symbols, and on the other, those who would sacrifice almost anything for union. For the most part both churches cordially seconded the efforts of the royal head of the church; only in Silesia did a Lutheran minority refuse to give way, which still maintains a separate existence.

1. The Evangelical Union.—Circumstances favoured this movement. Both in the Lutheran and in the Reformed church comparatively little stress was laid upon distinctive confessional doctrines, and pietism and rationalism, for different reasons, had taught the relative unimportance of dogma. And so a general accord was given to the king's proposal, at the Reformation centenary of A.D. 1817, to fortify the Protestant church by means of a Union of Lutherans and Calvinists. The new Book of Common Order of A.D. 1822, in the preparation of which the pious king, Frederick William III., had himself taken part, was indeed condemned by many as too high-church, even Catholicizing in its tendency. A revised edition in A.D. 1829, giving a wider choice of formularies, was legally authorized, and the union became an accomplished fact. There now existed in Prussia an evangelical national church with a common government and liturgy, embracing within it three different sections: a Lutheran, and a Reformed, which held to their distinctive doctrines, though not regarding these as a cause of separation, and a real union party, which completely abandoned the points of difference. But more and more the union became identified with doctrinal indifferentism and slighting of all church symbols, and those in whom the church feeling still prevailed were driven into opposition to the union (§ 193). The example of Prussia in seeking the union of the two churches was

followed by Nassau, Baden, Rhenish Bavaria, Anhalt, and to some extent in Hesse (§§ 194, 196).

2. The Lutheran Separation.—Though the union denied that there was any passing over from one church to another, it practically declared the distinctive doctrines to be unessential, and so assumed the standpoint of the Reformed church. Steffens (§ 174, 3), the friend of Scheibel of Breslau, who had been deprived of his professorship in A.D. 1832 for his determined opposition to the union, and died in exile in 1843 (§ 195, 2), headed a reaction in favour of old Lutheranism. Several suspended clergymen in Silesia held a synod at Breslau in A.D. 1835, to organize a Lutheran party, but the civil authorities bore so heavily upon them that most of them emigrated to America and Australia. Guericke of Halle, secretly ordained pastor, ministered in his own house to a small company of Lutheran separatists, was deprived of his professorship in A.D. 1835, and only restored in A.D. 1840, after he had apologised for his conduct. From A.D. 1838, the laws were modified by Frederick William IV., imprisoned clergymen were liberated in A.D. 1840, and a Lutheran church of Prussia independent of the national church was constituted by a general synod at Breslau in A.D. 1841, which received recognition by royal favour in A.D. 1845. The affairs are administered by a supreme council resident in Breslau, presided over by the distinguished jurist Huschke. Other separations were prevented by timely concessions on the part of the national church. The separatists claim 50,000 members, with fifty pastors and seven superintendents.

3. The Separation within the Separation.—Differences arose among the separate Lutherans, especially over the question of the visible church. The majority, headed by Huschke, defined the visible church as an organism of various offices and orders embracing even unbelievers, which is to be sifted by the divine judgment. To it belongs the office of church government, which is a *jus divinum*, and only in respect of outward form a *jus humanum*. The opposition understood visibility of the preaching of the word and dispensation of sacraments, and held that unbelievers belonged as little to the visible as to the invisible church. The distribution of orders and offices is a merely human arrangement without divine appointment, individual members are quite independent of one another, the church recognises no other government than that of the unfettered preaching of the word, and each pastor rules in his own congregation. Diedrich of Jabel and seven other pastors complained of the papistical assumptions of the supreme council, and at a general synod in A.D. 1860 refused to recognise the authority of that council, or of a majority of synods, and in A.D. 1861, along with their congregations, they formally seceded and constituted the so called Immanuel Synod.

§ 178.   EVANGELICAL CONFEDERATION.

The union had only added a third denomination to the two previously existing, and was the means of even further dissension and separation.   Thus the interests of Protestantism were endangered in presence of the unbelief within her own borders and the machinations of the ultramontane Catholics without.   An attempt was therefore made in A.D. 1840 to combine the scattered Protestant forces, by means of confederation, for common work and conflict with common foes.

1. **The Gustavus Adolphus Society.**—In A.D. 1832, on the two hundredth anniversary of the birth of the saviour of German Protestantism, on the motion of Superintendent Grossman of Leipzig, a society was formed for the help of needy Protestant churches, especially in Catholic districts.   At first almost confined to Saxony, it soon spread over Germany, till only Bavaria down to A.D. 1849, and Austria down to A.D. 1860, were excluded by civil enactment from its operations.   The masses were attracted by the simplicity of its basis, which was simply opposition to Catholicism, and the demagogical Friends of Light soon found supremacy in its councils.   Because of opposition to the expulsion of Rupp, in A.D. 1846, as an apostate from the principle of protestantism, great numbers with church leanings seceded, and attempted to form a rival union in A.D. 1847.   After recovering from the convulsions of A.D. 1848, under the wise guidance of Zimmermann of Darmstadt, the society regained a solid position.   In A.D. 1883 it had 1,779 branches besides 392 women's and 11 students' unions, and a revenue for the year of about £43,000.—The same feeling led to the erection of the Luther Monument at Worms.   This work of genius, designed by Rietschel, and completed after his death in A.D. 1857 by his pupils, and inaugurated on 25th June, A.D. 1868, represents all the chief episodes in the Reformation history.   It was erected at a cost of more than £20,000, raised by voluntary contributions, and the scheme proved so popular that there was a surplus of £2,000, which was devoted to the founding of bursaries for theological students.

2. **The Eisenach Conference.**—The other German states borrowed the idea of confederation from Prussia and Württemberg.   It took practical shape in the meetings of deputies at Eisenach, begun in A.D. 1852, and held for a time yearly, and afterwards every second year to consult together on matters of worship, discipline and constitution.   Beyond ventilating such questions the conference yielded no result.

8. The Evangelical Alliance.—An attempt was made in England, on the motion of Dr. Chalmers (§ 202, 7), at a yet more comprehensive confederation of all Protestant churches of all lands against the encroachments of popery and puseyism (§ 202, 2). After several preliminary meetings the first session of the Evangelical Alliance was held in London in August, A.D. 1846. Its object was the fraternizing of all evangelical Christians on the basis of agreement upon the fundamental truths of salvation, the vindication and spread of this common faith, and contention for liberty of conscience and religious toleration. Nine articles were laid down as terms of membership: Belief in the inspiration of Scripture, in the Trinity, in the divinity of Christ, in original sin, in justification by faith alone, in the obligatoriness of the two sacraments, in the resurrection of the body, in the last judgment, and in the eternal blessedness of the righteous and the eternal condemnation of the ungodly. It could thus include Baptists, but not Quakers. In A.D. 1855 it held its ninth meeting at the great Paris Industrial Exhibition as a sort of church exhibition, the representatives of different churches reporting on the condition of their several denominations. The tenth meeting, of A.D. 1857, was held in Berlin. The council of the Alliance, presided over by Sir Culling Eardley, presented an address to King Frederick William IV., in which it was said that they aimed a blow not only against the sadduceanism, but also against the pharisaism of the German evangelical church. The confessional Lutherans, who had opposed the Alliance, regarded this latter reference as directed against them. The king, however, received the deputation most graciously, while declaring that he entertained the brightest hopes for the future of the church, and urged cordial brotherly love among Christians. Though many distinguished confessionalists were members of the Alliance none of them put in an appearance. The members of the "Protestantenverein" (§ 180) would not take part because the articles were too orthodox. On the other hand, numerous representatives of pietism, unionism, Melanchthonianism, as well as Baptists, Methodists, and Moravians, crowded in from all parts, and were supported by the leading liberals in church and state. While there was endless talk about the oneness and differences of the children of God, about the universal priesthood, about the superiority of the present meeting over the œcumenical councils of the ancient church, about the want of spiritual life in the churches, even where the theology of the confessions was professed, etc., with denunciations of half-Catholic Lutheranism and its sacramentarianism and officialism, and many a true and admirable statement of what the church's needs are, Merle d'Aubigné introduced discord by the hearty welcome which he accorded his friend Bunsen, which was intensified by the passionate manner in

which Krummacher reported upon it. The gracious royal reception of the members of the Alliance, at which Krummacher gave expression to his excited feelings in the words, "Your Majesty, we would all fall not at your feet, but on your neck!" was described by his brother, Dr. F. W. Krummacher, as a sensible prelude to the solemn scenes of the last judgment. Sir Culling Eardley declared, "There is no more the North Sea." Lord Shaftesbury said in London that with the Berlin Assembly a new era had begun in the world's history; and others who had returned from it extolled it as a second Pentecost.

4. The Evangelical Church Alliance.—After the revolution of A.D. 1848, the most distinguished theologians, clergymen and laymen well-affected toward the church, sought to bring about a confederation of the Lutheran, Reformed, United, and Moravian churches. When they held their second assembly at Wittenberg, A.D. 1849, many of the strict Lutherans had already withdrawn, especially those of Silesia. The Lutheran congress, held shortly before at Leipzig under the presidency of Harless, had pronounced the confederation unsatisfactory. The political reaction in favour of the church had also taken away the occasion for such a confederation. Yet the yearly deliberations of this council on matters of practical church life did good service. An attempt made at the Berlin meeting of A.D. 1853 to have the *Augustana* adopted as the church confession awakened keen opposition. At the Stuttgart meeting of A.D. 1857 there were violent debates on foreign missions and evangelical Catholicity between the representatives of confessional Lutheranism who had hitherto maintained connection with the confederation and the unionist majority. The Lutherans now withdrew. The attempt made at the Berlin October assembly of A.D. 1871, amid the excitement produced by the glorious issue of the Franco-Prussian War and the founding of the new German empire with a Protestant prince, to draw into the confederation confessional Lutherans and adherents of the "Protestantenverein," in order to form a grand German Protestant national church, miscarried, and a meeting of the confederation in the old style met again at Halle in the following year. But it was now found that its day was past.

5. The Evangelical League.—At a meeting of the Prussian evangelical middle party in autumn, 1886, certain members, "constrained by grief at the surrender of arms by the Prussian government in the *Kulturkampf*," gathered together for private conference, and resolved in defence of the threatened interests of the evangelical church to found an "Evangelical League" out of the various theological and ecclesiastical parties. Prominent party leaders on both sides being admitted, a number of moderate representatives of all schools were invited to a consultative gathering at Erfurt. On January 15th, 1887, a call to join the membership of the league was issued. It was

signed by distinguished men of the middle party, such as Beyschlag,
Riehm of Halle, etc., moderate representatives of confessionalism and
the positive union, such as Kawerau of Kiel, Fricke of Leipzig, Witte,
Warneck, etc., and liberal theologians like Lipsius and Nippold o
Jena, etc.; and it soon received the addition of about 250 names. It
recognised Jesus Christ, as the only begotten Son of God, as the only
means of salvation, and professed the fundamental doctrines of the
Reformation. It represented the task of the League as twofold : on
the one hand the defending at all points the interests of the evangelical
church against the advancing pretensions of Rome, and, on the other
hand, the strengthening of the communal consciousness of the Christian evangelical church against the cramping influence of party, as
well as in opposition to indifferentism and materialism. For the
accomplishment of this task the league organized itself under the control of a central board with subordinate branches over all Germany,
each having a committee for representing its interests in the press, and
with annual general assemblies of all the members for common consultation and promulgating of decrees.

§ 179. LUTHERANISM, MELANCHTHONIANISM, AND CALVINISM.

Widespread as the favourable reception of the Prussian
union had been, there were still a number of Lutheran states
in which the Reformed church had scarcely any adherents,
e.g. Bavaria, Saxony, Hanover, Mecklenburg, and Schleswig-
Holstein ; and the same might be said of the Baltic Provinces and of the three Scandinavian kingdoms. Also in
Austria, France, and Russia the two denominations kept
apart ; and in Poland, the union of A.D. 1828 was dissolved
in A.D. 1849 (§ 206, 3). The Lutheran confessional reaction
in Prussia afforded stimulus to those who had thus stood
apart. In all lands, amid the conflict with rationalism, the
confessional spirit both of Lutheran and Reformed became
more and more pronounced.

1. Lutheranism within the Union.—After the Prussian State church
had been undermined by the revolution of A.D. 1848, an unsuccessful
attempt was made to have a pure Lutheran confessional church set
up in its place At the October assembly in Berlin, in A.D. 1871, an

ineffectual effort was made by the United Lutherans to co-operate with those who were unionists on principle. During the agitation caused by the May Laws (§ 197, 5) and the Sydow proceedings (§ 180, 4), the first general evangelical Lutheran conference was held in August, A.D. 1873, in Berlin. It assumed a moderate conciliatory tone toward the union, pronounced the efforts of the " Protestantenverein " (§ 180) an apostasy from the fundamental doctrines of the gospel, bewailed the issuing of the May Laws, protested against their principles, but acknowledged the duty of obedience, and concluded an address to the emperor with a petition on behalf of a democratic church constitution and civil marriage.—The literary organs of the United Lutherans are the " *Evang. Kirchenzeitung*," edited by Hengstenberg, and now by Zöckler, and the " *Allgem. konserv. Monatsschrift für die christl. Deutschl.*," by Von Nathusius.

2. **Lutheranism outside of the Union.**—A general Lutheran conference was held under the presidency of Harless, in July, A.D. 1868, at which the sentiments of Kliefoth, denouncing a union under a common church government without agreement about doctrine and sacraments, met with almost universal acceptance. At the Leipzig gathering of A.D. 1870, Luthardt urged the duty of firmly maintaining doctrinal unity in the Lutheran church. The assembly of the following year agreed to recognise the emperor as head of the church only in so far as he did not interfere with the dispensation of word and sacrament, admitted the legality of a merely civil marriage but maintained that despisers of the ecclesiastical ordinance should be subjected to discipline, that communion fellowship is to be allowed neither to Reformed nor unionists if fixed residents, but to unionists faithful to the confession if temporary residents, even without expressly joining their party; and also with reference to the October assembly of the previous year the union of the two Protestant churches of Germany under a mixed system of church government was condemned. The third general conference of Nüremburg, in A.D. 1879, dealt with the questions: Whether the church should be under State control or free? Whether the schools should be denominational or not? and in both cases decided in favour of the latter alternative.—Its literary organ is Luthardt's " *Allg. Luth. Kirchenzeitung.*"

3. **Melancthonianism and Calvinism.**—The Reformed church of Germany has maintained a position midway between Lutheranism and Calvinism very similar to the later Melanchthonianism. Ebrard indeed sought to prove that strict predestinarianism was only an excrescence of the Reformed system, whereas Schweitzer, purely in the interests of science (§ 182, 9, 16), has shown that it is its all-conditioning nerve and centre, to which it owes its wonderful vitality, force, and consistency. Heppe of Marburg went still further than Ebrard in his

attempt to combine Lutheranism and Calvinism in a Melanchthonian
church (§ 182, 16), by seeking to prove that the original evangelical
church of Germany was Melanchthonian, that after Luther's death
the fanatics, more Lutheran than Luther, founded the so-called
Lutheran church and completed it by issuing the Formula of Concord; that the Calvinizing of the Palatinate, Hesse, Brandenburg,
Anhalt was only a reaction against hyper- or pseudo-Lutheranism,
and that the restoration of the original Melanchthonianism, and the
modern union movement were only the completion of that restoration. Schenkel's earlier contributions to Reformation history moved
in a similar direction. Ebrard also, in A.D. 1851, founded a "*Ref.
Kirchenzeitung.*"—But even the genuine strict Calvinism had zealous
adherents during this century, not only in Scotland (§ 202, 7) and
the Netherlands (§ 200, 2), but also in Germany, especially in the
Wupperthal. G. D. Krummacher, from A.D. 1816 pastor in Elberfeld,
and his nephew F. W. Krummacher of Barmen, were long its chief
representatives. When Prussia sought in A.D. 1835 to force the
union in the Wupperthal, and threatened the opposing Reformed
pastors with deposition, the revolt here proved almost as serious as
that of the Lutherans in Silesia. The pastors, with the majority of
their people agreed at last to the union only in so far as it was in
accordance with the Reformed mode of worship. But a portion,
embracing their most important members, stood apart and refused
all conciliation. The royal Toleration Act of A.D. 1847 allowed them
to form an independent congregation at Elberfeld with Dr. Kohl-
brügge as their minister. This divine, formerly Lutheran pastor at
Amsterdam, was driven out owing to a contest with a rationalising
colleague, and afterwards, through study of Calvin's writings, became an ardent Calvinist. This body, under the name of the Dutch
Reformed church, constituted the one anti-unionist, strictly Calvinistic denomination in Prussia.—The De Cock movement (§ 200, 2), out
of which in A.D. 1830 the separate "Chr. Ref. Church of Holland"
sprang, spread over the German frontiers and led to the founding
there of the "Old Ref. Church of East Frisia and Bentheim," which
has now nine congregations and seven pastors.—At the meeting of the
Evangelical Alliance in New York in A.D. 1873, the Presbyterians
present resolved to convoke an œcumenical Reformed council. A
conference in London in A.D. 1875 brought to maturity the idea of
a Pan-Presbyterian assembly. The council is to meet every third
year; the members recognise the supreme authority of the Old and
New Testament in matters of faith and practice, and accept the
consensus of all the Reformed confessions. The first "General Presbyterian Council" met in Edinburgh from 3rd to 10th July, A.D. 1877,
about 300 delegates being present. The proceedings consisted in

unmeasured glorification of presbyterianism "drawn from the whole
Scripture, from the seventy elders of the Pentateuch to the twenty-four
elders of the Apocalypse." The second council met at Philadelphia
in A.D. 1880, and boasted that it represented forty millions of Presbyterians. It appointed a committee to draw up a consensus of the
confessions of all Reformed churches. The third council of 305 members met at Belfast in A.D. 1884, and after a long debate declined, by
a great majority, to adopt a strictly formulated consensus of doctrine
as uncalled for and undesirable, and by the reception of the Cumberland Presbyterians they even surrendered the Westminster Confession (§ 155, 1) as the only symbol qualifying for membership of
the council. The fourth council met in London in A.D. 1887.—An
œcumenical Methodist congress was held in London in A.D. 1881,
attended by 400 delegates.

§ 180.   The "Protestantenverein."

Rationalists of all descriptions, adherents of Baur's school,
as well as disciples of Hegel and Schleiermacher of the left
wing, kept far off from every evangelical union. But the
common negation of the tendencies characterizing the evangelical confederations and the common endeavour after a
free, democratic, non-confessional organization of the German Protestant church, awakened in them a sense of the
need of combination and co-operation. While in North Germany this feeling was powerfully expressed from A.D. 1854,
in the able literary organ the "*Protest. Kirchenzeitung*,"
in South Germany, with Heidelberg as a centre and Dean
Zittel as chief agitator, local "*Protestantenvereine*" were
formed, which combined in a united organization in the
Assembly of Frankfort, A.D. 1863. After long debates the
northern and southern societies were joined in one. In
June, A.D. 1865, the first general Protestant assembly was
held at Eisenach, and the nature, motive, and end of the
associations were defined. To these assemblies convened
from year to year members of the society crowded from
all parts of Germany in order to encourage one another to
persevere in spreading their views by word and pen, and to

take steps towards the founding of branch associations for disseminating among the people a Christianity which renounces the miraculous and sets aside the doctrines of the church.

1. **The Protestant Assembly.**—The first general German Protestant Assembly, composed of 400 clerical and lay notabilities, met at Eisenach in A.D. 1865, under the presidency of the jurist Bluntschli of Heidelberg and the chief court preacher Schwarz of Gotha. A peculiar lustre was given to the meeting by the presence of Rothe of Heidelberg. Of special importance was Schwarz's address on "The Limits of Doctrinal Freedom in Protestantism," which he sought not in the confession, not in the authority of the letter of Scripture, not even in certain so called fundamental articles, but in the one religious moral truth of Christianity, the gospel of love and the divine fatherhood as Christ taught it, expounded it in his life and sealed it by his death. In Berlin, Osnabrück, and Leipzig, the churches were refused for services according to the *Protestantenverein*. In A.D. 1868 fifteen heads of families in Heidelberg petitioned the ecclesiastical council to grant them the use of one of the city churches where a believing clergyman might conduct service in the old orthodox fashion. This request was refused by fifty votes against four. Baumgarten denounced this intolerance, and declared that unless repudiated by the union it would be a most serious stain upon its reputation. In A.D. 1877 he publicly withdrew from the society.

2. **The "Protestantenverein" Propaganda.**—The views of the union were spread by popular lectures and articles in newspapers and magazines. The "*Protestanten-Bibel*," edited by Schmidt and Holtzendorff in A.D. 1872, of which an English translation has been published, giving the results of New Testament criticism, "laid the axe at the root of the dogmatics and confessionalism," and proved that "we are still Christians though our conception of Christianity diverges in many points from that of the second century, and we proclaim a Christianity without miracles and in accordance with the modern theory of the universe." The success of such efforts to spread the broad theology has been greatly over-estimated. Enthusiastic partisans of the union claimed to have the whole evangelical world at their back, while Holtzendorff boasted that they had all thoughtful Germans with them.

3. **Sufferings Endured.**—In many instances members of the society were disciplined, suspended and deposed. In October, A.D. 1880, Beesenmeyer of Mannheim, on his appointment to Osnabrück, was examined by the consistory. He confessed an economic but not an

essential Trinity, the sinlessness and perfect godliness but not the divinity of Christ, the atoning power of Christ's death but not the doctrine of vicarious satisfaction. He was pronounced unorthodox, and so unfit to hold office. Schroeder, a pastor in the consistory of Wiesbaden in A.D. 1871, on his refusing to use the Apostles' Creed at baptism and confirmation, was deposed, but on appealing to the minister of worship, Dr. Falk, he was restored in the beginning of A.D. 1874. The Stettin consistory declined to ordain Dr. Hanne on account of his work "*Der ideale u. d. geschichtl. Christus*," and an appeal to the superior court and another to the king were unsuccessful. Several members of the church protested against the call of Dr. Ziegler to Liegnitz in A.D. 1873, on account of his trial discourse and a previous lecture on the authority of the Bible, and the consistory refused to sustain the call. The Supreme Church Council, however, when appealed to, declared itself satisfied with Ziegler's promise to take unconditionally the ordination vow, which requires acceptance of the fundamental doctrines of the gospel and not the peculiar theological system of the symbols.

4. The conflicts in Berlin were specially sharp. In A.D. 1872 the aged pastor of the so called New Church, Dr. Sydow, delivered a lecture on the miraculous birth of Jesus, in which he declared that he was the legitimate son of Joseph and Mary. His colleague, Dr. Lisco, son of the well-known commentator, spoke of legendary elements in the Apostles' Creed, and denied its authority. Lisco was reprimanded and cautioned by the consistory. Sydow was deposed. He appealed, together with twenty-six clergymen of the province of Brandenburg, and twelve Berlin pastors, to the Supreme Church Council. The Jena theologians also presented a largely signed petition to Dr. Falk against the procedure of the consistory, while the Weimar and Württemberg clergy sent a petition in favour of maintaining strict discipline. The superior court reversed the sentence, on the ground that the lecture was not given in the exercise of his office, and severely reprimanded Sydow for giving serious offence by its public delivery. At a Berlin provincial synod in A.D. 1877, an attack was made by pastor Rhode on creed subscription. Hossbach, preaching in a vacant church, declared that he repudiated the confessional doctrine of the divinity of Christ, regarded the life of Jesus in the gospels as a congeries of myths, etc. Some loudly protested and others as eagerly pressed for his settlement. The consistory accepted Rhode's retractation and annulled Hossbach's call. The Supreme Church Council supported the consistory, and issued a strict order to its president to suffer no departure from the confession. The congregation next chose Dr. Schramm, a pronounced adherent of the same party, who was also rejected. In A.D. 1879 Werner, biographer of Boniface, a more mode-

rate disciple of the same school, holding a sort of Arian position, received the appointment. When, in A.D. 1880, the Supreme Church Council demanded of Werner a clear statement of his belief regarding Scripture, the divinity and resurrection of Christ, and the Apostles Creed, and on receiving his reply summoned him to a conference at Berlin, he resigned his office.

5. The conflicts in Schleswig Holstein also caused considerable excitement. Pastor Kühl of Oldensworth had published an article at Easter, A.D. 1880, entitled, "The Lord is Risen indeed," in which the resurrection was made purely spiritual. He was charged with violating his ordination vow, sectaries pointed to his paper as proof of their theory that the state church was the apocalyptic Babylon, and petitions from 115 ministers and 2,500 laymen were presented against him to the consistory of Kiel. The consistory exhorted Kühl to be more careful and his opponents to be more patient. In the same year, however, he published a paper in which he denied that the order of nature was set aside by miracles. He was now advised to give up writing and confine himself to his pastoral work. A pamphlet by Decker on "The Old Faith and the New," was answered by Lühr, and his mode of dealing with the ordination vow was of such a kind as to lead pastor Paulsen to speak of it as a "chloroforming of his conscience."

§ 181. DISPUTES ABOUT FORMS OF WORSHIP.

During the eighteenth century the services of the evangelical church had become thoroughly corrupted and disordered under the influence of the "Illumination," and were quite incapable of answering to the Christian needs and ecclesiastical tastes of the nineteenth century. Whenever there was a revival in favour of the faith of their fathers, a movement was made in the direction of improved forms of worship. The Rationalists and Friends of Light, however, prevented progress except in a few states. Even the official Eisenach Conference did no more than prepare the way and indicate how action might afterwards be taken.

1. The Hymnbook.—Traces of the vandalism of the Illumination were to be seen in all the hymnbooks. The noble poet Ernst Moritz Arndt was the first to enter the lists as a restorer; and various attempts were made by Von Elsner, Von Raumer, Bunsen, Stier, Knapp,

Daniel, Harms, etc., to make collections of sacred songs answerable to the revived Christian sentiment of the people. These came to be largely used, not in the public services, but in family worship, and prepared the way for official revisal of the books for church use. The Eisenach Conference of A.D. 1853 resolved to issue 150 classical hymns with the old melodies as an appendix to the old collection and a pattern for further work. Only with difficulty was the resolution passed to make A.D. 1750 the *terminus ad quem* in the choice of pieces. Wackernagel insisted on a strict adherence to the original text and retired from the committee when this was not agreed to. Only in a few states has the Eisenach collection been introduced; *e.g.* in Bavaria, where it has been incorporated in its new hymnbook.

2. The Book of Chorales.—In A.D. 1814, Frederick William III. of Prussia sought to secure greater prominence to the liturgy in the church service. In A.D. 1817, Natorp of Münster expressed himself strongly as to the need of restoring the chorale to its former position, and he was followed by the jurist Thibaut, whose work on "The Purity of Tone" has been translated into English. The reform of the chorale was carried out most vigorously in Württemberg, but it was in Bavaria that the old chorale in its primitive simplicity was most widely introduced.

3. The Liturgy.—Under the reign of the Illuminists the liturgy had suffered even more than the hymns. The Lutherans now went back to the old Reformation models, and liturgical services, with musical performances, became popular in Berlin. Conferences held at Dresden did much for liturgical reform, and the able works and collections of Schöberlein supplied abundant materials for the practical carrying out of the movement.

4. The Holy Scriptures.—The Calw Bible in its fifth edition adopted somewhat advanced views on inspiration, the canon and authenticity, while maintaining generally the standpoint of the most reverent and pious students of scripture. Bunsen's commentary assumed a "mediating" position, and the "Protestant Bible" on the New Testament, translated into English, that of the advanced school. Besser's expositions of the New Testament books, of which we have in English those on John's gospel, had an unexampled popularity. The Eisenach Conference undertook a revision of Luther's translation of the Bible. The revised New Testament was published in A.D. 1870, and accepted by some Bible societies. The much more difficult task of Old Testament revision was entrusted to a committee of distinguished university theologians, which concluded its labours in A.D. 1881. A "proof" Bible was issued in A.D. 1883, and the final corrected rendering in A.D. 1886. A whole legion of pamphlets were now issued from all quarters. Some bitterly opposing any change in the

Luther-text, others severely criticising the work, so that the whole movement seems now at a standstill.[1]—In England, in May, 1885, the work of revision of the English version of the Bible, undertaken by order of convocation, was completed after fifteen years' labour, and issued jointly by the two universities of Oxford and Cambridge. The revised New Testament, prepared four years previously, had been telegraphed in short sections to America by the representative of the *New York Herald*, so that the complete work appeared there rather earlier than in England. But in the case of the Old Testament revision such freebooting industry was prevented by the strict and careful reserve of all concerned in the work. The revised New Testament had meanwhile never been introduced into the public services; whether the completed Bible will ever succeed in overcoming this prejudice remains to be seen.[2]

§ 182. PROTESTANT THEOLOGY IN GERMANY.

The real founder of modern Protestant theology, the Origen of the nineteenth century, is Schleiermacher. His influence was so powerful and manysided that it extended not merely to his own school, but also in almost all directions, even to the Catholic church, embracing destructive and constructive tendencies such as appeared before in Origen and Erigena. Alongside of the vulgar rationalism, which still had notable representatives, De Wette founded the new school of historico-critical rationalism, and Neander that of pietistic supernaturalism, which soon overshadowed the two older schools of rational and supra-rational supernaturalism. On the basis of Schelling's and Hegel's philosophy Daub founded the school of speculative theology with an evangelical tendency; but after Hegel's death it split into a right

---

[1] Strack, "The Work of Bible Revision in Germany," in *Expositor*, third series, vol. ii., pp. 178–187.

[2] See papers by Driver, Cheyne, Davidson, Kirkpatrick, in *Expositor* for 1886–1888, on various books in Revised Old Testament. Westcott, "Some Lessons of Revised Version of New Testament," in *Expositor*, third series, vol. v., pp. 81, 241. 453. Jennings and Lowe, "Revised Version of Old Testament: a Critical Estimate," in *Expositor*, third series, vol. ii., pp. 57, etc.

and left wing. As the former could not maintain its position, its adherents by-and-by went over to other schools; and the latter, setting aside speculation and dogmatics, applied itself to the critical investigation of the early history of Christianity, and founded the school of Baur at Tübingen. Schleiermacher's school also split into a right and left wing. Each of them took the union as its standard; but the right, which claimed to be the "German" and the "Modern" theology, wished a union under a consensus of the confessions, and sought to effect an accommodation between the old faith and the modern liberalism; whereas the left wished union without a confession, and unconditioned toleration of "free science." This latter tendency, however, secured greater prominence and importance from A.D. 1854, through combination with the representatives of the historico-critical and the younger generation of the Baurian school, from which originated the "free Protestant" theology. On the other hand, under the influence of pietism, there has arisen since A.D. 1830, especially in the universities of Erlangen, Leipzig, Rostock, and Dorpat, a Lutheran confessional school, which seeks to develop a Lutheran system of theology of the type of Gerhard and Bengel. A similar tendency has also shown itself in the Reformed church. The most recent theological school is that founded by Ritschl, resting on a Lutheran basis but regarded by the confessionalists as rather allied to the "free Protestant" theology, on account of its free treatment of certain fundamental doctrines of Lutheranism.— Theological contributions from Scandinavia, England, and Holland are largely indebted to German theology.

1. **Schleiermacher, A.D. 1768–1834.**—Thoroughly grounded in philosophy and deeply imbued with the pious feeling of the Moravians among whom he was trained, Schleiermacher began his career in A.D. 1807 as professor and university preacher at Halle, but, to escape French domination, went in the same year to Berlin, where by speech and writing he sought to arouse German patriotism. There he was appointed preacher in A.D. 1809, and professor in A.D. 1810, and continued

to hold these offices till his death in A.D. 1834. In A.D. 1799 he published five " *Reden über d. Religion.*" In these it was not biblical and still less ecclesiastical Christianity which he sought with glowing eloquence to address to the hearts of the German people, but Spinozist pantheism. The fundamental idea of his life, that God, "the absolute unity," cannot be reached in thought nor grasped by will, but only embraced in feeling as immediate consciousness, and hence that feeling is the proper seat of religion, appears already in his early productions as the centre of his system. In the following year, A.D. 1800, he set forth his ethical theory in five " Monologues " : every man should in his own way represent humanity in a special blending of its elements. The s dy and translation of Plato, which occupied him now for severa years, exercised a powerful influence upon him. He approached more and more towards positive Christianity. In a Christmas Addr ss in A.D. 1808 on the model of Plato's Symposium, he represents Christ as the divine object of all faith. In A.D. 1811 he published his " Short Outline of Theological Study," which has been tr nslated into English, a masterly sketch of theological encyclopædia. In A.D. 1821 he produced his great masterpiece, " *Der Chr. Glaube,*" which makes feeling the seat of all religion as immedir te consciousness of absolute dependence, perfectly expressed in Jesus Christ, whose life redeems the world. The task of do matics is to give scientific expression to the Christian consciousness as seen the life of the redeemed ; it has not to prove, but only to work out and exhibit in relation to the whole spiritual life what is already present as a fact of experience. Thus dogmatics and philosophy are quite distinct. He proves the evangelical Protestant character of the doctrines thus developed by quotations from the consensus of both confessions. Notwithstanding his protest, many of his contemporaries still found remnants of Spinozist pantheism. On certain points too, he failed to satisfy the claims of orthodoxy ; *e.g.* in his Sabellian doctrine of the Trinity, his theory of election, his doctrine of the canon, and his account of the beginning and close of our Lord's life, the birth and the ascension.[1]

2. The Older Rationalistic Theology.—The older, so-called vulgar rationalism, was characterized by the self-sufficiency with which it rejected all advances from philosophy and theology, science and national literature. The new school of historico-critical rationalism availed itself of every aid in the direction of scientific investigation. The father of the vulgar rationalism of this age was Röhr of Weimar, who exercised his ingenuity in proving how one holding such views

---

[1] "Schleiermacher's Life in Letters," translated by Rowan. London, 1860. Baur, "Religious Life in Germany," London, 1872, pp. 197 ff Dorner, "History of Protestant Theology," vol. ii., pp. 374-395.

might still hold office in the church. To this school also belonged
Paulus of Heidelberg, described by Marheineke as one who believes he
thinks and thinks he believes but was incapable of either; Wegscheider
of Halle, who in his "*Institutiones theol. Christ. dogmaticœ*" repudiates
miracles; Bretschneider of Gotha, who began as a supernaturalist and
afterwards went over to extreme rationalism; and Ammon of Dresden,
who afterwards passed over to rational supernaturalism.

3. The founder of Historico-critical Rationalism was De Wette; a
contemporary of Schleiermacher in Berlin University, but deprived of
office in A.D. 1819 for sending a letter of condolence to the mother of
Sands, which was regarded as an apology for his crime. From A.D.
1822 till his death in A.D. 1849 he continued to work unweariedly
in Basel. His theological position had its starting point in the
philosophy of his friend Fries, which he faithfully adhered to down
to the end of his life. His friendship with Schleiermacher had also a
powerful influence upon him. He too placed religion essentially in
feeling, which, however, he associated much more closely with knowledge and will. In the church doctrines he recognised an important
symbolical expression of religious truths, and so by the out and out
rationalist he was all along sneered at as a mystic. But his chief
strength lay in the sharp critical treatment which he gave to the
biblical canon and the history of the O.T. and N.T. His commentaries
on the whole of the N.T. are of permanent value, and contain his
latest thoughts, when he had approached most nearly to positive
Christianity. His literary career began in A.D. 1806 with a critical
examination of the books of Chronicles. He also wrote on the Psalms,
on Jewish history, on Jewish archæology, and made a new translation
of the Bible. His Introductions to the O.T. and N.T. have been translated into English.—Winer of Leipzig is best known by his "Grammar
of New Testament Greek," first published in A.D. 1822, of which several
English and American translations have appeared, the latest and best
that of Dr. Moulton, made in A.D. 1870, from the sixth German edition.
He also edited an admirable "*Bibl. Reallexicon*," and wrote a work
on symbolics which has been translated into English under the title
"A Comparative View of the Doctrines and Confessions of the Various
Communities of Christendom" (Edin., 1873).—Gesenius of Halle, who
died A.D. 1842, has won a high reputation by his grammatical and
lexicographical services and as author of a commentary on Isaiah.—
Hupfeld of Marburg and Halle, who died A.D. 1866, best known
by his work in four vols. on the Psalms, in his critical attitude
toward the O.T., belonged to the same party.—Hitzig of Zürich and
Heidelberg, who died A.D. 1875, far outstripped all the rest in genius
and subtlety of mind and critical acuteness. He wrote commentaries
on most of the prophets and critical investigations into the O.T

history.—Ewald of Göttingen, A.D. 1803–1875, whose hand was against
every man and every man's hand against him, held the position of
recognised dictator in the domain of Hebrew grammar, and uttered
oracles as an infallible expounder of the biblical books. In his
Journal for Biblical Science, he held an annual *auto da fe* of all the
biblico-theological literature of the preceding year; and, assuming
a place alongside of Isaiah and Jeremiah, he pronounced in every
preface a prophetic burden against the theological, ecclesiastical, or
political ill doers of his time. His exegetical writings on the poetical
and prophetical books of the O.T., his "History of Israel down to the
Post-Apostolic Age," and a condensed reproduction of his "Bible
Doctrine of God," under the title: "Revelation, its Nature and
Record " and " Old and New Testament Theology," have all appeared
in English translations, and exhibit everywhere traces of brilliant
genius and suggestive originality.[1]

4. Supernaturalism of the older type (§ 171, 8) was now represented
by Storr, Reinhard, Planck, Knapp, and Stäudlin. In Württemberg
Storr's school maintained its pre-eminence down to A.D. 1830.
Neander, Tholuck, and Hengstenberg may be described as the
founders and most powerful enunciators of the more recent Pietistic
Supernaturalism. Powerfully influenced by Schleiermacher, his colleague in Berlin, Neander, A.D. 1789–1850, exercised an influence such
as no other theological teacher had exerted since Luther and Melanchthon. Adopting Schleiermacher's standpoint, he regarded religion as
a matter of feeling: *Pectus est quod theologum facit.* By his subjective
pectoral theology he became the father of modern scientific pietism,
but it incapacitated him from understanding the longing of the age
for the restoration of a firm objective basis for the faith. He was
adverse to the Hegelian philosophy no less than to confessionalism.
Neander was so completely a pectoralist, that even his criticism was
dominated by feeling, as seen in his vacillations on questions of N.T.
authenticity and historicity. His "Church History," of which we have
admirable English translations, was an epoch-making work, and his
historical monographs were the result of careful original research.[2]—
Tholuck, A.D. 1799–1877, from A.D. 1826 professor at Halle, at first devoted
to oriental studies, roused to practical interests by Baron von Kottwitz
of Berlin, gave himself with all his wide culture by preaching,

---

[1] Cheyne, "Life and Works of Heinrich Ewald," in *Expositor*, third
series, vol. iv., pp. 241 ff., 361 ff.

[2] There are English translations of his "Life of Christ," "First
Planting of Christianity," "Antignostikus," "History of Christian
Dogmas," " Christian Life in the Early and Middle Ages," all published
by Bohn.

lecturing and conversing to lead his students to Christ. His scientific theology was latitudinarian, but had the warmth and freshness of immediate contact with the living Saviour. His most important works are apologetical and exegetical. In his "Preludes to the History of Rationalism" he gives curious glimpses into the scandalous lives of students in the seventeenth century ; and he afterwards confessed that these studies had helped to draw him into close sympathy with confessionalism. While always lax in his views of authenticity, he came to adopt a very decided position in regard to revelation and inspiration.—Hengstenberg, A.D. 1802–1869, from A.D. 1826 professor in Berlin, had quite another sort of development. Rendered determined by innumerable controversies, in none of which he abated a single hair's breadth, he looked askance at science as a gift of the Danaides, and set forth in opposition to rationalism and naturalism a system of theology unmodified by all the theories of modern times. Born in the Reformed church and in his understanding of Scripture always more Calvinist than Lutheran, rationalising only upon miracles that seemed to detract from the dignity of God, and in his later years inclined to the Romish doctrine of justification, he may nevertheless claim to be classed among the confessionalists within the union. He deserves the credit of having given a great impulse to O.T. studies and a powerful defence of O.T. books, though often abandoning the position of an apologist for that of an advocate. His "Christology of the Old Testament," in four vols., "Genuineness of the Pentateuch and Daniel," three vols., "Egypt and the Books of Moses," commentaries on Psalms, Ecclesiastes, Ezekiel, the Gospel of John, Revelation, and his "History of the Kingdom of God in the Old Testament," have all been translated into English.

5. The so called Rational Supernaturalism admits the supernatural revelation in holy scripture, and puts reason alongside of it as an equally legitimate source of religious knowledge, and maintains the rationality of the contents of revelation. Its chief representative was Baumgarten-Crusius of Jena. Of a similar tendency, but more influenced by æsthetic culture and refined feeling, and latterly inclining more and more to the standpoint of "free Protestantism," Carl Hase, after seven years' work in Tübingen, opened his Jena career in A.D. 1830, which he closed by resigning his professorship in A.D. 1883, after sixty years' labour in the theological chair. In his "Life of Jesus," first published A.D. 1829, he represents Christ as the ideal man, sinless but not free from error, endowed with the fulness of love and the power of pure humanity, as having truly risen and become the author of a new life in the kingdom of God, of which the very essence is most purely and profoundly expressed in the gospel of the disciple who lay upon the Master's heart. The latest revision

of this work, issued in A.D. 1876 under the title "*Geschichte Jesu*," treats the fourth gospel as non-Johannine in authorship and mythical in its contents, and explains the resurrection by the theory of a swoon or a vision. In his "*Hutterus Redivivus*," A.D. 1828, twelfth edition 1883, he seeks to set forth the Lutheran dogmatic as Hutter might have done had he lived in these days. This led to the publication of controversial pamphlets in A.D. 1834–1837, which dealt the deathblow to the *Rationalismus Vulgaris*. His "Church History," distinguished by its admirable little sketches of leading personalities, was published in A.D. 1834. and the seventh edition of A.D. 1854 has been translated into English.

6. **Speculative Theology.**—Its founder was Daub, professor at Heidelberg from A.D. 1794 till his death in A.D. 1836. Occupying and writing from the philosophical standpoints of Kant, Fichte, and Schelling successively, he published in A.D. 1816 "Judas Iscariot," an elaborate discussion of the nature of evil, but passed over in A.D. 1833, with his treatise on dogmatics, to the Hegelian position. He exerted great influence as a professor, but his writings proved to most unintelligible. —Marheineke of Berlin in the first edition of his "Dogmatics" occupied the standpoint of Schelling, but in the second set forth Lutheran orthodoxy in accordance with the formulæ of the Hegelian system.— After Hegel's death in A.D. 1831 his older pupils Rosenkrantz and Göschel sought to enlist his philosophy in the service of orthodoxy. Richter was the first to give offence, by his "Doctrine of the Last Things," in which he denounced the doctrine of immortality in the sense of personal existence after death. Strauss, A.D. 1808–1874, represented the "Life of Jesus," in his work of A.D. 1835, as the product of unintentional romancing, and in his "*Glaubenslehre*" of A.D. 1840, sought to prove that all Christian doctrines are put an end to by modern science, and openly taught pantheism as the residuum of Christianity. Bruno Bauer, after passing from the right to the left Hegelian wing, described the gospels as the product of conscious fraud, and Ludwig Feuerbach, in his "Essence of Christianity," A.D. 1841, set forth in all its nakedness the new gospel of self-adoration. The breach between the two parties in the school was now complete. Whatever Rosenkranz and Schaller from the centre, and Göschel and Gabler from the right, did to vindicate the honour of the system, they could not possibly restore the for ever shattered illusion that it was fundamentally Christian. Those of the right fell back into the camps of "the German theology" and the Lutheran confessionalism; while in the latest times the left has no prominent theological representative but Biedermann of Zürich.

7. **The Tübingen School.**—Strauss was only the advanced skirmisher of a school which was proceeding under an able leader to subject the

history of early Christianity to a searching examination. **Fred. Chr.**
Baur of Tübingen, A.D. 1792–1860, almost unequalled among his contemporaries in acuteness, diligence, and learning, a pupil of Schleiermacher and Hegel, devoted himself mainly to historical research
about the beginnings of Christianity. In this department he proceeded to reject almost everything that had previously been believed.
He denied the genuineness of all the New Testament writings, with
the exception of Revelation and the Epistles to the Romans, Galatians,
and Corinthians; treating the rest as forgeries of the second century,
resulting from a bitter struggle between the Petrine and Pauline
parties. This scheme was set forth in a rudimentary form in the
treatise on "The So-called' Pastoral Epistles of the Apostle Paul,"
A.D. 1835. His works, "Paul, the Apostle," and the "History of the
First Three Centuries," have been translated into English. He had
as collaborateurs in this work, Schwegler, Zeller, Hilgenfeld, Volkmar,
etc. Ritschl, who was at first an adherent of the school, made important concessions to the right, and in the second edition of his
great work, "*Die Entstehung d. alt-kath. Kirche,*" of A.D. 1857, announced himself as an opponent. Hilgenfeld of Jena, too, marked
out new lines for himself in New Testament Introduction and in
the estimate of early church doctrine, modifying in various ways
the positions of Baur. The labours of this school and its opponents
have done signal service in the cause of science.

8. **Strauss,** who had meanwhile occupied himself with the studies
of Von Hutten, Reimarus, and Lessing's "Nathan," feeling that the
researches of the Tübingen school had antiquated his "Life of Jesus,"
and stimulated by Renan's "Life of Jesus," written with French
elegance and vivacity, in which he described Christ as an amiable
hero of a Galilæan village story, undertook in 1864 a semi-jubilee
reproduction of his work, addressed to "the German people." This
was followed by a severe controversial pamphlet, "The Half and
the Whole," in which he lashed the halting attempts of Schenkel as
well as the uncompromising conservatism of Hengstenberg. He now
pointed out cases of intentional romancing in the gospel narratives;
the resurrection rests upon subjective visions of Christ's disciples.
His "Lectures on Voltaire" appeared in A.D. 1870, and in A.D. 1872 the
most radical of all his books, "The Old and the New Faith," which
makes Christianity only a modified Judaism, the history of the resurrection mere "humbug," and the whole gospel story the result of the
"hallucinations" of the early Christians. The question whether "we"
are still Christians he answers openly and honourably in the negative.
He has also surmounted the standpoint of pantheism. The religion
of the nineteenth century is *pancosmism,* its gospel the results of
natural science with Darwin's discoveries as its bible, its devotional

works the national classics, its places of worship the concert rooms, theatres, museums, etc. The most violent attacks on this book came from the *Protestantenverein*. Strauss had said, "If the old faith is absurd, then the modernized edition of the '*Protestantenverein*' and the school of Jena is doubly, trebly so. The old faith only contradicts reason, not itself; the new contradicts itself at every point, and how can it then be reconciled with reason?" [1]

9. The Mediating Theology.—This tendency originated from the right wing of the school of Schleiermacher, still influenced more or less by the pectoralism of Neander. It adopted in dogmatics a more positive and in criticism a more conservative manner. It earnestly sought to promote the interests of the union not merely as a combination for church government, but as a communion under a confessional consensus. Its chief theological organs were the "*Studien und Kritiken*," started in A.D. 1828, edited by Ullmann and Umbreit in Heidelberg, afterwards by Riehm and Köstlin in Halle, and the "*Jahrbücher für deutsche Theologie*" of Dorner and Leibner, A.D. 1856–1878.—Although the mediating theology sought to sink all confessional differences, denominational descent was more or less traceable in most of its adherents. Its leading representatives from the Reformed church were: Alexander Schweizer, who most faithfully preserved the critical tendency of Schleiermacher, and, in a style far abler and subtler than any other modern theologian, expounded the Reformed system of doctrine in its rigid logical consistency. In his own system he gives a scientific exposition of the evangelical faith from the unionist standpoint, with many pious reflections on Scripture and the confession as well as results of Christian experience, based upon the threefold manifestation of God set forth without miracle in the physical order of the world, in the moral order of the world, and in the historical economy of the kingdom of God.—Sack, one of the oldest and most positive of Schleiermacher's pupils, professor at Bonn, then superintendent at Magdeburg, wrote on apologetics and polemics. Hagenbach of Basel, A.D. 1801–1874, is well-known by his "Theological Encyclopædia and Methodology," "History of the Reformation," and "History of the Church in the Eighteenth and Nineteenth Centuries," all of which are translated into English.—John Peter Lange of Bonn, A.D. 1802–1884, a man of genius, imaginative, poetic, and speculative, with strictly positive tendencies, widely known by his "Life of Christ" and the commentary on Old and New Testament, edited and contributed to by him.—Dr. Philip

---

[1] Zeller, "David Frederick Strauss, in his Life and Writings." London, 1874. Translations: "Life of Jesus Critically Treated," 1846; "Life of Jesus for the German People," 1865; "The Old Faith and the New," 1874; "Ulrich von Hutten," 1874.

Schaff may also be named as the transplanter of German theology of the Neander-Tholuck type to the American soil. Born in Switzerland, he accepted a call as professor to the theological seminary of the German Reformed church at Mercersburg in 1843. He soon fell under suspicion of heresy, but was acquitted by the Synod of New York in 1845. In 1869 he accepted a call to a professorship in the richly endowed Presbyterian Union Theological Seminary of New York. Writing first in German and afterwards in English, his works treat of almost all the branches of theological science, especially in history and exegesis. He is also president of several societies engaged in active Christian work.

10. Among those belonging originally to the Lutheran church were Schleiermacher's successor in Berlin, Twesten, whose dogmatic treatise did not extend beyond the doctrine of God, a faithful adherent of Schleiermacher's right wing on the Lutheran side; Nitzsch, professor in Bonn A.D. 1822–1847, and afterwards of Berlin till his death in A.D. 1868, best known by his "System of Christian Doctrine," and his Protestant reply to Möhler's "Symbolism," a profound thinker with a noble Christian personality, and one of the most influential among the consensus theologians. Julius Müller of Halle, A.D. 1801–1878, if we except his theory of an ante-temporal fall, occupied the common doctrinal platform of the confessional unionists. His chief work, "The Christian Doctrine of Sin," is a masterpiece of profound thinking and original research. Ullmann, A.D. 1796–1865, professor in Halle and Heidelberg, a noble and peace-loving character, distinguished himself in the domain of history by his monograph on "Gregory Nazianzen," his "Reformers before the Reformation," and most of all by his beautiful apologetical treatise on the "Sinlessness of Jesus."— Isaac Aug. Dorner, A.D. 1809–1884, born and educated in Württemberg, latterly professor in Berlin, applied himself mainly to the elaborating of Christian doctrine, and gave to the world, in his "Doctrine of the Person of Christ," in A.D. 1839, a work of careful historical research and theological speculation. The fundamental ideas of his Christology are the theory favoured by the "German" theology generally of the necessity of the incarnation even apart from sin (which Müller strongly opposed), and the notion of the archetypal Christ, the God-Man, as the collective sum of humanity, in whom "are gathered the patterns of all several individualities." His "System of Christian Doctrine" formed the copestone of an almost fifty years' academical career. Christ's virgin birth is admitted as the condition of the essential union in Him of divinity and humanity; but the incarnation of the Logos extends through the whole earthly life of the Redeemer; it is first completed in his exaltation by means of his resurrection; it was therefore an operation of the Logos, as principle of all divine movement, *extra*

can nem. His "System of Christian Ethics" was edited after his death by his son.[1]—Richard Rothe, A.D. 1799–1867, appointed in A.D. 1823 chaplain to the Prussian embassy at Rome, where he became intimately acquainted with Bunsen. In A.D. 1828 he was made ephorus at the preachers' seminary of Wittenberg, and afterwards professor in Bonn and Heidelberg. Rothe was one of the most profound thinkers of the century, equalled by none of his contemporaries in the grasp, depth, and originality of his speculation. Though influenced by Schleiermacher, Neander, and Hegel, he for a long time withdrew like an anchoret from the strife of theologians and philosophers, and took up a position alongside of Oetinger in the chamber of the theosophists. His mental and spiritual constitution had indeed much in common with that great mystic. In his first important work, "*Die Anfänge der chr. Kirche,*" he gave expression to the idea that in its perfected form the church becomes merged into the state. The same thought is elaborated in his "Theological Ethics," a work which in depth, originality, and conclusiveness of reasoning is almost unapproached, and is full of the most profound Christian views in spite of its many heterodoxies. In his later years he took part in the ecclesiastical conflicts in Baden (§ 196, 3) with the *Protestantenverein* (§ 180, 1), and entered the arena of public ecclesiastical life.[2]—Beyschlag of Halle, in his "*Christologie d. N. T.,*" A.D. 1866, carried out Schleiermacher's idea of Christ as only man, not God and man but the ideal of man, not of two natures but only one, the archetypal human, which, however, as such is divine, because the complete representation of the divine nature in the human. From this standpoint, too, he vindicates the authenticity of John's Gospel, and from Romans ix.-xi. works out a "Pauline Theodicy."—Hans Lassen Martensen, A.D. 1808–1884, professor at Copenhagen, Bishop of Zealand and primate of Denmark, with high speculative endowments and a considerable tincture of theosophical mysticism, has become through his "Christian Dogmatics," "Christian Ethics," in three vols., etc., of a thoroughly Lutheran type, one of the best known theologians of the century.

11. Among Old Testament exegetes the most distinguished are: Umbreit, A.D. 1795–1860, of Heidelberg, who wrote from the supernaturalist standpoint, influenced by Schleiermacher and Herder, commentaries on Solomon's writings and those of the prophets, and on Job; Bertheau of Göttingen, of Ewald's school, wrote historico-critical and philological commentaries on the historical books; and

---

[1] Simon, "Isaac August Dorner," in *Presbyterian Review* for October 1887, pp. 569-616.

[2] Rothe, "Still Hours," translated by Miss Stoddard, with Introductory Essay on Rothe by Rev. J. Macpherson. London, 1886.

Dillmann, Hengstenberg's successor in Berlin, specially distinguished
for his knowledge of the Ethiopic language and literature, has written
critical commentaries on the Pentateuch and Job.—Among New Testament exegetes we may mention: Lücke of Göttingen, known by his
commentary on John's writings; Bleek, the able New Testament critic
and commentator on the Epistle to the Hebrews; Meyer, A.D. 1800–1873,
most distinguished of all, whose "Critical and Exegetical Commentary
on the New Testament," begun in A.D. 1832, in which he was aided by
Huther, Lunemann, and Düsterdieck, is well-known in its English
edition as the most complete exegetical handbook to the New Testament; Weiss of Kiel and Berlin, author of treatises on the doctrinal
systems of Peter and of John, "The Biblical Theology of the New
Testament," "Life of Christ," "Introduction to New Testament,"
revises and rewrites commentaries on Mark, Luke, John, and Romans,
in the last edition of the Meyer series.—A laborious student in the
domain of New Testament textual criticism was Constant. von Tischen-
dorff of Leipzig, A.D. 1815–1874, who ransacked all the libraries of
Europe and the East in the prosecution of his work. The publication
of several ancient codices, e.g. the Cod. Sinaiticus, a present from
the Sinaitic monks to the czar on the thousandth anniversary of
the Russian empire in A.D. 1862, the Cod. Vaticanus N.T., a new
edition of the LXX., the most complete collection of New Testament
apocrypha and pseudepigraphs, and finally a whole series of editions
of the New Testament (from A.D. 1841–1873 there appeared twenty-
four editions, of which the Editio Octava Major of 1872 is the most
complete in critical apparatus), are the rich and ripe fruits of his
researches. A second edition, compared throughout with the recen-
sions of Tregelles and Westcott and Hort, was published by Von
Gebhardt, and a third volume of Prolegomena was added by C. R.
Gregory. As a theologian he attached himself, especially in later
years, to the Lutheranism of his Leipzig colleagues, and on questions
of criticism and introduction took up a strictly conservative position
as seen in his well known tract, "When were our Gospels written?"

12. Among the university teachers of his time John Tob. Beck,
A.D. 1804–1878, assumed a position all his own. After a pastorate
of ten years he began in A.D. 1836 his academical career in Basel,
and went in A.D. 1843 to Tübingen, where he opposed to the teaching
of Baur's school a purely biblical and positive theology, with a success
that exceeded all expectations. A Württemberger by birth, nature
and training, he quite ignored the history of the church and its
dogmas as well as modern criticism, and set forth a system of theology
drawn from a theosophical realistic study of the Bible. He took little
interest in the excited movements of his age for home and foreign
missions, union, confederation, and alliances, in questions about litur-

gies, constitution, discipline, and confessions, in all which he saw only the form of godliness without the power. Better times could be hoped for only as the result of the immediate interposition of God. His " Pastoral Theology " and " Biblical Psychology " have been translated into English.

13. The Lutheran Confessional Theology.—Sartorius, A.D. 1797–1859, from A.D. 1822 professor in Dorpat, then from A.D. 1835 general superintendent at Königsberg, made fresh and vigorous attacks upon rationalism, and supported the union as preserving " the true mean " of Lutheranism. He is best known by his " Doctrine of Divine Love." Rudelbach,—a Dane by birth and finally settled in Copenhagen, occupying the same ground, became a violent opponent of the union. —Guericke of Halle, beginning as a pietist, passed through the union into a rigorous Lutheran, and joined Rudelbach in editing the journal afterwards conducted by Luthardt of Leipzig.—Alongside of these older representatives of Lutheran orthodoxy there arose a second generation which from A.D. 1840 has fallen into several groups. Their divergencies were mainly on two points: (1) On the place and significance of the clerical order, some viewing it as based on the general priesthood of believers and resting on the call of the congregation for the orderly administration of the means of grace, others regarding it as a divine institution, yet without adopting the Romanizing and Anglican theory of apostolic succession ; and (2) On the more important question of biblical prophecy, where one party maintained the spiritualistic, widely favoured since the time of Jerome, and another party, attaching itself to Crusius and Bengel, insisted upon a realistic interpretation.—At the head of the first group, which maintained the old Protestant theory of church and office and looked askance at chiliastic theories, supporting the old doctrines by all available materials from modern science, stands Harless, A.D. 1806–1879, professor in Erlangen and Leipzig, the chief ecclesiastical commissioner in Dresden, and finally at Munich. His theological reputation rests upon his " Commentary on Ephesians," A.D. 1835, his " Christian Ethics," A.D. 1842. Alongside of him Thomasius of Erlangen, A.D. 1802–1875, wrought in a similar direction.—Keil, A.D. 1807–1888, from A.D. 1833 professor in Dorpat, since A.D. 1858 living retired in Leipzig, of all Hengstenberg's students has most faithfully preserved his master's exegetical and critical conservatism. He began in A.D. 1861 in connexion with Delitzsch his " Old Testament Commentary " on strictly conservative lines. We have an English translation of that work, and also of his " Introduction to the Old Testament " and his " Old Testament Archæology."—Philippi, A.D. 1809–1882, son of Jewish parents, during his academic career in Dorpat, A.D. 1841–1852 exercised a powerful influence in securing for

strict Lutheranism a very widespread ascendency among the clergy
of Livonia. From A.D. 1852 till his death in A.D. 1882 he resided in
Rostock. As exegete and dogmatist, he has, like a John Gerhard
and Quenstedt of the nineteenth century, reproduced the Lutheran
theology of the seventeenth century, unmodified by the developments
of modern thought. He is known to English readers by his "Commentary on Romans." His chief work is " *Kirchl. Glaubenslehre*,"
in six vols.—Alongside of him, and scarcely less important, stands
Theodosius Harnack, who went from Dorpat in A.D. 1853 to Erlangen,
but returned to Dorpat in A.D. 1866, and retired in A.D. 1873. He has
written upon the worship of the church of the post-apostolic age, on
Luther's theology, and practical theology.

14. At the head of the second group, characterized by a decided
biblical realism and inclined to a biblical chiliasm, stands Von Hofmann
of Erlangen, A.D. 1810–1877, whose " *Weissagung und Erfüllung*," 1841,
represents the very antipodes of Hengstenberg's view of the Old
Testament, placing history and prophecy in vital relation to one
another, and studying prophecy in its historical setting. In his
" *Schriftbeweis* " we have an entirely new system of doctrine drawn
from Scripture, the doctrine of the atonement being set forth in quite
a different form from that generally approved, but vindicated by its
author against Philippi as "a new way of teaching old truth." In
his commentary on the New Testament, he takes up a conservative
position on questions of criticism and introduction.—Franz Delitzsch,
in Rostock, A.D. 1846, Erlangen, A.D. 1850, in Leipzig since A.D. 1867,
more intimately acquainted with rabbinical literature than any other
Christian theologian, became an enthusiastic adherent of Hofmann's
position. His theology, however, has a more decidedly theosophical
tendency, while his critical attitude is more liberal. He is well known
by his "Biblical Psychology," commentary on Psalms, Isaiah, Solomon's
writings, Job, Hebrews, and a new commentary on Genesis in which
he accepts many of the positions of the advanced school of biblical
criticism.—Luthardt of Leipzig in the domain of New Testament
exegesis and dogmatics works from the standpoint of Hofmann. His
"Commentary on John's Gospel," "Authorship of Fourth Gospel,"
and "Apologetical Lectures on the Fundamental, Saving and Moral
Truths of Christianity," are well known.—Hofmann's conception of
Old Testament doctrine is admirably carried out by Oehler, A.D. 1812–
1872, with learning and speculative power, in his "Theology of the
Old Testament," and in various important monographs on Old Testament doctrines.—The most important representatives of the third
group, which strongly emphasizes the extreme Lutheran theory of
the church and office, are Kliefoth of Schwerin, liturgist and biblical
commentator; and Vilmar, who opened his academic career at Marburg,

in 1856, with a controversial programme entitled "The Theology of
Facts against the Theology of Rhetoric." Vilmar's lectures, able,
though sketchy and incomplete, were published after his death in
A.D. 1868 by some of his disciples. To the same school belonged
Von Zezschwitz of Erlangen, A.D. 1825–1886, whose "*Catechetics*" is a
treasury of solid learning.

15. Among Lutheran theologians having little or nothing to do with
these controversial questions, Kahnis, A.D. 1814–1888, from A.D. 1850
orofessor at Leipzig, occupied a strict Lutheran confessional standpoint, diverging only in the adoption of a subordinationist doctrine
on the person of Christ, a Sabellian theory of the Trinity, and a theory
of the Lord's supper in some points differing from that of the strict
Lutherans. His historical sketches are vigorous and lively.—Zöckler
of Giessen and Greifswald has made important contributions to church
history, exegesis, and dogmatics, and especially to the theory and
history of natural theology. In 1886 he began the publication of a
short biblical commentary contributed to by the most distinguished
positive theologians, he himself editing the New Testament and
Strack the Old Testament. It is to be in twelve vols., and is being
translated into English.—Von Oetingen of Dorpat has devoted himself
to social problems and moral statistics.—Frank of Erlangen has proved
a powerful apologist for old Lutheranism, and in his "System of
Christian Evidence" has introduced a new branch of theology, in
which the subjective Christian certitude which the believer has with
his faith is made the basis of the scientific exposition of the truth
set forth in his "System of Christian Truth," a thoughtful and
speculative treatise on doctrine, followed by "The System of Christian
Morals" as the conclusion of his theological work.—Lutheran theology
had also zealous representatives in several distinguished jurists:
Göschel, president of the consistory of Magdeburg, who wrote against
Strauss, sought to derive profound Christian teaching from Goethe
and Dante, and wrote on the last things, and on man in respect of
body, soul, and spirit; Stahl, A.D. 1802–1861, professor of law at
Erlangen and Berlin, leader since A.D. 1849 of the high-church aristocratic reactionary party in the Prussian chamber, supported his
views by reference to the Scripture doctrine of the divine origin
of magisterial authority.

16. As zealous representatives of Reformed Confessionalism who set
aside the dogma of predestination and so show no antagonism to the
union, may be named: Heppe, opponent of Vilmar in Marburg, who
devoted much of his career as a historian to the undermining of
Lutheranism, then wrought upon the histories of provincial churches,
of Catholic mysticism and pietism, etc.; and Ebrard, A.D. 1818–1887
a brilliant believing theologian who combated rationalism and

Catholicism, professor from A.D. 1847 of Reformed theology at Erlangen, known by his "Gospel History: a Compendium of Critical Investigations in Support of the Historical Church of the Four Gospels," his "Apologetics," in 8 vols., "Commentary on Hebrews," etc.

17. **The Free Protestant Theology.**—This school originated in the left wing of Schleiermacher's following, and has as its literary organs, Hilgenfeld's *Zeitschrift* and the *Jahrbücher für prot. Theologie.*—The distinguished statesman, Von Bunsen, A.D. 1791–1860, ambassador at Rome and afterwards at London, at first stood at the head of the revival of the church interests and life; but in his "Church of the Future," conceived a constitutional idea on a democratic basis, for which he sought support in historical studies on the Ignatian age, etc., and the historical refutation of the orthodox Christology and trinitarianism. His elaborate work on "Egypt's Place in the World's History," full of arbitrary criticism, negative and positive, on the chronological and historical data of the Old Testament, seeks to show that, by restoring the Egyptian chronology, we for the first time make the Bible history fit into general history. "The Signs of the Times" comprise glowing philippics against the hierarchical pretensions of Papists and even more dangerous Lutherans, insists on Scripture being translated out of the Semitic into the Japhetic mode of speech, to which end he devoted his last great works, "God in History" and his "Bible Commentary," the latter finished after his death by Kamphausen and Holtzmann.—Schenkel, A.D. 1813–1885, professor at Heidelberg from A.D. 1851 till his resignation in A.D. 1884, from the right wing of the mediating school, through unionism and Melanchthonianism advanced to the standpoint of his "*Charakterbild Jesu,*" which strips Christ of all supernatural features, yet proclaims him the redeemer of the world, and strives to save his resurrection as a historical and saving truth, and explains his appearances after the resurrection as "real manifestations of the personality living and glorified after death." In later years he sought to draw yet more closely to positive Christianity. Keim of Zürich and Giessen, A.D. 1825-1878, the ablest of all recent historians of the life of Jesus, and with all his radicalism preserving some conservative tendencies, is best known by his "Jesus of Nazareth," in six vols.—Holtzmann of Heidelberg and Strassburg, passed from the mediating school over to that of Tübingen, from which in important points he has now departed.—To the same rank belongs Hausrath of Heidelberg, whose "History of the New Testament Times" is well known. Under the pseudonym of George Taylor he has composed several highly successful historical romances.—The organs of this school are Hilgenfeld's *Zeitschrift*, and since 1875 the Jena "*Jahrbücher für protest. Theologie.*"

18. **In the** Old Testament Department a liberal critical school has

arisen which has reversed the old relation of "the law and the prophets," treating the origin of the law as post-exilian, and as in not coming at the beginning, but at the end of the Jewish history. Reuss, whose "History of the New Testament Books" marked an epoch in New Testament introduction, was the first who moved in this direction, in his lectures begun at Strassburg in A.D. 1834, the results of which are given us in his "History of the Theology of the Apostolic Age" and in his "History of the Canon." Meanwhile Vatke of Berlin had, in A.D. 1835, undertaken to prove that the patriarchal religion was pure Semitic nature worship, and that the prophets were the first to raise it into a monotheistic Jehovism. Little success attended his efforts. Greater results were obtained by Reuss' two pupils, Graf in A.D. 1866, and Kayser in A.D. 1874. The most brilliant exposition of this theory was given by Julius Wellhausen of Greifswald, transferred in A.D 1882 to the Philosophical Faculty of Halle, in his "History of Israel." In his "Prolegomena to History of Israel," and article "Israel" in "Encyclopœdia Britannica," he gives expression with clearness and force to his radical negative criticism, and develops a purely naturalist conception of the Old Testament. Professor Kuenen of Leyden transplanted these views to the Netherlands, and Robertson Smith has introduced them into Scotland and England, while in Germany they are taught by a number of the younger teachers, Stade in Giessen, Merx in Heidelberg, Smend in Basel, etc. And now at last in A.D. 1882 the venerable master of the school, Edward Reuss, has himself in his "Geschichte d. h. Schr. d. A. Test." given a brilliant and in many points modified exposition of these radical theories. The history of Israel, according to him, divides itself into the four successive periods of the heroes, of the prophets, of the priests, and of the scribes, characterized respectively by individualism, idealism, formalism, and traditionalism. Even before the close of prophetism the priestly influence began to assert itself, but it was only in the post-exilian period under the domination of the priests that the construction and codification of the law began to make impression on the Jewish people. So too in the age of the kings there existed a Levitical tradition about rites and worship, which traced back its first outlines to the time of Moses, though at this period there could have been no written official codex of any kind. In regard to Moses, we are to think not only of his person as historical, but also of his career as that of a man inspired by the divine spirit and recognised as such by his contemporaries and fellow-countrymen.—Also Wellhausen, who has hitherto concerned himself only with the critical introduction to the Old Testament books, not with their historical or theological interpretation, supplied this defect to some extent by his "Prolegomena to the History of Israel." He admits that much of the history of Israel related in the Old Testament is credible. He even goes so far as to allow that this history was a preparation and forerunner of Christianity, but without miracle and prophecy, and without any immediate interposition of God in the affairs of Israel.

19. Among the most distinguished free-thinking dogmatists of recent times, Biedermann of Zürich, A.D. 1819–1885, has occupied the most advanced position. His principal work, "*Christliche Dogmatik,*" A.D. 1869, defined God and the origin of the world as the self-development of the Absolute Idea according to the Hegelian scheme, recognises in the person of Christ the first realization of the Christian principle of the divine sonship in a personal life, then proceeds with free exposition of the Scripture and church doctrines, and combats openly the doctrines of the church and through them also those of Scripture, as setting religion purely in the domain of the imagination.—Lipsius of Leipzig, Kiel, and Jena, in his earliest treatise on the Pauline Doctrine of Justification in A.D. 1853, held the position of the mediating theology, but under the influence of Kant, Hegel, and Baur has been led to adopt the standpoint of the "Free Protestant" school. His history of gnosticism and his researches in early apocryphal literature are important contributions to our knowledge of primitive Christianity. His "*Lehrbuch d. ev. prot. Dogmatik,*" 1876, 2nd ed. 1879, on the basis of Kant and Schleiermacher, fixing the limits of science with the former, and maintaining with the latter the necessity of religious faith and life, not rejecting metaphysics generally, but only its speculations on God and divine things lying quite outside of human experience, seeks from the common faith of the Christian church of all ages, as it is expressed in the Scriptures and in the confessions, by the application of the freest subjective criticism of the letter of revelation, to secure a theory of the world in harmony with modern views.— Pfleiderer, Twesten's successor in Berlin, in his "Paulinism," "Influence of Paul on Development of Christianity" and "History of the Philosophy of Religion," occupies more the Hegelian speculative standpoint than that of Kantian criticism.

20. Ritschl and his School.—Ritschl, 1822–1889, from A.D. 1846 in Bonn, from A.D. 1864 in Göttingen, on his withdrawal from the Tübingen party, applied himself to dogmatic studies and founded a school, the adherents of which, divided into right and left wings, have secured quite a number of academical appointments. After the completion of his great dogmatic work on "Justification and Reconciliation," Ritschl resumed his historical studies in a "History of Pietism," which he traces back through the persecuted anabaptists of the Reformation age to the Tertiaries of the Franciscan order and the mysticism of St. Bernard. He earnestly maintains his adherence to the confessions of

the Lutheran church, and regards it as the task of his life to disentangle the pure Lutheran doctrine from the accretions of scholastic metaphysics. Even more decidedly than Schleiermacher, he banishes all philosophy from the domain of theology. The grand significance of Kant's doctrine of knowledge, with its assertion of the incomprehensibility of all transcendent truth except the ethical postulates of God, freedom and immortality, as set forth in a more profound manner by Lotze, is indeed admitted, but only as a methodological basis of all religious inquiries, and with determined rejection of every material support from Kant's construction of religion within the limits of the pure reason. Ritschl rather pronounces in favour of the formal principle of Protestantism, and declares distinctly that all religious truth must be drawn directly from Scripture, primarily from the New Testament as the witness of the early church uncorrupted by the Platonic-Aristotelian metaphysic, but also secondarily from the Old Testament as the record of the content of revelation made to the religious community of Israel. The truthfulness of the biblical, especially of the New Testament, system of truth, rests, however, not on any theory of inspiration, but on its being an authentic statement of the early church of the doctrine of Christ, inasmuch as to this witness the necessary degree of *fides humana* belongs. Ritschl's Christology rests on the witness of Christ to himself in the synoptists, through which he proclaims himself the one prophet who in the divine purpose of grace for mankind has received perfect consecration, sent by God into the world to represent the founding of the kingdom of God on earth foreshadowed in the Old Testament revelation ; but no attempt is made to explain how Christ became possessed of the secrets of the divine decree. To him, as the first and only begotten Son of God, standing in essential union with the Father, belongs the attribute of deity and the right of worship. But of an eternal pre-existence of Christ we can speak only in so far as this is meant of the eternal gracious purpose of God to redeem the world through him by means of the complete unfolding of the kingdom of God in the fellowship of love. Whatever goes beyond this in the fourth gospel, its Johannine authenticity not being otherwise contested, as well as in Paul's epistles and in the Epistle to the Hebrews, resulted from the necessity felt by their writers for assigning a sufficient reason for the assumption of such incomparable glory on the part of Christ. As the archetype of humanity destined for the kingdom of God, Christ is the original object of the divine love, so that the love of God to the members of his kingdom comes to them only through him. And as the earthly founding, so also the heavenly completion, of the kingdom of God is assigned to Christ, and hence after his resurrection all power was given to him, of the transcendent exercise of which, however, we can know nothing. The universality of human sin is admitted by Ritschl as a fact of experience, but he despairs of reaching any dogmatic statement as to the origin of sin through the temptation of a superhuman evil power. But that sin is inherited and as original guilt is under the condemnation of God, is not taught or pre-supposed by the teaching either of Christ or of the apostles. Redemption (reconciliation and justification) consists in the forgiveness of sins, by which the guilt that estranges from God is removed and the sinner is restored into the fellowship of the kingdom of God. Forgiveness, however, is not given on condition of the vicarious penal sufferings of Christ, whose sufferings and death are of significance rather because his life and works were a complete fulfilment of his calling, and witnessed to as such by God's raising him from the dead. Justification secures the reception of the penitent sinner into the fellowship of the kingdom of God, preached and perfectly developed by Christ, and the sonship enjoyed in its membership, prefigured in Christ himself, which contains in itself the desire as well as the capacity to do good works out of love to God.—The school of Ritschl is represented in Göttingen by its founder and by Schultz and Wendt, in Marburg by Herrmann, in Bonn by Bender, in Giessen by Gottschick and Katten-busch, in Strassburg by Lobstein, in Basel by Kaftan, formerly of Berlin.[1]

21. Opponents and critics of the school of Ritschl, especially from the confessional Lutheran ranks, have appeared in considerable numbers. Luthardt of Leipzig in A.D. 1878 opened the campaign against Ritschilianism, followed by Bestmann, charging it with undermining Christianity. The Hanoverian synod of A.D. 1882 decided by a large majority that the scientific results of theological science must be ruled by the confessions of the evangelical church. The chief theme at the following Hanoverian Pentecost Conference was the "Incarnation of the Son of God," the discussion being led by Professor Dieckhoff of Rostock, against whom no voice was raised in favour of the views of Ritschl. Not long after, Professor Fricke of Leipzig published a lecture given by him at the Meissen Conference, on the Present Relations of Metaphysics and Theology, followed by utterances of Kübel of Tübingen, Grau of Königsberg, Kreibig and H. Schmidt at Berlin, all unfavourable to Ritschl's theology.—The main objections are, according to Bestmann: idolatry of Kant, depreciation of the religious factor in Christianity in favour of the ethical by laying out a moral foreground without providing a dogmatic background, reducing the objective fundamental truths of the confession into subjective ethical ideas, etc.;

---

[1] Galloway, "The Theology of Ritschl," in *Presbyterian Review* for April, 1889, pp. 192-209.

according to Luthardt: Ritschl's position that it does not matter so much what the facts of the Christian faith are in themselves, as what they mean for us, makes his whole dogmatic system hang in the air, if in Christianity we have to do not with what God, Christ, the resurrection are, but only what significance we attach to them, Christianity is stript of all importance, the significance of a thing must have its foundation in the thing itself, etc.; according to Dieckhoff: Ritschl on his accepting the divinity of Christ lays down the rule that the special content of what is meant by the term divinity must be transferable to the believer, and so for Ritschl, Christ is a mere man who in his person was the first to represent a relation to God which is destined for all men in like measure, etc.; according to Fricke: new Kantian scepticism with regard to ideals and transcendentals, reducing religious elements to moral, with Ritschl's removal of all metaphysical facts the chief verities of our Christian faith are taken away, at least in the scientific form in which we have them, *e.g.* the doctrine of the Trinity, our Christology, our theory of satisfaction, in place of which comes the Catholic *justitia infusa*, etc.; according to Münchmayer: "the object of justification with Ritschl is not the individual but the community, it is no act of God upon the individual but an eternal purpose of God for the community, its effect on the individual is not objective divine forgiveness of guilt but a subjective act of incorporation of the individual into the redeemed community; Christ and his work are not the ground of justification, but only the means of revealing the eternal justifying will of God, and therefore finally a continuation of the historical work of Christ by means of his church takes the place of the personal intercession of the exalted Redeemer for the penitent sinner." Kreibig and Schmidt express themselves in a similar manner.—Ritschl has not himself undertaken any reply, but his disciples have sought to remove what they regard as misunderstandings, and generally to vindicate the system of their master.

22. **Writers on Constitutional Law and History.**—The most distinguished writers on the constitutional law of the church are Eichhorn and Dove of Göttingen, Jacobsen of Königsberg, Wasserschleben of Giessen, Richter and Hinschius of Berlin, Friedberg of Leipzig, who belong to the unionist party; while Bickell of Marburg, Mejer of Göttingen and Hanover, Von Scheuerl of Erlangen, and Sohm of Strassburg belong to the confessional Lutherans.—Of ecclesiastical historians (§ 5, 4, 5) the number is so great that we cannot even enumerate their names.—The "*Theologische Literaturzeitung*" of Schürer and Harnack is a liberal scientific journal, distinguished for its fair criticisms by writers whose names are given.

§ 183. HOME MISSIONS.

In regard to home mission work, the Protestant church long lagged behind the Catholic, which had wrought vigorously through its monkish orders. England first entered with zeal into the field, especially dissenters and members of the low church party, and subsequently also the high church ritualistic party (§ 202, 1, 3), which now takes an active interest in this work. Germany, in view of the scanty means at the disposal of the pietists and the church party, made noble efforts. In other continental countries, but especially in North America, much was done for home missions. Soon the whole Protestant world began to organize benevolent and evangelistic institutions. The laborious Wichern, in A.D. 1849, went through all Germany to arouse interest in home missions, and started a yearly congress on the subject in Wittenberg. Till his death in A.D. 1881, Wichern continued to direct this congress and further the interests which it represented.

1. Institutions.—The earliest charity school was that founded at Düsselthal by Count Recke-Volmarstein, in A.D. 1816, followed by Zeller's at Beuggen in A.D. 1820. One of the most famous of these institutions was the Rauhe Haus of Wichern, at Horn, near Hamburg, A.D. 1833.[1] Fliedner's Deaconess Institute at Kaiserswerth is the pride of the evangelical church. It has now 190 branches, with 625 sisters, in the four continents. There are many independent institutions modelled upon it in Germany, England, Sweden, Norway, Denmark. Russia, and France. In A.D. 1881 there were in Germany 31, and in the cities of other lands 22, principal deaconess institutions of this German order, with 4,751 sisters and 1,491 fields of labour outside of the institution. The original institute of Kaiserswerth comprises a hospital with 600 patients, a refuge for fallen women and liberated prisoners, an orphanage for girls, a seminary for governesses, and a home for female imbeciles.[2] Löhe founded the deaconess institute of

---

[1] Series of papers in *Good Words* for 1860, pp. 377 ff.

[2] Fleming Stevenson, "The Blue Flag of Kaiserswerth," in *Good Words* for 1861, pp. 121 ff., 143 ff,

Neuendettelsau, on strict Lutheran principles, with hospital, girls' school, and asylum for imbecile children. In France a most successful institution was founded by pastor Bost of Laforce, in A.D. 1848, for foundlings, imbeciles, and epileptics. In England, George Müller, a poor German student of Halle, a pupil of Tholuck, beginning in A.D. 1832, founded at Bristol five richly endowed orphanages after the pattern of that of A. H. Francke, in which thousands of destitute street children have been educated, and for this and other purposes has spent nearly £1,000,000 without ever asking any one for a contribution, acting on the belief that "the God of Elijah still lives." The London City Mission employs 600 missionaries. In New York, since A.D. 1855, about 60,000 street children have been placed, by the Society for Poor Children, in Christian families, and 21 Industrial schools are maintained with 10,000 scholars.—Tract Societies in London, Hamburg, Berlin, etc., send out millions of tracts for Christian instruction and awakening. The Society for North Germany successfully pursues a similar work ; the Calw Publication Society circulates Christian textbooks with woodcuts at a remarkably small price. In Berlin the Evangelical Book Society issues reprints of the older tracts on practical divinity. Christian women, like the English Quakeress Elizabeth Fry, the noble Amalie Sieveking of Hamburg, Miss Florence Nightingale, the heroine of the Crimean war, and the brave Maria Simon of Dresden, who organized the female nursing corps of the wars of 1866, 1870, 1871, helped on the work of home missions in all lands, especially in the departments of tending the poor and the sick.

2. The Order of St. John, secularized in A.D. 1810, was reorganized by Frederick William IV. in A.D. 1852 into an association for the care of the sick and poor. Under a grand-master it has 350 members and 1,500 associates. Its revenues are formed from entrance fees and annual contributions. It has thirty hospitals. In A.D. 1861 it founded a hospital for men in Beyrout during the persecution of Christians in Syria, and in A.D. 1868 gave aid during the famine that followed the typhus epidemic in East Prussia, and did noble service in the wars of A.D. 1864, 1866, and 1870.

3. The Itinerant Preacher Gustav Werner in Württemberg.—Abandoning his charge in A.D. 1840, Werner began his itinerant labours, and during the year formed more than a hundred groups of adherents over all Württemberg. His preaching was allegorical and eschatological, and avoided the doctrines of satisfaction and justification. On his repudiating the Augsburg Confession, the church boards refused to recognise him, and he went hither and thither preaching a Christian communism. In A.D. 1842 he bought a site in Reutlingen, built a house, and founded a school for eighty children. In order to develop his views of carrying on industrial arts on a Christian basis,

he bought, in A.D. 1850, the paper factory at Reutlingen for £4,000, and subsequently transferred it to Dettingen on a larger scale, at an outlay of £20,000. By A.D. 1862 he had established no less than twenty-two branches, in which manufacturing was carried on, with institutions of all kinds for education, pastoral work, rescuing the lost and raising the fallen. Each member lives and works for the whole; none receives wages; surplus income goes to increase the number and extent of the institutions. Vast multitudes of sunken and destitute families have been by these means restored to respectable social positions and to a moral religious life.

4. Bible Societies.—The Bible societies constitute an independent branch of the home mission. Modern efforts to circulate Scripture began in England. As a necessary adjunct to missionary societies, the great British and Foreign Bible Society was founded in London in A.D. 1804, embracing all Protestant sects, excepting the Quakers. It circulates Bibles without note or comment. The Apocryphal controversy of A.D. 1825–1827 resulted in the society resolving not to print the Apocrypha in its issues. In consequence of this decision, fifty German societies, including the present society of Berlin, seceded. The New York Association, founded in A.D. 1817, is in thorough accord with the London society. The Baden Missionary Society revived the discussion in A.D. 1852 by making it the subject of essay for a prize, which was won by the learned work of Keerl, who, along with the stricter Lutherans, condemned the Apocrypha. The other side was taken by Stier and Hengstenberg, and most of the consistories advised adherence to the old practice, as all misunderstanding was prevented by Luther's preface and the prohibition against using passages from the Apocrypha as sermon texts.—Bible societies altogether have issued during the century 180,000,000 Bibles and New Testaments in 324 different languages.[1]

§ 184. Foreign Missions.

Protestant zeal for missions to the heathen has gone on advancing since the end of last century (§ 172, 5). Missionary societies increase from year to year. In A.D. 1883 there were seventy independent societies with innumerable branches, which contribute annually about £1,500,000, or five times as much as the Romish church, and maintain

---

[1] Owen, "History of the First Ten Years of the Bible Society." 8 vols. London, 1816.

2,000 mission stations, 2,940 European and American missionaries, and 1,000 ordained native pastors and 25,000 native teachers and assistants, having under their care 2,214,000 converts from heathenism. In missionary enterprise England holds the first place, next comes America, and then Germany. Among Protestant sects the Methodists and Baptists are most zealous in the cause of missions, and the Moravian Brethren have wrought most successfully in this department. The missions also did much to prepare the way for the suppression of the slave trade by the European powers in A.D. 1830, and the emancipation of all slaves in the British possessions in A.D. 1834, at a cost of £20,000,000. The noble English philanthropist, William Wilberforce, unweariedly laboured for these ends.—Also in England, Germany, Russia, and France new associations were formed for missions to the Jews, and the work was carried on with admirable patience, though the visible results were very small.

1. Missionary Societies.—The great American Missionary Society was founded at Boston in A.D. 1810, the English Wesleyan in A.D. 1814, the American Methodist in A.D. 1819, the American Episcopal in A.D. 1820, and the Society of Paris in A.D. 1824. The new German societies were on confessional lines: that of Basel in A.D. 1816, of Berlin in A.D. 1823, the Rhenish with the mission seminary at Barmen in A.D 1829, the North German, on the basis of the Augsburg Confession, in A.D. 1836. The Dresden Society, which resumed the old Lutheran work in the East Indies (§ 167, 9), founded a seminary at Leipzig in A.D. 1849, in order to get the benefit of the university. Lutheran societies, mostly affiliated with that of Leipzig, were started in Sweden, Denmark, Norway, Russia, Bavaria, Hanover, Mecklenburg, Hesse, and America. The Neuendettelsau Institute wrought through the Iowa Synod among the North American Indians, and through the Immanuel Synod among the aborigines of Australia. The Hermannsburg institute under Harms prosecuted mission work with great zeal. In A.D. 1853, Harms sent out in his own mission ship eight missionaries and as many Christian colonists. It has been objected to this mission, that endeavours after social elevation and industrial training have driven to the background the main question of individual conversion.

—The advanced liberal school in Switzerland and Germany sought in A.D. 1883 to start a mission on their own particular lines. They do not propose any opposition to existing agencies, and intend to make their first experiment among the civilized races of India and Japan.

2. **Europe and America.**—The Swedish mission in Lapland (§ 160, 7) was resumed in A.D. 1825 by Stockfleth. The Moravians carried on their work among the Eskimos in Greenland, which had now become a wholly Christian country, and also in Labrador, which was almost in the same condition. The chaplain of the Hudson Bay Company, J. West, founded a successful mission in that territory in A.D. 1822 Among the natives and negro slaves in the British possessions, the United States, and West Indies, Moravians, Methodists, Baptists, and Anglican Episcopalians patiently and successfully carried on the work. Among the natives and bush negroes, descendants of runaway slaves, in Guiana, the Moravians did a noble work.—Catholic South America remained closed against Protestant missions. But the ardent zeal of Capt. Allen Gardiner led him to choose the inhospitable shores of Patagonia as a field of labour. He landed there in A.D. 1850 with five missionaries, but in the following year their corpses only were found. The work, however, was started anew in A.D. 1856, and prosecuted with success under the direction of an Anglican bishop.

3. **Africa.**—The Moravians have laboured among the Hottentots, the Berlin missionaries among the wild Corannas, and the French Evangelical Society among the Bechuanas. Hahn of Livonia is the apostle of the Hereros. On the East Coast the London Missionary Society has wrought among the warlike Kaffirs, and other British societies are labouring in Natal among the Zulus. On the West Coast the English colony of Sierra Leone was founded for the settling and Christianizing of liberated slaves, and farther south is Liberia, a similar American colony; both in a flourishing condition, under the care of Methodists, Baptists, and Anglican Episcopalians. The Basel missionaries labour on the Gold Coast, Baptists in Old Calabar, and the American and North German Societies on the Gaboon River.— The London missionaries won Radama of Madagascar to Christianity in A.D. 1818, but his successor Ranavalona instituted a bloody perse- cution of the Christians in A.D. 1835, during which David Jones, the apostle of the Malagassy, suffered martyrdom in A.D. 1843. In the island of Mauritius, where there is an Anglican bishop, many Mala- gassy Christians found refuge. After the queen's death in A.D. 1861, her Christian son Radama II. recalled the Christian exiles and the missionaries. He soon became the victim of a palace revolution. His wife and successor Rosaherina continued a heathen till her death in A.D. 1868, but put no obstacle in the way of the gospel. But her

cousin Ranavalona II. overthrew the idol worship, was baptized in A.D. 1869, and in the following year burned the national idols. Protestantism now made rapid strides, till interrupted by French Jesuit intrigues, which have been favoured by the recent French occupation.

4. Livingstone and Stanley have made marvellous contributions to our geographical knowledge of Central Africa and to Christian missions there. The Scottish missionary, David Livingstone, factory boy, afterwards physician and minister, wrought, A.D. 1840-1849, under the London Missionary Society in South Africa, and then entered on his life work of exploration in Central Africa. During his third exploring journey into the interior in A.D. 1865 as a British consul, he was not heard of for a whole year. H. M. Stanley, of the *New York Herald*, was sent in A.D. 1871, and found him in Ujiji on Lake Tanganyiká. Livingstone died of dysentery on the southern bank of this lake in A.D. 1873. Still more important was Stanley's second journey, A.D. 1874-1877, which yielded the most brilliant scientific results, and was epoch-making in the history of African missions. He got the greatest potentate in those regions, King Mtesa of Uganda, who had been converted by the Arabs to Mohammedanism, to adopt Christianity and permit a Christian church to be built in his city. Stanley's letters from Africa roused missionary fervour throughout England. The Church Missionary Society in A.D. 1877 set up a mission station in the capital, and put a steamer on the Victoria Nyanza. The church services were regularly attended, education and the work of civilization zealously prosecuted, Sunday labour and the slave trade prohibited, etc. French Jesuits entered in A.D. 1879, insinuating suspicions of the English missionaries into the ear of the king, and the machinations of the Arab slave-dealers made their position dangerous. Missionaries arrived by way of Egypt with flattering recommendations from the English foreign secretary in the name of the queen. But the traders, by means of an Arabic translation of a letter purporting to be from the English consul at Zanzibar, cast suspicion on the document as a forgery, and represented its bearers as in the pay of the hostile Egyptians. Mtesa's wrath knew no bounds, and only his favour for the missionary physician saved the mission and led him to send an embassy of three chiefs and two missionaries to England in June, A.D. 1879, to discover the actual truth. His anger meanwhile cooled, and the work of the mission was resumed. He was preparing to put an utter end to the national heathenism, when suddenly a report spread that the greatest of all the Lubaris or inferior deities, that of the Nyanza Lake, had become incarnate in an old woman, in order to heal the king and restore the ancient religion. The whole populace was in an uproar;

Mtesa, under threat of deposition, restored heathenism, with human sacrifice, man stealing, and the slave trade. Then the Lubari excitement cooled down. Mtesa, moved by a dream, declared himself again a Mohammedan, and converted the Christian church into a mosque. The English missionaries, stripped of all means, starved, and subjected to all sorts of privations, did not flinch. At last, in January, A.D. 1881, the embassy, sent eighteen months before to England, reached home again, and, by the story of their reception, caused a revulsion of feeling in favour of the English mission, which again flourished under the protection of the king. But Mtesa died in 1884. His son and successor, Mwanga, a suspicious, peevish young despot, addicted to all forms of vice, began again the most cruel persecution, of which Bishop Hannington, sent out from England, with fifty companions, were the victims. Only four escaped.

5. Asia.—The most important mission field in Asia is India. The old Lutheran mission there had great difficulties to contend against: the system of caste distinctions, the proud self-sufficiency of the pantheistic Brahmans, the politico-commercial interests of the East India Company, etc. The Leipzig Society has sixteen stations among the Tamuls, and alongside are English, American, and German missionaries of every school. The Gossner Society works among the Kohls of Chota Nagpore, where a rival mission has been started by the puseyite bishop of Calcutta, Dr. Milman, to which, in A.D. 1868, six of the twelve German missionaries and twelve of the thirty-six chapels were transferred. The Basel missionaries labour in Canara and Malabar. The military revolt in Northern India in A.D. 1857 interrupted missionary operations for two years; but the work was afterwards resumed with great vigour. The Christian benevolence shown during the famine of A.D. 1878, in which three millions perished, made a great impression in favour of the Protestant church. In the preceding years throughout all India only between 5,000 and 10,000 souls were annually added; but in A.D. 1878 the number of new converts rose to 100,000, and in A.D. 1879 there were 44,000.—The island of Ceylon was, under Portuguese and Dutch rule, in great part nominally Christianized; but when compulsion was removed under British rule, this sham profession was at an end. Multitudes fell back into heathenism, and in the first ten years of the British dominion 900 new idol temples were erected. From A.D. 1812 Baptist, Methodist, and Anglican missionaries have toiled with small appearance of fruit. In Farther India the American missionaries have wrought since A.D. 1813. Judson and his heroic wife did noble work among the Karens and the Burmans. Also in Malacca, Singapore, and Siam the Protestant missions have had brilliant success. The work in Sumatra has been retarded by the opposition of the Malays

and deadly malarial fever. The preaching of the gospel was eminently successful in Java, where since A.D. 1814 Baptist missionaries and agents of the London Society have wrought heroically. In Celebes the Dutch missionaries found twenty Christian congregations of old standing, greatly deteriorated for want of pastoral care, but still using the Heidelberg Catechism. At Banjermassin, in A.D. 1835 the Rhenish Society founded their first station in Borneo. and wrought not unsuccessfully among the heathen Dyaks. But in A.D. 1859 a rebellion of the Mohammedan residents led to the expulsion of the Dutch and the murder of all Christians. Only a few of the missionaries escaped martyrdom, and subsequently settled in Sumatra.

6. The work in China began in A.D. 1807, when the London Missionary Society settled Morrison in Canton, where he began the study of the language and the translation of the Bible. Gutzlaff of Pomerania, in A.D. 1826, conceived the plan of evangelizing China through the Chinese converts, but, though he continued his efforts till his death in A.D. 1854, the scheme failed through the unworthiness of many of the professors. The war against the opium traffic, A.D. 1839–1842, opened five ports to the mission, and led to the transference of Hongkong to the English. The Chinese mission now made rapid strides; but the interior was still untouched. The conflict between the governor of Canton and the English, French, and Americans, and the chastisement administered to the Chinese in A.D. 1857, led the emperor, in A.D. 1858, to make a treaty with the three powers and also with Russia, by which the whole land was opened up for trade and missions, and full toleration granted to Christianity. Popular hatred of strangers, and especially of missionaries, however, occasioned frequently bloody encounters, and in A.D. 1870 there was a furious outburst directed against the French missionaries. During a terrible famine in North China, in A.D. 1878, when more than five millions perished, the heroic and self-sacrificing conduct of the missionaries brought them into high favour. Throughout China there are now 320 organized Christian congregations with 50,000 adherents under 238 foreign missionaries.—After seclusion for three centuries, Japan, about the same time as China, was opened by treaty to European and American commerce, notwithstanding the opposition of the old feudal nobility, the so-called Daimios. In A.D. 1871 the mikado's government succeeded in overcoming completely the power of the daimios and setting aside the shiogun or military vizier, who had exercised supreme executive power. European customs were introduced, but the rigorous enactments against native converts to Christianity were still enforced. A cruel persecution of native Christians was carried on in A.D. 1867, but the Protestant missionaries continued to work unweariedly, preparing dictionaries and reading books. The Buddhist

priests sought to get up a rival mission to send agents to America and Europe, whereas many of the leading newspapers expressed the opinion that Japan must soon put Christianity in the place of Buddhism as the state religion.

7. **Polynesia and Australia.**—The flourishing Protestant church of Tahiti, the largest and finest of the Society Islands (§ 172, 5), suffered from the appearance of two French Jesuits in A.D. 1836. When Queen Pomare compelled them to withdraw, the French government, resenting this as an indignity to their nation, sent a fleet to attack the defenceless people, proclaimed a French protectorate, and introduced not only Catholic missionaries, but European vices. Amid much persecution, however, the Protestants held their own. In December, 1880, Pomare V. resigned, and the Society Islands became a dependency of France.—In the south-east groups great opposition was shown, but in the north-west Christianity made rapid progress. The island of Raiatea was the centre of the South Sea missions. There from A.D. 1819 John Williams, the apostle of the South Seas, wrought till he met a martyr's death in A.D. 1839. He went from place to place in a mission ship built by his own hands. The Harvey Group were Christianized in A.D. 1821, and the Navigator Group in A.D. 1830. The French took the Marquesas Islands in A.D. 1838, and introduced Catholic missionaries. The attempt to evangelize the New Hebrides led to the death of Williams and two of his companions. Missionaries of the London Society, A.D. 1797–1799, had failed in the Friendly Islands through the savage character of the natives, but in A.D. 1822 the Methodists made a successful start. The gospel was carried thence to Fiji, which is now under British rule. Both groups have become almost wholly Christianized. The Sandwich Islands form a third mission centre, wrought by the American board. Kamehameha I. gladly adopted the elements of Christian civilization, though rejecting Christianity : while his successor Kamehameha II. in A.D. 1829 abolished tabu and overthrew the idol temples. In A.D. 1851 Christianity was adopted as the national religion. The work was more difficult in New Zealand, where the Church Missionary Society, represented by Samuel Marsden, the apostle of New Zealand, began operations in A.D. 1814. For ten years the position of the missionaries was most hazardous; yet they held on, and the conversion of the most bloodthirsty of the chiefs did much to advance their cause. In New Guinea the London Society has been making steady progress. Among the stolid natives of the continent of New Holland, the so called Papuans, the labours of the Moravians since A.D. 1849 have not yielded much fruit. Since A.D. 1875 the German-Australian Immanuel Synod, supported by Neuendettelsau, has laboured for the conversion of the heathen in the inland districts.

8. Missions to the Jews.—In A.D. 1809 the London Society for Promoting Christianity among the Jews (§ 172, 5) was formed by a union of all denominations, but soon passed into the hands of the Anglicans. By the circulation of the Scriptures and tracts, and by the sending out of missionaries, mostly Jewish converts, the work was persevered in amid many discouragements. In A.D. 1818 Poland was opened to its missionaries, and there some 600 Jews were baptized. The society carried on its operations also in Germany, Holland, France, and Turkey. The work in Poland was interrupted by the Crimean war, and was not resumed till A.D. 1875. In Bessarabia Faltin has laboured successfully among the Jews since A.D. 1860. He was joined in the work in A.D. 1867 by the converted Rabbi Gurland, who had studied theology at Halle and Berlin. In A.D. 1871 Gurland accepted a call to similar work in Courland and Lithuania, and since A.D. 1876 has been Lutheran pastor at Mitau. In A.D. 1841 the evangelical bishopric of St. James was founded in Jerusalem by the English and Prussian governments conjointly, presentations to be made alternately, but the ordination to be according to the Anglican rite. The first bishop was Alexander, a Jewish convert. He died in A.D. 1845 and was succeeded by the zealous missionary Gobat, elected by the Prussian government. He died in A.D. 1879 and was succeeded by Barclay, who died in A.D. 1881. It was now again Prussia's turn to make an appointment. The English demand to have Lutheran ministers ordained successively deacon, presbyter, and bishop had given offence, and so no new appointment has been made. In June 1886 the English-Prussian compact was formally cancelled and a proposal made to found an independent Prussian Evangelical bishopric.

9. Missions among the Eastern Churches.—In A.D. 1815 the Church Missionary Society founded a missionary emporium in the island of Malta, as a tract depôt for the evangelizing the East; and in A.D. 1846 the Malta Protestant College was erected for training native missionaries, teachers, physicians, etc., for work in the various oriental countries. In the Ionian islands, in Constantinople, and in Greece, British and American missionaries began operations in A.D. 1819 by erecting schools and circulating the scriptures. At first the orthodox clergy were favourable, but as the work progressed they became actively hostile, and only two mission schools in Syra and Athens were allowed to continue. In Syria the Americans made Beyrout their head quarters in A.D. 1824, but the work was interrupted by the Turco-Egyptian conflicts. Subsequently, however, it flourished more and more, and, before the Syrian massacre of A.D. 1860 (§ 207, 2), there were nine prosperous stations in Syria. The founding of the Jerusalem bishopric in A.D. 1841, and the issuing of the Hatti-Humayun in A.D. 1856 (§ 207, 2), induced the Church Missionary Society to make more vigorous efforts which, however, were afterwards abandoned for want of success. Down to the outbreak of the persecution of Syrian Christians in A.D. 1860, this society had five flourishing stations. From A.D. 1831 the Americans had wrought zealously and successfully among the Armenians in Constantinople and neighbourhood, but in A.D. 1845 the Armenian patriarch excited a violent persecution which threatened the utter overthrow of the work. The British ambassador, Sir Stratford de Redcliffe, however, insisted upon the Porte recognising the rights of the Protestant Armenians as an independent religious denomination, and since then the missions have prospered. Among the Nestorians in Turkey and Persia the Americans, with Dr. Grant at their head, began operations in A.D. 1834; but through Jesuit intrigues the suspicions of the Kurds and Turks were excited, and in A.D. 1843 and 1846 a war of extirmination was waged against the mountain Nestorians, which annihilated the Protestant missions among them. Operations, however, have been recommenced with encouraging success. Among the deeply degraded Copts in Egypt, and extending from them into Abyssinia, the Moravians had been working without any apparent result from A.D. 1752 to A.D. 1783. In A.D. 1826 the Church Missionary Society, under German missionaries trained at Basel (Gobat, Irenberg, Krapf, etc.), took up the work, till it was stopped by the government in A.D. 1837. In A.D. 1855 the Basel missionaries began again to work in Abyssinia with the approval of king Theodore. This state of things soon changed. Theodore's ambition was to conquer Egypt and overthrow Islam. But when in A.D. 1863 this scheme only called forth threats from London and Paris. he gave loose rein to his natural ferocity and put the English consul and the German missionaries in chains. By means of an armed expedition in A.D. 1868, England compelled the liberation of the prisoners, and Theodore put an end to his own life. After the withdrawal of the English the country was desolated by civil wars, and at the close of these troubles in A.D. 1878 the mission resumed its operations.

III.—Catholicism in General.

§ 185. THE PAPACY AND THE STATES OF THE CHURCH.

The papacy, humiliated but not destroyed by Napoleon I., was in A.D. 1814 by the aid of princes of all creeds restored to the full possession of its temporal and spiritual authority, and amid many difficulties it reasserted for the most part successfully its hierarchical claims in the Catholic states and in those whose Protestantism and Catholicism were alike tolerated. Many severe blows indeed were dealt to the papacy even in the Roman states by revolutionary movements, yet political reaction generally by-and-by put the church in a position as good if not better than it had before. But while on this side the Alps, especially since the outbreak of A.D. 1848, ultramontanism gained one victory after another in its own domain, in Italy, it suffered one humiliation after another; and while the Vatican Council, which put the crown upon its idolatrous assumptions (§ 189, 3), was still sitting, the whole pride of its temporal sovereignty was shattered: the States of the Church were struck out of the number of the European powers, and Rome became the capital and residence of the prince of Sardinia as king of United Italy. But reverence for the pope now reached a height among catholic nations which it had never anywhere attained before.

1. The First Four Popes of the Century.—Napoleon as First Consul of the French Republic, in A.D. 1801 concluded a concordat with Pius VII., A.D. 1800–1823, who under Austrian protection was elected pope at Venice, whereby the pope was restored to his temporal and spiritual rights, but was obliged to abandon his hierarchical claims over the church of France (§ 203, 1). He crowned the consul emperor of the French at Paris in A.D. 1804, but when he persisted in the assertion of his hierarchical principles, Napoleon in A.D. 1808 entered the papal territories, and in May, A.D. 1809, formally repudiated the donation of "his predecessor" Charlemagne. The pope treated the offered payment of two million francs as an insult, threatened the emperor with the ban, and in July, A.D. 1809, was imprisoned at Savona, and in A.D. 1812 was taken to Fontainebleau. He refused for a time to give canonical institution to the bishops nominated by the emperor, and though at last he yielded and agreed to reside in France, he soon withdrew his concession, and the complications of A.D. 1813 constrained the emperor, on February 14th, to set free the pope and the Papal States. In May the pope again entered Rome. One of his first official acts was the restoration of the Jesuits by the bull *Sollicitudo omnium*, as by the unanimous request of all Christendom. The Congregation of the Index was again set up, and during the course of the year 737 charges of heresy were heard before the tribunal of the holy office. All sales of church property were pronounced void, and 1,800

monasteries and 600 nunneries were reclaimed. In A.D. 1815 the pope formally protested against the decision of the Vienna Congress, especially against the overthrow of the spiritual principalities in the German empire (§ 192, 1). Equally fruitless was his demand for the restoration of Avignon (§ 165, 15). In A.D. 1816 he condemned the Bible societies as a plague to Christendom, and renewed the prohibition of Bible translations. His diplomatic schemes were determined by his able secretary Cardinal Consalvi, who not only at the Vienna Congress, but also subsequently by several concordats secured the fullest possible expression to the interests and claims of the curia. —His successor was Leo XII., A.D. 1823–1829, who, more strict in his civil administration than his predecessor, condemned Bible societies, renewed the Inquisition prosecutions, for the sake of gain celebrated the jubilee in A.D. 1825, ordered prayers for uprooting of heresy rebuilt the Ghetto wall of Rome, overturned during the French rule (§ 95, 3), which marked off the Jews' quarter, till Pius IX. again threw it down in A.D. 1846. After the eight months' reign of Pius VIII., A.D. 1829–1830, Gregory XVI., A.D. 1831–1846, ascended the papal throne, and sought amid troubles at home and abroad to exalt to its utmost pitch the hierarchical idea. In A.D. 1832 he issued an encyclical, in which he declared irreconcilable war against modern science as well as against freedom of conscience and the press, and his whole pontificate was a consistent carrying out of this principle. He encountered incessant opposition from liberal and revolutionary movements in his own territory, restrained only by Austrian and French military interference, A.D. 1832–1838, and from the rejection of his hierarchical schemes by Spain, Portugal, Prussia, and Russia.[1]

2. Pius IX., A.D. 1846-1878.—Count Mastai Feretti in his fifty-fourth year succeeded Gregory on 16th June, and took the name of Pius IX. While in ecclesiastical matters he seemed willing to hold by the old paths and distinctly declared against Bible societies, he favoured reform in civil administration and encouraged the hopes of the liberals who longed for the independence and unity of Italy. But this only awakened the thunder storm which soon burst upon his own head. The far resounding cry of the jubilee days, "*Evviva Pio Nono!*" ended in the pope's flight to Gaeta in November, 1848; and in February, 1849, the Roman Republic was proclaimed. The French Republic, however, owing to the threatening attitude of Austria, hastened to take Rome and restore the temporal power of the pope. Amid the convulsions of Italy, Pius could not return to Rome till

---

[1] Wiseman, "Recollections of the Last Four Popes." 3 vols. London, 1858. Mendham, "Index of Prohibited Books by order of Gregory XVI." London, 1840

April, 1850, where he was maintained by French and Austrian bayonets. Abandoning his liberal views, the pope now put himself more and more under the influence of the Jesuits, and his absolutist and reactionary politics were directed by Card. Antonelli. From his exile at Gaeta he had asked the opinion of the bishops of the whole church regarding the immaculate conception of the blessed Virgin, to whose protection he believed that he owed his safety. The opinions of 576 were favourable, resting on Bible proofs: Genesis iii. 15, Song of Sol. iv. ., ·2, and Luke i. 28; but some French and German bishops were strongly opposed. The question was now submitted for further consideration to various congregations, and finally the consenting bishops were invited to Rome to settle the terms of the doctrinal definition of the new dogma. After four secret sessions it was acknowledged by acclamation, and on 8th December, 1854 (§ 104, 7), the pope read in the Sixtine chapel the bull *Ineffabilis* and placed a brilliant diadem on the head of the image of the queen of heaven. The disciples of St. Thomas listened in silence to this aspersion of their master's orthodoxy; no heed was paid to two isolated individual voices that protested; the bishops of all Catholic lands proclaimed the new dogma, the theologians vindicated it, and the spectacle-loving people rejoiced in the pompous Mary-festival. The pope's next great performance was the encyclical, *Quanta cura*, of December 8th, 1864, and the accompanying syllabus cataloguing in eighty-four propositions all the errors of the day, by which not only the antichristian and anti-ecclesiastical tendencies, but also claims for freedom of belief and worship, liberty of the press and science, the state's independence of the church, the equality of the laity and clergy in civil matters, in short all the principles of modern political and social life, were condemned as heretical. Three years later the centenary of Peter (§ 16, 1) brought five hundred bishops to Rome, with other clergy and laymen from all lands. The enthusiasm for the papal chair was such that the pope was encouraged to convoke an œcumenical council. The jubilee of his consecration as priest in A.D. 1869 brought him congratulatory addresses signed by one and a half millions, filled the papal coffers, attracted an immense number of visitors to Rome, and secured to all the votaries gathered there a complete indulgence. On the Vatican Council which met during that same year, see § 189.[1]

3. The Overthrow of the Papal States.—In the Peace of Villafranca of 1859, which put an end to the short Austro-French war in Italy, a confederation was arranged of all the Italian princes under the

---

[1] Legge, "Pius IX. to the Restoration of 1850." 2 vols. London, 1872. Trollope, "Life of Pius IX." 2 vols. London, 1877. Shea, "Life and Pontificate of Pius IX." New York, 1877.

honorary presidency of the pope for drawing up the future constitution of Italy. During the war the Austrians had vacated Bologna, but the French remained in Rome to protect the pope. The revolution now broke out in Romagna. Victor Emanuel, king of Sardinia, was proclaimed dictator for the time over that part of the Papal States and a provisional government, was set up. In vain did the pope remind Christendom in an encyclical of the necessity of maintaining his temporal power, in vain did he thunder his *excommunicatio major* against all who would contribute to its overthrow. A pamphlet war against the temporal power now began, and About's letters in the *Moniteur* described with bitter scorn the incapacity of the papal government. In his pamphlet, "*Le Pope et le Congrès*," Laguéron-nière proposed to restrict the pope's sovereignty to Rome and its neighbourhood, levy a tax for the support of the papal court on all Catholic nations, and leave Rome undisturbed by political troubles. On December 31st, 1859, Napoleon III. exhorted the pope to yield to the logic of facts and to surrender the provinces that refused any longer to be his. The pope then issued a rescript in which he declared that he could never give up what belonged not to him but to the church. The popular vote in Romagna went almost unanimously for annexation to Sardinia, and this, in spite of the papal ban, was done. A revolution broke out in Umbria and the March of Ancona, and Victor Emanuel without more ado attached these states also to his dominion in A.D. 1860, so that only Rome and the Campagna were retained by the pope, and even these only by means of French support. At the September convention of A.D. 1864 Italy undertook to maintain the papal domain intact, to permit the organization of an independent papal army, and to contribute to the papal treasury; while France was to quit Roman territory within at the latest two years. The pope submitted to what he could not prevent, but still insisted upon his most extreme claims, answered every attempt at conciliation with his stereotyped *non possumus*, and in A.D. 1866 proclaimed St. Catherine of Siena (§ 112, 4) patron of the "city." When the last of the French troops took ship in A.D. 1866 the radical party thought the time had come for freeing Italy from papal rule, and roused the whole land by public proclamation. Garibaldi again put himself at the head of the movement. The Papal State was soon encircled by bands of volunteers, and insurrections broke out even within Rome itself. Napoleon pronounced this a breach of the September convention, and in A.D. 1867 the volunteers were utterly routed by the French at Mentana. The French guarded Civita Vecchia and fortified Rome. But in August, 1870, their own national exigencies demanded the withdrawal of the French troops, and after the battle of Sedan the Italians to a man insisted on having Rome as their capital, and Victor Emanuel acquiesced. The pope sought help far and near from Catholic and non-Catholic powers, but he received only the echo of his own words, *non possumus.* After a four hours' cannonade a breach was made in the walls of the eternal city, the white flag appeared on St. Angelo, and amid the shouts of the populace the Italian troops entered on September 20th, 1870. A plebiscite in the papal dominions gave 133,681 votes in favour of annexation and 1,507 against; in Rome alone there were 40,785 for and only 46 against. The king now issued the decree of incorporation; Rome became capital of united Italy and the Quirinal the royal residence.

4. The Prisoner of the Vatican, A.D. 1870-1878.—The dethroned papal king could only protest and utter denunciations. No result followed from the adoption of St. Joseph as guardian and patron of the church, nor from the solemn consecration of the whole world to the most sacred heart of Jesus, at the jubilee of June 16th, A.D. 1875. The measures of A.D. 1871, by which Cavour sought to realize his ideal of a "free church in a free state," were pronounced absurd, cunning, deceitful, and an outrage on the apostles Peter and Paul. By these measures the rights and privileges of a sovereign for all time had been conferred on the pope: the holiness and inviolability of his person, a body-guard, a post and telegraph bureau, free ambassadorial communication with foreign powers, the *ex-territoriality* of his palace of the Vatican, embracing fifteen large saloons, 11,500 rooms, 236 stairs, 218 corridors, two chapels, several museums, archives, libraries, large beautiful gardens, etc., as also of the Lateran and the summer palace of Castle Gandolpho, with all appurtenances, also an annual income, free from all burdens and taxes, of three and a quarter million francs, equal to the former amount of his revenue, together with unrestricted liberty in the exercise of all ecclesiastical rights of sovereignty and primacy, and the renunciation of all state interference in the disposal of bishoprics and benefices. The right of the inferior clergy to exercise the *appellatio ab abusu* to a civil tribunal was set aside, and of all civil rights only that of the royal *exequatur* in the election of bishops, *i.e.* the mere right of investing the nominee of the curia in the possession of the revenues of his office, was retained.—To the end of his life Pius every year returned the dotation as an insult and injury, and "the starving holy father in prison, who has not where to lay his head," received three or four times more in Peter's pence contributed by all Catholic Christendom. Playing the *rôle* of a prisoner he never passed beyond the precincts of the Vatican. He reached the semi-jubilee of his papal coronation in A.D. 1871, being the first pope who falsified the old saying, *Annos Petri non videbit.* He rejected the offer of a golden throne and the title of "the great," but he accepted a Parisian lady's gift of a golden crown of thorns. In support of the

prison myth, straws from the papal cell were sold in Belgium for half a franc per stalk, and for the same price photographs of the pope behind an iron grating. As once on a time the legend arose about the disciple whom Jesus loved that he would not die, so was it once said about the pope; and on his eighty-third birthday, in A.D. 1874, a Roman Jesuit paper, eulogising the moral purity of his life, put the words in his mouth, "Which of you convinceth me of sin?" But he himself by constantly renewed rescripts, encyclicals, briefs, allocutions to the cardinals and to numerous deputations from far and near, unweariedly fanned the flame of enthusiasm and fanaticism throughout papal Christendom, and thundered threatening prophecies not only against the Italian, but also against foreign states, for with most of them he lived in open war. A collection of his "Speeches delivered at the Vatican" was published in 1874, commented on by Gladstone in the *Contemporary Review* for January, 1875, who gives abundant quotations showing papal assumptions, maledictions, abuse and mis-understanding of the Scriptures with which they abound. On the fiftieth anniversary of the pope's episcopal consecration, in June 1877, crowds from all lands assembled to offer their congratulations, with costly presents and Peter's pence amounting to sixteen and a half million francs. He died February 8th, 1878, in the eighty-sixth year of his age and thirty-second of his pontificate. His heirs claimed the unpaid dotations of twenty million lire, but were refused by the courts of law.[1]—His secretary Antonelli, descended from an old brigand family, who from the time of his stay at Gaeta was his evil demon, predeceased him in A.D. 1876. Though the son of a poor herdsman and woodcutter, he left more than a hundred million lire. His natural daughter, to the great annoyance of the Vatican, sought, but without success, in the courts of justice to make good her claims against her father's greedy brothers.

5. Leo XIII.—After only two days' conclave the Cardinal-archbishop of Perugia, Joachim Pecci, born in A.D. 1810, was proclaimed on February 20th, 1878, as Leo XIII. In autograph letters he intimated his accession to the German and Russian emperors, but not to the king of Italy, and expressed his wish for a good mutual understanding. To the government of the Swiss Cantons he declared his hope that their ancient friendly relations might be restored. At Easter, 1878, he issued an encyclical to all patriarchs, primates, archbishops, and bishops, in which he required of them that they should earnestly entreat the mediation of the "immaculate queen of heaven" and the intercession of St. Joseph, "the heavenly shield of the church," and

---

[1] Geffcken, "Church and State," vol. ii., pp. 269-293: "The Italian Question and the Papal States."

also failed not to make prominent the infallibility of the apostolic
chair, and to condemn all the errors condemned by his predecessors,
emphasizing the necessity of restoring the temporal power of the pope,
and confirming and renewing all the protests of his predecessor Pius
IX., of sacred memory, against the overthrow of the Papal States.
On the first anniversary of his elevation he proclaimed a universal
jubilee, with the promise of a complete indulgence. He still persisted
in the prison myth of his predecessor, and like him sent back the
profferred contribution of his "jailor." In the conflicts with foreign
powers inherited from Pius, as well as in his own, he has employed
generally moderate and conciliatory language.—He has not hesitated
to take the first step toward a good understanding with his opponents,
for which, while persistently maintaining the ancient principles of
the papal chair, he makes certain concessions in regard to subordinate matters, always with the design and expectation of seeing
them outweighed on the other side by the conservation of all the
other hierarchical pretensions of the curial system. It was, however,
only in the middle of A.D. 1885 that it became evident that the pope
had determined, without allowing any misunderstanding to arise
between himself and his cardinals, to break through the trammels
of the irreconcilable zealots in the college. And indeed after the
conclusion of the German *Kulturkampf* (§ 197, 13, 15), brought about
by these means, in an allocution with reference thereto addressed to
the cardinals in May, 1887, he gave an unexpected expression to his
wish and longing in regard to an understanding with the government
on the Italian question, which involved an utter renunciation of his
predecessor's dogged *Non possumus*, the attitude hitherto unfalteringly
maintained. "Would that peaceful counsels," says he, "embracing all
our peoples should prevail in Italy also, and that at last once that
unhappy difference might be overcome without loss of privilege to the
holy see!" Such harmony, indeed, is only possible when the pope "is
subjected to no authority and enjoys perfect freedom," which would
cause no loss to Italy, "but would only secure its lasting peace and
safety." That he counts upon the good offices of the German emperor
for the effecting of this longed-for restoration of such a *modus vivendi*
with the Italian government, he has clearly indicated in his preliminary communications to the Prussian centre exhorting to peace
(§ 197, 14). The *Moniteur de Rome* (§ 188, 1), however, interpreted
the words of the pope thus: "Italy would lose nothing materially or
politically, if it gave a small corner of its territory to the pope, where
he might enjoy actual sovereignty as a guarantee of his spiritual
independence."—On Leo's contributions to theological science see
§ 191, 12; on his attitude to Protestantism and the Eastern Church,
see § 175, 2, 4. He expressed himself against the freemasons in an

encyclical of A.D. 1884 with even greater severity than Pius. Consequently the Roman Inquisition issued an instruction to all bishops throughout the Catholic world requiring them to enjoin their clergy in the pulpit and the confessional to make it known that all freemasons are *eo ipso* excommunicated, and by Catholic associations of every sort, especially by the spread of the third order of St. Francis (§ 186, 2), the injunction was carried out. At the same time a year's reprieve was given to the freemasons, during which the Roman heresy laws, which required their children, wives, and relatives to denounce them to all clergy and laymen, were to be suspended. Should the guilty, however, allow this day of grace to pass, these laws were to be again fully enforced, and then it would be only for the pope to absolve them from their terrible sin.

§ 186. VARIOUS ORDERS AND ASSOCIATIONS.

The order of the Jesuits restored in A.D. 1814 by Pius VII. impregnated all other orders with its spirit, gained commanding influence over Pius IX., made the bishops its agents, and turned the whole Catholic church into a Jesuit institution. An immense number of societies arose aiming at the accomplishment of home mission work, inspired by the Jesuit spirit and carrying out unquestioningly the ultramontane ideas of their leaders. Also zeal for foreign missions on old Jesuit lines revived, and the enthusiasm for martyrdom was due mainly to the same cause.

1. **The Society of Jesus and Related Orders.**—After the suppression of their order by Clement XIV. the Jesuits found refuge mainly among the Redemptorists (§ 165, 2), whose headquarters were at Vienna, from which they spread through Austria and Bavaria, finding entrance also into Switzerland, France, Belgium, and Holland, and after 1848 into Catholic Prussia, as well as into Hesse and Nassau. The Congregation of the Sacred Heart was founded by ex-Jesuits in Belgium in A.D. 1794, and soon spread in Austria and Bavaria.—The restored Jesuit order was met with a storm of opposition from the liberals. The July revolution of A.D. 1830 drove the Jesuits from France, and when they sought to re-establish themselves, Gregory XVI., under pressure of the government, insisted that their general should abolish the French institutions in A.D. 1845. An important branch of the order had settled in Catholic Switzerland, but the unfavourable issue

of the Separated Cantons' War of 1847 drove its members out of that refuge. The revolution of 1848 threatened the order with extinction, but the papal restoration of A.D. 1850 re-introduced it into most Catholic countries. Since then the sons of Loyola have renewed their youth like the eagle. They have forced their way into all lands, even in those on both sides of the ocean that had by legislative enactments been closed against them, spreading ultramontane views among Catholics, converting Protestants, and disseminating their principles in schools and colleges. Even Pius IX., under whose auspices Aug. Theiner had been allowed, in A.D. 1853, in his "History of the Pontificate of Clement XIV." to bring against them the heavy artillery drawn from "the secret archives of the Vatican," again handed over to them the management of public instruction, and surrendered himself even more and more to their influence, so that at last he saw only by their eyes, heard only with their ears, and resolved only according to their will.[1] The founding of the Italian kingdom under the Prince of Sardinia in A.D. 1860 led to their expulsion from all Italy, with the exception of Venice and the remnants of the Papal States. When, in A.D. 1866, Venice also became an Italian province, they migrated thence into the Tyrol and other Austrian provinces, where they enjoyed the blessings of the concordat (§ 198, 2). Spain, too, on the expulsion of Queen Isabella in A.D. 1868, and even Mexico and several of the States of Central and Southern America, drove out the disciples of Loyola. On the other hand, they made brilliant progress in Germany, especially in Rhenish Hesse and the Catholic provinces of Prussia. But under the new German empire the Reichstag, in A.D. 1872, passed a law suppressing the Jesuits and all similar orders throughout the empire (§ 197, 4). They were also formally expelled from France in A.D. 1880 (§ 203, 6). Still, however, in A.D. 1881 the order numbered 11,000 members in five provinces, and according to Bismarck's calculation in A.D. 1872 their property amounted to 280 million thalers. In A.D. 1853 John Beckx of Belgium was made general. He retired in A.D. 1884 at the age of ninety, Anderlady, a Swiss, having been appointed in A.D. 1883 his colleague and successor.—The hope which was at first widely entertained that Leo XIII. would emancipate himself from the domination of the order seems more and more to be proved a vain delusion. In July, 1886, he issued, on the occasion of a new edition of the institutions of the order, a letter to Anderlady, in which he, in the most extravagant manner, speaks of the order as having performed the most signal services "to the church and society," and confirms anew everything that his predecessors had said and done in its favour, while expressly

---

[1] Geffcken, "Church and State." vol. ii., pp. 286-288.

and formally he recalls anew anything that any of them had said and done against it.

2. Other Orders and Congregations.—After the storms of the revolution religious orders rapidly recovered lost ground. France decreed, on November 2nd, 1789, the abolition of all orders, and cloisters and in 1802, under Napoleon's auspices, they were also suppressed in the German empire and the friendly princes indemnified with their goods. Yet on grounds of utility Napoleon restored the Lazarists, as well as the Sisters of Mercy, whose scattered remnants he collected in A.D. 1807 in Paris into a general chapter, under the presidency of the empress-mother. But new cloisters in great numbers were erected specially in Belgium and France (in opposition to the law of 1789, which was unrepealed), in Austria, Bavaria, Prussia, Rhenish Hesse, etc., as also in England and America. In 1849 there were in Prussia fifty monastic institutes; in 1872 there were 967. In Cologne one in every 215, in Aachen one in every 110, in Münster one in every sixty-one, in Paderborn one in every thirty-three, was a Catholic priest or member of an order. In Bavaria, between 1831 and 1873 the number of cloisters rose from 43 to 628, all, with the exception of some old Benedictine monasteries, inspired and dominated by the Jesuits. Even the Dominicans, originally such determined opponents, are now pervaded by the Jesuit spirit. The restoration of the Trappist order (§ 156, 8) deserves special mention. On their expulsion from La Trappe in A.D. 1791 the brothers found an asylum in the Canton Freiburg, and when driven thence by the French invasion of A.D. 1798, Paul I. obtained from the czar permission for them to settle in White Russia, Poland, and Lithuania. But expelled from these regions again in A.D. 1800 they wandered through Europe and America, till after Napoleon's defeat they purchased back the monastery of La Trappe, and made it the centre of a group of new settlements throughout France and beyond it.—Besides regular orders there were also numerous congregations or religious societies with communal life according to a definite but not perpetually binding rule, and without the obligation of seclusion, as well as brotherhoods and sisterhoods without any such rule, which after the restoration of A.D. 1814 in France and after A.D. 1848 in Germany, were formed for the purposes of prayer, charity, education, and such like. From France many of these spread into the Rhine Provinces and Westphalia.—In Spain and Portugal (§ 205, 1, 5) all orders were repeatedly abolished, subsequently also in Sardinia and even in all Italy (§ 204, 1, 2), and also in several Romish American states (§ 209, 1, 2), as also in Prussia and Hesse (§ 197, 8, 15). Finally the third French Republic has enforced existing laws against all orders and congregations not authorized by the State (§ 206, 6).—On the 700th anniversary of the birth of St. Francis, in

September, 1882, Leo XIII. issued an encyclical declaring the institute of the Franciscan Tertiaries (§ 98, 11) alone capable of saving human society from all the political and social dangers of the present and future, which had some success at least in Italy.

Of what inhuman barbarity the superiors of cloisters are still capable is shown *instar omnium* in the horrible treatment of the nun Barbara Ubryk, who, avowedly on account of a breach of her vow of chastity, was confined since A.D. 1848 in the cloister of the Carmelite nuns at Cracow in a dark, narrow cell beside the sewer of the convent, without fire, bed, chair, or table. It was only in A.D. 1869, in consequence of an anonymous communication to the law officers, that she was freed from her prison in a semi-animal condition, quite naked, starved, and covered with filth, and consigned to an asylum. The populace of Cracow, infuriated at such conduct, could be restrained from demolishing all the cloisters only by the aid of the military.

8. The Pius Verein.—A society under the name of the Pius Verein was started at Mainz in October, 1848, to further Catholic interests, advocating the church's independence of the State, the right of the clergy to direct education, etc. At the annual meetings its leading members boasted in grossly exaggerated terms of what had been accomplished and recklessly prophesied of what would yet be achieved. At the twenty-eighth general assembly at Bonn in A.D. 1881, with an attendance of 1,100, the same confident tone was maintained. Windhorst reminded the Prussian government of the purchase of the Sibylline books, and declared that each case of breaking off negotiations raised the price of the peace. Not a tittle of the ultramontane claims would be surrendered. The watchword is the complete restoration of the *status quo ante*. Baron von Loë, president of the Canisius Verein, concluded his triumphant speech with the summons to raise the membership of the union from 80,000 to 800,000, yea to 8,000,000; then would the time be near when Germany should become again a Catholic land and the church again the leader of the people. At the assembly at Düsseldorf in A.D. 1883, Windhorst declared, amid the enthusiastic applause of all present, that after the absolute abrogation of the May laws the centre would not rest till education was again committed unreservedly to the church. In the assembly at Münster in A.D. 1885, he extolled the pope (notwithstanding all confiscation and imprisoning for the time being) as the governor and lord of the whole world. The thirty-third assembly at Breslau in A.D. 1886, with special emphasis, demanded the recall of all orders, including that of the Jesuits.

4. The various German unions gradually fell under ultramontane influences. The Borromeo Society circulated Catholic books inculcating ultramontane views in politics and religion. The Boniface

Union, founded by Martin, Bishop of Paderborn, aided needy Catholic congregations in Protestant districts. Other unions were devoted to foreign missions, to work among Germans in foreign lands, etc. In all the universities such societies were formed. In Bavaria patriot peasant associations were set on foot, as a standing army in the conflict of the ultramontane hierarchy with the new German empire. For the same purpose Bishop Ketteler founded in A.D. 1871 the Mainz Catholic Union, which in A.D. 1814 had 90,000 members. The Görres Society of 1876 (§ 188, 1) and the Canisius Society of 1879 (§ 151, 1) were meant to promote education on ultramontane lines.—In Italy such societies have striven for the restoration of the temporal power and the supremacy of the church over the State. The unions of France were confederated in A.D. 1870, and this general association holds an annual congress. The several unions were called "*œuvres.*" The *Œuvre du Vœu National*, e.g., had the task of restoring penitent France to the "sacred heart of Jesus" (§ 188, 12); the *Œuvre Pontifical* made collections of Peter's pence and for persecuted priests; the *Œuvre de Jesus-Ouvrier* had to do with the working classes, etc.

5. The knowledge of the omnipotence of capital in these days led to various proposals for turning it to account in the interests of Catholicism. The Catholic Bank schemes of the Belgian Langrand-Dumonceau in 1872 and the Munich bank were pure swindles; and that of Adele Spitzeder 1869–1872, pronounced "holy" by the clergy and ultramontane press, collapsed with a deficit of eight and a quarter million florins.—Archbishop Purcell of Cincinnati invited church members to avoid risk to bank with him. He invested in land, advanced money for building churches, cloisters, schools, etc., and in A.D. 1878 found himself bankrupt with liabilities amounting to five million dollars. He then offered to resign his office, but the pope refused and gave him a coadjutor, whereupon the archbishop retired into a cloister where he died in his eighty-third year. In the *Union Générale* of Paris, founded in 1876, which came to a crash in 1882, the French aristocracy, the higher clergy and members of orders lost hundreds of millions of francs.

6. The Catholic Missions.—The impulse given to Catholic interests after 1848 was seen in the zeal with which missions in Catholic lands, like the Protestant Methodist revival and camp-meetings (§ 208, 1), began to be prosecuted. An attempt was thus made to gather in the masses, who had been estranged from the church during the storms of the revolution. The Jesuits and Redemptorists were prominent in this work. In bands of six they visited stations, staying for three weeks, hearing confessions, addressing meetings three times a day, and concluding by a general communion.

7. Besides the Propaganda (§ 156. 9), fourteen societies in Rome,

three in Paris, thirty in the whole of Catholic Christendom, are
devoted to the dissemination of Catholicism among Heretics and
Heathens. The Lyons Association for the spread of the faith, insti-
tuted in 1822, has a revenue of from four to six million francs.
Specially famous is the Picpus Society, so called from the street in
Paris where it has its headquarters. Its founder was the deacon
Coudrin, a pupil of the seminary for priests at Poictiers broken up in
A.D. 1789. Amid the evils done to the church and the priests by the
Revolution, in his hiding-place he heard a divine call to found a
society for the purpose of training the youth in Catholic principles,
educating priests, and bringing the gospel to the heathen "by atoning
for excesses, crimes, and sins of all kinds by an unceasing day and
night devotion of the most holy sacrament of the altar." Such a
society he actually founded in A.D. 1805, and Pius VII. confirmed it
in A.D. 1817. The founder died in A.D. 1837, after his society had
spread over all the five continents. Its chief aim henceforth was
missions to the heathen. While the Picpus society, as well as the
other seminaries and monkish orders, sent forth crowds of missionaries, other societies devoted themselves to collecting money and
engaging in prayer. The most important of these is the Lyonese
Society for the spread of the faith of A.D. 1822. The member's weekly
contribution is 5 cents, the daily prayer-demand a paternoster, an
angel greeting, and a "St. Francis Xavier, pray for us." The
fanatical journal of the society had a yearly circulation of almost
250,000 copies, in ten European languages. The popes had showered
upon its members rich indulgences.—After Protestant missions had
received such a powerful impulse in the nineteenth century, the
Catholic societies were thereby impelled to force in wherever success
had been won and seemed likely to be secured, and wrought with all
conceivable jesuitical arts and devices, for the most part under the
political protection of France. The Catholic missions have been most
zealously and successfully prosecuted in North America, China, India,
Japan, and among the schismatic churches of the Levant. Since 1837
they have been advanced by aid of the French navy in the South Seas
(§ 184, 7) and in North Africa by the French occupation of Algiers,
and most recently in Madagascar. In South Africa they have made
no progress.—In A.D. 1837–1839 a bloody persecution raged in Tonquin
and Cochin China; in A.D. 1866 Christianity was rooted out of Corea,
and over 2,000 Christians slain; two years later persecution was
renewed in Japan. In China, through the oppressions of the French,
the people rose against the Catholics resident there. This movement
reached a climax in the rebellion of 1870 at Tientsin, when all French
officials, missionaries, and sisters of mercy were put to death, and the
French consulate, Catholic churches and mission houses were levelled

to the ground. Also in Further India since the French war of A.D.
1883 with Tonquin, over which China claimed rights of suzerainty,
the Catholic missions have again suffered, and many missionaries
have been martyred.

§ 187. LIBERAL CATHOLIC MOVEMENTS.

Alongside of the steady growth of ultramontanism from
the time of the restoration of the papacy in A.D. 1814, there
arose also a reactionary movement, partly of a mystical-
irenical, evangelical-revival and liberal-scientific, and partly
of a radical-liberalistic, character. But all the leaders in
such movements sooner or later succumbed before the
strictly administered discipline of the hierarchy. The Old
Catholic reaction (§ 190), on the other hand, in spite of
various disadvantages, still maintains a vigorous existence.

1. Mystical-Irenical Tendencies.—J. M. Sailer, deprived in A.D. 1794 of
his office at Dillingen (§ 165, 12), was appointed in A.D. 1799 professor
of moral and pastoral theology at Ingolstadt, and was transferred to
Landshut in A.D. 1800. There for twenty years his mild and conciliatory as well as profoundly pious mysticism powerfully influenced
crowds of students from South Germany and Switzerland. Though
the pope refused to confirm his nomination by Maximilian as Bishop
of Augsburg in A.D. 1820, he so far cleared himself of the suspicion
of mysticism, separatism, and crypto-calvinism, that in A.D. 1829 no
opposition was made to his appointment as Bishop of Regensburg.
Sailer continued faithful to the Catholic dogmatic, and none of his
numerous writings have been put in the Index. Yet he lay under
suspicion till his death in A.D. 1832, and this seemed to be justified
by the intercourse which he and his disciples had with Protestant
pietists. His likeminded scholar, friend, and vicar-general, the Suf-
fragan-bishop Wittmann, was designated his successor in Regensburg,
but he died before receiving papal confirmation. Of all his pupils
the most distinguished was the Westphalian Baron von Diepenbrock,
over whose wild, intractable, youthful nature Sailer exercised a magic
influence. In A.D. 1823 he was ordained priest, became Sailer's secretary, remaining his confidential companion till his death, was made
vicar-general to Sailer's successor in A.D. 1842, and in A.D. 1845 was
raised to the archiepiscopal chair of Breslau, where he joined the
ultramontanes, and entered with all his heart into the ecclesiastico-
political conflicts of the Würzburg episcopal congress (§ 192, 4).

His services were rewarded by a cardinal's hat from Pius IX. in A.D. 1850. His pastoral letters, however, as well as his sermons and private correspondence, show that he never altogether forgot the teaching of his spiritual father. He delighted in the study of the mediæval mystics, and was specially drawn to the writings of Suso.

2. Evangelical-Revival Tendencies.—A movement much more evangelical than that of Sailer, having the doctrine of justification by faith alone as its centre, was originated by a simple Bavarian priest, Martin Boos, and soon embraced sixty priests in the diocese of Augsburg. The spiritual experiences of Boos were similar to those of Luther. The words of a poor old sick woman brought peace to his soul in A.D. 1790, and led him to the study of Scripture. His preaching among the people and his conversations with the surrounding clergy produced a widespread revival. Amid manifold persecutions, removed from one parish to another, and flying from Bavaria to Austria and thence into Rhenish Prussia, where he died in A.D. 1825 as priest of Sayn, he lighted wherever he went the torch of truth. Even after his conversion Boos believed that he still maintained the Catholic position, but was at last to his own astonishment convinced of the contrary through intercourse with Protestant pietists and the study of Luther's works. But so long as the mother church would keep him he wished not to forsake her.[1] So too felt his like-minded companions Gossner and Lindl, who were expelled from Bavaria in A.D. 1829 and settled in St. Petersburg. Lindl, as Provost of South Russia, went to reside in Odessa, where he exercised a powerful influence over Catholics and Protestants and among the higher classes of the Russians. The machinations of the Roman Catholic and Greek churches caused both Gossner and Lindl to leave Russia in A.D. 1824. They then joined the evangelical church, Lindl in Barmen and Gossner in Berlin. Lindl drifted more and more into mystico-apocalyptic fanaticism; but Gossner, from A.D. 1829 till his death in A.D. 1858 as pastor of the Bohemian church in Berlin, proved a sincere evangelical and a most successful worker.—The Bavarian priest Lutz of Carlshuld, influenced by Boos, devoted himself to the temporal and spiritual well-being of his people, preached Christ as the saviour of sinners, and exhorted to diligent reading of the Bible. In A.D. 1831, with 600 of his congregation, he joined the Protestant church; but to avoid separation from his beloved people, he returned again after ten months, and most of his flock with him, still retaining his evangelical convictions. He was not, however, restored to office, and subsequently in A.D. 1857, with three Catholic priests of the diocese, he attached himself to the Irvingites, and was with them excommunicated.

---

[1] Bridges, "Life of Martin Boos." London, 1836.

3. **Liberal-Scientific Tendencies.**—Von Wessenberg, as vicar-general of the diocese of Constance introduced such drastic administrative reforms as proved most distasteful to the nuncio of Lucerne and the Romish curia. He also endeavoured unsuccessfully to restore a German national Catholic church. In the retirement of his later years he wrote a history of the church synods of the fifteenth and sixteenth centuries, which gave great offence to the ultramontanes.— Fr. von Baader of Munich expressed himself so strongly against the absolutism of the papal system that the ultramontane minister, Von Abel, suspended his lectures on the philosophy of religion in A.D. 1838. He gave still greater offence by his work on Eastern and Western Catholicism, in which he preferred the former to the latter.[1] The talented Hirscher of Freiburg more interested in what is Christian than what is Roman Catholic, could not be won over to yield party service to the ultramontanes. They persecuted unrelentingly Leop. Schmid, whose theosophical speculation had done so much to restore the prestige of theology at Giessen, and had utterly discredited their pretensions. When his enemies successfully opposed his consecration as Bishop of Mainz in A.D. 1849, he resigned his professorship and joined the philosophical faculty. Goaded on by the venomous attacks of his opponents he advanced to a more extreme position, and finally declared " that he was compelled to renounce the specifically Roman Catholic church so long as she refused to acknowledge the true worth of the gospel."

4. **Radical-Liberalistic Tendencies.**—The brothers Theiner of Breslau wrote in A.D. 1828 against the celibacy of the clergy; but subsequently John attached himself to the German-Catholics, and in A.D. 1833 Augustine returned to his allegiance to Rome (§ 191, 7).—During the July Revolution in Paris, the priest Lamennais, formerly a zealous supporter of absolutism, became the enthusiastic apostle of liberalism His journal *L'Avenir*, A.D. 1830–1832, was the organ of the party, and his *Paroles d'un Croyant*, A.D. 1834, denounced by the pope as unutterably wicked, made an unprecedented sensation. The endeavour however, to unite elements thoroughly incongruous led to the gradual breaking up of the school, and Lamennais himself approximated more and more to the principles of modern socialism. He died in A.D. 1854. One of his most talented associates on the staff of the *Avenir* was the celebrated pulpit orator Lacordaire, A.D. 1802–1861. Upon Gregory's denunciation of the journal in A.D. 1832 Lacordaire submitted to Rome, entered the Dominican order in A.D. 1840, and wrote a life of Dominic

---

[1] Hamberger, "Sketch of the Character of the Theosophy of Baader," translated in *American Presbyterian and Theological Review*, 1869.

in which he eulogised the Inquisition; but his eloquence still attracted crowds to *Notre Dame.* Ultimately he fell completely under the influence of the Jesuits.

5. **Attempts at Reform in Church Government.**—In A.D. 1861 Liverani, pope's chaplain and apostolic notary, exposed the scandalous mismanagement of Antonelli, the corruption of the sacred college, the demoralization of the Roman clergy, and the ambitious schemes of the Jesuits, recommended the restoration of the holy Roman empire, not indeed to the Germans, but to the Italians: the pope should confer on the king of Italy by divine authority the title and privileges of Roman emperor, who, on his part, should undertake as papal mandatory the political administration of the States of the Church. But in A.D. 1873 he sought and obtained papal forgiveness for his errors. The Jesuit Passaglia expressed enthusiastic approval of the movements of Victor Emanuel and of Cavour's ideal of a "free church in a free state." He was expelled from his order, his book was put into the Index, but the Italian Government appointed him professor of moral philosophy in Turin. At last he retracted all that he had said and written. In the preface to his popular exposition of the gospels of 1874, the Jesuit father Curci urged the advisability of a reconciliation between the Holy See and the Italian government, and expressed his conviction that the Church States would never be restored. That year he addressed the pope in similar terms, and refusing to retract, was expelled his order in A.D. 1877. Leo XIII. by friendly measures sought to move him to recant, but without success. The condemnation of his books led to their wider circulation. In A.D. 1883 he charged the Holy See with the guilt of the unholy schism between church and state; but in the following year he retracted whatever in his writings the pope regarded as opposed to the faith, morals, and discipline of the Catholic church.

6. **Attempts to Found National Catholic Churches.**—After the July Revolution of A.D. 1830 the Abbé Chatel of Paris had himself consecrated bishop of a new sect by a new-templar dignitary (§ 210, 1) and became primate of the French Catholic Church, whose creed recognised only the law of nature and viewed Christ as a mere man. After various congregations had been formed, it was suppressed by the police .D. 1842. The Abbé Helsen of Brussels made a much more earnest endeavour to lead the church of his fatherland from the antichrist to the true Christ. His Apostolic Catholic Church was dissolved in A.D. 1857 and its remnants joined the Protestants. The founding of the German Catholic Church in A.D. 1844 promised to be more enduring. In August of that year, Arnoldi, Bishop of Treves, exhibited the holy coat preserved there, and attracted one and a half millions of pilgrims to Treves (§ 188, 2). A suspended priest, Ronge, in a letter

to the bishop denounced the worship of relics, seeking to pose as the Luther of the nineteenth century. Czerski of Posen had in August, 1844 seceded from the Catholic church, and in October founded the "Christian Catholic Apostolic Church," whose creed embodied the negations without the positive beliefs of the Protestant confessions, maintaining in other respects the fundamental articles of the Christian faith. Ronge meanwhile formed congregations in all parts of Germany, excepting Bavaria and Austria. A General Assembly held at Leipzig in March, 1845, brought to light the deplorable religious nihilism of the leaders of the party. Czerski, who refused to abandon the doctrine of Christ's divinity, withdrew from the conference, but Ronge held a triumphal procession through Germany. His hollowness, however, became so apparent that his adherents grew ashamed of their enthusiasm for the new reformer. His congregations began to break up; many withdrew, several of the leaders threw off the mask of religion and adopted the *rôle* of political revolutionists. After the settlement that followed the disturbances of A.D. 1848 the remnants of this party disappeared.[1]

7. The inferior clergy of Italy, after the political emancipation of Naples from the Bourbon domination in A.D. 1860, longed for deliverance from clerical tyranny, and founded in A.D. 1862 a society with the object of establishing a national Italian church independent of the Romish curia. Four Neapolitan churches were put at the disposal of the society by the minister Ricasoli, but in 1865, an agreement having been come to between the curia and the government, the bishops were recalled and the churches restored. Thousands, to save themselves from starvation, gave in their submission, but a small party still remained faithful. Encouraged by the events of 1870 (§§ 135, 3; 189, 3), they were able in 1875 to draw up a "dogmatic statement" for the "Church of Italy independent of the Roman hierarchy," which indeed besides the Holy Scriptures admitted the authority of the universal church as infallible custodian and interpreter of revealed truth, but accepted only the first seven œcumenical councils as binding. In the same year Bishop Turano of Girgenti excommunicated five priests of the Silician town Grotta as opponents of the syllabus and the dogma of infallibility. The whole clergy of the town, numbering twenty-five, then renounced their obedience to the bishop, and with the approval of the inhabitants declared themselves in favour of the "statement." North of Rome this movement made little progress; but in 1875 three villages of the Mantuan diocese claimed the ancient privilege of choosing their own priest,

---

[1] Laing, "Notes on the Rise, Progress, etc., of the German Catholic Church of Ronge and Czerski." London, 1845.

and the bishop and other authorities were obliged to yield. The Neapolitan movement, however, as a whole seems to be losing itself in the sand.

8. The Frenchman, Charles Loyson, known by his Carmelite monkish name of *Père Hyacinthe*, was protected from the Jesuits by Archbishop Darboy when he inveighed against the corruptions of the church, and even Pius IX. on his visit to Rome in 1868 treated him with favour. The general of his order having imposed silence on him, he publicly announced his secession from the order and appeared as a "preacher of the gospel," claiming from a future General Council a sweeping reform of the church, protesting against the falsifying of the gospel of the Son of God by the Jesuits and the papal syllabus. He was then excommunicated. In A.D. 1871 he joined the German Old Catholics (§ 190,1); and though he gave offence to them by his marriage, this did not prevent the Old Catholics of Geneva from choosing him as their pastor. But after ten months, because "he sought not the overthrow but the reform of the Catholic church, and reprobated the despotism of the mob as well as that of the clergy, the infallibility of the state as well as that of the pope," he withdrew and returned to Paris, where he endeavoured to establish a French National Church free of Rome and the Pope. The clerical minister Broglie, however, compelled him to restrict himself to moral-religious lectures. In February, 1879, he built a chapel in which he preaches on Sundays and celebrates mass in the French language. He sought alliance with the Swiss Christian Catholics, whose bishop, Herzog, heartily reciprocated his wishes, and with the Anglican church, which gave a friendly response. But that this "seed corn" of a "Catholic Gallican Church" will ever grow into a fully developed plant was from the very outset rendered more than doubtful by the peculiar nature of the sower, as well as of the seed and the soil.

§ 188. CATHOLIC ULTRAMONTANISM.

The restoration of the Jesuit order led, during the long pontificate of Pius IX., to the revival and hitherto unapproached prosperity of ultramontanism, especially in France, whose bishops cast the Gallican Liberties overboard (§§ 156, 3; 203, 1), and in Germany, where with strange infatuation even Protestant princes gave it all manner of encouragement. Even the lower clergy were trained from their youth in hierarchical ideas, and under the despotic rule of their bishops, and a reign of terror carried on by spies and secret courts, were constrained to continue the profession of the strictest absolutism.

1. **The Ultramontane Propaganda.**—In France ultramontanism revived with the restoration. Its first and ablest prophet was Count de Maistre, A.D. 1754–1821, long Sardinian ambassador at St. Petersburg. He wrote against the modern views of the relations of church and state, supporting the infallibility, absolutism, and inviolability of the pope. He was supported by Bonald, Chateaubriand, Lamartine, Lamennais, Lacordaire, and Montalembert. Only Bonald maintained this attitude. Between him and Chateaubriand a dispute arose over the freedom of the press; Lamennais and Lacordaire began to blend political radicalism with their ultramontanism; Lamartine involved himself in the February revolution of 1848 as the apostle of humanity; and Montalembert took up a half-way position. In 1840 Louis Veuillot started the *Univers Religieux* in place of the *Avenir*, in which, till his death in 1883, he vindicated the extremest ultramontanism.—In Germany ultramontane views were disseminated by romancing historians and poets mostly converts from Protestantism. Görres, professor of history in Munich, represented the Reformation as a second fall, and set forth the legends of ascetics in his " History of Mysticism " as sound history. The German bishops set themselves to train the clergy in hierarchical views, and by a rule of terror prevented any departure from that theory. The ultramontanising of the masses was carried on by missions, and by the establishment of brotherhoods and sisterhoods. In the beginning of A.D. 1860 there were only thirteen ultramontane journals with very few subscribers, while in January, 1875, there were three hundred. The most important was *Germania*, founded at Berlin in 1871.—The *Civiltà Cattolica* of Rome was always revised before publication by Pius IX., and under Leo XIII. a similar position is held by the *Moniteur de Rome*, while the *Osservatore Romano* and the *Voce della verità* have also an official character.

2. **Miracles.**—Prince Hohenlohe went through many parts of Germany, Austria, and Hungary, performing miraculous cures; but his day of favour soon passed, and he settled down as a writer of ascetical works.—Pilgrimages to wonder-working shrines were encouraged by reports of cures wrought on the grand-niece of the Bishop of Cologne (§ 193, 1), cured of knee-joint disease before the holy coat of Treves (§ 187, 6). Subjected to examination, the pretended seamless coat was found to be a bit of the gray woollen wrapping of a costly silk Byzantine garment 1½ feet broad and 1 foot long.

3. **Stigmatizations.**—In many cases these marks were found to have been fraudulently made, but in other cases it was questionable whether we had not here a pathological problem, or whether hysteria created a desire to deceive or pre-disposed the subject to being duped under clerical influence. Anna Cath. Emmerich, a nun of Dülmen in Westphalia, in 1812, professed to have on her body bloody wound-marks of the Saviour. For five years down to her death in 1824, the poet Brentano sat at her feet, venerating her as a saint and listening to her ecstatic revelations on the death and sufferings of the Redeemer and his mother. Overberg, Sailer, and Von Stolberg were also satisfied of the genuineness of her revelations and of the miraculous marking of her body. The physician Von Drussel examined the wound-prints and certified them as miraculous; but Bodde, professor of chemistry at Münster, pronounced the blood marks spots produced by dragon's-blood. Competent physicians declared her a hysterical woman in-capable of distinguishing between dream and reality, truth and lies, honesty and deceit. Others famous in the same line were Maria von Wörl, Dominica Lazzari, and Crescentia Stinklutsch; also Dorothea Visser of Holland and Juliana Weiskircher from near Vienna.

4. Of a very doubtful kind were the miraculous marks on Louise Lateau, daughter of a Belgian miner. On 24th April, 1868, it is said she was marked with the print of the Saviour's wounds on hands, feet, side, brow, and shoulders. In July, A.D. 1868, she fell into an ecstasy from which she could be awakened only by her bishop or one author-ized by him. Trustworthy physicians, after a careful medical exami-nation, reported that she laboured under a disease which they pro-posed to call "stigmatic neuropathy." Chemical analysis proved the presence of food which had been regularly taken, probably in a som-nambulistic trance. In the summer of 1875 her sister for a time put an end to the affair by refusing the clergy entrance into the house, and she was then obliged to eat, drink, and sleep like other Christians, so that the Friday bloody marks disappeared. But now, say ultramon-tane journals, Louise became dangerously ill, and clergy were called in to her help, and the marks were again visible. Her patron Bishop Dumont of Tournay being deposed by the pope in 1879, she took part against his successor, and was threatened with excommunication. (§ 200, 7). She was now deserted by the ultramontanes and Belgian clergy, and treated as a poor, weak-minded invalid. She died neglected and in obscurity in A.D. 1883.

5. Of pseudo-stigmatizations there has been no lack even in the most recent times. In 1845 Caroline Beller, a girl of fifteen years, in Westphalia, was examined by a skilful physician. On Thursday he laid a linen cloth over the wound prints, and sure enough on Friday it was marked with blood stains; but also strips of paper laid under

without her knowledge, were pricked with needles. The delinquent now confessed her deceit, which she had been tempted to perpetrate from reading the works of Francis of Assisi, Catherine of Siena, and Emmerich. Theresa Städele in 1849, Rosa Tamisier in 1851, and Angela Hupe in 1863, were convicted of fraudulently pretending to have stigmata. The latter was proved to have feigned deafness and lameness for a whole year, to have diligently read the writings of Emmerich in 1861, to have shown the physician fresh bleeding wounds on hands, feet, and side, and to have affirmed that she had neither eaten nor drunk for a year. Four sisters of mercy were sent to attend her, and they soon discovered the fraud. In 1876 the father confessor of Ernestine Hauser was prosecuted for damages, having injured the girl's health by the severe treatment to which she was subjected in order to induce ecstasy and obtain an opportunity for impressing the stigmata. Sabina Schäfer of Baden, in her eighteenth year, had for two years borne the reputation of a wonder working saint, who every Friday showed the five wound prints, and in ecstasy told who were in hell and who in purgatory. She professed to live without food, though often she betook herself to the kitchen to pray alone, and even carried food with her to give to her guardian angel to carry to the distant poor. When under surveillance in 1880 she sought to bribe her guardian to bring her meat and drink, fragments of food were found among her clothes, and also a flask with blood and an instrument for puncturing the skin. She confessed her guilt, and was sentenced by the criminal court of Baden to ten weeks' imprisonment. The ultramontane *Pfälzer Bote* complained that so-called liberals should ruthlessly encroach on the rights of the church and the family.

6. **Manifestations of the Mother of God in France.**—The most celebrated of these manifestations occurred in 1858 at Lourdes, where in a grotto the Virgin repeatedly appeared to a peasant girl of fourteen years, almost imbecile, named Bernadette Soubirous, saying "Je suis l'Immaculée Conception," and urging the erection of a chapel on that spot. A miracle-working well sprang up there. Since 1872 the pilgrimages under sanction of the hierarchy have been on a scale of unexampled magnificence, and the cures in number and significance far excelling anything heard of before.—At the village of La Salette in the department of Isère, in 1846 two poor children, a boy of fifteen and a girl of eleven years, saw a fair white-dressed lady sitting on a stone and shedding tears, and, lo, from the spot where her foot rested sprang up a well, at which innumerable cures have been wrought. The epidemic of visions of the Virgin reached a climax in Alsace Lorraine in 1872. In a wood near the village of Gereuth crowds of women and children gathered, professing to see visions of the mother of God ; but when the police appeared to protect the forest, the

manifestation craze spread over the whole land, and at thirty-five stations almost daily visions were enjoyed. The epidemic reached its crisis in Mary's month, May, 1874, and continued with intervals down to the end of the year. In some cases deceit was proved; but generally it seemed to be the result of a diseased imagination and self-deception fostered by speculative purveyors and the ultramontane press and clergy.

7. **Manifestations of the Mother of God in Germany.**—In the summer of 1876 three girls of eight years old in the village of Marpingen, in the department of Treves, saw by a well a white-robed lady, with the halo over her head and with a child in her arms, who made herself known as the immaculate Virgin, and called for the erection of a chapel. A voice from heaven said, This is my beloved Son, etc. There were also processions and choirs of angels, etc. The devil, too, appeared and ordered them to fall down and worship him. Thousands crowded from far and near, and the water of the fountain wrought miraculous cures. The surrounding clergy made a profitable business of sending the water to America, and the *Germania* of Berlin unweariedly sounded forth its praises. Before the court of justice the children confessed the fraud, and were sentenced to the house of correction; and though on technical grounds this judgment was set side, the supreme court of appeal in 1879 pronounced the whole thing scandalous and disgraceful swindle.—Weichsel, priest of Dittrichswald Ermland, who gained great reputation as an exorcist, made a pilgrimage to Marpingen in the summer of 1877, and on his return gave such an account of what he had seen to his communicants' class that first one and then another saw the mother of God at a maple tree, which also became a favourite resort for pilgrims.

8. **Canonizations.**—When in 1825 Leo XII. canonized a Spanish monk Julianus, who among other miracles had made roasted birds fly away off the spit, the Roman wits remarked that they would prefer a saint who would put birds on the spit for them. St. Liguori was canonized by Gregory XVI. in 1839. Pius IX. canonized fifty-two and beatified twenty-six of the martyrs of Japan. The Franciscans had sought from Urban VIII. in 1627 canonization for six missionaries and seventeen Japanese converts martyred in 1596 (§ 150, 2), but were refused because they would not pay 52,000 Roman thalers for the privilege. Pius IX. granted this, and included three Jesuit missionaries. At Pentecost, 1862, the celebration took place, amid acclamations, firing of cannons, and ringing of bells. In 1868 the infamous president of the heretic tribunal Arbúes (§ 117, 2) received the distinction. The number of *doctores ecclesiæ* was increased by Pius IX. by the addition of Hilary of Poitiers in 1851, Liguori in 1870, and Francis de Sales in 1877. And Leo XIII. canonized four new saints,

the most distinguished of whom was the French mendicant, Bened
Jos. Labre, who after having been dismissed by Carthusians, Cistercians, and Trappists as unteachable, made a pilgrimage to Rome,
where he stayed fifteen years in abject poverty, and died in 1783 in
his thirty-sixth year.

9. Discoveries of Relics.—The Roman catacombs continued still to
supply the demand for relics of the saints for newly erected altars.
Toward the end of A.D. 1870 the Archbishop of St. Iago de Compostella
(§ 88, 4) made excavations in the crypt of his cathedral, in consequence of an old tradition that the bones of the Apostle James the
Elder, the supposed founder of the church, had been deposited there,
and he succeeded in discovering a stone coffin with remains of a
skeleton. The report of this made to Pius IX. gave occasion to the
appointment of a commission of seven cardinals, who, after years of
minute examination of all confirmatory historical, archæological,
anatomical, and local questions, submitted their report to Leo XIII.,
whereupon, in November, 1884, he issued an "Apostolic Brief," by
which he (without publishing the report) declared the unmistakable
genuineness of the discovered bones as *ex constanti et pervulgato apud
omnes sermone jam ab Apostolorum œtate memoriœ prodita*, pronounced
the relics generally *perennes fontes*, from which the *dona cœlestia* flow
forth like brooks among the Christian nations, and calls attention to
the fact that it is just in this century, in which the power of darkness
has risen up in conflict against the Lord and his Christ, these and
also many other relics "*divinitus*" have been discovered, as *e.g.* the
bones of St. Francis, of St. Clara, of Bishop Ambrose, of the martyrs
Gervasius and Protasius, of the Apostles Philip and James the Less,
the genuineness of which had been avouched by his predecessors Pius
VII. and Pius IX.

10. The blood of St. Januarius, a martyr of the age of Diocletian,
liquefies thrice a year for eight days, and on occasion of earthquakes
and such-like calamities in Naples, the blood is brought in two
vials by a matron near to the head of the saint; if it liquefies the
sign is favourable to the Neapolitans, if it remains thick unfavourable; but in either case it forms a powerful means of agitation in
the hands of the clergy. Unbelievers venture to suggest that this
precioso sangue del taumaturgo S. Gennaro is not blood, but a mixture
that becomes liquid by the warmth of the hand and the heat of the
air in the crowded room, some sort of cetaceous product coloured red.

11. About 100 clergy, twenty colour-bearers, 150 musicians, 10,000
leapers, 3,000 beggars, and 2,000 singers take part in the Leaping
Procession at Echternach in Luxemburg, which is celebrated yearly
on Whit-Tuesday. It was spoken of in the sixteenth century as an
ancient custom. After an "exciting" sermon, the procession is formed

in rows of from four to six persons bound together by pocket-handker-
chiefs held in their hands; Wilibrord's dance is played, and all jump
in time to the music, five steps forward and two backward, or two
backward and three forward, varied by three or four leaps to the
right and then as many to the left. Thus continually leaping the
procession goes through the streets of the city to the parish church,
up the sixty-two steps of the church stair and along the church aisles
to the tomb of Wilibrord (§ 78, 3). The dance is kept up incessantly
for two hours. The performers do so generally because of a vow, or
as penance for some fault, or to secure the saint's intercession for the
cure of epilepsy and convulsive fits, common in that region, mainly
no doubt owing to such senseless proceedings. The origin of the
custom is obscure. Tradition relates that soon after the death of
Wilibrord a disease appeared among the cattle which jumped incessantly in the stalls, till the people went leaping in procession to
Wilibrord's tomb, and the plague was stayed! But the custom is
probably a Christian adaptation of an old spring festival dance of
pagan times (§ 75, 3; comp. 2 Sam. vi. 14).

12. The Devotion of the Sacred Heart.—Even after the suppression
of the Jesuit order the devotion of the Sacred Heart (§ 156, 6) was
zealously practised by the ex-Jesuits and their friends. On the
restoration of the order numerous brotherhoods and sisterhoods,
especially in France, devoted themselves to this exercise, and the
revanche movement of A.D. 1870 used this as one of its most powerful
instruments. Crowds of pilgrims flocked to Paray le Monial, and
there, kneeling before the cradle of Bethlehem, they besought the
sacred heart of Jesus to save France and Rome, and the refrain of all
the pilgrim songs, "*Dieu, de la clemence . . . sauvez Rome et la
France au nom du sacré-cœur*," became the spiritual Marseillaise of
France returning to the Catholic fold. From the money collected
over the whole land a beautiful church *du Sacré-Cœur* has been
erected on Montmartre in Paris. The gratifying news was then
brought from Rome that the holy father had resolved on July 16th,
1875, the twenty-ninth anniversary of his ascending the papal throne
and the two hundredth anniversary of the great occurrences at Paray
le Monial, that the whole world should give adoration to the sacred
heart. In France this day was fixed upon for the laying of the
foundation stone of the church at Montmartre, and the Archbishop
of Cologne, Paul Melchers, commanded Catholic Germany to show
greater zeal in the adoration of the sacred heart, "ordained by divine
revelation" two hundred years before.

13. Ultramontane Amulets.—The Carmelites adopted a brown, the
Trinitarians a white, the Theatines a blue, the Servites a black, and
the Lazarites a red, scapular, assured by divine visions that the

wearing of them was a means of salvation. A tract, entitled "*Gnaden und Ablässe des fünffachen Skapuliers*," published by episcopal authority at Münster in 1872, declared that any layman who wore the five scapulars would participate in all the graces and indulgences belonging to them severally. The most useful of all was the Carmelite scapular, impenetrable by bullets, impervious to daggers, rendering falls harmless, stilling stormy seas, quenching fires, healing the possessed, the sick, the wounded, etc.—The Benedictines had no scapulars, but they had Benedict-medals, from which they drew a rich revenue. This amulet first made its appearance in the Bavarian Abbey of Metten. The tract, entitled, "*St. Benediktusbüchlein oder die Medaille d. h. Benediktus*," published at Münster in 1876, tells how it cures sicknesses, relieves toothache, stops bleeding at the nose, heals burns, overcomes the craving for drink, protects from attacks of evil spirits, restrains skittish horses, cures sick cattle, clears vineyards of blight, secures the conversion of heretics and godless persons, etc.—In A.D. 1878 there appeared at Mainz, with approval of the bishop, a book in its third edition, entitled, "*Der Seraphische Gürtel und dessen wunderbare Reichtümer nach d. Franz. d. päpstl. Hausprälaten Abbé v. Segur*," according to which Sixtus V. in 1585 founded the Archbrotherhood of the Girdle of St. Francis. It also affirms that whoever wears this girdle day and night and repeats the six enjoined paternosters, participates in all the indulgences of the holy land and of all the basilicas and sanctuaries of Rome and Assisi, and is entitled to liberate 1,000 souls a day from purgatory.—Great miracles of healing and preservation from all injuries to body and soul, property and goods, are attributed by the Jesuits to the "*holy water of St. Ignatius*" (§ 149, 11), the sale of which in Belgium, France, and Switzerland has proved to them a lucrative business. But the mother of God has herself favoured them with a still more powerful miracle-working water in the fountains of Lourdes and Marpingen.

14. We give in conclusion a specimen of Ultramontane pulpit eloquence. A Bavarian priest, Kinzelmann, said in a sermon in 1872: "We priests stand as far above the emperor, kings, and princes as the heaven is above the earth. . . . Angels and archangels stand beneath us, for we can in God's stead forgive sins. We occupy a position superior to that of the mother of God, who only once bare Christ, whereas we create and beget him every day. Yea, in a sense, we stand above God, who must always and everywhere serve us, and at the consecration must descend from heaven upon the mass," etc.—An apotheosis of the priesthood worthy of the Middle Ages.

§ 189. THE VATICAN COUNCIL.[1]

Immediately after Pius IX. had, at the centenary of St. Peter in 1867, given a hint that a general council might be summoned at an early date, the *Civiltà Cattolica* of Rome made distinct statements to the effect that the most prominent questions for discussion would be the confirming of the syllabus (§ 185, 2), the sanctioning of the doctrine of papal absolutism in the spirit of the bull *Unam sanctam* of Boniface VIII. (§ 110, 1), and the proclamation of papal infallibility. The *Civiltà* had already taught that " when the pope thinks, it is God who thinks in him." When the council opened on the day of the immaculate conception, December 8th, 1869, all conceivable devices of skilful diplomacy were used by the Jesuit Camarilla, and friendly cajoling and violent threatening on the part of the pope, in order to silence or win over, and, in case this could not be done, to stifle and suppress the opposition which even already was not inconsiderable in point of numbers, but far more important in point of moral, theological, and hierarchical influence. The result aimed at was secured. Of the 150 original opponents only fifty dared maintain their opposition to the end, and even they cowardly shrank from a decisive conflict, and wrote from their respective dioceses, as their Catholic

---

[1] Manning, "The True History of the Vatican Council." London, 1877. Pomponio Leto, "The Vatican Council, being the impressions of a contemporary (Card. Vitelleschi), translated from the Italian with the original documents." London, 1876. Quirinus, "Letters from Rome on the Council." London, 1870. Janus, "The Pope and the Council." London, 1869. Bungener, "Rome and the Council in the Nineteenth Century." Edinburgh, 1870. Arthur, "The Pope, the Kings, and the People, a History of the Movement to make the Pope Governor of the World, 1864–1871." 2 vols. London, 1877. Acton, ' History of the Vatican Council." London, 1871. Friedrich, "*Documenta ad illum. Conc. Vat.*" Nördling, 1871. Martin (Bishop of Paderborn), "*Omnium Conc. Vat. quœ ad doctr. et discipl. pertin. docum. Collectio*" 1873.

faith obliged them to do, notifying their most complete acquiescence.

1. **Preliminary History of the Council.**—When Pius IX. on the centenary of St. Peter made known to the assembled bishops his intention to summon a general council, they expressed their conviction that by the blessing of the immaculate Virgin it would be a powerful means of securing unity, peace, and holiness. The formal summons was issued on the day of St. Peter and St. Paul of the following year, June 29th, 1868. The end for which the council was convened was stated generally as follows : The saving of the church and civil society from all evils threatening them, the thwarting of the endeavours of all who seek the overthrow of church and state, the uprooting of all modern errors and the downfall of all godless enemies of the apostolical chair. In Germany the Catholic General Assembly which met at Bamberg soon after this declared that from this day a new epoch in the world's history would begin, for "either the salvation of the world would result from this council, or the world is beyond the reach of help." This hopefulness prevailed throughout the whole Catholic world. Fostered by the utterances of the *Civiltà Cattolica*, the excitement grew from day to day. The learned bishop *in partibus* Maret, dean of the theological faculty of Paris, now came forward as an eloquent exponent of the Gallican liberties ; even the hitherto so strict Catholic, the Count Montalembert, to the astonishment of everybody, assumed a bold and independent attitude in regard to the council, and energetically protested in a publication of March 7th, 1870, six days before his death, against the intrigues of the Jesuits and the infallibility dogma which it was proposed to authorize. But the greatest excitement was occasioned by the work "*Der Papst und das Konzil*," published in Leipzig, 1869, under the pseudonym *Janus*, of which the real authors were Döllinger, Friedrich, and Huber of Munich, who brought up the heavy artillery of the most comprehensive historical scholarship against the evident intentions of the curia. The German bishops gathered at the tomb of St. Boniface at Fulda in September, 1869, and issued from thence a general pastoral letter to their disturbed flocks, declaring that it was impossible that the council should decide otherwise than in accordance with holy Scripture and the apostolic traditions and what was already written upon the hearts of all believing Catholics. Also the papal secretary, Card. Antonelli, quieted the anxiety of the ambassadors of foreign powers at Rome by the assurance that the Holy See had in view neither the confirming of the syllabus nor the affirming of the dogma of infallibility. In vain did the Bavarian premier, Prince Hohenlohe, insist that the heads of other governments should combine in taking measures to prevent any

encroachment of the council upon the rights of the state. The great powers resolved to maintain simply a watchful attitude, and only too late addressed earnest expostulations and threats.

2. The Organization of the Council.—Of 1,044 prelates entitled to take part in the council 767 made their appearance, of whom 276 were Italians and 119 bishops *in partibus*, all pliable satellites of the curia, as were also the greater number of the missionary bishops, who, with their assistants in the propaganda, were supported at the cost of the holy father. The sixty-two bishops of the Papal States were doubly subject to the pope, and of the eighty Spanish and South American bishops it was affirmed in Rome that they would be ready at the bidding of the holy father to define the Trinity as consisting of four persons. Forty Italian cardinals and thirty generals of orders were equally dependable. The Romance races were represented by no less than 600, the German by no more than fourteen. For the first time since general councils were held was the laity entirely excluded from all influence in the proceedings, even the ambassadors of Catholic and tolerant powers. The order of business drawn up by the pope was arranged in all its details so as to cripple the opposition. The right of all fathers of the council to make proposals was indeed conceded, but a committee chosen by the pope decided as to their admissibility. From the special commissions, whose presidents were nominated by the pope, the drafts of decrees were issued to the general congregation, where the president could at will interrupt any speaker and require him to retract. Instead of the unanimity required by the canon law in matters of faith, a simple majority of votes was declared sufficient. A formal protest of the minority against these and similar unconstitutional proposals was left quite unheeded. The proceedings were indeed taken down by shorthand reporters, but not even members of council were allowed to see these reports. The conclusions of the general congregation were sent back for final revision to the special commissions, and when at last brought up again in the public sessions, they were not discussed, but simply voted on with a *placet* or a *nonplacet*. The right transept of St. Peter's was the meeting place of the council, the acoustics of which were as bad as possible, but the pope refused every request for more suitable accommodation. Besides, the various members spoke with diverse accents, and many had but a defective knowledge of Latin. Although absolute secresy was enjoined on pain of falling into mortal sin, under the excitement of the day so much trickled out and was in certain Romish circles so carefully gathered and sifted, that a tolerably complete insight was reached into the inner movements of the council. From such sources the author of the "*Römischen Briefe*," supposed to have been Lord Acton, a friend and scholar of Döllinger, drew the material for his account, which

carried by trusty messengers beyond the bounds of the Papal State reached Munich, and there, after careful revision by Döllinger and his friends, were published in the *Augsburg Allg. Zeitung.* Also Prof. Friedrich of Munich, who had accompanied Card. Hohenlohe to Rome as theological adviser, collected what he could learn in episcopal and theological circles in a journal which was published at a later date.

3. The Proceedings of the Council.—The first public session of December 8th, 1869, was occupied with opening ceremonies; the second, of January 6th, with the subscription of the confession of faith on the part of each member. The first preliminary was the *schema* of the faith, the second that on church discipline. Then followed the *schema* on the church and the primacy of the pope in three articles: the legal position of the church in reference to the state, the absolute supremacy of the pope over the whole church on the principles of the Pseudo-Isidore (§ 87, 2) and the assumptions of Gregory VII., Innocent III. and Boniface VIII., reproduced in the principal propositions of the syllabus (§ 184, 2), and the outlines of a catechism to be enforced as a manual for the instruction of youth throughout the church. On March 6th there was added by way of supplement to the *schema* of the church a fourth article in the form of a sketch of the decree of infallibility. Soon after the opening of the council an agitation in this direction had been started. An address to the pope emanating from the Jesuit college petitioning for this was speedily signed by 400 subscribers. A counter address with 137 signatures besought the pope not to make any such proposal. At the head of the agitation in favour of infallibility stood archbishops Manning of Westminster, Deschamps of Mechlin, Spalding of Baltimore, and bishops Fessler of St. Pölten, secretary of the council, Senestrey of Regensburg, the "overthrower of thrones" (§ 197, 1), Martin of Paderborn, and, as bishop *in partibus,* Mermillod of Geneva. Among the leaders of the opposition the most prominent were cardinals Rauscher of Vienna, Prince Schwarzenberg of Prague and Matthieu of Besançon, Prince-bishop Förster of Breslau, archbishops Scherr of Munich, Melchers of Cologne, Darboy of Paris, and Kenrick of St. Louis, the bishops Ketteler of Mainz, Dinkel of Augsburg, Hefele of Rottenburg, Strossmayer of Sirmium, Dupanloup of Orleans, etc.—Owing to the discussions on the Schema of the Faith there occurred on March 22nd a stormy scene, which in its wild uproar reminds one of the disgraceful *Robber Synod of Ephesus* (§ 52, 4). When Bishop Strossmayer objected to the statement made in the preamble, that the indifferentism, pantheism, atheism, and materialism prevailing in these days are chargeable upon Protestantism, as contrary to truth, the furious fathers of the majority amid shouts and roars, shaking of their fists

rushed upon the platform, and the president was obliged to adjourn the sitting. At the next session the objectionable statement was withdrawn and the entire *schema* of the faith was unanimously adopted at the third public sitting of the council on April 24th. The Schema of the Church came up for a consideration on May 10th. The discussion turned first and mainly on the fourth article about the infallibility of the pope. Its biblical foundation was sought in Luke xxii. 32, its traditional basis chiefly in the well-known passage of Irenæus (§ 34, 8) and on its supposed endorsement by the general councils of Lyons and Florence (§ 67, 4, 6), but the main stress was laid on its necessarily following from the position of the pope as the representative of Christ. The opposition party had from the outset their position weakened by the conduct of many of their adherents who, partly to avoid giving excessive annoyance to the pope, and partly to leave a door open for their retreat, did not contest the correctness of the doctrine in question, but all the more decidedly urged the inopportuneness of its formal definition as threatening the church with a schism and provocative of dangerous conflicts with the civil power. The longer the decision was deferred by passionate debates, the more determinedly did the pope throw the whole weight of his influence into the scales. By bewitching kindliness he won some, by sharp, angry words he terrified others. He denounced opponents as sectarian enemies of the church and the apostolic chair, and styled them ignoramuses, slaves of princes, and cowards. He trusted the aid of the blessed Virgin to ward off threatened division. To the question whether he himself regarded the formulating of the dogma as opportune, he answered : " No, but as necessary." Urged by the Jesuits, he confidently declared that it was notorious that the whole church at all times taught the absolute infallibility of the pope ; and on another occasion he silenced a modest doubt as to a sure tradition with the dictatorial words, *La tradizione sono io*, adding the assurance, "As Abbáte Mastai I believe in infallibility, as pope I have experienced it." On July 13th the final vote was called for in the general congregation. There were 871 who voted simply *placet*, sixty-one *placet juxta modum*, *i.e.* with certain modifications, and eighty-eight *non placet.* After a last hopeless attempt by a deputation to obtain the pope's consent to a milder formulating of the decree, Bishop Ketteler vainly entreating on his knees, to save the unity and peace of the church by some small concession, the fifty hitherto steadfast members of the minority returned home, after emitting a written declaration that they after as well as before must continue to adhere to their negative vote, but from reverence and respect for the person of the pope they declined to give effect to it at a public session. On the following day, July 18th, the fourth and last public sitting was held : 547 fathers voted *placet* and only two, Riccio of Cajazzo and Fitzgerald of Little Rock, *non placet*. A violent storm had broken out during the session and amid thunder and lightning, Pius IX., like "a second Moses" (Exod. xix. 16), proclaimed in the *Pastor œternus* the absolute plenipotence and infallibility of himself and all his predecessors and successors.—It was on the evening preceding the proclamation of this new dogma that Napoleon III. proclaimed war with Prussia, in consequence of which the pope lost the last remnants of temporal sovereignty and every chance of its restoration. Under the influence of the fever-fraught July sun, the council now dwindled down to 150 members, and, after the whole glory of the papal kingdom had gone down (§ 185, 3), on October 20th, its sittings were suspended until better times. The *schema* of discipline and the preliminary sketch of a catechism were not concluded; a subsequently introduced *schema* on apostolic missions was left in the same state; and a petition equally pressed by the Jesuits for the defining of the corporeal ascension of Mary had not even reached the initial stage.

4. Acceptance of the Decrees of the Council.—All protests which during the council the minority had made against the order of business determined on and against all irregularities resulting from it, because not persisted in, were regarded as invalid. Equally devoid of legal force was their final written protest which they left behind, in which they expressly declined to exercise their right of voting. And the assent which they ultimately without exception gave to the objective standpoint of the law and the faith of the Catholic church, was not in the least necessary in order to make it appear that the decisions of the council, drawn up with such unanimity as had scarcely ever before been seen, were equally valid with any of the decrees of the older councils. Thus the bishops of the minority, if they did not wish to occasion a split of unexampled dimensions and incalculable complications, quarrels, and contentions in the church that boasted of a unity which had hitherto been its strength and stay, could do nothing else than yield at the twelfth hour to the pope's demand that "*sacrificio dell' intelletto*" which at the eleventh hour they had refused. The German bishops, who had proved most steadfast at the council, were now in the greatest haste to make their submission. Even by the end of August, at Fulda, they joined their infallibilist neighbours in addressing a pastoral letter, in which they most solemnly declared that all true Catholics, as they valued their soul's salvation, must unconditionally accept the conclusions of the council unanimously arrived at which are in no way prejudiced by the "differences of opinion" elicited during the discussion. At the same time they demanded of theological professors, teachers of religion, and clergymen throughout the dioceses a formal acceptance of these decrees as the inviolable standpoint of their

doctrinal teaching; they also took measures against those who refused
to yield, and excommunicated them. Even Bishop Hefele, who did
not sign this pastoral and was at first determined not to yield nor
swerve, at last gave way. In his pastoral proclaiming the new dogma
he gave it a quite inadmissible interpretation: As the infallibility of
the church, so also that of the pope as a teacher, extends only to the
revealed doctrines of faith and morals, and even with reference to
them only the definitions proper and not the introductory statements,
grounds, and applications, belong to the infallible department. But
subsequently he cast himself unreservedly into the arms of his
colleagues assembled once again at Fulda in September, 1872, where
he also found his like-minded friend, Bishop Haneberg of Spires. Yet
he forbore demanding an express assent from his former colleagues
at Tübingen and his clergy, and thus saved Württemberg from a
threatened schism. Strossmayer held out longest, but even he at last
threw down his weapons. But many of the most cultured and
scholarly of the theological professors, disgusted with the course events
were taking, withdrew from the field and continued silently to hold
their own opinions. The inferior clergy, for the most part trained by
ultramontane bigots, and held in the iron grasp of strict hierarchical
discipline, passed all bounds in their extravagant glorification of the
new dogma. And while among the liberal circles of the Catholic
laity it was laughed at and ridiculed, the bigoted nobles and the
masses who had long been used to the incensed atmosphere of an
enthusiastic adoration of the pope, bowed the knee in stupid devotion
to the papal god. But the brave heart of one noble German lady
broke with sorrow over the indignity done by the Vatican decree and
the characterlessness of the German bishops to the church of which
to her latest breath she remained in spirit a devoted member. Amalie
von Lasaulx, sister of the Munich scholar Ernst von Lasaulx (§ 174, 4),
from 1849 superioress of the Sisters of Mercy in St. John's Hospital at
Bonn, lay beyond hope of recovery on a sick-bed to which she had been
brought by her self-sacrificing and faithful discharge of the duties of
her calling, when there came to her from the lady superior of the
order at Nancy the peremptory demand to give in her adhesion to the
infallibility dogma. As she persistently and courageously withstood
all entreaties and threats, all adjurations and cruelly tormenting
importunings, she was deposed from office and driven from the scene
of her labours, and when, soon thereafter, in 1872, she died, the habit
of her order was stripped from her body. The Old Catholics of Bonn,
whose proceedings she had not countenanced, charged themselves
with securing for her a Christian burial.—No state as such has recognised the council. Austria answered it by abolishing the concordat
and forbidding the proclamation of the decrees. Bavaria and Saxony

refused their *placet*; Hesse, Baden, and Württemberg declared that the conclusions of the council had not binding authority in law. Prussia indeed held to its principle of not interfering in the internal affairs of the Catholic church, but, partly for itself, partly as the leading power of the new German empire, passed a series of laws in order to resume its too readily abandoned rights of sovereignty over the affairs of the Catholic church, and to insure itself against further encroachments of ultramontanism upon the domain of civil life (§ 197). The Romance states, on the other hand, pre-eminently France, were prevented by internal troubles and conflicts from taking any very decisive steps.

§ 190. THE OLD CATHOLICS.

A most promising reaction, mainly in Germany, led by men highly respected and eminent for their learning, set in against the Vatican Council and its decrees, in the so-called Old Catholic movement of the liberal circles of the Catholic people, which went the length, even in 1873, of establishing an independent and well organized episcopal church. Since then, indeed, it has fallen far short of the all too sanguine hopes and expectations at first entertained ; but still within narrower limits it continues steadily to spread and to rear for itself a solid structure, while carefully, even nervously, shrinking from anything revolutionary. More in touch with the demands of the *Zeitgeist* in its reformatory concessions, yet holding firmly in every particular to the positive doctrines of orthodoxy, the Old Catholic movement has made progress in Switzerland, while in other Catholic countries its success has been relatively small.

1. **Formation and Development of the Old Catholic Church in the German Empire.**—In the beginning of August, 1870, the hitherto exemplary Catholic professor Michelis of Braunsberg (§ 191, 6), issued a public charge against Pius IX. as a heretic and devourer of the church, and by the end of August several distinguished theologians (Döllinger and Friedrich of Munich, Reinkens, Weber, and Baltzer of Breslau, Knoodt of Bonn, and the canonist Von Schulte of Prague) joined him at Nuremberg in making a public declaration that the Vatican Council could not be regarded as œcumenical, nor its new dogma as a Catholic

doctrine. This statement was subscribed to by forty-four Catholic professors of the university of Munich with the rector at their head, but without the theologians. Similarly, too, several Catholic teachers in Breslau, Freiburg, Würzburg, and Bonn protested, and still more energetically a gathering of Catholic laymen at Königswinter. Besides the Breslau professors already named, the Bonn professors Reusch, Langen, Hilgers, and Knoodt refused to subscribe the council decrees at the call of their bishop; whereas the Munich professors, with the exception of Döllinger and Friedrich, yielded. A repeated injunction of his archbishop in January, 1871, drew from Döllinger the statement that he as a Christian, a theologian, a historian, and a citizen, was obliged to reject the infallibility dogma, while at the same time he was prepared before an assembly of bishops and theologians to prove that it was opposed to Scripture, the Fathers, tradition, and history. He was now literally overwhelmed with complimentary addresses from Vienna, Würzburg, Munich, and almost all other cities of Bavaria; and an address to government on the dangers to the state threatened by the Vatican decrees that lay at the Munich Museum, was quickly filled with 12,000 signatures. On April 14th, Döllinger was excommunicated, and Professor Huber sent an exceedingly sharp reply to the archbishop. After several preliminary meetings, the first congress of the Old Catholics was held in Munich in September, 1871, attended by 500 deputies from all parts of Germany. A programme was unanimously adopted which, with protestation of firm adherence to the faith, worship, and constitution of the ancient Catholic church, maintained the invalidity of the Vatican decrees and the excommunication occasioned by them, and, besides recognising the Old Catholic church of Utrecht (§ 165, 8), expressed a hope of reunion with the Greek church, as well as of a gradual progress towards an understanding with the Protestant church. But when at the second session the president, Dr. von Schulte, proposed the setting up of independent public services with regular pastors, and the establishing as soon as possible of an episcopal government of their own, Döllinger contested the proposal as a forsaking of the safe path of lawful opposition, taking the baneful course of the Protestant Reformation, and tending toward the formation of a sect. As, however, the proposal was carried by an overwhelming majority, he declined to take further part in their public assemblies and retired more into the background, without otherwise opposing the prevailing current or detaching himself from it. The second congress was held at Cologne in the autumn of 1872. From the episcopal churches of England and America, from the orthodox church of Russia, from France, Italy, and Spain, were sent deputies and hearty friendly greetings. Archbishop Loos of Utrecht, by the part which he took in the congress cemented more closely the union with the Old Catholics of Holland. Even the German "*Protestantenverein*" was not unrepresented. A committee chosen for the purpose drew up an outline of a synodal and congregational order, which provides for the election of bishops at an annual meeting at Pentecost of a synod, of which all the clergy are members and to which the congregations send deputies, one for every 200 members. Alongside of the bishop stands a permanent synodal board of five priests and seven laymen. The bishop and synodal board have the right of vetoing doubtful decrees of synod. The choice of pastors lies with the congregation; its confirmation belongs to the bishop. In July, 1873, a bishop was elected in the Pantaleon church of Cologne by an assembly of delegates, embracing twenty-two priests and fifty-five laymen. The choice fell upon Professor Reinkens, who, as meanwhile Bishop Loos of Utrecht had died, was consecrated on August 11th, at Rotterdam, by Bishop Heykamp of Deventer, and selected Bonn as his episcopal residence.

2. The first synod of the German Old Catholics, consisting of thirty clerical and fifty-nine lay members, met at Bonn in May, 1874. It was agreed to continue the practice of auricular confession, but without any pressure being put upon the conscience or its observance being insisted upon at set times. Similarly the moral value of fasting was recognised, but all compulsory abstinence, and all distinctions of food as allowable and unallowable, were abolished. The second synod, with reference to the marriage law, took the position that civil regular marriages ought also to have the blessing of the church; only in the case of marriages with non-Christians and divorced parties should this be refused. The third synod introduced a German ritual in which the exorcism was omitted, while the Latin mass was provisionally retained. The fourth synod allowed to such congregations as might wish it the use of the vernacular in several parts of the service of the mass. At all these synods the lay members had persistently repeated the proposal to abolish the obligatory celibacy of the clergy. But now the agitation, especially on the part of the Baden representatives, had become so keen, that at the fifth synod of 1878, in spite of the warning read by Bishop Reinkens from the Dutch Old Catholics, who threatened to withdraw from the communion, the proposal was carried by seventy-five votes against twenty-two. The Bonn professors, Langen and Menzel, foreseeing this result, had absented themselves from the synod, Reusch immediately withdrew and resigned his office as episcopal vicar-general, Friedrich protested in the name of the Bavarian Old Catholics. Reinkens, too, had vigorously opposed the movement; whereas Knoodt, Michelis, and Von Schulte had favoured it. The synod of 1883 resolved to dispense the supper in both kinds to members of the Anglican church residing

.n Germany, but among their own members to follow meanwhile the usual practice of *communio sub una.* The number of Old Catholic congregations in the German empire is now 107, with 38,507 adherents and 56 priests.—Even at their first congress the German Old Catholics, in opposition to the unpatriotic and law-defying attitude of German ultramontanism, had insisted upon love of country and obedience to the laws of the state as an absolute Christian duty. Their newly chosen bishop Reinkens, too, gave expression to this sentiment in his first pastoral letter, and had the oath of allegiance administered him by the Prussian, Baden, and Hessian governments. But Bavaria felt obliged, on account of the terms of its concordat, to refuse. At first the Old Catholics had advanced the claim to be the only true representatives of the Catholic church as it had existed before July 18th, 1870. At the Cologne congress they let this assumption drop, and restricted their claims upon the state to equal recognition with "the New Catholics," equal endowments for their bishop, and a fair proportion of the churches and their revenues. Prussia responded with a yearly episcopal grant of 16,000 thalers; Baden added about 6,000. It proved more difficult to enforce their claim to church property. A law was passed in Baden in 1874, which not only guaranteed to the Old Catholic clergy their present benefices and incomes, freed them from the jurisdiction of the Romish hierarchy, and gave them permission to found independent congregations, but also granted them a mutual right of possessing and using churches and church furniture as well as sharing in church property according to the numerical proportion of the two parties in the district. A similar measure was introduced into the Prussian parliament, and obtained the royal assent in July, 1875. Since then, however, the interest of the government in the Old Catholic movement has visibly cooled. In Baden, in 1886 the endowment had risen to 24,000 marks.

3. The Old Catholics in other Lands.—In Switzerland the Old, or rather, as it has there been called, the Christian, Catholic movement, had its origin in 1871 in the diocese of Basel-Solothurn, whence it soon spread through the whole country. The national synod held at Olten in 1876 introduced the vernacular into the church services, abolished the compulsory celibacy of the clergy and obligatory confession of communicants, and elected Professor Herzog bishop, Reinkens giving him episcopal consecration. In 1879 the number of Christian Catholics in German Switzerland amounted to about 70,000, with seventy-two pastors. But since then, in consequence of the submission of the Roman Catholics to the church laws condemned by Pius IX, they have lost the majority in no fewer than thirty-nine out of the forty-three congregations of Canton Bern, and therewith the privileges attached. A proposal made in the grand council of the canton

1883 for the suppression of the Christian Catholic theological faculty in the University of Bern, which has existed since 1874, was rejected by one hundred and fifty votes against thirteen.—In Austria, too, strong opposition was shown to the infallibility dogma. At Vienna the first Old Catholic congregation was formed in February, 1872, under the priest Anton; and soon after others were established in Bohemia and Upper Austria. But it was not till October, 1877, that they obtained civil recognition on the ground that their doctrine is that which the Catholic church professed before 1870. In June, 1880, they held their first legally sanctioned synod. The provisional synodical and congregational order was now definitely adopted, and the use of the vernacular in the church services, the abolition of compulsory fasting, confession, and celibacy, as well as of surplice fees, and the abandoning of all but the high festivals, were announced on the following Sunday. The bitter hatred shown by the Czechs and the ultramontane clergy to everything German has given to the Old Catholic movement for some years past a new impulse and decided advantage.—In France the Abbé Michaud of Paris lashed the characterlessness of the episcopate and was excommunicated, and the Abbés Mouls and Junqua of Bordeaux were ordered by the police to give up wearing the clerical dress. Junqua, refusing to obey this order, was accused by Cardinal Donnet, Bishop of Bordeaux, before the civil court, and was sentenced to six months' imprisonment. Not till 1879 did the ex-Carmelite Loyson of Paris lay the foundation of a Catholic Gallican church, affiliated with the Swiss Old Catholics (§ 187, 8).—In Italy since 1862, independently of the German movement, yet on essentially the same grounds, a national Italian church was started with very promising beginnings, which were not, however, realized (§ 187, 7). Rare excitement was caused throughout Italy by the procedure of Count Campello, canon of St. Peter's in Rome, who in 1881 publicly proclaimed his creed in the Methodist Episcopal chapel, there renouncing the papacy, and in a published manifesto addressed to the cathedral chapter justified this step and made severe charges against the papal curia; but soon after, in a letter to Loyson, he declared that he, remaining faithful to the true Catholic church, did not contemplate joining any Protestant sect severed from Catholic unity, and in a communication to the Old Catholic Rieks of Heidelberg professed to be in all points at one with the German Old Catholics. Accordingly he sought to form in Rome a Catholic reform party, whose interests he advocated in the journal *Il Labaro*. The pope's domestic chaplain, Monsignor Savarese, has adopted a similar attitude. In December, 1883, he was received by the pastor of the American Episcopal church at Rome into the Old Catholic church on subscribing the Nicene Creed. In 1886 they were joined by another domestic chaplain of the pope, Monsignor Renier

formerly an intimate friend of Pius IX., who publicly separated himself from the papal church, and with them took his place at the head
of a Catholic "*Congregation of St. Paul*" in Rome.—Also the Episcopal *Iglesia Española* in Spain (§ 205, 4), and the Mexican *Iglesia de
Jesus* (§ 209, 1), must be regarded as essentially of similar tendencies
to the Old Catholics.

§ 191. CATHOLIC THEOLOGY, ESPECIALLY IN GERMANY.

Catholic theology in Germany, influenced by the scientific
spirit prevailing in Protestantism, received a considerable
impulse. From latitudinarian Josephinism it gradually rose
toward a strictly ecclesiastical attitude. Most important
were its contributions in the department of dogmatic and
speculative theology. Besides and after the schools of
Hermes, Baader, and Günther, condemned by the papal
chair, appeared a whole series of speculative dogmatists
who kept their speculations within the limits of the church
confession. Also in the domain of church history, Catholic
theology, after the epoch-making productions of Möhler and
Döllinger, has aided in reaching important results, which,
however, owing to the "tendency" character of their researches, demand careful sifting. Least important are their
contributions to biblical criticism and exegesis. In general,
however, the theological *docents* at the German universities
give a scientific character to their researches and lectures
in respect of form and also of matter, so far as the Tridentine limits will allow. But the more the Jesuits obtained
influence in Germany, the more was that scholasticism, which
repudiated the German university theology and opposed it
with perfidious suspicions and denunciations, naturalized,
especially in the episcopal seminaries, while it was recommended by Rome as the official theology. The attempt,
however, at the Munich Congress of Scholars in 1863 to
come to an understanding between the two tendencies failed,
owing to the contrariety of their principles and the opposition

of the Jesuits.—Outside of Germany, French theology, especially in the department of history, manifested a praiseworthy activity. In Spain theology has never outgrown the period of the Middle Ages. In Italy, on the other hand, the study of Christian antiquities flourished, stimulated by recent discoveries of treasures in catacombs, museums, archives, and libraries.

1. **Hermes and his School.**—The Bonn professor, George Hermes, influenced in youth by the critical philosophy, passed the Catholic dogma of Trent, assured it would stand the test, through the fire of doubt and the scrutiny of reason, because only what survives such examination could be scientifically vindicated. He died in A.D. 1831, and left a school named after him, mainly in Treves, Bonn, and Breslau. Gregory XVI. in 1835 condemned his writings, and the new Archbishop of Cologne, Droste-Vischering, forbad students at Bonn attending the lectures of Hermesians. These made every effort to secure the recall of the papal censure. Bsaun and Elvenich went to Rome, but their declaration that Hermes had not taught what the pope condemned profited them as little as a similar statement had the Jansenists. There now arose on both sides a bitter controversy, which received new fuel from the Prusso-Cologne ecclesiastical strife (§ 193, 1). Finally in 1844 professors Braun and Achterfeld of Bonn were deprived of office by the coadjutor-Archbishop Geistel, and the Prussian government acquiesced. The professors of the Treves seminary and Baltzer of Breslau, the latter influenced by Günther's theology, retracted.—A year before Hermes' condemnation the same pope had condemned the opposite theory of Abbe Bautain of Strassburg, that the Christian dogmas cannot be proved but only believed, and that therefore all use of reason in the appropriation of the truths of salvation is excluded. Bautain, as an obedient son of the church, immediately retracted, "*laudabiliter se subjecit.*"

2. **Baader and his School.**—Catholic theology for a long time paid no regard to the development of German philosophy. Only after Schelling, whose philosophy had many points of contact with the Catholic doctrine, a general interest in such studies was awakened as forming a speculative basis for Catholicism. To the theosophy of Schelling based on that of the Görlitz shoemaker (§ 160, 2), Francis von Baader, professor of speculative dogmatics at Munich, though not a professional theologian, but a physician and a mineralogist, attached himself. In his later years he went over completely to ultramontanism. His scholar Franz Hoffmann of Würzburg has given an exposition of

Baader's speculative system. At Giessen this system was represented by Leop. Schmid (§ 187, 3). All the Catholic adherents of this school are distinguished by their friendly attitude toward Protestantism.

3. Günther and his School.—A theology of at least equal speculative power and of more decidedly Catholic contents than that of Baader, was set forth by the secular priest Anton Günther of Vienna, a profound and original thinker of combative humour, sprightly wit, and a roughness of expression sometimes verging upon the burlesque. He recognised the necessity of going up in philosophical and theological speculation to Descartes, who held by the scholastic dualism of God and the creature, the Absolute and the finite, spirit and nature, while all philosophy, according to him, had been ever plunging deeper into pantheistic monism. Thence he sought to solve the two problems of Christian speculation, creation and incarnation, and undertook a war of extermination against " all monism and semimonism, idealistic and realistic pantheism, disguised and avowed semipantheism," among Catholics and Protestants. His first great work, " *Vorschule zur Spekul. Theologie*," published in 1828, treating of the theory of creation and the theory of incarnation, was followed by a long series of similar works. His most eminent scholars were Pabst, doctor of medicine in Vienna, who gave clear expositions of his master's dark and aphoristic sayings, and Veith, who popularized his teachings in sermons and practical treatises. Some of the Hermesians, such as Baltzer of Breslau, entered the rank of his scholars. The historico-political papers, however, charged him with denying the mysteries of Christianity, rejecting the traditional theology, etc., and Clemens, a *privatdocent* of philosophy in Bonn, became the mouthpiece of this party. Thus arose a passionate controversy, which called forth the attention of Rome. We might have expected Günther to meet the fate of Hermes twenty years before; but the matter was kept long under consideration, for strong influence from Vienna was brought to bear on his behalf. At last in January, 1857, the formal reprobation of the Güntherian philosophy was announced, and all his works put in the Index. Günther humbly submitted to the sentence of the church. So too did Baltzer. But being suspected at Rome, he was asked voluntarily to resign. This Baltzer refused to do. Then Prince-Bishop Förster called upon the government to deprive him; and when this failed, he withdrew from him the *missio canonica* and a third of his canonical revenues, and in 1870, on his opposing the infallibility dogma, he withheld the other two-thirds. His salary from the State continued to be paid in full till his death in A.D. 1871.

4. John Adam Möhler.—None of all the Catholic theologians of recent times attained the importance and influence of Möhler in his short life of forty-two years. Stimulated to seek higher scientific culture

by the study mainly of Schleiermacher's works and those of other Protestants, and putting all his rich endowments at the service of the church, he won for himself among Catholics a position like that of Schleiermacher among Protestants. His first treatise of 1825, on the unity of the church, was followed by his "Athanasius the Great," and the work of his life, the "Symbolics" of 1832, in its ninth edition in 1884, which with the apparatus of Protestant science combats the Protestant church doctrine and presented the Catholic doctrine in such an ennobled and sublimated form, that Rome at first seriously thought of placing it in the Index. Hitherto Protestants had utterly ignored the productions of Catholic theology, but to overlook a scientific masterpiece like this would be a confession of their own weakness. And in fact, during the whole course of the controversy between the two churches, no writing from the Catholic camp ever caused such commotion among the Protestants as this. The ablest Protestant replies are those of Nitsch and Baur. In 1835 Möhler left Tübingen for Munich; but sickness hindered his scientific labours, and, in 1838, in the full bloom of manhood, the Catholic church and Catholic science had to mourn his death. He can scarcely be said to have formed a school; but by writings, addresses, and conversation he produced a scientific ferment in the Catholic theology of Germany, which continued to work until at last completely displaced by the scholasticism reintroduced into favour by the Jesuits.

5. John Jos. Ignat. von Döllinger.—Of all Catholic theologians in Germany, alongside of and after Möhler, by far the most famous on either side of the Alps was the church historian Döllinger, professor at Munich since 1826. His first important work issued in that same year was on the "Doctrine of the Eucharist in the First Three Centuries." His comprehensive work, "The History of the Christian Church," of 1833 (4 vols., London, 1840), was not carried beyond the second volume; and his "Text-book of Church History" of 1836, was only carried down to the Reformation. The tone of his writings was strictly ecclesiastical, yet without condoning the moral faults of the popes and hierarchy. Great excitement was produced by his treatise on "The Reformation," in which he gathered everything that could be found unfavourable to the Reformers and their work, and thus gained the summit of renown as a miracle of erudition and a master of Catholic orthodoxy. Meanwhile in 1838 he had taken part in controversies about mixed marriages (§ 193, 1), and in 1843 over the genuflection question (§ 195, 2), with severely hierarchical pamphlets. As delegate of the university since 1845 he defended with brilliant eloquence in the Bavarian chamber the measures of the ultramontane government and the hierarchy, became in 1847 Provost of St. Cajetan, but was also in the same year involved in the overthrow

of the Abel ministry, and was deprived of his professorship. In the following year he was one of the most distinguished of the Catholic section in the Frankfort parliament, where he fought successfully in the hierarchical interest for the unconditional freedom and independence of the church. King Maximilian II. restored him to his professorship in 1849. From this time his views of confessional matters became milder and more moderate. He first caused great offence to his ultramontane admirers at Easter, 1861, when he in a series of public lectures delivered one on the Papal States then threatened, in which he declared that the temporal power of the pope, the abuses of which he had witnessed during a journey to Rome in 1857, was by no means necessary for the Catholic church, but was rather hurtful. The papal nuncio, who was present, ostentatiously left the meeting, and the ultramontanes were beside themselves with astonishment, horror, and wrath. Döllinger gave some modifying explanations at the autumn assembly of the Catholic Union at Munich in 1861. But soon thereafter appeared his work, "The Church and the Churches" (London, 1862), which gave the lecture slightly modified as an appendix. The "Fables respecting the Popes of the Middle Ages" (London, 1871), was as little to the taste of the ultramontanes. Indeed in these writings, especially in the first named, the polemic against the Protestant Church had all its old bitterness; but he is at least more just toward Luther, whom he characterizes as "the most powerful man of the people, the most popular character, which Germany ever possessed." And while he delivers a glowing panegyric on the person of the pope, he lashes unrelentingly the misgovernment of the Papal States. At the Congress of Scholars at Munich he contended for the freedom of science. Döllinger as president of the congress sent the pope a telegram which satisfied his holiness. But the Jesuits looked deeper, and immediately "*il povero Döllinger*" was loaded by the *Civiltà Cattolica* with every conceivable reproach. In A.D. 1868 nominated to the life office of imperial councillor, he voted with the bishops against the liberal education scheme of the government. But his battle against the council and infallibility made the rent incurable, and his angry archbishop hurled against him the great excommunication. Then Vienna made him doctor of philosophy, Marburg, Oxford, and Edinburgh gave him LL.D., and the senate of his university unanimously elected him rector in 1871. But his tabooed lecture room became more and more deserted. He took no prominent part in the organizing of the Old Catholic church (§ 190, 1), but all the more eagerly did he seek to promote its union negotiations (§ 175, 6).

6. The Chief Representatives of Systematic Theology.—Klee, A.D. 1800–1840, of Bonn and Munich, was a positivist of the old school, and

during the Hermesian controversy a supporter of the theology of the curia. Hirscher, 1788–1865, of Freiburg, numbered by the liberals as one of their ornaments and by the fanatical ultramontanes as a heretic, did much to promote a conciliatory and moderate Catholicism, equally free from ultramontane and rationalistic tendencies, abandoning nothing essential in the Catholic doctrine. Hilgers, the Hermesian, afterwards joined the Old Catholics of Bonn. Staudenmaier and Sengler of Freiburg and Berlage of Münster held a distinguished rank as speculative theologians. In the same department, Kuhn and Drey of Tübingen, Ehrlich of Prague, Deutinger of Dillingen, a disciple of Schelling and Baader, and as such persecuted, though a pious believing Catholic, Oischinger of Munich, who in despair at the proclamation of the Vatican decree suddenly stopped his fruitful literary activity, Dieringer of Bonn, who for the same reason not only ceased to write but also in 1871 resigned his professorship and retired to a small country pastorate, and finally, Hettinger of Würzburg, best known by his "*Apologie d. Christenthums.*"—While the above-named, though suspected and opposed by the scholastic party, strove to preserve intact their ecclesiastical Catholic character, other representatives of this tendency by their struggles against scholasticism and then against the Vatican Council, were driven away from their orthodox position. Thus Frohschammer of Munich, when his treatise on "The Origin of the Soul," in which he supported the theory of Generationism in opposition to the Catholic doctrine of creationism, and other works were placed in the Index, asked for a revision on the ground that he taught nothing contrary to Catholic doctrine. He was stripped of all his clerical functions, and students were prohibited attending his lectures. He protested, and his rooms were more crowded than ever. Subsequently, however, repudiated even by the Old Catholics, he drifted more and more, not only from the church, but even from belief in revelation. Against Strauss' last work he wrote a tract in which he sought to prove that "the old faith is indeed untenable," but that also "the new science" cannot take its place, that a "new faith" must be introduced by going back to the Christianity of Christ. Michelis, a man of wide culture in the department of natural science and philology, as well as theology and philosophy, had in his earlier position as professor in Paderborn, Münster, and Braunsberg, supported by word and pen a strictly ecclesiastical tendency; but the Vatican Council made him one of the first and most zealous leaders of the Old Catholic movement. His most important work is his "Catholic Dogmatics," of 1881, in which the Old Catholic conception of Christianity is represented as the purified higher unity of the Protestant and Vatican systems of doctrine.

7. **The Chief Representatives of Historical Theology.**— The first place

after Möhler and Döllinger belongs to Möhler's scholar Hefele, from 1840 professor at Tübingen and from 1869 Bishop of Rottenburg, distinguished by the liberal spirit of his researches. His treatises on the Honorius controversy made him one of the most dangerous opponents of the infallibility dogma, to which, however, he at last submitted (§ 189, 4). His most important work is the "History of the Councils." Hase criticised the second edition of the work, severely but not without sufficient grounds, by saying that in it "the bishop chokes the scholar." Werner of Vienna is a prolific writer in the department of the history of theological literature; while Bach of Munich and the Dominican Denifle have written on the mediæval mystics, the latter also on the universities of the Middle Ages. Hergenröther of Würzburg, by his monograph on "Photius and the Greek Schism," written in the interests of his party, and by his polemic against the anti-Vatican movement, and specially by his "Handbook of Church History," rendered such service to the papacy and the papal church, that Leo XIII. in 1879 made him a cardinal and librarian of the Vatican, with the task of reorganizing the library.—Among the Old Catholics, Friedrich of Munich, besides his historical account of the Vatican Council, had written on Wessel, Huss, and the church history of Germany. Huber of Munich, whose "Philosophy of the Church Fathers" of 1859 was put in the Index, while his much more liberal work on Erigena of 1861 passed without censure, in later years wrote an exhaustive account of the Jesuit order and a critical reply to Strauss' "Old and New Faith." Pichler of Munich, by his conscientious research and criticism, drew down upon him the papal censure, and his book on the "History of the Division of the Eastern and Western Churches" had the honour of being placed in the Index. His later studies and writings estranged him more and more from Romanism, inspired him with the idea of a national German church, and fostered in him a love for the *Protestantenverein* movement; but his unbridled bibliomania while assistant in the Royal Library of St. Petersburg in 1871, brought his public career to a sad and shameful end. The Old Catholic Professor Langen of Bonn, wrote a four-volume work against the Vatican dogma, discussed the "Trinitarian Doctrinal Differences between the Eastern and Western Churches," in the interests of a union with the Greek church, and published an able monograph on "John of Damascus," as well as a thorough and impartial "History of the Roman Church down to Nicholas I.," two vols., 1881, 1885.—In Rome the Oratorian Aug. Theiner atoned for the literary errors of his youth (§ 187, 4) by his zealous vindication of papal privileges. His chief works were the continuation of the "*Annales Ecclesiastici*" of Baronius, and the editing of the historical documents of the various Christian nations. The

Jesuits charged him with giving the anti-Vaticanists aid from the library and sought to influence the pope against him so as to deprive him of his office of prefect of the Vatican archives. He was suspended from his duties, and though he still retained his title and occupied his official residence in the Vatican, the doors from it into the library were built up. His edition of the "Acts of the Council of Trent," which was commenced, was also prohibited. But he succeeded in making a transcript at Agram in Croatia, where in 1874 a portion of it, the official protocol of the secretary of the Council, Massarelli, was printed by the help of Bishop Strossmayer in an elegant style but abbreviated, and therefore unsatisfactory. Cardinal Angelo Mai, as principal Vatican librarian, distinguished himself by his palimpsest studies in old classical as well as patristic literature. And quite worthy of ranking with either in carefulness, diligence, and patience was De Rossi, who has laboured in the department of Christian archæology, and is well known by his great work, " *Roma sotteranea cristiana*," published in 1864 ff.—Xavier Kraus, when his " Handbook " had been adversely criticised, hastened to Rome, submitted all his utterances to the judgment of the pope, and proclaimed on his return that in the next edition he would explain what had been misunderstood and withdraw what was objected to. The question now rises, whether the more recent work of Xav. Funk can escape a similar censure.

Among Catholic writers on canon law the most notable are Walters of Bonn, Phillips of Vienna, Von Schulte of Prague and Bonn, who till the Vatican Council was one of the most zealous advocates of the strict Catholic tendency, since then openly on the side of the opposition, a keen supporter, and by word and pen a vigorous promoter, of the Old Catholic movement, and Vering of Prague, who occupies the ultramontane Vatican standpoint.

8. The Chief Representatives of Exegetical Theology. — Hug of Freiburg, in his "Introduction," occupies the biblical but ecclesiastically latitudinarian attitude of Jahn. Leaving dogma unattacked and so himself unattacked, Mövers of Breslau, best known by his work on the Phœnicians, a Richard Simon of his age, developed a subtlety of destructive criticism of the canon and history of the Old Testament which astonished even the father of Protestant criticism, De Wette. Kaulen of Bonn wrote an "Introduction to the Old and New Testament " in a fairly scientific spirit from the Vatican standpoint; while Maier of Freiburg, wrote an introduction to the New Testament and commentaries on some New Testament books.—The Old Catholic Reusch of Bonn wrote "Introduction to the Old Testament," and "Nature and the Bible " (2 vols., Edin., 1886). Sepp of Munich, silent since 1867. began his literary career with a " Life of Christ," a " History of

the Apostles," etc., in the spirit of the romantic mystical school of Görres. His "Sketch of Church Reform, beginning with a Revision of the Bible Canon," caused considerable excitement. With humble submission to the judgment of his church, he demanded a correction of the Tridentine decrees on Scripture in accordance with the results of modern science, but the only response was the inclusion of his book in the Index.

9. **The Chief Representatives of the New Scholasticism.**—The official and most masterly representative of this school for the whole Catholic world was the Jesuit Perrone, 1794–1876, professor of dogmatics of the *Collegium Romanum*, the most widely read of the Catholic polemical writers, but not worthy to tie the shoes of Bellarmin, Bossuet, and Möhler. In his "*Prælectiones Theologicæ*," nine vols., which has run through thirty-six editions, without knowing a word of German, he displayed the grossest ignorance along with unparalleled arrogance in his treatment of Protestant doctrine, history, and personalities (§ 175, 2). The German Jesuit Kleutgen who, under Pius IX., was the oracle of the Vatican in reference to German affairs, introduced the new Roman scholasticism by his work "*Die Theologie der Vorzeit*," into the German episcopal seminaries, whose teachers were mostly trained in the *Collegium Germanicum* at Rome. Alongside of Perrone and Kleutgen, in the domain of morals, the Jesuit Gury holds the first place, reproducing in his works the whole abomination of probabilism, *reservatio mentalis*, and the old Jesuit casuistry (§ 149, 10), with the usual lasciviousness in questions affecting the sexes. Among theologians of this tendency in German universities we mention next Denzinger of Würzburg, who seeks in his works "to lead dogmatics back from the aberrations of modern philosophic speculations into the paths of the old schools." His zealous opposition to Güntherism did much to secure its emphatic condemnation.

10. **The Munich Congress of Catholic Scholars, 1863.**— In order if possible to heal the daily widening cleft between the scientific university theologians and the scholastic theologians of the seminaries, and bring about a mutual understanding and friendly co-operation between all the theological faculties, Döllinger and his colleague Haneberg summoned a congress at Munich, which was attended by about a hundred Catholic scholars, mostly theologians. After high mass, accompanied with the recitation of the Tridentine creed, the four days' conference began with a brilliant presidential address by Döllinger "On the Past and Present of Catholic Theology." The liberal views therein enunciated occasioned violent and animated debates, to which, however, it was readily admitted as a religious duty that all scientific discussions and investigations should yield to the dogmatic claims of the infallible authority of the church, as thereby the true freedom

of science can in no way be prejudiced. A telegraphic report to the pope drawn up in this spirit by Döllinger was responded to in a similar manner on the same day with the apostolic blessing. But after the proceedings *in extenso* had become known, a papal brief was issued which burdened the permission to hold further yearly assemblies with such conditions as must have made them utterly fruitless. They were indeed acquiesced in with a bad grace at the second and last congress at Würzburg in 1864, but the whole scheme was thus brought to an end.

11. **Theological Journals.**—The most severely scientific journal of this century is the Tübingen *Theol. Quartalschrift,* which, however, since the Vatican Council has been struggling to maintain a neutral position between the extremes of the Old and the New Catholicism. In order if possible to displace it the Jesuits Wieser and Stenstrup of Innsbruck started in 1877 their *Zeitschrift für Kath. Theologie.* The ably conducted *Theol. Litteraturblatt,* started in 1866 by Prof. Reusch of Bonn, had to be abandoned in 1878, after raising the standard of Old Catholicism.

12. **The Popes and Theological Science.**—What kind of theology Pius **IX.** wished to have taught is shown by his proclaiming St. Liguori (§ 165, 2) and St. Francis de Sales (§ 157, 1) *doctores ecclesiæ.* Leo **XIII.**, on the other hand, in 1879 recommended in the encyclical *Æterni patris,* in the most urgent way, all Catholic schools to make the philosophy of the angelical Aquinas (§ 103, 6) their foundation, founded in 1880 an " Academy of St. Thomas Aquinas," three out of its thirty members being Germans, Kleutgen, Stöckl, and Morgott, and gave 300,000 lire out of Peter's pence for an edition of Aquinas' works with the commentaries of "the most eminent expositors," setting aside "all those books which, while professing to be derived from St. Thomas are really drawn from foreign and unholy sources "; *i.e.,* in accordance with the desires of the Jesuits, omitting the strictly Thomist expositors (§ 149, 13), and giving currency only to Jesuit interpretations. No wonder that the Jesuit General Beckx in such circumstances submitted himself " humbly," being praised for this by the pope as a saint. But a much greater, indeed a really great, service to the documentary examination of the history of the Christian church and state has been rendered by the same pope, undoubtedly at the instigation of Cardinal Hergenröther, by the access granted not only to Catholic but also to Protestant investigators to the exceedingly rich treasures of the Vatican archives. Though still hedged round with considerable limitations, the concession seems liberality itself as compared with the stubborn refusal of Pius IX. to facilitate the studies of any inquirer. With honest pride the pope could inscribe on his bust placed in the library: " *Leo XIII. Pont. Max. historiæ*

studiis consulens tabularii arcana reclusit a 1880."—But what the ends
were which he had in view and what the hopes that he cherished,
is seen from the rescript of August, 1883, in which he calls upon
the cardinals De Luca, Pitra, and Hergenröther, as prefects of the
committee of studies, of the library and archives, while proclaiming
the great benefits which the papacy has secured to Italy, to do their
utmost to overthrow "the lies uttered by the sects" on the history of
the church, especially in reference to the papacy, for, he adds, "we
desire that at last once more the truth should prevail." Therefore
archives and library are to be opened to pious and learned students
"for the service of religion and science in order that the historical
untruths of the enemies of the church which have found entrance
even into the schoolbooks should be displaced by the composition of
good writings. The firstfruits of the zeal thus stimulated were the
"*Monumenta ref. Lutheranœ ex tabulariis S. Sedis,*" Ratisbon, 1883,
published by the assistant keeper of the archives P. Balan as an ex-
tinguisher to the Luther Jubilee of that year. But this performance
came so far short of the wishes and expectations of the Roman zealots
that by their influence the editor was removed from his official
position. The next attempt of this sort was the edition by Hergenröther of the papal *Regesta* down to Leo X.

IV.—Relation of Church to the Empire and to the States.

§ 192. The German Confederation.

The Peace of Luneville of 1801 gave the deathblow to
the old German empire, by the formal cession of the left
bank of the Rhine to France, indemnifying the secular
princes who were losers by this arrangement with estates
and possessions on the right of the Rhine, taken from the
neutral free cities of the empire and the secularized ecclesiastical principalities, institutions, monasteries, and orders.
An imperial commission sitting at Regensburg arranged
the details of these indemnifications. They were given expression to by means of the imperial commission's decree or
recess of 1803. The dissolution of the constitution of the
German empire thus effected was still further carried out
by the Peace of Presburg of 1805, which conferred upon the

princes of Bavaria, Württemberg, and Baden, in league with
Napoleon, full sovereignty, and to the two first named the
rank of kings, and was completed by the founding of the
Confederation of the Rhine of 1806, in which sixteen German
princes formally severed themselves from the emperor and
empire and ranked themselves as vassals of France under
the protectorate of Napoleon. Francis II., who already in
1804 had assumed the title of Emperor of Austria as Francis
I., now that the German empire had actually ceased to exist,
renounced also the name of German emperor. The unhappy
proceedings of the Vienna Congress of the German Confederation and its permanent representation in the Frankfort
parliament during 1814 and 1815, after Napoleon's twice
repeated defeat, led finally to the Austro-Prussian war of
1866.

1. The Imperial Commission's Decree, 1803.—The significance of this
for church history consists not merely in the secularization of the
ecclesiastical principalities and corporations, but even still more in
the alteration caused thereby in the ecclesiastical polity of the territorial governments. With the ecclesiastical principalities the most
powerful props of the Catholic church in Germany were lost, and
Protestantism obtained a decided ascendency in the council of the
German princes. The Catholic prelates were now simply paid servants of the state, and thus their double connexion with the curia
and the state brought with it in later times endless entanglements
and complications. On the other hand, in states hitherto almost exclusively Protestant, e.g. Württemberg, Baden, Hesse, there was a
great increase of Catholic subjects, which attracted but little serious
attention when the confessional particularism in the consciousness of
the age was more unassuming and tolerant than ever it has been
before or since.

2. The Prince-Primate of the Confederation of the Rhine.—Baron Carl
Theod. von Dalberg, distinguished for his literary culture and his
liberal patronage of art and science, was made in 1802 Elector of
Mainz and Lord High Chancellor of the German empire. When by
the recess of 1803 the territories of the electorate on the left of the
Rhine were given over to France and those on the right secularized,
the electoral rank was abolished. The same happened with respect
to the lord high chancellorship through the creation of the Rhenish

Confederation. Dalberg was indemnified for the former by the favour of Napoleon by the gift of a small territory on the right of the Rhine, and for the latter by the renewal of the prince-primacy of the Confederation of the Rhine with a seat in the Federal council. He still retained his episcopal office and fixed its seat at Regensburg. The founding of a metropolitan chapter at Regensburg embracing the whole domain of the Rhenish Confederation he did not succeed in carrying out, and in 1813 he felt compelled to surrender also his territorial possessions. His spiritual functions, however, as Archbishop of Regensburg, he continued to discharge until his death in 1817.

8. The Vienna Congress and the Concordat.—The Vienna Congress of 1814, 1815, had assigned it the difficult task of righting the sorely disturbed political affairs of Europe and giving a new shape to the territorial and dynastic relations. But never had an indispensably necessary redistribution of territory been made more difficult or more complicated by diplomatic intrigues than in Germany. Instead of the earlier federation of states, the restoration of which proved impossible, the federal constitution of June 8th, 1815, created under the name of the German Confederation a union of states in which all members of the confederation as such exercised equal sovereign rights. Their number then amounted to thirty-eight, but in the course of time by death or withdrawal were reduced to thirty-four. The new distribution of territory, just as little as the Luneville Peace, took into account confessional homogeneity of princes and territories, so that the combination of Catholic and Protestant districts with the above referred to consequences, occurred in a yet larger measure. But the federal constitution secured in Article XVI. full toleration for all Christian confessions in the countries of the confederation. The claims of the Romish curia, which advanced from the demand for the restoration of all ecclesiastical principalities and the return of all impropriated churches and monasteries to their original purposes, to the demand for the restoration of the holy Roman-German empire in the mediæval and hierarchical sense, as well as the solemn protest against its conclusions laid upon the table of the congress by the papal legate Consalvi, were left quite unheeded. But also a proposal urgently pressed by the vicar-general of the diocese of Constance, Baron von Wessenberg (§ 187, 3), to found a German Catholic national church under a German primate found no favour with the congress; and an article recommended by Austria and Prussia to be incorporated in the acts of the confederation by which the Catholic church in Germany endeavoured to secure a common constitution under guarantee of the confederation, was rejected through the opposition of Bavaria. And since in the Frankfort parliament neither Wessenburg with his primacy and national church idea nor Consalvi with a comprehensive

concordat answering to the wishes of the curia, was able to carry through a measure, it was left to the separate states interested to make separate concordats with the pope. Bavaria concluded a concordat in 1817 (§ 195, 1); Prussia in 1821 (§ 193, 1). Negotiations with the other German states fell through owing to the excessiveness of the demands of the hierarchy, or led to very unsatisfactory results, as in Hanover in 1824 (§ 194, 1) and the states belonging to the ecclesiastical province of the Upper Rhine in 1837 (§ 196, 1). In the time of re-action against the revolutionary excesses of 1848 the curia first secured any real advance. Hesse-Darmstadt opened the list in 1854 with a secret convention (§ 196, 4); then Austria followed in 1855 with a model concordat (§ 198, 2) which served as the pattern for the concordats with Württemberg in 1857 (§ 196, 6), and with Baden in 1859 (§ 196, 2), as well as for the episcopal convention with Nassau in 1861 (§ 196, 4). But the revived liberal current of 1860 swept away the South German concordats; the Vatican Council by its infallibility dogma gave the deathblow to that of Austria, and the German "*Kulturkampf*" sent the Prussian concordat to the winds, and only that of Bavaria remained in full force.

4. **The Frankfort Parliament and the Würzburg Bishops' Congress of 1848.**—As in the March diets of 1848 the magic word "freedom" roused throughout Germany a feverish excitement, it found a ready response among the Catholics, whose church was favoured in the highest degree by the movement. In the Frankfort parliament the ablest leaders of Catholic Germany had seats. Among the Catholic population there were numerous religio-political societies formed (§ 186, 3), and the German bishops, avowedly for the celebration of the 600th anniversary of the building of Cologne cathedral, set alongside of the Frankfort people's parliament a German bishops' council. After they had at Frankfort declared themselves in favour of unconditional liberty of faith, conscience, and worship, the complete independence of all religious societies in the ordering and administering of their affairs, but also of freeing the schools from all ecclesiastical control and oversight, as well as of the introduction of obligatory civil marriage, the bishops' council met in October at Würzburg under the presidency of Archbishop Geissel of Cologne with nineteen episcopal assistants and several able theological advisers. In thirty-six sessions they reached the conclusion that complete separation between church and state is not to be desired so long as the state does not refuse to the church the place of authority belonging to it. On the other hand, by all means in their power they are to seek the abrogation of the *placet* of the sovereign, the full independence of ecclesiastical legislation, administration and jurisdiction, with the abolition of the *appellatio tanquam ab abusu*, the direction and oversight of the public schools as

well as the control of religious instruction in higher schools to be given only by teachers licensed for the purpose by the bishops, and finally to demand permission to erect educational institutions of their own of every kind, etc., and to forward a copy of these decisions to all German governments. The main object of the Würzburg assembly to secure currency for their resolutions in the new Germany sketched out at the Frankfort parliament, was indeed frustrated by that parliament's speedy overthrow. Nevertheless in the several states concerned it proved of great and lasting importance in determining the subsequent unanimous proceedings of the bishops.

§ 193. PRUSSIA.

To the pious king Frederick William III. (1797-1840) it was a matter of heart and conscience to turn to account the religious consciousness of his people, re-awakened by God's gracious help during the war of independence, for the healing of the three hundred years' rent in the evangelical church by a union of the two evangelical confessions. The jubilee festival of the Reformation in 1817 seemed to him to offer the most favourable occasion. The king also desired to see the Catholic church in his dominions restored to an orderly and thriving condition, and for this end concluded a concordat with Rome in 1821. But it was broken up in 1836 over a strife between canon and civil law in reference to mixed marriages. Frederick William IV. was dominated by romantic ideas, and his reign (1840-1858), notwithstanding all his evangelical Christian decidedness, was wanting in the necessary firmness and energetic consistency. In the Catholic church the Jesuits were allowed unhindered to foster ultramontane hierarchical principles, and in the evangelical church the troubles about constitution, union, and confession could not be surmounted either by its own proper guardian, the episcopate, or by the superior church councils created in 1850. And although the notifications of William I. on his entrance upon the sole government in 1858 were hailed by the liberals as giving assurance that a new era had dawned in the development of the evangelical national church, this hope proved to be premature. With the exaltation of the victory-crowned royal house of Prussia to the throne of the newly erected German Empire on January 18th, 1871, a new era was actually opened for ecclesiastical developments and modifications throughout the land.

1. **The Catholic Church to the Close of the Cologne Conflict.**—The government of Frederick William III. entered into negotiations with the papal curia, not so much for the old provinces in which everything was going well, but rather in the interests of the Rhine provinces annexed in 1814, whose bishops' sees were vacant or in need of circumscription. The first Prussian ambassador to the Roman curia (1816–1823) was the famous historian Niebuhr. Although a true Protestant and keen critic and restorer of the history of old pagan Rome he was no match for the subtle and skilful diplomacy of Consalvi. In presence of the claims of the curia he manifested to an almost incredible extent trustful sympathy and acquiescence, even taking to do with matters that lay outside of Prussian affairs, eagerly silencing and opposing any considerations suggested from the other side. A complete concordat, however, defining in detail all the relations between church and state was not secured, but in 1821 an agreement was come to, with thankful acknowledgment of the "great magnanimity and goodness" shown by the king, by the bull *De salute animarum*, sanctioned by the king through a cabinet order ("in the exercise of his royal prerogative and without detriment to these rights"), according to which two archbishoprics, Cologne and Posen, and six bishoprics, Treves, Münster, Paderborn, Breslau, Kulm, and Ermeland, with a clerical seminary, were erected in Prussia and furnished with rich endowments. The cathedral chapter was to have the free choice of the bishop; but by an annexed note it was recommended to make sure in every such election that the one so chosen would be a *grata persona* to the king. The union thus effected between church and state was of but short duration. The decree of Trent forbade Catholics to enter into mixed marriages with non-Catholics. A later papal bull of 1741, however, permitted it on condition of an only passive assistance of the clergy at the wedding and an engagement by the parents to train up the children as Catholics. The law of Prussia, on the other hand, in contested cases made all the children follow the religion of their fathers. As this was held in 1825 to apply to the Rhine provinces, and as the bishops there had, in 1828, appealed to the pope, Pius VIII. when negotiations with the Prussian ambas-

sador Bunsen (1824–1838) proved fruitless, issued in 1830 a brief which permitted Catholic priests to give the ecclesiastical sanction to mixed marriages only when a promise was given that the children should be educated as Catholics, but otherwise to give only passive assistance. When all remonstrances failed to overcome the obstinacy of the curia, the government turned to the Archbishop of Cologne, Count Spiegel, a zealous friend and promoter of the Hermesian theology (§ 191, 1), and arranged in 1834 a secret convention with him, which by his influence all his suffragans joined. In it they promised to give such an interpretation to the brief that its observance would be limited to teaching and exhortation, but would by no means extend to the obligation of submitting the children to Catholic baptism, and that the mere *assistentia passiva* would be resorted to as rarely as possible, and only in cases where absolutely required. Spiegel died in November, 1835. In 1836 the Westphalian Baron Clement Droste von Vischering was chosen as his successor. Although before his elevation he had unhesitatingly agreed to the convention, soon after his enthronization he strictly forbad all the clergy celebrating any marriage except in accordance with the brief, and blamed himself for having believed the agreement between convention and brief affirmed by the government, and having only subsequently on closer examination discovered the disagreement between the two. At the same time, in order to give effect to the condemnation that had been meanwhile passed on the Hermesian theology, he gave orders that at the confessional the Bonn students should be forbidden to attend the lectures of Hermesians. When the archbishop could not be prevailed on to yield, he was condemned in 1837 as having broken his word and having incited to rebellion, and sent to the fortress of Minden. Gregory XIV. addressed to the consistory a fulminating allocution, and a flood of controversial tracts on either side swept over Germany. Görres designated the archbishop "the Athanasius of the nineteenth century." The government issued a state paper justifying its procedure, and the courts of law sentenced certain refractory priests to several years' confinement in fortresses or prisons. The moderate peaceful tone of the cathedral chapter did much to quell the disturbance, supporting as it did the state rather than the archbishop. The example of Cologne encouraged also Dunin, Archbishop of Gnesen and Posen, to issue in 1838 a pastoral in which he threatened with suspension any priest in his diocese who would not yield unconditional obedience to the papal brief. For this he was deposed by the civil courts and sentenced to half a year's imprisonment in a fortress, but the king prevented the execution of the sentence. But Dunin fled from Berlin, whither he had been ordered by the king, to Posen, and was then brought in 1839 to the fortress of Kolberg. While matters were in this state Frederick William IV.

came to the throne in 1840. Dunin was immediately restored, after promising to maintain the peace. Droste also was released from his confinement with public marks of respect, but received in 1841, with his own and the pope's approval, in the former Bishop of Spires, Geissel, a coadjutor, who in his name and with the right of succession administered the diocese. The government gave no aid to the Hermesians. The law in regard to mixed marriages continued indeed in force, but was exercised so as to put no constraint of conscience upon the Catholic clergy. Of his own accord the king declined further exercise of the royal prerogative, allowing the bishops direct intercourse with the papal see, whereas previously all correspondence had to pass through royal committees, with this proviso by the minister Eichhorn, "that this display of generous confidence be not abused," and with the expectation that the bishops would not only communicate to the government the contents of their correspondence with the pope, but also the papal replies which did not deal exclusively with doctrine, and would not speak and act against the wish and will of the government. But Geissel, recommended by Louis of Bavaria to his son-in-law Frederick William IV. instead of Baron von Diepenbrock (§ 187, 1) who was first thought of, by his skilful and energetic manœuvring, going on from victory to victory, raised ultramontanism in Prussia to the very summit of its influence and glory.

2. The Golden Age of Prussian Ultramontanism, 1841-1871.—In the Cologne-Posen conflict Rome had won an almost complete victory, and with all its satellites now thought only of how it might in the best possible manner turn this victory to account, in which the all too trustful government sought to aid it to the utmost. This movement received a further impulse in the revolution of 1848 (§ 192, 4). In Prussia as well as in other German lands, and there in a special degree, the Catholic church managed to derive from the revolutionary movements of those times, and from the subsequent reaction, substantial advantage. The constitution of 1850 declared in Article xv.: "The evangelical and the Roman Catholic Church as well as every other religious society regulates and administers its affairs independently "; in Article xvi.: "The correspondence of religious societies with their superiors is unrestricted, the publication of ecclesiastical ordinances is subject only to those limitations which apply to all other documents"; in Article xviii.: "The right of nomination, proposal, election, and institution to spiritual office, so far as it belongs to the state, is abolished "; and in Article xxiv.: "The respective religious societies direct religious instruction in the public schools." Under the screen of these fundamental privileges the Catholic episcopate now claimed one civil prerogative after another, emancipated itself wholly from the laws of the state, and, on the plea that God must be obeyed

rather than man, made the canon law, not only in purely ecclesiastical
but also in mixed matters, the only standard, and the decision of the
pope the final appeal. At last nothing was left to the state but the
obligation of conferring splendid endowments upon the bishops,
cathedral chapters, and seminaries for priests, and the honour of being
at home the executioner of episcopal tyranny, and abroad the avenger
of every utterance unfavourable to the doctrine and worship, customs
and enactments of the Catholic church. With almost incredible infatuation the Catholic hierarchy was now regarded as a main support
of the throne against the revolutionary tendencies of the age and as
the surest guarantee for the loyalty of subjects in provinces predominantly Catholic. Under protection of the law allowing the
formation of societies and the right of assembling, the order of Jesuits
set up one establishment after another, and made up for defects or
insufficient energy of ultramontane pastoral work, agitation and
endeavour at conversion on the part of other peaceably disposed parish
priests, by numerous missions conducted in the most ostentatious
manner (§ 186, 6). Although according to Article xiii. of the constitution religious societies could obtain corporative rights only by
special enactments, the bishops, on their own authority, without regarding this provision, established religious orders and congregations
wherever they chose. As these were generally placed under foreign
superiors male or female, to whom in Jesuit fashion unconditional
obedience was rendered, each member being "like a corpse," without
any individual will, they spread without hindrance, so that continually new cloisters and houses of the orders sprang up like mush-
rooms over the Protestant metropolis (§ 186, 2). Education in Catholic
districts fell more and more into the hands of religious corporations,
and even the higher state educational institutions, so far as they dealt
with the training of the Catholic youth (theological faculties,
gymnasia, and Training schools), were wholly under the control of
the bishops. From the boys' convents and priests' seminaries, erected
at all episcopal residences, went forth a new generation of clergy
reared in the severest school of intolerance, who, first of all acting as
chaplains, by espionage, the arousing of suspicion and talebearing, were
the dread of the old parish priests, and, as "chaplains at large," stirred
up fanaticism among the people, and secured the Catholic press to
themselves as a monopoly. For the purposes of Catholic worship and
education the government had placed state aid most liberally at their
disposal, without requiring any account from the bishops as to their
disposal of the money. Although the number of Catholics in the
whole country was only about half that of the Protestants, the endowment of the Catholic was almost double that of the evangelical church.
The civil authority readily helped the bishops to enforce any spiritual

penalties, and thus the inferior clergy were brought into absolute dependence upon their spiritual superiors. In the government department of Public Worship, from 1840 to 1848 under the direction of Eichhorn, there was since 1841 a subsection for dealing with the affairs of the Catholic church which, although restricted to the guarding of the rights of the king over against the curia and that of the state over against the hierarchy, came to be in an entirely opposite sense "the civil department of the pope in Prussia." Under Von Mühler's ministry, 1862-1872, it obtained absolute authority which it seems to have exercised in removing unfavourable acts and documents from the imperial archives. And thus the Catholic church, or rather the ultramontane party dominant in it since 1848, grew up into a power that threatened the whole commonwealth in its very foundations.— By the annexation of Hanover, Hesse, and Nassau in 1866, four new bishoprics, those of Hildesheim, Osnabrück, Fulda and Limburg were added to the previous eight.—Continuation § 197.

3. The Evangelical Church in Old Prussia down to 1848.—On the accomplishment of the union by Frederick William III. and the confusions arising therefrom, see § 177. Frederick William IV. on his accession declared his wish in reference to the national evangelical church, that the supreme control of the church should be exercised only in order to secure for it in an orderly and legal way the independent administration of its own affairs. The realization of this idea, after a church conference of the ordinary clergy from almost all German states had been held in Berlin without result, was attempted at Berlin by a general synod, opened on Whitsunday, 1846. The synod at its eighteenth session entered upon the consideration of the difficult question of doctrine and the confession. The result of this was the approval of an ordination formula drawn up by Dr. Nitzsch (§ 182, 10), according to which the candidate for ordination was to make profession of the great fundamental and saving truths instead of the church confession hitherto enforced. And since among these fundamental truths the doctrines of creation, original sin, the supernatural conception, the descent into hell and the ascension of Christ, the resurrection of the body, the last judgment, everlasting life and everlasting punishment were not included, and therefore were not to enforced, since further by this ordination formula the special confessions of Lutheran and Reformed were really set aside, and therewith the existence of a Lutheran as well as a Reformed church within the union seemed to be abolished, a small number of decided Lutherans in the synod protested ; still more decided and vigorous protests arose from outside the synod, to which the *Evang. Kirchenzeitung* opened its columns. The government gave no further countenance to the decisions of the synod, and opponents exercised their wit upon

the unfortunate *Nicænum* of the nineteenth century, which as a *Nitzschenum* had fallen into the water. In March, 1847, the king issued a patent of toleration, by which protection was assured anew to existing churches, but the formation of new religious societies was allowed to all who found not in these the expression of their belief.

4. The Evangelical Church in Old Prussia, 1848-1872.—When the storms of revolution broke out in 1848, the new minister of worship, Count Schwerin, willingly aided in reorganizing the church according to the mind of the masses of the people by a constitutional synod. But before it had met the reaction had already set in. The transition ministry of Ladenberg was assured by consistories and faculties of the danger of convoking such a synod of representatives of the people. Instead of the synod therefore a Supreme Church Council was assembled at Berlin in 1850, which, independent of the ministry, and only under the king as *præcipuum membrum ecclesiæ*, should represent the freedom of the church from the state as something already realized. On March 6th, 1852, the king issued a cabinet order, in consequence of which the Supreme Church Council administered not only the affairs of the evangelical national church as a whole, but also was charged with the interests of the Lutheran as well as the Reformed church in particular, and was to be composed of members from both of those confessions, who should alone have to decide on questions referring to their own confession. On the *Itio in partes* thus required in this board, only Dr. Nitzsch remained over, as he declared that he could find expression for his religious convictions in neither of the two confessions, but only in a consensus of both. The difficulty was overcome by reckoning him a representative equally of both denomination. Encouraged by such connivance in high places to entertain still bolder hopes, the Lutheran societies in 1853 presented to the king a petition signed by one hundred and sixty one clergymen, for restoring Lutheran faculties and the Lutheran church property. But this called forth a rather unfavourable cabinet order, in which the king expressed his disapproval of such a misconception of the ordinances of the former year, and made the express declaration that it never was his intention to break up or weaken the union effected by his father, that he only wished to give the confession within the union the protection to which it was undoubtedly entitled. After this the separate Lutheran interest so long highly favoured fell into manifest and growing disfavour. Still the ministerial department of worship under Von Raumer, 1850-1858, continued to conduct the affairs of schools and universities in the spirit of the ecclesiastical orthodox reaction, and issued the endless school regulations conceived in this spirit of the privy councillor Stiehl. The Supreme Church Council also exhibited a rare activity and passed many wholesome ordinances

The evangelical church won great credit by the care it took of its members scattered over distant lands, in supplying them with clergy and teachers. The evident favour with which Frederick William IV. furthered the efforts of the Evangelical Alliance of 1857 (§ 178, 8) was the last proof of decided aversion from the confessional movement which he was to be allowed to give. A long and hopeless illness, of which he died in 1861, obliged him to resign the government to his brother William I. When this monarch in October, 1855, began to rule in his own name, he declared to his newly appointed ministers that it was his firm resolve that the evangelical union, whose beneficent development had been obstructive to an orthodoxy incompatible with the character of the evangelical church, and which had thus almost caused its ruin, should be maintained and further advanced. But in order that the task might be accomplished, the organs for its administration must be carefully chosen and to some extent changed. All hypocrisy and formalism, which that orthodoxy had fostered, is wherever possible to be removed. The "new era," however, marked by the appearance of liberal journals, by no means answered to the expectations which those words excited. The ministry of Von Bethmann-Hollweg, 1858-1862, filled some theological and spiritual offices in this liberal spirit; Stahl withdrew from the Supreme Church Council; the proceedings against the free churches, as well as the severe measures against the re-marriage of divorced parties, were relaxed. But the marriage law laid down by the ministry with permission of civil marriage was rejected by the House of Peers, and the hated school regulations had to be undertaken by the minister himself. The ecclesiastically conservative ministry of Von Mühler, 1862-1872, which, however, wanted a fixed principle as well as self-determined energy of will, and was therefore often vacillating and losing the respect of all parties, was utterly unfit to realize these expectations. The Supreme Church Council published in 1867 the outlines of a provincial synodal constitution for the six East Provinces which were still without this institution, which the Rhine Provinces and Westphalia had enjoyed since 1835. For this purpose he convened in autumn, 1869, an extraordinary provincial synod, which essentially approved the sketch submitted, whereupon it was provisionally enacted.

5. The Evangelical Church in Old Prussia, 1872-1880.—After the removal of Von Mühler, the minister of worship, in January, 1872, his place was taken by Dr. Falk, 1872-1879. The hated school regulations were now at last set aside and replaced by new moderate prescriptions, conceived in an almost unexpectedly temperate spirit. On September 10th, 1873, the king issued a congregational and synodal constitution for the eastern provinces, with the express statement that the position

of the confession and the union should thereby be in no way affected. It prescribed that in every congregation presided over by a pastor, elected by the ecclesiastically qualified church members, *i.e.* those of honourable life who had taken part in public worship and received the sacraments, there should be a church council of from four to twelve persons, and for more important matters, *e.g.* the election of a pastor, a congregational committee of three times the size, half of which should be reappointed every third year. To the district synod, presided over by the superintendent, each congregation sends as delegates besides the pastor a lay representative chosen by the church council from among its members or from the congregational committee. According to the same principle the District Synods choose from their members a clerical and a lay representative to the provincial synod, to which also the evangelical theological faculty of the university within the bounds sends a deputy, and the territorial lord nominates a number of members not exceeding a sixth part of the whole. The general synod, in which also the two western provinces, the Rhenish and Westphalian, take part, consists of one hundred and fifty delegates from the provincial synods, and thirty nominated by the territorial lords, to which the faculties of theology and law of the six universities within the bounds send each one of their members. Although this royal decree had proclaimed itself final, and only remitted to an Extraordinary General Synod to be called forthwith the task of arranging for future ordinary general synods, yet at the meeting of this extraordinary synod in Berlin, on November 24th, 1875, a draft was submitted of a constitution modified in various important points. Of the three demands of the liberal party now violently insisted upon—(1) Substitution of the "filter" system in the election of provincial and general synod members for that of the community electorate. (2) Strengthening of the lay element in all synods; and (3) Abolition of the equality of small village communities with large town communities—the first was by far the most important and serious in its consequences, but the other two bore fruit through the decree that two-thirds of the members of the district and provincial synods should be laymen, and the other one-third should be freely elected to the district synod from the populous town communities, for the provincial synods from the larger district synods. Also in reference to the rights belonging to the several grades of synods, considerable modifications were made, whereby the privileges of communities were variously increased (*e.g.* to them was given the right of refusing to introduce the catechisms and hymn-books sanctioned by the provincial synods), while those of the district and provincial synods were lessened in favour of the general synod, and those of the latter again in favour of the high church council and

the minister of public worship. After nearly four weeks' discussion the bill without any serious amendments was passed by the
assembly, and on January 20th, 1876, received the royal assent and
became an ecclesiastical law. But in order to give it also the rank of
a law of the state, a decision of the States' Parliament on the relation
of church and state was necessary. The parliament had already in
1874, when the original congregational and synodal constitution was
submitted to it, in order to advance the movement, approved only the
congregational constitution with provisional refusal of everything
going beyond that. In May, 1876, the bill already raised by the king
into an ecclesiastical law, passed both houses of parliament, and had
here also some amendments introduced with the effect of increasing
and strengthening the prerogative of the state. The main points in
the law as then passed are these: The general synod, whose members
undertake to fulfil their duties agreeably to the word of God and the
ordinances of the evangelical national church, has the task of maintaining and advancing the state church on the basis of the evangelical
confession. The laws of the state church must receive its assent, but
any measure agreed upon by it cannot be laid before the king for his
sanction without the approval of the minister of public worship. It
meets every sixth year; in the interval it, as well as the provincial
synods, is represented by a synodal committee chosen from its members. The head of the church government is the Supreme Church
Council, whose president countersigns the ecclesiastical laws approved
by the king. The right of appointing to this office lies with the
minister of public worship; in the nomination of other members the
president makes proposals with consent of the minister. Taxation of
the general synod for parliamentary purposes needs the assent of the
minister of state, and must, if it exceeds four per cent. of the class
and income tax, be agreed to by the Lower House, which also annually
has to determine the expenditure on ecclesiastical administration.

6. When preparations were being made for the extraordinary
general synod, the king had repeatedly given vigorous expression to
his positive religious standpoint, and from the proposed lists of members for that synod submitted by the minister of public worship all
names belonging to the *Protestantenverein* were struck out. Still
more decidedly in 1877 did he show his disapproval in the Rhode-
Hossbach troubles (§ 180, 4), by declaring his firm belief in the
divinity of Christ, and when the then president of the Brandenburg
consistory, Hegel, tendered his resignation, owing to differences with
the liberal president of the Supreme Church Council, Hermann, the
king refused to accept it, because he could not then spare any such
men as held by the apostolic faith. In May, 1878, Hermann was at
last, after repeated solicitations, allowed to retire, Dr. Hermes, member

of the Supreme Church Council, was nominated his successor, and the positive tendency of the Supreme Church Council was strengthened by the admission of the court preachers, Kögel and Baur. His proposals again disagreeing with the royal nominations for the provincial synod and for the First Ordinary General Synod of autumn, 1879, led the minister of public worship, Dr. Falk, at last, after repeated solicitation, to accept his resignation. It was granted him in July, 1879, and the chief president of the province of Silesia, Von Puttkamer, a more decided adherent of the positive union party, was named as his successor; but in June, 1881, he was made minister of the interior, and the undersecretary of the department of public worship, Von Gossler, was made minister. The general synod, October 10th till November 3rd, consisted of fifty-two confessionalists, seventy-six positive-unionists, fifty-six of the middle party or evangelical unionist, and nine from the ranks of the left, the *Protestantenverein;* three confessionalists, twelve positive-unionists, and fifteen of the middle party were nominated by the king. The measures proposed by the Supreme hurch Council: (1) A marriage service without reference to the preceding civil marriage, with two marriage formulæ, the first a joint promise, the second a benediction; (2) A disciplinary law against despisers of baptism and marriage, which threatened such with the loss of all ecclesiastical electoral rights, and eventually with exclusion from the Lord's supper and sponsor rights; and (3) A law dealing with *Emeriti,* were adopted by the synod and then approved by the king. On the other hand a series of independent proposals conceived in the interests of the high-church party remained in suspense. The last effected elections for the general synod committee resulted in the appointment of three positive-unionist members, including the president, two confessionalists, and two of the middle party.[1]

7. The Evangelical Church in the Annexed Provinces.—In 1866 the provinces of Hanover, Hesse and Schleswig-Holstein were incorporated with the kingdom of Prussia. In these political particularism, combined with confessional Lutheranism, suspicion of every organized system of church government as intended to introduce Prussian unionism, even to the extreme of open rebellion, led to violent conflicts. The king, indeed, personally gave assurance in Cassel, Hanover and Kiel that the position of the church confession should in no way be endangered. "He will indeed support the union where it already existed as a sacred legacy to him from his forefathers; he

[1] Geffcken, "Church and State," vol. ii. pp. 501–531. Smith, "The Falk Legislation from the Political Point of View," in the *Theological Review* for October, 1875.

also hopes that it may always make further progress as a witness to the grand unity of the evangelical church; but compulsion is to be applied to no man." The consistories of these provinces were still to continue independent of the Supreme Church Council. But the ministerial order for the restoration of representative synodal constitution increasingly prevailed, although the wide-spread suspicion and individual protests against the system of church government, such as the temporary prohibition of the Marburg consistory of the mission festival, as avowedly used for agitation against the intended synodal constitution, helped to intensify the bitterness of feeling. But on the other hand many preachers by their unbecoming pulpit harangues, and their refusal to take the oath of allegiance or service, to pray in church for their new sovereign, and to observe the general holiday appointed to be held in 1869 on November 10th (Luther's birthday), etc., compelled the ecclesiastical authorities to impose fines, suspension, penal transportation, and deposition. In the Lutheran Schleswig-Holstein a new congregational constitution was introduced in 1869 by the minister Von Mühler, as the basis of a future synodal constitution, which was adopted by the *Vorsynode* of Rendsburg in 1871, preserving the confessional status laid down, without discussion. In 1878 an advance was made by the institution of district or provostship synods, and in February, 1880, the first General Synod was held at Rendsburg. As in Old Prussia so also here the conservative movement proved victorious. The laity obtained majorities in all synods, and the supremacy of the state was secured by the subordination of the church government under the minister of public worship.

8. In Hanover, where especially Lichtenberg, president of the upper consistory, and Uhlhorn, member of the upper consistory (since 1878 abbot of Loccûm), although many Lutheran extremists long remained dissatisfied, temperately and worthily maintained the independence and privileges of the Lutheran church, the first national synod could be convened and could bring to a generally peaceful conclusion the question of the constitution only in the end of 1869, after the preliminary labour of the national synod committee. In 1882 the Reformed communities of 120,000 souls, hitherto subject to Lutheran consistories, obtained an independent congregational and synodal constitution. Against the new marriage ordinance enacted in consequence of the civil marriage law (§ 197, 5), Theod. Harms (brother, and from 1865 successor of L. Harms, § 184, 1), pastor and director of Hermannsburg missionary seminary, rebelled from the conviction that civil marriage did not deserve to be recognised as marriage. He was first suspended, then in 1877 deposed from office, and with the most of his congregation retired and founded a separate Lutheran community, to which subsequently fifteen other small congregations of 4,000 souls

were attached. As teacher and pupils of the seminary made it a zealous propaganda for the secession, the missionary journals and missionary festivals were misused for the same purpose, and as Harms answered the questions of the consistory in reference thereto, partly by denying, partly by excusing, that court, in December, 1878, forbad the missionary collections hitherto made throughout the churches at Epiphany for Hermannsburg, and so completely broke off the connection between the state church and the institution which had hither-been regarded as "its pride and its preserving salt." A reaction has since set in in favour of the seminary and its friends on the assurance that the interests of the separation would not be furthered by the seminary, and that several other objectionable features, *e.g.* the frequent employment in the mission service of artisans without theological training, the sending of them out in too great numbers without sufficient endowment and salary, so that missionaries were obliged to engage in trade speculations, should be removed as far as possible; but since the seminary life was always still carried on upon the basis of ecclesiastical secession, it could lead to no permanent reconciliation with the state church. Harms died in 1885. His son Egmont was chosen his successor, and as the consistory refused ordination, he accepted consecration at the hands of five members of the Immanuel Synod at Magdeburg.

9. In Hesse the ministry of Von Mühler sought to bring about a combination of the three consistories of Hanau, Cassel, and Marburg, as a necessary vehicle for the introduction of a new synodal constitution. In the province itself an agitation was persistently carried on for and against the constitutional scheme submitted by the ministers, which wholly ignored the old church order (§ 127, 2), which, though in the beginning of the seventeenth century through the ecclesiastical disturbances of the time (§ 154, 1), it had passed out of use, had never been abrogated and so was still legally valid. A *Vorsynode* convened in 1870 approved of it in all essential points, but conventions of superintendents, pastoral conferences and lay addresses protested, and the Prussian parliament, for which it was not yet liberal enough, refused the necessary supplies. As these after Von Mühler's overthrow were granted, his successor, Dr. Falk, immediately proceeded in 1873 to set up in Cassel the court that had been objected to so long. It was constituted after the pattern of the Supreme Church Council, of Lutheran, Reformed, and United members with *Itio in partes* on specifically confessional questions. The clergy of Upper Hesse comforted themselves with saying that the new courts in which the confessions were combined, if not better, were at least no worse than the earlier consistories in which the confessions were confounded; and they felt obliged to yield obedience to them, so long as they did not

demand anything contradictory the Lutheran confession. On the other hand, many of the clergy of Lower Hesse saw in the advance from a merely eventual to an actual blending of the confessional status in church government an intolerable deterioration. And so forty-five clergymen of Lower and one of Upper Hesse laid before the king a protest against the innovation as destructive of the confessional rights of the Hessian church contrary to the will of the supreme majesty of Jesus Christ. They were dismissed with sharp rebuke, and, with the exception of four who submitted, were deposed from office for obstinate refusal to obey. There were about sixteen congregations which to a greater or less extent kept aloof from the new pastors appointed by the consistories, and without breaking away from the state church wished to remain true to the old pastor " appointed by Jesus Christ himself."—In autumn, 1884, the movement on behalf of the restoration of a presbyterial and synodal constitution of the Hessian evangelical church, which had been delayed for fourteen years, was resumed. A sketch of a constitution, which placed it under three general superintendents (Lutheran, Reformed, United) and thirteen superintendents, and, for the fair co-operation of the lay element in the administration of church affairs (the confession status, however, being beyond discussion), provided suitable organs in the shape of presbyteries and synods, with a predominance of the lay element, was submitted to a *Vorsynode* that met on November 12th, consisting of two divisions, like a Lower and Upper House, sitting together. The first division, as representative of the then existing church order, embraced, in accordance with the practice of the old Hessian synods, all the members of the consistory, *i.e.* the nine superintendents and thirteen pastors elected by the clergy ; the second, consisting at least of as many lay as clerical members, was chosen by the free election of the congregation. The royal assent was given to the decrees of the *Vorsynode* in the end of December, 1885, and the confessional status was thereby expressly guaranteed.

§ 194. The North German smaller States.

In most of the smaller North German states, owing to the very slight representation of the Reformed church, which was considerable only in Bremen, Lippe-Detmold, and a part of Hesse and East Friesland, the union met with little favour. Yet only in a few of those provinces did a sharply marked confessional Lutheranism gain wide and general acceptance. This was so especially and most decidedly in Mecklenburg, but also in Hanover, Hesse, and Saxony. On the other hand, since the close of 1860, in almost all those smaller states a determined demand was made for a representative synodal constitution, securing the due co-operation of the lay element.—The Catholic church was strongest in Hanover, and next come some parts of Hesse, which had been added to the ecclesiastical province of the Upper Rhine (§ 196, 1), but in the other North German smaller states it was only represented here and there.

1. The **Kingdom of Saxony.**—The present kingdom of Saxony, formerly an electoral principality, has had Catholic princes since 1679 (§ 153, 1), but the Catholic church could strike its roots again only in the immediate neighbourhood of the court. Indeed those belonging to it did not enjoy civil and religious equality until 1807, when this distinction was set aside. The erection of cloisters and the introduction of monkish orders, however, continued even then forbidden, and all official publications of the Catholic clergy required the *placet* of the government. The administration of the evangelical church, so long as the king is Catholic, lies, according to agreement, in the hands of the ministers commissioned *in evangelicis*. Although several of these have proved defenders of ecclesiastical orthodoxy, the rationalistic Illumination became almost universally prevalent not only among the clergy but also among the general populace. Meanwhile a pietistic reaction set in, especially powerful in Muldenthal, where Rudelbach's labours impressed on it a Lutheran ecclesiastical character. The religious movement, on the other hand, directed by Martin Stephan, pastor of the Bohemian church in Dresden, came to a sad and shameful end. As representative and restorer of strict Lutheran views he had wrought successfully in Dresden from 1810, but, through the adulation of his followers, approaching even to worship, he fell more and more deeply into hierarchical assumption and neglect of self-vigilance. When the police in 1837 restricted his nightly assemblies, without, however, having discovered anything immoral, and suspended him from his official duties, he called upon his followers to emigrate to America. Many of them, lay and clerical, blindly obeyed, and founded in 1835, in Missouri, a Lutheran church communion (§ 208, 2). Stephan's despotic hierarchical assumptions here reached their fullest height; he also gave his lusts free scope. Women oppressed or actually abused by him at length openly pro-

claimed his shame in 1839, and the community excommunicated him. He died in A.D. 1846. Taught by such experiences, and purged of the Donatist-separatist element, a church reaction against advancing rationalism made considerable progress under a form of church that favoured it, and secured also influential representatives in members of the theological faculty of the university of Leipzig distinguished for their scientific attainments. After repeated debates in the chamber over a scheme of a new ecclesiastical and synodal order submitted by the ministry, the first evangelical Lutheran state synod met in Dresden, in May, 1871. On the motion of the government, the law of patronage was here modified so that the patron had to submit three candidates to the choice of the ecclesiastical board. It was also decided to form an upper or state consistory, to which all ecclesiastical matters hitherto administered by the minister of public worship should be given over; the control of education was to remain with the ministry, and the state consistory was to charge itself with the oversight only of religious instruction and ethico-religious training. The most lively debates were those excited by the proposal to abolish the obligation resting upon all church teachers to seem to adhere to the confession of the Lutheran church, led by Dr. Zarncke, the rector of the state university. The commission of inquiry sent down, under the presidency of Professor Luthardt, demanded the absolute withdrawal of this proposal, which aimed at perfect doctrinal freedom. On the other hand, Professor G. Baur made the mediate proposal to substitute for the declaration on oath, the promise to teach simply and purely to the best of his knowledge and according to conscience the gospel of Christ as it is contained in Scripture, and witnessed in the confessions of the Lutheran church. And as even now Luthardt, inspired by the wish not to rend the first State Synod at its final sitting by an incurable schism, agreed to this suggestion, it was carried by a large majority. In consequence of this decision, a number of " Lutherans faithful to the confession," withdrew from the State church, and on the anniversary of the Reformation in 1871, constituted themselves into an Evangelical Lutheran Free Church, associated with the Missouri synod (§ 208, 2), from which, on the suggestion of some of the members of the community who had returned from America, they chose for themselves a pastor called Ruhland. There were five such congregations in Saxony: at Dresden, Planitz, Chemnitz, Frankenberg, and Krimmitschau, to which some South German dissenters at Stenden, Wiesbaden, Frankfort, and Anspach attached themselves.

2. The Saxon Duchies.—The Stephan emigration had also decoyed a number of inhabitants from Saxe-Altenburg. In a rescript to the Ephorus Ronneburg, in 1838, the consistory traced back this separatist movement to the fact that the religious needs of the congregations

found no satisfaction in the rationalistic preaching, and urged a more earnest presentation from the pulpit of the fundamental and central doctrines of evangelical Christianity. This rescript was the subject of violent denunciation. The government took the opinion of four theological faculties on the procedure of the consistory and its opponents, who published it simply with the praise and blame contained therein, and thus prevented any investigation. Also in Weimar and Gotha the rationalism of Röhr and Bretschneider, which had dominated almost all pulpits down to the middle of the century, began gradually to disappear, and the more recent parties of Confessional, Mediation, and Free Protestant theology to take its place. The last named party found vigorous support in the university of Jena. A petition addressed to it in 1882 from the Thuringian Church Conference of Eisenach, to call to Jena also a representative of the positive Lutheran theology, was decidedly refused, and, in a controversial pamphlet by Superintendent Braasch, condemned as "the Eisenach outrage" (*Attentat*). In Meiningen the *Vorsynode* convened there in 1870 sanctioned the sketch of a moderately liberal synodal constitution submitted to it, which placed the confession indeed beyond the reach of legislative interference, but also secured its rights to free inquiry. The first State Synod, however, did not meet before 1878. In Weimar the first synod was held in 1873, the second in 1879.

3. The Kingdom of Hanover.—Although the union found no acceptance in Hanover, after the overthrow of the rationalism of the *ancien régime*, the union theology became dominant in the university. The clergy, however, were in great part carried along by the confessional Lutheran current of the age. The Preachers' Conference at Stade in 1854 took occasion to call the attention of the government to the "manifest divergence" between the union theology of the university and the legal and actual Lutheran confession of the state church, and urged the appointment of Lutheran teachers. The faculty, on the other hand, issued a memorial in favour of liberty of public teaching, and the curators filled the vacancies again with union theologians. When in April, 1862, it was proposed to displace the state catechism introduced in 1790, which neither theologically nor catechetically satisfied the needs of the church, by a carefully sifted revision of the Walther catechism in use before 1790, approved of by the Göttingen faculty, the agitation of the liberal party called forth an opposition, especially in city populations, which expressed itself in insults to members of consistories and pastors, and in almost daily repeated bloody street fights with the military, and obliged the government at last to give way.—The negotiations about a concordat with Rome reached no further in 1824 than obtaining the circumscription bull *Impensa Romanorum*, by which the Catholic church obtained two bishoprics, those of Hildesheim

and Osnabrück.—In 1886, Hanover was incorporated with the kingdom of Prussia (§ 193, 8).

4. Hesse.—Landgrave Maurice, 1592–1627, had forced upon his territories a modified Melanchthonian Calvinism (§ 154, 1), but a Lutheran basis with Lutheran modes of viewing things and Lutheran institutions still remained, and the Lutheran reaction had never been completely overcome, not even in Lower Hesse, although there the name of the Reformed Church with Reformed modes of worship had been gradually introduced in most of the congregations. The communities of Upper Hesse and Schmalcald, however, by continuous opposition saved for the most part their Lutheranism, which in 1648 was guaranteed to them anew by the Darmstadt Recess, and secured an independent form of church government in the Definitorium at Marburg. The union movement, which issued from Prussia in 1817, met with favour also in Hesse, but only in the province of Hanau in 1818 got the length of a formal constituting of a church on the basis of the union. In 1821, however, the elector issued the so-called Reorganization edict, by which the entire evangelical church of the electorate, without any reference to the confession status, but simply in accordance with the political divisions of the state, was put under the newly instituted consistories of Cassel, Marburg, and Hanau, in the formation of which the confession of the inhabitants had not been considered. The Marburg Definitorium indeed protested, but in vain, against this despotic act, which was felt a grievance, less on account of the wiping out of the confession than on account of the loss of independent church government which it occasioned. The government appointed pastors, teachers and professors without enquiring much about their confession. In 1838 the hitherto required subscription of the clergy to the confessional writings, the Augsburg Confession and its Apology, was modified into a formula declaring conscientious regard for them. But in this Bickell, professor of law at Marburg, saw a loss to the church in legal status, an endangering of the evangelical church; the theological professor, Hupfeld, also in the further course of the controversy took his side, while the advocate, Henkel, in Cassel, as a popular agitator opposed him and demanded a State Synod for the formal abolishing of all symbolical books. The government ignored both demands, and the vehement conflict was quieted by degrees. With 1850 a new era began in the keen controversy over the question, which confession, whether Lutheran or Reformed, was legally and actually that of the state. The ministry of Hassenpflug from 1850, which suppressed the revolution, considered it as legally the Lutheran, and determined the ecclesiastical arrangements in this sense, and in this course Dr. Vilmar, member of the Consistory, was the minister's right hand But the elector was from

the beginning personally opposed to this procedure, and on the overthrow of the ministry in 1855, Vilmar (died 1868) was also transferred to a theological professorship at Marburg. This, however, only gave a new impulse to the confessional Lutheran movement in the state, for the spirit and tendency of the highly revered theological teacher powerfully influenced the younger generation of the Hessian clergy. In consequence of the German war, Hesse was annexed to Prussia in 1866 (§ 193, 9).—On the Catholic church in this state, compare § 196, 1.

5. Brunswick, Oldenburg, Anhalt, and Lippe-Detmold.—Much ado was made also in Brunswick over the introduction of a new constitution for the Lutheran state church in 1869, and at last in 1871 a synodal ordinance was passed by which the State Synod, consisting of fourteen clerical and eighteen lay members, was to meet every four years, so as not to be a too offensive factor in the ecclesiastical administration and legislation, which therefore has left untouched the content of the confession. The first synod of 1872 began by rejecting the injunction to open the sessions with prayer and reading of scripture. Oldenburg, which in 1849, by a synod whose membership had been chosen by the original electorate, had been favoured with a democratic church constitution wholly separate from the state, accepted in 1854 without opposition a new constitution which restored the headship of the church to the territorial lords, the administration of the church to a Supreme Church Council and ecclesiastical legislation to a State Synod consisting of clerical and lay members.—The prince in the exercise of his sovereign rights gave a charter in 1878 to the evangelical church of the Duchy of Anhalt to a synodal ordinance which, though approved by the *Vorsynode* of 1876, had been rejected by parliament, and afterwards it gained the assent of the national representatives.—In the Reformed Lippe-Detmold there were in 1844 still five preachers who, wearied of the illuminationist catechism of the state church, had gone back to the Heidelberg catechism and protested against the abolition of acceptance on oath of the symbols, as destructive of the peace of the church. The democratic church constitution of 1851, however, was abrogated in 1854, and instead of it, the old Reformed church order of 1684 was again made law. At the same time, religious pardon and equality were guaranteed to Catholics and Lutherans. The first Reformed State Synod was constituted in 1878.

6. Mecklenburg.—Mecklenburg-Schwerin from 1848 was in possession of a strictly Lutheran church government under the direction of Kliefoth, and its university at Rostock had decidedly Lutheran theologians. When the chamberlain Von Kettenburg, on going over to the Catholic church, appointed a Catholic priest on his estate, the government in 1852, on the ground that the laws of the state did not allow Catholic services which extended beyond simple family worship, held

that he had overstepped the limits. A complaint, in reference thereto, presented to the parliament and then to the German *Bund*, was in both cases thrown out. Even in 1863 the Rostock magistrates refused to allow tower and bells in the building of a Catholic church.—An extraordinary excitement was caused by the removal from office in January, 1858, of Professor M. Baumgarten of Rostock. An examination paper set by him on 2 Kings xi. by which the endeavour was made to win scripture sanction for a violent revolution, obliged the government even in 1856 to remove him from the theological examination board. At the same time his polemic addressed to a pastoral conference at Parchim, against the doctrine of the Mecklenburg state catechism on the ceremonial law, especially in reference to the sanctification of the Sabbath, increased the distrust which the clergy of the state, on account of his writings, had entertained against his theological position as one which, from a fanatical basis, diverged on all sides into fundamental antagonism to the confession and the ordinances of the Lutheran state church. The government finally deposed him in 1858 (leaving him, however, in possession of his whole salary, also of the right of public teaching), on the ground and after the publication of a judgment of the consistory which found him guilty of heretical alteration of all the fundamental doctrines of the Christian faith and the Lutheran confession, and sought to prove this verdict from his writings. As might have been foreseen, this step was followed by a loud outcry by all journals; but even Lutherans, like Von Hofmann Von Scheurl, and Luthardt, objected to the proceedings of the government as exceeding the law laid down by the ecclesiastical ordinance and the opinion of the consistory as resting upon misunderstanding, arbitrary supposition and inconsequent conclusion.

§ 195. BAVARIA.

Catholic Bavaria, originally an electorate, but raised in 1806, by Napoleon's favour, into a royal sovereignty, to which had been adjudged by the Vienna Congress considerable territories in Franconia and the Palatine of the Rhine with a mainly Protestant population, attempted under Maximilian Joseph (IV.) I., after the manner of Napoleon, despotically to pass a liberal system of church polity, but found itself obliged again to yield, and under Louis I. became again the chief retreat of Roman Catholic ecclesiasticism of the most pronounced ultramontane pattern. It was under the noble and upright king, Maximilian II., that the evangelical church of the two divisions of the kingdom, numbering two-thirds of the population, first succeeded in securing the unrestricted use of their rights. Nevertheless, Catholic Bavaria remained, or became, the unhappy scene cf the wildest demagogic agitation of the Catholic clergy and of the Bavarian "Patriots" who played their game, whose patriotism consisted only in mad hatred of Prussia and fanatical ultramontanism. Yet King Louis II., after the brilliant successes of the Franco-German war, could not object to the proposal of November 30th, 1870, to found a new German empire under a Prussian and therefore a Protestant head.

1. The Bavarian Ecclesiastical Polity under Maximilian I., 1799-1825.— Bavaria boasted with the most unfeigned delight after the uprooting of Protestantism in its borders as then defined (§ 151, 1), that it was the most Catholic, *i.e.* the most ultramontane and most bigoted, of German-speaking lands, and, after a short break in this tradition by Maximilian Joseph III. (§ 165, 10), went forth again with full sail, under Charles Theodore, 1777-1779, on the old course. But the thoroughly new aspect which this state assumed on the overthrow of the old German empire, demanded an adapting territorially of the civil and ecclesiastical life in accordance with the relations which it owed to its present political position. The new elector Maximilian Joseph IV., who as king styled himself Maximilian I., transferred the execution of this task to his liberal, energetic, and thoroughly fear-less minister, Count Montgelas, 1799-1817. In January, 1802, it was enacted that all cloisters should be suppressed, and that all cathedral foundations should be secularized; and these enactments were imme-diately carried out in an uncompromising manner. Even in 1801 the qualification of Protestants to exercise the rights of Bavarian citizens was admitted, and a religious edict of 1803 guaranteed to all Christian confessions full equality of civil and political privileges. To the clergy was given the control of education, and to the gymnasia and universities a considerable number of foreigners and Protestants received appointments. In all respects the sovereignty of the state over the church and the clergy was very decidedly expressed, the episcopate at all points restricted in its jurisdiction, the training of the clergy regulated and supervised on behalf of the state, the patronage of all pastorates and benefices usurped by the government, even public worship subjected to state control by the prohibition

of superstitious practices, etc. But amid many other infelicities of
this autocratic procedure was specially the gradual dying out of the
old race of bishops, which obliged the government to seek again
an understanding with Rome; and so it actually happened in June,
1817, after Montgelas' dismissal, that a concordat was drawn up.
By this the Roman Catholic apostolic religion secured throughout
the whole kingdom those rights and prerogatives which were due
to it according to divine appointment and canonical ordinances,
which, strictly taken, meant supremacy throughout the land. In
addition, two archbishoprics and seven bishoprics were instituted,
the restoration of several cloisters was agreed to, and the unlimited
administration of theological seminaries, the censorship of books, the
superintendance of public schools and free correspondence with the
holy see were allowed to the bishops. On the other hand, the king
was given the choice of bishops (to be confirmed by the pope), the
nomination of a great part of the priests and canons, and the *placet*
for all hierarchical publications. After many vain endeavours to
obtain amendments, the king at last, on October 17th, ratified this
concordat; but, to mollify his highly incensed Protestant subjects, he
delayed the publication of it till the proclamation of the new civil
constitution on May 18th following. The concordat was then adopted
as an appendage to an edict setting forth the ecclesiastical supremacy
of the state, securing perfect freedom of conscience to all subjects,
as well as equal civil rights to members of the three Christian confessions, and demanding from them equal mutual respect. The irre-
concilableness of this edict with the concordat was evident, and the
newly appointed bishops as well as the clerical parliamentary deputies,
declared by papal instruction that they could not take the oath to
the constitution without reservation, until the royal statement of
Tegernsee, September 21st, that the oath taken by Catholic subjects
simply referred to civil relations, and that the concordat had also the
validity of a law of the state, induced the curia to agree to it. But
the government nevertheless continued to insist as before upon the
supremacy of the state over the church, enlarged the claims of the
royal *placet*, put the free intercourse with Rome again under state
control, arbitrarily disposed of church property and supervised the
theological examinations of the seminarists, made the appointment of
all clergy dependent on its approbation, and refused to be misled in
anything by the complaints and objections of the bishops.

2. The Bavarian Ecclesiastical Polity under Louis I., 1825-1848.—
Zealous Catholic as the new king was, he still held with unabated
tenacity to the sovereign rights of the crown, and the extreme ultramontane ministry of Von Abel from 1837 was the first to wring from
him any relaxations, *e.g.* the reintroduction of free intercourse between

the bishops and the holy see without any state control. But it could not obtain the abolition of the *placet*, and just as little the eagerly sought permission of the return of the Jesuits. On the other hand the allied order of Redemptorists was allowed, whose missions among the Bavarian people, however, the king soon made dependent on a permission to be from time to time renewed. His tolerant disposition toward the Protestants was shown in 1830, by his refusing the demand of the Catholic clergy for a Reverse in mixed marriages, and recognising Protestant sponsors at Catholic baptisms. But yet his honourable desire to be just even to the Protestants of his realm was often paralysed, partly by his own ultramontane sympathies, partly and mainly by the immense influence of the Abel ministry, and the religious freedom guaranteed them by law in 1818 was reduced and restricted. Among other things the Protestant press was on all sides gagged by the minister, while the Catholic press and preaching enjoyed unbridled liberty. Great as the need was in southern Bavaria the government had strictly forbidden the taking of any aid from the *Gustavus Adolphus Verein*. Louis saw even in the name of this society a slight thrown on the German name, and was specially offended at its vague, nearly negative attitude towards the confession. Yet he had no hesitation in affording an asylum in Catholic Bavaria to the Lutheran confessor Scheibel (§ 177, 2) whom Prussian diplomacy had driven out of Lutheran Saxony, and did not prevent the university of Erlangen, after its dead orthodoxy had been reawakened by the able Reformed preacher Krafft (died 1845), becoming the centre of a strict Lutheran church consciousness in life as well as science for all Germany. The adoration order of 1838, which required even the Protestant soldiers to kneel before the host as a military salute, occasioned great discontent among the Protestant population, and many controversial pamphlets appeared on both sides. When finally the parliament in 1845 took up the complaint of the Protestants, a royal proclamation followed by which the usually purely military salute formerly in use was restored. In 1847 the ultramontane party, with Abel at its head, fell into disfavour with the king, on account of its honourable attitude in the scandal which the notorious Lola Montez caused in the circle of the Bavarian nobility; but in 1848 Louis was obliged, through the revolutionary storm that burst over Bavaria, to resign the crown.

3. The Bavarian Ecclesiastical Polity under Maximilian II., 1848-1864, and Louis II. (died 1886).—Much more thoroughly than his father did Maximilian II. strive to act justly toward the Protestant as well as the Catholic church, without however abating any of the claims of constitutional supremacy on the part of the state. In consequence of the Würzburg negotiations (§ 192, 4), the Bavarian bishops assembled at Freysing, in November, 1850, presented a memorial, by which they

demanded the withdrawal of the religious edict included in the constitution of 1818, as in all respects prejudicial to the rights of the church granted by the concordat, and set forth in particular those points which were most restrictive to the free and proper development of the catholic church. The result was the publication in April, 1852, of a rescript which, while maintaining all the principles of state administration hitherto followed, introduced in detail various modifications, which, on the renewal of the complaints in 1854, were somewhat further increased as the fullest and final measure of surrender.—The change brought about in 1866 in the relation of Bavaria to North Germany led the government under Louis II. to introduce liberal reforms, and the offensive and defensive alliance which the government concluded with the heretical Prussia, the failure of all attempts on the outbreak of the Franco-Prussian war to force it in violation of treaty to maintain neutrality, and then to prevent Bavaria becoming part of the new German empire founded in 1871 at the suggestion of her own king, roused to the utmost the wrath of the Bavarian clerical patriots. In the conflicts of the German government, in 1872, against the intolerable assumptions, claims and popular tumults of the ultramontane clergy, the department of public worship, led by Lutz, inclined to take an energetic part. But this was practically limited to the passing of the so-called *Kanzelparagraphen* (§ 197, 4) in the *Reichstag.* Comp. § 197, 14.

4. Attempts at Reorganization of the Lutheran Church.—Since 1852, Dr. von Harless (§ 182, 13), as president of the upper consistory at Munich, stood at the head of the Lutheran church of Bavaria. Under his presidency the general synod at Baireuth in 1853 showed a vigorous activity in the reorganization of the church. On the basis of its proceedings the upper consistory ordered the introduction of an admirable new hymnbook. This occasioned considerable disagreement. But when, in 1856, the upper consistory issued a series of enactments on worship and discipline, a storm, originating in Nuremberg, burst forth in the autumn of that same year, which raged over the whole kingdom and attacked even the state church itself. The king was assailed with petitions, and the spiritual courts went so far in faintheartedness as to put the acceptance and non-acceptance of its ordinances to the vote of the congregations. Meanwhile the time had come for calling another general synod (1857). An order of the king as head of the church abolished the union of the two state synods in a general synod which had existed since 1849, and forbad all discussion of matters of discipline. Hence instead of one, two synods assembled, the one in October at Anspach, the other in November at Baireuth. Both, consisting of equal numbers of lay and clerical members, maintained a moderate attitude, relinquishing none of the

privileges of the church or the prerogatives of the upper consistory, and yet contributed greatly to the assuaging of the prevalent excitement. Also the lay and clerical members of the subsequent reunited general synods held every fourth year for the most part co-operated successfully on moderate church lines. The synod held at Baireuth in 1873 unanimously rejected an address sent from Augsburg inspired by "Protestant Union" sympathies, as to their mind "for the most part indistinct and where distinct unevangelical."

5. The Church of the Union in the Palatine of the Rhine.—In the Bavarian Palatine of the Rhine the union had been carried out in 1818 on the understanding that the symbolical books of both confessions should be treated with due respect, but no other standard recognised than holy scripture. When therefore the Erlangen professor, Dr. Rust, in 1832 appeared in the consistory at Spires and the court for that time had endeavoured to fill up the Palatine union with positive Christian contents, 204 clerical and lay members of the Diocesan Synod presented to the assembly of the states of the realm, opportunely meeting in 1837, a complaint against the majority of the consistory. As this memorial yielded practically no result, the opposition wrought all the more determinedly for the severance of the Palatine church from the Munich Upper Consistory. This was first accomplished in the revolutionary year 1848. An extraordinary general synod brought about the separation, and gave to the country a new democratic church constitution. But the reaction of the blow did not stop there. The now independent consistory at Spires, from 1853 under the leadership of Ebrard, convened in the autumn of that year a general synod, which made the *Augustana Variata* of 1540 as representing the consensus between the *Augustana* of 1530 and the Heidelberg as well as the Lutheran catechism, the confessional standard of the Palatine church, and set aside the democratic election law of 1848. When now the consistory, purely at the instance of the general synod of 1853, submitted to the diocesan synod in 1856 the proofs of a new hymnbook, the liberal party poured out its bitter indignation upon the system of doctrine which it was supposed to favour. But the diocesan synods admitted the necessity of introducing a new hymnbook and the suitability of the sketch submitted, recommending, however, its further revision so that the recension of the text might be brought up to date and that an appendix of 150 new hymns might be added. The hymnbook thus modified was published in 1859, and its introduction into church use left to the judgment of presbyteries, while its use in schools and in confirmation instruction was insisted upon forthwith. This called forth protest after protest. The government wished from the first to support the synodal decree, but in presence of growing disturbance, changed i⁴ ⁴⁴⁴ ⁴ ⁻ commended the consistory

to observe decided moderation so as to restore peace, and in February 1861, called a general synod which, however, in consequence of the prevailingly strict ecclesiastical tendencies of its members, again expressed itself in favour of the new hymnbook. Its conclusions were meanwhile very unfavourably received by the government. Ebrard sought and obtained liberty to resign, and even at the next synod, in 1869, the consistory went hand in hand with the liberal majority.

§ 196. THE SOUTH GERMAN SMALLER STATES AND RHENISH ALSACE AND LORRAINE.

The Protestant princely houses of South Germany had by the Lüneville Peace obtained such an important increase of Catholic subjects, that they had to make it their first care to arrange their delicate relations by concluding a concordat with the papal curia in a manner satisfactory to state and church. But all negotiations broke down before the exorbitant claims of Rome, until the political restoration movements of 1850 led to modifications of them hitherto undreamed of. The concordats concluded during this period were not able to secure enforcement over against the liberal current that had set in with redoubled power in 1860, and so one thing after another was thrown overboard. Even in the Protestant state churches this current made itself felt in the persistent efforts, which also proved successful, to secure the restoration of a representative synodal constitution which would give to the lay element in the congregations a decided influence.

1. **The Upper Rhenish Church Province.**—The governments of the South German States gathered in 1818 at Frankfort, to draw up a common concordat with Rome. But owing to the utterly extravagant pretensions nothing further was reached than a new delimitation in the bull " *Provida sollersque*," 1821, of the bishoprics in the so-called Upper Rhenish Church Province: the archbishopric of Freiburg for Baden and the two Hohenzollern principalities, the bishoprics of Mainz for Hesse-Darmstadt, Fulda for Hesse-Cassel, Rottenburg for Württemberg, Limburg for Nassau and Frankfort; and even this was given effect to only in 1827, after long discussions, with the provision

(bull *Ad dominicæ gregis custodiam*) that the choice of the bishops should issue indeed from the chapter, but that the territorial lord might strike out objectionable names in the list of candidates previously submitted to him. The actual equality of Protestants and Catholics which the pope had not been able to allow in the concordat, was now in 1830 proclaimed by the princes as the law of the land. Papal and episcopal indulgences had to receive approval before their publication; provincial and diocesan synods could be held only with approval of the government and in presence of the commissioners of the prince; taxes could not be imposed by any ecclesiastical court: appeal could be made to the civil court against abuse of spiritual power; those preparing for the priesthood should receive scientific training at the universities, practical training in the seminaries for priests, etc. The pope issued a brief in which he characterized these conditions as scandalous novelties, and reminded the bishops of Acts v. 29. But only the Bishop of Fulda followed this advice, with the result that the Catholic theological faculty at Marburg was after a short career closed again, and the education of the priests given over to the seminary at Fulda. Hesse-Darmstadt founded a theological faculty at Giessen in 1830; Baden had one already in Freiburg, and Würtemberg had in 1817 affiliated the faculty at Ellwanger with the university of Tübingen, and endowed it with the revenues of a rich convent. In all these faculties alongside of rigorous scientific exactness there prevailed a noble liberalism without the surrender of the fundamental Catholic faith. The revolutionary year, 1848, first gave the bishops the hope of a successful struggle for the unconditional freedom of the church. In order to enforce the Würzburg decrees (§ 192, 4), the five bishops issued in 1851 a joint memorial. As the governments delayed their answer, they declared in 1852 that they would immediately act as if all had been granted them; and when at last the answer came, on most points unfavourable, they said in 1853, that, obeying God rather than man, they would proceed wholly in accordance with canon law.

2. The Catholic Troubles in Baden down to 1873.—The Grand Duchy of Baden, with two-thirds of its population Catholic, where in 1848 the revolution had shattered all the foundations of the state, and where besides a young ruler had taken the reins of government in his hands only in 1852, seemed in spite of the widely prevalent liberality of its clergy, the place best fitted for such an attempt. The Archbishop of Freiburg, Herm. von Vicari, in 1852, now in his eighty-first year, began by arbitrarily stopping, on the evening of May 9th, the obsequies of the deceased grand-duke appointed by the Catholic Supreme Church Council for May 10th, prohibiting at the same time the saying of mass for the dead (*pro omnibus defunctis*) usual at

Catholic burials, but in Baden and Bavaria hitherto not refused even to Protestant princes. More than one hundred priests, who disobeyed the injunction, were sentenced to perform penances. In the following year he openly declared that he would forthwith carry out the demands of the episcopal memorial, and did so immediately by appointing priests in the exercise of absolute authority, and by holding entrance examinations to the seminary without the presence of royal commissioners as required by law. As a warning remained unheeded, the government issued the order that all episcopal indulgences must before publication be subscribed by a grand-ducal special commissioner appointed for the purpose. Against him, as well as against all the members of the Supreme Church Council, the archbishop proclaimed the ban, issued a fulminating pastoral letter, which was to have been read with the excommunication in all churches, and ordered preaching for four weeks for the instruction of the people on these matters. At the same time he solemnly protested against all supremacy of the state over the church. The government drove the Jesuits out of the country, forbad the reading of the pastoral, and punished disobedient priests with fines and imprisonment. But the archbishop, spurred on by Ketteler, Bishop of Mainz, advanced more boldly and recklessly than ever. In May, 1854, the government introduced a criminal process against him, during the course of which he was kept prisoner in his own house. The attempts of his party to arouse the Catholic population by demonstrations had no serious result. At the close of the investigation the archbishop was released from his confinement and continued the work as before. The government, however, still remained firm, and punished every offence. In June, 1855, however, a provisional agreement was published, and finally in June, 1859, a formal concordat, the bull *Æterni patris*, was concluded with Rome, its concessions to the archbishop almost exceeeding even those of Austria (§ 198, 2). In spite of ministerial opposition the second chamber in March, 1860, brought up the matter before its tribunal, repudiated the right of the government to conclude a convention with Rome without the approbation of the states of the realm, and forbad the grand-duke to enforce it. He complied with this demand, dismissed the ministry, insisted, in answer to the papal protest, on his obligation to respect the rights of the constitution, and on October 9th, 1860, sanctioned jointly with the chambers a law on the legal position of the Catholic and Protestant churches in the state. The archbishop indeed declared that the concordat could not be abolished on one side, and still retain the force of law, but in presence of the firm attitude of the government he desisted, and satisfied himself with giving in 1861 a grudging acquiescence, by which he secured to himself greater independence than before in regard to imposing of dues and administration of the church property. Conflicts with the archbishop, however, and with the clerical minority in the chamber, still continued. The archbishop died in 1868. His see remained vacant, as the chapter and the government could not agree about the list of candidates; the interim administration was carried on by the vicar-general, Von Kübel (died 1881), as administrator of the archdiocese, quite in the spirit of his predecessor. The law of October 9th, 1860, had prescribed evidence of general scientific culture as a condition of appointment to an ecclesiastical office in the Protestant as well as the Catholic church. Later ordinances required in addition: Possession of Baden citizenship, having passed a favourable examination on leaving the university, a university course of at least two and half years, attendance upon at least three courses of lectures in the philosophical faculty, and finally also an examination before a state examining board, within one and half years of the close of the university curriculum, in the Latin and Greek languages, history of philosophy, general history, and the history of German literature (later also the so called *Kulturexamen*). The Freiburg curia, however, protested, and in 1867 forbad clergy and candidates to submit to this examination or to seek a dispensation from it. The result was, that forthwith no clergymen could be definitely appointed, but up to 1874 no legal objection was made to interim appointments of parochial administrators. The educational law of 1868 abolished the confessional character of the public schools. In 1869 state recognition was withdrawn from the festivals of Corpus Christi, the holy apostles, and Mary, as also, on the other hand, from the festivals of Maundy Thursday and Good Friday. In 1870 obligatory civil marriage was introduced, while all compulsion to observe the baptismal, confirmational, and funeral rites of the church was abolished, and a law on the legal position of benevolent institutions was passed to withdraw these as much as possible from the administration of the ecclesiastical authorities. On the subsequent course of events in Baden, see § 197, 14.

3. The Protestant Troubles in Baden.—The union of the Lutheran and Reformed churches was carried out in the Grand Duchy of Baden in 1821. It recognised the normative significance of the *Augustana*, as well as the Lutheran and Heidelberg catchisms, in so far as by it the free examination of scripture as the only source of Christian faith, is again expressly demanded and applied. A synod of 1834 provided this state church with union-rationalistic agenda, hymnbook, and catechism. When there also a confessional Lutheran sentiment began again in the beginning of 1850 to prevail, the church of the union opposed this movement by gensdarmes, imprisonment and fines. The pastor Eichhorn, and later also the pastor Ludwig, with

a portion of their congregations left the state church and attached themselves to the Breslau Upper Church Conference, but amid police interference could minister to their flocks only under cloud of night. After long refusal the grand-duke at last in 1854 permitted the separatists the choice of a Lutheran pastor, but persistently refused to recognise Eichhorn as such. Pastor Haag, who would not give up the Lutheran distribution formula at the Lord's supper, was after solemn warning deposed in 1855. On the other hand the positive churchly feeling became more and more pronounced in the state church itself. In 1854 the old rationalist members of the Supreme Church Council were silenced, and Ullmann of Heidelberg was made president. Under his auspices a general synod of 1855 presented a sketch of new church and school books on the lines of the union consensus, with an endeavour also to be just to the Lutheran views. The grand-duke confirmed the decision and the country was silent. But when in 1858 the Supreme Church Council, on the ground of the Synodal decision of 1855, promulgated the general introduction of a new church book, a violent storm broke out through the country against the liturgical novelties contained therein (extension of the liturgy by confession of sin and faith, collects, responses, Scripture reading, kneeling at the supper, the making a confession of their faith by sponsors), the Heidelberg faculty, with Dr. Schenkel at its head, leading the opposition in the Supreme Church Council. Yet Hundeshagen, who in the synod had opposed the introduction of a new agenda, entered the lists against Schenkel and others as the apologist of the abused church book. The grand-duke then decided that no congregation should be obliged to adopt the new agenda, while the introduction of the shorter and simpler form of it was recommended. The agitations those awakened caused its rejection by most of the congregations. Meanwhile in consequence of the concordat revolution in 1860, a new liberal ministry had come into power, and the government now presented to the chambers a series of thoroughly liberal schemes for regulating the affairs of the evangelical church, which were passed by large majorities. Toward the end of the year the government, by deposing the Supreme Church Councillor Heintz, began to assume the patronage of the supreme ecclesiastical court. Ullmann and Bähr tendered their resignations, which were accepted. The new liberal Supreme Church Council, including Holtzmann, Rothe, etc., now published a sketch of a church constitution on the lines of ecclesiastical constitutionalism, which with slight modifications the synod of July, 1861, adopted and the grand-duke confirmed. It provided for annual diocesan synods of lay and clerical members, and a general synod every five years. The latter consists of twenty-four clerical and twenty-four lay members, and six chosen by the grand-duke, besides the prelate, and is represented in the interval by a standing committee of four members, who have also a seat and vote in the Supreme Church Council.—Dr. Schenkel's "*Leben Jesu*" of 1864 led the still considerable party among the evangelical clergy who adhered to the doctrine of the church to agitate for his removal from his position as director of the Evangelical Pastors' Seminary at Heidelberg; but it resulted only in this, that no one was obliged to attend his lectures. The second synod, held almost a year behind time in 1867, passed a liberal ordination formula. At the next synod in 1871, the orthodox pietistic party had evidently become stronger, but was still overborne by the liberal party, whose strength was in the lay element. Meanwhile a praiseworthy moderation prevailed on both sides, and an effort was made to work together as peaceably as possible.—In Heidelberg a considerable number attached to the old faith, dissatisfied with the preaching of the four "Free Protestant" city pastors, after having been in 1868 refused their request for the joint use of a city church for private services in accordance with their religious convictions (§ 180, 1), had built for this purpose a chapel of their own, in which numerously attended services were held under the direction of Professor Frommel of the gymnasium. When a vacancy occurred in one of the pastorates in 1880, this believing minority, anxious for the restoration of unity and peace, as well as the avoidance of the separation, asked to have Professor Frommel appointed to the charge. At a preliminary assembly of twenty-one liberal church members this proposal was warmly supported by the president, Professor Bluntschli, by all the theological professors, with the exception of Schenkel and eighteen other liberal voters, and agreed to by the majority of the two hundred liberals constituting the assembly. But when the formal election came round the proposal was lost by twenty-seven to fifty-one votes.

4. Hesse-Darmstadt and Nassau.—In 1819 the government of the Grand Duchy of Hesse recommended the union of all Protestant communities under one confession. Rhenish Hesse readily agreed to this, and there in 1822 the union was accomplished. In the other provinces, however, it did not take effect, although by the rationalism fostered at Giessen among the clergy and by the popular current of thought in the communities, the Lutheran as well as the Reformed confession had been robbed of all significance. But since 1850 even there a powerful Lutheran reaction among the younger clergy, zealously furthered by a section of the aristocracy of the state, set in, especially in the district on the right bank of the Rhine, which has eagerly opposed the equally eager struggles of the liberal party to introduce a liberal synodal representative constitution for the evangelical church of the whole state. These endeavours, however,

were frustrated, and at an extraordinary state synod of 1873, on all controverted questions, the middle party gave their vote in favour of the absorptive union. The state church was declared to be the united church. The clause that had been added to the government proposal: "Without prejudice to the status of the confessions of the several communities," was dropped ; the place of residence and not the confession was that which determined qualifications in the community; the ordination now expressed obligation to the Reformation confessions generally, etc. The members of the minority broke off their connection with the synod, and seventy-seven pastors presented to the synod a protest against its decisions. The grand-duke then, on the basis of these deliberations, gave forthwith a charter to the church constitution, in which indeed the Lutheran, Reformed, and United churches were embraced in one evangelical state church with a common church government; but still also, by restoring the phrase struck out by the synod from § 1, the then existing confessional status of the several communities was preserved and the confession itself declared beyond the range of legislation. Yet fifteen Lutheran pastors represented that they could not conscientiously accept this, and the upper consistory hastened to remove them from office shortly before the shutting of the gates, *i.e.*, before July 1st, 1875, when by the new law (§ 197, 15) depositions of clergy would belong only to the supreme civil court. The opposing congregations now declared, in 1877, their withdrawal from the state church, and constituted themselves as a " free Lutheran church in Hesse."—The Catholic church in the Grand Duchy of Hesse, had under the peaceful bishops of Mainz, Burg (died 1833) and Kaiser (died 1849), caused the government no trouble. But it was otherwise after Kaiser's death. Rome rejected Professor Leopold Schmid of Giessen, favoured at Darmstadt and regularly elected by the chapter (§ 187, 3), and the government yielded to the appointment of the violent ultramontane Westphalian, Baron von Ketteler. His first aim was the extinction of the Catholic faculty at Giessen (§ 191, 2); he rested not until the last student had been transferred from it to the newly erected seminary at Mainz (1851). No less energetic and successful were his endeavours to free the Catholic church from the supremacy of the state in accordance with the Upper Rhenish episcopal memorial. The Dalwigk ministry, in 1854, concluded a "provisional agreement" with the bishop, which secured to him unlimited autonomy and sovereignty in all ecclesiastical matters, and, to satisfy the pope with his desiderata, these privileges were still further extended in 1856. To this convention, first made publicly known in 1860, the ministry, in spite of all addresses and protests, adhered with unfaltering tenacity, although long convinced of its consequences. The political events of 1886, however, led the grand-duke in September of that year to abrogate the hateful convention. But the minister as well as the bishop considered this merely to refer to the episcopal convention of 1850, and treated the agreement with the pope of 1856 as always still valid. So everything went on in the old way, even after Ketteler's supreme influence in the state had been broken by the overthrow of Dalwigk in 1871. Comp. § 197, 15.—The Protestant church in the Duchy of Nassau attached itself to the union in 1817. The conflict in the Upper Rhenish church overflowed even into this little province. The Bishop of Limburg, in opposition to law and custom, appointed Catholic clergy on his own authority, and excommunicated the Catholic officers who supported the government, while the government arrested the temporalities and instituted criminal proceedings against bishop and chapter. After the conclusion of the Württemberg and Baden concordats, the government showed itself disposed to adopt a similar way out of the conflict, and in spite of all opposition from the States concluded in 1861 a convention with the bishop, by which almost all his hierarchical claims were admitted. Thus it remained until the incorporation of Nassau in the Prussian kingdom in 1866.

5. In Protestant Württemberg a religious movement among the people reached a height such as it attained nowhere else. Pietism, chiliasm, separatism, the holding of conventicles, etc., assumed formidable dimensions; solid science, philosophical culture, and then also philosophical and destructive critical tendencies issuing from Tübingen affected the clergy of this state. Dissatisfaction with various novelties in the liturgy, the hymnbook, etc., led many formally to separate from the state church. After attempts at compulsion had proved fruitless, the government allowed the malcontents under the organizing leadership of the burgomaster, G. W. Hoffman (died 1846), to form in 1818 the community of Kornthal, with an ecclesiastical and civil constitution of its own after the apostolic type. Others emigrated to South Russia and to North America (§ 211, 6, 7). Out of the pastoral work of pastor Blumhardt at Möttlingen, who earnestly preached repentance, there was developed, in connection with the healing of a demoniac, which had been accompanied with a great awakening in the community, the "gift" of healing the sick by absolution and laying on of hands with contrite believing prayer. Blumhardt, in order to afford this gift undisturbed exercise, bought the Bad Boll near Göppingen, and officiated there as pastor and miraculous healer in the way described. He died in 1880.—After the way to a synodal representation of the whole evangelical state church had been opened up in 1851 by the introduction, according to a royal ordinance, of parochial councils and diocesan synods, the consistory having also in 1858 published a scheme referring thereto, the whole

business was brought to a standstill, until at last in 1867, by means of a royal edict, the calling of a State Synod consisting of twenty-five clerical and as many lay members was ordered, and consequently in February, 1869, such a synod met for the first time. Co-operation in ecclesiastical legislation was assigned to it as its main task, while it had also the right to advise in regard to proposals about church government, also to make suggestions and complaints on such matters, but the confession of the evangelical church was not to be touched, and lay entirely outside of its province. A liberal enactment with regard to dissenters was sanctioned by the chamber in 1870.

6. The Catholic Church in Württemberg.—Even after the founding of the bishopric of Rottenberg the government maintained strictly the previously exercised rights of sovereignty over the Catholic church, to which almost one-third of the population belonged, and the almost universally prevalent liberalism of the Catholic clergy found in this scarcely any offence. A new order of divine service in 1837, which, with the approval of the episcopal council, recommended the introduction of German hymns in the services, dispensing the sacraments in the German language, restriction of the festivals, masses, and private masses, processions, etc., did indeed cause riots in several places, in which, however, the clergy took no part. But when in 1837, in consequence of the excitement caused throughout Catholic Germany by the Cologne conflict (§ 193, 1), the hitherto only isolated cases of lawless refusal to consecrate mixed marriages had increased, the government proceeded severely to punish offending clergymen, and transported to a village curacy a Tübingen professor, Mack, who had declared the compulsory celebration unlawful. Called to account by the nuncio of Munich for his indolence in all these affairs and severely threatened, old Bishop Keller at last resolved, in 1841, to lay before the chamber a formal complaint against the injury done to the Catholic church, and to demand the freeing of the church from the sovereignty of the state. In the second chamber this motion was simply laid *ad acta*, but in the first it was recommended that the king should consider it. The bishop, however, and the liberal chapter could not agree as to the terms of the demand, contradictory opinions were expressed, and things remained as they were. But Bishop Keller fell into melancholy and died in 1845. His successor took his stand upon the memorial and declaration of the Upper Rhenish bishops, and immediately in 1853 began the conflict by forbidding his clergy, under threats of severe censure, to submit as law required to civil examinations. The government that had hitherto so firmly maintained its sovereign rights, under pressure of the influence which a lady very nearly related to the king exercised over him, gave in without more ado, quieted the bishop first of all by

a convention in 1854, and then entered into negotiations with the
Roman curia, out of which came in 1857 a concordat proclaimed by
the bull *Cum in sublimi*, which, in surrender of a sovereign right of
the state over the affairs of the church, far exceeds that of Austria
(§ 198, 2).   The government left unheeded all protests and petitions
from the chambers for its abolition.   But the example of Baden and
the more and more decided tone of the opposition obliged the government at last to yield.   The second chamber in 1861 decreed the
abrogation of the concordat, and a royal rescript declared it abolished.
In the beginning of 1862 a bill was submitted by the new ministry
and passed into law by both chambers for determining the relations of
the Catholic church to the state.   The royal *placet* or right of permitting or refusing, is required for all clerical enactments which are
not purely inter-ecclesiastical but refer to mixed matters; the theological endowments are subject to state control and joint administration; boys' seminaries are not allowed; clergymen appointed to office
must submit to state examination; according to consuetudinary
rights, about two-thirds of the benefices are filled by the king, one-
third by the bishops on reporting to the civil court, which has the
right of protest; clergy who break the law are removable by the civil
court, etc.   The curia indeed lodged a protest, but the for the most
part peace-loving clergy reared, not in the narrowing atmosphere of
the seminaries but amid the scientific culture of the university, in
the halls of Tübingen, submitted all the more easily as they found
that in all inter-ecclesiastical matters they had greater freedom and
independence under the concordat than before.

7. The Imperial Territory of Alsace and Lorraine since 1871.—After
Alsace with German Lorraine had again, in consequence of the Franco-
Prussian war, been united to Germany and as an imperial territory
had been placed under the rule of the new German emperor, the
secretary of the Papal States, Cardinal Antonelli, in the confident
hope of being able to secure in return the far more favourable conditions, rights and claims of the Catholic church in Prussia with the
autocracy of the bishops unrestricted by the state, declared in a letter
to the Bishop of Strassburg, that the concordat of 1801 (§ 203, 1) was
annulled.   But when the imperial government showed itself ready to
accept the renunciation, and to make profit out of it in the opposite
way from that intended, the cardinal hasted in another letter to explain how by the incorporation with Germany a new arrangement had
become necessary, but that clearly the old must remain in force until
the new one has been promulgated.   Also a petition of the Catholic
clergy brought to Berlin by the bishop himself, which laid claim to
this unlimited dominion over all Catholic educational and benevolent
institutions, failed of its purpose.   The clergy therefore wrought for

this all the more zealously by fanaticizing the Catholic people in favour of French and against German interests. On the epidemic about the appearance of the mother of God called forth in this way, see § 188, 7. In 1874 the government found itself obliged to close the so-called "little seminaries," or boys' colleges, on account of their fostering sentiments hostile to the empire. Yet in 1880 the newly appointed imperial governor, Field-marshal von Manteuffel (died 1885), at the request of the States-Committee, allowed Bishop Räss of Strassburg to reopen the seminary at Zillisheim, with the proviso that his teachers should be approved by the government, and that instruction in the German language should be introduced. Manteuffel has endeavoured since, by yielding favours to the France-loving Alsatians and Lorrainers, and to their ultramontane clergy, to win them over to the idea of the German empire, even to the evident sacrifice of the interests of resident Germans and of the Protestant church. But such fondling has wrought the very opposite result to that intended.

§ 197. The so-called Kulturkampf in the German Empire.[1]

Ultramontanism had for the time being granted to the Prussian state, which had not only allowed it absolutely free scope but readily aided its growth throughout the realm (§ 193, 2), an indulgence for that offence which is in itself unatoneable, having a Protestant dynasty. Pius IX. had himself repeatedly expressed his satisfaction at the conduct of the government. But the league which Prussia made in 1866 with the "church-robbing Sub-alpine," i.e. Italian, government, was not at all to the taste of the curia. The day of Sadowa, 3rd July, 1866, called from Antonelli the mournful cry, *Il mondo cessa*, "The world has gone to ruin," and the still more glorious day of Sedan, 2nd September, 1870, completely put the bottom out of the Danaid's vessel of ultramontane forbearance and endurance. This day, 18th January, 1871, had as its result the overthrow of the temporal power of the papacy as well the establishment of a

[1] Geffcken, "Church and State." 2 vols. London, 1877. Vol. ii. pp. 488-531.

new and hereditary German empire under the Protestaɪt dynasty of the Prussian Hohenzollerns. German ultramontanism felt itself all the more under obligation to demand from the new emperor as the first expiation for such uncanonical usurpation, the reinstatement of the pope in his lost temporal power. But when he did not respond to this demand, the ultramontane party, by means of the press favourable to its claims, formally declared war against the German empire and its governments, and applied itself systematically to the mobilization of its entire forces. But the empire and its governments, with Prussia in the van, with unceasing determination, supported by the majority of the States' representatives, during the years 1871–1875 proceeded against the ultramontanes by legislative measures. The execution of these by the police and the courts of law, owing to the stubborn refusal to obey on the part of the higher and lower clergy, led to the formation of an opposition, commonly designated after a phrase of the Prussian deputy, Professor Virchow, "*Kulturkampf*," which was in some degree modified first in 1887. The imperial chancellor, Prince Bismarck, uttered at the outset the confident, self-assertive statement, " We go not to Canossa,"—and even in 1880, when it seemed as if a certain measure of submission was coming from the side of the papacy, and the Prussian government also showed itself prepared to make important concessions, he declared, " We shall not buy peace with Canossa medals ; such are not minted in Germany." Since 1880, however, the Prussian government with increasing compliance from year to year set aside and modified the most oppressive enactments of the May laws, so as actually to redress distresses and inconveniences occasioned by clerical opposition to these laws, without being able thereby to obtain any important concession on the part of the papal curia, until at last in 1887, after the government had carried concession to the utmost limit, the pope put his seal to definitive terms of peace by admitting the right of giving information on the part of the bishops regarding appointments to vacant pastorates, as well as the right of protest on the part of the government against those thus nominated.

1. The Aggression of Ultramontanism.—Even in the revolution year, 1848, German ultramontanism, in order to obtain what it called the freedom of the church, had zealously seconded many of the efforts of democratic radicalism. Nevertheless, in the years of reaction that followed, it succeeded in catching most of the influential statesmen on the limed twig of the assurance that the episcopal hierarchy, with its unlimited sway over the clergy and through them over the feelings of the people, constituted the only certain and dependable bulwark against the revolutionary movements of the age, and this idea prevailed down to 1860, and in Prussia down to 1871. But the overthrow of the concordat in Baden, Württemberg and Darmstadt by the states of the realm after a hard conflict, the humiliation of Austria in 1866 and the growth in so threatening a manner since of the still heretica Prussia, produced in the whole German episcopate a terrible apprehension that its hitherto untouched supremacy in the state would be at an end, and in order to ward off this danger it was driven into agitations and demonstrations partly secret and partly open. On 8th October, 1868, the papal nuncio in Munich, Monsignor Meglia, uttered his inmost conviction regarding the Württemberg resident thus: "Only in America, England, and Belgium does the Catholic church receive its rights ; elsewhere nothing can help us but the revolution." And on 22nd April, 1869, Bishop Senestray of Regensburg declared plainly in a speech delivered at Schwandorff: "If kings will no longer be of God's grace, I shall be the first to overthrow the throne. . . . Only a war or revolution can help us in the end." And war at last came, but it helped only their opponents. Although at its outbreak in 1870 the ultramontane party in South Germany, especially in Bavaria, for the most part with unexampled insolence expressed their sympathy with France, and after the brilliant and victorious close of the war did everything to prevent the attachment of Bavaria to the new German empire, their North German brethren, accustomed to the boundless compliance of the Prussian government, indulged the hope of prosecuting their own ends all the more successfully under the new regime. Even in November, 1870, Archbishop Ledochowski of Posen visited the victorious king of Prussia at Versailles, in order to interest him personally in the restoration of the Papal States. In February, 1871, in the same place. fifty-six Catholic deputies of the

Prussian parliament presented to the king, who had meanwhile been
proclaimed Emperor of Germany, a formal petition for the restoration
of the temporal power of the pope, and soon afterwards a deputation
of distinguished laymen waited upon him " in name of all the Catho
lics of Germany," with an address directed to the same end. The
Bavarian Fatherland (Dr. Sigl) indeed treated it with scorn as a
" belly-crawling-deputation, which crawled before the magnanimous
hero-emperor, beseeching him graciously to use said deputation as
his spittoon." And the *Steckenberger Bote*, inspired by Dr. Ketteler,
declared : " We Catholics do not entreat it as a favour, but demand it
as our right. . . . Either you must restore the Catholic church to all
its privileges or not one of all your existing governments will endure."
At the same time as the insinuation was spread that the new German
empire threatened the existence of the Catholic church in Germany, a
powerful ultramontane election agitation in view of the next Reichstag was set on foot, out of which grew the party of the " Centre,"
so called from sitting in the centre of the hall, with Von Ketteler,
Windthorst, Mallinkrodt (died 1874), and the two Reichenspergers,
as its most eloquent leaders. Even in the debate on the address in
answer to the speech from the throne this party demanded intervention, at first indeed only diplomatic, in favour of the Papal States.
In the discussion on the new imperial constitution A. Reichensperger
sought to borrow from the abortive German landowners' bill of 1848,
condemned indeed as godless by the syllabus (§ 185, 2), principles that
might serve the turn of ultramontanism regarding the unrestricted
liberty of the press, societies, meetings, and religion, with the most
perfect independence of all religious communities of the State.
Mallinkrodt insisted upon the need of enlarged privileges for the
Catholic church owing to the great growth of the empire in Catholic
territory and population. All these motions were rejected by the
Reichstag, and the Prussian government answered them by abolishing in July, 1871, the Catholic department of the Ministry of Public
Worship, which had existed since 1841 (§ 193, 2). The *Genfer
Korrespondenz*, shortly before highly praised by the pope, declared :
If kings do not help the papacy to regain its rights, the papacy must
also withdraw from them and appeal directly to the hearts of the
people. " Understand ye the terrible range of this change ? Your
hours, O ye princes, are numbered ! " The Berlin *Germania* pointed
threateningly to the approaching *revanche* war in France, on the
outbreak of which the German empire would no longer be able
to reckon on the sympathy of its Catholic subjects ; and the *Ellwanger kath. Wochenblatt* proclaimed openly that only France is able
to guard and save the Catholic church from the annihilating pro-
jects of Prussia. And in this way the Catholic people throughout all

Germany were roused and incited by the Catholic press, as well as from the pulpit and confessional, in home and school, in Catholic monasteries and nunneries, in mechanics' clubs and peasants' unions, in casinoes and assemblies of nobles. Bishop Ketteler founded expressly for purposes of such agitations the Mainz Catholic Union, in September, 1871, which by its itinerant meetings spread far and wide the flame of religious fanaticism; and a Bavarian priest, Lechner, preached from the pulpit that one does not know whether the German princes are by God's or by the devil's grace.

2. Conflicts Occasioned by Protection of the Old Catholics, 1871-1872.— That the Prussian government refused to assist the bishops in persecuting the Old Catholics, and even retained these in their positions after excommunication had been hurled against them, was regarded by those bishops as itself an act of persecution of the Catholic church. To this opinion they gave official expression, under solemn protest against all encroachments of the state upon the domain of Catholic faith and law, in a memorial addressed to the German emperor from Fulda, on September 7th, 1871, but were told firmly and decidedly to keep within their own boundaries. Even before this Bishop Krementz of Ermeland had refused the *missio canonica* to Dr. Wollmann, teacher of religion at the Gymnasium of Braunsberg, on account of his refusing to acknowledge the dogma of infallibility, and had forbidden Catholic scholars to attend his instructions. The minister of public worship, Von Mühler, decided, because religious instruction was obligatory in the Prussian gymnasia, that all Catholic scholars must attend or be expelled from the institution. The Bavarian government followed a more correct course in a similar case that arose about the same time; for it recognised and protected the religious instructions of the anti-infallibilist priest, Renftle in Mering, as legitimate, but still allowed parents who objected to withhold their children from it. And in this way the new Prussian minister, Falk, corrected his predecessor's mistake. But all the more decidedly did the government proceed against Bishop Krementz, when he publicly proclaimed the excommunication uttered against Dr. Wollmann and Professor Michelis, which had been forbidden by Prussian civil law on account of the infringement of civil rights connected therewith according to canon law. As the bishop could not be brought to an explicit acknowledgment of his obligation to obey the laws of the land, the minister of public worship on October 1st, 1872, stripped him of his temporalities. But meanwhile a second conflict had broken out. The Catholic field-provost of the Prussian army and bishop *in partibus*, Namszanowski, had under papal direction commanded the Catholic divisional chaplain, Lünnemann of Cologne, on pain of excommunication, to discontinue the military worship in the garrison chapel.

which, by leave of the military court, was jointly used by the Old Catholics, and so was desecrated. He was therefore brought before a court of discipline, suspended from his office in May, 1872, and finally, by royal ordinance in 1873, the office of field-provost was wholly abolished.

3. Struggles over Educational Questions, 1872-1873.—In the formerly Polish provinces of the Prussian kingdom the Polonization of resident Catholic Germans had recently assumed threatening proportions. The archbishop of Posen and Gnesen, Count Ledochowski, whom the pope during the Vatican Council appointed primate of Poland, was the main centre of this agitation. In the Posen priest seminary he formed for himself, in a fanatically Polish clergy, the tools for carrying it out, and in the neighbouring Schrimm he founded a Jesuit establishment that managed the whole movement. Where previously Polish and German had been preached alternately, German was now banished, and in the public schools, the oversight of which, as throughout all Prussia, lay officially in the hands of the clergy, all means were used to discourage the study of the German language, and to stamp out the German national sentiment. But even in the two western provinces the Catholic public schools were made by the clerical school inspectors wholly subservient to the designs of ultramontanism. In order to stem such disorder the government, in February, 1872, sanctioned the School Inspection Law passed by the parliament, by which the right and duty of school inspection was transferred from the church to the state, so that for the sake of the state the clerical inspectors hostile to the government were set aside, and where necessary might be replaced by laymen. A pastoral letter of the Prussian bishops assembled at Fulda in April of that year complained bitterly of persecution of the church and unchristianizing of the schools, but advised the Catholic clergy under no circumstances voluntarily to resign school inspection where it was not taken from them. By a rescript of the minister of public worship in June, the exclusion of all members of spiritual orders and congregations from teaching in public schools was soon followed by the suppression of the Marian congregations in all schools, and it was enjoined in March, 1873, that in Polish districts, where other subjects had been taught in the higher educational institutions in the German language, this also would be obligatory in religious instruction. Ledochowski indeed directed all religious teachers in his diocese to use the Polish language after as they had done before, but the government suspended all teachers who followed his direction, and gave over the religious instruction to lay teachers. The archbishop now erected private schools for the religious instruction of gymnasial teachers, and the government forbad attendance at them.

4. The Kanzelparagraph and the Jesuit Law, 1871-1872.—While thus the Prussian government took more and more decided measures against the ultramontanism that had become so rampant in its domains, on the other hand, its mobile band of warriors in cassock, dress coat, and blouse did not cease to labour, and the imperial government passed some drastic measures of defence applicable to the whole empire. At the instance of the Bavarian government, which could not defend itself from the violence of its "patriots," the Federal Council asked the Reichstag to add a new article to the penal code of the empire, threatening any misuse of the pulpit for political agitation with imprisonment for two years. The Bavarian minister of public worship, Lutz, undertook himself to support this bill before the Reichstag. "For several decades," he said, "the clergy in Germany have assumed a new character; they are become the simple reflection of Jesuitism." The Reichstag sanctioned the bill in December, 1871. Far more deeply than this so-called Kanzelparagraph, the operation of which the agitation of the clergy by a little circumspection could easily elude, did the Jesuit Law, published on July 4th, 1872, cut into the flesh of German ultramontanism. Already in April of that year had a petition from Cologne demanding the expulsion of the Jesuits been presented to the Reichstag. Similar addresses flowed in from other places. The Centre party, on the other hand, organized a regular flood of petitions in favour of the Jesuits. The Reichstag referred both to the imperial chancellor, with the request to introduce a law against the movements of the Jesuits as dangerous to the State. The Federal Council complied with this request, and so the law was passed which ordained the removal of the Jesuits and related orders and congregations, the closing of their institutions within six months, and prohibited the formation of any other orders by their individual members, and the government authorised the banishment of foreign members and the interning of natives at appointed places. A later ordinance of the Federal Council declared the Redemptorists, Lazarists, Priests of the Holy Ghost, and the Society of the Heart of Jesus to be orders related to the Society of Jesus. Those affected by this law anticipated the threatened interning by voluntarily removing to Belgium, Holland, France, Turkey, and America.

5. The Prussian Ecclesiastical Laws, 1873-1875.—In order to be able to check ultramontanism, even in its pædagogical breeding places, the episcopal colleges and seminaries, and at the same time to restrict by law the despotic absolutism of the bishops in disciplinary and beneficiary matters, the Prussian government brought in other four ecclesiastical bills, which in spite of violent opposition on the part of the Centre and the Old Conservatives, were successively passed by both houses of parliament, and approved by the king on May 11th,

12th, 13th, and 14th, 1873. Their most important provisions are: As a condition for admission to a spiritual office the state requires citizenship of the German empire, three years' study at a German university, and, besides an exit gymnasial examination preceding the university course, a state examination in general knowledge (in philosophy, history, and German literature), in addition to the theological examination. The episcopal boys' seminaries and colleges are abolished. The priest seminaries, if the minister of worship regards them as fit for the purpose, may take the place of the university course, but must be under regular state inspection. The candidates for spiritual offices, which must never be left vacant more than a year, are to be named to the chief president of the province, and he can for cogent reasons lodge a protest against them. Secession from the church is freely allowed, and releases from all personal obligations to pay ecclesiastical dues and perform ecclesiastical duties. Excommunication is permissible, but can be proclaimed only in the congregation concerned, and not publicly. The power of church discipline over the clergy can be exercised only by German superiors and in accordance with fixed processional procedure. Corporal punishment is not permissible, fines are allowed to a limited extent, and restraint by interning in so-called *Demeriti* houses, but only at furthest of three months, and when the party concerned willingly consents. Church servants, whose remaining in office is incompatible with the public order, can be deposed by civil sentence. And as final court of appeal in all cases of complaint between ecclesiastical and civil authorities as well as within the ecclesiastical domain, a royal court of justice for ecclesiastical affairs is constituted, whose proceedings are open and its decision final.—But even the May Laws soon proved inadequate for checking the insolence of the bishops and the disorders among the Catholic population occasioned thereby. In December, 1873, therefore, by sovereign authority there was prescribed a new formula of the episcopal Oath of Allegiance, recognising more distinctly and decisively the duty of obedience to the laws of the state. Then next a bill was presented to the parliament, which had been kept in view in the original constitution, demanding obligatory civil marriage and abolition of compulsory baptism, as well as the conducting of civil registration by state officials. In February, 1874, it was passed into law. On the 20th and 21st May, 1874, two other bills brought in for extending the May Laws of the previous year, in consequence of which a bishop's see vacated by death, a judicial sentence, or any other cause, must be filled within the space of a year, and the chapter must elect within ten days an episcopal administrator, who has to be presented to the chief president, and to undertake an oath to obey the laws of the state. If the chapter does not fulfil these requirements, a lay commissioner will be appointed to administer the affairs of the diocese. During the episcopal vacancy, all vacant pastorates, as well as all not legally filled, can be at once validly supplied by the act of the patron, and, where no such right exists, by congregational election. Parochial property, on the illegal appointment of a pastor, is given over to be administered by a lay commissioner.—The empire also came to the help of the May Laws by an imperial enactment of May 4th, 1874, sanctioned by the emperor, which empowers the competent state government to intern all church officers discharged from their office and not yielding submission thereto, as well as all punished on account of incompetence in their official duties, and, if this does not help, to condemn them to loss of their civil rights and to expulsion from the German federal territory.—Also in its next session the imperial house of representatives again gave legislative sanction to the *Kulturkampf;* for in January, 1875, it passed a bill presented by the Federal Council on the deposition on oath as to personal rank, and on divorce with obligatory civil marriage, which, going far beyond the Prussian civil law of the previous year, and especially ridding Bavaria of its strait-jacket canon marriage law enforced by the concordat, abolished the spiritual jurisdiction in favour of that of the civil courts, and gave it to the state to determine the qualifications for, as well as the hindrances to, divorce, without, however, touching the domain of conscience, or entrenching in any way upon the canon law and the demands of the church.

6. Opposition in the States to the Prussian May Laws.—Bishop Martin of Paderborn had even beforehand refused obedience to the May Laws of 1873. After their promulgation, all the Prussian bishops collectively declared to the ministry that "they were not in a position to carry out these laws," with the further statement that they could not comply even with those demands in them which in other states by agreement with the pope, are acknowledged by the church because they are administered in a one-sided way by the state in Prussia. On these lines also they proceeded to take action. First of all, the refractoriness of several of the seminaries drew down upon them the loss of endowment and of the right of representation; and in the next place, the refusal of the bishops to notify their appointment of clergymen led to their being frequently fined, while the church books and seals were taken away from clergymen so appointed, all the official acts performed by them were pronounced invalid in civil law, and those who performed them were subjected to fines. But here, too, again Bishop Martin, well skilled in church history (he had been previously professor of theology in Bonn), had beforehand in a pastoral instructed his clergy that "since the days

of Diocletian there had not been seen so violent a persecution of the name of Jesus Christ." Soon after this Archbishop Ledochowski, in an official document addressed to the Chief President of Poland, compared the demand to give notification of clerical appointments with the demand of ancient Rome upon Christian soldiers to sacrifice to the heathen gods. And by order of the pope prayers were offered in all churches for the church so harshly and cruelly persecuted. And yet the whole "persecution" then consisted in nothing more than this, that a newly issued law of the state, under threat of fine in case of disobedience, demanded again of the bishops paid by the state what had been accepted for centuries as unobjectionable in the originally Catholic Bavaria, and also for a long while in France, Portugal, and other Romish countries, what all Prussian bishops down to 1850 (§ 193, 2) had done without scruple, what the bishops of Paderborn and Münster even had never refused to do in the extra-Prussian portion of these dioceses (Oldenburg and Waldeck), as also the Prince-Bishop of Breslau, since the issuing of the similar Austrian May Laws (§ 198, 4) in the Austro-Silesian part of his diocese, what the episcopal courts of Württemberg and Baden had yielded to, although in almost all these states the demand referred to broke up the union with the papal curia. Yet before a year had passed the cases of punishment for these offences had so increased that the only very inadequate fines that could be exacted by the seizure of property had to be changed into equivalent sentences of imprisonment. The first prelate who suffered this fate was Archbishop Ledochowski, in February, 1874. Then followed in succession : Eberhard of Treves, Melchers of Cologne, Martin of Paderborn, and Brinkmann of Münster. The ecclesiastical court of justice expressly pronounced deposition against Ledochowski in April, 1874 ; against Martin in January, 1875, and against the Prince-Bishop Förster of Breslau in October, 1875, who alone had dared to proclaim in his diocese the encyclical *Quod nunquam* (Par. 7). But the latter had even beforehand withdrawn the diocesan property to the value of 900,000 marks to his episcopal castle, Johannisberg, in Austro-Silesia, where with a truly princely income from Austrian funds he could easily get over the loss of the Prussian part of his revenues. Martin, who had been interned at Wesel, fled in August, 1875, under cloud of night, to Holland, from whence he transferred his agitations into Belgium, and finally to London (died 1879). Ledochowski found a residence in the Vatican. Brinkmann was deposed in March, and Melchers in June, 1876, after both had beforehand proved their enjoyment of martyrdom by escaping to Holland. Eberhard of Treves anticipated his deposition from office by his death in May, 1876. Blum of Limburg was deposed in June, 1877, and Beckmann of Osnabrück died in 1878.—In the Prussian parliament and German Reichstag the Centre party, supported by Guelphs, Poles, and the Social Democrats, had meanwhile with anger, scorn, and vituperation, with and without wit, fought not only against all ecclesiastical, but also against all other legislative proposals, whose acceptance was specially desired by the government. And all the representatives of the ultramontane press within and without Europe vied with one another in violent denunciation of the ecclesiastical laws, and in unmeasured abuse of the emperor and the empire. But almost without exception the Roman Catholic officials in Prussia, as well as the Protestants and Old Catholics, carried out "the Diocletian persecution of Christians" in the judicial and police measures introduced by the church laws. A number of Catholic notables of the eastern provinces of their own accord, in a dutiful address to the emperor, expressly accepted the condemned laws, and won thereby the nickname of "State Catholics." The great mass of the Catholic people, high and low, remained unflinchingly faithful to the resisting clergy in, for the most part, only a passive opposition, although even, as the Berlin *Germania* expressed it, "the Catholic rage at the Bismarckian ecclesiastical polity could condense itself into one Catholic head" in a murderous attempt on the chancellor in quest of health at Kissingen, on July 13th, 1874. It was the cooper, Kullmann, who, fanaticised by exciting speeches and writings in the Catholic society of Salzwedel, sought to take vengeance, as he himself said, upon the chancellor for the May Laws and "the insult offered to his party of the Centre."—In the further course of the Prussian *Kulturkampf*, however, fostered by the aid of the confessional, the insinuating assiduity of the clerical press, and the all-prevailing influence of the thoroughly disciplined Catholic clergy over the popish masses, the Centre grew in number and importance at the elections from session to session, so that from the beginning of 1880, by the unhappy division of the other parties in the Reichstag as well as Chamber, it united sometimes with the Conservatives, sometimes and most frequently with the Progressionists and Democrats renouncing the *Kulturkampf*, and was supported on all questions by Poles, Danes, Guelphs, and Alsatian-Lorrainers, as clerical interest and ultramontane tactics required, in accordance with the plan of campaign of the commander-in-chief, especially of the quondam Hanoverian minister, Windthorst, dominated far more by Guelphic than by ultramontane tendencies. The Centre was thus able to turn the scale, until, at least in the Reichstag, after the dissolution and new election of 1887, its dominatory power was broken by the closer combination of the conservative and national liberal parties.

7. **Share in the Conflict taken by the Pope.**—Pius IX. had congratu-

lated the new emperor in 1871, trusting, as he wrote, that his efforts
directed to the common weal "might bring blessing not only to
Germany, but also to all Europe, and might contribute not a little
to the protection of the liberty and rights of the Catholic religion."
And when first of all the Centre party, called forth by the election
agitation of German ultramontanism, opened its politico-clerical
campaign in the Reichstag, he expressed his disapproval of its
proceedings upon Bismarck's complaining to the papal secretary
Antonelli. Yet a deputation of the Centre sent to Rome succeeded
in winning over both. In order to build a bridge for the securing
an understanding with the curia, now that the conflict had grown
in extent and bitterness, the imperial government in May, 1⁰⁷⁻,
appointed the Bavarian Cardinal Prince Hohenlohe to the vacant
post of ambassador to the Vatican. But the pope, with offensive recklessness, rejected the well-meant proposal, and forbade the cardinal
to accept the imperial appointment. From that time he gave free
and public expression on every occasion to his senseless bitterness
against the German empire and its government. In an address to
the German Reading Society at Rome in July, 1872, he allowed
himself to use the most violent expressions against the German
chancellor, and closed with the prophetic threatening: " Who knows
but the little stone shall soon loose itself from the mountain (Dan.
ii. 34), which shall break in pieces the foot of the colossus ? " But
even this diatribe was cast in the shade by the Christmas allocution
of that year, in which he was not ashamed to characterize the procedure of the German statesmen and their imperial sovereign as
" *impudentia*." And after the publication of the first May Laws he
addressed a letter to the emperor, in which, founding upon the fact
that even the emperor like all baptized persons belonged to him
the pope, he cast in his teeth that "all the measures of his government for some time aimed more and more at the annihilation or
Catholicism," and added the threatening announcement that these
measures against the religion of Jesus Christ can have no other result
than the overthrow of his own throne." The emperor in his answer
made expressly prominent his divinely appointed call as well as his
own evangelical standpoint, and with becoming dignity and earnestness decidedly repudiated the unmeasured assumptions of the papacy,
and published both letters. In the same style of immoderate pretension the pope again, in November, 1875, in one encyclical after
another, gave vent to his anger against emperor and empire, especially
its military institutions. In place of the deposed and at that time
imprisoned archbishop, Ledochowski, he appointed in 1874 a native
apostolic legate, who was at last ascertained to be the Canon
Kurowski, when he was in October, 1875, condemned to two years'

imprisonment. But the pope took the most decided and successful step by the Encyclical Quod nunquam, of 5th February, 1875, addressed to the Prussian episcopate, in which he characterized the Prussian May Laws as "not given to free citizens to demand a reasonable obedience, but as laid upon slaves, in order to force obedience by fears of violence," and, "in order to fulfil the duties of his office," declared quite openly to all whom it concerns and to the Catholics throughout the world: "*Leges illas irritas esse, utpote quæ divinæ Ecclesiæ constitutioni prorsus adversantur*"; but upon those "godless" men who make themselves guilty of the sin of assuming spiritual office without a divine call, falls *eo ipso* the great excommunication. On the other hand he rewarded, in March, 1875, Archbishop Ledochowski, then still in prison, but afterwards, in February, 1876, settled in Rome, for his sturdy resistance of those laws, with a cardinal's hat, and to the not less persistent Prince-Bishop Förster of Breslau he presented on his jubilee as priest the archiepiscopal pall. In the next Christmas allocution he romanced about a second Nero, who, while in one place with a lyre in his hand he enchanted the world by lying words, in other places appeared with iron in his hand, and, if he did not make the streets run with blood, he fills the prisons, sends multitudes into exile, seizes upon and with violence assumes all authority to himself. Also to the German pilgrims who went in May, 1877, to his episcopal jubilee at Rome, he had still much that was terrible to tell about this "modern Attila," leaving it uncertain whether he intended Prince Bismarck or the mild, pious German emperor himself.

8. **The Conflict about the Encyclical Quod nunquam of 1875.**—By this encyclical the pope had completely broken up the union between the Prussian state and the curia, resting upon the bull *De salute animarum* (§ 193, 1); for he, bluntly repudiating the sovereign rights of the civil authority therein expressly allowed, by pronouncing the laws of the Prussian state invalid, authorized and promoted the rebellion of all Catholic subjects against them. The Prussian government now issued three new laws quickly after one another, cutting more deeply than all that went before, which without difficulty received the sanction of all the legislative bodies. I. The so called Arrestment Act (*Sperrgesetz*) of April 22nd, 1875, which ordered the immediate suspension of all state payments to the Roman Catholic bishoprics and pastorates until those who were entitled to them had in writing or by statement declared themselves ready to yield willing obedience to the existing laws of the state. II. A law of May 31st, 1875, ordering the Expulsion of all Orders and such like Congregations within eight months, the minister of public worship, however, being authorized to extend this truce to four years in the case of institutions devoted to

the education of the young, while those which were exclusively hospital and nursing societies were allowed to remain, but were subject to state inspection and might at any time be suppressed by royal order. III. A law of June 12th, 1875, declaring the formal Abrogation of the Fifteenth, Sixteenth, and Eighteenth Articles of the Constitution (§ 193, 2). And finally in addition there came the enforcement during this session of the Chamber of laws previously introduced on the rights of the Old Catholics (§ 190, 2), and, on June 20th, 1875, on the administration of church property in Catholic parishes. The latter measures aimed at withdrawing the administration referred to from the autocratic absolutism of the clergy, and transferring it to a lay commission elected by the community itself, of which the parish priest was to be a member, but not the president. Although the Archbishop of Cologne in name of all the bishops before its issue had solemnly protested against this law, because by it " essential and inalienable rights of the Catholic church were lost," and although the recognition of it actually involved recognition of the May Laws and the ecclesiastical court of justice, yet all the bishops declared themselves ready to co-operate in carrying out the arrangements for surrendering the church property to the administration of a civil commission. They thus indeed secured thoroughly ultramontane elections, but at the same time put themselves into a position of self-contradiction, and admitted that the one ground of their opposition to the May Laws, that they were one-sidedly wrought by the state was null and void.

9. Papal Overtures for Peace.—Leo XIII., since 1878, intimated his accession to the Emperor William, and expressed his regret at finding that the good relations did not continue which formerly existed between Prussia and the holy see. The Emperor's answer expressed the hope that by the aid of his Holiness the Prussian bishops might be induced to obey the laws of the land, as the people under their pastoral care actually did; and afterwards while in consequence of the attempt on his life of June 2nd, 1873, he lay upon a sickbed, the crown prince on June 10th answered other papal communications by saying, that no Prussian monarch could entertain the wish to change the constitution and laws of his country in accordance with the ideas of the Romish church; but that, even though a thorough understanding upon the radical controversy of a thousand years could not be reached, yet the endeavour to preserve a conciliatory disposition on both sides would also for Prussia open a way to peace which had never been closed in other states. Three weeks later the Munich nuntio Masella was at Kissingen and conferred with the chancellor, Prince Bismarck, who was residing there, about the possibility of a basis of reconciliation. Subsequently negotiations were continued at

Gastein, and then in Vienna with the there resident nuntio Jacobini, but were suspended owing to demands by the curia to which the state could not submit. Still the pope attempted indirectly to open the way for renewed consultation, for he issued a brief dated February 24th, 1880, to "Archbishop Melchers of Cologne" (deposed by the royal court of justice), in which he declared his readiness to allow to the respective government boards notification of new elected priests before their canonical institution. Thereupon a communication was sent to Cardinal Jacobini that the state ministry had resolved, so soon as the pope had actually implemented this declaration of his readiness, to make every effort to obtain from the state representatives authority to set aside or modify those enactments of the May Laws which were regarded by the Romish church as harsh. But the pope received this compromise of the government very ungraciously and showed his dissatisfaction by withdrawing his concession, which besides referred only to the unremovable priests, therefore not to *Hetzkaplane* and succursal or assistant priests, and presupposed the obtaining the "*agrément*," i.e. the willingly accorded consent, of the state, without by any means allowing the setting aside of the party elected.

10. **Proof of the Prussian Government's willingness to be Reconciled, 1880–1881.**—Notwithstanding this brusque refusal on the part of the papal curia, the government, at the instance of the minister of public worship, Von Puttkamer (§ 193, 6), resolved in May, 1880, to introduce a bill which gave a wide discretionary power for moderating the unhappy state of matters that had prevailed since the passing of the May Laws, throughout Catholic districts, where 601 pastorates stood wholly vacant and 584 partly so, and nine bishoprics, some by death and others by deposition. Although the need of peace was readily admitted on both sides, the Liberals opposed these "Canossa proposals" as far too great; the Centre, Poles, and Guelphs as far too small. Yet it obtained at last in a form considerably modified, through a compromise of the conservatives with a great part of the national liberals the consent of both chambers. This law, sanctioned on July 14th, 1880, embraced these provisions : 1. The royal court shall no longer depose from office any church officers, but simply pronounce incapable of administering the office ; 2–4. The ministry of the state is authorized to give the episcopal administrator charged by the church with the interim administration of a vacant bishopric a dispensation from the taking of the prescribed oath; further, an administration by commission of ecclesiastical property may be revoked as well as appointed ; also state endowments that had been withdrawn are to be restored for the benefit of the whole extent of the diocese ; 5. Spiritual official acts of a duly appointed clergyman by way merely of assis-

tance in another vacant parish are to be allowed ; 6. The minister of the interior and of public worship are empowered to approve of the erection of new institutions of religious societies which are devoted wholly to the care of the sick, as to allow revocably to them the care and nurture of children not yet of school age ; and more recently added were 7, the particular, according to which Articles 2, 3, and 4 cease to operate after January 1st, 1882. The government was particularly careful to carry out the provisions temporarily recognised in Article 8, for the restoration of orderly episcopal administration by regularly elected episcopal administrators in bishoprics made vacant by death. Fulda, which was longest vacant, from October, 1873, had to be left out of account, since in that case there was only one member of the chapter left and so a canonical election was impossible. But without difficulty in March, 1881, the Vicar-General Dr. Höting for Osnabrück and Canon Drobe for Paderborn, without taking the oath of allegiance, succeeded in obtaining independent administration of the property as well as the restoration of state pay for the entire dioceses, though they did not give the notification required by the May Laws for the interim administration. In October, 1881, the deposed Prince Bishop Förster of Breslau died, and the suffragan bishop, Gleich, elected by the chapter, undertook with consent of the government the office of episcopal administrator.—Meanwhile the pope, by a hearty letter of congratulation to the emperor on his birthday, March 22nd, had given new life to the suspended peace negotiations. And now also, when the respective chapters transferred their right of election to the pope, the orderly appointments of the Canon Dr. Korum of Metz, a pupil of the Jesuit faculty of Innspruck, very warmly recommended by Von Manteuffel, governor of Alsace and Lorraine, to the episcopal see of Treves, in August, 1881, of Vicar-General Kopp of Hildesheim to Fulda in December, 1881, of the episcopal administrators Höting and Drobe, in March and May, 1882, respectively to Osnabrück and Paderborn, were duly carried into effect. For Breslau the chapter drew up a list of seven candidates, but the government pointed out the Berlin provost, Rob. Herzog, as a mild and conciliatory person. The chapter now laid its right of election in the hands of the pope, and in May, 1882, Herzog was raised to the dignity of prince-bishop. There now remained vacant only the sees of Cologne, Posen, Limburg and Münster, which had been emptied by the depositions of the civil courts.— Meanwhile, too, the negotiations carried on at the instance of the government by privy councillor Von Schlözer, with the curia at Rome for the restoration of the embassy to the Vatican had been brought to a close. The chamber voted for this purpose an annual sum of 90,000 marks, and Schlözer himself was appointed to the post in March, 1882.

11. Conciliatory Negotiations, 1882–1884.—With January 1st, 1882, the three enactments of the July law of 1880, which might be enforced at the discretion of the government, ceased to operate. Von Gossler, minister of public worship since June, 1881, on behalf of government, introduced a new bill into the Chamber on January 16th, 1882, for their re-enactment and extension, which by a compromise between the Conservatives and the Centre, after various modifications secured a majority in both houses. This second revised law embraced the following points: 1. Renewal of the three above-named enactments till April 1st, 1884; 2. Restoration of the "Bishop's Paragraph," lost in 1880, in this new form: If the king has pardoned a bishop set aside by the ecclesiastical court, he becomes again the bishop of his diocese recognised by the state; 3. The setting aside of the examination in general knowledge (*Kulturexamen*) for those who bring a certificate of having passed the Gymnasium exit examination, or have attended with diligence lectures on philosophy, history and German literature during a three years' course at a German university, or at a Prussian seminary of equal rank, and have given proof of this by presenting evidence to the chief president; 4. The setting aside of the rights of the patron and congregation of themselves filling the vacant pastorates during a vacancy in the episcopal see. The new law obtained royal sanction on May 31st, 1882. But its two most important articles, 2 and 3, remained for a long time a dead letter, and even Article 1 was only carried out by the resumption of the state emoluments for the Hohenzollerns and the five newly instituted bishoprics (Par. 10), but not for the other seven. But the ill humour of the ultramontane Hotspurs was raised to the boiling point by the fate of the bill introduced by the Centre into the Reichstag to set aside the Expatriation Law of May 4th, 1874, which seemed to the government indispensable on account of its applicability to the agitations against the empire of the Polish clergy. This bill, after violent debates, was carried on January 18th, 1882, by a two-thirds majority; but it was cast out by the Federal Council on June 6th, almost unanimously, only Bavaria and Reuss *jüngere Linie* voting in its favour. This was the result mainly of the failure of all the attempts of Von Schlözer to render the government's concessions acceptable to the papal curia.— On the other hand, the government of its own accord brought in a third revision scheme in June, 1883, by which it sought to relieve as far as possible the troubles of the Catholic church. By adopting this law: (1) The obligation of notification on the part of the bishops and the right of the state to protest on the change of temporary assistants and substitutes into regular spiritual officers, were abolished; as also (2) the competence of the court for ecclesiastical affairs in appeals against the protest of the chief president, which now therefore, according to the generally prevailing rule, are referred to the minister of worship, the whole ministry, the parliament, the king; (3) the immunity from punishment in the execution of their office guaranteed in Article 5 of the July law of 1880 (Par. 10) was extended to all spiritual offices whether vacant or not; (4) the ordaining of individual candidates in vacant dioceses by bishops recognised by the state was declared to be legal. In spite of repeated declarations of the curia that it could and would agree to the notification only after a previous sufficient guarantee of perfectly free training of the clergy and free administration of the spiritual office, the king while residing at the Castle of Mainau on Lake Constance, on July 11th, 1883, sanctioned the so-called Mainau Law that had passed both houses, and on the 14th, the minister of public worship demanded that the Prussian bishops, without making notification, should fill up vacancies in pastorates by appointing assistants, and should name those candidates who were eligible for such appointment under the conditions of the May Law of the previous year (Par. 3). The pope at last, in September, 1883, allowed the dispensation required, but for that time only and without prejudice for the future. By the end of May, 1,884 applications had been made to the senior of the Prussian episcopate appointed to receive such, Marnitz of Kulm, by 1,443 clergymen, of whom the government rejected only 178 who had studied at the Jesuit institutions of Rome, Louvain, and Innsbrück.—In December, 1883, Bishop Blum of Limburg, and in January, 1884, Brinkmann of Münster were restored by royal grace, and for both dioceses, as well as for Ermeland, Kulm and Hildesheim, and at last also on March 31st, shortly before the closing of the door, even for Cologne, in this case, however, revocably, the arrest of salaries ceased, so that only the two archiepiscopal sees of Cologne and Posen remained vacant, and only Posen continued bereft of its endowments. On the other hand the government allowed the three discretionary enactments that were in operation till April 1st, 1884, to lapse without providing for their renewal. Also the proposal for abolishing the Expatriation Law of November, 1884, introduced anew by the Centre and again adopted by the Reichstag by a great majority, was thrown out by the Federal Council; but in the beginning of December, on the opening of the new Reichstag, it was again brought in by the Centre and passed, but was left quite unnoticed by the Federal Council. The repeated motions of the Centre for payment of the bishops' salaries from the state exchequer, as well as for immunity to those who read mass and dispensed the sacraments, were again thrown out by the House of Deputies in April, 1885.

12. Resumption on both sides of Conciliatory Measures, 1885–1886.— The next subject of negotiation with the curia was the re-institution of the archiepiscopal see of Posen-Gnesen. In March, 1884, the pope

had nominated Cardinal Ledochowski secretary of the committee on petitions, in which capacity he had to remain in Rome. He now declared himself willing to accept Ledochowski's resignation of the archbishopric if the Prussian government would allow a successor who would possess the confidence of the holy see as well as of the Polish inhabitants of the diocese. But of the three noble Polish chauvinists submitted by the Vatican the government could accept none. Since further no agreement could be reached on the question of the bishop's obligation to make notification and the state's right to protest, the negotiations were for a long time at a standstill, and were repeatedly on the point of being broken off. But from the middle of 1885, a conciliatory movement gained power, through the counsels of the more moderate party among the cardinals. Archbishop Melchers, who lived as an exile in Maestricht, was called to Rome, and as a reward for his assistance was made cardinal, and the pope consecrated as his successor in the archbishopric of Cologne, Bishop Krementz of Ermeland (Par. 2), who also was acknowledged by the Prussian government and introduced to Cologne on December 15th, 1885, with great pomp, with 20,000 torches and twenty bands of music. After a long list of candidates had been set aside by one side and the other, some here, some there, the pope at last fell from his demand for one of Polish nationality, and in March, 1886, appointed to the vacant see Julius Dinder, dean of Königsberg, a German by nation but speaking the Polish language.—Meanwhile at other points advance was made in the peaceful, yea, even friendly, relations between the pope and the Prussian government. The diplomatist Leo showed his admiring regard for the diplomatist Bismarck by sending him a valuable oil-painting of himself by a Münich master, and the latter astonished the world by making the pope umpire in a threatening conflict with Spain on the possession of the Caroline islands. His decision on the main question was indeed in favour of Spain, but not unimportant concessions were also made to Germany. The pope sent the prince two Latin poems as *pretium affectionis*, and conferred upon him, the first Protestant that had ever been so honoured, at the close of 1885 or beginning of 1886, the highest papal order, the insignia of the Order of Christ, with brilliants, after the cardinal secretary of state Jacobini as president of the papal court of arbitration had been rewarded with the Prussian order of the Black Eagle, and the other members of the court with other high Prussian orders; and at the end of April, 1886, the German emperor sent the pope himself thanks for his mediation, with an artistic and costly Pectoral (§ 59, 7) worth 10,000 marks.—The government had, meanwhile, on February 15th, 1886, brought in a new proposal of revision of church polity, the fourth, and in order to secure the advice of a distinguished representative of the

Prussian episcopate, called Bishop Kopp of Fulda to the House of
Peers. But as his demands for concessions, suggested to him, not by
the pope, but by the Centre, went far beyond what was proposed, they
were for the most part decidedly opposed by the minister of worship
and rejected by the house. The law confirmed by the king on May
24th, 1886, made the following changes: Complete abolition of the
examination in general culture; freeing of the seminaries recognised
by the minister as suitable for clerical training, as well as faculties
established in universities, seminaries and gymnasia from any special
state inspection (as laid down in the May Laws), and subjecting such
to the common laws affecting all similar educational institutions.
Removal of restrictions requiring ecclesiastical disciplinary procedure to be only before German ecclesiastical courts; Abolition of the
Court for Ecclesiastical Affairs and transference of its functions partly
to the ministry of worship, which now as court of appeal in matters
of church discipline dealt only with those cases which entailed a loss
or reduction of official income, partly to the Berlin supreme court,
which has jurisdiction in case of a breach of the law of the state by a
church officer as well as in case of a refusal to fulfil the oath of obedience; The discretionary enactments of the government of 1880 (Par.
10) are again enforced and the modifications of these in Article 6 of
that law are extended to all other institutions engaged on the home
propaganda; All reading of private masses and dispensing of sacraments are no longer subjected to the infliction of penalties.—Some
weeks before royal sanction was given to this law, Cardinal Jacobini
had, at the instance of the pope, expressed his profound satisfaction
with the success of the advice in the House of Peers, as also particularly at the prospect of other concessions promised by the government. In an official communication to the president of the House of
Deputies, he proposed the addition that the notification of new appointments to vacant pastorates should begin from that date. In August
there followed, on the part of the government, the hitherto refused
dispensation for those trained by the Jesuits in Rome and Innsbrück,
and in November, with consent of the minister of public worship,
the re-opening of the episcopal seminaries at Fulda and Treves.

13. Definitive Conclusion of Peace, 1887.—In February, 1887, the state
journal published a new form of oath for the bishops, sanctioned by
royal ordinance, in which the obligation hitherto enforced "to conscientiously observe the laws of the state," was omitted, and the as-
severation added, "that I have not, by the oath, taken to his Holiness
the pope and the church, undertaken any obligation which can be in
conflict with the oath of fidelity as a subject of his Royal Majesty."—
The promised fifth revision, meanwhile accepted by the pope in its
several particulars and acknowledged by him as sufficient basis for a

definitive peace, was on February 13th, 1887, contrary to precedent, first laid before the House of Peers. Bishop Kopp proposed a great number of changes and additions, of which several of a very important nature were accepted. The most important provisions of this law, which was passed on April 29th, 1887, are the following: The obligation on bishops to make notification applies only to the conferring of a spiritual office for life, and the right of protest by the state must rely upon a basis named and belonging to the civil domain; All state compulsion to lifelong reinstatement in a vacant office is unlawful; The previously insured immunity for reading mass and dispensing the sacraments is now applied to members of all spiritual orders again allowed in the kingdom; The duty of ecclesiastical superiors to communicate disciplinary decisions to the Chief President is given up. Those orders and congregations which devote themselves to aiding in pastoral work, the administering of Christian benevolence, and, on Bishop Kopp's motion, those which engage in educational work in girl's high schools and similar institutions, as well as those which lead a private life, are to be allowed and are to be also restored to the enjoyment of their original possessions; The training of missionaries for foreign work and the erection of institutions for this purpose are to be permitted to the privileged orders and congregations.—Bishop Kopp, and also the pope, with lively gratitude, accepted these ordinances as making the reconciliation an accomplished fact; but they also expressed the hope that the success of this peaceful arrangement will be such as shall lead to further important concessions to the rightful claims of the Catholic church. After this conclusive revision, besides the extremely contracted obligation of notification by the bishops and the almost completely insignificant right of civil protest, there remain of the *Kulturkampf* laws only: the *Kanzelparagraph*, the Jesuit and the exile enactments (all of them imperial and not Prussian laws), and the abrogation of the three articles of the Prussian constitution (Par. 8). Insignificant as the concessions of the papal curia may seem in comparison to the almost complete surrender of the Prussian government, it can hardly be said that Bismarck has been untrue to his promise not to go to Canossa. With him the main thing ever was to restore within the German empire the peace that was threatened by thunderclouds gathering from day to day in the political horizon in east and west, and thus, as also by nurturing and developing the military forces, to set aside the danger of war from without. But for this end, the sovereignty of the Centre, which hampered him on every side, allying itself with all elements in the Chamber and Reichstag hostile to the government and the empire, must be broken. But this was possible only if he succeeded in breaking up the unhallowed artificial amalgamation of Catholic church interests for which the Centre con-

tended with the political tendencies of the party hostile to the empire,
by recognising those interests in a manner satisfactory to the pope
and to all right-minded loyal German Catholics, and so estranging
them from the political schemes of the leader of the Centre. This
indeed would have scarcely been possible with Pius IX., but with the
much clearer and sharper Leo XIII. there was hope of success. And
the statesmanlike insight and self-denial of the prince succeeded,
though at first only in a limited measure, and this was a much more
important gain for the state than the papal concessions of episcopal
notification and the state's right of protest.—When in the beginning
of 1887, at the same time that the fear was greatest of a war with
France and Russia, the renewal and enlargement of the military
budget, hitherto for seven years, was necessary, and its refusal by the
Centre and its adherents was regarded as certain, Bismarck prevailed
on the pope to intervene in his favour. The pope did it in a confidential communication to the president of the Centre, in which he urged
acceptance of the septennial act in the Reichstag for the security of
the Fatherland and the conserving of peace on the continent, expressly
referring to the friendly and promising attitude of the imperial
government to the papacy and the Catholic church. But the president
kept the communication secret from the members of his party, and
they continued strenuously and unanimously opposed to the Septennate.
The Reichstag was consequently dissolved. The pope now published
his correspondence with the leaders of the Centre, thirty-seven Rhenish
nobles separated from the party, and the new elections to the Reichstag
were mainly favourable to the government. Although the Deputy
Windthorst as chief leader of the Prussian *Ecclesia militans* had on
every occasion protested his and his party's profoundest reverence for
and conditional submission to every expression of the papal will, and
shortly before (§ 186, 3) had styled the pope "Lord of the whole
world," he opposed himself, as he had done on the Septennate question,
on the fifth revision of the ecclesiastical laws, to the will of the infallible pope by publishing a memorial proving the absolute impossibility
of accepting this proposed law, which, however, this time also he failed
to carry out.

14. Independent Procedure of the other German Governments.—(1)
Bavaria's energy in the struggle against ultramontanism (Par. 4) soon
cooled. Yet in 1873 the Redemptorists were instructed to discontinue
their missionary work (§ 186, 6), and all theological students were
forbidden to attend the Jesuit German College at Rome (§ 151, 1).
Also in 1875, the jubilee processions organized by the episcopate
without obtaining the royal *Placet* were inhibited.—(2) Württemberg,
which since 1862 possessed more civil jurisdiction over Catholic church
affairs and exercised it more freely (§ 196, 6) than Prussia laid claim

to in 1873, could all the more easily maintain ecclesiastical peace, since its peaceful Bishop Hefele (§ 189, 3, 4; 191, 7) avoided all occasion of conflict and strife.—(3) In Baden the *Kulturkampf* that had here previously broken out (§ 196, 2) was continued all the more keenly. In 1873 public teaching, holding of missions and assisting in pastoral work, had been refused to all religious orders and fraternities. But the main blow, followed by the comprehensive church legislation of February 19th, 1874, which closed all boys' seminaries and episcopal institutions, allowed none to hold a clerical office or discharge any ecclesiastical function without a three years' course at a German university and a state examination in general culture (§ 196, 2), strictly forbad all influencing of public elections by the clergy, and made deposition follow the second conviction of a church officer. The expedient hitherto resorted to of appointing mere deputy priests so as to avoid the examination, was consequently frustrated. The rapid increase of vacant pastorates, after five years' opposition, at last moved the episcopal curia to sue for peace at the hands of the government, and when the latter showed an exceedingly conciliatory spirit, the curia with consent of the pope in February, 1880, withdrew its prohibition of the request for dispensation from the state examination, and the government now on its part with the Chambers passed a law, by which the obligation to undergo this examination was abolished, and the certificate of the exit examination, three years' attendance at a German university, and diligent attention to at least three courses of the philosophical faculty, was held as sufficient evidence of general culture. The Baden *Kulturkampf* seems to have been definitely concluded by the election and recognition of Dr. Orbin to the see of Freiburg, vacant for fourteen years, when he. without scruple took the oath of allegiance. This, however, did not check, far less put an end to the tumults of the fanatical ultramontane Irredenta.

15.—(4) Hesse-Darmstadt in 1874 followed the example of Prussia and Baden in excluding all spiritual orders from teaching in public schools, and on April 23rd, 1875, issued five ecclesiastical laws which were directed to restoring under penal sanctions the state of the law, which before 1850 (§ 196, 4) had been unquestioned. Essentially in harmony with the Prussian May Laws of 1873 and 1874, they go beyond these in several particulars. All clergymen receiving appointments, *e.g.*, must have gone through a full university course; all religious orders and congregations were to be allowed to die out; public roads and squares could be used for ecclesiastical festivals only by permission of the government to be renewed on each occasion. The "contentious" Bishop Ketteler of Mainz, who stirred up the fire to the utmost with the Prussian brand, and had kindled also a similar flame in Hesse over the proposal of this law. held still that it saw martyrdom at a distance was the better part, and carefully avoided any overt act of disobedience. But he immediately refused to co-operate in restoring the Catholic theological faculty at Giessen, and the government consequently abandoned the idea. The Mainz see after Ketteler's death in 1877 remained long vacant, as the government felt obliged to reject the electoral list submitted by the chapter. A candidate satisfactory to the Vatican and the government was only found in May, 1886, in the person of Dr. Haffner, a member of the chapter. After Prussia had concluded its definitive peace with Rome, the Hessian government, in May, 1887, laid before the house of representatives a revision of ecclesiastical legislation of 1875, like that of Prussia, only not going so far, for which meanwhile the approval of the papal curia had been obtained. It agrees to the erection of a Catholic clerical seminary, and Catholic students' residences in this seminary and in the state-gymnasia; erection of independent boys' institutions preparatory to the seminary for priests is, however, still refused; the existing duty of bishops to make notification, and the right of the state to protest in regard to appointments to vacant pastorates are also retained. There is no word of rehabilitating religious orders and congregations, nor of any limitation of the law about the exercise of ecclesiastical punishment and means of discipline.—(5) Last of all among the German states affected by the *Kulturkampf*, the kingdom of Saxony, with only 73,000 Catholic inhabitants, at the instance of the second Chamber in 1876, came forward with a Catholic church law modelled upon the Prussian May Laws, with its several provisions modified, in spite of the contention of the talented heir to the throne, Prince George, that the power of the state in relation to the Catholic church could only be determined by a concordat with the Roman curia.

§ 198. AUSTRIA-HUNGARY.

To the emperor of Austria there was left, after the reorganization of affairs by the Vienna Congress, of the Roman empire, only the name of defender of the papal see, and the Catholic church, and the presidency of the German Federal Council. The remnants of the Josephine ecclesiastical constitution were gradually set aside and Catholicism firmly established as the state religion; yet the government asserted its independence against all hierarchical claims, and granted, though only in a very limited degree, toleration to Protestantism. The revolution year 1848 removed indeed some of these limits, but the period of reaction that followed gave, by means of a concordat concluded with the curia in 1855, to the ultramontane hierarchy of the country an unprecedented power in almost all departments of civil life, and prejudicial also to the interests of the Protestant church. After the disastrous issue of the Italian war in 1859, and still more that of the German war in 1866, the government was obliged to make an honest effort to introduce and develop liberal institutions. And after an imperial patent of 1861 had secured religious liberty, self-administration, and equal rights to the Protestant church, the constitutional legislation of 1868 freed Catholic as well as Protestant civil, educational, and ecclesiastical matters from the provisions of the concordat that most seriously threatened them, and by the declaration of papal infallibility in 1870 the government felt justified in regarding the entire concordat as antiquated and declaring it abolished. In its place a Catholic church act was passed by the state in 1874. But the *Kulturkampf* struggle which was thus made imminent also for Austria was avoided by pliancy on both sides.

1. **The Zillerthal Emigration.**—In the Tyrolese Zillerthal the knowledge of evangelical truth had spread among several families by means of Protestant books and Bibles. When the Catholic clergy from 1826 had pushed to its utmost the clerical guardianship by means of auricular confession, an opposition arose which soon from the refusal to confess passed on to the rejection of saint worship, masses for the dead, purgatory, indulgences, etc., and ended in the formal secession of many to the evangelical church in 1830, with a reference to the Josephine edict of toleration. The emperor Francis I., to whom on the occasion of his visit to Innsbrück in 1832 they presented their petition, promised them toleration. But the Tyrolese nobles protested, and the official decision, given at last in 1834, ordered removal to Transylvania or return to the Catholic church. The petitioners now applied, as those of Salzburg had previously done (§ 165, 4), by a deputation to the king of Prussia, who, after by diplomatic communications securing the emperor's consent to emigration, assigned them his estate of Erdmannsdorf in Silesia for colonization. There now the

exiles, 399 in number, settled in 1837, and, largely aided by the royal munificence, founded a new Zillerthal.

2. The Concordat.—After the revolution year 1848, the government were far more yielding toward the claims of the hierarchy than under the old Metternich *régime*. In April, 1850, an imperial patent relieved the papal and episcopal decrees of the necessity of imperial approval, and on August 18th, 1855, a concordat with the pope was agreed to, by which unprecedented power and independence was granted to the hierarchy in Austria for all time to come. The first article secured to the Roman Catholic religion throughout the empire all rights and privileges which they claimed by divine institution and the canon law. The others gave to the bishops the right of unrestricted correspondence with Rome, declared that no papal ordinance required any longer the royal *placet*, that prelates are unfettered in the discharge of their hierarchical obligations, that religious instruction in all schools is under their supervision, that no one can teach religion or theology without their approval, that in catholic schools there can be only catholic teachers, that they have the right of forbidding all books which may be injurious to the faithful, that all cases of ecclesiastical law, especially marriage matters, belong to their jurisdiction, yet the apostolic see grants that purely secular law matters of the clergy are to be decided before a civil tribunal, and the emperor's right of nomination to vacant episcopal sees is to continue, etc. The inferior clergy, who were now without legal protection against the prelates, only reluctantly bowed their necks to this hard yoke; the liberal Catholic laity murmured, sneered, and raged, and the native press incessantly urged a revision of the concordat, the necessity of which became ever more apparent from concessions made meanwhile willingly or grudgingly to the "Non-Catholics." But only after Austria, by the issue of the German war of 1866, was restricted to her own domain, and finally freed from the drag of its ultramontane Italian interests, found herself obliged to make every effort to reconcile the opposing parties within her own territories, could these views prove successful. But since the government nevertheless held firmly by the principle that the concordat, as a state contract regularly concluded between two sovereigns, could be changed only by mutual consent, the liberal majority of the house of deputies resolved to make it as harmless as possible by means of domestic legislation, and on June 11th, 1867, the deputy Herbst moved the appointment of a committee for drawing up three bills for restoring civil marriage, emancipation of schools from the church, and equality of all confessions in the eye of the law. The motion was carried by a hundred and thirty-four votes against twenty-two. The Cisleithan (*i.e.* Austrian excluding Hungary) episcopate, with Cardinal Rauscher of

Vienna at their head, presented an address to his apostolic majesty demanding the most rigid preservation of the concordat, denouncing civil marriage as concubinage, and the emancipation of schools as their dechristianizing. An imperial autograph letter to Rauscher rebuked with earnest words the inflammatory proceedings of the bishops, and at the same time the ultramontane ambassador to Rome, Baron Hübner, was recalled. After the arrangement with Hungary was completed, the first Cisleithan, the so-called Burger, ministry was constituted under the presidency of Prince Auersperg, composed of the most distinguished leaders of the parliamentary majority. All the three bills were passed by a large majority, and obtained imperial sanction on May 25th, 1868. The papal nuncio of Vienna protested, the pope in an allocution denounced the new Austrian constitution as *nefanda sane* and the three confessional laws as *abominabiles leges.* "We repudiate and condemn these laws," he says, "by apostolic authority, as well as everything done by the Austrian government in matters of church policy, and determine in the exercise of the same authority that these decrees with all their consequences are and shall be null and void." But all Vienna, all Austria held jubilee, and the Chancellor von Beust rejected with energy the assumptions of the curia over the civil domain. The bishops indeed issued protests and inflammatory pastorals, and forbad the publication of the marriage act, but submitted to the threats of compulsion by the supreme court, and Bishop Rudigier of Linz, who went furthest in inciting to opposition, was in 1869 taken into court by the police, and sentenced to twelve days' imprisonment, but pardoned by the emperor. Toward the Vatican Council Austria assumed at first a waiting policy, then in vain remonstrated, warned, threatened, and finally, on July 30th, 1870, after the proclamation of infallibility, declared that the concordat was antiquated and abolished, because by this dogma the position of one of the contracting parties had undergone a complete change.

3. **The Protestant Church in Cisleithan Austria.**—Down to 1848 Protestantism of both confessions in Austria enjoyed only a very limited toleration. The storms of this year first set aside the hated official name of "Non-Catholics," and won permission for Protestant places of worship to have bells and towers. But the repeated petitions for permission to found branches of the *Gustavus Adolphus Union,* the persistently maintained law that Catholic clergymen, even after they had formally become Protestants, could not marry, because the *character indelibilis* of priestly consecration attached itself even to apostates, and many such facts, prove that the government was far from intending to grant to the Protestants civil equality with the Catholics. But the unfortunate result of the Sardinian-French war

of 1859, and the fear thereby increased of the falling asunder of the whole Austrian federation, induced the government to address itself earnestly to the introduction of liberal institutions, and also to do justice to the Protestant church. The presidency of the two Protestant consistories in Vienna, hitherto given to a Catholic, was now assigned to a Protestant; meetings of the Gustavus Adolphus Union were now allowed, and a share was given to the Protestant party in the ministry of public worship by the appointment of three evangelical councillors. After the entrance on office of the liberal minister Von Schmerling, an imperial patent was issued on April 8th, 1864, by which unrestricted liberty of faith, independent administration of all ecclesiastical, educational, and charitable matters, free election of pastors, even from abroad, full exercise of civil and political rights, and complete equality with Catholics was given to the Protestants of the German and Slavonian crown territories. Also in 1868, under the reactionary ministry of Belcredi, on the expiry of the legal term of the Evangelical Supreme Church Council, it was reorganized, two evangelical school councillorships were created, and the pecuniary position of the evangelical clergy considerably improved. But in spite of all privileges legally granted to the evangelical church, it continued in many cases, in presence of the concordat, which down to 1870 still remained in force, exposed to the whims and caprice, sometimes of the imperial courts, sometimes of the Catholic clergy.

4. The Clerical Landtag Opposition in the Tyrol.—In the Tyrol, after the publication of the imperial patent of April, 1861, a violent movement was set on foot by clerical agitation. The Landtag, by a great majority, pronounced the issuing of it the most serious calamity which the country, hitherto honest, true, and happy in its undivided attachment to the Catholic faith, could have suffered, and concluded that Non-Catholics in the Tyrol should only by way of dispensation be allowed, but that publicity of Protestant worship and formation of Protestant congregations should be still forbidden. The Schmerling ministry, indeed, refused to confirm these resolutions. The agitation of the clergy, however, which fanned in all possible ways the fanaticism of the people, grew from year to year, until at last the Belcredi ministry of 1866 came to an agreement with the Landtag, sanctioned by the emperor, according to which the creation of an evangelical landed proprietary in the Tyrol was not indeed formally forbidden, but permission for an evangelical to possess land had in each case to be obtained from the Landtag. The ecclesiastical laws of 1868 next called forth new conflicts. Twice was the Landtag closed because of the opposition thus awakened, until finally in September, 1870, the estates took the oath to the new constitution with reservation of conscience. But now, when in December, 1875, the ministry of

worship gave approval to the formal constituting of two evangelical
congregations in the Tyrol, at Innsbrück and Meran, the clerical
press was filled with burning denunciations, and the majority of the
Landtag meeting in the following March thought to give emphasis
to their protest by leaving the chamber, and so bringing the assembly
to a sudden close. In June, 1880, the three bishops of the Tyrol
uttered in the Landtag a fanatical protest against the continuance of
the meanwhile established congregations, which the Landtag majority
renewed in July, 1883.

5. **The Austrian Universities.**—Stremayr, minister of public worship,
introduced in 1872 a scheme of university reorganization, by which
the exclusively Catholic character which had hitherto belonged to
the Austrian universities, especially those of Vienna and Prague,
should be removed. Up to this time a Non-Catholic could there
obtain no sort of academical degree, but this was now to be obtain-
able apart from any question of confession. The office of chancellor,
held by the archbishops of Prague and Vienna, was restricted to the
theological faculty, to the state was assigned the right of nominating
all professors, even in the theological faculty, and the German language was recommended as the medium of instruction. Candidates
of theology have to pass through a full and comprehensive course of
theological science in a three years' university curriculum, before
they can be admitted into an episcopal seminary for practical training. In spite of the opposition of the superior clergy, the bill passed
even in the House of Peers, and became law in 1873.—In Innsbrück,
where according to ancient custom the rector was chosen from the
four faculties in succession, the other faculties protested against
the election when, in 1872, the turn came to the theological (Jesuit)
faculty, and they carried their point. The new organization law
gave the choice of rector to the whole professoriate, and a subsequent
imperial order withdrew from the general of the Jesuits the right of
nominating all theological professors.—Much was done, too, for the
elevation of the evangelical theological faculty in Vienna by bringing
able scholars from Germany, by giving a right to the promotion to
the degree of doctor of theology, etc. But its incorporation in the
university, though often moved for, was hindered by the continued
opposition of the Catholic theologians as well as philosophers, and in
1873 it did not meet with sufficient support in the House of Peers.
Even the use of certain halls in the university buildings, promised by
the minister, could not yet be obtained.

6. **The Austrian Ecclesiastical Laws, 1874-1876.**—At last the government in January, 1874, introduced the long-promised Catholic church
legislation into the Reichstag, intended to supply blanks occasioned
by the setting aside of the concordat. Its main contents are these:

I. The concordat, hitherto only ̣iplomatically dealt with, is now legislatively annulled; the bishops have to present all their manifestoes not before but upon publication to the state government for its cognisance; every vacancy of an ecclesiastical office, as well as every new appointment to such, is to be notified to the civil court, which can raise objections against such appointment within thirty days; the minister of worship then decides on the admissibility or inadmissibility of the candidate; legal deposition of a church officer involves withdrawal of the emoluments; the performance of unusual practices in public worship of a demonstrative character can be prohibited by the civil court; any misuse of ecclesiastical authority in restraining any one from obeying the laws of the land or from exercising his civil rights is strictly interdicted. **II.** The ecclesiastical revenues and the income of the cloisters are subjected to a progressive taxation on behalf of a religious fund, mainly for improving the condition of the lower clergy, for which the episcopate hitherto, in spite of all entreaties, had done practically nothing. **III.** Newly formed religious societies received state recognition if their denomination and principles contain nothing contrary to law and morality or offensive to those of another faith. **IV.** The state grants or refuses its approval of the establishment of spiritual orders, congregations, and ecclesiastical societies; institutions and legacies for them amounting to over three thousand gulden require state sanction; any member is free to quit any order; all orders must report annually on the personal changes and disciplinary punishments that have taken place; at any time when occasion calls for it they may be subjected to a visitation by the civil court.[1]—In vain did the pope by an encyclical seek to rouse the episcopate to violent opposition, in vain did he adjure the emperor in a letter in his own hand not to suffer the church to be put into such disgraceful bondage; the House of Deputies approved the four bills, and the emperor in May, 1874, confirmed at least the first three, while the fourth was being debated in the House of Peers. The bishops now issued a joint declaration that they could obey these laws only in so far as they "were in harmony with the demands of justice as stated in the concordat." But it did not go to the length

---

[1] The Austrian May Laws were in some respects more sweeping than the Prussian (§ 197, 5); but the former were framed with reference to the police, the latter with reference to the law. In Prussia the decision, judgment, and sentence in all cases of contravention and collision were assigned to the court of law; in Austria they were assigned to the court of administration, in the last instance to the minister. The Austrian laws could thus be urged and ignored at pleasure.

of actual conflict. Neither to the pope and episcopate, nor to the government was such a thing convenient at the time. Hence the attitude of reserve on both sides, which kept everything as it had been. And when notwithstanding Bishop Rudigier of Linz, threatened with fines on account of his refusal to notify the newly appointed priests, appealed to the pope, he obtained through the Vienna nuncio permission to yield on this point, " *non dissentit tolerari posse.*" But all the more urgently did the nuncio strive to prevent the passing of the sweeping cloister law. In January, 1876, it was passed in the House of Peers with modifications, to which, however, the emperor refused his assent. Also the revised marriage law of the same date, which removed the hindrances to marriage incorporated even in the book of civil law, and no longer recognised differences of religion, Christians and non-Christians, the remarriage of separated parties of whom at the time of the first marriage only one party belonged to the Catholic church, higher consecration and the vows of orders, did not pass the House of Peers.

7. The Protestant Church in the Transleithan Provinces.—In Hungary since 1833 the Reichstag had by bold action won for the Protestants full equality with the Catholics, but in consequence of the revolution, the military lordship of the Protestant Haynau in 1850 again put in fetters all independent life in both Protestant churches. The Haynau decree was, indeed, again abrogated in 1854, but full return to the earlier autonomy of the church, in spite of all petitions and deputations, could never be regained, all the less as Hungary in all too decided a manner rejected the constitutional proposals submitted by the Government in 1856. The liberal imperial patent of September 1st, 1859, which secured independent administration and development to the Protestant church in the crown possessions of Hungary, got no better reception. In the German-Slavonian districts of North Hungary, as well as in Croatia, Slavonia, and Austrian Servia, it was greeted with jubilation and gratitude, but the Magyar Hungarians declined on many, for the most part frivolous, grounds, mainly because it emanated from the emperor, and did not originate in an autonomous synod. When the government showed its intention of going forward with it, the opposition was carried to the utmost extreme, so that the emperor was obliged temporarily to suspend proceedings in May, 1860. Still the ecclesiastical joined with the political movement continued to increase until in 1867 the imperial chancellor, Von Beust, succeeded in quieting both for a time by the Hungarian Agreement. On June 8th of that year, the emperor, Francis Joseph, on ratifying the agreement, was solemnly crowned King of Hungary. The hated patent had been shortly before revoked by an imperial edict, with the direction to order church matters in a constitutional way. After a

complete reconciliation, at a General Protestant Convention in December, 1867, with the Patent congregations, hitherto denounced as unpatriotic, it was concluded that to the state belonged only a right of protection and oversight of the church, which is autonomous in all its internal affairs, but to all confessions perfect freedom in law, and that there should be not a separate religious legislation for each, but a common one for all confessions. A committee first appointed in 1873 for this purpose, with the motto, "A Free Church in a Free State," constituted, and then adjourned *ad kalendas Græcas.*

§ 199. SWITZERLAND.

The Catholic church of Switzerland, after long continued troubles, obtained again a regular hierarchical organization in 1828. Since that time the Jesuits settled there in crowds, and assumed to themselves in most of the Catholic cantons the whole direction of church and schools. The unfortunate issue of the cantonal war of 1847 led indeed to their banishment by law, but, favoured by the bishops, they knew how still to re-enter by back doors and secretly to regain their earlier influence. The city of Calvin was the centre of their plots, not only for Switzerland, but also for all Cisalpine Europe, until at last the overstrained bow broke, and the Swiss governments became the most decided and uncompromising opponents of the ultramontane claims. In 1873 the papal nuncio, in consequence of a papal encyclical insulting the government, was banished.—In Protestant Switzerland, besides the destructive influence of the Illumination, antagonistic to the church, and radical liberalism, there appeared a soil receptive of pietism, separatism, and fanaticism, whose first cultivation has been ascribed to Madame Krüdener (§ 176, 2). In the Protestant church of German Switzerland the religious and theological developments stood regularly in lively connexion with similar movements in Germany, while those in the French cantons received their impulse and support from France and England. From France, to which they were allied by a common language, they learned the unbelief of the encyclopædists (§ 165, 14), while travelling Englishmen and those residing in the country for a longer period introduced the fervour and superstition of Methodism and other sects.

1. **The Catholic Church in Switzerland till 1870.**—The ecclesiastical superintendence of Catholic Switzerland was previously subject to the neighbouring foreign bishoprics. But for immediate preservation of its interests the curia had appointed a nunciature at Lucerne in 1588. When now, in 1814, the liberal Wessenberg (§ 187, 8), already long suspected of heresy, was called as coadjutor to Constance, the nuncio manœuvred with the Catholic confederates till these petitioned the pope for the establishment of an independent and national bishopric. But when each of the cantons interested claimed to be made the episcopal residence negotiations were at last suspended, and in 1828 six small bishoprics were erected under immediate control of Rome. At the end of 1833 the diocesan representatives of Basel and St. Gall assembled in Baden to consult about the restoration of a national Swiss Metropolitan Union and a common state church constitution for securing church and state against the encroachments of the Romish hierarchy. But Gregory XIV. condemned the articles of conference here agreed upon, which would have given to Switzerland only what other states had long possessed, as false, audacious, and erroneous, destructive of the church, heretical, and schismatic, and among the Catholic people a revolt was stirred up by ultramontane fanaticism, under the influence of which the whole action was soon frustrated. On the occasion of a revision of the constitution of the canton of Aargau, a revolt, led by the cloisters, broke out in 1841. But the rebels were defeated, and the grand council resolved upon the closing of all cloisters, eight in number. Complaint made against this at the diet was regarded as satisfied by the Aargau Agreement of 1843 restoring three nunneries. An opposition was organized against the revision of the constitution of Canton Lucerne in 1841. The liberal government was overthrown, and the new constitution, in which the state insisted on its *placet* in ecclesiastical matters and the granting of cantonal civil rights to those only who professed attachment to the Roman Catholic church, was submitted to the pope for approval. At last, in 1844, the academy of Lucerne was given over to the Jesuits, for which Joseph Leu, the popular agitator, as member of the grand council, had wrought unweariedly since 1839. In Canton Vaud the parties of old or clerical and young Switzerland contended with one another for the mastery. The latter suffered an utter defeat in 1844, and the constitution which was then carried allowed the right of

public worship only to the Catholic church. In consequence of this victory of the clerical party Catholic Switzerland with Lucerne at its head became a main centre of ultramontanism and Jesuitism. At the diet of 1844, indeed, Aargau, supported by numerous petitions from the people, moved for the banishment of all Jesuits from all Switzerland, but the majority did not consent. The Jesuit opponents expelled from Lucerne now organized twice over a free volunteer corps to overthrow the ultramontane government and force the expulsion of the Jesuits, but on both occasions, in 1844 and 1845, it suffered a sore defeat. In face of the threateningly growing increase of the excitement, which made them fear a decisive intervention of the diet, the Catholic cantons formed in 1845 a separate league (*Sonderbund*) for the preservation of their faith and their sovereign rights. This proceeding, irreconcilable with the Act of Federation, led to a civil war. The members of the *Sonderbund* were defeated, the ultramontane governments had to resign, and the Jesuits departed in 1847. The new Federal constitution which Switzerland adopted in 1848, secured unconditional liberty of conscience and equality of all confessions, and the expulsion of the Jesuits in terms of the law. But since that time ultramontanism has gained the supremacy in Catholic Switzerland, and in spite of the existing law against the Jesuits all the threads of the ultramontane clerical movements in Switzerland were in the Jesuits' hands. These were never more successful than in Canton Geneva, where the radical democratic agitator Fazy leagued himself closely with ultramontanism to compass the destruction of the old Calvinistic aristocracy, and by bringing in large numbers the lower class Catholics from the neighbouring France and Savoy he obtained a considerable Catholic majority in the canton, and in the capital itself made Catholics and Protestants nearly equal.

2. The Geneva Conflict, 1870-1883.—The Catholic church of Canton Geneva, on the founding of the six Swiss bishoprics by a papal bull, had been incorporated "for all time to come," after the style of the concordat, with the bishopric of Freiburg-Lausanne. But the government made no objection when the newly elected priest of Geneva, Mermillod, a Jesuit of the purest water, assumed the title and rank of an episcopal vicar-general for the whole canton. But when in 1864 the pope nominated him bishop of Hebron *in partibus* and auxiliary bishop of Geneva, it made a protest. Nevertheless, when, in the following year, Bishop Marilley of Freiburg by papal orders transferred to him absolute power for the canton with personal responsibility, and in 1870 formally renounced all episcopal rights over it, so that the pope now appointed the auxiliary bishop independent bishop of Geneva, it was evident a step had been taken that could not be recalled. The government renewed its protest and made it more vehement, in conse-

quence of which, in January, 1873, by a papal brief which was first officially communicated to the government after it had already been proclaimed from all Catholic pulpits, Mermillod was appointed apostolic vicar-general with unlimited authority for Canton Geneva, and the district was thus practically made a Catholic mission field. A demand made of him by the state to resign this office and title and divest himself of every episcopal function, was answered by the declaration that he would obey God rather than man. The *Bund* then expelled him from Federal territory until he would yield to that demand. From Ferney, where he settled, he unceasingly stirred up the fire of opposition among the Genevan clergy and people, but the government decidedly rejected all protests, and by a popular vote obtained sanction for a Catholic church law which restricted the rights of the diocesan bishop who might reside in Switzerland, but not in Canton Geneva, and without consent of the government could not appoint there any episcopal vicar, and transferred the election of priests and priests' vicars to the congregations. The next elections returned Old Catholics, since the Roman Catholic population did not acknowledge the law condemned by the pope and took no part in the voting. By decision of the grand council of 1875 the abolition of all religious corporations was next enacted, and all religious ceremonies and processions in public streets and squares forbidden. Leo XIII. made an attempt to still the conflict, for in 1879 he gave Bishop Marilley the asked for discharge, and confirmed his elected successor, Cosandry as bishop of Freiburg, Lausanne, and Geneva, without however removing Mermillod from his office of vicar apostolic of Geneva. But this actually took place after the death of Cosandry in 1882 by the appointment of Mermillod as his successor in 1883. As he now ceased to style himself a vicar apostolic, the Federal council removed the decree of banishment as the occasion of it had ceased, but left each canton free as to whether or not it should accept him as bishop. Freiburg, Neuenburg, and Vaud accepted him, and Mermillod had a brilliant entry into Freiburg, which he made his episcopal residence. But Geneva refused to recognise him, because it had already officially attached itself to the Old Catholic Bishop Herzog of Berne, and Mermillod went so far in his ostentatious love of peace as to declare that he would not in future enter Genevan territory.

8. **Conflict in the Diocese of Basel-Soleure, 1870-1880.**—Bishop Lachat of Soleure, whose diocese comprised the Cantons Bern, Soleure, Aargau, Basel, Thurgau, Lucerne, and Zug, had been previously in conflict with the diocesan conference, *i.e.* the delegates of the seven cantons entrusted with the oversight of the ecclesiastical administration, on account of introducing the prohibited handbook on morals of the Jesuit Gury (§ 191, 9), which ended in the closing of the

seminary aided by the government, and the erection of a new semi-nary at his own cost. Although the diocesan conference next forbad the proclamation of the new Vatican dogma, the bishop threatened excommunicated Egli in Lucerne in 1871, and Geschwind in Starr-kirch in 1872, who refused. The conference ordered the withdrawal of this unlawful act, and on the bishop's refusal, deposed him in January, 1873. The dissenting cantons, Lucerne and Zug, indeed declared that after as well as before they would only recognise Lachat as lawful bishop, the chapter refused to make the required election of administrator of the diocese, the clergy in Soleure and in Bernese Jura without exception took the side of the bishop, as also by means of a popular vote the great majority of Catholics in Thurgau. But amid all this the conference did not yield in the least. Lachat was compelled by the police to quit his episcopal residence, and with-drew to a village in Canton Lucerne. The council of the Bernese government resolved to recall the refractory clergy of the Jura, took their names off the civil register and forbad them to exercise any clerical functions. The outbreaks incited by rebel clergy in the Jura were put down by the military, sixty-nine clergymen were exiled, and, so far as the means allowed, replaced by liberal successors introduced by the Old Catholic priest Herzog (§ 190, 3) in Olten. In November 1875, permission to return home was granted to the exiles in conse-quence of the revised Federal constitution of 1874, according to which the banishment of Swiss burghers was no longer allowed. The Bernese government felt all the more disposed to carry out this enactment of the National Council, as it believed that it had obtained the legal means for checking further rebellion and obstinacy among those who should return. On January, 1874, by popular vote a law was sanctioned reorganizing the whole ecclesiastical affairs of the Canton Bern. By it all clergy, Catholic as well as Protestant, are ranked as civil officers, the choice of whom rests with the congregations, the tenure of office lasting for six years. All purely ecclesiastical affairs for the canton rest in the last instance with a synod of the particular denomination. for the several congregations with a church committee, both composed of freely elected lay and clerical members. But if a dispute in a particular congregation should arise about a synodal decree, the con-gregational assembly decides on its validity or non-validity for the particular congregation. All decrees of higher church courts and pastorals must have state approval, which must never be refused on dogmatic grounds. If a congregation splits over any question, the majority claims the church property and pastor's emoluments, etc. And this law was next extended in October 31st, 1875, in the matter of penal law by the so-called Police Worship Law. It imposes heavy fines up to 1000 francs or a year's imprisonment for any clerical agitation against the law, institutions or enactments of the civil courts, as well as for every outbreak of hostilities against members of other religious bodies, refuses to allow any interference of foreign spiritual superiors without leave granted by government in each particular case, forbids all processions and religious ceremonies outside of the fixed church locality, etc. In the same year the first Catholic Cantonal Synod declared its attachment to the Christian or Old Catholic church of Switzerland. But it was otherwise after the newly elected Grand Council of the canton of its own accord, on September 12th, 1878, granted the returned Jura clergy complete amnesty for all the past, and on the assumption of future submission to existing laws of state, recognised them again eligible for election to spiritual offices which had previously been denied them. Not only did the Roman Catholic people regularly take part in elections of priests, church councils, and synods, undoubtedly with the approval of the new pope Leo XIII., who had in February addressed a conciliatory letter to the members of the Federal Council, but also the extremest of the Jura now submitted without scruple to the new election required by the law, and won therein for the most part the majority of votes. In the Catholic Cantonal Synod convened in Bern, in January, 1880, were found seventy-five Roman Catholics and only twenty-five Old Catholic deputies. The latter were naturally defeated in all controversies. The synod declared that the connexion with the Christian Catholic national bishopric was annulled, that auricular confession was obligatory, that marriages of priests were forbidden, etc. Since now the law assigns the state pay of the priest as well as all the church property in the case of a split to the majority for the time being, the inevitable consequence was that Old Catholics of the Jura district were deprived of all share in these privileges, and had to make provision for their own support. Also in Canton Soleure, the law that all pastors must be re-elected after the expiry of six years, came in force in 1872, and then the thirty-two Roman Catholic clergymen concerned were with only two exceptions re-elected, while, on the other hand, the Old Catholic priest Geschwind of Starrkirch was rejected.—But all efforts to restore the bishopric of Basel-Soleure came to grief over the person of Bishop Lachat, whom the curia would not give up and the Federal Council would not again allow, until at last a way out of the difficulty was found. The canton Tessin, which previously in church matters belonged to the Italian dioceses of Milan and Como, was, in 1859, by decree of the Federal Council, detached from these. But Tessin insisted on the founding of a bishopric of its own, while the Federal Council wished to join it to the bishopric of Chur. Thus the matter remained undecided, till in September, 1884, the papal curia came to an understanding with the Federal Council

that Lachat should be appointed vicar-apostolic for the newly founded
bishopric of Tessin, and that to the vacated bishopric of Basel-Soleure
the "learned as well as mild" Provost Fiala of Soleure should be
called. In this way all the cantons referred to, with the exception of
Bern, were won.[1]

4. The Protestant Church in German Switzerland.—Among all the
German cantons, Basel (§ 172, 5), which unweariedly prosecuted the
work of home and foreign missions, fell most completely under
the influence of rationalism and then of the liberal Protestant
theology. While pietism obtained powerful support and encouragement in its missionary institutions and movements, and there, though
developing itself on Reformed soil, assumed, in consequence of its
manifold connection with Germany, a colour almost more Lutheran
than Reformed, the university by eminent theological teachers of
scientific ability represented the Mediation school in theology of a
predominently Reformed type. In the Canton Zürich, on the other
hand, the advanced theology, theoretical and practical, obtained an
increasing and finally an almost exclusive mastery in the university
and church. But yet, when in 1839 the Grand Council called Dr.
David Strauss to a theological professorship, the Zürich people rose
to a man against the proposal, the appointment was not enforced, the
Grand Council was overthrown, and Strauss pensioned. The victory
and ascendency of this reaction, however, was not of long continuance. Theological and ecclesiastical radicalism again won the upper
hand and maintained it unchecked. In the other German cantons
the most diverse theological schools were represented alongside of one
another, yet with steadily increasing advantage to liberal and radical
tendencies. The theological faculty at Bern favoured mainly a
liberal mediation theology, and an attempt of the orthodox party in
1847, to set aside the appointment of Professor E. Zeller by means of
a popular tumult, miscarried. From 1860 ecclesiastical liberalism
prevailed in German Protestant Switzerland, frequently going the
length of the extremest radicalism and showing its influence even in
the cantonal and synodal legislation. The starting of the "Zeitstim-
men für d. ref. Schweiz," in 1859, by Henry Lang, who had fled in
1848 from Württemberg to Switzerland, and died in 1876 as pastor
in Zürich, marked an epoch in the history of the radical liberal movement in Swiss theology. In Fred. Langhans, since 1876 professor
at Bern, he had a zealous comrade in the fight. During 1864–1866,
Langhans published a series of violent controversial tracts against
the pietistic orthodox party in Switzerland, which zealously prosecuted foreign missions, and in 1866 he founded the *Swiss Reform*

[1] Geffcken, "Church and State," vol. ii., pp. 469–488.

Union, while Alb. Bitzius, son of the writer known as Jer. Gotthelf (§ 174, 8) started as its organ the " *Reformblätter aus d. bernischen Kirche,*" which was subsequently amalgamated with the *Zeitstimmem.* —After more or less violent conflicts with pietistic orthodoxy, still always pretty strongly represented, especially in the aristocracy, the emancipation of the schools from the church and the introduction of obligatory civil marriage were accomplished in most cantons, even before the revised Federal constitution of 1874 and the marriage law of 1875 gave to these principles legal sanction throughout the whole of Switzerland. In almost all Protestant cantons the re-election or new election to all spiritual offices every six years was ordained by law, in many the freeing of the clergy from any creed subscription with the setting aside of confessional writings as well as of the orthodox liturgy, hymnbooks and catechisms was also carried, and the withdrawing of the Apostles' Creed from public worship and from the baptismal formula was enjoined. The Basel synod in 1883, by thirty-six to twenty-seven votes, carried the motion to make baptism no longer a condition of confirmation ; and although the Zürich synod in 1882 still held baptism obligatory for membership in the national church, the Cantonal Council in 1883, on consulting the law of the church, overturned this decision by 140 against 19 votes.

5. The Protestant Church in French Switzerland.—The French philosophy of the eighteenth century had given to the Reformed church of Geneva a prevailingly rationalistic tendency. Notwithstanding, or just because of this, Madame Krüdener, in 1814, with her conventicle pietism, found an entrance there, and won in the young theologian Empaytaz a zealous supporter and an apostle of conversion preaching. In the next year a wealthy Englishman, Haldane, appeared there as the apostle of methodistic piety, and inspired the young pastor Malan with enthusiasm for the revival mission. Empaytaz and Malan now by speech and writing charged the national church with defection from the Christian faith, and won many zealous believers as adherents, especially among students of theology. The *Vénérable Compagnie* of the Geneva clergy, hitherto resting on its lees in rationalistic quiet, now in 1817 thought it might still the rising storm by demanding of theological candidates at ordination the vow not to preach on the two natures in Christ, original sin, predestination, etc., but thereby they only poured oil on the fire. The adherents of the daily increasing evangelical movement withdrew from the national church, founded free independent communities and *Réunions* under the banner of the restoration of Calvinistic orthodoxy, and were by their enemies nicknamed *Momiers,* i.e. mummery traders or hypocrites. The government imprisoned and banished their leaders, while the mob, unchecked, heaped upon them all manner of abuse. The persecution came to an end in 1830. Thereafter settling down in quiet moderation, it founded in 1831 the *Société évangélique*, which, in 1832, established an *Ecole de Théologie*, and became the centre of the Free church evangelical movement. From that time the *Eglise libre* of Geneva has existed unmolested alongside of the *Eglise Nationale*, and the opposition at first so violent has been moderated on both sides by the growth of conciliatory and mediating tendencies. Since 1850, two divergent parties have arisen within the bosom of the free church itself, which without any serious conflict continued alongside of one another, until in May, 1883, the majority of the presbytery resolved to make a peaceful separation, the stricter forming the congregation of the *Pelisserie*, and the more liberal that of the *Oratoire*. At the same time a committee was appointed to draw up a confession upon which both could unite in lasting fellowship. But when this failed, a formal and complete separation was agreed upon at the new year.—From Geneva the Methodist revival spread to Vaud. The religious movement got a footing, especially in Lausanne. The Grand Council, however, did not allow the contemplated formation of an independent congregation, and in 1824 forbad all "sectarian" assemblies, while the mob raged even more wildly than at Geneva against the "*Momiers.*" The excitement increased when, in 1839, by decision of the Grand Council, the Helvetic Confession was abrogated. When in 1845 a revolutionary radical government came into office at Lausanne, the refusal of many clergymen to read from the pulpit a political proclamation, caused a thorough division in the church, for the preachers referred to were in a body driven out of the national church. A Free church of Vaud now developed itself alongside of the national church, sorely oppressed and persecuted by the radical government, and spread into other Swiss cantons. It owed its freedom from sectarian narrowness mainly to the influence of the talented and thoroughly independent Alex. Vinet, who devoted his whole energies and brilliant eloquence to the interests of religious freedom and liberty of conscience and to the struggle for the separation of church and state. Vinet was from 1817 teacher of the French language and literature in Basel, then from 1837 to 1845 professor of practical theology at Lausanne, but on the reconstruction of the university he was not re-elected. He died in 1847.[1]—In the canton Neuchatel the State Council in 1873 introduced a law, which granted unconditional liberty of conscience, freedom in teaching and worship without any sort of restriction on clergy, teachers and congregations

---

[1] R. J. Sandeman, "Alexander Vinet" in "Evangelical Succession Lectures," Third Series, Edinburgh, 1884. Dorner, "History of Protestant Theology," ii., 470, 478.

The Grand Council by forty-seven votes to forty-six gave it its sanction, notwithstanding the almost unanimous protest of the evangelical synod, and refused to appeal to a popular vote. When an appeal to the Federal Council proved fruitless, somewhere about one half of the pastors, including the theological professors and all the students, left the state church, and formed an *Eglise libre;* while the other half regarded it as their duty to remain in the national church so long as they were not hindered from preaching God's word in purity and simplicity. Both parties had a common meeting point in the *Union évangélique,* and a law originally passed in favour of the Old Catholics, which secured to all seceders a right to the joint use of their respective churches, proved also of advantage to the Free church.—The canton Geneva issued, in 1874, a Protestant law of worship, which with dogma and liturgy also threw overboard ordination, and maintained that the clergy are answerable only to their conscience and their electors. Yet at the new election of the consistory in 1879, at the close of the legal term of four years, the evangelical and moderate party again obtained the supremacy, and a law introduced by the radical party in the Grand Council, demanding the withdrawal of the budget of worship and the separation of church and state, was, on July 4th, 1880, thrown out by universal popular vote, by a majority of 9,000 to 4,000.

§ 200. HOLLAND AND BELGIUM.

Among the most serious mistakes in the new partition of states at the Vienna Congress was the combining in one kingdom of the United Netherlands the provinces of Holland and Belgium, diverse in race, language, character, and religion. The contagion of French Revolution of July, 1830, however, caused an outbreak in Brussels, which ended in the separation of Catholic Belgium from the predominantly Protestant Holland. Belgium has since then been the scene of unceasing and changeful conflicts between the liberal and ultramontane parties, whose previous combination was now completely shattered. And while, on the other hand, in the Reformed state church of Holland, theological studies, leaning upon German science, have taken a liberal and even radical destructive course, the not inconsiderable Roman

Catholic population has fallen, under Jesuit leading, **more** and more into bigoted obscurantism.

1. The United Netherlands.—The constitution of the new kingdom created in 1814 guaranteed unlimited freedom to all forms of worship and complete equality of all citizens without distinction of religious confession. Against this the Belgian episcopate protested with bishop Maurice von Broglie, of Ghent, at their head, who refused, in 1817, the prayers of the church for the heretical crown princess and the *Te Deum* for the newborn heir to the throne. As he went so far as to excite the Catholic people on all occasions against the Protestant government, the angry king, William I., summoned him to answer for his conduct before the court of justice. But he eluded inquiry by flight to France, and as guilty of high treason was sentenced to death, which did not prevent him from his exile unweariedly fanning the flames of rebellion. The number of cloisters grew from day to day and also the multitude of clerical schools and seminaries, in which the Catholic youth was trained up in the principles of the most violent fanaticism. The government in 1825 closed the seminaries, expelled Jesuit teachers, forbad attendance at Jesuit schools abroad, and founded a college at Louvain, in which all studying for the church were obliged to pass through a philosophical curriculum. The common struggle for maintaining the liberty of instruction promised by the constitution made political radicalism and ultramontanism confederates, and the government, intimidated by this combination, agreed, in a concordat with the pope in 1827, to modify the obligatory into a facultative attendance at Louvain College. The inevitable consequence of this was the speedy and complete decay of the college. But the confederacy of the radicals and ultramontanes continued, directing itself against other misdeeds of the government, and was not broken up until in 1830 it attained its object by the disjunction of Belgium and Holland.

2. The Kingdom of Holland.—In the prevailingly Reformed national church rationalism and latitudinarian supernaturalism had to such an extent blotted out the ecclesiastical distinctions between Reformed, Remonstrants, Mennonites, and Lutherans, that the clergy of one party would unhesitatingly preach in the churches of the others. Then rose the poet Bilderdijk, driven from political into religious patriotism, to denounce with glowing fury the general declension from the orthodoxy of Dort. Two Jewish converts of his, the poet and apologist Isaac da Costa, and the physician Cappadose, gave him powerful support. A zealous young clergyman, Henry de Cock, was theological mouthpiece of the party. Because he offended church

order, especially by ministering in other congregations, he was suspended and finally deposed in 1834. The greater part of his congregation and four other pastors with him formally declared their secession from the unfaithful church, as a return to the orthodox Reformed church. As separatists and disturbers of public worship, they were fined and imprisoned, and were at last satisfied with the recognition granted them of royal grace in 1839, as a separate or Christian Reformed Church. It consists now of 364 congregations, embracing about 140,000 souls, with a flourishing seminary at Kampen. The Reformed State Church, with three-fourths of all the Protestant population, persevered in and developed its liberalistic tendencies. The State Synod of 1883 expressly declared that the Netherland Reformed Church demands from its teachers not agreement with all the statements of the confessional writings, but only with their spirit, gist, and essence; and the synod of 1877, by the vote of a majority, stated that no sort of formulated confession should be required even of candidates for confirmation. Yet even amid such proceedings from various sides, a churchly and evangelical reaction of considerable importance set in. Three great parties within the state church carried on a life and death struggle with one another: (1) The Strict Calvinists, whose leader is Dr. Kuyper, formerly pastor in Amsterdam; (2) The so-called Middle Party, which falls into two divisions: the, just about expiring, Ethical Irenical Party, with the Utrecht professor Van Oosterzee (died 1882), and the Evangelical Party with the Gröningen professor Hofstede de Groot, since 1872 Emeritus, as leaders, of which the former, subordinating the confession, regards the Christian life as the main thing in Christianity, and the latter declares itself prepared to take the gospel alone for its creed and confession; and (3) The so-called Modern Party, which, with Professors Scholten and Kuenen as leaders, has its centre at Leyden, and in theology carries out with reckless energy the destructive critical principles of the school of Baur and Wellhausen (§ 182, 7, 18). The "*Moderns*" are also the founders and leaders of the "*Protestant Federation*" after the German model (§ 180), with its annual assemblies since 1873, in opposition to which a "*Confessional Union*" holds its annual meetings at Utrecht, and operates by means of evangelists and lay preachers in places where there are only "Modern" pastors. The higher and cultured classes in the congregations mostly favour the Gröningen and some also the Leyden school, but the great majority of the middle and lower classes are adherents of Kuyper, and have frequently secured majorities in the Congregational Church Council. —The Dutch school law of 1856 banished every sort of confessional religious education from public schools supported by the state, and so called forth the erection of numerous denominational schools independent of the state, and the founding of a "*Union for Christian Popular Education*," which has spread through the whole country. The university law sanctioned, after violent debates in the chamber, in 1876, establishes in place of the old theological faculties, professorships for the science of religion generally, with the exception of dogmatics and practical theology, and left it with the Reformed State Synod to care for these two subjects, either in a theological seminary or by founding for itself the two theological professorships in the universities and supporting them from the sums voted for the state church. The synod decided on the latter course, and appointed to the new chairs men of moderate liberal views. The adherents of the strict Calvinistic party, however, founded a Free Reformed University at Amsterdam, which was opened in autumn, 1880. Its first rector was Kuyper.—The Lutheran Church of fifty congregations and sixty-two pastors, with about 60,000 souls, has also had since 1816 a theological seminary. In it neological tendencies prevail.

3. The founding of the Free University at Amsterdam, referred to above, led to a series of violent conflicts which threatened to break up the whole Reformed church of the Netherlands by a wild schism. The Reformed State Synod, consisting mainly of Gröningen theologians, but also numbering many members belonging to the Modern or Leyden school, and constituting the supreme ecclesiastical court, had, in spite of its eleventh rule, which makes "the maintenance of the doctrine" a main task of all church government, for a long time admitted the principle of unfettered freedom of teaching, and ordained that even evidence of orthodoxy on the part of candidates for confirmation would no longer be regarded as a condition of their acceptance, their examination referring only to their knowledge, the examining clergy and not the assisting elders being judges in this matter. When now the Free University had been founded in direct opposition to the synod, the latter resolved to reject all its pupils at the examination of candidates, and when, in the summer of 1885, its first student presented himself, actually carried out this resolution. Thereupon the university transferred the examination to a committee, elected by itself, consisting of orthodox Reformed pastors and elders, and a small village congregation agreed to elect the candidate for its poorly endowed, and so for seventeen years vacant, pastorate. But the synod refused him ordination. Therefore the director of a strict Calvinistic Gymnasium, formerly a pastor, performed the ceremony, and the congregation announced its secession from the synodal union. At the same time in Amsterdam a second conflict arose over the question of candidates for confirmation. Three pastors of the "modern" school demanded the elders subject to them, among them Dr. Kuyper, to take part as required in the examining of their

candidates; but these refused to give their assistance, because the previous training had not been according to Scripture and the confession, and also the majority of the church council approved of this refusal, as the parents had complained, and declared that the certificate of morality demanded by other pastors could be made out only if candidates for confirmation had previously formally and solemnly confessed their genuine and hearty faith in Jesus Christ as the only and all-sufficient Saviour, which these, however, in accordance with the Dutch practice of the eighteenth century, declined to do. The controversy was carried by appeal through all the church courts, and finally the State Synod ordered the church council to make delivery of the certificates within six weeks on pain of suspension. But this was brought about before the expiry of that period by the outbreak of a far more serious conflict over matters of administration. In Amsterdam the administration of church property lay with a special commission, responsible to the church council, consisting of members, one half from the church council and the other half from the congregations. If in the beginning of January, 1886, the threatened suspension and deposition of the church council should be carried out, in accordance with proper order until the appointment of a new council all the rights of the same, therefore also that of supervising that commission, would fall to the "classical board" (§ 143, 1) as the next highest court. In order to avoid this, the fateful resolution was passed on December 14th, 1885, to alter § 41 of the regulations, so that, if the church council in the discharge of its duty to govern the community in accordance with God's word and the legalized church confession, it would be so hindered therein that it might feel in conscience obliged to obey God rather than man and accept suspension and deposition, and a church council should be appointed, the administrative commission would be obliged to remain subject, not to this, but to the original commission. The "classical board" annulled this resolution, suspended on January 4th, 1886, for continued obstinacy the previous church council, and constituted itself, pending decision on the part of discipline, interim administrator of all its rights and duties. The suspended majority, however, called a meeting for the same day, and when it found the doors of its meeting place closed, sent for a locksmith to break them open. They were prevented by the police, who then, by putting on a safety lock, strengthening the boards of the door by mailed plates, and setting a watch, greatly reduced the chances of an entrance. But the opposition sent to the watchers a letter by a policeman demanding that the representatives of the church council should be allowed to pass; upon which these, regarding it as an order of the police, withdrew. They then had the mailed plates sawn through, took possession of the hall and the archives and treasure box lying there, and refused admissior to the classical board. While then the question of law and possession was referred to the courts of law, and there the final decision would not be given before the lapse of a year, the disciplinary procedure took its course through all the ecclesiastical courts and ended in the deposition of all resisting elders and pastors. The latter preached now to great crowds in hired halls. From the capital the excitement increased by means of violent publications on both sides, spread over the whole land and produced discord in many other communities. Wild and uproarious tumults first broke out in Leidendorf, a suburb of Leyden. The pastor and the majority of the church council refused to enter on their congregational list two girls who had been confirmed by liberal churchmen elsewhere, and with by far the greater part of the congregation seceded from the synodal union. The classical board now, in July, 1886, declared the pastorate vacant, and ordered that a regular interim service should be conducted on Sundays by the pastors of the circuit. The uproar among the people, however, was thereby only greatly increased, so that the civil authorities were obliged to protect the deputed preachers, by a large military escort, from rude maltreatment, and to secure quiet during public worship by a company of police in church. And similar conflicts soon broke out on like occasions and with similar consequences in many other places throughout all parts of the land. In December, 1886, the Amsterdam church council also declared its secession from the state church, and a numerously attended " Reformed Church Congress " at Amsterdam, in January, 1887, summoned by Kuyper in the interests of the crowd of seceders, resolved to accept the decision of the law in regard to church property.[1]

4. Even after the separation of Belgium there was still left a considerable number of Catholics, about three-eighths of the population, most numerous in Brabant, Limburg, and Luxemburg, and these were, as of old, inclined to the most bigoted ultramontanism. This tendency was greatly enhanced when the new constitutional law of 1848 announced the principle of absolute liberty of belief, in consequence of which the Jesuits crowded in vast numbers, and the pope in 1853 organized a new Catholic hierarchy in the land, with four bishops and an archbishop at Utrecht, under the control of the propaganda. The Protestant population went into great excitement over this. The liberal ministry of Thorbecke was obliged to resign, but the chambers at length sanctioned the papal ordinance, only securing

---

[1] Cairns, " The Present Struggle in the National Church of Holland," in *Presbyterian Review* for January, 1888, pp. 87-108. Wicksteed, " The Ecclesiastical Institutions of Holland." London.

the Protestant population against its misapplication and abuse.—On the withdrawal of the French in 1814 there were only eight cloisters remaining; but in 1861 there were thirty-nine for monks and 137 for nuns, and since then the number has considerably increased.— The Dutch Old Catholics (§ 165, 8), on account of their protest against the dogma of the Immaculate Conception (§ 185, 2), enjoined upon the Catholic church by the pope, were anew excommunicated, and joined the German Old Catholics in rejecting the decrees of the Vatican Council (§ 190, 1).

5. **The Kingdom of Belgium.**—Catholic Belgium obtained after its separation from Holland a constitution by which unlimited freedom of religious worship and education, and the right of confessing opinion and of associating, were guaranteed, and to the state was allowed no interference with the affairs of the church beyond the duty of paying the clergy. Also in Leopold I., 1830–1865, of the house of Saxe-Coburg, it had a king who though himself a Protestant was faithful to the constitution, and, according to agreement, had his children trained up in the Roman Catholic church. The confederacy of radicalism and ultramontanism, however, was broken by the irreconciliable enmity and violent conflict in daily life and in the chambers among clerical and liberal ministers. The ultramontanes founded at Louvain in 1834 a strictly Catholic university, which was under the oversight of the bishops and the patronage of the Virgin; while the liberals promoted the erection of an opposition university for free science at Brussels. That the Jesuits used to the utmost for their own ends the liberty granted them by the constitution by means of missions and the confessional, schools, cloisters, and brotherhoods of every kind, is what might have been expected. But liberalism also knew how to conduct a propaganda and to bring the clergy into discredit with the educated classes by unveiling their intrigues, legacy-hunting, etc., while these exercised a great influence chiefly upon bigoted females. The number of cloisters, which on the separation from Holland amounted only to 280, had risen in 1880 in that small territory to 1,559, with 24,672 inmates, of whom 20,645 were nuns.

6. After the ultramontane party had enjoyed eight years of almost unchallenged supremacy, the Malou ministry favourable to it was overthrown in June, 1878, and a liberal government, under the presidency of Frère-Orban, took its place. Then began the Kulturkampf in Belgium. The charge of public education was taken from the ministry of the interior, and a special minister appointed in the person of Van Humbeeck. He began by changing all girls' schools under the management of sisters of spiritual orders into communal schools, and in January, 1879, brought in a bill for reorganizing

elementary education, which completely secularized the schools; deprived the clergy of all official influence over them, and relegated religious instruction to the care of the family and the church, the latter, however, having the necessary accommodation allowed in the school buildings. The chambers approved the bill, and the king confirmed it, in spite of all protests and agitation by the clergy. The clerical journals put a black border on their issue which published it; the provincial councils under clerical influence nullified as far as possible all money bequests for the public schools, and the bishops assembled in August at Mechlin resolved to found free schools in all communities, and to refuse absolution to all parents who entrusted their children to state schools and all teachers in them, in order thus to cause a complete decay of the public schools, which indeed happened to this extent that within a few months 1,167 communal schools had not a single Catholic scholar. On complaint being made by the government to Leo XIII., he expressed through the Brussels nuncio his regret and disapproval of the proceedings of the bishops, but, on the other hand, he not only privately praised them on account of their former zeal in opposing the school law, but also incited them to continued opposition. When this double dealing of the curia was discovered, the government in June, 1880, broke off all diplomatic relations with the Vatican by recalling their ambassador and giving the nuncio his passports. The ministerial president publicly in the chamber of deputies characterized the action of the Holy See as "*fourberie.*" Whereupon the pope at the next consistory called princes and peoples as witnesses of this insult. In May, 1882, the results of the inquiry into clerical incitements against the public was read in the chamber, where such startling revelations were made as these Priests taught the children that they should no longer pray for the king when he had committed the mortal sin of confirming the school law; the ministers are worse than murderers and true Herods; a priest even taught children to pray that God might cause their "liberal" parents to die, etc. Amid such conflicts the Catholic party in parliament split into the parties of the *Politici,* who were willing to submit to the constitution, and that of the *Intransigenti,* who, under the direction of the bishops and the university of Louvain, held high above everything the standard of the syllabus. The latter fought with such passionateness, that the pope felt obliged in 1881 to enjoin upon the episcopate " that prudent attitude" which the church in such cases always maintains in " enduring many evils" which for the time cannot be overcome. But undeterred, the government continued to restrict the claims of the clergy, so far as these were not expressly guaranteed by the constitution.—In June, 1884, as the result of the elections for the chamber of deputies, the clerical party again were in power. Malou was once more at the head of a ministry in favour of the clericals, caused the king to dissolve the senate, and in the new elections won there also a majority for his party. No sooner were they in power than the clerical ministry, in conjunction with the majority in the chambers, proceeded with inconsiderate haste, amid the most violent, almost daily repeated explosions from the now intensely embittered liberal and radical section of the population, which only seemed to increase their zeal, to employ their absolute power to the utmost in the interest of clericalism. The restoration of diplomatic relations with the papal curia in the spirit of absolute acquiescence in its schemes was the grand aim of the reaction, as well as a new school law by which the schools were completely given over again to the clergy and the orders. But when at the next communal elections a liberal majority was returned, and protests of the new communal councils poured in against the school law on behalf of the vast number of state certificated teachers reduced by it to hunger and destitution, the Malou ministry found itself obliged to resign in October, 1884. Its place was taken by the moderate ultramontane Beernaert ministry, which sought indeed to quiet the excitement by mild measures, but held firmly in all essential points to the principles of its predecessor.

7. An exciting episode in the Belgium *Kulturkampf* is presented by the appearance of Bishop Dumont of Tournay, who, previously an enthusiastic admirer of Pius IX. and a vigorous defender of the infallibility dogma, also a zealous patron of stigmatization miracles at Bois d'Haine (§ 188, 4), now suddenly turned round on the school question and refused to obey the papal injunction. For this he was first suspended, and then in 1880 formally deposed by the pope. He afterwards wrote letters in the most advanced liberal journals with violent denunciations of the pope, whom he would not recognise as pope, but only as Bishop of Rome, and so styled him not Leo, but only Pecci. In these letters Dumont makes the interesting communication that the virgin Louise Lateau, favoured of God, has threatened with excommunication the "intruder" Durousseaux, nominated by the pope as his successor, because she continues to reverence Dumont as the only legitimate Bishop of Tournay. The Vatican pronounced him insane, and the chapter appealed to the civil authorities to have him declared incapable in the sight of the law, which, however, they refused, because they could not regard Dumont's insanity as proved. On the other hand, Dumont refused to renounce his episcopal office, and accused Durousseaux of having by night, with the help of a locksmith, obtained entrance to his episcopal palace, and having taken forcible possession of a casket lying there, which, besides the diocesan property to the value of five millions, contained also about one and a

nalf millions of his own private means. Pending the issue of the conflict, as to which of the two should be regarded as the true bishop, the palace was now officially sealed up. The attempt to arrest the robbed casket had to be abandoned, because meanwhile the canon Bernard, as keeper of the treasures of the diocese, had fled with its contents to America. He was, however, on legal warrant imprisoned in Havanna and brought back to Belgium in 1882. In April, 1884, the dispute of the bishops was definitively closed by the judgment of the supreme tribunal, according to which Dumont, having been legitimately deposed, has no more claim to the title and revenues of his earlier office; and in 1886 the supreme court of appeal at Brussels condemned Bernard "on account of serious breach of trust" to three years' imprisonment.

8. The Protestant Church was represented in Belgium only by small congregations in the chief cities and some Reformed Walloon village congregations. But for several decades, by the zealous exertions of the Evangelical Society at Brussels with thirty-four pastors and evangelists, the work of evangelization not only among Catholic Walloons, but also among the Flemish population, has made considerable progress, notwithstanding all agitation and incitement of the people by the Catholic clergy, so that several new evangelical congregations, consisting mostly of converts, have been formed. In two small places indeed the whole communities, roused by episcopal arbitrariness, have gone over.—The pastor Byse employed by the Evangelical Society at Brussels has taken up the idea that all men by the fall have lost their immortality, and that it could be restored again by faith in Christ, while all the unreconciled are given over to annihilation, the second death of Revelation ii. 11, xx. 15. So long as he maintained this theory merely as a private opinion the society took no offence at it, but when he began to proclaim it in his preaching and in his instruction of the young, and declined to yield to all advice on the matter, the synod of 1882 resolved upon his dismissal. But a great part of his congregation still remain faithful to him.

§ 201. THE SCANDINAVIAN COUNTRIES.

Notwithstanding the common Scandinavian-national and Lutheran-ecclesiastical basis on which the civil and religious life is developed, it assumed in the three Scandinavian countries a completely diversified course. While in Denmark the civil life bore manifold traces of democratic tendencies and thereby the relations between church and

state were loosened, Sweden, with a tenacity almost unparalleled in Protestant countries, has for a long period held
fast in exclusive attachment to the idea of a state church.
On the other hand Denmark was far more open to influences
from without hostile to the church, on the one side those
of rationalism, on the other, those of the anti-ecclesiastical
sects, especially of the Baptists and Mormons, than Sweden,
which in its certainly barren, if not altogether dead orthodoxy till after the middle of the century was almost hermetically sealed against all heterogeneous influences, but
yet could not altogether over-master the pietistically or
methodistically coloured movements of religious yearning
that arose among her own people. Norway, again, although
politically united with Sweden, has, both in national character and in religious development, shown its more intimate
relationship with Denmark.

1. Denmark.—From the close of last century rationalism has had a
home in Denmark. In 1825 Professor Clausen, a moderate adherent
of the neological school, published a learned work on the opposition
of "Catholicism and Protestantism," identifying the latter with
rationalism. First of all in that same year Pastor Grundtvig (died
1872), "a man of poetic genius, and skilled in the ancient history of
the land," inspired with equal enthusiasm for the old Lutheranism
of his fathers and for patriotic Danism, entered the lists and replied
with powerful eloquence, lamenting the decay of Christianity and the
church. He was condemned by the court of justice as injurious,
after he had during the process resigned his pastoral office. A like
fate befell the orientalist Lindberg, who charged Clausen with the
breach of his ordination vow. The adherents of Grundtvig met for
mutual edification in conventicles, until at last in 1832 he obtained
permission again to hold public services. Not less influential was the
work of Sören Kierkegaard (died 1855), who, largely in sympathy with
Grundtvig, without ecclesiastical office, in his writings earnestly pled
for a living subjective piety and unweariedly maintained an uncompromising struggle against the official Christianity of the secularized
clergy. The wild, unmeasured Danomania of 1848–1849, during the
military conflict with Germany, drew opponents together and made
them friends. Grundtvig declaimed against everything German,
and of the two factors, which he had formerly regarded as the pivots

on which universal history turned, Danism and Lutheranism, he now let go Lutheranism as of German origin. He therefore proposed the abrogation of the distinctive German-Lutheran confessions, placed the Apostles' Creed before and above the Bible and, pressing in a one-sided manner the doctrine of baptismal grace, demanded a "joyous Christianity," denied the necessity of continued preaching and exercise of repentance, and wished especially to introduce into the schools the Norse mythology as introductory to the study of Christianity. His adherents wrought with the anti-church party for the abolition of the union of church and state. The Danish constitutional law of 1849 abolished the confessional churches of the state church, and Catholics, Reformed, Moravians, and Jews were granted equal civil rights with the Lutherans. Since then the Catholic church has made slow but steady progress in the country, and the increasing Baptist movement was also favoured by a law of the Volkthing of 1857, which abolished compulsory baptism, and only required the enrolment of all children in the church books of their respective districts within the period of one year. Civil marriage had also been granted to dissenters in 1851, and in 1868 the peculiar institution of "electing communities" was founded, by means of which twenty families from one or more parishes which declare themselves dissatisfied with the pastors appointed them, may, without leaving the national church, form an independent congregation under pastors chosen by themselves and maintained at their own cost. The Schleswig-Holstein revolution in 1848, occasioned enormous confusion and disturbance in the ecclesiastical conditions of the district. Over a hundred German pastors were expelled and forty-six Schleswig parishes deprived of the use of the German language in church and school. In 1864 both provinces were at last by the Austrian and Prussian alliance rent from the Danish government, and in consequence of the German war of 1866 were incorporated with Prussia.

2. Sweden.—In Sweden there was formed in 1803, in opposition to the barren orthodoxy of the state church, a religious association which, if not altogether free of pietistic narrowness, was yet without any heretical doctrinal tendency, and exercised a quiet and wholesome influence. From the diligent *reading* of Scripture and the works of Luther that prevailed among its members it obtained the name of *Läsare*. The state proceeded against its members with fines and imprisonment, according to the old conventicle law of 1726, and the mob treated them with insults and violence. But in 1842 a fanatical tendency began to show itself under the leadership of a peasant, Erich Jansen, who induced many "*Readers*" to quit the church and to cast into the fire even Luther's Postils and Catechism as quite superfluous alongside of Holy Scripture. They mostly emigrated to

America in 1846. The law of the land since 1686 threatened every Swede who seceded from the Lutheran state church with imprisonment and exile, loss of civil privileges and the right of inheritance. As might therefore be supposed the French Marshal Bernadotte, who in 1818, under the name of Charles XIV., ascended the throne of Sweden, had been previously in 1810 obliged to repudiate the Catholic confession. Even in 1857 the Reichstag rejected a royal proposal to set aside the Secession as well as the Conventicle Act. But in the very next year, the holding of conventicles under clerical supervision, and in 1860, the secession to other ecclesiastical denominations, were allowed by law. The constitution of 1865 still indeed made adherence to the Lutheran confession a condition of qualification for a seat in either of the chambers. The Reichstag of 1870 at last sanctioned the admission of all Christian dissenters and also of Jews to all offices of state as well as to the membership of the Reichstag. On behalf of dissenters, especially of the numerous Baptists and Methodists, the right of civil marriage was granted in 1879. In 1877, Waldenström, head-master of the Latin school at Gefle, without ecclesiastical ordination, began zealously and successfully by speech and writings (to secure the widest possible circulation of which a joint stock company with large capital was formed) to work for the revival of the Christian life in the Lutheran national church. He vigorously contended against the church doctrine of atonement and justification, repudiating the idea of vicarious penal suffering, and broke through all church order by allowing the sacrament of the Lord's supper to be dispensed by laymen. He thus put himself, with his numerous following, directed by lay preachers in their own prayer meetings and mission halls, into direct opposition to the church, but by the wise forbearance of the ecclesiastical authorities he has not yet been formally ejected.[1]

3. Norway.—In Norway, toward the end of last century, rationalism was dominant in almost all the pulpits, and only a few remnants of Moravian revivalism raised a voice against it. But in 1796, a simple unlearned peasant Hans Nielsen Hauge, then in his twenty-fifth year, made his appearance as a revival preacher, creating a mighty spiritual movement that spread among the masses throughout the whole land. He had obtained his own religious knowledge from the study of old Lutheran practical theology, and arising at a period of extraordinary spiritual excitement, "his call," as Hase says, "to be a prophet was like that of the herdsman of Tekoa." From 1799 he continued itinerating for five years, persecuted, reproached, and calumniated by the

---

[1] Lumsden, "Sweden, its Religious State and Prospects." London, 1855.

rationalistic clergy, ten times cast into prison, under a law of 1741, which forbad laymen to preach, and then set free, until he had gone over all Norway even to its farthest and remotest corners, preaching unweariedly everywhere in houses and in the open air often three or four times a day, and nourishing besides the flame which he had kindled by voluminous writings and an extensive correspondence. He directed his preaching not only against the rationalism of the state clergy, but also against the antinomian religion of feeling, of " Blood and Wounds " theology introduced in earlier days by the Moravians, with a one-sided emphasis and exaggeration indeed, but still in all essentials maintaining the basis and keeping within the lines of Lutheran orthodoxy. In 1804 he was charged with tendencies dangerous to church and state, obtaining money from peasants on false pretences, inciting the people against the clergy, etc., and again cast into prison. The trial this time was carried on for ten years, until at last in 1814 the supreme court sentenced him on account of his invectives against the clergy to pay a fine, but pronounced him not guilty on the other charges. Broken down in spirit and body by his long imprisonment, he could not think of engaging again in his former work. He died in 1824. Numerous peasant preachers, however, issuing from his school were ready to go forth in his footsteps, and till this day the salutary effects of his and their activity are seen in wide circles. The law of 1741 which had been made to tell against them was at last abrogated by the Storthing in 1842. In 1845 the right of forming Christian sects was recognised, and in 1851 even the Jews were allowed the right of settlement previously refused them, and the security of all civil privileges. Since that time even in Norway the Catholic church has made considerable progress : in June, 1878, it had eleven churches and fourteen priests.

§ 202. GREAT BRITAIN AND IRELAND.

During the course of the century a breach from without was made upon the stronghold of the Anglican established church and its legal standing throughout the United Kingdom. The strong coherence of the Anglican episcopal church had already been weakened internally by the rise within its own bosom of High, Low, and Broad tendencies. The advance of the first-named party to tractarianism and ritualism opened the door to Romish sympathies, while in the last-named school German rationalism and criticism found favour, and the low church party was not ashamed to go hand-in-hand with the evangelical pietistic and methodistic tendencies of the dissenters. There followed numerous conversions to Rome, especially from the aristocratic ranks of the upper ten thousand. The Emancipation Act of 1829 opened the door to both Houses of Parliament to the Catholics, and in 1858 the same privileges were extended to the Jews. Also the bulwarks which the state church had in the old universities of Oxford and Cambridge were undermined, and in 1871 were completely overthrown by the legal abolition of all confessional tests. Down to 1869 the hierarchy of the episcopal state church, though clearly alien to the country, maintained its legal position in Catholic Ireland, till at last the Irish Church Bill brought it there to an end. Repeatedly have bills been introduced in the House of Commons, though hitherto without success, by members of the incessantly agitating Liberation Society, to disestablish the churches of England, Scotland, and Wales.[1]

1. The Episcopal State Church.—The two opposing parties of the state church corresponded to the two political parties of Tories and Whigs. The *high church party*, which has its most powerful representatives in the aristocracy, holds aloof from the dissenters, seeks to maintain the closest connexion between church and state, and eagerly contends for the retention of all old ecclesiastical forms and ordinances in constitution, worship, and doctrine. On the other hand the *evangelical or low church party*, which is more or less methodistically inclined, holds free intercourse with dissenters, associating with them in home and foreign mission work, etc., and with various shades of differences advocates the claims of progress against those of immobility, the independence of the church against its identification with the state, the evangelical freedom and general priesthood of believers against orthodoxy and hierarchism. From their midst arose a move-

---

[1] Stoughton, "Religion in England during the First Half of the Present Century, with a Postscript on Subsequent Events." 2 vols., London 1876. Molesworth, "History of England from 1830 to 1874." 8 vols., London

ment in 1871, occasioned by the Oxford "Essays and Reviews" and
the works of Bishop Colenso, which resulted in the publication, under
the authority of the bishops, of the "Speaker's Commentary," so-called
because suggested by Denison, who had long been speaker of the
House of Commons. It is a learned, thoroughly conservative commentary on the whole Bible by the ablest theologians of England.
On the revision of the English translation of the Bible see § 181, 4.
Besides these two parties, however, there has arisen a third, the broad
church party. It originated with the distinguished poet and philosopher, Coleridge (died 1834), and includes many of the most excellent
and scholarly of the clergy, especially those most eminent for their
acquaintance with German theology and philosophy. They do not
form an organized ecclesiastical party like the evangelicals and high
church men, but endeavour not only to overcome the narrowness and
severity of the former, but also to secure a broader basis and a wider
horizon for theology as well as for the church.[1]—The struggle for
the legalizing of marriage with a deceased wife's sister has been energetically pressed since 1850, but though the House of Common has
repeatedly passed the bill, it has been hitherto by small majorities,
under the influence of the bishops, rejected by the House of Lords.—
A non-official Pan-Anglican Council of English bishops from all parts
of the world, excluding the laity and inferior clergy, with pre-
eminently anti-Romish and anti-ritualistic tendencies, was held in
London in 1867 (cf. § 175, 5). When it met the second time in 1878,
it was attended by nearly one hundred bishops, one of them a negro.
Of the three weeks' debates and their results, however, no detailed
account has been published.

2. The Tractarians and Ritualists.—The activity of the dissenters
and the episcopal evangelical party's attachment to them stirred up
the adherents of the high church party to vigorous guarding of their
interests, and drove them into a one-sided exaggerated accentuation of
the Catholic element. The centre of this movement since 1833 was
the university of Oxford. Its leaders were Professors Pusey and
Newman, its literary organ the *Tracts for the Times*, from which the
party received the name of Tractarians. This was a series of ninety
treatises, published 1833-1841, on the basis of Anglo-Catholicism, which
sought, while holding by the Thirty-nine Articles, to affirm with
equal decidedness the genuine Protestantism over against the Roman
papacy, and, in the importance which it attached to the apostolical
succession of the episcopate and priesthood and the apostolical tradi-

---

[1] Littledale, "Church Parties," art. in the *Contemporary Review* for
July, 1874, pp. 287-320. Mozley, "Reminiscences of Oriel College."
London, 1882.

tion for the interpretation of Scripture, the genuine Catholicism over against every form of ultra-Protestantism. In this way, too, their dogmatics in all the several doctrines, as far as the Thirty-nine Articles would by any means allow, was approximated to the Roman Catholic doctrine, and indeed by-and-by passed over entirely to that type of doctrine. Newman's Tract 90 caused most offence, in which, with thoroughly jesuitical sophistry, it was argued that the Thirty-nine Articles were capable of an explanation on the basis of which they might be subscribed even by one who occupied in regard to the church doctrine and practice an essentially Roman Catholic standpoint. The university authorities now felt obliged to declare publicly that the tracts were by no means sanctioned by them, and that especially the application of the principles of Tract 90 to the conduct of students in the matter of subscription of the Thirty-nine Artices is not allowable. Bishop Bagot of Oxford, hitherto favourable to the tractarians, refused to permit the continued issue of the tracts. The other bishops also for the most part spoke against them in their pastorals, and a flood of controversial pamphlets roused the wrath of the non-Catholic populace. But on the other hand tractarianism still found favour among the higher clergy and the aristocracy. In 1845 Newman went over to the Catholic church, and has since led a retired life devoted to theological study. Pius IX. paid him no attention, but in 1879 Leo XIII. acknowledged and rewarded his services to the Catholic church by elevating him to the rank of cardinal. The majority of the tractarians disapproved of Newman's step and remained in the Anglican church. Thus acted Pusey (died 1882), the recognised leader of the party, after whom they were now called Puseyites. Many, however, followed Newman's example, so that by the end of 1846 no less than one hundred and fifty clergymen and prominent laymen were received into the widely opened door of the Catholic church.[1]—The following twelve years, 1846–1858, were occupied by two dogmatico-ecclesiastical conflicts vitally affecting the interests of the tractarians. (1) The Gorham Case. The Thirty-nine Articles took essentially Lutheran ground in treating of baptism, recognising it as a vehicle of regeneration and divine sonship, and the tractarians laid uncommonly great stress upon this article. So also the Bishop of Exeter, Dr. Philpotts, refused to institute the Rev. Cornelius Gorham because of his views on this subject. Gorham accused him before the Archbishop of Canterbury, but the Court of Arches decided in favour of the bishop. The Court of Appeal, however, the judicial committee of the Privy Council, annulled the

---

[1] Newman, "*Apologia pro Vita Sua.*" London, 1864. **Weaver,** "Puseyism, a Refutation and Exposure," London, 1843.

episcopal judgment, and ordered that Gorham should be installed in his office. In vain did Philpotts, by a protest before the Court of Queen's Bench, and then before the Court of Common Pleas, against the jurisdiction of the Privy Council in this case, in vain, too, did Blomfield, Bishop of London, insist upon the revival of Convocation, which for one and a half centuries had been inoperative as a spiritual parliament with upper and lower houses, and in vain did a tractarian assembly of more than 1,500 distinguished clergymen and laymen lodge a solemn protest. The judgment of the Privy Council stood, and Gorham was inducted to his office in 1850. Many of the protesters now went over to the Catholic church, and about 600 others, like the Puritan Pilgrim Fathers 230 years before (§ 143, 4), under ecclesiastical oppression, emigrated to New Zealand.—(2) The Denison Eucharist Case.—The Puseyite Archdeacon Denison of Taunton, in the diocese of Bath and Wells, had in 1851 in open defiance of the Thirty-nine Articles, which represent Calvin's views of the Lord's Supper, affirmed in preaching and writing that unbelievers as well as believers eat and drink the body and blood of the Lord. Over this he was involved in a sharp discussion with a neighbouring clergyman called Ditcher. In 1854 Ditcher accused Denison before his bishop, who, after vain efforts to reconcile the parties, referred the matter to the Court of Arches, which sought, but in vain, to end the strife by compromise. Ditcher now in 1856 brought his complaint before the *Queen's Bench* which obliged the archbishop to take up the matter again. A commission appointed by him declared that the complaint was quite justifiable, and threatened Denison, when he refused any sort of retractation, with deposition. But the Court of Appeal in 1858 stayed the judgment on the ground of a technical error in procedure, and Denison remained in office.

3. From the middle of 1850 the tractarians, who had hitherto confined themselves to the development of the Romanizing system of doctrine, began to apply its consequences to the church ritual and the Christian life, and so won for themselves the name of Ritualists, which has driven out their earlier designation. Wherever possible they showed their Catholic zeal by introducing images, crucifixes, candles, holy water, mass dresses, mass bells, and boy choristers, urged the restoration of the seven sacraments, especially of extreme unction, auricular confession, the sacrificial theory and Corpus Christi day, of prayers for the dead and masses for souls, invocation of saints and the blessed Virgin; they also praised celibacy and monasticism, etc. Ritualism has from the first shown singular skill in party organization. The *English Church Union*, founded in 1860, has now nearly 200,000 members, of these about 3,000 clergymen and 50 bishops, and it embraces 300 branches over the whole domain of

the Anglican church. Numerous brotherhoods and sisterhoods, guilds and orders, organized after the style of Roman Catholic monasticism, promote the interests of ritualism, and zealously prosecute home and foreign mission work. The *Confraternity of the Blessed Sacrament* originated in 1862, was able in 1882 to celebrate Corpus Christi day in 250 churches along with the Romish church, dispensing only with the procession. The *Society of the Holy Cross*, founded in 1873 consists only of priests, and forms a kind of directory for all branches of the ritualistic propaganda. The *English Order of St. Augustine* has a threefold division, into spiritual brothers who are preparing for priests' orders, lay brothers who are being qualified as lay preachers, both under the strictest vows, and a sort of tertiaries, who are free from vows. Among the sisterhoods which already supply nurses to all the great hospitals of the capital, the most important is that called "by the name of Jesus." They take, like the Beguines of the middle ages, the three vows, but not as binding for life. By the ultra high church party the genuine apostolic succession of the ordination of the first Protestant archbishop, Matthew Parker, and so the genuineness of all subsequent ordinations going back to him, were doubted; three Anglican bishops are said to have had episcopal consecration anew conferred on them by a Greek Catholic bishop. The reckless and wilful procedure of the ritualists in imitating the Roman Catholic ritual in public worship called forth frequent violent disturbances at their services, and noisy crowds flocked to their churches. Most frequent and violent were the riots in 1859 and 1860 in the parish of St. George's, London, where scarcely any service was held without disgraceful scenes of hissing, whistling, stamping, and cries of "No popery." The offscouring of all London flocked to the Sunday services as to a public entertainment. Instead of hymns, street songs were sung, instead of responses blasphemous cries were shouted forth, while cushions and prayer-books were hurled at the altar decorations, etc. These unseemly proceedings were caused by the ritualistic rector, Bryan King, who had introduced the objectionable ceremonial, and obstinately continued it in spite of the decided opposition and protests of his colleague, Mr. Allen. King's removal in 1860 first put an end to these disturbances, which police interference proved utterly unable to check. The ritualistic *Church Union*, called into existence by these proceedings, was opposed by an anti-ritualistic *Church Association*, and from both multitudes of complaints and appeals were brought before the ecclesiastical and civil tribunals. The first case they brought up was that of Rev. A. H. MacConochie, of Holborn. who, having been admonished by the ecclesiastical courts on account of his ritualistic practices in 1867, appealed to the Privy Council. And although this court decided in 1869 that all ceremonies not authorized by the prayer-book are to be regarded as forbidden, he and his followers continued to act on the principle that whatever is not there expressly prohibited ought to be permitted. The *Public Worship Regulation Bill*, introduced by Archbishop Tait, and passed by Parliament, which legislatively determined the procedure in ritualistic cases, did not prevent the constant advance of this movement. The *Court of Arches* now issued a suspension against the accused, and condemned them to prison when they continued to officiate, until they declared themselves ready to obey or to demit their office. Tooth of Hatcham, Dale of London, Enraght of Bordesdale, and Green of Miles Platting were actually sent to prison in 1880. But the first three were soon liberated by the Court of Appeal finding some technical flaw in the proceedings against them, while Green, in whose case no such flaw appeared, lay in confinement for twenty months. The ritualists still persistently continued their practice, and their opponents renewed their prosecutions; these were followed by appeals to the higher courts, presenting of petitions to both the Houses of Parliament, addresses with vast numbers of signatures for and against to the Archbishop of Canterbury, to Convocation which had meanwhile been restored, to the Cabinet, to the Queen, etc. The result was that many cases were abandoned, some obnoxious parties transferred elsewhere, and a very few deposed.

4. Liberalism in the Episcopal Church.—The more liberal tendency of the broad church party had also many supporters who scrupled not to pass beyond the traditional bounds of English orthodoxy. In opposition to the orthodoxy zealousy inculcated at Oxford, rationalism found favour at the rival university of Cambridge, and vigorous support was given to the views of the Tübingen school of Baur in the London *Westminster Review*. And even in high church Oxford, there were not wanting teachers in sympathy with the critical and speculative rationalism of Germany. Great excitement was caused in 1860 by the "*Essays and Reviews*," which in seven treatises by so many Oxford professors contested the traditional apologetics and hermeneutics of English theology, and set a sublimated rationalism in its place. In Germany these not very important treatises would probably have excited little remark, but in the English church they roused an unparalleled disturbance; more than nine thousand clergymen of the episcopal church protested against the book, and all the bishops unanimously condemned it. The excitement had not yet subsided when from South Africa oil was poured upon the flames. Bishop Colenso of Natal (died 1883), who had zealously carried on the mission there, but had openly expressed the conviction that it is unwise, unscriptural, and unchristian to make repudiation by Caffres living in polygamy, of all their wives but one, a condition of baptism, had

occasioned still greater offence by publishing in 1863 in seven vols. a prolix critical disquisition on the Pentateuch and the Book of Joshua, in which he contested the authenticity and unconditional credibility of these books by arguments familiar long ago but now quite antiquated and overthrown in Germany. During a journey to England undertaken for his defence he was excommunicated and deposed by a synod of the South African bishops in Capetown. The Privy Council, as supreme ecclesiastical court in England, cleared him, as well as the authors of the Essays, from the charge of heresy. An important aid for the dissemination of liberal religious views is afforded by the Hibbert Lectureship. Robert Hibbert (died 1849), a wealthy private gentleman in London, assigned the yearly interest of a considerable sum for "the spreading of Christianity in its simplest form as well as the furthering of the unfettered exercise of the individual judgment in matters of religion." The Hibbert trustees are eighteen laymen who dispense the revenues in supplementing the salaries of poorly paid clergymen of liberal views, in providing bursaries for theological students at home and abroad, and in other such like ways, but since 1878 especially, by advice of distinguished scholars, in the endowment of annual courses of lectures, afterwards published, on subjects in the domain of philosophy, biblical criticism, the comparative science of religion and the history of religion. The first Hibbert Lecturer was the celebrated Oxford professor, Max Müller, in 1878. Among other lecturers may be named Renan of Paris in 1880; Kuenen of Leyden in 1882; Pfleiderer of Berlin, in 1885. The battle waged with great passionateness on both sides since 1869 for and against the removal of the Athanasian Creed, or at least its anathemas, from the liturgy has not yet been brought to any decided result.

5. **Protestant Dissenters in England.**—Down nearly to the end of the eighteenth century all the enactments and restrictions of the Toleration Act of 1689 (§ 155, 3) continued in full force. But in 1779 the obligation of Protestant dissenters to subscribe the Thirty-nine Articles was abolished, and the acknowledgment of the Bible as God's revealed word substituted. The right of founding schools of their own, hitherto denied them, was granted in 1798. In 1813 the Socinians were also included among the dissenters who should enjoy these privileges. After a severe struggle the *Corporation and Test Acts* were set aside in 1826, affording all dissenters entrance to Parliament and to all civil offices. The necessity of being married and having their children baptized in an episcopal church was removed by the Marriage and Registration Act of 1836 and 1837, and divorce suits were removed from the ecclesiastical to a civil tribunal in 1857. In 1868 compulsory church rates for the episcopal parish church were abolished. Lord Russell's University Bill of 1854, by restricting sub-

scription of the Thirty-nine Articles to the theological students, opened the universities of Oxford and Cambridge to dissenters, while the University Tests Bill of 1871 made the adherents of all religious confessions eligible for all university honours and emoluments at both seminaries. Thus one restriction after another was removed, so that at last the episcopal church has nothing of her exclusive privileges left beyond the rank and title of a state church, and the undiminished possession of all her ancient property, from which her prelates draw princely revenues.

6. Scotch Marriages in England.—The saints of the English Revolution had indeed resolved in 1653 to introduce civil marriage (§ 162, 1). But the reaction under Cromwell set this unpopular law aside. and the Restoration made marriage by an Anglican clergyman, even for dissenters, an indispensable condition of legal recognition. But in no country, especially among the higher orders, were private marriages, without the knowledge and consent of the family, so frequent as here, and clergymen were always to be found unscrupulous enough to celebrate such weddings in taverns or other convenient places. When an end had been put to such irregularities on English soil by an Act of Parliament of 1753, lovers seeking secret marriage betook themselves to Scotland. In that country there prevailed, and still prevails, the theory that a declaration of willingness on both sides constitutes a perfectly valid marriage. The Scottish ecclesiastical law indeed requires church proclamation and ceremony, but failure to observe this requirement is followed only by a small pecuniary fine. Fugitive English couples generally made the necessary declaration before a blacksmith at Gretna-Green, who was also justice of the peace in this small border village, and were then legitimately married people according to Scottish law. Only in 1856 were all marriages performed in this manner without previous residence in Scotland pronounced by Act of Parliament invalid.

7. The Scottish State Church.—The Presbyterian Church of Scotland, from the beginning strictly Calvinistic in constitution, doctrine and practice, has, generally speaking, preserved this character. Only in recent times has the endeavour of the so-called *Moderates* to introduce a milder type of doctrine won favour. The Established Church, as a national church properly so-called and recognised by law, dates from the political union of England and Scotland in the kingdom of Great Britain in 1707, and the Anglican Episcopal Church there was then reduced to a feebly represented dissenting denomination. Patronage, set aside indeed in the Reformation age, but restored under Queen Anne in 1712, and since then, in spite of all opposition from the stricter party, continued, because often misused to secure the intrusion of inacceptable ministers upon congregations, gave occasion to

repeated secessions. Thus the *Secession Church* broke off in 1732, and the *Relief Church* in 1752, the latter going beyond the former's protest against patronage by unconditional repudiation of Erastianism, *i.e.* the theory of the necessary connection of Church and State (§ 144, 1), and the assertion of the spiritual independence of the church, and expressed firmly the principles of Voluntaryism, *i.e.* the payment of all ecclesiastical officers, etc., by voluntary contributions. Both parties united in 1847 in the *United Presbyterian Church*, which now embraces one-fifth of the population.—Twice that number joined the secession of the Free Church in 1843. The General Assembly of the Church of Scotland granted to congregations in 1834 the right of vetoing presentations to vacancies. The civil courts, however, upheld the absolute right of patrons, and at the Assembly of 1843 about two hundred of the most distinguished ministers, with the great Dr. Chalmers (died 1847) at their head, left the state church, and, as *Non-Intrusionists*, founded the *Free Church of Scotland*, which at its own cost formed new parishes and distinguished itself by Christian zeal in every direction. It differs from the *United Presbyterian Church* in restricting its opposition to the abuse of patronage, without repudiating right off every sort of state aid and endowment as unevangelical. But even to it the law passed in 1846, granting to all congregations the right of veto, seemed now no longer a sufficient motive to return to the state church. Even when in 1874, parliament, at the call of the government, formally abolished the rights of patronage through all Scotland and gave to the congregations the right of choosing their own ministers, the General Assembly of the Free Church by a great majority refused to reunite with the state church brought so near it, because it conceded to the civil courts unwarrantable interference with its internal affairs, especially the right of suspending its clergy.[1]

8. Scottish Heresy Cases.—The Glasgow presbytery lodged before the United Presbyterian Synod in Edinburgh of 1878 a charge against the Rev. Fergus Ferguson of heresy, because his teaching was in conflict with the church doctrine of the atonement in saying that sinners, apart from Christ's intervention, would not suffer eternal

---

[1] The very confused, wholly inadequate, and in some points positively incorrect statements in the above paragraph may be supplemented and amended by reference to the following literature: Buchanan, "Ten Years' Conflict." 2 vols. Edin., 1852. Moncrieff, "Vindication of the Claim of Right." Edin., 1877. Moncrieff, "The Free Church Principle: its Character and History." Edin., 1888. Mackerrow, "History of the Secession Church." Glasgow, 1841.

punishment but extinction, and that the same fate still lay before unbelievers and the impenitent. After five days' violent discussion, the majority of the synod, while strongly dissenting from his views and urging him to avoid it in his preaching and catechising, resolved to retain him in office as having proved his adherence to the orthodox doctrine of the atonement. But when, at next year's synod, the Rev. D. Macrae of Gourock asserted that, in spite of the Westminster Confession, it was allowable for ministers to deny the eternity of punishment, and would not promise to preach otherwise, he was unanimously deposed.—Far more exciting and long continued were the proceedings begun in the Free Church in 1876, against Professor Robertson Smith of Aberdeen, who was charged before his presbytery with offensive statements about angels, but especially with contradicting the inspiration of Scripture by contesting the Mosaic authorship of Deuteronomy. After various proposals of deposition, suspension, rebuke, acquittal, had been made, the General Assembly of 1880, after much deliberation and discussion, by a majority found the charge of heterodoxy not proven, but earnestly exhorted the accused to greater circumspection and moderation, and the decision was greeted with thundering applause from the students and waving of handkerchiefs from the ladies present. But when, very soon after this acquittal, several other contributions by him appeared in the *Encyclopædia Britannica*, on the Hebrew Language and Literature, and Haggai, in the spirit of the Wellhausen criticism (§ 182, 18), as also an article on Animal Worship among the Arabians and in the Old Testament, in the *Journal of Philology*, the *Commission* sitting in Edinburgh reinstituted proceedings against him. In October, 1880, Smith vindicated before that court his scientific attitude toward the Old Testament, maintaining that a moderate criticism of the biblical books was reconcilable with the maintenance of their inspired authority. The majority of the Commission, however, voted for his expulsion from his chair. Smith protested both against the competence and against the judgment of the Commission, but declared himself ready to submit to the judgment of the General Assembly. Meanwhile he accepted an invitation from Glasgow to deliver public lectures there on the Old Testament, which were received with extraordinary favour. This course was published under the title: "*The Old Testament in the Jewish Church*." The General Assembly of May, 1881, now decided by a large majority to remove him from his academical chair, with retention of his license and his professor's salary, which latter, however, Smith declined. But his numerous sympathizers presented him with a scientific library worth £3,000, and promised an annual stipend equal to his former salary. In 1883 he received the appointment as Professor of Arabic in Cambridge, and the large revenues of that office allowed him to decline the offer of his friends.[1]

9. The Catholic Church in Ireland.—The Catholic inhabitants of Ireland under Protestant proprietors, and forced to pay tithes for the support of the Protestant clergy, were always deprived of civil rights. In 1809 O'Connell (died 1847), an agitator of great popular eloquence, placed himself at the head of the oppressed people, in order in a constitutional way to secure religious and political freedom and equality. At last, in 1829, the Emancipation Bill, supported by Peel and Wellington, was passed, which on the basis of the formal declaration of the whole Catholic episcopate that papal infallibility and papal sovereignty in civil matters was not part of the Catholic faith nor could be joined therewith either in Ireland or anywhere else in the Catholic world, gave to Catholics admission to parliament and to all civil and military appointments. But the hated tithes remained, and were enforced, when refused, by military force. After long debates in both houses of parliament, the Tithes Bill was adopted in 1838, which transferred the tithe as a land-tax from tenants to proprietors, which, however, was only a postponing of the question. It was thus regarded by O'Connell. He declared that justice for Ireland could only be got by abolishing the legislative union with Great Britain existing since 1800, and restoring her independent parliament. For this purpose he organized the Repeal Association. In 1840 another no less powerful popular agitator arose in the person of the Irish Capuchin, Father Mathew, the apostle of temperance, who with unparalleled success persuaded thousands of those degraded by drink to take vows of abstinence from spirituous liquors. He kept apart from all political agitation, but the fruits of his exertions were all in its favour. O'Connell in 1843 organized monster meetings, attended by hundreds of thousands. The government had him tried, the jury found him guilty, but the House of Lords quashed the conviction and liberated him from prison in 1844. The Peel ministry now sought to soothe the excitement by passing in 1845 the Legacy Act, which allowed Catholics to hold property in their own names, and the Maynooth Bill, by which the theological seminary at Maynooth received a rich endowment from the State. Continued famine, and consequent emigration of several hundreds of thousands to America and Australia, relieved Ireland of a considerable portion of its Catholic population, while Protestant missions

---

[1] Smith's appointment was to the Lord Almoner's Professorship, with a merely nominal salary; but he was afterwards elected to the more remunerative office of University librarian, and more recently has succeeded Prof. Wright in the Chair of Arabic in the University

by Bible and tract circulation and by schools had some success in
evangelizing those who remained.   On November 5th, 1855, the
anniversary of the Gunpowder Plot, the Redemptorists at Kingstown,
near Dublin, erected and burnt a great bonfire in the public streets
of Bibles which they had seized, and the primate archbishop of
Ireland justified it by reference to the example of the believers at
Ephesus (Acts xix. 19).

10. The Fenian movement, originating among the American Irish,
which since 1863 created such terror among the English, was the
result of political rather than religious agitation.   Although this
movement failed in its proper end, namely the complete separation
of Ireland from England, it yet forced upon the government the
conviction of the absolute necessity of meeting the just demands of
the Irish by thorough-going reforms and putting an end to the
oppressions which the native farmers suffered at the hands of foreign
landowners, and the grievances endured by the Catholic church by
the maintenance of the Anglican church established in Ireland.
The carrying out of these reforms was the service rendered by the
Gladstone ministry.   By the Irish Land Bill of 1870 the land question
was solved according to the demands of justice, and by the Irish
Church Bill of 1869, which deprived the Anglican church in Ireland
of the character of a state church and put it on the same footing
as other denominations, the church question was similarly settled.
The dignitaries of the Anglican church thus lost their position as
state officials and their seats in the House of Lords.   The rich property of the hitherto established church was calculated and applied
partly to compensating for losses caused by this reform, partly to
creating benevolent institutions for the general good.   But neither
the Church Bill, nor the Land Bill, nor the Universities Bill, which
in 1880 founded by state aid a Catholic university in Dublin, secured
the reconciliation of the Irish.   "Eternal hatred of England" was
and is the battle cry; "Ireland for the Irish, and only for them,"
is their watchword.   In order to carry out this scheme an Irish
"National League" was formed, and innumerable secret "Moon-
lighters," under the supposed leadership of "Captain Moonshine,"
committed atrocities by burning farm steadings and mutilating
cattle, murdering and massacring by dagger and revolver, petroleum
and dynamite, and directed their operations against the representatives of the government, against proprietors who sought rent, against
tenants who paid rent, against officials who endeavoured to enforce
it, and against everything that was, or was called, English.   In order
to cut at the root of this lawlessness, which by proclamation of a state
of siege was only restricted, not overthrown, the government of 1881
passed further agrarian reforms: All tenant rights were to be pur-

chased by the surplus of the fund formed by the disestablishment of the Irish church, and where this did not suffice, by state grants, and the right to conclude contracts for rent and to determine its amount was transferred from the proprietors to a newly-constituted land court, without whose permission, after the lapse of the fifteen years' term, no rent contract could be made. But even this did not stop almost daily repeated murders and acts of destruction. The government now sought the aid of the pope through the mediation of a Catholic member of parliament on a visit to Rome; but these merely confidential negotiations led to no considerable result. In May, 1883, the curia, on the occasion of a collection promoted by the National League as a magnificent national present to the great (Protestant) leader of the agitation, Mr. Parnell, in a circular letter, forbad "*proprio motu*," the bishops in the strictest manner taking any part in the movement, and urged them to dissuade their members from doing so. But only Archbishop McCabe of Dublin (died 1885), from the first an opponent of the League, issued a pastoral against it to be read in all the pulpits of his diocese. The other bishops ignored the papal command, and among the Catholic people the opinion obtained that they owed to the pope obedience in spiritual but not in political matters. The collections for the Parnell fund were continued with redoubled zeal. The attempts of dynamitards, supplied with materials by their American compatriots, and other agrarian offences have not yet been finally stopped.

11. The Catholic Church in England and Scotland.—The Emancipation Act, passed mainly for the relief of the Irish, naturally also benefited English Catholics, who in 1791 had been allowed to hold Catholic services. Led by the numerous accessions of Puseyites to entertain the most extravagant hopes, Pius IX. in 1850 issued a bull, by which the Roman Catholic hierarchy in England was reinstituted with twelve suffragan bishoprics under one archbishop of Westminster. The bull occasioned great excitement in the Protestant population (*Anti-Papal Aggression*), and the *Ecclesiastical Titles Bill* forbade the use of ecclesiastical titles not sanctioned by the law of the land. After the first excitement had passed, the Catholic bishops, at their head the learned and brilliant and zealous ultramontane Cardinal Archbishop Wiseman (died 1865), and his successor, surpassing him, if not in genius and learning, at least in ultramontane zeal, the Puseyite convert Manning, made a cardinal in 1875, used with impunity their condemned titles, until in 1871 the Ecclesiastical Titles Bill was formally revoked by act of parliament. Conversions in noble families were particularly numerous in the later decades. Since 1850 the number of Catholics in England and Scotland has quadrupled. This has been caused in great part by Irish emigration,

for the middle and lower ranks of the English have scarcely been affected by the conversion fever, which as the latest form of the fitful humour of the English had so rich a harvest in the families of the nobility. In 1780 all London had only one Catholic place of worship, the chapel of the Sardinian embassy, which on June 2nd of that year was wrecked and burnt by a raging mob. Now the English capital has two episcopal dioceses, ninety-four Catholic churches and chapels (besides about 900 Anglican churches) with 313 clergymen, and forty-four cloisters. In the House of Lords sit twenty-eight Roman Catholic peers, and in both countries there are forty-seven Catholic baronets. Since 1847 England has a specifically Catholic university at Kensington, under the episcopate, and with the pope as its supreme head, which, however, with its poor staff of teachers and its expensive course attracts but a few of the Catholic youth of England. Since the Anti-Papal Aggression of 1850 failed, the Protestant people have shown themselves comparatively indifferent to such assumptions of the papacy.—In the Act of Union of 1707 (§ 155, 3), Scotland was guaranteed the absolute exclusion of every sort of Roman Catholic hierarchy for all time to come. But in recent times the number of its Catholic inhabitants so greatly increased, that Pius IX. in his last years, not unaided by the English government, eagerly urged the re-establishment of the hierarchy, and Leo XIII. was able at his first consistory of the college of cardinals in March, 1878, to make appointments to the two newly-erected archdioceses and their bishoprics. On the following Easter Sunday the allocution relating thereto was read in all Catholic churches in Scotland. The restoration was thus carried out in spite of all protests and demonstrations of Scottish Protestants.

12. German Lutheran Congregations in Australia.—Besides the dominant Anglican church, emigration has led to the formation of a considerable number of German Lutheran congregations, which are distributed in three synods. 1. The Victoria Synod was founded in 1352 by pastor Göthe. It adopted at first the union platform. but subsequently attached itself more decidedly to the Lutheran confession. 2. Pastor Karch, who in 1830 emigrated with a number of Prussian Lutherans, in order to avoid the union, laid the foundation of the Immanuel Synod. Since 1875 it has been supplied with preachers from the missionary institute of Neuendettelsau. It is distinguished by its missionary zeal for the conversion of the natives, pursues with special interest the study of the prophetic word, and makes chiliasm an open question which need not rend the church. 3. The South Australian Synod, on the other hand, is the decided opponent of any sort of chiliasm, and has assumed an attitude of violent antagonism to the Immanuel Synod

§ 203. FRANCE.

In France, lauded as the eldest daughter of the church after the overthrow of the first Empire, ultramontanism, under the secret and open co-operation of the Jesuits, has ever arisen with revived youth and vigour out of all the political convulsions which have since passed over the land. And though indeed Gallicanism seemed again to obtain strength under the second Empire and, down to the close of that period, found many able champions among learned theologians like Bishop Maret (§ 189, 1), and even among exalted prelates like the noble Archbishop Darboy of Paris, a martyr of his office under the Commune (§ 212, 4). its influence faded gradually, and in the latest phase of France's political development, the third republic, seems utterly to have disappeared, so that even the "*Kulturkampf*" which broke out in 1879 could not give it life again.— The number of Protestant churches and church members, in spite of bloody persecutions during the Bourbon restoration, and many arbitrary restrictions by Catholic prefects under the citizen king and the second Empire, by numerous accessions of whole congregations and groups of congregations through zealous evangelization efforts, by means of school instruction, itinerant preaching, and Bible colportage, has increased during the century fourfold. In the Reformed church the opposition of methodistically tinctured orthodoxy, reinforced from England and French Switzerland, and rationalistic freethinking, led to sharp conflicts. Also in the Lutheran church, more strongly influenced by Germany, similar discussions arose, but a more conciliatory spirit prevailed and violent struggles were avoided.

1. The French Church under Napoleon I.—In 1801 Napoleon as Consul concluded with Pius VII. a Concordat which, adopting the concordat of Francis I. (§ 111, 14), abandoning the pragmatic sanction of Bourges, and only haggling about the limits to be fixed for the two

powers, gave no consideration to the idea of a wholesome internal reform of the French Church: Catholicism is the acknowledged religion of the majority of the French people; the church property belongs to the state, with the obligation to maintain the clergy and ordinances; the clergy who had taken the oath and those who were expatriated were all to resign, but were eligible for election; new boundaries were to be marked out for the episcopal dioceses with reference to the political divisions of the country; the government elects and the pope confirms the bishops, and these, with approval of the government, appoint the priests. The one-sided Organic Articles of the first Consul of 1802, which were annexed to the publication of the Concordat as a code of explanatory regulations, made any proclamation of papal orders and decrees of all foreign councils dependent on previous permission of the government, as also the calling of synods and consultative assemblies of the clergy. They further ordained that all official services of the clergy should be gratuitous, and transferred to the civil council the right and duty of strict inquiry into any clerical breach of civil laws and any misuse or excessive exercise of clerical authority. The thirty-first article, however, created that unhappy order of *Desservants* or curates, the result of which was that interim appointments were made to most of the benefices in order to squeeze state pay in supplement to the inadequate ecclesiastical endowments, and so their holders were at the absolute mercy of the bishops who could transport or dispense with them at any moment. For further particulars about the friendly and hostile relations of Napoleon and the pope, see § 185, 1. By an imperial decree of 1810, the four articles of the Gallican Church (§ 156, 8) were made laws of the Empire; and a French National Council of 1811 sought to complete the reconstruction of the church according to Napoleon's ideas, but proved utterly incapable for such a task, and was therefore dissolved by the emperor himself.—To pacify the Protestants, dissatisfied with the Concordat, amid flattering acknowledgment of their services to the state, to science and to the arts, an appendix was attached to the Organic Articles, securing to them liberty of religious worship and political and municipal equality with Catholics. For training ministers for the Reformed Church a theological seminary was founded at Montauban, and for Lutherans an academy with a seminary at Strassburg. Napoleon also afterwards proved himself on every occasion ready to help the Protestants. He was equally forward in recognising public opinion in France. The National Institute of France in 1804 offered a prize for an essay on the influence of Luther's Reformation on the formation and advance of European national life, and awarded it to the treatise of the Catholic physician

Villers (*Essai sur l'influence de la réf. de Luther*, etc.), which in all respects glorified Protestantism. Even the Catholic clergy during the first Empire exhibited an easy temper and tolerance such as was never shown before or since. The obligatory civil marriage law introduced by the Revolution in 1792, obtained place in the *Code Napoléon* in 1804, and was with it introduced in Belgium and the provinces of the Rhine.[1]

2. The Restoration and the Citizen Kingdom.—The Charter of the Bourbon Restoration under Louis XVIII. (1814–1824) and Charles X. (1824–1830) made Catholicism the state religion and granted toleration and state protection to the other confessions. A new concordat concluded with Pius VII. in 1817, by which that of Napoleon of 1801, with the Organic Articles of the following year, were abrogated, and the state of matters previous to 1789 restored, was so vigorously opposed by the nation, that the ministry were obliged to withdraw the measure introduced in both chambers for giving it legislative sanction. Ultramontanism, however, in its baldest form, steadily favoured by the government, soon prevailed among the clergy to such an extent that any inclination to Gallicanism was denounced as heresy and intolerance of Protestantism lauded as piety. In southern France the rekindled hatred of the Catholic mob against the Reformed broke out in 1815 in brutal and bloody persecution. The government kept silence till the indignation of Europe obliged it to put down the atrocities, but the offenders were left unpunished. Connivance in such lawlessness on the part of the government contributed largely to its overthrow in the July revolution of 1830. The Catholic Church then lost again the privilege of a state religion, and the hitherto persecuted and oppressed Protestants obtained equal rights with the Catholics. But even under the new constitutional government of Orleans, ultramontanism soon reasserted itself. The Protestants had to complain of much injury and injustice from Catholic prefects, and the Protestant minister Guizot claimed for France the protectorate of the whole Catholic world. The Reformed Church meanwhile flourished, though vacillating between methodistic narrowness and rationalistic shallowness, growing both inwardly and outwardly, and also the Lutheran communities, which outside of Alsace were only thinly scattered, enjoyed great prosperity. In the February revolution of 1848 the Catholic clergy readily yielded obedience to the citizen king Louis Philippe, and, on the ground that the Catholic church is suited to any form of government which only

---

[1] Jarvis, "The Gallican Church and the Revolution," pp. 324–395. London, 1882.

grants liberty to the church, did not refuse their benediction to the tree of freedom with the sovereign people at the barricades.

3. The Catholic Church under Napoleon III.—Louis Napoleon, as president of the new republic (1848–1852), and still more decidedly as emperor (1852–1870), inclined to follow the traditions of his uncle, regarded the concordat of 1801 as still legally in force and seemed specially anxious to arouse zeal for the Gallican liberties. Although his bayonets secured the pope's return to Rome (§ 185, 2) and even afterwards supported his authority there, he did not fulfil the heart's wish of the emperor by the people's grace to place the imperial crown upon his head in his own person. Severely strained relations between the imperial court and the episcopate resulted in 1860 from a pamphlet against the papacy inspired by the government (§ 185, 3). Dupanloup, Bishop of Orleans, was one of the oldest and most determined defenders of the interests of the papal see, and from Poitiers the emperor was pretty openly characterized as a second Pilate. The government did not venture directly to interfere between the two, but reminded the bishops that the emperor's differences with the pope referred only to temporal affairs. It also forbade the forming of separate societies for the collecting of Peter's pence, and dissolved the societies of St. Vincent, instituted for benevolent purposes, but misused for ultramontane agitations. When Archbishop Desprez of Toulouse, like his predecessors in 1662 and 1762, on May 16th, 1862, with pompous phrases of piety appointed the jubilee festival of the "*fait glorieux*," by which at Toulouse three hundred years before, by means of shameful treachery and base breach of pledges 4,000 Protestants were murdered (§ 139, 15), a shout of indignation rose from almost all French journals and the government forbade the ceremonial. It also refused permission to proclaim the papal encyclical with the syllabus (§ 185, 2) and condemned several bishops who disobeyed for misuse of their office. Under the influence of the ultramontane empress Eugenie, however, the relation of the government to the curia and the higher clergy of the empire, since the one could not do without the other, became more friendly and intimate, till the day of Sedan, September 2nd, 1870, put an end to the Napoleonic empire and the temporal power of the papacy which it had maintained.

4. The Protestant Churches under Napoleon III.—After the revolution of 1848, the Lutherans at an assembly in Strassburg and the Reformed in Paris consulted about a new organization of their churches. But as the latter resolved in order to maintain constitutional union amid doctrinal diversity, entirely to set aside symbol and dogma, pastor Fr. Monod and Count Gasparin, the noble defenders of French Protestantism, lodged a protest, and with thirty congregations of the strict party constituted a new council at Paris in 1849, independent of

the state, as the *Union des églises évangéliques de France* with biennial synods.   Louis Napoleon gave to the Reformed Church a central council in Paris with consistories and presbyteries ; to the Lutheran, an annual general consistory as a legislative court and a standing directory as an administrative court.   The Lutheran theological faculty at Strassburg with its vigorous unconfessional science represents the westernmost school of Schleiermacher's theology.   The academy at Montauban, with Adolph Monod at its head, represents Reformed orthodoxy, not strictly confessional but coloured by methodistic piety, and Coquerel in Paris, was the head of the rationalistic party of the Reformed national church.   The lead in the reaction against rationalism since 1830 has been taken by the *Société évangélique* at Paris, which, aiming at the Protestantising of France, and using for this end Bible colportage, tract distribution, the sending out of evangelists, school instruction, etc., has developed an extraordinarily restless and successful activity.   It has been powerfully supported by the evangelical society of Geneva.   The number of Protestant clergymen in France has steadily risen, and almost every year in and out of the Catholic population new evangelical congregations have been formed, in spite of endless difficulties put in the way by Catholic courts.   In Strassburg, in 1854, the Jesuits persuaded the Catholic prefects to recall and arrest the revenues of the former St. Thomas institute, which since the Reformation had been applied to the maintenance of a Protestant gymnasium.   The prefect of Paris, however, was instructed to desist from his claims.   In the speech from the throne in 1858, the emperor declared that the government secured for Protestants full liberty of worship, without forgetting, however, that Catholicism is the religion of the majority, and the *Moniteur* commented on this imperial speech so evidently in the spirit of the *Univers*, that the prefects could not be in doubt how to understand it.   By General Espinasse, who, after the Orsini attempt on the emperor's life in 1858, officiated for a long time as Minister of the Interior, the prefects were expressly instructed, to extend their espionage of the ill-affected press to the proceedings of the evangelical societies, and to prohibit the colportage of Protestant Bibles.   On a change of minister, however, the latter enactment was withdrawn, and only agents of foreign Bible societies were interfered with.   By an imperial decree of 1859, the right of permitting of the opening of new Protestant churches and chapels was taken from the local courts and transferred to the imperial council of state.   For every Protestant congregation, so soon as it numbered 400 souls, the legal state salary for the clergymen would be paid.

5. **The Catholic Church in the Third French Republic.**—The Gambetta government, the national vindication of the 4th September, 1870, resigned its power in February, 1871, into the hands of the National

Assembly elected by the whole nation, which, although through clerical influence upon the electors predominantly monarchical and clerical, appointed the old Voltairean Thiers (died, 1877), formerly ministerial president under Louis Philippe, as alone qualified for the difficult post of president of the republic. In the necessary second vote,
indeed, there was a considerable increase of the republican and as
such thoroughly anti-clerical party; but even in its ranks it was
admitted that the establishment of France as leader of all Europe
in the fight against ultramontanism and the co-operation therein
of the clergy were the absolutely indispensable means for the
political *Revanche*, after which the hearts of all Frenchmen longed
as the hart for the water streams. A petition from five bishops
and other dignitaries to the National Assembly for the restoration
of the temporal power of the pope was set aside as inopportune.
But Archbishop Guibert of Paris, without asking the government,
proclaimed the infallibility dogma, and the minister of instruction,
Jules Simon, contented himself with warning the episcopate in a
friendly way against any further illegal steps of that kind. The
clerical party was also successful in its protest to the National Assembly against the education law, which by raising the standard of
instruction, placing it under the supervision of the state and making
inspection of schools obligatory, proposed to put an end to the terrible
ignorance of the French people as the chief cause of their deep decay
Bishop Dupanloup of Orleans was appointed president of the commission for examining it, and so its fate was sealed. Meanwhile the
people, by frequent manifestations of the Virgin, were roused to a
high pitch of religious excitement. Crowds of pilgrims encouraged
by miraculous healings flocked to our Lady of La Salette, at Lourdes,
etc. (§ 188, 6), and the consecration of *Notre Dame de la Deliverance* at
Bayeux was celebrated as a brilliant national festival. When in
May, 1873, Thiers gave way before the machinations of his opponents
and, under the new president, Marshal Macmahon, the thoroughly
clerical ministry of the Duc de Broglie got the helm of affairs, the
pilgrimage craze, mariolatry and ultramontane piety, aided by the
prefects and mayors, increased to an unparalleled extent among all
ranks. Under the Buffet ministry of 1875 the influence of clericalism
was unabated. To him it owed its most important acquisition, the
right of creating free Catholic universities wholly independent of the
State, with the privilege of conferring degrees. But when in 1876 the
new elections for the National Assembly gave an anti-clerical majority,
Buffet was obliged to resign. The new Dufaure ministry, with the
Protestant Waddington as minister of instruction, declared indeed
that it continued the liberty of instruction, but decidedly refused the
right of conferring degrees. The proposal to this effect met with the

hearty support of the new chamber of deputies. But all the greater was the jubilation of the clericals when the senate by a small majority refused its consent, and all the more eagerly was the founding of new free Catholic universities carried on, at Paris, Angers, Lyons, Lille and Toulouse, but notwithstanding every effort they only attracted a very small number of scholars,—in 1879, when they flourished most, at all the five there were only 742 students.

6. The French " Kulturkampf," 1880. — The Dufaure ministry was succeeded in December, 1876, by the semi-liberal ministry of Jules Simon, which again was driven out in a summary fashion by president Macmahon on May 16th, 1877, and replaced, on the dissolution of the chamber, by a clerical ministry under Duc de Broglie. But in the newly elected chamber the republican anti-clerical majority was so overwhelming that Macmahon, on January 30th, 1879, abandoning his motto of government, *J'y suis et j'y reste*, was at last obliged, between the alternatives offered him by Gambetta, *Se soumettre ou se démettre*, to choose the latter. His successor was Grévy, president of the Chamber, who entrusted the protestant Waddington with the forming of a new ministry in which Jules Ferry was minister of instruction. Ferry brought in a bill in March to abolish the representation of the clergy in the High Council of Education by four archiepiscopal deputies, continuing indeed the free Catholic universities, but requiring their students to enroll in a state university which alone could hold examinations and give degrees, and finally enacting by Article 7 that the right of teaching in all educational institutions should be refused to members of all religious orders and congregations not recognised by the state. The chamber deputies accepted this bill without amendment on July 9th, but the senate on March 7th, 1880, after passing six articles refused to adopt the seventh. On March 29th, the president of the republic issued on his own authority two decrees, based indeed upon earlier enactments (1789–1852), gone into desuetude indeed, but never abrogated (§ 186, 2), demanded the dissolution of the Society of Jesus, containing 1,480 members in 56 institutions, within three months, and insisted that the orders and congregations not recognised by the State, embracing 14,033 sisters in 602 institutions and 7,444 brothers in 384 institutions, in the same time should by production of their statutes and rules seek formal recognition or else be broken up. A storm of protests on the part of the bishops greeted these " *March Decrees*," and riotous demonstrations made before the Minister of Instruction at his residence at Lille expressed the protests of the students of the Catholic university there. The pope now broke his reserve and by a nuncio sent the president of the republic a holograph letter in which he declared that he must interfere on behalf of the Jesuits and the threatened orders, because they were indispensably

necessary to the wellbeing of the church. He did not wish that they should have recourse to unlawful means, but it must be understood that they would appeal to the courts for protection of their threatened civil liberties. When therefore on the morning of June 30th the police began their work of expelling the Jesuits from their houses, these lodged a complaint before the courts of invasion of their domestic peace and infringement of their personal liberty. Their schools were closed on August 31st, the end of the school year; meanwhile they had taken the precaution to transfer most of them to such as would be ready afterwards to restore them. The enforcement of the second of the March Decrees against the other orders was delayed for a while. A compromise proposed by the episcopate, favoured by the pope and not absolutely rejected even by the minister Freycinet, Waddington's successor, according to which instead of the required application for recognition all these orders should sign a declaration of loyalty, undertaking to avoid all participation in political affairs and to do nothing opposed to existing order, brought about the overthrow of this ministry in September, 1880, by the machinations from other motives of the president of the chamber and latent dictator, Leon Gambetta. At the head of the new ministry was Ferry, who held the portfolio of instruction, and under him the carrying out of the second March Decree began on October 16th, 1880. Up to the meeting of the chamber in November 261 monasteries had been vacated: the rest, as from the first all female congregations, were spared, so that France with its colonies and mission stations still number 4,288 male and 14,990 female settlements of spiritual orders, the former with about 32,000, the latter with about 166,200 inmates.— The expulsion of the Jesuits, as well as the more recent of the other orders, was, however, stoutly opposed. The police told off for this duty found doors shut and barricaded against them or defended by fanatical peasants and mobs of shrieking women, so that they had often to be stormed and broken up by the military. Still more threatening than this opposition was the reaction which began to assert itself at the instance of the almost thoroughly ultramontane jurists of the country, a survival of the times of Napoleon III. and Macmahon. An advocate Rousse, who publicly stated the opinion that the March Decrees were illegal and therefore not binding, was supported by 2,000 attorneys and over 200 corporations of attorneys and by many distinguished university jurists. More than 200 state officials and many judiciary and police officers, together with several officers of the army, tendered their resignations so as to avoid taking part in the execution of the decrees. When it became clear that unfavourable verdicts would be given by the courts invoked by the Jesuits against the executors of the decree, as indeed was soon actually done by several courts, the government lodged an appeal against their competence before the tribunal of conflicts which also actually in regard to all such cases pronounced them incompetent and their decisions therefore null and void; but the complainers insisted that their complaints should be taken to a Council of State as the only court suitable to deal with charges against officials, which, as might be expected, was not done.

7. In the future course of the French "Kulturkampf" the most important proceedings of the government were the following: The abolition of the institute of military chaplains, highly serviceable in ultramontanizing the officers, was carried out in 1880, as well as the requirement that the clergy and teachers should give military service for one year, and subsequently also military escorts to the Corpus Christi procession were forbidden. In 1880 the Municipal Council of Paris, with the concurrence of the prefect of the Seine, forbad the continuance of the beautiful building of the church of the Heart of Jesus begun in 1875 on Montmartre (§ 188, 12), confiscating the site that had been granted for it. In 1881 the churchyards were relieved of their denominational character, and the following year the right of managing them, with permission of merely civil interment without the aid of a clergyman, was transferred from the ecclesiastical to the civil authorities. By introducing in 1880 high schools for girls with boarding establishments an end was put to the education of girls of the upper ranks in nunneries, which had hitherto been the almost exclusive practice. Far more sweeping was the School Act brought in by the radical minister of worship, Paul Bert, and first enforced in October, 1886, which made attendance compulsory, relegated religious instruction wholly to the church and home, and absolutely excluded all the clergy from the right of giving any sort of instruction in the public schools, and demanded the removal of all crucifixes and other religious symbols from the school buildings. In December, 1884, a tax was imposed on the property of all religious orders, also the state allowance for the five Catholic seminaries with only thirty-seven students was withdrawn, and many other important deductions made upon the budget for Catholic worship, which at first the senate opposed, but at last agreed to. The Divorce Bill frequently introduced since 1881, which permitted parties to marry again, and gave disposal of the matter to the civil court, got the assent of the senate only in the end of July, 1884. The clericals were also greatly offended by the decree passed in May, 1885, which closed the church of St. Genoveva, the former Pantheon, as a place of worship and made it again a burial place for distinguished Frenchmen. This resolution was first carried out by placing there the remains of Victor Hugo. Amid these and many other injuries to its interests the Roman curia, concentrat-

ing all its energies upon the German "Kulturkampf," endeavoured to keep things back in a moderate way. Yet in July, 1883, the pope addressed to president Grévy a friendly but earnest remonstrance, which he treated simply as a private letter and, without communicating it officially to his cabinet, answered that apart from parliament he could not act, but that so far as he and his ministry were able they would seek to avoid conflict with the holy see. And in fact the government, especially after the overthrow of the Gambetta ministry in 1882, often successfully opposed the proposal of the radical chamber, *e.g.* the separation of church and state, the abrogation of the concordat, the recall of the embassy to the V tican, the abolition of religious oaths in the proceedings of the courts, the stopping of the state subvention of a million francs for payment of salaries in seminaries for priests, etc.

8. **The Protestant Churches under the Third Republic.** — Since the French Reformed began to emulate their Catholic countrymen in wild Chauvinism, fanatical hatred of Germany and unreasoning enthusiasm for the *Revanche*, they were left by the advancing clerical party unmolested in respect of life, confession and worship during the time of war. The Lutherans on the other hand, consisting, although on French territory, mainly of German emigrants and settlers, even their French members not so disposed to Chauvinistic extravagance, were obliged to atone for this double offence by expulsion from house and home and by various injuries to their ecclesiastical interests. After the conclusion of peace, especially under Thiers' moderate government, this fanaticism gradually cooled down, so that the expelled Germans returned and the churches and institutions that had been destroyed were restored, so far as means would allow. By the decree of Waddington, the minister of instruction, of date March 27th, 1877, instead of the theological faculty of Strassburg, now lost for the French Lutheran church, one for both Protestant churches was founded in Paris.—The Lutheran Church, in consequence of the cession of Alsace-Lorraine, had only sixty-four out of 278 pastorates and six out of forty-four consistories remaining. At the general synod convened at Paris, in July, 1872, by the government for reorganizing the Lutheran church it was resolved: To form two inspectorates independent of each other—Paris, predominantly orthodox, Mömpelgard, predominantly liberal; the general assembly, which meets every third year alternately at Mömpelgard and Paris, to consist of delegates from both. The two inspectorates are to correspond in administrative matters directly with the minister of public instruction, but in everything referring to confession, doctrine, worship and discipline, the general assembly is the supreme authority. In regard to the confessional question they agreed to the statement

that the holy Scripture is the supreme authority in matters of faith, and the Augsburg Confession the basis of the legal constitution of the church. An express undertaking on the part of the clergy to this effect is not, however, insisted upon. Only in 1879 could this constitution obtain legal sanction by the State, and that only after considerable modification in the direction of liberalism, especially in reference to electoral qualification. In consequence of this the first ordinary general assembly held in Paris in May, 1881, found both parties in a conciliatory mood.—The Reformed Church, with about 500 pastorates and 105 consistories, summoned by order of government a newly constituted General Assemby at Paris, in June, 1872. Prominent among the leaders of the orthodox party was the aged ex-minister Guizot; the leaders of the liberals were Coquerel and Colani. The former supported the proposal of Professor Bois of Montauban, who insisted on the frank and full confession of holy Scripture as the sovereign authority in matters of faith, of Christ as the only Son of God, and of justification by faith as the legal basis of instruction, worship and discipline; while the latter protested against every attempt to lay down an obligatory and exclusive confession. The orthodox party prevailed and the dissenters who would not yield were struck off the voting lists. When now in consequence of the complaint of the liberal party the summoning of an ordinary general assembly was refused by the government, the orthodox party repeatedly met in "official" provincial and general assemblies without state sanction. The council of state then declared all decisions regarding voting qualifications passed by the synod of 1872 to be null and void, the minister of worship, Ferry, ordered the readmission of electors struck from the lists, and his successor Bert legalized, by a decree of March 25th, 1882, the division of the Parisian consistorial circuit into two independent consistories of Paris and Versailles, moved for by the liberal party but opposed by the orthodox. But upon the elections for the new consistory of Paris, ordered in spite of all protests, and for the presbyteries of the eight parishes assigned to it, contrary to all expectation, in seven of these the elections with great majorities were in favour of the orthodox. and the first official document issued by the new consistory was a solemn protest against the decree to which it owed its existence. Under such circumstances the government as well as the liberal party had no desire for the calling of an official general assembly, and the latter resolved at a general assembly at Nimes, in October, 1882, to institute official synods of their own for consultation and protection of their own interests.

§ 204. ITALY.

In Italy matters returned to their old position after the restoration of 1814. But liberalism, aiming at the liberty and unity of Italy, gained the mastery, and where for the time it prevailed, the Jesuits were expelled, and the power of the clergy restricted; where it failed, both came back with greatly increased importance. The arms of Austria and subsequently also of France stamped out on all sides the revolutionary movements. Pius IX., who at first was not indisposed, contrary to all traditions of the papacy, to put himself at the head of the national party, was obliged bitterly to regret his dealings with the liberals (§ 185, 2). Sardinia, Modena and Naples put the severest strain upon the bow of the restoration, while Parma and Tuscany distinguished themselves by adopting liberal measures in a moderate degree. Sardinia, however, in 1840 came to a better mind. Charles Albert first broke ground with a more liberal constitution, and in 1848 proclaimed himself the deliverer of Italy, but yielded to the arms of Austria. His son Victor Emanuel II. succeeded amid singularly favourable circumstances in uniting the whole peninsula under his sceptre as a united kingdom of Italy governed by liberal institutions.

1. **The Kingdom of Sardinia.**—Victor Emanuel I. after the restoration had nothing else to do but to recall the Jesuits, to hand over to them the whole management of the schools, and, guided and led by them in everything, to restore the church and state to the condition prevailing before 1789. Charles Felix (1821–1831) carried still further the absolutist-reactionary endeavours of his predecessor, and even Charles Albert (1831–1849) refused for a long time to realize the hopes which the liberal party had previously placed in him. Only in the second decade of his reign did he begin gradually to display a more liberal tendency, and at last in 1848 when, in consequence of the French Revolution, Lombardy rose against the Austrian rule, he placed himself at the head of the national movement for freeing Italy

from the yoke of strangers. But the king gloried in as "the sword of Italy" was defeated and obliged to abdicate. Victor Emanuel II. (1849-1878) allowed meanwhile the liberal constitution of his father to remain and indeed carried it out to the utmost. The minister of justice, Siccardi, proposed a new legislative code which abolished all clerical jurisdiction in civil and criminal proceedings, as also the right of asylum and of exacting tithes, the latter with moderate compensation. It was passed by parliament and subscribed by the king in 1850. The clergy, with archbishop Fransoni of Turin at their head, protested with all their might against these sacrilegious encroachments on the rights of the church. Fransoni was on this account committed for a month to prison and, when he refused the last sacrament to a minister, was regularly sentenced to deposition and banishment from the country. Pius IX. thwarted all attempts to obtain a new concordat. But the government went recklessly forward. As Fransoni from his exile in France continued his agitation, all the property of the archiepiscopal chair was in 1854 sequestered and a number of cloisters were closed. Soon all penalties in the penal code for spreading non-Catholic doctrines were struck out and non-Catholic soldiers freed from compulsory attendance at mass on Sundays and festivals. The chief blow now fell on March 2nd, 1855, in the Cloister Act, which abolished all orders and cloisters not devoted to preaching, teaching, and nursing the sick. In consequence 331 out of 605 cloisters were shut up. The pope ceased not to condemn all these sacrilegious and church robbing acts, and when his threats were without result, thundered the great excommunication in July, 1855, against all originators, aiders, and abettors of such deeds. Among the masses this indeed caused some excitement, but it never came to an explosion.

2. **The Kingdom of Italy.**—Amid such vigorous progress the year 1859 came round with its fateful Franco-Italian war. The French alliance had not indeed, as it promised, made Italy free to the Adriatic, but by the peace of Villafranca the whole of Lombardy was given to the kingdom of Sardinia as a present from the emperor of the French. In the same year by popular vote Tuscany, including Modena and Parma, and in the following year the kingdom of the two Sicilies, as well as the three provinces of the States of the Church, revolted and were annexed, so that the new kingdom of Italy embraced the whole of the peninsula, with the exception of Venice, Rome and the Campagna. Prussia's remarkable successes in the seven days' German war of 1866 shook Venice like ripe fruit into the lap of her Italian ally, and the day of Sedan, 1870, prepared the way for the addition of Rome and the Campagna (§ 185, 3).—In Lombardy and then also in Venice, immediately after they had been taken possession of, the concordat with Austria was abrogated and the Jesuits expelled. Ecclesiastical tithes

on the produce of the soil were abolished throughout the whole kingdom, begging was forbidden the mendicant friars as unworthy of a spiritual order, ecclesiastical property was put under state control and the support of the clergy provided for by state grants. In 1867 the government began the appropriation and conversion of the church property; in 1870 all religious orders were dissolved, with exception for the time being of those in Rome, wherever they did not engage in educational and other useful works. In May, 1873, this law was extended to the Roman province, only it was not to be applied to the generals of orders in Rome. Nuns and some monks were also allowed to remain in their cloisters situated in unpeopled districts. The amount of state pensions paid to monks and nuns reached in 1882 the sum of eleven million lire, at the rate of 330 lire for each person. The abolition of the theological faculties in ten Italian universities in 1873, because these altogether had only six students of theology, was regarded by the curia rather as a victory than a defeat. The newly appointed bishops were forbidden by the pope to produce their credentials for inspection in order to obtain their salaries from the government. The loss of temporalities thus occasioned was made up by Pius IX. out of Peter's pence flowing in so abundantly from abroad; each bishop receiving 500 and each archbishop 700 lire in the month. Leo XIII., however, felt obliged in 1879, owing to the great decrease in the Peter's pence contributions, to cancel this enactment and to permit the bishops to accept the state allowance. In consequence of the civil marriage law passed in 1866 having been altogether ignored by the clergy, nearly 400,000 marriages had down to the close of 1878 received only ecclesiastical sanction, and the offspring of such parties would be regarded in the eye of the law as illegitimate. To obviate this difficulty a law was passed in May, 1879, which insisted that in all cases civil marriage must precede the ecclesiastical ceremony, and clergymen, witnesses and parties engaging in an illegal marriage should suffer three or six months' imprisonment; but all marriages contracted in accordance merely with church forms before the passing of this law might be legitimized by being entered on the civil register. —Finally in January, 1884, the controversy pending since 1873 as to whether the rich property of the Roman propaganda (§ 156, 9) amounting to twenty million lire should be converted into state consols was decided by the supreme court in favour of the curia, which had pronounced these funds international because consisting of presents and contributions from all lands. But not only was the revenue of the propaganda subjected to a heavy tax, but also all increase of its property forbidden. In vain did the pope by his nuncios call for the intervention of foreign nations. None of these were inclined to meddle in the internal affairs of Italy. The curia now devised the plan of affiliating a number of societies outside of Italy to the propaganda for receiving and administering donations and presents.

3. The Evangelization of Italy.—Emigrant Protestants of various nationalities had at an early date, by the silent sufferance of the respective governments, formed small evangelical congregations in some of the Italian cities; in Venice and Leghorn during the seventeenth century, at Bergamo in 1807, at Florence in 1826, at Milan in 1847. Also by aid of the diplomatic intervention of Prussia and England, the erection of Protestant chapels for the embassy was allowed at Rome in 1819, at Naples in 1825, and at Florence in 1826. When in 1848 Italy's hopes from the liberal tendencies of Pius IX. were bitterly disappointed, Protestant sympathies began to spread far and wide through the land, even among native Catholics, fostered by English missionaries, Bibles and tracts, which the governments sought in vain to check by prisons, penitentiaries and exile. Persecution began in 1851 in Tuscany, where, in spite of the liberty of faith and worship guaranteed by the constitution of 1848, Tuscan subjects taking part in the Italian services in the chapel of the Prussian embassy at Florence were punished with six months' hard labour, and in the following year the pious pair Francesco and Rosa Madiai were sentenced to four years' rigorous punishment in a penitentiary for the crime of having edified themselves and their household by reading the Bible. In vain did the Evangelical Alliance remonstrate (§ 178, 8), in vain did even the king of Prussia intercede. But when, stirred up by public opinion in England, the English premier Lord Palmerston offered to secure the requirement of Christian humanity by means of British ships of war, the grand-duke got rid of both martyrs by banishing them from the country in 1853. In proportion as the union of Italy under Victor Emanuel II. advanced, the field for evangelistic effort and the powers devoted thereto increased. So it was too since 1860 in Southern Italy. But when in 1866 a Protestant congregation began to be formed at Barletta in Naples, a fanatical priest roused a popular mob in which seventeen persons were killed and torn in pieces. The government put down the uproar and punished the miscreants, and the nobler portion of the nation throughout the whole land collected for the families of those murdered. The work of evangelization supported by liberal contributions chiefly from England, but also from Holland, Switzerland, and the German *Gustav-Adolf-Verein* (§ 178, 1), advanced steadily in spite of occasional brutal interferences of the clergy and the mob, so that soon in all the large cities and in many of the smaller towns of Italy and Sicily there were thriving and flourishing little evangelical congregations of converted native Catholics, numbering as many as 182 in 1882.

4. The chief factor in the evangelization of Italy as far as the

southern coast of Sicily was the old **Waldensian Church,** which for three hundred years had occupied the Protestant platform in the spirit of Calvinism (§ 139, 25). Remnants consisting of some 200,000 souls still survived in the valleys of Piedmont, almost without protection of law amid constant persecution and oppressions (§ 153, 5), moderated only by Prussian and English intervention. But when Sardinia headed Italian liberalism in 1848 religious liberty and all civil rights were secured to them. A Waldensian congregation was then formed in the capital, Turin, which was strengthened by numerous Protestant refugees from other parts of Italy. But in 1854 a split occurred between the two elements in it. The new Italian converts objected, not altogether without ground, against the old Waldensians that by maintaining their church government with its centre in the valleys, the so-called "Tables" and their old forms of constitution, doctrine and worship, much too contracted and narrow for the enlarged boundaries of the present, they thought more of Waldensianizing than of evangelizing Italy. Besides, their language since 1630, when a plague caused their preachers and teachers to withdraw from Geneva, had been French, and the national Italian pride was disposed on this domain also to unfurl her favourite banner "*Italia farà da se.*" The division spread from Turin to the other congregations. At the head of the separatists, afterwards designated the "*Free Italian Church*" (*Chiesa libera*), stood Dr. Luigi Desanctis, a man of rich theological culture and glowing eloquence, who, when Catholic priest and theologian of the inquisition at Rome, became convinced of the truth of the evangelical confession, joined the evangelical church at Malta in 1847 and wrought from 1852 with great success in the congregation at Turin. After ten years' faithful service in the newly formed free church he felt obliged, owing to the Darbyite views (§ 211, 11) that began to prevail in it, to attach himself again in 1864 to the Waldensians, who meanwhile had been greatly liberalised. He now officiated for them till his death in 1869 as professor of theology at Florence, and edited their journal *Eco della verità*. This journal was succeeded in 1873 by the able monthly *Rivista Cristiana*, edited at Florence by Prof. Emilio Comba.—After Desanctis left the *Chiesa libera* its chief representative was the ex-Barnabite father Alessandro Gavazzi of Naples. Endowed with glowing eloquence and remarkable popularity as a lecturer, he appeared at Rome in 1848 as a politico-religious orator, attached himself to the evangelical church in London in 1850, and undertook the charge of the evangelical Italian congregation there. He returned to Italy in 1860 and accompanied the hero of Italian liberty, Garibaldi, as his military chaplain, preaching to the people everywhere with his leonine voice with equal enthusiasm of Victor Emanuel as the only saviour of Italy and of Jesus Christ as the only Saviour of sinners.

He then joined the *Chiesa libera*, and, as he himself obtained gradually fuller acquaintance with evangelical truth, wrought zealously in organizing the congregations hitherto almost entirely isolated from one another.   At a general assembly at Milan in 1870, deputies from thirty-two congregations drew up a simple biblical confession of faith, and in the following year at Florence a constitutional code was adopted which recognised the necessity of the pastoral office, of annual assemblies, and a standing evangelization committee.   They now took the name "Unione della Chiesa libere in Italia."   The predominantly Darbyist congregations, which had not taken part in these constitutional assemblies, have since formed a community of their own as Chiesa Cristiana, depending only on the immediate leading of the Holy Spirit, rejecting every sort of ecclesiastical and official organization, and denouncing infant baptism as unevangelical.—Besides these three national Italian churches, English and American Methodists and Baptists carry on active missions.   On May 1st, 1884, the evangelical denominations at a general assembly in Florence, with the exception only of the Darbyist *Chiesa Cristiana*, joined in a confederation to meet annually in an "Italian Evangelical Congress" as a preparation for ecclesiastical union.   When, however, the various Methodist and Baptist denominations began to check the progress of the work of union, the two leading bodies, the Waldensians and the Free Church party, separated from them.   A committee chosen from these two sketched at Florence in 1885 a basis of union, according to which the Free Church adopted the confession and church order of the Waldensians, subject to revision by the joint synods, their theological school at Rome was to be amalgamated with the Waldensian school at Florence, and the united church was to take the name of the "Evangelical Church of Italy."   But a Waldensian synod in September, 1886, resolved to hold by the ancient name of the "Waldensian Church."   Whether the "Free Church" will agree to this demand is not yet known.

§ 205. SPAIN AND PORTUGAL.

No European country has during the nineteenth century been the scene of so many revolutions, outbreaks and civil wars, of changes of government, ministries and constitutions, sometimes of a clerical absolutist, sometimes of a democratic radical tendency, and in none has revolution gone so unsparingly for the time against hierarchy, clergy and monasticism, as in unfortunate Spain.   Portugal too passed through similar struggles, which, however, did not prove so dreadfully disordering to the commonwealth as those of Spain.

1. **Spain under Ferdinand VII. and Maria Christina.**—Joseph Bonaparte (1808–1813) had given to the Spaniards a constitution of the French pattern, abolishing inquisition and cloisters. The constitution which the Cortes proclaimed in 1812 carried out still further the demands of political liberalism, but still declared the apostolic Roman Catholic religion as alone true to be the religion of the Spanish nation and forbad the exercise of any other. Ferdinand VII., whom Napoleon restored in December, 1813, hastened to restore the inquisition, the cloisters and despotism, especially from 1815 under the direction of the Jesuits highly esteemed by him. The revolution of 1820 indeed obliged him to reintroduce the constitution of 1812 and to banish the Jesuits; but scarcely had the feudal clerical party of the apostolic Junta with their army of faith in the field and Bourbon French intervention under the Duke of Angoulême again made his way clear, than he began to crush as before by means of his Jesuit Camarilla every liberal movement in church and state. But all the more successful was the reaction of liberalism in the civil war which broke out after Ferdinand's death under the regency of his fourth wife, the intriguing Maria Christina (1833–1837). The revolution now erected an inquisition, but it was one directed against the clergy and monks, and celebrated its *autos de fe*, but these were in the form of spoliation of cloisters and massacres of monks. Ecclesiastical tithes were abolished, all monkish orders suspended, the cloisters closed, ecclesiastical goods declared national property, and the papal nuncio sent over the frontier. A threatening papal allocution of 1841 only increased the violence of the Cortes, and when Gregory XVI. in 1842 pronounced all decrees of the government null and void, it branded all intercourse with Rome as an offence against the state.

2. **Spain under Isabella II., 1843–1865.**—Ferdinand VII., overlooking the right of his brother Don Carlos, had, by abolishing the Salic law, secured the throne to Isabella, his own and Maria Christina's daughter. After the Cortes of 1843 had declared Isabella of age in her thirteenth year, the Spanish government became more and more favourable to the restoration. After long negotiations and vacillations under constantly changing ministries a concordat was at last drawn up in 1851, which returned the churches and cloisters that had not been sold, allowed compensation for what had been sold, reduced the number of bishoprics by six, put education and the censorship of the press under the oversight of the bishops, and declared the Catholic religion the only one to be tolerated. But although in 1854 the Holy Virgin was named generalissima of the brave army and her image at Atocha had

been decorated by the queen with a band of the Golden Fleece, a revolution soon broke out in the army which threatened to deal the finishing stroke to ultramontanism. Meanwhile it had not fully permeated the republican party. The proposal of unrestricted liberty to all forms of worship was supported by a small minority, and the new constitution of 1855 called upon the Spanish nation to maintain and guard the Catholic religion which "the Spaniards profess"; yet no Spaniard was to be persecuted on account of his faith, so long as he did not commit irreligious acts. A new law determined the sale of all church and cloister property, and compensation therefore by annual rents according to the existing concordat. Several bishops had to be banished owing to their continued opposition; the pope protested and recalled his legates. Clerical influence meanwhile regained power over the queen. The sale of church and cloister property was stopped, and previous possessors were indemnified for what had been already sold. Owing to frequent change of ministry, each of which manifested a tendency different from its predecessor, it was only in 1859 that matters were settled by a new concordat. In it the government admitted the inalienability of church property, admitted the unrestricted right of the church to obtain new property of any kind, and declared itself ready to exchange state paper money for property that had fallen into decay according to the estimation of the bishops. The queen proved her Catholic zeal at the instigation of the nun Patrocinio by fanatical persecution of Protestants, and hearty but vain sympathies for the sufferings of the pope and the expatriated Italian princes. Pius IX. rewarded Isabella, who seemed to him adorned with all the virtues, by sending her in 1868 the consecrated rose at a time when she was causing public scandal more than ever by her private life, and by her proceedings with her paramour Marforio had lost the last remnant of the respect and confidence of the Spanish nation. Eight months later her reign was at an end. The provisional government now ordered the suppression of the Society of Jesus, as well as of all cloister and spiritual associations, and in 1869 the Cortes sanctioned the draught of a new civil constitution, which required the Spanish nation to maintain the Catholic worship, but allowed the exercise of other forms of worship to strangers and as cases might arise even to natives, and generally made all political and civil rights independent of religious profession.

8. Spain under Alphonso XII., 1875–1885.—When Isabella's son returned to Spain in January, 1875, in his seventeenth year, he obtained the blessing of his sponsor the pope on his ascending the throne, promised to the Catholic church powerful support, but also to non-Catholics the maintenance of liberty of worship. How he meant to perform both is shown by a decree of 10th February, 1875, which,

abolishing the civil marriage law passed by the Cortes in 1870, gave back to the Catholic church the administration of marriage and matters connected therewith ; for all persons living in Spain, however, " who professed another than the true faith," as well as for " the bad Catholics," to whom ecclesiastical marriage on account of church censures is refused, liberty was given to contract a civil marriage; but this did not apply to apostate priests, monks, and nuns, to whom any sort of marriage is for ever refused, and whose previously contracted marriages are invalid, without, however, affecting the legitimacy of children already born of such connections.—Against the draught of the new constitution, whose eleventh article indeed affords toleration to all dissenting forms of worship, but prohibits any public manifestation thereof outside of their place of worship and burial grounds, Pius IX. protested as infringing upon the still existing concordat in its "noblest" part, and aiming a serious blow at the Catholic church. The Cortes, however, sanctioned it in 1876.

4. The Evangelization of Spain.—A number of Bibles and tracts, as well as a religious paper in Spanish called *el Albo*, found entrance into Spain from the English settlement at Gibraltar, without Spain being able even in the most flourishing days of the restoration to prevent it, and evangelical sympathies began more or less openly to be expressed. Franc. Ruat, formerly a lascivious Spanish poet, who was awakened at Turin by the preaching of the Waldensian Desanctis, and by reading the Bible had obtained knowledge of evangelical truths, appeared publicly after the publication of the new constitution of 1855 as a preacher of the gospel in Spain. The reaction that soon set in, however, secured for him repeated imprisonments, and finally in 1856 sentence of banishment for life. He then wrought for several years successfully in Gibraltar, next in London, afterwards in Algiers among Spanish residents, till the new civil constitution of 1868 allowed him to return to Spain, where, in the service of the German mission at Madrid, he gathered around him an evangelical congregation, to which he ministered till his death in 1878. While labouring in Gibraltar he won to the evangelical faith among others the young officer Manuel Matamoros, living there as a political refugee. This noble man, whose whole career, till his death in exile in 1866, was a sore martyrdom for the truth, became the soul of the whole movement, against which the government in 1861 and 1862 took the severest measures. By intercepted correspondence the leaders and many of the members of the secret evangelical propaganda were discovered and thrown into prison. The final judgment condemned the leaders of the movement to severe punishment in penitentiaries and the galleys. Infliction of these sentences had already begun when the queen found herself obliged, by a visit to Madrid in

1863 of a deputation of the Evangelical Alliance (§ 178, 3), consisting of the most distinguished and respected Protestants of all lands, to commute them to banishment.—After Isabella's overthrow in 1868, permission was given for the building of the first Protestant church in Madrid, where a congregation soon gathered of more than 2,000 souls. In Seville an almost equally strong congregation obtained for its services what had been a church of the Jesuits. Also at Cordova a considerable congregation was collected, and in almost all the other large cities there were largely attended places of worship. Several of those banished under Isabella, who had returned after her overthrow, Carrasco, Trigo, Alhama, and others, increased by new converts who had received their theological training at Geneva, Lausanne, etc., and supported by American, English and German fellow-labourers, such as the brothers F. and H. Fliedner, wrought with unwearied zeal as preachers and pastors, for the spreading and deeper grounding of the gospel among their countrymen. With the restoration of the monarchy in 1875, the oppression of the Protestants was renewed with increasing severity. The widest possible interpretation was given to the prohibition of every public manifestation of dissenting worship in Article XI. of the constitution. The excesses and insults of the mob, whose fanaticism was stirred up by the clergy, were left unpunished and uncensured. Even the most sorely abused and injured Protestants were themselves subjected to imprisonment as disturbers of the peace. No essential improvement in their condition resulted from the liberal ministry of Sagasta in 1881. Nevertheless the number of evangelical congregations continued steadily though slowly to increase, so that now they number more than sixty, with somewhere about 15,000 native Protestant members.—Besides these an *Iglesia Española* arose in 1881, consisting of eight congregations, which may be regarded to some extent as a national Spanish counterpart to the Old Catholicism of Germany. Its founder and first bishop is Cabrera, formerly a Catholic priest, who, after having wrought from 1868 in the service of the Edinburgh (Presbyterian) Evangelization Society as preacher in Seville, and then in Madrid, received in 1880 episcopal consecration from the Anglican bishop Riley of Mexico (§ 209, 1), then visiting Madrid. Although thus of Anglican origin, the church directed by him wishes not to be Anglican, but Spanish episcopal. It attaches itself therefore, while accepting the thirty-nine Articles of the Anglican Church, in the sketch of its order of service in the Spanish language, more to the old Mozarabic ritual (§ 88, 1) than to the Anglican liturgy.[1]

---

[1] Borrow, "The Bible in Spain." 2 vols. London, 1843.

5. The Church in Portugal.—Portugal after some months followed the example of the Spanish revolution of 1820. John VI. (1816–1826) confirmed the new constitution, drawn up after the pattern of the democratic Spanish constitution of 1812, enacting the seizure of church property and the suppression of the monasteries. But a counter revolution, led by the younger son of the king, Dom Miguel, obliged him in 1823 to repudiate it and to return to the older constitution. But he persistently resisted the reintroduction of the Jesuits. After his death in 1826, the legitimate heir, Pedro I. of Brazil, abandoned his claims to the Portuguese throne in favour of his daughter Donna Maria II. da Gloria, then under a year old, whom he betrothed to his brother Dom Miguel. Appointed regent, Dom Miguel took the oath to the constitution, but immediately broke his oath, had himself proclaimed king, recalled the Jesuits, and, till his overthrow in 1834, carried on a clerical monarchical reign of terror. Dom Pedro, who had meanwhile vacated the Brazilian throne, as regent again suppressed all monkish orders, seized the property of the church, and abolished ecclesiastical tithes, but died in the same year. His daughter Donna Maria, now pronounced of age and proclaimed queen (1834–1853), amid continual revolutions and changes of the constitution, manifested an ever-growing inclination to reconciliation with Rome. In 1841 she negotiated about a concordat, and showed herself so submissive that the pope rewarded her in 1842 with the consecrated golden rose. But the liberal Cortes resisted the introduction of the concordat, and maintained the right of veto by the civil government as well as the rest of the restrictions upon the hierarchy, and the *Codigo penal* of 1882 threatened the Catholic clergy with heavy fines and imprisonment for every abuse of their spiritual perogatives and every breach of the laws of the State. In 1857 a concordat was at last agreed to, which, however, was adopted by the representatives of the people not before 1859, and then only by a small majority. Its chief provisions consist in the regulating of the patronage rights of the crown in regard to existing and newly created bishoprics. The relation of government to the curia, however, still continued strained. The constitution declares generally that the Catholic Apostolic Romish Church is the state religion. A Portuguese who passes over from it to another loses thereby his civil rights as a citizen. Yet no one is to be persecuted on account of his religion. The erection of Protestant places of worship, but not in church form, and also of burial grounds, where necessary, is permitted.—Evangelization has made but little progress in Portugal. The first evangelical congregation, with Anglican episcopal constitution, was founded at Lisbon by a Spanish convert, Don Angelo Herrero de Mora, who in the service of the Bible Society had edited a revision of the old Spanish Bible in New York, and had there been naturalized as an American citizen. Consisting originally of American and English Protestants, about a hundred Spanish and Portuguese converts have since 1868 gradually attached themselves to it, the latter after they had been made Spanish instead of Portuguese subjects. After the pattern of this mother congregation, two others have been formed in the neighbourhood of Lisbon and one at Oporto.

§ 206. RUSSIA.

The Russian government since the time of Alexander I. has sought amid many difficulties to advance the education and enlightenment of the people, and to elevate the orthodox church by securing a more highly cultured clergy, and to increase its influence upon the life of the people; a task which proved peculiarly difficult in consequence of the wide-spread anti-ecclesiastical spirit (§ 210, 3) and the incomparably more dangerous antichristian Nihilism (§ 212, 6).—The Catholic church, mainly represented in what had before been the kingdom of Poland, had, in consequence of the repeated revolutionary agitation of the Poles, in which the clergy had zealously taken part by stirring up fanaticism among the people and converting their religion and worship into a vehicle of rebellion, so compromised itself that the government, besides taking away the national political privileges, reduced more and more the rights and liberties granted to the church as such.—The prosperous development of the evangelical church in Russia, which, through the absolutely faultless loyalty of its members, had hitherto enjoyed the hearty protection of the government, in 1845 and 1846, and afterwards in 1883, in consequence of numerous conversions among Esthonian and Livonian peasants, was checked by incessant persecutions.

1. The Orthodox National Church.—The evangelical influences introduced from the West during the previous century, especially among the higher clergy, found further encouragement under Alexander I.,

A.D. 1801–1825. Himself affected by the evangelical pietism of Madame Krüdener (§ 176, 2), he aimed at the elevation of the orthodox church in this direction, founded clerical seminaries and public schools, and took a lively interest in Bible circulation among the Russian people. But under Nicholas I., A.D. 1825–1855, a reaction proceeding from the holy synod set in which unweariedly sought to seal the orthodox church hermetically against all evangelical influences. Also during the reign of Alexander II., A.D. 1855–1881, a reign singularly fruitful in civil reforms, this tendency was even more rigidly illustrated, while with the consent and aid of the holy synod every effort was put forth to improve the church according to its own principles. Specially active in this work was Count Tolstoi, minister of instruction and also procurator of the holy synod. A committee presided over by him produced a whole series of useful reforms in 1868, which were approved by the synod and confirmed by the emperor. While the inferior clergy had hitherto formed an order by themselves, all higher ranks of preferment were now opened to them, but, on the other hand, the obligation of priests' sons to remain in the order of their fathers was abolished. The clamant abuse of putting mere clerks and sextons to do the work of priests was also now put a stop to, and training in clerical seminaries or academies was made compulsory. Previously only married men could hold the offices of deacon and priest; now widowers and bachelors were admitted, so soon as they reached the age of forty years. In order to increase the poor incomes many churches had not their regular equipment of clergy, and instead of the full set of priest, deacon, sub-deacon, reader, sexton, and doorkeeper, in the poorer churches there were only priest and reader. Order was restored to monastic life, now generally grown dissolute, by a fixed rule of a common table and uniform dress, etc. In 1860 an Orthodox Church Society for Missions among the peoples of the Caucasus, and in 1866 a second for Pagans and Mohammedans throughout the empire, were founded, both under the patronage of the empress. The Russian church also cleverly took advantage of political events to carry on missionary work in Japan (§ 184, 6). A society of the "Friends of Intellectual Enlightenment," founded in St. Petersburg in 1872, aimed chiefly at the religious improvement of the cultured classes in the spirit of the orthodox church by means of tracts and addresses, while agreeing with foreign confessions as to the nature and characteristics of the true church. Under Alexander III., since A.D. 1881, the emperor's former tutor Pobedownoszew, with the conviction of the incomparable superiority of his church, and believing that by it and only by it could the dangerous commotions of the present be overcome (§ 212, 6) and Russia regenerated, as procurator of the holy synod has zealously wrought in this direction.—But meanwhile a new impulse was given to the evangelical movement in aristocratic circles by Lord Radstock, who appeared in St. Petersburg in 1870. The addresses delivered by him in French in the salons of the fashionable world won a success scarcely to be looked for. The most famous gain was the conversion of a hitherto proud, worldly, rich and popular Colonel of the Guards, called Paschcow, who now turned the beautiful ball-room of his palatial residence into a prayer-meeting room, and with all the enthusiasm of a neophyte proclaimed successfully among high and low the newly won saving truth in a Biblical evangelical spirit, though not without a methodistic flavour. The excitement thus created led to police interference, and finally, when he refused to abstain from spreading his religious views among the members of the orthodox church by the circulation of evangelical tracts in the Russian language, he was, at the instigation of the holy synod and its all powerful procurator, banished first from St. Petersburg and then in 1884 from the empire, whereupon he withdrew to London.

2. The Catholic Church.—After the Greeks in the old West Russian provinces (§ 151, 3), who had been forcibly united to Rome in 1596, had again in 1772, in consequence of the first partition of Poland, come under Russian rule, the government sought to restore them also to the orthodox national church. This was first accomplished under Nicholas I., when at the synod of Polosk in 1839 they themselves spontaneously expressed a wish to be thus reunited with the mother church. Rome thus lost two million members. But the allocution directed against this robbery by Gregory XVI. was without effect, and the public opinion of Europe saw a case of historical justice in this reunion, though effected not without severe measures against those who proved obstinate and rebellious. Yet there always remained a considerable remnant, about one-third of a million, under the bishop of Chelun, in the Romish communion. But even these in 1875, after many disturbances with the prelate Popiel at their head, almost wholly severed their connection with the pope, and were again received into the bosom of the orthodox national church. In a memorial addressed to the emperor for this purpose, they declared they were led to this on the one hand by the continual endeavour of the curia and its partisans, by Latinizing their old Greek liturgy and Polandizing the people, to overthrow their old Russian nationality, and on the other hand, by their aversion to the new papal dogmas of the immaculate conception of Mary and the infallibility of the pope. —The insurrection of the Poles against Russian rule in 1830, which even Pope Gregory XVI. condemned, bore bitter fruits for the Catholic church of that country. The organic statute of 1832 indeed secured

anew to the Poles religious liberty, but the bishops were prohibited holding any direct communication with Rome, the clergy deprived of all control over the schools, and the Russian law regarding mixed marriages made applicable to that province. By an understanding with the curia in 1847 the choice of the bishops was given to the emperor, their canonical investiture to the pope. The mildness with which Alexander II. treated the Poles and the political troubles in the rest of Europe fostered the hope of restoring the old kingdom of Poland. Reckless demonstrations were made in the beginning of 1861, pilgrimages to the graves of the martyrs of freedom were organized, political memorial festivals were celebrated in churches, a general national mourning was enjoined, mourning services were held, revolutionary songs were sung in churches, etc. The Catholic clergy headed the movement and canonized it as a religious duty. In vain the government sought to put it down by making liberal concessions, in vain they applied to Pius IX. to discountenance it. When in October the country lay in a state of siege, and the military forced their way into the churches to apprehend the ringleaders of rebellion, the episcopal administrator, Bialobezeski, denounced that as church profanation, had all the Catholic churches in Warsaw closed, and answered the government's request to reopen them by making extravagant demands and uttering proud words of defiance. The military tribunal sentenced him to death, but the emperor commuted this to one year's detention in a fortress, with loss of all his dignities and orders. Meanwhile the eyes of the pope had at length been opened. He now confirmed the government's appointment cf Archbishop Felinsky, who entered Warsaw in February, 1862, and reopened the churches. After the suppression of the revolt in 1864, almost all cloisters, as nurseries of revolution, were abolished; in the following year the whole property of the church was taken in charge by the State, and the clergy supported by state pay. The pope, enraged at this, gave violent expression to his feelings to the Russian ambassador at Rome during the New Year festivities of 1866, whereupon the government completely broke off all relations with the curia. Consequently in 1867 all the affairs of the Catholic church were committed to the clerical college at St. Petersburg, and intercourse between the clergy and the pope prohibited. Hence arose many conflicts with Catholic bishops, whose obstinacy was punished by their being interned in their dioceses. In 1869 the Russian calendar was introduced, and Russian made the compulsory language of instruction. But in 1870 greater opposition was offered to the introduction of Russian in the public services by means of translations of the common Polish prayer and psalm-books. Pietrowitsch, dean of Wilna, read from the pulpit the ukase referring to this matter, but then cast it together with the Russian translations into the flames, with violent denunciations of the government, and gave information against himself to the governor-general. He was agreeably to his own desire imprisoned, and then transported to Archangel. The same sentence was pronounced against several other obstinate prelates and clergy, among them Archbishop Felinsky, and thus further opposition was stamped out.—Leo XIII. soon after entering on his pontificate in 1878 took the first step toward reconciliation. His efforts reached a successful issue first in February, 1883. The deposed prelates were restored from their places of banishment, with promise of a liberal pension, and were allowed to choose their residences as they pleased, only not within their former dioceses. In their stead the pope consecrated ten new bishops nominated by the emperor, who amid the jubilation of the people entered their episcopal residences. With reference to the Roman Catholic seminaries and clerical academies at Warsaw, the curia granted to the government the right of control over instruction in the Russian language, literature and history, but committed instruction in canonical matters solely to the bishops, who, after obtaining the approval of the government, appointed the rector and inspector and canonical teachers. Vacant pastorates were filled by the bishops, and only in the case of the more important was the approval of the government required. As to the language to be used, it was resolved that only where the people speak Russian were the clergy obliged to employ that language in preaching and in their pastoral work.

3. The Evangelical Church.—The Lutheran church in Russia, comprising two and a half millions of Germans, Letts, Esthonians and Finns, is strongest in Livonia, Esthonia and Courland, is the national church in Finland, and is also largely represented in Poland, in the chief cities of Russia, and in the numerous German colonies in South Russia. In 1832 it obtained, for the Baltic provinces and the scattered congregations in central Russia, a church constitution and service book, the latter on the basis of the old Swedish service book, the former requiring all religious teachers in church and school to accept the Formula of Concord. Annual provincial synods have the initiative in calling in, when necessary for legislative purposes, the aid of the general synod.—In Poland the Reformed and Lutheran churches were in 1828 united under one combined consistory. By an imperial ukase of 1849, however, the independent existence of both churches was restored. Protestants enjoyed all civil rights and had absolute liberty in the exercise of their religion; but in central Russia down to recent times, when a more liberal spirit began to prevail, they were prohibited putting bells in their churches. The old prohibition of evangelical preaching and the teaching of religion in the Russian

tongue also continued; but the attempt made for some decades in St. Petersburg and the surrounding district to preach the gospel to Germans who had lost their mother tongue, in the Russian language, has been hitherto ungrudgingly allowed by the government. Quitting the national church or returning from it to a church that had been left before, is visited by severe penalties, and children of mixed marriages, where one parent belongs to the national orthodox church, are claimed by law for that church. Only Finland counts among her privileges the right of assigning children of mixed marriages to the church of the father. The Lutheran church in Livonia, with the island of Oesel, suffered considerable, and according to the law of the land irreparable, loss by the secession of sixty or seventy thousand Letts and Esthonians to the orthodox church under the widespread delusion that thereby their economic position would be improved. Disillusions and regret came too late, and the ever increasing desire for restoration to the church forsaken in a moment of excitement could only obtain arbitrary and insufficient satisfaction in Lutheran baptism of infants seemingly near death, and in permission at irregular intervals and without previous announcement to sit at the Lord's Table according to the Lutheran rite. In 1865, not indeed legislatively but administratively, the contracting of mixed marriages in the Baltic provinces was permitted without the enforcement of the legal enactment requiring that the children should be trained in the Greek church. In Esthonia, however, in 1883 there was a new outbreak of conversions in Leal, where five hundred peasants went over to the orthodox church, declaring their wish to be of the same faith as the emperor and the whole of the Russian people. By imperial decree in 1885 the suspension of the law against withdrawing again from the national church, which had existed for twenty years, was abolished. At the instigation of Pobedownoszew the Imperial Council granted an annual subsidy of 100,000 roubles for furthering orthodoxy in the Baltic provinces. No evangelical church could be built in these provinces without the approval of the orthodox bishop of the diocese, and any evangelical pastor who should dissuade a member of his church from his purpose of joining the orthodox church, was liable to punishishment.—In order to supply the want of churches and schools, preachers and teachers in the Lutheran congregations of Russia, a society was formed in 1858 similar to the *Gustav-Adolfs-Verein*, under the supervision of the General Consistory of St. Petersburg, which has laboriously and zealously endeavoured to improve the condition of the oppressed church.[1]

---

[1] Lendrum, " *Ecclesia Pressa:* or, the Lutheran Church in the Baltic Provinces," in *The Theological Review and Free Church College Quar-*

§ 207. GREECE AND TURKEY.

In the spirited struggle for liberty Greece freed herself from the tyranny of the Turkish Mohammedan rule and obtained complete civil independence. But the same princes representing all the three principal Christian confessions, who in 1830 gave their sanction to this emancipation within lamentably narrow limits, in 1840 conquered again the Holy Land for the Turks out of the hands of a revolting vassal. And so inextricable were, and still are, the political interests of the Christian States of Europe with reference to the East, that in the London parliament of 1854 it could be affirmed that the existence of Turkey in a condition of utter impotence was so necessary, that if it did not exist, it would require to be created. On two occasions has Russia called out her whole military force to emancipate from the Turkish yoke her Slavic brethren of a common race and common faith, without being able to give the finishing blow to the "sick man" who had the protection of European diplomacy.

1. The Orthodox Church of Greece.—Deceived in their expectations from the Vienna Congress, the Greeks tried to deliver themselves from Turkish tyranny. In 1814 a *Hetairia* was formed, branches of which spread over the whole land and fostered among the people ideas of freedom. The war of independence broke out in 1821. Its first result was a fearful massacre, especially in Constantinople. The patriarch Gregorius with his whole synod and about 30,000 Christians were in three months with horrid cruelty murdered by the Turks. The London Conference of 1830 at last declared Greece an independent state, and an assembly of Greek bishops at Nauplia in 1833 freed the national church of Greece from the authority of the patriarch of Constantinople, who was under the control of Turkey. Its supreme direction was committed to a permanent Holy Synod at Athens, instituted by the king but in all internal matters absolutely independent. The king must belong to the national church, but otherwise all

terly, vol. ii. 310–330. C. H. H. Wright. "The Persecution of the Lutheran Church in the Baltic Provinces of Russia," in the *British and Foreign Evangelical Review*, January, 1887

religions are on the same footing. Meanwhile the orthodox church is fully represented, the Roman Catholic being strongest, especially in the islands. The University of Athens, opened in 1856 with professors mostly trained in Germany, has not been unsuccessful in its task even in the domain of theology.

2. **Massacre of Syrian Christians, 1860.**—The Russo-Turkish war ending in the beginning of 1856, in which France and England, and latterly also Sardinia took the part of the sick man, left the condition of the Christians practically unchanged. For though the Hatti Humayun of 1856 granted them equal civil rights with the Moslems, this, however well meant on the part of the Sultan of that time, practically made no improvement upon the equally well meant Hatti Sherif of Gülhane of 1839. The outbreak of 1860 also proved how little effect it had in teaching the Moslems tolerance towards the Christians. Roused by Jesuit emissaries and trusting to French support, the Maronites of Lebanon indulged in several provoking attacks upon their old hereditary foes the Druses. These, however, aided by the Turkish soldiery were always victorious, and throughout all Syria a terrible persecution against Christians of all confessions broke out, characterized by inhuman cruelties. In Damascus alone 8,000, in all Syria 16,000 Christians were murdered, 3,000 women taken to the harems, and 100 Christian villages destroyed. After the massacre had been stopped, 120,000 Christians wandered about without food, clothing, or shelter, and fled hither and thither in fear of death. Fuad Pasha was sent from Constantinople to punish the guilty, and seemed at first to proceed to business energetically; but his zeal soon cooled, and French troops, sent to Syria to protect the Christians, were obliged, yielding to pressure from England, where their presence was regarded with suspicion, to withdraw from the country in June, 1861.

3. **The Bulgarian Ecclesiastical Struggle.**—The Bulgarian church, with somewhere about two and a half million souls, was from early times subject to the patriarch of Constantinople (§ 73, 3), who acted toward it like a pasha. He sold the Bulgarian bishoprics and archbishoprics to the highest bidders among the Greek clergy, who were quite ignorant of the language of the country, and had only one end in view, namely to recoup themselves by extorting the largest possible revenue. No thought was given to the spiritual needs of the Bulgarians, preaching was wholly abandoned, the liturgy was read in a language unknown to the people. It was therefore not to be wondered at that the Bulgarian church was for years longing for its emancipation and ecclesiastical independence, and made every effort to obtain this from the Porte. Turkey, however, sympathized with the patriarch till the revolt in Crete in 1866–1869 and threatening political movements in

Bulgaria broke out. Then at last in 1870 the sultan granted the establishment of an independent Slavic ecclesiastical province under the designation of the Bulgarian Exarchate, with liberty to attach itself to the other Slavic provinces upon a two-thirds majority of votes. The patriarch Gregorius protested, but the Sublime Porte would not thereby be deterred, and in May, 1872, Anthimos the Exarch elect was installed. The patriarch and his synod now stigmatized *Phyletism*, the struggle for a national church establishment, as accursed heresy, and excommunicated the exarch and the whole Bulgarian church. Only the patriarch Cyril of Jerusalem dissented, but he was on that account on his return home treated with indignity and abuse and was deposed by a synod at Jerusalem.

4. The Armenian Church.—To the Gregorian-Armenian patriarch at Constantinople (§ 64, 3), equally with his orthodox colleague (§ 67, 7), had been assigned by the Sublime Porte civil jurisdiction as well as the primacy over all members of his church in the Turkish empire. When now in 1830, at the instigation of France, an independent patriarchate with equal rights was granted to the United Armenians (§ 72, 2), the twofold dependence on the Porte and on the Roman curia created difficulties, which in the meantime were overcome by giving the patriarch, who as a Turkish official exercised civil jurisdiction, a primacy with the title of archbishop as representative of the pope. The United Armenians, like the other united churches of the East, had from early times enjoyed the liberty of using their ancient liturgy, their old ecclesiastical calendar, and their own church constitution with free election of their bishops and patriarchs, and these privileges were left untouched down to 1866. But when in that year the Armenian Catholic patriarch died, the archbishop Hassun was elected patriarch, and then a fusion of the two ecclesiastical powers was brought about, which was expected to lead to absolute and complete subjection under papal jurisdiction and perfect assimilation with the Romish constitution and liturgy, at the same time Hassun with a view to securing a red hat showed himself eager and zealous in this business. By the bull *Reversurus* of 1867 Pius IX. claimed the right of nominating the patriarchs of all united churches of the East, of confirming bishops chosen by these patriarchs, in cases of necessity even choosing these himself, and deciding all appeals regarding church property. But the Mechitarists of St. Lazzaro (§ 164, 2) had already discovered the intriguing designs of France and made these known among their countrymen in Turkey. These now, while Monsignore Hassun was engaged combating the infallibility dogma at the Vatican Council of 1870, drove out his creatures and constituted themselves into a church independent of Rome, without however, joining the Gregorian-Armenians. The influence of France being meanwhile crippled by the Prussian victory, the Porte acquiesced in the accomplished fact, confirmed the appointment of the newly chosen patriarch Kupelian, and refused to yield to the pope's remonstrances and allocutions. In 1874, however, it also recognised the Hassun party as an independent ecclesiastical community, but assigned the church property to the party of Kupelian, and banished Hassun as a fomenter of disturbance, from the capital. The hearty sympathies which on the outbreak of the Russo-Turkish war the Roman curia expressed so loudly and openly for the victory of the crescent over the schismatic Russian cross, made the Sublime Porte again regard the Hassunites with favour, so that Hassun in September, 1877, returned to Constantinople, where the churches were given over to his party and a great number of the Kupelianists were won over to his side. He was eagerly aided not only by the French but also by the Austrian ambassador, and the patriarch Kupelian, now sorely persecuted from every side, at last resigned his position and went in March, 1879, to Rome to kneel as a penitent before the pope. By an irade of the sultan, Hassun was now formally restored, and in 1880 he was adorned with a red hat by Leo XIII. Shortly before this the last of the bishops of the opposing party, with about 30,000 souls, had given in his submission.

5. The Berlin Treaty, 1878.—Frequent and severe oppression, refusal to administer justice, and brutal violence on the part of the Turkish government and people toward the defenceless vassals drove the Christian states and tribes of the Balkan peninsula in 1875 into a rebellion of desperation, which was avenged, especially in Bulgaria in 1876, by scandalous atrocities upon the Christians. When the half-hearted interference of European diplomacy called forth instead of actual reforms only the mocking sham of a pretended free representative constitution, Russia held herself under obligation in 1877 to avenge by arms the wrongs of her brethren by race and creed, but owing to the threats of England and Austria could not fully reap the fruits of her dearly bought victory as had been agreed upon in the Treaty of San Stefano. By the Berlin Conference, however, of 1878 the principalities of Roumania, Servia, and Montenegro, hitherto under the suzerainty of Turkey, were declared independent, and to them, as well as to Greece, at the cost of Turkey, a considerable increase of territory was granted, the portion between the Balkans and the Danube was formed into the Christian principality of Bulgaria under Turkish suzerainty, but East Roumelia, south of the Balkans, now separated from Bulgaria, obtained the rank of an autonomous province with a Christian governor-general. To Thessaly, Epirus, and Crete were granted administrative reforms and throughout the European territory left to the Porte it was stipulated that full religious

and political rights be granted to members of all confessions. The administration of Bosnia and Herzegovina was given over to Austria, and that of Cyprus, by means of a separate treaty, to England. The greater part of Armenia, lying in Asia, belongs to Russia.

§ 208. The United States of America.[1]

The Republic of the United States of America, existing since the Declaration of Independence in 1776, and recognised by England as independent since the conclusion of Peace in 1783, requires of her citizens no other religious test than belief in one God. Since the settlers had often left their early homes on account of religious matters, the greatest variety of religious parties were gathered together here, and owing to their defective theological training and their practical turn of mind, they afforded a fruitful field for religious movements of all sorts, among which the revivals systematically cultivated by many denominations play a conspicuous part. The government does not trouble itself with religious questions, and lets every denomination take care of itself. Preachers are therefore wholly dependent on their congregations, and are frequently liable to dismissal at the year's end. Yet they form a highly respected class, and nowhere in the Protestant world is the tone of ecclesiastical feeling and piety so prevailingly high. In the public schools, which are supported by the State, religious instruction is on principle omitted. The Lutheran and Catholic churches have therefore founded parochial schools; the other denominations seek to supply the want by Sunday schools. The candidates for the ministry are trained in colleges and in numerous theological seminaries.

---

[1] Baird, "Religion in the United States." Glasgow, 1844. "Progress and Prospects of Christianity in the United States." London, 1851. Gorrie, "Churches and Sects in the United States." New York, 1850.

1. **English Protestant Denominations.**—The numerous Protestant denominations belong to two great groups, English and German. Of the first named the following are by far the most important: (1) **The Congregationalists** are the descendants of the Pilgrim Fathers who emigrated in 1620 (§ 143, 4). They profess the doctrines of the Westminster Confession (§ 155, 1).—(2) **The Presbyterians**, of Scotch origin, have the same confession as the Congregationalists, but differ from them by having a common church government with strict Synodal and Presbyterial constitution. By rejecting the doctrine of predestination the Cumberland Presbyterians in 1810 formed a separate body and have since grown so as to embrace in the south-western states 120,000 communicants.—(3) **The Anglican Episcopal Church** is equally distinguished by moderate and solid churchliness. Even here, however, Puseyism has entered in and the Romish church has made many proselytes. But when at the general conference of the Evangelical Alliance at New York in 1873, bishop Cummins of Kentucky took part in the administration of the Lord's Supper in the Presbyterian church and was violently attacked for this by his Puseyite brethren, he laid the foundation of a "Reformed Episcopal Church," in which secession other twenty-five Episcopal ministers joined. They regard the episcopal constitution as an old and wholesome ordinance but not a divine institution, also the Anglican liturgy and *Book of Common Prayer*, though capable of improvement, while they recognise the ordinations of other evangelical churches as valid, and reject as Puseyite the doctrine of a special priesthood of the clergy, of a sacrifice in the eucharist, the presence of the body and blood of Christ in the elements, and of the essential and invariable connection between regeneration and baptism.— (4) The Episcopal Methodists in America formed since 1784 an independent body (§ 169, 4). Their influence on the religious life in the United States has been extraordinarily great. They have had by far the most to do with the revivals which from the first they have carried to a wonderful pitch with their protracted meetings, inquiry meetings, camp meetings, etc. They reached their climax in the camp meetings which, under the preaching mostly of itinerant Methodist preachers frequently in the forest under the canopy of heaven, produced religious awakening among the multitudes gathered from all around. Day and night without interruption they continued praying, singing, preaching, exhorting; all the horrors of hell are depicted, the excitement increases every moment, penitent wrestlings with sighs, sobs, groans, convulsions and writhings, occur on every side; grace comes at last to view; loud hallelujahs, thanksgivings and ascription of praise by the converted mix with the moanings of those on "the anxious bench" pleading for grace, etc. In San Francisco in 1874

there were "*Baby-Revivals*," at which children from four to twelve years of age, who trembled with the fear of hell, sang penitential hymns, made confession of sin, and wrote their names on a sheet in order to engage themselves for ever for Jesus. Since 1847 the Methodist church had been divided into two hostile camps, a southern and a northern. The first named tolerated slavery, while the members of the latter were decided abolitionists and excommunicated all slave-owners as unworthy of the name of Christian. Another party, the Protestant Methodists, has blended the episcopal and congregational constitution.—(5) The Baptists are split up into many sects. The most numerous are the Calvinistic Baptists. Their activity in proselytising is equally great with their zeal for missions to the heathen. In opposition to them the Free-Will Baptists are Arminian and the Christian Baptists have adopted Unitarian views.[1]

2. The German Lutheran Denominations.—The German emigration to America began in Penn's time. In the organization of church affairs, besides Zinzendorf and the Herrnhut missionaries, a prominent part was taken by the pastor Dr. Melchior Mühlenberg (died 1787), a pupil of A. H. Francke, and the Reformed pastor Schlatter from St. Gall; the former sent by the Halle Orphanage, the latter by the Dutch church. The Orphanage sent many earnest preachers till rationalism broke in upon the society. As at the same time the stream of German emigration was checked almost completely for several decades, and so all intercourse with the mother country ceased, crowds of Germans, impressed by the revivals, went over to the Anglo-American denominations, and in the German denominations themselves along with the English language entered also English Puritanism and Methodism. In 1815 German emigration began again and grew from year to year. At the synod of 1857 the Lutheran church with 8,000 pastors divided into three main divisions: (1) The American Lutheran church had become in language, customs, and doctrine thoroughly Anglicised and Americanized; Zwinglian in its doctrine of the sacraments, it was Lutheran in scarcely anything but the name, until in its chief seminary at Gettysburg in Pennsylvania in 1850 a reaction set in in favour of genuine Lutheran and German tendencies. (2) A greatly attenuated Lutheranism with unionistic sympathies and frequent abandonment of the German language also found expression in the congregations of the Old Pennsylvanian Synod. (3) On the other hand, the strict Lutheran church held tenaciously to the exclusive use of the German language and the genuine Lutheran confession.

---

[1] Stevens, "History of the Episcopal Methodist Church in North America." Philadelphia, 1868. Gorrie, "History of the Episcopal Methodist Church in the United States." New York, 1881.

The Prussian emigration with Grabau and the Saxon Lutheran settlers with Stephan constituted its backbone (§ 194, 1). To them a number of Bavarian Lutherans attached themselves who had emigrated under the leadership of Löhe, whose missionary institute at Neuendettelsau supplied them with pastors. The Saxon Lutherans were meanwhile grouped together in the Missouri Synod, which Löhe's missionaries also joined, so that it soon acquired much larger proportions than the Buffalo Synod formed previously by the Prussian Lutherans under Grabau. But very soon the two synods had a violent quarrel over the idea of office and church which, owing to the reception by the Missouri Synod of several parties excommunicated by the Buffalo Synod, led to the formal breach of church fellowship between the two parties. The Missouri Synod, with Dr. Walther at its head, attached all importance to sound doctrine; the clerical office was regarded as a transference of the right of the congregation and excommunication as a congregational not a clerical act. The Buffalo Synod, on the other hand, in consequence of serious conflict with pietistic elements, had been driven into an overestimation of external order, of forms of constitution and worship, and of the clerical office as of immediately divine authority, and carried this to such a length as led to the dissolution of the synod in 1877. Löhe's friends, who had not been able to agree with either party, formed themselves into the Synod of Iowa, with their seminary at Wartburg under Fritschel. On all questions debated between the synods they took a mediating position. The Missourians, however, would have nothing to do with them, while those of Buffalo long maintained tolerably friendly relations with them. But the historical view of the symbols taken by the Iowans, their inclination toward the new development of Lutheran theology, and above all their attitude toward biblical chiliasm, which they wished to treat as an open question, seemed to those of Buffalo, as well as to the Missourians, a falling away from the church confession, and led to their excommunication by that party also.—In opposition to all this splitting up into sections a General Council of the Lutheran Church in America was held in 1866, which sought to combine all Lutheran district synods, of which twelve, out of fifty-six, with 814 clergymen, joined it, Iowa assuming a friendly and Missouri a distinctly hostile attitude. The ninth assembly at Galesburg in Illinois in 1875 laid down as its fundamental principle, "Lutheran pulpits only for Lutheran preachers, and Lutheran altars only for Lutheran communicants." The native Americans, however, insisted upon exceptions being allowed, e.g. in peril of death, etc. On the question of the limits of these exceptions, however, subsequent assemblies have not been able to agree.

3. But also in the Synodal Conference founded and led by the

Missouri Synod, embracing five synods, doctrinal controversies sprang up in 1860. A large number with Dr. Walther at their head held a strict doctrine of predestination which they regarded as the mark of genuine Lutheranism. God has, they taught, chosen a definite number of men from eternity to salvation; these shall and must be saved. Salvation in Christ is indeed offered to all, but God secures it only for His elect, so that they are sure of it and cannot lose it again, not indeed *intuitu fidei* but only according to His sovereign grace. Even one of the elect may seem temporarily to fall from grace, but he cannot die without returning into full possession of it. Prof. Fritschel protested against this in 1872 as essentially Calvinistic, and opposition also arose in the Missouri Pastoral Conference. Prof. Asperheim, of the seminary of the Norwegian Synod at Madison in Wisconsin, who first pronounced against it in 1876, was deprived of his office and obliged to withdraw from the synod. The controversy broke out in a violent form at the conferences of about 500 pastors held at Chicago in 1880 and at Milwaukee three months later in 1881, at the former of which Prof. Stellhorn of Fort Wayne, at the latter Prof. Schmidt of Madison, offered a vigorous opposition. Walther closed the conference with the words: "You ask for war, war you shall have." The result was that the whole of the Ohio Synod and a large portion of the Norwegian Wisconsin Synod, broke away from communion with the Missouri Synod.—Walther and his adherents went so far in their fanaticism as to pronounce not only their American opponents but all the most distinguished Lutheran theologians of Germany, Philippi as well as Hofmann, Luthardt as well as Kahnis, Vilmar as well as Thomasius, Harms as well as Zöckler, etc., bastard theologians, semipelagians, synergists and rationalists, and to refuse church fellowship not only with all Lutheran national churches in Europe, but also with German Lutheran Free Churches, which did not unconditionally attach themselves to them. These Missouri separatist communities, though everywhere quite unimportant, are in Europe strongest in the kingdom of Saxony; they have also a few representatives in Nassau, Baden, Württemberg, Bavaria and Hesse.

4. **German-Reformed and other German-Protestant Denominations.**—The German-Reformed church has its seminary at Mercersburg in Pennsylvania. Its confession of faith is the Heidelberg Catechism, its theology an offshoot of German evangelical union theology, but with a distinctly positive tendency. Although the union theology there prevailed among the Reformed as well as the Lutherans, a German Evangelical Church Union was formed at St. Louis in 1841 which wished to set aside the names Reformed and Lutheran. It established a seminary at Marthasville in Missouri. The Herrnhuters are also represented in America. Several German Methodist sects have re-

cently sprung up: 1. The "United Brethren in Christ," with 500 preachers, founded by a Reformed preacher Otternbein (died 1813). 2. The "Evangelical Communion," commonly called *Albrechtsleute*, founded by Jac. Albrecht, originally a Lutheran layman, whom his own followers ordained in 1803, with 500 or 600 preachers working zealously and carrying on mission work also in Germany (§ 211, 1). 3. The Weinbrennians or Church of God, founded by an excommunicated Reformed pastor of that name in 1839. They carry the Methodist revivalism to the most extravagant excess and are also fanatical opponents of infant baptism

5. The Catholic Church.—A number of English Catholics under Lord Baltimore settled in Maryland in 1634. The little community grew and soon filled the land. There alone in the whole world did the Roman Catholic church though dominant proclaim the principle of toleration and religious equality. Consequently Protestants of various denominations crowded thither, outnumbered the original settlers, and rewarded those who had hospitably received them with abuse and oppression. The Catholics were also treated in other states as idolaters and excluded from public offices and posts of honour. Only after the Declaration of Independence in 1783 was this changed by the sundering of the connection of church and state and the proclamation of absolute religious liberty. The number of Catholics was greatly increased by numerous emigrations, specially from Ireland and Catholic Germany. They now claim seven million members, with a cardinal at New York, 13 archbishops, 64 bishops, about 7,000 churches and chapels. A beautiful cathedral was erected in New York in 1879, the immense cost of which, exceeding all expectation, was at last defrayed by very unspiritual and unecclesiastical methods, *e.g.* lotteries, fairs, dramatic exhibitions, concerts, and even dearly sold kisses, etc. The Roman Catholics have also a university at St. Louis, 80 colleges, and 300 cloisters.

§ 209. THE ROMAN CATHOLIC STATES OF SOUTH AMERICA.

To the predominantly Protestant North America the position of the Roman Catholic states of South America forms a very striking contrast. Nowhere else was the influence and power of the clergy so wide-spread and deeply rooted, nowhere else has the depravation of Catholicism reached such a depth of superstition, obscurantism, and fanaticism. During the second and third decades of our century the Spanish states, favoured by the revolutionary movement in the mother country, one after another asserted their independence, and the Portuguese Brazil established herself as an independent empire under the legitimate royal prince of Portugal, Pedro I. in 1822. Although the other new states adopted a republican constitution, they could not throw aside the influence of the Catholic clergy and carry out the principles of religious freedom proclaimed in their constitutions. The Catholicism of the creoles, half-castes, and mulattoes was of too bigoted a kind and the power of the clergy too great to allow any such thing. Mexico went furthest in the attempt, and Brazil, under Dom Pedro II. from 1831, astonished the world by the vigorous measures of its government in 1874 against the assumptions of the higher clergy.—In spite of all hindrances a not inconsiderable number of small evangelical congregations have been formed in Romish America, partly through emigration and partly by evangelization.

1. **Mexico.**—Of all the American states, Mexico, since its independence in 1823, has been most disturbed by revolutions and civil wars. The rich and influential clergy, possessing nearly a half of all landed property, was the factor with which all pretenders, presidents and rulers had to reckon. After most of the earlier governments had supported the clergy and been supported by them, the ultimately victorious liberal party under president Juarez shook off the yoke in 1859. He proclaimed absolute religious freedom, introduced civil marriage, abolished cloisters, pronounced church possessions national property and exiled the obstinate bishops. The clerical party now sought and obtained foreign aid. Spain, France and England joined in a common military convention in 1861 in supporting certain claims of citizens repudiated by Juarez. Spain and England soon withdrew their troops, and Napoleon III. openly declared the purpose of his interference to be the strengthening of the Latin race and the monarchical principle in America. At his instigation the Austrian Grand-Duke Maximilian was elected emperor, and that prince, after receiving the pope's blessing in Rome, began his reign in 1864. Distrusted by all parties as a stranger, in difficulties with the curia and clergy because he opposed their claims to have their most extravagant

privileges restored, shamefully left in the lurch by Napoleon from fear of the threatening attitude of the North American Union, and then sold and betrayed by his own general Bazaine, this noble but unfortunate prince was at last sentenced by Juarez at a court-martial to be shot in 1867. Juarez now maintained his position till the end of his life in 1872, and strictly carried out his anticlerical reforms. After his death clericalism again raised her head, and the Jesuits expelled from Guatemala swarmed over the land. Yet constitutional sanction was given to the Juarez legislation at the congress of 1873. The Jesuits were driven across the frontiers, obstinate priests as well as a great number of nuns, who had gathered again in cloisters and received novices, were put in prison.—Also Evangelization advanced slowly under sanction of law, though regarded with disfavour by the people and interfered with often by the mob. It began in 1865 with the awakening of a Catholic priest Francisco Aguilar and a Dominican monk Manuel Aguas, through the reading of the Scriptures. They laid the foundation of the "*Iglesia de Jesus*" of converted Mexicans, with evangelical doctrine and apostolic-episcopal constitution, which has now 71 congregations throughout the whole country with about 10,000 souls. This movement received a new impulse in 1869, when a Chilian-born Anglican episcopal minister of a Spanish-speaking congregation in New York, called Riley, took the control of it and was in 1879 consecrated its bishop. Besides this independent "*Church of Jesus*" North American missionaries of various denominations have wrought there since 1872 with slow but steady success.

2. In the Republics of Central and Southern America, when the liberal party obtained the helm of government through almost incessant civil wars, religious freedom was generally proclaimed, civil marriage introduced, the Jesuits expelled, cloisters shut up, etc. But in Ecuador, president Moreno, aided by the clergy, concluded in 1862 a concordat with the curia by which throughout the country only the Catholic worship was tolerated, the bishops could condemn and confiscate any book, education was under the Jesuits, and the government undertook to employ the police in suppressing all errors and compelling all citizens to fulfil all their religious duties. And further the public resolved in 1873, although unable to pay the interest of the national debt, to hand over a tenth of all state revenues to the pope. But Moreno was murdered in 1875. The Jesuits, who were out of favour, left Quito. The tithe hitherto paid to the pope was immediately withheld, and in 1877 the concordat was abrogated. As Ecuador in Moreno, so Peru at the same time in Pierola had a dictator after the pope's own heart. The republic had his misgovernment to thank for one defeat after another in the war with Chili.— Bolivia in 1872 declared that the Roman Catholic religion alone

would be tolerated in the country, and suffered, in common with Peru annihilating defeats at the hand of Chili.—When at St. Iago in Chili, during the festival of the Immaculate Conception in 1863, the Jesuit church La Compania was burnt and in it more than 2,000 women and children consumed, the clergy pronounced this disaster an act of grace of the blessed Virgin, who wished to give the country a vast number of saints and martyrs. But here, too, the conflicts between church and state continued. In 1874 the Chilian episcopate pronounced the ban against the president and the members of the national council and of the Lower House who had favoured the introduction of a new penal code which secured liberty of worship, but it remained quite unheeded. When then the archiepiscopal chair of St. Iago became vacant in 1878, the pope refused on any condition to confirm the candidate appointed by the government. After the decisive victory over Peru and Bolivia, the government again in December, 1881, urgently insisted upon their presentation. The curia now sent to Chili, avowedly to obtain more accurate information, an apostolic delegate who took advantage of his position to stir up strife, so that the government was obliged to insist upon his recall. As the curia declined to do so, his passports were sent to the legate in January, 1883, and a presidential message was addressed to the next congress which demanded the separation of the church and state, with the introduction of civil marriage and register of civil station, as the only remaining means for putting down the confusion caused by papal tergiversation. The result of the long and heated debates that followed was the promulgation of a law by which Catholicism was deprived of the character of the state religion and the perfect equality of all forms of worship was proclaimed.—Guatemala in 1872 expelled the Jesuits whose power and wealth had become very great. In 1874 the president Borrias opened a new campaign against the clergy by forbidding them to wear the clerical dress except when discharging the duties of their office, and closing all the nunneries.—In Venezuela, in 1872, Archbishop Guevara of Caracas, who had previously come into collision with the government by favouring the rebels, forbade his clergy taking part in the national festival, and put the cathedral in which it was to be celebrated under the interdict. Deposed and banished on this account, he continued from the British island of Trinidad his endeavours to stir up a new rebellion. The president, Guzman Blanco, after long fruitless negotiations with the papal nuncio, submitted in May, 1876, to the congress at St. Domingo the draft of a bill, which declared the national church wholly independent of Rome. The congress not only homologated his proposals, but carried them further, by abolishing the episcopal hierarchy and assigning its revenues to the national exchequer, for education. Now at last the Roman curia agreed to the deposition of Guevara and confirmed the nomination of his previously appointed successor. But president Blanco now asked congress to abolish the law, and this was agreed to.—In the United States of Colombia since 1853, and in the Argentine Republic since 1865, perfect liberty of faith and worship have been constitutionally secured. From the latter state the Jesuits had been banished for a long time but had managed to smuggle themselves in again. When in the beginning of 1875 Archbishop Aneiros of Buenos Ayres addressed to the government which favoured the clerical party rather than to the congress which was the only competent court, a request to reinvest the Jesuits with the churches, cloisters, and properties held by them before their expulsion, a terrible outbreak took place, which the archbishop intensified to the utmost by issuing a violent pastoral. A mob of 30,000 men, convened by the students of the university, wrecked the palace of the archbishop, then attacked the Jesuit college, burnt all its furniture and ornaments on the streets and by means of petroleum soon reduced the building itself to flames. Only with difficulty did the military succeed in preventing further mischief. In October, 1884, the papal nuncio was expelled, because, when the government decidedly refused his request to prevent the spread of Protestant teaching and to place Sunday schools under the oversight of the bishops, he replied in a most violent and passionate manner. About the same time the republic of Costa-rica issued a law forbidding all religious orders, pronouncing all vows invalid, and threatening banishment against all who should contravene these enactments, and also an education act which forbade all public instruction apart from that provided by the State.

3. Brazil.—In Brazil down to 1884, the " Catholic Apostolic Roman Religion " was, according to the constitution, the religion of the empire. But from 1828 there was a Protestant congregation in Rio de Janeiro, and through the inland districts, in consequence of immigration, there were 100 small evangelical congregations, with twenty-five ordained pastors, whose forms of worship were of various kinds. In earlier times Protestant marriage was regarded as concubinage, but in 1851 a law was passed which gave it civil recognition. But the bishops held to their previous views and demanded of married converts a repetition of the ceremony. Since 1870, however, the government has energetically opposed the claims of the clergy who wished only to acknowledge the authority of Rome. Protestant marriages were pronounced equally legitimate with Catholic marriages, no civil penalties are incurred by excommunication, all papal bulls are subject to the approval of the government, and it was insisted that announcement should be made of all clergy nominated. The clergy considered freemasonry the chief source of all this liberal current.

and against it therefore they directed all their forces. The pope assisted by his brief of May, 1873, condemning freemasonry. At the head of the rebel prelates stood Don Vitalis Gonsalvez de Oliveira, bishop of Olinda and Pernambuco. He published the papal brief without asking the imperial permission, pronounced the ban upon all freemasons and suspended the interdict over all associations which refused to expel masonic brothers from their membership. In vain the government demanded its withdrawal. It then accused him of an attack upon the constitution. The supreme court ordered his detention, and he was placed in the state prison at Rio de Janeiro in January, 1874. The trial ended by his being sentenced to four years' imprisonment, which the emperor as an act of grace commuted to detention in a fortress, and set him free in a year and a half. In consequence of this occurrence the Jesuits were, in 1874, expelled the country. The increasing advent of monks and nuns from Europe led the government, in 1884, to appoint a commission to carry out the law already passed in 1870, for the secularization of all monastic property after providing pensions for those entitled to support. In the same year all naturalized non-Catholics were pronounced eligible for election to the imperial parliament and to the provincial assemblies. The members belonging to the evangelical churches now number about 50,000, of whom 30,000 are Germans.[1]

V.—Opponents of Church and of Christianity.

§ 210. SECTARIANS AND ENTHUSIASTS IN THE ROMAN CATHOLIC AND ORTHODOX RUSSIAN DOMAINS.

It cannot be denied that since the Tridentine attempt to define the church doctrine far fewer sects condemning the church as such have sprung from Roman Catholicism than from Protestantism. Yet such phenomena are not wanting in the nineteenth century. Their scarcity is abundantly made up for by the numberless degenerations and errors (§ 191) which the Catholic church or its representatives in

---

[1] A full account of the recent development of Protestantism in Brazil is given in an article in the *Presbyterian Review* for January, 1889, pp. 101–106, "The Organization of the Synod of Brazil," by Dr. J. Aspinwall Hodge.—On 15th November, 1889, the emperor was expelled and a republic proclaimed.

the higher and lower grades of the clergy not only fell into but actually provoked and furthered, and thus encouraged an unhealthy love for religious peculiarities. Were the absence of new heretical, sectarian and fanatical developments something to be gloried in for itself alone, the Eastern church, with its absolute stability, would obtain this distinction in a far higher degree. In the Russian church, however, the multitude of sects which amid manifold oppressions and persecutions continue to exist to the present day, in spite of many persistent and even condemnable errors, witnesses to a deep religious need in the Russian people.

1. Sects and Fanatics in the Roman Catholic Domain (§ 187, 6–8, § 190). —On the Catholic Irvingites see § 211, 10.—(1) The Order of New Templars sprang from the Freemasons (§ 172, 2). Soon after their establishment in France the Jesuits sought to carry out their own hierarchical ideas. The fable of an uninterrupted connection between freemasonry as a "temple of humanity" and the Templars of the Middle Ages, and the introduction therewith in their secret ceremonies of exercises, borrowed from the chivalry of romance, afforded a means toward this end. The idea was started in the Jesuit college at Claremont and was approved and accepted by the local lodge. In A.D. 1754 a great number of their noble members, who were disgusted with the Jesuit templar farce, withdrew in order as "New Templars" to continue the old order in the spirit of modern times. In consequence, however, of the revolution that broke out in A.D. 1789 they could no longer hold their ground as a band of nobles. Napoleon favoured the reorganization of the order freed from those limits. The day of Molay's death (§ 112, 7) was publicly celebrated with great pomp in Paris, A.D. 1808 and the order spread among all French populations. On the Bourbon restoration the grand-master was, at the instigation of the Jesuits, cast into prison and the order suppressed. After the July revolution he was liberated and a new temple was opened in Paris in A.D. 1833. The show-loving Parisians for a long time took pleasure in the peculiar rites and costume of the templars. When this interest declined the order passed out of view. Its religion, which professed to be a primitive revelation carried down in the Greek and Egyptian mysteries, from which Moses borrowed, then further developed by Christ and transmitted in esoteric tradition by John and his successors the grand-masters of the templars, taught a divine

trinity of being, act and consciousness, the eternity of the world alongside of God and an indwelling of God in man. It declared the Roman
Catholic church to be the only true Christianity (*église chrétienne
primitive*). Its sacred book consisted of an apocryphal gospel of John
in accordance with its own notions.—(2) On the communistic society
of St. Simonians, which also sprang up in France, see § 212, 2.—(3) St.
Simon's secretary was Aug. Comte, the founder of the Positivist philosophical school (§ 174, 2) and he maintained intimate relations with
his master all through life. In his later years he undertook by carrying his philosophical doctrine into the practical domain to sketch
out a "religion of humanity," and thus became the founder of a
Positivist religious sect. The men of science indeed who had adopted
his philosophical principles (Littré, Renan, Taine, Lewes, Leslie
Stephens, Tyndall, Huxley, Draper, etc.), repudiate it; but in the
middle and lower ranks some were found longing for an object of
worship, who endeavoured on the basis of his *Calendrier positiviste* and
Catechisme positiviste to form a religious society for the worship of
humanity. His festival calendar divides the year into thirteen months
of four weeks each, named after the thirteen great benefactors of mankind (among whom Christ does not appear), while the weeks are named
after lesser heroes. By the profound veneration of woman, which
savours greatly of Mariolatry, as well as by the fantastic worship of
heroes, geniuses and scholars, which is a mimicry of the popish saint
worship, and by the adoption of a sacerdotalism like that of Catholicism, this religion of humanity shows itself to be an antichristian
growth on Roman Catholic soil.

2.—(4) Thomas Pöschl, in the second decade of the century, presents
an instance of a degeneration of originally pietistic tendencies into
mischievous fanaticism. A Catholic priest at Ampfelwang near Linz,
he sought under the influence of Sailer's mysticism to awaken in his
congregation a more lively Christianity by means of prayer meetings
and the circulation of tracts, in which he proclaimed the approaching
end of the world. When the district in which he lived was, in 1814,
attached to Austria, he was committed to prison, and his followers
accepted as their leader the peasant Jos. Haas, who led them further
still into fanatical excesses. His fanaticism at length went so far
that on Good Friday of 1817 a young maiden belonging to their party
suffered a voluntary death after the example of Christ for her brothers
and sisters. Pöschl professed the deepest horror at this cruel deed
for which he was blamed. He died in close monastic confinement in
1837.—(5) The Antinomian sect of the Antonians, most numerous in the
Canton Bern, had its beginning among the Roman Catholics. Its
founder was Antoni Unternährer, born and reared at Shüpfheim, near
Lucerne, in the Catholic faith. From 1802 he resided at Amfoldingen,

near Thun, where he stood in high repute among the peasants as a
quack doctor, gave himself out as the son of God a second time become man, and proclaimed by word and writing the perfect redemption
from the curse of the law by the introduction of the true freedom of
the sons of God, which was to show itself first of all in the absolutely
unrestricted intercourse of the sexes. After two years' confinement
in a house of correction he was banished from the Canton Bern and
transported to his native place, where, abandoning all pastoral duties,
he died in a police cell in 1814. The sect, which had meanwhile
spread widely, and at Gsteig near Interlaken had obtained a new leader
in the person of Benedict Schori, a third incarnation of Christ, could
not be finally suppressed, notwithstanding the liberal use of the
prison, till the beginning of 1840. Even at this day scattered remnants of Antonians are to be found in Canton Bern.—(6) When the
Austrian constitution of 1849 gave unconditional religious toleration,
the Bohemian Adamites (§ 115, 5), of whom remnants under the mask of
Catholicism had continued down to the nineteenth century, ventured
again publicly to engage in proselytising efforts. An official enquiry
instituted on this occasion declared that the sect, consisting of Bohemian peasants and artisans, had its headquarters among the mystics
of the Krüdener school, that its religious doctrine was a mixture of
communism, freethinking and quietism, and that its members were in
their ordinary public life blameless, but that in their secret nightly
assemblies, where they dispensed with clothes, they celebrated orgies
regardless of marriage or relationship.—(7) David Lazzaretti, formerly
a carrier in Tuscany, appeared in his native place after an absence of
several years, in 1872, declaring that he was descended from a natural
son of Charlemagne and had been entrusted by the Apostle Peter with
a message to the pope, pointing to a cross that had been burnt upon
his brow by the apostle himself. He startled those of the Vatican,
where he was quite unknown, by declaring that the bones of his an-
cestors lay under the ruins of an old Franciscan cloister in Sabina, of
whose existence nobody was aware, the discovery of which seemed to
vouch for his claims. These were all the more readily admitted when
it was found that he made the restoration of the Pope's temporal
power his main task. The number of his adherents, mostly peasants,
soon increased immensely, reaching, it is said, 40,000. On Monte
Labro they built a church with a strong " David's Tower," over which
" St. David " appointed two priests who, when they had made certain
changes in worship at the call of the prophet, were excommunicated
by the bishop. David now began to spread his socialistic and communistic ideas. He insisted that his adherents should surrender their
goods to him as representative of the society, and promised down to
December 31st, 1890, the introduction of community of goods through-

out Italy and afterwards in other countries. In Arcidosso, the prophet's birthplace, a beginning was to be made, but in its overthrow on August 18th, 1878, he met his death, and his befooled followers waited in vain for the fulfilment of his dying promise that he would rise again on the third day.

3. **Russian Sects and Fanatics.**—After the attempt under Nicholas I. at the forcible conversion of the Raskolniks, especially the purely schismatic Starowerzians or Old Believers (§ 163, 10), had proved fruitless, the government of Alexander II. by patience and concession took a surer way to reconciliation and restoration. In October, 1874, their marriages, births and deaths, which had hitherto been without legal recognition, were put on the regular register and so their lawful rights of inheritance were secured. Under Alexander III. in 1883 an imperial decree was issued, which gave them permission to celebrate divine service after their own methods in their chapels, which had not before the legal standing of churches, and declared them also eligible for public appointments.— To the Duchoborzians (§ 166, 2), sorely oppressed under Catherine II. and Paul I., Alexander I., after they had laid before him the confession which they had adopted, granted toleration, but assigned them a separate residence in the Taurus district. Under Nicholas I. they were to the number of 8,000 transported to the Transcaucasian mountains in 1841, where they were called Duchoborje.—The Württemberg Pietist colonists of South Russia originated among the peasants the widespread sect of the Stundists soon after the abolition of serfdom in 1863. The originator of those separatist meetings for the study of Scripture, which led first of all to the condemnation of image worship and making the sign of the cross as unbiblical, and subsequently to a complete withdrawal from the worship of the orthodox church and the forming of conventicles, was the peasant and congregational elder Ratusny of Osnowa near Odessa, to whom, at a later period, with equal propagandist zeal, the peasant Balabok attached himself. The latter was, in 1871, sentenced to one year's imprisonment at Kiev and the loss of civil rights, and in 1873, at Odessa, a great criminal prosecution was instituted against Ratusny and all the other leaders of the sect, which, however, after proceeding for five years ended in a verdict of acquittal. A process started in 1878 against the so-called Schaloputs had a similar issue. This sect, spread most widely among the Cossacks of Cuban, rejects the Old Testament, the sacraments and the doctrine of the resurrection, but believes in a continued effusion of the Holy Spirit upon the prophets of the church who have prepared themselves for their vocation by complete abstinence from flesh and spirituous liquor as well as by incessant prayer and frequent fasting.

4. About the middle of the eighteenth century among the " *Men of*

God," the strict interpretation of the prescriptions of their founder
Danila Filipow (§ 163, 10) had led many to abstain wholly from sexual
relations; when a peasant Andrew Selivanov appeared as a reformer
and founded the sect of the Skopzen or mutilators, who, building on
misinterpreted passages of Scripture (Matt. v. 28–30, xix. 12; Rev.
xiv. 4) insisted upon the destruction of sexual desire by castration and
excision of the female breasts, generally performed under anæsthetics,
as a necessary condition of entrance into the kingdom of heaven. The
first Skopzic congregation was gathered round him in the village of
Sosnowka. The " men of God " enraged at his success denounced him
to the government. He was punished with the knout and condemned
in 1774 to hard labour at Irkutzk. The idea that Peter III., who died
in 1762, was still alive, then widely prevailed. The " men of God " had
also adopted this opinion, and proclaimed him their last-appearing
Christ, who would soon return from his hiding-place to call to account
all unbelievers. Selivanov, who knew of this, now gave himself out
for the exiled monarch, and was accepted as such by his adherents
in his native place. When Paul I., Peter's son, assumed the reins of
government in 1796, a Skopzic merchant of Moscow told him secretly
that his father was living at Irkutzk under the name of Selivanov
The emperor therefore brought him to Petersburg and shut him up as
an imbecile in an asylum. After Paul's death, however, his adherents
obtained his release. He now lived for eighteen years in honour at
Petersburg, till in 1820 the court again interfered and had him confined in a cloister at Suzdal, where after some years he died. Sorely
persecuted by Nicholas I. many of his followers migrated to Moldavia
and Walachia where they, dwelling in separate quarters at Jassy,
Bucharest and Galatz, lived as owners of coach-hiring establishments,
and by rich presents obtained proselytes. Still more vigorously was
the propaganda carried on in the Moscow colonies on the Sea of Azov.
There in Morschansk lived the spiritual head of all Russian Skopzen,
the rich merchant Plotizyn. After the government got on the track
of this society, Plotizyn's house was searched and a correspondence
revealing the wide extension of the sect was found, together with a
treasure of several, some say as much as thirty, millions of roubles,
which, however, in great part again disappeared in a mysterious
manner. Plotizyn and his companions were banished to Siberia and
sentenced to hard labour, the less seriously implicated to correction in
a cloister.—The secret doctrine of the Skopzen so far as is known is as
follows: God had intended man to propagate not by sexual intercourse but by a holy kiss. They broke this command and this constituted the fall. In the fulness of time God sent his Son into the
world. The central point of his preaching transmitted to us in a
greatly distorted form was the introduction of the baptism of fire

(Matt. iii. 11), *i.e.* mutilation by hot irons for which, in consideration of human weakness, a baptism of castration may be substituted (Matt. xix. 12). Origen is regarded by them as the greatest saint of the ancient church; to his example all saints conformed who are represented as beardless or with only a slight beard. The promised return of the Christ (in this alone diverging from the doctrine of the "men of God"), took place in the person of the emperor Peter III. whom an unstained virgin bore, who was called the empress Elizabeth Petrovna. The latter after some years transferred the government to a lady of the court resembling her and retired into private life under the name of Akulina Ivanovna, where she still remains invisible behind golden walls, waiting for the things that are to come. Her son Peter III., who had also himself undergone the baptism of fire, escaped the snares of his wife, reappeared under the name of Selivanov, performed many miracles and converted multitudes, obtained as a reward the knout, and was at last sent to Siberia. Emperor Paul recalled him and was converted by him. Under Alexander I. he was again arrested and imprisoned in the cloister of Suzdal. But he was conveyed thence by a divine miracle to Irkutzk, where he now lives in secret, whence at his own time he shall return to judge the living and the dead.—They kept up an outward connection with the state church although they regarded it as the apocalyptic whore of Babylon. In their own secret services inspired psalms were sung, and after exciting dances prophecies were uttered.[1]

§ 211. SECTARIES AND ENTHUSIASTS IN THE PROTESTANT DOMAIN.

The United States of America with their peculiar constitution formed the favourite ground for the gathering and moulding of sects during this age. There, besides the older colonies of Quakers, Baptists and Methodists from England, we meet with Swedenborgianism and Unitarianism, while Baptists and Methodists began to send missionaries into Europe, and from England the Salvation Army undertook a campaign for the conquest of the world. But also on the European continent independent fanatical developments made their appearance.—A new combination of communism

---

[1] Hepworth Dixon, "Free Russia." 2 vols. London, 1870. Heard, "The Russian Church and Russian Dissent." 2 vols. London, 1887.

with religious enthusiasm is represented by the Harmonists and by the Perfectionists in North America. The Grusinian Separatists and the Bavarian Chiliasts are millenarians of German extraction, of whom the former sought deliverance from the prevailing antichristian spirit in removal from, and the latter in removal to, South Russia. The Amen churches sought to gather God's people of the Jewish Christian communities together in Palestine, while the so-called German Temple sought to gather the Gentile Christians. As Latter Day Saints, besides the Adventists, the Darbyites established themselves on an independent basis; the Irvingites, with revival of the apostolic offices and charisms, and their American caricature, the Mormons, with the addition of socialistic and fantastic gnostic tendencies. The religion of the Taiping rebellion in China presented the rare phenomenon of a national Chinese Christianity of native growth, and a still rarer manifestation is met with in American-European spiritualism with pretended spirit revelations from the other world.

1. The Methodist Propaganda.—From 1850 the American Methodists, both the Albrechtsleute (§ 208, 4) and the Episcopal Methodists, have sent out numerous missionaries, mostly Germans into Germany, whose zeal has won considerable success among the country people. In North-West Germany Bremen is their chief station, whence they have spread to Sweden, Central and Southern Germany, and Switzerland, and have stations in Frankfort, Carlsruhe, Heilbronn, and Zürich.—Of a more evanescent character was the attempt made on Germany by the so-called Oxford Holiness Movement. In 1866 the North American Methodists celebrated their centenary in New York by the appointment of a great revival and holiness committee, in which were also members of many other denominations. Among them the manufacturer, Pearsall Smith, of Philadelphia, converted in 1871, exhibited extraordinary zeal. In September, 1874, he held at Oxford great revival meetings, from which the designation of the Oxford movement had its origin. By some Germans there present his opinions were carried to Germany. In spring, 1875, he began his second European missionary tour. While his two companions, the revivalists Moody and Sankey, travelled through England for the

conversion of the masses, Smith went to Germany, and proceeding from Berlin on to Switzerland, gave addresses in English, that were interpreted, in ten of the large cities. The most pious among clergy and laity flocked from far and near to hear him. The new apostle's journey became more and more a triumphal march. He was lauded as a reformer called to complete the work of Luther; as a prophet, who was to fructify the barren wastes of Germany with the water of life. The core of his doctrine was: Perfect holiness and the attainment of absolute perfection, not hereafter, but now! now! now! with the constant refrain: "*Jesus saves me now*"; not remission of sins through justification by faith in the atoning efficacy of Christ's blood, which only avails for outward sinful actions, but immediate extinction of sins by Christ in us, proved in living, unfaltering, inner, personal experience, etc. By a great international and interconfessional meeting at Brighton, lasting for ten days, in June, 1875, at which many German pastors, induced by the payment of travelling expenses, were present, the crown was put upon the work. But at the height of his triumph, under the daily increasing tension and excitement the apostle of holiness showed himself to be a poor sinful son of man, for he strayed into errors, "if not practically, at least theoretically," which his admirers at first referred to mental aberration, but which they hid from the eyes of the world under a veil of mystery. Toward the end of the Brighton conference he declared to his hearers: "Thus plunge into a life of divine unconcern!" and, "All Europe lies at my feet." And in subsequent private conversations he developed a system of ethics that "would suit Utah rather than England," to which he then so conformed his own conduct that his admirers, "although satisfied of the purity of his own intentions," were obliged energetically to repudiate and with all speed send away across the sea the man whom their own unmeasured adulation had deceived.

2. The Salvation Army.—An extremely fantastic caricature of English Methodism is the Salvation Army. The Methodist evangelist, William Booth, who in 1865 founded in one of the lowest quarters of London a new mission station, fell upon the idea in 1878, in order to make an impression on the rude masses, to give his male and female helpers a military organisation, discipline and uniform, and with military banners and music to undertake a campaign against the kingdom of the devil. The General of the Salvationists is Booth himself, his wife is his adjutant, his eldest daughter field-marshal; his fellow-workers male and female are his soldiers, cadets and officers of various ranks; chief of the staff is Booth's eldest son. Their services are conducted according to military forms; their orchestra of trombone, drum and trumpet is called the Hallelujah Brass Band.

Their journal, with an issue of 400,000, is the *War Cry;* another for children, is *The Little Soldier*, in which Jane, four years old, dilates on the experiences of her inner life; and Tommy, eleven years old, is sure that, having served the devil for eleven years, he will now fight for King Jesus; and Lucy, nine years old, rejoices in being washed in the blood of the Lamb. The army attained its greatest success in England. Its numerous "prisoners of war" from the devil's army (prostitutes, drunkards, thieves, etc.) are led at the parade as trophies of war, and tell of their conversion, whereupon the command of the general, "Fire a Volley," calls forth thousands of hallelujahs. Liberal collections and unsought contributions, embracing several donations of a £1,000 and more, are given to the General, not only to pay his soldiers, but also to rent or to purchase and fit up theatres, concert halls, circuses, etc., for their meetings, and to build large new "barracks." Its wonderful success has secured for the army many admirers and patrons, even in the highest ranks of society. Queen Victoria herself testified to Mrs. Booth her high satisfaction with her noble work. At the Convocation, too, in the Upper as well as the Lower House, distinguished prelates spoke favourably of its methods and results, and so encouraged the formation of a Church Army, which, under the direction of the mission preacher Aitken, pursues similar ways to those of the Salvation Army, without, however, its spectacular displays, and has lately extended its exertions to India. The temperance party after the same model has formed a Blue Ribbon Army, the members of which, distinguished by wearing a piece of blue ribbon in the buttonhole, confine themselves to fighting against alcohol. In opposition to it public-house keepers and their associates formed a Yellow Ribbon Army, which has as its ensign the yellow silk bands of cigar bundles. Soon after the first great success of the Salvation Army, a Skeleton Army was formed out of the lowest dregs of the London mob, which, with a banner bearing the device of a skeleton, making a noise with all conceivable instruments, and singing obscene street songs to sacred melodies, interrupted the marches of the Salvation, and afterwards of the Church, Army: throwing stones, filthy rotten apples and eggs, and even storming and demolishing their "barracks."—In 1880 a detachment of the Salvation Army, with Railton at its head, assisted by seven Hallelujah Lasses, made a first campaign in America, with New York as its head-quarters. In the following year, under Miss Booth, it invaded France, where it issues a daily bulletin, "*En Avant.*" In 1882 it appeared in Australia, then in India, where Chunder Sen, the founder of the Brama-Somaj, showed himself favourable. In Switzerland it broke ground in 1882, in Sweden in 1884, and in Germany, at Stuttgart, in November, 1886. Africa, Spain, Italy, etc., followed in succession. These foreign corps outside of England also found considerable success. Almost everywhere they met with opposition, the magistrates often forbidding their meetings, and inflicting fines and imprisonment, and the mob resorting to all sorts of violent interference. Nowhere were both sorts of opponents so persistent as in Switzerland in 1883 and 1884, especially in Lausanne, Geneva, Neuenburg, Bern, Beil, etc. Although General Booth himself at the annual meeting in April, 1884, boasted that £393,000 had been collected during the past year for the purposes of the army, and over 846 barracks in eighteen countries of the world had been opened, and now even spoke of strengthening the army by establishing a Salvation Navy, the increasing extravagances caused by the army itself, as well as the far greater improprieties of those more or less associated with it, has drawn away many of its former supporters.

3. **Baptists and Quakers.**—Baptist sympathies and tendencies often appeared in Germany apart from an anti-ecclesiastical pietism or mysticism. But this aberration first assumed considerable proportions when a Hamburg merchant, Oncken, who had been convinced by his private Bible reading of the untenableness of infant baptism, was baptized by an American baptist in 1834, and now not only founded the first German baptist congregation in Hamburg, but also proved unwearied in his efforts to extend the sect over all Germany and Scandinavia by missions and tract distribution. Oncken died in 1884. Thus gradually there were formed about a hundred new Baptist German congregations in Mecklenburg, Brandenburg (Berlin), Pomerania, Silesia, East Prussia (Memel, Tilsit, etc.), Westphalia, Wupperthal, Hesse, Württemberg and Switzerland. In Sweden (250 congregations with 18,000 souls) they were mainly recruited from the "Readers," who after 1850 went over in crowds (§ 201, 2). They also found entrance into Denmark and Courland, but in all cases almost exclusively among the uncultured classes of labourers and peasants. After long but vain attempts at suppression by the governments during the reactionary period of 1850, they obtained under the liberal policy of the next two decades more or less religious toleration in most states. They called themselves the society of "baptized Christians," and maintained that they were "the visible church of the saints," the chosen people of God, in contrast to the "hereditary church and the church of all and sundry," in which they saw the apocalyptic Babylon. Even the Mennonites who "sprinkle," instead of immersing, "all," *i.e.* without proper sifting, they regard as a "hereditary" church. With the Anglo-American Baptists they do indeed hold fellowship, but take exception to them in several points, especially about open communion.—A peculiar order of Baptists has arisen in Hungary in the Nazarenes or Nazirites, or as they call them-

selves: "Followers of Christ." Founded in 1840 by Louis Hencfey, originally a Catholic smith, who had returned home from Switzerland, the sect obtained numerous adherents from all three churches, most largely from the Reformed church, favoured perhaps by the not yet altogether extinguished reminiscences of the Baptist persecutions of the eighteenth century (§ 163, 2). They practised strict asceticism, refused to take oaths or engage in military service, and kept the bare Puritan forms of worship, in which any one was allowed to preach whom the Holy Spirit enlightened. Their congregations embraced weak and strong friends, and also weak and strong brethren. The strong friends after receiving baptism joined the ranks of weak brethren, and then again became strong brethren on their admission to the Lord's Supper. The church officers were singers, teachers, evangelists, elders, and bishops.—In North America Quakerism, under the influence of increasing material prosperity, had lost much of its primitive strictness in life and manners. The more lax were styled *Wet-*, and their more rigorous opponents *Dry-Quakers*. Enthusiasm over the American War of Independence of 1776-1783, spreading in their ranks, led to further departures from the rigid standard of early times. Those who took weapons in their hands were designated *Fighting Quakers*. The General Assembly disapproved but tolerated these departures; neither the Wet nor the Fighting Quakers were excommunicated, but they were not allowed any part in the government of the community. In 1822 a party appeared among them, led by Elias Hicks, which carried the original tendency of Quakerism to separate itself from historical Christianity so far as to deny the divinity of Christ, and to allow no controlling authority to Scripture in favour of the unrestricted sway of reason and conscience. This departure from the traditions of Quakerism, however, met with vigorous opposition, and the protesting party, known as *Evangelical Friends*, pronounced more decidedly than ever for the authority of Scripture. In England, notwithstanding the wealth and position of its adherents, Quakerism, since the second half of the eighteenth century, has suffered a slow but steady decrease, while even in America, to say the least, no advance can be claimed. In Holland, Friesland, and Holstein, Quaker missionaries had found some success among the Mennonites, without, however, forming any separate communities. In 1786 some English Quakers succeeded in winning a small number of proselytes in Hesse, who in 1792, under the protection of the prince of Waldeck, formed a little congregation at Friedersthal, near Pyrmont, which still maintains its existence.—On the sects of Jumpers and Shakers, variously related to primitive, fanatical Quakerism, see § 170, 7.[1]

---

[1] Rowntree, "Quakerism Past and Present." London, 1859.

4. Swedenborgians and Unitarians.—In the nineteenth century Swedenborgianism has found many adherents. In England, Scotland and North America the sect has founded many missionary and tract societies. In Württemberg the procurator Hofacker and the librarian Tafel, partly by editions and translations of the writings of Swedenborg, partly by their own writings, were specially zealous in vindicating and spreading their views. A general conference of all the congregations in Great Britain and Ireland in 1828 published a confession of faith and catechism, and thirteen journals (three English, seven American, Tafel's in German, one Italian and one Swedish) represent the interests of the party. The liberal spirit of modern times has in various directions introduced modifications in its doctrine. Its Sabellian opposition to the church doctrine of the Trinity and its Pelagian opposition to the doctrine of justification, have been retained, and its spiritualising of eschatological ideas has been intensified, but the theosophical magical elements have been wholly set aside and scarcely any reference is ever made to revelations from the other world.—From early times the Unitarians had a well ordered and highly favoured ecclesiastical institution in Transylvania (§ 163, 1). But in England the law still threatened them with a death sentence. This law had not indeed for a long time been carried into effect, and in 1813 it was formally abrogated. There are now in England about 400 small Unitarian congregations with some 300,000 souls. The famous chemist Jos. Priestly may be regarded as the founder of North American Unitarianism (§ 171, 1), although only after his death in 1804 did the movement which he represented spread widely through the country. Then in a short time hundreds of Unitarian congregations were formed. Their most celebrated leaders were W. Ellery Channing, who died in 1842, and Theodore Parker, who died in 1860, both of Boston.

5. Extravagantly Fanatical Manifestations. — The English woman Johanna Southcote declared that she was the "woman in the sun" of Revelation xii. or the Lamb's wife. In 1801 she came forth with her prophecies. Her followers, the New Israelites or Sabbatarians, so called because they observed the Old Testament law of the Sabbath, founded a chapel in London for their worship. A beautiful cradle long stood ready to receive the promised Messiah, but Johanna died in 1814 without giving birth to him.—A horrible occurrence, similar to that recorded in § 210, 2, took place some years later, in 1823, in the village of Wildenspuch in Canton Zürich. Margaret Peter, a peasant's daughter, excited by morbid visions in early youth, was on this account expelled from Canton Aargau, and was carried still farther in the direction of extreme mysticism by the vicar John Ganz, by whom she was introduced to Madame de Krüdener (§ 176, 2). Amid continual heavenly visions and revelations, as well as violent conflicts with the devil and his evil spirits, she gathered a group of faithful followers, by whom she was revered as a highly gifted saint, among them a melancholy shoemaker, Morf, whom Ganz introduced to her. The spiritual love relationship between the two in an unguarded hour took a sensual form and led to the birth of a child, which Morf's forbearing wife after successfully simulating pregnancy adopted as her own. This deep fall, for which she wholly blamed the devil, drove her fanaticism to madness. The ridiculous proceedings in her own house, where for a whole day she and her adherents beat with fists and hammers what they supposed to be the devil, led the police to interfere. But before orders arrived from Zürich, she found refuge in an asylum, and there the end soon came. Margaret assured her followers that in order that Christ might fully triumph and Satan be overthrown, blood must be shed for the salvation of many thousand souls. Her younger sister Elizabeth voluntarily allowed herself to be slain, and she herself with almost incredible courage allowed her hands and feet to be nailed to the wood and then with a stroke of the knife was killed, under the promise that she as well as her sister should rise again on the third day. The tragedy ended by the apprehension and long confinement of those concerned in it.—The sect of Springers in Ingermannland had its origin in 1818. Arising out of a religious excitement not countenanced by the church authorities, they held that each individual needed immediate illumination of the Holy Spirit for his soul's salvation. So soon as they believed that this was obtained, the presence of the Spirit was witnessed to by ecstatic prayer, singing and shouting joined with handshaking and springing in their assemblies. The special illumination required as its correlate a special sanctification, and this they sought not only in repudiation of marriage, but also in abstinence from flesh, beer, spirits and tobacco. The "holy love," prized instead of marriage, however, here also led to sensual errors, and the result was that many after the example of the Skopzen (§ 210, 4) resorted to the surer means of castration.—Among the Swedish peasants in 1842 appeared the singular phenomenon of the Crying Voices (*Röstar*). Uneducated laymen, and more particularly women and even children, after convulsive fits broke out into deep mutterings of repentance and prophesyings of approaching judgment. The substance of their proclamations, however, was not opposed to the church doctrine, and the criers were themselves the most diligent frequenters of church and sacrament.—In the beginning of 1870 the wife of a settler at Leonerhofe, near San Leopoldo in Brazil, Jacobina Maurer, became famous among the careless colonists of that region as a pious miracle-working prophetess. In religious assemblies which she originated, she gave forth her fantastic revelations based upon allegorical interpretations of Scripture, and founded a congregation of the "cloot" with a communistic constitution, in which she assumed to herself all church offices as the Christ come again. Rude abuse and maltreatment of these "Muckers" on the part of the "unbelieving," and the interference of the police, who arrested some of the more zealous partisans of the female Christ, brought the fanaticism to its utmost pitch. Jacobina now declared it the duty of believers to prepare for the bliss of the millennium by rooting out all the godless. Isolated murders were the prelude of the night of horror, June 25th-26th, 1874, on which well organized Mucker-bands, abundantly furnished with powder and shot, went forth murdering and burning through the district for miles around. The military sent out against them did not succeed in putting down the revolt before August 2nd, after the prophetess with many of her adherents had fallen in a fanatically brave resistance.

6. **Christian Communistic Sects.**—The only soil upon which these could flourish was that of the Free States of North America. Besides the small Shaker communities (§ 170, 7) still surviving in 1858, the following new fraternities are the most important: 1. The Harmonites The dissatisfaction caused among the Württemberg Pietists by the introduction of liturgical innovations led to several migrations in the beginning of the century. Geo. Rapp, a simple peasant from the village of Iptingen, went to America in 1803 or 1804 with about six hundred adherents, and settled in the valley of Connoquenessing, near Pittsburg in Pennsylvania. As a fundamental principle of this "Harmony Association," which honoured father Rapp as autocratic patriarch, prophet and high priest, and with him believed in the near approach of the second advent, the community of goods holds a prominent place. By diligence and industry in agriculture, labour and manufactures, they reached great prosperity under the able leadership of their patriarch. In 1807 the community, by a resolution of its own to which Rapp agreed, resolved to abstain from marriage, so that henceforth no children were born nor marriages performed. A falling off in numbers was made up in 1817 by new arrivals from Württemberg and afterwards by the adoption of children. Industrial reasons led the community in 1814 to colonize Wabashthal in Indiana, where they built the town of Harmony, which, however, in 1823, on account of its unhealthy situation, they sold to the Scotchman Robert Owen (§ 212, 8), and then founded for themselves the town of Economy, not far from Pittsburg, where they still reside. In 1831 an adventurer, Bernard Müller, appeared among them, who, at Offenbach, had, for a long time, under the name of Proli, played a brilliant part as a prophet called to establish universal spiritual monarchy, and then, when in danger from the courts of law, had fled to America. In Economy

where he passed himself off as Count Maximilian von Leon, persecuted on account of his belief in the second coming, he found as such a hearty welcome, and within a year, by his agitation for the reintroduction of marriage and worldly enjoyments, drew away a third part of the community, embracing 250 souls. The dissentients with 105,000 dollars from the common purse withdrew and settled under the leadership of the pseudo-count as a New Jerusalem society in the neighbouring village of Philippsburg. But the new patriarch conducted himself so riotously that he was obliged in 1833 to flee to Louisiana, where in the same year he died of cholera. His people now in deep distress turned to Dr. Keil, a mystic come from Prussia, who reorganised them after the pattern of Rapp's communistic society, but with liberty to marry, and brought them to a prosperous condition in two colonies mainly founded by him at Bethel in Missouri and Aurora in Oregon. Economy, too, flourished in spite of the heavy losses it sustained, so that now the common property of the populace, which through celibacy had been reduced to about eighty persons, amounts to eight million dollars. Father Rapp died in 1847, in his ninetieth year, confident to the end that he would guide his church unto the hourly expected advent of Christ.—2. When in 1831 a wave of revival passed over North America, J. H. Noyes, an advocate's assistant, applied himself to the study of the Bible and became the founder of a new sect, the Bible Communists or Perfectionists of the Oneida Society. He taught that the promised advent of Christ took place spiritually soon after the destruction of Jerusalem; by it the kingdom of Adam was ended and the kingdom of God in the heart of those who knew and received him was established. The official churches were only state churches, but the true church was scattered in the hearts of individual saints, until Noyes collected and organized it into a Bible family. For them there is no more law, for laws are for sinners and the saints no longer sin. Each saint can do and suffer whatever the Spirit of God moves him to. All the members of the congregation constitute one family, live, eat, and work together. Goods, wives and children are in common. It lies with the wife to accept or refuse the approaches of a man. But soon this proclaimed freedom from law sent everything into confusion and disunion; schism—apostasy prevailed. But Father Noyes now saved his church from destruction by introducing a correction to this freedom from law in *Sympathy*, i.e. in the agreement of all members of the family. The odium which fell upon the community from without on account of its "complex marriages," induced him at last in August, 1879, although he still always maintained the soundness of his principle of free love and its final victory over prejudice, to ordain the introduction of monogamic marriages, and the community acquiesced. With

regard to community of goods, meals and children, however, they kept
to the old lines. The parent community has its seat at Lenox in
Oneidabach in New York State. Alongside of it are three daughter
communities. They have their prophets and prophetesses, but no
ritual service and no Sunday. Their employment (they number
about 300 souls) is mainly fruit culture and the manufacture of snares
of every kind for wild and other animals.[1]

7. **Millenarian Exodus Communities.—1. The Georgian Separatists.** The
stream of Württemberg emigrants above referred to turned also
toward Southern Russia. The settlers in Transcaucasian Georgia in
the long absence of regular pastors fell into fanatical separation, which
the clergy who followed in 1820 could not overcome. Under the
direction of three elders (one of them an old woman) as representing
the Holy Trinity, they lived quietly, refused to baptize their children,
to give their dead burial according to the rites of the church,
to call in physicians in sickness, and at last rejected the marriage
relation. In 1842 their female elder, Barbara Spohn, wife of a cart-
wright, appeared in the rôle of a prophet, proclaiming the near approach of the end of the world and calling upon her followers to pass
through the wilderness to the promised land, there to enter into the
millenial kingdom. They were to take with them no money, no bread,
etc., but only a staff; their clothes and shoes would not wear old in
the desert, they could eat manna and quails, and in the holy land
Christ would dress them in the bridal robe. The government sought
in vain to bring them to reason and to obstruct their way, when about
three hundred of them wished at Pentecost, 1843, to start on their
journey. They were allowed to send three men to Constantinople and
Palestine to seek permission from the Turkish government to settle
in a spot near Jerusalem. But these returned before the close of the
year with the news, that Palestine is not the land that would suit
them. This brought the majority to their senses and they rejoined
the church.—2. Equally unfortunate was the attempt at colonization made in 1878 by some Bavarian Chiliasts. The pastor Clöter in
Illenschwang had for a long time in the " *Brüderbote*," edited by him,
urged the emigration of believers to South Russia, where, according to
his exposition of the apocalyptic prophecy, a secure place of refuge
had been provided by God for believers of the last times during the
near approaching persecutions of antichrist. In June, 1878, the tailor
Minderlein with his family and nineteen other persons started to go

---

[1] Dixon, "New America." 2 vols., 8th edition. London, 1869.
Nordhoff, "The Communistic Societies of the United States." London 1874.

thither. Minderlein died by the way, and his companions after enduring great hardships were obliged to return, and reached Nuremberg again in October, absolutely destitute. Clöter, however, was not discouraged by this misfortune. In December he called his adherents from Bavaria, Württemberg and Switzerland, together to a conference at Stuttgart, where they formed themselves into the "German Exodus Church." In the summer, 1880, Clöter himself travelled to South Russia and thought that he found in the Crimea the fittest place of refuge. On his return he was banished, but after some days liberated, though deprived of his clerical office. A final stop was then put to the exodus movement.

8.—3. The Amen Community owed its feeble existence to a Christian Jew, Israel Pick of Bohemia. Believing that he was not required in baptism to renounce his Judaism, but that rather thereby he first became a true Jew, through a onesided interpretation of Old Testament promises to his nation, he wished to found a colony of the people of God in the Holy Land on Jewish-Christian principles. The whole Mosaic law, excluding the observance of the Sabbath and circumcision, was to be the basis, together with baptism and the Lord's Supper, of ecclesiastical and civil organization. He succeeded in winning a few converts here and there, to whom he gave the name of the Amen Community, because in Christ (the אֱלֹהֵי אָמֵן Isa. lxv. 16) all the prophecies of the old covenant are Yea and Amen. Its chief seat was at Munich-Gladbach. In 1859 Pick travelled to Palestine in order to choose a spot for the settlement of his followers and there all trace of him was lost.—4. The founder of the German Temple Communities in Palestine was Chr. Hoffmann, brother of General Superintendent Hoffmann of Berlin, and son of the founder of the Kornthal Community (§ 196, 5), in connection with Chr. Paulus, nephew of the well known Heidelberg professor Paulus (§ 182, 2). In 1854 they issued an invitation to a conference at Ludwigsburg, for consultation about the means for gathering the people of God in Palestine. A great crowd of believers from all parts, numbering some 10,000 families, was to embark for the holy land to form there a new people of God which, on the foundation of prophets and apostles, should strictly practise the public law of the old covenant in all points of civil administration, including the laws of the sabbath and the jubilee. The conference besought of the German League that it would use its influence with the Sultan to secure permission for colonization with self-government and religious freedom. As the German League simply declined the request, the committee bought the estate of Kirschenhardthof near Marbach, in order there temporarily and in a small way to form a social commonwealth observing the Mosaic law. In 1858 Hoffmann went with two of his followers to Jerusalem in order to look out a place there suitable for their purpose. The result was unsatisfactory. Therefore he issued in 1861 a summons to take part in a German Temple. Consequently a number of men from Württemberg, Bavaria, and Baden, Protestants and Catholics, forsook their churches, ordained priests and elders, and appointed Hoffmann their bishop and held regular synods. The final aim of this procedure, however, was always still to find a settlement in Palestine and erect a temple in Jerusalem which, according to prophecy, is to form the central sanctuary for the whole world. Colonization in the East was tried as a means to this end. Since 1869 there have been five organized colonies, with a Temple Chief and a congregational school, embracing about 1,000 souls, established in Palestine, viz. at Jaffa, Haifa, Sarona, Beyrout, and in 1878 even in Jerusalem, whither the original colony at Jaffa was transferred. The German Imperial Government refused indeed in 1879 to give the recognition sought for to the civil and political organization of the Palestinian colonies, as in a foreign country beyond its jurisdiction, but granted to its Lyceum at Jerusalem a yearly contribution of 1,500 marks and to the schools of Jaffa, Haifa and Sarona from 650 to 1,000. In 1875 Hoffmann published at Stuttgart a large apologetical and polemical work, "*Occident und Orient*," which contained many thoughtful remarks. But since then, in the central organ of all the Temple Communities inspired by him, the "*Süddeutsche Warte*," he has openly and distinctly attached himself to Ebionitic rationalism, by denying and opposing the fundamental evangelical doctrine of the trinity, redemption, and the sacraments. These theological views, however, were by no means shared in by all the Templars, and caused a split in the community, one section at Haifa with the chief templar there, Hardegg, at its head, separating from the central body as an independent "Imperial Brotherhood." The seceders, joined by many German and American templar friends, again drew nearer to the Evangelical church and ultimately became reconciled with it. But Hoffmann has, in his last work, *Bibelforschungen* i. ii.: *Röm.- u. Kol. br., Jerus.* 1882, 1884, carried his polemic against the church doctrine to the utmost extreme of cynical abuse. He died in December, 1885. At the head of the denomination now stands his fellow-worker Paulus. From year to year several drop back into the Evangelical church so that the community is evidently approaching extinction.

9. **The Community of "the New Israel."**—The Jewish advocate Jos. Rabinowitsch at Kishenev in Bessarabia, who had long occupied himself with plans for the improvement of the spiritual and material circumstances of his fellow-countrymen, at the outbreak of the persecution of the Jews in 1882 in South Russia eagerly urged their return to the holy land of their fathers and himself undertook a

journey of inspection. There definite shape seems to have been given
to the long cherished thought of seeking the salvation of his people
in an independent national attachment to their old sacred historical
development, broken off 1850 years before, by acknowledging the
Messiahship of Jesus. At least after his return he gave expression
to the sentiment, based on Romans xi.: "The keys of the holy land
are in the hands of our brother Jesus," which, in consequence of the
high esteem in which he was held by his countrymen, was soon re-
echoed by some 200 Jewish families. His main endeavour now was
the formation of independent national Jewish-Christian communities,
after the pattern of the primitive church of Jerusalem, as "*New
Israelites*," observing all the old Jewish rites and ordinances com-
patible with New Testament apostolic preaching and reconcilable
with modern civil and social conditions. The Torah, the prophets of
the Old Testament and the New Testament writings, are held as absolutely binding, whereas the Talmud and the post-apostolic Gentile
Christian additions to doctrine, worship, and constitution are not so
regarded. Jesus, Rabinowitsch teaches, is the true Messiah who, as
Moses and prophets foretold, was born as Son of David by the Spirit
of God and in the power of that Spirit lived and taught in Israel,
then for our salvation suffered, was crucified and died, rose from the
dead, and ascended to the right hand of the Father in heaven. The
trinity of persons in God as well as the two natures in Christ he
rejects, as not taught in the New Testament and originating in Gentile
Christian speculation. Baptism and the Lord's Supper (and that
"according to the example of Christians of the pure Evangelical
confession in England and Germany") are recognised as necessary
means of grace; but the Lord's Supper is to be, according to its institution, a real meal with the old Jewish prayers. As to the doctrine
of the Supper, Rabinowitsch agrees with the views of the Lutheran
church. Circumcision and the observance of the Sabbath and the
feasts (especially the Passover), are retained, not indeed as necessary
to salvation, therefore not binding on Gentile Christians, but pa-
triotically observed by Jewish-Christians as signs of their election
from and before all nations as the people of God. In January, 1885,
with consent of the Russian Government, the newly-erected synagogue
of "the holy Messiah Jesus Christ" for the small congregation of
Rabinowitsch's followers at Kishenev was solemnly opened, the
Russian church authorities, the Lutheran pastor Fultin and many
young Jews taking part in the service. Soon afterwards Rabinowitsch received Christian baptism in the chapel of the Bohemian
church at Berlin at the hands of Prof. Mead of Andover, probably in
recognition of the aid sent from America.—A Jewish-Christian religious communion with similar tendencies has been formed in the

South Russian town of Jellisawetgrad under the designation of a "*Biblical Spiritual Brotherhood.*"

10. The Catholic Apostolic Church of the Irvingites.—Edward Irving, 1792–1834, a powerful and popular preacher of the Scotch-Presbyterian church in London, maintained the doctrine that the human nature of Christ like our own was affected by original sin, which was overcome and atoned for by the power of the divine nature. At the same time he became convinced that the spiritual gifts of the apostolic church could and should still be obtained by prayer and faith. A party of his followers soon began to exercise the gift of tongues by uttering unintelligible sounds, loud cries, and prophecies. His presbytery suspended him in 1832 and the General Assembly of the Church of Scotland excommunicated him. Rich and distinguished friends from the Episcopal church, among them the wealthy banker, Drummond, afterwards prominent as an apostle (died 1859), rallied round the man thus expelled from his church, and gave him the means to found a new church, but, in spite of Irving's protests, brought with them high church puseyite tendencies, which soon drove out the heretical as well as the puritanic tendencies, and modified the fanatical element into a hierarchical and liturgical formalism. The restoration of the office of apostle was the characteristic feature of the movement. After many unsuccessful attempts they succeeded by the divine illumination of the prophets in calling twelve apostles, first and chief of whom was the lawyer Cardale (died 1877). By the apostles, as chief rulers and stewards of the church, evangelists and pastors (or angels, Rev. ii. 1, 8, etc.) were ordained in accordance with Eph. iv. 11; and subordinate to the pastors, there were appointed six elders and as many deacons, so that the office bearers of each congregation embraced thirteen persons, after the example of Christ and His twelve disciples. In London seven congregations were formed after the pattern of the seven apocalyptic churches (Rev. i. 20). Prominent among their new revelations was the promise of the immediately approaching advent of the Lord. The Lord, who was to have come in the lifetime of the first disciples and so was looked for confidently by them, delayed indefinitely His return on account of abounding iniquity and prevented the full development of the second apostolate designed for the Gentiles and meanwhile represented only by Paul, because the church was no longer worthy of it. Now at last, after eighteen centuries of degradation, in which the church came to be the apocalyptic Babylon and ripened for judgment, the time has come when the suspended apostolate has been restored to prepare the way for the last things. Very confidently was it at first maintained that none of their members should die, but should live to see the final consummation. But after death had removed so many from among them, and even the apostles

one after another, it was merely said that those are already born who should see the last day. It may come any day, any hour. It begins with the first resurrection (Rev. xx. 5) and the "changing" of the saints that are alive (the wise virgins, *i.e.* the Irvingites), who will be caught up to the Lord in the clouds and in a higher sphere be joined with the Lord in the marriage supper of the Lamb. They are safely hidden while antichrist persecutes the other Christians, the foolish virgins, who only can be saved by means of painful suffering, and executes judgment on Babylon. This marks the end of the Gentile church; but then begins the conversion of the Jews, who, driven by necessity and the persecution of sinful men, have sought and found a refuge in Palestine. After a short victory of antichrist the Lord visibly appears among the risen and removed. The kingdom of antichrist is destroyed, Satan is bound, the saints live and reign with Christ a thousand years on the earth freed from the curse. Thereafter Satan is again let loose for a short time and works great havoc. Then comes Satan's final overthrow, the second resurrection and last judgment. Their liturgy, composed by the apostles, is a compilation from the Anglican and Catholic sources. Sacerdotalism and sacrifice are prominent and showy priestly garments are regarded as requisite. Yet they repudiate the Romish doctrine of the bloodless repetition of the bleeding sacrifice, as well as the doctrine of transubstantiation. But they strictly maintain the contribution of the tenth as a duty laid upon Christians by Heb. vii. 4. Their typical view of the Old Testament history and legislation, especially of the tabernacle, is most arbitrary and baseless. Their first published statement appeared in 1836 in an apostolic "*Letter to the Patriarchs, Bishops, and Presidents of the Church of Christ in all Lands, and to emperors, kings, and princes of all baptized nations,*" which was sent to the most prominent among those addressed, even to the pope, but produced no result. After this they began to prosecute their missionary work openly. But they gave their attention mainly to those already believers, and took no part in missions to the heathen, as they were sent neither to the heathen nor to unbelievers, but only to gather and save believers. In their native land of England, where at first they had great success, their day seems already past. In North America they succeeded in founding only two congregations. They prospered better in Germany and Switzerland, where they secured several able theologians, chief of all Thiersch, the professor of Theology in Marburg, the Tertullian of this modern Montanism (died 1885), and founded about eighty small congregations with some 5,000 members, chief of which are those of Berlin, Stettin, Königsberg, Leipzig, Marburg, Cassel, Basel, Augsburg, etc. Even among the Catholic clergy of Bavaria this movement found response; but that was checked by a series of depositions and excommunications during 1857.—In 1882 the Lutheran pastor Alpers of Gehrden in Hanover was summoned to appear before the consistory to answer for his Irvingite views. He denied the charge and referred to his good Lutheran preaching. As, however, he had taken the sacramental "sealing" from Irvingite apostles, the court regarded this as proof of his having joined the party and so deposed him.[1]

11. The Darbyites and Adventists.—Related on the one hand to Irvingism by their expectation of the immediately approaching advent and by their regarding themselves as the saints of the last time who would alone be saved, the Darbyites, on the other hand, by their absolute independentism form a complete contrast to the Irvingite hierarchism. John Darby, 1800–1882, first an advocate, then a clergyman of the Anglican church, breaking away from Anglicanism, founded between 1820 and 1830 a sectarian, apocalyptic, independent community at Plymouth (whence the name Plymouth Brethren), but in 1838 settled in Geneva, and in 1840 went to Canton Vaud, where Lausanne and Vevey have become the headquarters of the sect. All clerical offices, all ecclesiastical forms are of the evil one, and are evidence of the corruption of the church. There is only one office, the spiritual priesthood of all believers, and every believer has the right to preach and dispense the sacraments. Not only the Catholic, but also the Protestant church is a "Balaam Church," and since the departure of the apostles no true church has existed. In doctrine they are strictly Calvinistic.[2]—The Adventists. Regarding the 2,300 days of Dan. viii. 14 as so many years, W. Miller of New York and Boston proclaimed in 1833 that the second advent would take place on the night of October 23rd, 1847, and convinced many thousands of the correctness of his calculations. When at last the night referred to arrived the believers continued assembled in their tabernacles waiting, but in vain, for the promise (Matt. xxiv. 30, 31; 1 Cor. xv. 52; 1 Thess. iv. 16, 17), at "the voice of the archangel and the trump of God to be caught up in the clouds to meet the Lord in the air." This miscalculation, however, did not shake the Adventists' belief in the near approach of the Lord, but their number rather increased from year to year. Most zealous in propagating their views by journals and tracts, evangelists and missionaries, is a branch of the sect founded by James White of

---

[1] Oliphant, "Life of Ed. Irving." 3rd edition. London, 1865. Carlyle, in "Miscellaneous Essays." Brown, "Personal Reminiscences of Ed. Irving," in *Expositor*. 3 ser., vol. vi., pp. 216, 257. Miller, "History and Doctrine of Irvingism," 2 vols. London, 1878.

[2] Darby, "Personal Recollections." London, 1881.

Michigan, whose adherents, because they keep the Sabbath in place of the Lord's Day, are called *Seventh Day Adventists*.

12. The Mormons or Latter Day Saints.—Jos. Smith, a broken down farmer of Vermont, who took to knavish digging for hid treasures, affirmed in 1825, that under direction of divine revelations and visions, he had excavated on Comora hill in New York State, golden tablets in a stone kist on which sacred writings were engraved. A prophet's spectacles, *i.e.*, two pierced stones which as a Mormon Urim and Thummim lay beside them, enabled him to understand and translate them. He published the translation in "the Book of Mormon." According to this book, the Israelites of the ten tribes had migrated under their leader, Lehi, to America. There they divided into two peoples; the ungodly Lamanites, answering to the modern Redskins, and the pious Nephites. The latter preserved among them the old Israelitish histories and prophecies, and through miraculous signs in heaven and earth obtained knowledge of the birth of Christ that had meanwhile taken place. Toward the end of the fourth century after Christ, however, the Lamanites began a terrible war of extermination against the Nephites, in consequence of which the latter were rooted out with the exception of the prophet Mormon and his son Moroni. Mormon recorded his revelations on the golden tablets referred to, and concealed them as the future witness for the saints of the last days on the earth. Smith proclaimed himself now called on of God, on the basis of these documents and the revelations made to him, to found the church of *The Latter Day Saints*. The widow of a preacher in New York proved indeed that the Book of Mormon was almost literally a plagiarism from a historico-didactic romance written by her deceased husband, Sal. Spaulding. The MS. had passed into the hands of Sidney Rigdon, formerly a Baptist minister and then a bookseller's assistant, subsequently Smith's right-hand man. But even this did not disturb the believers. In 1831 Smith with his followers settled at Kirtland in Ohio. To avoid the daily increasing popular odium, he removed to Missouri, and thence to Illinois, and founded there, in 1840, the important town of Nauvoo with a beautiful temple. By diligence, industry and good discipline, the wealth, power and influence of their commonwealth increased, but in the same proportion the envy, hatred and prejudices of the people, which charged them with the most atrocious crimes. In 1844, to save bloodshed the governor ordered the two chiefs, Jos. and Hiram Smith, to surrender to voluntary imprisonment awaiting a regular trial. But furious armed mobs attacked the prison and shot down both. The roughs of the whole district then gathered in one great troop, destroyed the town of Nauvoo, burned the temple and drove out the inhabitants. These, now numbering 15,000 men, in several suc-

cessive expeditions amid indescribable hardships pressed on "through the wilderness" over the Rocky Mountains, in order to erect for themselves a Zion on the other side. Smith's successor was the carpenter, Brigham Young. The journey occupied two full years, 1845–1847. In the great Salt Lake basin of Utah they founded *Salt Lake City*, or the New Jerusalem, as the capital of their wilderness state *Deseret.* The gold digging of the neighbouring state of California did not allure them, for their prophet told them that to pave streets, build houses and sow fields was better employment than seeking for gold So here again they soon became a flourishing commonwealth.

13. In common with the Irvingites, who recognised in them their own diabolic caricature, the Mormons restored the apostolic and prophetic office, insisted upon the continuance of the gift of tongues and miracles, expected the speedy advent of the Lord, reintroduced the payment of tithes, etc. But what distinguished them from all Christian sects was the proclamation of polygamy as a religious duty, on the plea that only those women who had been "sealed" to a Latter-day Saint would share in the blessedness of life eternal. This was probably first introduced by Young in consequence of a new "divine revelation," but down to 1852 kept secret and denied before "the Gentiles." The ambiguous book of Mormon was set meanwhile more and more in the background, and the teachings and prophecies of their prophet brought more and more to the front. "The Voice of Warning to all Nations" of the zealous proselyte Parly Pratt, formerly a Campbellite preacher, exercised a great influence in spreading the sect. But the most gifted of them all was Orson Pratt, Rigdon's successor in the apostolate. To him mainly is ascribed the construction of its later, highly fantastic religious system which, consisting of elements gathered from Neoplatonism, gnosticism, and other forms of theosophical mysticism, embraces all the mysteries of time and eternity. Its fundamental ideas are these: There are gods without number; all are polygamists and their wives are sharers of their glory and bliss. They are the fathers of human souls who here on earth ripen for their heavenly destiny. Jesus is the first born son of the highest god by his first wife; he was married on earth to Mary Magdalene, the sisters Martha and Mary and other women. Those saints who here fulfil their destiny become after death gods, while they are arranged according to their merit in various ranks and with prospect of promotion to higher places. At the end of this world's course, Jesus will come again, and, enthroned in the temple of Salt Lake City, exercise judgment against all "Gentiles" and apostates, etc.—The constitution of the Mormon State is essentially theocratic. At the head stood the president, **Brigham Young**, as prophet, patriarch, and priest-king, in whose

hands are all the threads of the spiritual as well as secular administration. A high council alongside of him, consisting of seventy
members, as also the prophets and apostles, bishops and elders, and
generally the whole richly organized hierarchy, are only the pliable
instruments of his all-commanding will. Every one on entering the
society surrenders his whole property, and after that contributes a
tenth of his yearly income and personal labour to the common purse
of the community. Soon numerous missionaries were sent forth who
crossed the Atlantic, and attained great success, especially in Scotland,
England and Scandinavia, but also in North-West Germany and
in Switzerland. On removing the misunderstanding that prevailed
about their social and political condition, and supplying the penni-
less out of the rich immigration fund with the means to make
the journey, they persuaded great crowds of their new converts to
accompany them to Utah.

14. In 1849 the Mormons had asked Congress for the apportioning
of the district colonized by them as an independent and autonomous
" State " in the union, but were granted, in 1850, only the constitution
of a " territory " under the central government at Washington, and
the appointment of their patriarch, Young, as its governor. Accustomed to absolute rule, in two years he drove out all the other
officers appointed by the union. He was then deprived of office, but
the new governor, Col. Sefton, appointed in 1854, with the small
armament supplied him could not maintain his position and
voluntarily retired. When afterwards in 1858 Governor Cumming,
appointed by president Buchanan, entered Utah with a strong
military force, Young armed for a decisive struggle. A compromise,
however, was effected. A complete amnesty was granted to the
saints, the soldiers of the union entered peacefully into the Salt-Lake
City, and Young assumed tolerably friendly relations with the
governor, who, nevertheless, by the erection of a fort commanding the
city made the position safe for himself and his troops. On the outbreak of the war of Secession in 1861 the troops of the union were for
the most part withdrawn. But all the more energetically did the
central government at the close of the war in 1865 resolve upon the
complete subjugation of the rebel saints, having learnt that since
1852 numerous murders had taken place in the territory, and that
the disappearance of whole caravans of colonists was not due to
attacks of Indians, who would have scalped their victims, but to a
secret Mormon fraternity called Danites (Judges xviii.), brothers of
Gideon (Judges vi. ff.) or Angels of Destruction, which, obedient to the
slightest hint from the prophet, had undertaken to avenge by bloody
terrorism any sign of resistance to his authority, to arrest any
tendency to apostasy, and to guard against the introduction of any

foreign element. The Union Pacific Railway opened in 1869 deprived the "Kingdom of God" of its most powerful protection, its geographical isolation, while the rich silver mines discovered at the same time in Utah, peopled city and country with immense flocks of "Gentiles." The nemesis, which brought the Mormon bishop Lee, twenty years after the deed, under the lash of the high court of justiciary as involved in the horrible massacre of a large party of emigrants at Mountain Meadows in 1857, would probably have also befallen the prophet himself as the main instigator of this and many other crimes had he not by a sudden death two months later, in his seventy-fifth year, escaped the jurisdiction of any earthly tribunal (died 1877). A successor was not chosen, but supreme authority is in the hands of the college of twelve apostles with the elder John Taylor at their head.—Repeated attempts made since 1874 by the United States authorities by penal enactments to root out polygamy among the Mormons have always failed, because its actual existence could never be legally proved. The witness called could or would say nothing, since the "sealing" was always secretly performed, and the women concerned denied that a marriage had been entered into with the accused, or if one confessed herself his married wife she refused to give any evidence about his domestic relations.—Recently a split has occurred among the Mormons. By far the larger party is that of the "Salt Lake Mormons," which holds firmly by polygamy and all the other institutions introduced by Young and since his time. The other party is that of the Kirtland, or Old Mormons, headed by the son of their founder, Jos. Smith, who had been passed over on account of his youth, which repudiates all these as unsupported novelties and restores the true Mormonism of the founder. The Old Mormons not only oppose polygamy, but also all more recently introduced doctrines. They are called Kirtland Mormons from the first temple built by their founder at Kirtland in 1814, which having fallen into ruins, was restored by Geo. Smith, jun., and became the centre of the Old Mormon denomination. In April 1885 they held there their first synod, attended by 200 deputies.[1]

15. The Taepings in China.—Hung-sen-tsenen, born in 1813 in the province of Shan-Tung, was destined for the learned profession but failed in his examination at Canton. There he first, in 1833, came into contact with Protestant missionaries, whose misunderstood words awakened in him the belief that he was called to perform great things.

Stenhouse, "An Englishwoman in Utah, the story of a Life's Experience in Mormonism." 2nd ed. London, 1880. Gunnison, "The Mormons New York, 1884, Burton, "The City of the Saints." London, 1861.

At the same time he there got possession of some Christian Chinese tracts. Failing in his examination a second time in 1837, he fell into a dangerous illness and had a series of visions in which an old man with a golden beard appeared, handing to him the insignia of imperial rank, and commanding him to root out the demons. After his recovery he became an elementary teacher. A relative called Li visited him in 1843. The Christian tracts were again sought out and carefully studied. Sen now recognised in the old man of his visions the God of the Christians and in himself the younger brother of Jesus. The two baptized one another and won over two young relatives to their views. Expelled from their offices, they went in 1844 to the province of Kiang Se as pencil and ink sellers, preached diligently the new doctrine and founded numerous small congregations of their sect. The American missionaries at Canton heard of the success of their preaching, and Sen accepted an invitation to join them in 1847. The missionary Roberts had a great esteem for him and intended to baptize him, when in consequence of stories spread about him their relations became strained. Sen now returned in 1848 to his companions in Kiang Se, who had diligently and successfully continued their preaching. In 1850 they began to attract attention by the violent destruction of idols. When now all the remnants of a pirate band joined them as converts, they were in common with these persecuted by the government and proclaimed rebels. The expulsion of the hated Mantshu dynasty, which two hundred years before had displaced the Ming dynasty, and the overthrow of idolatry were now their main endeavour, and in 1857 they organized under Sen a regular rebellion for the setting up of a Taeping dynasty, i.e., of universal peace. The Taeping army advanced unhindered, all Mantschu soldiers who fell into its hands were massacred, and of the inhabitants of the provinces conquered, only those were spared who joined their ranks. In March, 1853, they stormed the second capital of the empire, Nankin, the old residence of the Ming dynasty. There Sen fixed his residence and styled himself Tien-Wang, the Divine Prince. He assigned to ten subordinate princes the government of the conquered provinces, almost the half of the immense empire. Thousands of bibles were circulated; the ten commandments proclaimed as the foundation of law, many writings, prayers and poems composed for the instruction of the people, and these with the bible made subjects of examination for entrance to the learned order. An Arian theory of the trinity was set forth; the Father is the one personal God, whose likeness in bodily human form Sen strictly forbade, destroying the Catholic images as well as the Chinese idols. Jesus is the firstborn son of God, yet not himself God, sent by the Father into the world in order to enlighten it by his doctrine and to redeem it by his atoning sufferings. Sen, the younger brother of Jesus, was sent into the world to spread the doctrine of Jesus and to expel the demons, the Mantschu dynasty. Reception takes place through baptism. The Lord's Supper was unknown to them. Bloody and bloodless offerings were still tolerated. The use of wine and tobacco was forbidden; the use of opium and trafficking in it were punished with death. But polygamy was sanctioned. Saturday, according to the Old Testament, was their holy day. Their service consisted only of prayer, singing and religious instruction; but also written prayers were presented to God by burning.

16. Sen himself had no more visions after 1837. But other ecstatic prophets arose, the eastern prince Yang and the western prince Siao The revelations of the latter were comparatively sober, but those of the former were in the highest degree blasphemously fanatical. He declared himself the Paraclete promised by Jesus, and taught that God himself, as well as Jesus, had a wife with sons and daughters. He was at the same time a brave and successful general, and the mass of the Taepings were enthusiastically attached to him. Sen humbly yielded to the extravagances of this fanatic, even when Yang sentenced him to receive forty lashes. Sen's overthrow was already resolved upon in Yang's secret council, when Sen took courage and gave the northern prince secret orders to murder Yang and his followers in one night. This was done, and Sen was weak enough to allow the executioner of his secret order to be publicly put to death so as to appease the excited populace. But he thus again in 1856 became master of the situation.—One of the oldest apostles of Sen, his near relative Hung Yin, had been turned off at Hong Kong. He there attached himself to the Basel missionary, Hamberg, who in 1852 baptized him and made him his native helper. In hope of winning his cousin to the true Christian faith, he travelled in 1854 to Nankin, which however he did not reach till January, 1859. Sen received him gladly and made him his war minister. But his efforts to introduce a purer Christianity among the Taepings were unsuccessful, for he tried the slippery way of accommodation, and under pressure from Sen set up for himself a harem. In October, 1860, on Sen's repeated invitation, his former teacher, the missionary Roberts of Nankin, arrived and was immediately made minister for foreign affairs. The Shanghai missionaries, several of whom visited Nankin, had interesting interviews with Yin in 1860, but not with the emperor, as they refused to go on their knees before him. They were encouraged by Yin to hope for a future much needed purifying of Taeping Christianity. Yang's revelations, however, held their ground after as well as before, and were increased by further absurdities. To such crass fanaticism was now added the inhuman cruelty with which they massacred the

vanquished and wasted the conquered cities and districts. Had the European powers ranged themselves in a friendly and peaceful attitude alongside of the Taepings, China might now have been a Christian empire. Instead of this the English, on account of the extreme opposition of the Taepings to the opium traffic, took up a hostile position toward them, while they were also in disfavour with the French, who had been denounced by them as idolaters on account of their Romish image worship. Down to the beginning of 1862, however, Yin's influence had prevented any hostile proceedings against the Europeans in spite of many provocations given. But after that the Taepings refused them any quarter. Roberts fled by night to save his life. Against disciplined European troops the rebels could not hold their ground. One city *ter another was taken from them, and at last, in July 1864, their capital Nankin. Sen was found poisoned in his burning palace.[1]

17. The Spiritualists.—The shoemaker's apprentice, An ew Jackson Davis of Poughkeepsie on the Hudson, in his nineteenth year fell into a magnetic sleep and composed his first work, "The Principles of Nature, Her Divine Revelations and a Voice to Mankind," in 1845. He declared its utterances to be spiritual revelations from the other world. But his later writings composed in working hours made the same claim, especially the five volume work, "Great Harmonia, being a Philosophical Revelation of the Natural, Spiritual, and Celestial Universe," 1850 ff. Both went through numerous editions and were translated into German. The great spiritual manifestation promised in the first work was not long delayed. In a house bought by the family of Fox in Hydesville in New York State a spectral knocking was often heard. Through the intercourse which the two youngest daughters, aged nine and twelve years, had with the ghosts, the skeleton of a murdered five years' old child of a pedlar was discovered buried in the cellar, and when the family soon thereafter left the house, the ghosts went with them and continued their communications by table turning, table rapping, table writing, etc. The thing now became epidemic. Hundreds and thousands of male and female *mediums* arose and held an extremely lively and varied intercourse with innumerable departed ones of earlier and later times. The believers soon numbered millions, including highly educated persons of all ranks, even such exact chemists as Mapes and Hare. An abundant literature in books and journals, as well as Sunday services, frequent camp-meetings and annual congresses formed a propaganda for the alleged

---

[1] Wilson, "The 'Ever-Victorious Army': a History of the Chinese Campaign under Lieut.-Col. C. G. Gordon, and of the Suppression of the Taeping Rebellion." Edinburgh.

spiritualism, which soon found its way across the ocean and won enthusiastic adherents for all confessions in all European countries, especially in London, Paris, Brussels, St. Petersburg, Vienna, Dresden, Leipzig, etc. They now broke up into two parties called respectively Spiritualists and Spiritists. The former put in the foreground physical experiments with astonishing results and miraculous effects; the latter, with the Frenchman Allan Kardec (*Rivail*) as their leader, give prominence to the teaching of spirits by direct communication. The former in reference to the origin of the human soul held by the theory of traducianism; the latter to that of pre-existence in connection with a doctrine of re-incarnation of spirits by reason of growing purity and perfection. The latter see in Christ the incarnation of a spirit of the highest order; the former merely the purest and most perfect type of human nature. But neither admit the real central truth of Christianity, the reconciliation of sinful humanity with God in Christ. Both evaporate the resurrection into a mere spectral spirit manifestation; and the disclosures and utterances of the spirits with both are equally trivial, silly, and vain.— In England the famous palæontologist and collaborateur of Darwin, Alfr. Russel Wallace, and the no less celebrated physicist Wm. Crookes, are apologists of spiritualism. The latter declared in 1879 that to the three well-known conditions of matter, solid, fluid and gaseous, should be added a fourth, "radiant," and that there is the borderland where force and matter meet. And in Germany the acute Leipzig astrophysicist Fr. Zöllner, after a whole series of spiritualistic séances conducted by the American medium Slade in 1877 and 1878 had been carefully scrutinized and tested by himself and several of his most accomplished scientific colleagues, was convinced of the existence and reality of higher "four dimension" space in the spirit world, to which by reason of its fourth dimension the power belonged of passing through earthly bodily matter. The philosophers I. H. Fichte of Stuttgart and Ulrici of Halle have admitted the reality of spiritualistic communications and allege them as proofs of immortality. Among German theologians Luthardt of Leipzig regards it all as the work of demons who take advantage for their own ends of the moral-religious dissolution of the modern world and its consequent nerve shaking that prevails, just as in the ancient world in the beginnings of Christianity. Zöckler of Greifswald finds an analogy between it and the demoniacal possession of New Testament times; so too Martensen in his "Jacob Boehme," and on the Catholic side W. Schneider; while Splittgerber refers most of the manifestations in question to a merely subjective origin in "the right side of the human soul life," but puts the materialization of spirits in the category of delusive jugglery. Spiritualism has scarcely rallied from the

obloquy cast upon it by the unmasking of the tricks of the famous
medium Miss Florence Cook in London in 1880 and of the distinguished spirit materialiser Bastian by the Grand-duke John of
Austria in 1884.[1]

18. To the domain of unquestionable illusion belongs also the
spiritualistic movement of Indian Theosophism or Occultism. The
American Col. Olcott of New York had already moved for twenty-
two years in spiritualist circles when in 1874 he met with Madame
Blavatsky, widow of a Russian general who had been governor of
Erivan in Armenia. She professed to have been from her eighth year
in communication with spirits, then to have had secret intercourse
with the Mahatmas, i.e. spirits of old Indian penitents, during a
seven years' residence on the Himalayas. She now promised to introduce the colonel to them. Olcott and Blavatsky founded at New
York in 1875 a society for research in the department of the mystic
sciences, travelled in 1878 to Further India and Ceylon, and settled
finally in Madras, whence by word and writing they proclaimed
through the whole land theosophism or occultism as the religion
of the future, which, consisting in a medley of Hinduism and Buddhism, enriched by spiritualistic revelations of Mahatmas, vouched
for by spiritualistic signs and miracles and conformed to the most
recent philosophical and scientific researches in America and Europe,
aimed at heaping contempt upon Christianity and finally driving
it from the field. As fanatical opponents of Christian missions in
India they were strongly supported by the Brahman and Buddhist
hierarchy, and soon obtained for the theosophical society founded
by them not only numerous adherents from among the natives,
but also many Englishmen befooled by their spiritualistic swindle.
As apostle and literary pioneer of the new religion appeared an
Anglo-Indian called Sinnett. In spring, 1884, Madame Blavatsky
and Col. Olcott went on a propagandist tour to Europe, where, in
England, France, Austria, and Hungary, they won many converts,
while Col. Olcott at Elberfeld and Madame Blavatsky at Odessa
founded branches of their theosophical society.—But meanwhile in

---

[1] Edmonds, "American Spiritualism." 2 vols. New York, 1858.
Cox, "Spiritualism answered by Science." London, 1872. Crookes,
"Spiritualism and Science." London, 1874. Wallace, "A Defence
of Spiritualism." London, 1874. Owen, "The Debatable Land."
New York, 1872. Carpenter, "Mesmerism, Spiritualism, etc., Histori-
cally and Scientifically Considered." London, 1877. Mahan, "The
Phenomena of Spiritualism Scientifically Explained and Exposed."
London, 1875. Horne, "Incidents in His Life." London, 1863.
"Lights and Shadows of Spiritualism." London, 1877.

India affairs assumed a threatening aspect. Blavatsky on her departure had entrusted the keys of her dwelling and her mysterious cabinet with its various panels, falling doors, etc., to Mr. and Mrs. Coulomb, who had been hitherto her assistants in all her juggleries. Madame Coulomb, however, quarrelled with the board of theosophists at Madras, and revenged herself by placing in the hands of the Scottish mission letters addressed by Blavatsky to herself and her husband which supplied evidence that all her spiritualistic manifestations were only common tricks. In addition she gave public exhibitions in which she demonstrated to the spectators *ad oculos* the spiritual manifestations of the Mahatmas, and subsequently published an " Account of My Acquaintanceship with Madame Blavatsky, 1872-1884," with discoveries of her earlier rogueries. Meanwhile the swindler had herself in December, 1884, returned to Madras in company with several believers gathered up in England, among others a young English clergyman, Leadbeater, who some days previously in Ceylon had formally adopted Buddhism. The theosophists now demanded that the reputed cheat and deceiver should be brought before a civil court. The president, however, declared that the investigations and judgment of a profane court of law could not be accepted to the mysteries of occultism, but promised a careful examination by a commission appointed by himself, and Blavatsky thought it advisable " for the restoration of her health in a cooler climate " to make off from the scene of conflict.[1]

§ 212. ANTICHRISTIAN SOCIALISM AND COMMUNISM.

While the antichristian spirit of the age breaks out in various theoretical forms in our literature, there also abound social and communistic movements of a practical kind. Socialism and communism both aim at a thorough-going reform of the rights of property and possession in strict proportion to the labour spent thereon. They are, however, distinguished in this, that while communism declares war against all private property and demands absolute community of goods, socialism, at least in its older and nobler forms, proceeding from the idea of precise correspondence between capital and labour, seeks to have expression given to this in fact. From the older socialism, which endeavoured to reach

---

[1] Sinnett, " Esoteric Buddhism." London. 1883.

its end in a peaceful way within the existing lines of civil order, a later social democracy is to be distinguished by its decidedly politico-revolutionary character and tendency to attach itself more to communism. This modern socialism thinks to open the way to the realization of its hare-brained ideas by the confusion and overthrow of existing law and order.

1. **The Beginnings of Modern Communism.**—As early as 1796 Babeuf published in Paris a communistic manifesto which maintained the thesis that natural law gives all men an equal right to the enjoyment of all goods. His ideas were subsequently systematized and developed by Fourier, Proudhon, Cabet, and Louis Blanc in France, and by Weibling and Stirner in Germany. In a treatise of 1840 Proudhon answered the question, *Qu'est-ce que la propriété?* in words which afterwards became proverbial, and formed the motto of communism : *La propriété c'est le vol.* But the mere negation of property affords no permanent standing ground. All altars must be thrown down ; all religion rooted out as the plague of humanity ; the family and marriage, as the fountain of all selfishness, must be abolished ; all existing governments must be overthrown ; all Europe must be turned into one great social democracy. A secret communistic propaganda spread over all western Europe, had its head centres in Belgium and Switzerland, crossed the Alps and the Pyrenees, as well as the Channel, and found a congenial soil even in Russia.

2. **St. Simonism.**—The Count St. Simon of Paris, reduced to poverty by speculation, proposed by means of a thorough organization of industry to found a new and happy state of things in which there would be pure enjoyment without poverty and care. An attempted suicide, which led however to his death in 1825, made him in the eyes of his disciples a saviour of the world. The July revolution of 1830 gave to the new universal religion, which reinstated the flesh in its long lost rights and sought to assign to each individual the place in the commonwealth for which he was fitted, some advantage. "Father" Enfantin, whom his followers honoured as the highest revelation of deity, contended with pompous phrases and in fantastic style for the emancipation of woman and against the unnatural institution of marriage. But St. Simonism soon excited public ridicule, was pronounced immoral by the courts of justice, and the remnants of its votaries fled from the scorn of the people and the vengeance of the law to Egypt, where they soon disappeared.

3. **Owenists and Icarians.**—The Scotch mill-owner Rob. Owen went

in 1829 to America, in order there, unhindered by religious prejudices, clerical opposition, and police interference, to work out on a large scale his socialistic schemes for improving the world, which in a small way he believed he had proved already among his Scotch mill-operatives. He bought for this purpose from the Württemberger Rapp the colony of Harmony (§ 211, 6); but wanting the necessary capital for the socialistic commonwealth there established, and failing to realize his expectations, discontent, disorder, and opposition got the upperhand, and in 1826 Owen was obliged to abandon all his property. He now returned to England, and addressed himself in treatises, tracts, and lectures to the working classes of the whole land, in order to win them over to his ideas. A vast brotherhood for mutual benefit and for the enjoyment of their joint earnings was to put an end to earth's misery, which the positive religions had not lessened but only increased. In 1836, in the great industrial cities socialist unions with nearly half a million members were formed, with their head centre and annual congress at Birmingham. The practical schemes of Owen, however, had no success in England, and his societies no permanency. He died in 1858.—Still more disastrous was the fate of the Icarian Colony, founded in Texas in 1848 by the Frenchman Stephen Cabet, author of "*Voyage en Icarie, Roman philos. et social,*" 1840, as an attempt to realize his communistic-philanthropic ideas on the other side the Atlantic. The colonists soon found their sanguine hopes bitterly disappointed, and hurled against their leader reproaches and threats. Some ex-Icarians accused him in 1849 before the Paris police-court as a swindler, and he was condemned to two years' imprisonment and five years' loss of civil privileges. Cabet now hastened to France, and on appeal obtained reversion of his sentence in 1851. Returning to America, he founded a new Icarian colony at Nauvoo in Illinois. But there, too, everything went wrong, and a revolt of the colonists obliged him to flee. He died in 1856.[1]

4. The International Working-Men's Association.—Local and national working-men's unions with a socialistic organization had for a long time existed in England, France, and Germany. The idea of a union embracing the whole world was first broached at the great London Exhibition in 1862, and at a conference in London on September 28th, 1864, at which all industrial countries of Europe were represented, it assumed a practical shape by the founding of a universal international working-men's association. Its constitution was strictly centralistic. A directing committee in London, Carl Marx of Treves, formerly

---

[1] Sargent, "Rob. Owen and his Social Philosophy." London, 1860 Nordhoff, "Communistic Societies in the United States." London 1875.

Privatdocent of philosophy at Bonn, standing at its head as dictator, represented the supreme legislative and governing authority, while alongside of it a general standing council held the administrative and executive power. The latter was divided into eight sections, English, American, French, German, Belgian, Dutch, Italian, and Spanish, and annual international congresses at Geneva, Lausanne, Brussels, Basel, and the Hague gave opportunity for general consultation on matters of common interest. Reception as members was granted by the giving of a diploma after six months' trial, and involved unconditional obedience to the statutes and ordinances of the central authorities and the payment of an annual fee. The number of members, not, however, exclusively drawn from the working classes, is said to have reached two and a half millions. The society adopted the current socialistic and communistic ideas and tendencies. The religious principle of the association was therefore: atheism and materialism; the political: absolute democracy; the social: equal rights of labour and profit, with abolition of private property, hereditary rights, marriage, and family; and as means for realizing this programme, unaccomplishable by peaceable methods, revolution and rebellion, fire and sword, poison, petroleum and dynamite. Such means have been used already in various ways by the international throughout the Romance countries; but specially in the brief Reign of Terror of the Paris Commune, March and April, 1871, in the relatively no less violent attempted revolt at Alcoy in Southern Spain in July, 1878. But meanwhile differences appeared within the society, which were formulated at the Hague Congress in 1872, and led to splits, which greatly lessened its unity, influence, and power to do mischief, so that this congress may perhaps be regarded as the first beginning of its end.[1]

5. German Social Democracy.—**Ferd. Lassalle**, son of a rich Jewish merchant of Breslau, after a full course of study in philosophy and law, began in 1848 to take a lively part in the advanced movements of the age, and when he found among the liberal citizens no favour for his socialistic ideas turned exclusively to the working classes. In answer to the question as to what was to be done, by the central committee of a working-men's congress at Leipzig, he wrought out in 1863 with great subtlety in an open letter the fundamental idea of his universal redemption. All plans of self-help to relieve the distress of working men hitherto proposed (specially that of Schulze-Delitzsch) break down over the "iron economic law of wages," in consequence of

---

[1] Onslow-Yorke, "The Secret History of the International Working-Men's Association." London, 1872. Lissagaray, "History of the Commune of 1871." Translated by Aveling. London, 1886.

which under the dominion of capital and the large employers of labour wages are always with fatalistic necessity reduced to the point indispensable for supplying a working man's family with the absolute necessaries of life. The working classes, however, have the right according to the law of nature to a full equivalent for their labour, but in order to reach this they must be their own undertakers, and where self-help is only a vain illusion, state help must afford the means. By insisting on the right to universal suffrage the working classes have obtained a decided majority in the legislative assemblies, and there secured a government of the future in accordance with their needs. On these principles the Universal German Society of Working Men was constituted, with Lassalle as its president, which position he held till his death in a duel in 1864. Long internal disputes and personal recriminations led to a split at the Eisenach Congress in 1869. The malcontents founded an independent "Social Democratic Working-Men's Union," under the leadership of Bebel and Liebknecht, which, particularly successful in Saxony, Brunswick, and South Germany, represents itself as the German branch of the "International Working-Men's Association." It adhered indeed generally to Lassalle's programme, but objected to the extravagant adulation claimed for Lassalle by their opponents, the proper disciples of Lassalle, who had Hasenclaver as their leader and Berlin as their headquarters, substituted a federal for a centralistic organization, and instead of a great centralised government in the future desired rather a federal republic embracing all Europe. But both declared equally in favour of revolution; they vied with one another in bitter hatred of everything bearing the name of religion; and wrought out with equal enthusiasm their communistic schemes for the future. At the Gotha Congress of 1875 a reconciliation of parties was effected. The social-democratic agitation thus received a new impulse and assumed threatening proportions. Yet it required such extraordinary occurrences as the twice attempted assassination of the aged emperor, by Hodel on May 11th, and Nobiling on June 2nd, 1878, to rouse the government to legislative action. On the basis of a law passed in October, 1878, for two and a half years (but in May, 1880, continued for other three and a half years, and in May, 1884, and again in April, 1886, on each occasion extended to other two years), 200 socialist societies throughout the German empire were suppressed, sixty-four revolutionary journals, circulated in hundreds of thousands and with millions of readers, and about 800 other seditious writings, were forbidden. But that the social-democratic organization and agitation was not thereby destroyed is proved by the fact that in August, 1880, in an uninhabited Swiss castle lent for the purpose, in Canton Zürich, a congress was held, attended by fifty-six German socialists, with greetings by letter from sympathisers in all European countries, which among other things passed the resolution unanimously, no longer as had been agreed upon at Gotha, to seek their ends by lawful methods, as by the law of the socialists impossible, but by the way of revolution.—On the other hand, the German Imperial Chancellor Prince Bismarck in the Reichstag, 1884, fully admitted the "right of the worker to work," as well as the duty of the state to ameliorate the condition of working men as far as possible, and in three propositions: "Work for the healthy workman, hospital attendance to the sick, and maintenance to the invalided," granted all that is asked for by a healthy social policy.

6. Russian Nihilism.—In Russia, too, notwithstanding a strictly exercised censorship, the philosophico-scientific gospel of materialism and atheism found entrance through the writings of Moleschott, Feuerbach, Büchner, Darwin, etc. (§ 174, 3), especially among the students. In 1860, Nihilism, springing from this seed, first assumed the character of a philosophical and literary movement. It sought the overthrow of all religious institutions. Then came the women's question, claiming emancipation for the wife. The example of the Paris Commune of 1871 contributed largely to the development of Nihilistic idealism, its political revolutionary socialism. The Nihilist propaganda, like an epidemic, now seized upon the academic youth, male and female, was spread in aristocratic families by tutors and governesses, won secret disciples among civil servants as well as officers of the army and navy, and was enthusiastically supported by ladies in the most cultured and exalted ranks. In order to spread its views among the people, young men and women disguised in peasant's dress went out among the peasants and artisans, lived and wrought like them, and preached their gospel to them in their hours of rest. But their efforts failed through the antipathy and apathy of the lower orders, and the energetic interference of the government by imprisonment and banishment thinned the ranks of the propagandists. But all the more closely did those left bind themselves together under their central leaders as the "Society for Country and Freedom," and strove with redoubled eagerness to spread revolutionary principles by secretly printing their proclamations and other incendiary productions, and scattering them in the streets and houses. On January 24th, 1878, the female Nihilist *Vera Sassulitsch* from personal revenge dangerously wounded with a revolver General Trepoff, the dreaded head of the St. Petersburg police. Although she openly avowed the deed before the court and gloried in it, she was amid the acclamations of the public acquitted. This was the hour when Nihilism exercised its fellest terrorism. The fair, peaceful phrase, "To work, fight. suffer, and die for the people," was silenced; it was now, sword and

fire, dagger and revolver, dynamite and mines for all oppressors of the people, but above all for the agents of the police, for their spies, for all informers and apostates. An "executive committee," unknown to most of the conspirators themselves, issued the death sentence ; the lot determined the executioner, who himself suffered death if he failed to accomplish it. What was now aimed at was the assassination of higher state officials ; then the sacred person of the emperor. Three bold attempts at assassination miscarried ; the revolver shot of Solowjews on April 14th, 1879 ; the mine on the railway near Moscow that exploded too late on November 30th, 1879 ; the horrible attempt to blow up the Winter Palace with the emperor and his family on February 17th, 1880 ; but the fourth, a dynamite bomb thrown between the feet of the emperor on March 13th, 1881, destroyed the life of this noble and humane monarch, who in 1861–1863 had freed his people from the yoke of serfdom. As for years nothing more had been heard of Nihilist attempts, it was hoped that the government had succeeded in putting down this diabolical rebellion, but in 1887 the news spread that an equally horrible attempt had been planned for the sixth anniversary of the assassination of Alexander II., but fortunately timely precautions were taken against it.

CHRONOLOGICAL TABLES.

A.D.   *FIRST CENTURY.*

14–37. The Emperor Tiberius, § 22, 1.
41–54. The Emperor Claudius, § 22, 1.
    44. Execution of James the Elder, § 16.
    51. The Council at Jerusalem, § 18, 1.
54–68. The Emperor Nero, § 23, 1.
    61. Paul's Arrival at Rome, § 15.
    63. Stoning of James the Just, § 16, 8.
    64. Persecution of Christians in Rome, § 22, 1
66–70. Jewish War, § 16.
81–96 The Emperor Domitian, § 22, 1.

SECOND CENTURY.

98–117. The Emperor Trajan, § 22, 2.
    115. (?) Ignatius of Antioch, Martyr, § 22, 2.
117–138. The Emperor Hadrian, § 22, 2. Basilides, Valentinus, § 22, 2, 4.
132–135. Revolt of Barcochba, § 25.
Abt.150. Celsus, § 23, 3. Marcion, § 27, 11.
138–161. The Emperor Antoninus Pius, § 22, 2.
    155. Paschal Controversy between Polycarp and Amicetus, § 87, 2.
161–180. The Emperor Marcus Aurelius, § 22, 3.
    165. Justin Martyr, § 80, 9.
    166. (155 ?) Martyrdom of Polycarp, § 22, 3.
    172. (156 ?) Montanus appears as a Prophet, § 40, 1.
    177. Persecution of Christians at Lyons and Vienne, § 22, 8.
    178. Irenæus made Bishop of Lyons, § 81, 2.
180–192. The Emperor Commodus, § 22, 3.
    196. Paschal Controversy between Victor and Polycrates, § 87, 2.

THIRD CENTURY.

A.D.

202. Tertullian becomes Montanist, § 40, 2. Pantænus dies § 31, 4.

220. Clement of Alexandria dies, § 31, 4.

235. Settlement of the Schism of Hippolytus, § 41, 1.

235–238. The Emperor Maximinus Thrax, § 22, 4.

243. Ammonius Saccus dies, § 25, 2.

244. Arabian Synod against Beryllus, § 33, 7.

249–251. The Emperor Decius, § 22, 5.

250. The Schism of Felicissimus, § 41, 2.

251. The Novatian Schism, § 41, 8.

253–260. The Emperor Valerian, § 22, 5.

254. Origen dies, § 31, 5.

255–256. Controversy about Heretics' Baptism, § 35, 5.

258. Cyprian dies, § 31, 11.

260–268. The Emperor Gallienus. The Toleration Edict, § 22, 5.

262. Synod at Rome against Sabellius and Dionysius of Alexandria, § 33, 7.

269. Third Synod of Antioch against Paul of Samosata, § 33, 8.

276. Mani dies, § 29, 1.

284–305. The Emperor Diocletian, § 22, 6.

FOURTH CENTURY.

303. Beginning of Diocletian Persecution, § 22, 6.

306. Synod of Elvira, § 38, 3 ; 45, 2. Meletian Schism in Egypt, § 41, 4. Constantius Chlorus dies, § 22, 7.

311. Galerius dies, § 22, 6.

312. Constantine's Expedition against Maxentius, § 22, 7. Donatist Schism in Africa, § 63, 1.

313. Edict of Milan, § 22, 7.

318. Arius is Accused, § 50, 1.

323–337. Constantine the Great, Sole Ruler, § 42, 2.

325. First Œcumenical Council at Nicæa, § 50, 1.

330–415. Meletian Schism at Antioch, § 50, 8.

335. Synod at Tyre, § 50, 2.

336. Athanasius Exiled. Arius dies, § 50, 2.

341. Council at Antioch, § 50, 2.

343. Persecution of Christians under Shapur II., § 64, 2.

344. Synod at Sardica, § 46, 3 ; 50, 2.

346. Council at Milan against Photinus, § 50, 2.

348. Ulfilas, Bishop of the Goths, § 76, 1.

350–361. Constantius, Sole Ruler, § 42, 2.

351. First Council at Sirmium against Marcellus, § 50, 2.

A.D.

357. Second Council at Sirmium, Homoians, § 50, 3.
358. Third Council at Sirmium, § 50, 3.
359. Synods at Seleucia and Rimini, § 50, 3.
361–363. Emperor Julian the Apostate, § 42, 3.
362. Synod at Alexandria against Athanasius, § 50, 4.
366–384. Damasus I., Bishop of Rome, § 46, 4.
368. Hilary of Poitiers dies, § 47, 14.
373. Athanasius dies, § 47, 3.
379. Basil the Great dies, § 47, 4.
379–395. Theodosius the Great, Emperor, § 42, 4.
380. Synod at Saragossa, § 54, 2.
381. Second Œcumenical Council at Constantinople. § 50, 4.
        Ulfilas dies, § 76, 1.
384–398. Siricius, Bishop of Rome, § 46, 4.
385. Priscillian beheaded at Treves, § 54, 2.
390. Gregory Nazianzen dies, § 47, 4.
391. Destruction of the Serapeion at Alexandria, § 42, 6.
393. Council at Hippo Rhegius, § 59, 1.
397. Ambrose dies, § 47, 15.
399. Rufinus Condemned at Rome as an Origenist, § 51, 2.
400. Martin of Tours dies, § 47, 15.

FIFTH CENTURY.

402–417. Innocent I. of Rome, § 46, 5.
403. Synodus ad Quercum, § 51, 3. Epiphanius dies, § 47, 10.
407. Chrysostom dies, § 47, 8.
408–450. Theodosius II. in the East, § 52, 3.
411. *Collatio cum Donatistis*, § 63, 1.
412. Synod at Carthage against Cœlestius, § 53, 4.
415. Synods at Jerusalem and Diospolis against Pelagius, § 53, 4.
416. Synods at Mileve and Carthage against Pelagius, § 53, 4.
418. General Assembly at Carthage, § 53, 4. Roman Schism of
        Eulalius and Bonifacius, § 46, 6.
420. Jerome dies, § 47, 16. Persecution of Christians under
        Behram V., § 64, 2.
422–432. Cœlestine I., Bishop of Rome, § 46, 6.
428. Nestorius is made Patriarch of Constantinople, § 52, 3.
429. Theodore of Mopsuestia dies, § 47, 9. The Vandals in North
        Africa, § 76, 3.
430. Cyril's Anathemas, § 52, 3. Augustine dies, § 47, 18.
431. Third Œcumenical Council at Ephesus, § 52, 3.
432. St. Patrick in Ireland, § 77, 1. John Cassianus dies, § 47, 21.

A.D.

440–461. Leo I., the Great, § 46, 7; 47, 22.

444. Cyril of Alexandria dies, § 47, 6. Dioscurus succeeds Cyril, § 52, 4.

445. Rescript of Valentinian III., § 46, 7.

448. Eutyches excommunicated at Constantinople, § 52, 4.

449. Robber Synod at Ephesus, § 52, 4. Attack of Angles and Saxons upon Britain, § 77, 4.

451. Fourth Œcumenical Synod at Chalcedon, § 52, 4.

457. Theodoret dies, § 47, 9.

475. Semipelagian Synods at Arles and Lyons, § 53, 5.

476. Overthrow of the West Roman Empire, § 46, 8; 76, 6. Monophysite Encyclical of Basiliscus, § 52, 5.

482. Henoticon of the Emperor Zeno, § 52, 5. Severinus dies, § 76, 6.

484–519. The Thirty-five Years' Schism between the East and West, § 52, 5.

492–496. Gelasius I., Bishop of Rome, § 46, 8; 47, 22.

496. Battle of Zülpich. Clovis baptized, § 76, 9.

SIXTH CENTURY.

502. Synodus Palmaris, § 46, 8.

517. Council at Epaon, § 76, 5.

527–565. Justinian I., Emperor, § 46, 9; 52, 6.

529. Synods at Oranges and Valence, § 53, 5. Monastic Rule of Benedict of Nursia, § 85. Suppression of the University of Athens, § 42, 4.

533. The Theopaschite Controversy, § 52, 6. Overthrow of the Vandal Empire, § 76, 3.

544. Condemnation of the "Three Chapters," § 52, 6.

553. Fifth Œcumenical Council at Constantinople, § 52, 6.

554. Overthrow of the Ostrogoth Empire in Italy, § 76, 7.

563. Council at Braga, § 54, 2. St. Columba among the Picts and Scots, § 77, 2.

567. Founding of the Exarchate of Ravenna, § 46, 9.

568. The Longobards under Alboin in Italy, § 76, 8.

589. Council at Toledo under Reccared, § 76, 2. Columbanus and Gallus in the Vosges Country, § 77, 7.

590–604. Gregory I., the Great, § 46, 10; 47, 22.

595. Gregory of Tours dies, § 90, 2.

596. Augustine goes as Missionary to the Anglo-Saxons, § 77, 4.

597. St. Columba dies, § 77, 2. Ethelbert baptized, § 77, 4.

SEVENTH CENTURY.

A.D.

606. Emperor Phocas recognises the **Roman Primacy**, § 46, 10.
611–641. Heraclius, Emperor, § 52, 8.
615. Columbanus dies, § 77, 7.
622. Hejira, § 65.
625–638. Honorius I., Pope, § 46, 11.
636. Isidore of Seville dies, § 90, 2.
637. Omar conquers Jerusalem, § 65.
638. Monothelite Ecthesis of Heraclius, **§ 52, 8.**
640. Omar conquers Egypt, § 65.
642–668. Constans II., Emperor, § 52, 8.
646. St. Gallus dies, § 78, 1.
648. The Typus of Constans II., § 52, 8.
649–653. Martin I., Pope, § 46, 11.
649. First Lateran Council under Martin I., **§ 52, 8.**
652. Emmeran at Regensburg, § 78, 2.
657. Constantine of Mananalis, § 71, 1.
662. Maximus Confessor, dies, § 47, 13.
664. Synod at Streoneshalch (*Syn. Pharensis*), § 77, 6.
668–685. Constantinus Pogonnatus, § 52, 8; 71, 1.
677. Wilfrid among the Frisians, § 78, 3.
678–682. Agatho, Pope, § 46, 11.
680. Sixth Œcumenical Council at Constantinople (**Trullanum I.**),
    § 52, 8.
690. Wilibrord among the Frisians, § 78, 3.
692. Concilium Quinisextum (Trullanum II.), § 63, 8.
696. Rupert in Bavaria (Salzburg), § 78, 2.

EIGHTH CENTURY.

711. The Saracens conquer Spain, § 81.
715–731. Pope Gregory II., § 66, 1; 78, 4.
716. Winifrid goes to the Frisians, § 78, 4.
717–741. Leo III., the Isaurian, Emperor, § 66, 1.
718. Winifrid in Rome, § 78, 4.
722. Winifrid in Thuringia and Hesse, § 78, 4.
723. Winifrid a second time at Rome, consecrated Bishop, etc.,
    § 78, 4.
724. Destruction of the Wonder-working Oak at Geismar, § 78, 4
726. Leo's First Edict against Image Worship, § 66, 1.
730. Leo's Second Edict against Image Worship, § 66, 1.
731. Gregory III., Pope, § 66, 1; 78, 4; 82, 1.

A.D.

732. Boniface, Archbishop and Apostolic Vicar, § 78, 4. Battle at Poitiers, § 81. Separation of Illyria from the Roman See by Leo the Isaurian, § 66, 1

735. The Venerable Bede dies, § 90, 2.

739. Wilibrord dies, § 78, 8.

741. Charles Martel dies, § 78, 5. Gregory III. dies. Leo the Isaurian dies.

741–752. Pope Zacharias, § 78, 5, 7; 82, 1.

741–775. Constantinus Copronymus, Emperor, § 66, 2.

742. Concilium Germanicum, § 78, 5.

743. Synod at Liptinä, § 78, 5; 86, 2.

744. Synod at Soissons, § 78, 5.

745. Boniface, Archbishop of Mainz, § 78, 5.

752. Childeric III. deposed, Pepin the Short, King, § 78, 5; 82, 1.

754. Iconoclastic Council at Constantinople, § 66, 2. Pepin's donation to the Chair of St. Peter, § 82, 1.

755. Boniface dies, § 78, 7.

Abt.760. Rule of St. Chrodegang of Metz, § 84, 4.

767. Synod at Gentilliacum, § 91, 2; 92, 1.

768–814. Charlemagne, § 82, 2, 4; 90, 1, etc.

772–795. Pope Hadrian I., § 82, 2.

772. Destruction of Eresburg, § 78, 9.

774. Charlemagne's donation to the Chair of St. Peter, § 82, 2.

785. Wittekind and Alboin are baptized, § 78, 9.

787. Seventh Œcumenical Council at Nicæa, § 66, 8. Founding of Cloister and Cathedral Schools, § 90, 1.

790. *Libri Carolini*, § 92, 1.

792. Synod at Regensburg, § 91, 1.

794. General Synod at Frankfort, § 91, 1; 92, 1.

795–816. Leo III., Pope, § 82, 8.

799. Alcuin's disputation with Felix at Aachen, § 91, 1.

800. Leo III. crowns Charlemagne, § 82, 8.

NINTH CENTURY.

804. End of the Saxon War, § 78, 9. Alcuin dies, § 90, 8.

809. Council at Aachen, on the *Filioque*, § 91, 2.

813–820. Leo the Armenian, Emperor, § 66, 4.

814–840. Louis the Pious, § 82, 4.

817. Reformation of Monasticism by Benedict of Aniane, § 85, 2.

820–829. Michael Balbus, Emperor, § 66, 4.

825. Synod at Paris against Image Worship, § 92, 1.

826. Theodorus Studita dies, § 66, 4. Ansgar in Denmark, § 80, 1.

A.D.

827. Establishment of Saracen Sovereignty in Sicily, § 81.

829–842. Theophilus, Emperor, § 66, 4.

833. Founding of the Archbishopric of Hamburg, § 80, 1.

835. Synod at Didenhofen, § 82, 4.

839. Claudius of Turin dies. Agobard of Lyons dies, § 90, 4.

840–877. Charles the Bald, § 90, 1.

842. Feast of Orthodoxy, § 66, 4. Theodora recommends the out rooting of the Paulicians, § 71, 1.

843. Compact of Verdun, § 82, 5.

844. Eucharist Controversy of Paschasius Radbertus, § 91, 3.

845–882. Hincmar of Rheims, § 83, 2 ; 90, 5.

847. Archbishopric of Hamburg-Bremen, § 80, 1

848. Synod of Mainz against Gottschalk, § 91, 5.

850–859. Persecution of Christians in Spain, § 81, 1.

851–852. The Decretals of the Pseudo-Isidore, § 87, 2, 3.

853. Synod of Quiersy. *Capitula Carisiaca*, § 91, 5.

855. Synod at Valence in favour of Gottschalk, § 91, 5.

856. Rabanus Maurus dies, § 90, 4.

858–867. Pope Nicholas I., § 82, 7.

858. Photius, Patriarch of Constantinople, § 67, 1.

859. Synod of Savonnières, § 91, 5.

861. Methodius goes to the Bulgarians, § 78, 3.

863. Cyril and Methodius go to Moravia, § 79, 2.

865. Ansgar dies, § 80, 1.

866. Encyclical of Photius, § 67, 1.

867–886. Basil the Macedonian, Emperor, § 67, 1.

867–872. Hadrian II., Pope, § 82, 7.

869. Eighth Œcumenical Council of the Latins at Constantinople § 67, 1.

870. Treaty of Mersen, § 82, 5.

871. Basil the Macedonian puts down the Paulicians, § 71, 1. Borziwoi and Ludmilla baptized, § 79, 3.

871–901. Alfred the Great, § 90, 9.

875. John VIII. crowns Charles the Bald Emperor, § 82, 8.

879. Eighth Œcumenical Council of the Greeks at Constantinople, § 67, 1.

886–911. Leo the Philosopher, Emperor, § 67, 2.

891. Photius dies, § 67, 1.

TENTH CENTURY.

910. Abbot Berno founds Clugny, § 98, 1.

911. The German Carolingians die out, § 82, 8.

911–918. Conrad I., King of the Germans, § 96, 1.

A.D.

914–928. Pope John X., § 96, 1.

919–936. Henry I., King of the Germans, § 96, 1

934. Henry I. enforced toleration of Christianity in Denmark, § 93, 2.

936–973. Otto I., Emperor, § 96, 1.

942. Odo of Clugny founds the Clugniac Congregation, § 98, 1.

950. Gylas of Hungary baptized, § 93, 8.

955. Olga baptized in Constantinople, § 78, 4.

960. Atto of Vercelli dies, § 100, 3.

962. Founding of the Holy Roman Empire of the German Nation, § 96, 1.

963. Synod at Rome deposes John XII., § 96, 1.

966. Miecislaw of Poland baptized, § 93, 7.

968. Founding of Archbishopric of Magdeburg, § 93, 9.

970. Migration of Paulicians to Thrace, § 71, 1.

973–983. Otto II., Emperor, § 96, 2.

974. Ratherius of Verona dies, § 100, 3.

983–1002. Otto III., Emperor, § 96, 2, 3.

983. Mistewoi destroys all Christian establishments among the Wends, § 93, 9.

987. Hugh Capet is made King of France, § 96, 2.

988. Wladimir Christianizes Russia, § 78, 4.

992–1025. Boleslaw Chrobry of Poland, § 93, 7.

996–999. Pope Gregory V., § 96, 2.

997–1038. Stephen the Saint, § 93, 8.

997. Adalbert of Prague, Apostle of Prussia, dies, § 93, 13.

999–1003. Pope Sylvester II., § 96, 3.

1000. Olaf Tryggvason dies, § 93, 4.

Christianity introduced into Iceland and Greenland, § 93, 5.

Stephen of Hungary secures the throne, § 93, 8.

ELEVENTH CENTURY.

1002–1024. Henry II., Emperor, § 96, 4.

1008. Olaf Skautkoning of Sweden baptized, § 93, 3.

1009. Bruno martyred, § 93, 13.

1012–1024. Pope Benedict VIII., § 96, 4.

1014–1036. Canute the Great, § 93, 2.

1018. Romuald founds the Camaldulensian Congregation, § 98, 1.

1024–1039. Conrad II., Emperor, § 96, 4.

1030. Olaf the Thick of Norway dies, § 93, 4.

1031. Overthrow of the Ommaides in Spain, § 95, 2.

TWELFTH CENTURY.

A.D.

1128. Second Missionary Journey of Otto of Bamberg, § 98, 10.

1130–1143. Pope Innocent II., § 96, 13.

1135. Rupert of Deutz dies, § 102, 8.

1139. Tenth Œcumenical Council (Second Lateran), § 96, 13.

1141. Synod at Sens condemns Abælard's writings, § 102, 2.
    Hugo St. Victor dies, § 102, 4.

1142. Abælard dies, § 102, 2.

1143. Founding of the Roman Commune, § 96, 13.

1145–1153. Pope Eugenius III., § 96, 13.

1146. Fall of Edessa, § 94, 2.

1147. Second Crusade. Conrad III. Louis VII., § 94, 2.

1149. Henry of Lausanne dies, § 108, 7.

1150. *Decretum Gratiani*, § 99, 5.

1152–1190. Frederick I., Barbarossa, § 96, 14.

1153. Bernard of Clairvaux dies, § 102, 8.

1154. Vicelin dies, § 93, 9.

1154–1159. Hadrian IV., Pope, § 96, 14.

1155. Arnold of Brescia put to death, § 96, 14.

1156. Peter the Venerable dies, § 98, 1. Founding of Carmelite
    Order, § 98, 3.

1157. Introduction of Christianity into Finland, § 93, 11.

1159–1181. Pope Alexander III., § 96, 15, 16.

1164. Peter the Lombard dies, § 102, 5. Council of Clarendon,
    § 96, 16.

1167. Council at Toulouse (Cathari), § 108, 2.

1168. Christianity of the Island of Rügen, § 93, 10.

1169. Gerhoch of Reichersberg dies, § 102, 6, 7.

1170. Thomas Becket murdered, § 96, 16. Founding of the
    Waldensian sect, § 108, 10.

1176. Battle of Legnano, § 6, 15.

1179. Eleventh Œcumenical Council (Third Lateran), § 96, 15.

1180. John of Salisbury dies, § 102, 9.

1182. Maronites are attached to Rome, § 73, 8.

1184. Meinhart in Livonia, § 93, 12.

1187. Saladin conquers Jerusalem, § 94, 3.

1189. Third Crusade. Frederick Barbarossa, § 94, 3.

1190–1197. Henry VI., Emperor, § 96, 16.

1190. Founding of Order of Teutonic Knights, § 98, 8.

1194. Eustathius of Thessalonica dies, § 68, 5.

1198–1216. Pope Innocent III., § 96, 17, 18.

THIRTEENTH CENTURY.

A.D.

1202. Joachim of Floris dies, § 108, 5. Founding of Order of the Brothers of the Sword, § 93, 12. Genghis Khan destroys Kingdom of Prester John, § 72, 1.

1204–1261. Latin Empire in Constantinople, § 94, 4.

1207. Stephen Langton, Archbishop of Canterbury, § 96, 18.

1208. Peter of Castelnau slain, § 109, 1.

1209–1229. Albigensian Crusade, § 109, 1.

1209. Council of Paris against Sect of Amalrich of Bena § 108, 4.

1212. Battle at Tolosa, § 95, 2.

1213. John Lackland receives England as a Papal Fief, § 96, 18

1215–1250. Frederick II., Emperor, § 96, 17, 19, 20.

1215. Twelfth Œcumenical Council (Fourth Lateran), § 96, 18.

1216. Confirmation of the Dominican Order, § 98, 5.

1216–1227. Pope Honorius III., § 96, 19.

1217. Fourth Crusade. Andrew II. of Hungary, § 94, 4.

1223. Confirmation of Franciscan Order, § 98, 8.

1226. Francis of Assisi dies, § 98, 8.

1226–1270. Louis IX., the Saint, § 94, 6 ; 93, 15.

1227–1241. Pope Gregory IX., § 96, 19.

1228. Fifth Crusade. Frederick II., § 94, 5. Settlement of the Teutonic Knights in Prussia, § 93, 13.

1229. Synod at Toulouse, § 109, 2.

1231. St. Elizabeth dies, § 105, 3.

1232. Inquisition Tribunal set up, § 109, 2.

1233. Conrad of Marburg slain, § 109, 8.

1234. Crusade against Stedingers, § 109, 3.

1237. Union of the Order of Sword with that of Teutonic Knights, § 98, 8.

1243–1254. Pope Innocent IV., § 96, 20.

1245. Thirteenth Œcumenical Council (first of Lyons), § 96, 20. Alexander of Hales died, § 103, 4.

1248. Foundation stone of Cathedral of Cologne laid, § 104, 11. Sixth Crusade, Louis IX., § 94, 6.

1253. Robert Grosseteste dies, § 103, 1.

1254. Condemnation of the "Introductorius in evangelium æternum," § 108, 5.

1260. First Flagellant Campaign in Perugia, § 107, 1.

1260–1282. Michael Palæologus, Emperor, § 67, 4.

1261–1264. Urban IV., Pope, § 96, 20.

1262. Arsenian Schism, § 70, 1.

1268. Conradin on the Scaffold, § 96, 20.

A.D.

1269. Pragmatic Sanction of Louis IX., § 96, **21.**

1270. Seventh Crusade, Louis IX., § 94, 6.

1271–1276. Pope Gregory X., § 96, 21.

1272. Italian Mission to the Mongols. Marco Polo § 93, **15.** David of Augsburg dies, § 103, 10. Bertholdt of Regensburg dies, § 104, 1.

1273–1291. Rudolph of Hapsburg, Emperor, § 96, 21, 22.

1274. Fourteenth Œcumenical Council (second of Lyons), § 96, 21. Thomas Aquinas dies, § 103, 6. Bonaventura dies, § 103, 4.

1275. Strassburg Minster, § 104, 13.

1280. Albert the Great dies, § 103, **5.**

1282. Sicilian Vespers, § 96, 22.

1283. Prussia subdued, § 93, 13.

1286. Barhabraeus dies, § 72, 2.

1291. Fall of Acre, § 94, 6. John of Montecorvino **among the** Mongols, § 93, 16.

1294. Roger Bacon dies, § 103, 8.

1294–1303. Boniface VIII., Pope, § 110, **1.**

1296. Bull *Clericis laicos*, § 110, 1.

1300. First Roman Jubilee, § 117. Lollards at Antwerp, § **116,** **2.** Gerhard Segarelli burnt, § 108, 8.

FOURTEENTH CENTURY.

1302. Bull *Unam Sanctam*, § 110, **1.**

1305–1314. Pope Clement V., § 110, 2.

1307. Dolcino burnt, § 108, 4.

1308. Duns Scotus dies, § 113, 1.

1309–1377. Residence of Popes at Avignon, § 110, 2–4.

1311–1312. Fifteenth Œcumenical Council at Vienne, § 110, 2. Suppression of Templar Order, § 112, 7.

1314–1347. Louis the Bavarian, Emperor, § 110, 3, **4.**

1315. Raimund Lullus dies, § 93, 17; 103, **5.**

1316–1334. Pope John XXII., § 110, 3; 112, 2.

1321. Dante dies, § 116, 6.

1322. Split in the Franciscan Order, § 112, **2.**

1327. Meister Eckhart dies, § 114, 1.

1334–1342. Pope Benedict XII., § 110, 4.

1335. Bishop Hemming in Lapland, § 93, **11.**

1338. Electoral Union at Rhense, § 110, 5.

1339. Union negotiations at Avignon. Barlaam, § **67, 5.**

1340. Nicholas of Lyra dies, § 113, 7.

1341–1351. Hesychast Controversy in Constantinople, § 69, 1.

A.D.

1342–1352. Pope Clement VI., § 110, 4.

1346–1378. Charles IV., Emperor, § 110, 4.

1347. Rienzi, § 110, 4. Emperor Louis dies, § 110, 4.

1348. Founding of University of Prague, § 119, 8.

1348–1350. Black Death. Flagellant Campaign, § 116, 8.

1349. Thomas Bradwardine dies, § 113, 2.

1352–1362. Pope Innocent VI., § 110, 4.

1356. Charles IV. issues the Golden Bull, § 110, 4.

1360. Wiclif against the Begging Friars, § 119, 1.

1361. John Tauler dies, § 114, 2.

1362–1370. Pope Urban V., § 110, 4.

1366. Henry Suso dies, § 114, 5.

1367–1370. Urban V. in Rome, § 110, 4.

1369. John Paläologus passes over to the Latin Church, § 67, 5.

1370–1378. Pope Gregory XI., § 110, 4.

1374. Dancers, § 116, 8.

1377. Return of the Curia to Rome, § 110, 4.

1378–1417. Papal Schism, § 110, 6.

1380. Catharine of Siena dies, § 112, 4.

1384. Wiclif dies, § 119, 1. Gerhard Groot dies, § 112, 9.

1386. Introduction of Christianity into Lithuania, § 93, 14.

1400. Florentius Radewin dies, § 112, 9.

FIFTEENTH CENTURY.

1402. Hus becomes Preacher in the Bethlehem Chapel, § 119, 8.

1409. Œcumenical Council at Pisa, § 110, 6.[1] Withdrawal of the Germans from Prague, § 119, 8.

---

[1] From the fifteenth century the numbering of the General Councils is so variable and uncertain that even Catholic historians are not agreed upon this point. They are at one only about this, that the anti-papal councils claiming to be œcumenical, of Pisa A.D. 1409, Basel A.D. 1438, and Pisa A.D. 1511, should be designated schismatical "*Conciliabula*." Hefele, in his "History of the Councils," counts eighteen down to the Reformation. He makes the Constance Council in its first and last sessions the sixteenth, but does not count the middle session held without the pope. He makes that of Basel the seventeenth down to A.D. 1438 with its papal continuation at Ferrara and Florence. Finally, as eighteenth he gives the fifth Lateran Council of A.D. 1512–1517. But others strike Basel and Constance out of the list altogether; and many, especially the Gallicans, reject also the fifth Lateran Council, because occupied with matters of slight or merely local interest.

A.D.

1410–1415. John XXIII., Pope, § 110, 7.

1410–1437. Sigismund, Emperor, § 110, 7, 8.

1412. Traffic in Indulgences in Bohemia, § 119, 4.

1413. Papal Ban against Hus, § 119, 4.

1414–1418. Sixteenth Œcumenical Council at Constance, § 110, 6 119, 5.

1415. Hus obtains the crown of martyrdom, § 119, 5.

1416. Jerome of Prague martyred, § 119, 5.

1417–1431. Pope Martin V., § 110, 7.

1420. Calixtines and Taborites, § 119, 7.

1423. General Councils at Pavia and Siena, § 110, 7.

1424. Ziska dies, § 119, 7.

1425. Peter D'Ailly dies, § 118, 8.

1429. Gerson dies, § 118, 8.

1431–1447. Pope Eugenius IV., § 110, 7.

1431–1449. Seventeenth Œcumenical Council at Basel, § 110, 8; 119 5–7.

1433. Basel Compacts, § 119, 7.

1434. Overthrow of Hussites at Böhmischbrod, § 119, 7.

1438. Papal Counter-Council at Ferrara, § 110, 8. Pragmatic Sanction of Bourges, § 110, 9.

1439. Council at Florence, § 67, 6.

1448. Concordat of Vienna, § 110, 9.

1453. Fall of Constantinople, § 67, 6.

1457. Laurentius Valla dies, § 120, 1.

1458–1464. Pope Pius II., § 110, 11.

1459. Congress of Princes at Mantua, § 110, 10.

1464–1471. Pope Paul II., § 110, 11.

1467. Convention of Bohemian Brethren at Lhota, § 119, 8.

1471. Thomas à Kempis dies, § 114, 5.

1471–1484. Sixtus IV., Pope, § 110, 11.

1483. Luther born on November 10th, § 122, 1. Spanish Inquisition, § 117, 1. Close of *Corpus juris canonici*, § 99, 5.

1484–1492. Innocent VIII., Pope, § 110, 11.

1484. Zwingli born January 1st, § 130, 1. Bull *Summis deside-rantes*, § 117, 4.

1485. Rudolph Agricola dies, § 120, 8.

1489. John Wessel dies, § 119, 10.

1492–1503. Alexander VI., Pope, § 110, 12.

1492. Fall of Granada, § 95, 2.

1493–1519. Maximilian I., Emperor, § 110, 13.

1497. Melanchthon born, § 122, 5.

1498. Savonarola sent to the stake. § 119, 11.

SIXTEENTH CENTURY.

A.D.

1502. Founding of University of Wittenberg, § 122, 1.

1503-1513 Pope Julius II., § 110, 13.

1506. Rebuilding of St. Peter's at Rome, § 115, 13.

1508. Luther becomes Professor at Wittenberg, § 122, 1

1509. Calvin born on July 10th, § 138, 2.

1509-1547. Henry VIII. of England, § 139, 4.

1511. Luther's journey to Rome, § 122, 1.   Council at Pisa, § 110, 13.

1512. Luther made Doctor of the Holy Scriptures and Preacher, § 112, 1.

1512-1517. Fifth Lateran Council, § 110, 13, 14.

1513-1521. Pope Leo X., § 110, 14.

1514. Reuchlin's contest with the Dominicans, § 120, 4.

1516. *Epistolæ Obscur. virorum*, § 120, 5.   Erasmus edits the New Testament, § 120, 6.   Zwingli preaches at Mariä Einsiedeln, § 130, 1.

1517. Luther's Theses, October 31st, § 122, 2.

1518. Luther at Heidelberg and before Cajetan at Augsburg, § 122, 3.   Melanchthon Professor at Wittenberg, § 122, 5.

1519. Miltitz, § 122, 3.   Disputation at Leipzig, § 122, 4.   Zwingli in Zürich, § 130, 1.   Olaf and Laurence Peterson in Sweden, § 139, 1.

1519-1556. Emperor Charles V., § 123, 5.

1520. Bull of Excommunication against Luther, § 123, 2.   Christian II. in Denmark, § 139, 2.

1521. Luther at Worms, § 123, 7.   Melanchthon's *Loci*, § 124, 1.   Beginning of Reformation in Riga, § 139, 3.

1521-1522. The Wartburg Exile, § 123, 8.

1522. The Prophets of Zwickau in Wittenberg, § 124, 1.   Reuchlin dies, § 120, 4.

1522-1523. Pope Hadrian VI., § 126, 1.

1523. Thomas Münzer in Allstädt, § 124, 4.   Luther's contest with Henry VIII., § 125, 3.   First Martyrs, Voes and Esch, § 128, 1.   Sickingen's defeat, § 124, 2.

1523-1534. Pope Clement VII., § 149, 1.

1524. Staupitz dies, § 112, 2.   Carlstadt in Orlamünde, § 124, 3.   Erasmus against Luther, § 125, 2.   Diet of Nuremberg, § 126, 2.   Regensburg League, § 126, 3.   Hans Tausen in Denmark, § 139, 2.   Founding of Theatine Order, § 149, 7.

1525. Eucharist Controversy, § 131, 1.   Luther's Marriage, § 129.   Albert of Prussia, Hereditary Duke, § 126, 4.   Founding of the Capuchin Order, § 149, 7.

1525–1532. John the Constant, Elector of Saxony, § 124, 5.

    1526. Synod at Hamburg, § 127, 2. Torgau League, § 126, 5. Diet at Spires, § 126, 6. Disputation at Baden, § 130, 6.

    1527. Diet at Odense, § 139, 2; and at Westerås, § 139, 1.

    1528. The Pack incident, § 132, 1. Disputation at Bern, § 130, 7.

    1529. Church Visitation of Saxony, § 127, 1. Diet at Spires, § 132, 3. Marburg Conference, § 132, 4. First Peace of Cappel, § 130, 9.

    1530. Diet at Augsburg. *Conf. Augustana*, June 25th, § 132, 6, 7.

    1531. Schmalcald League, § 133, 1. Zwingli dies. Second Peace of Cappel, § 130, 10.

1532–1547. John Frederick the Magnanimous, Elector of Saxony, § 133, 2.

    1532. Religious Peace of Nuremberg, § 133, 2. Farel at Geneva, § 138, 1. Henry VIII. renounces authority of the Pope, § 139, 4.

    1534. Luther's complete Bible Translation, § 129, 1. Reformation in Württemberg, § 133, 3.

1534–1535. Anabaptist Troubles in Münster, § 133, 6.

1534–1549. Pope Paul III., § 149, 2.

    1535. Vergerius in Wittenberg, § 134, 1. Calvin's *Institutio rel. Christ.*, § 138, 5.

    1536. Erasmus dies, § 120, 6. Wittenberg Concord, § 133, 8. Calvin in Geneva, § 138, 2. Diet at Copenhagen, § 139, 2. Menno Simons baptized, § 147, 1.

    1537. Schmalcald Articles, § 134, 1. Antinomian Controversy, § 141, 1.

    1538. Nuremberg League, § 134, 2. Calvin Expelled from Geneva, § 138, 3.

    1539. Outbreak at Frankfort, § 134, 3. Reformation in Albertine Saxony, § 134, 4. Joachim II. reforms Brandenburg, § 134, 5. Diet at Odense, § 139, 2.

    1540. The Society of Jesus, § 149, 8. Double Marriage of the Landgrave, § 135, 1. Religious Conferences at Spires, Hagenau, and Worms, § 135, 2.

    1541. Carlstadt dies, § 124, 3. Interim of Regensburg, § 135, 3. Naumburg Episcopate, § 135, 5. Calvin returns to Geneva, § 138, 3, 4.

    1542. Reformation in Brunswick, § 135, 6. National Assembly at Bonn, § 135, 7. Francis Xavier in the East Indies, § 150, 1. Roman Inquisition, § 139, 23.

    1544. Diet at Spires, Peace of Crespy, Wittenberg Reformation § 135, 9. Diet at Westerås, § 139, 1.

A.D.

1545. Synod at Erdöd, § 139, 20.

1545-1547. Nineteenth Œcumenical Council at Trent, § 136, 4; 149, 2.

1546. Regensburg Conference: Murder of John Diaz, § 135, 10. Luther dies, February 18th, § 135, 11. **Reformation in** the Palatinate, § 135, 6.

1546-1547. Schmalcald War, § 136.

1547-1553. Edward VI. of England, § 139, 5.

1547. Hermann of Cologne resigns, § 136, 2.

1548-1572. Sigismund Augustus, of Poland, § 139, 18.

1548. Interim of Augsburg, § 136, 5. Adiaphorist **Controversy,** § 141, 5. Priests of the Oratory, § 149, 7.

1549. *Consensus Tigurinus,* § 138, 7. Andrew Osiander at Königsburg, § 141, 2. Jesuit Mission in Brazil, § 150, 3. The first Jesuits in Germany (Ingolstadt), § 151, 2.

1550-1555. Pope Julius III., § 136, 8.

1550. Brothers of Mercy, § 149, 7.

1551. Resumption of Tridentine Council, § 136, 8; 149, 2.

1552. Compact of Passau, § 137, 3. Outbreak of Crypto-Calvinist Controversy, § 141, 9. Francis Xavier dies, § 150, 1.

1553-1558. Mary the Catholic of England, § 139, 5.

1553. Elector Maurice dies, § 137, 4. Servetus burnt, § 148, 2.

1554. *Consensus Pastorum Genevensium,* § 138, 7. John Frederick the Magnanimous dies, § 137, 3.

1555. Religious Peace of Augsburg, § 137, 5. Outbreak of Synergist Controversies, § 141, 7.

1555-1598. Philip II. of Spain, § 139, 21.

1556-1564. Ferdinand I., Emperor, § 137, 8.

1556. Loyola dies, § 149, 8.

1557. National Assembly at Clausenburg and *Confessio Hungarica*, § 139, 20.

1558. Frankfort Recess, § 141, 11.

1558-1603. Elizabeth of England, § 139, 6.

1559. Gustavus Vasa's Mission to the Lapps, § 142, 7. *Confessio Gallicana*, § 139, 14. The English Act of Uniformity, § 139, 6.

1560-1565. Pope Pius IV., § 149, 2.

1560. *Confessio Scotica*, § 139, 9. John a Lasco dies, § 139, 18. Calvinizing of the Palatinate, § 144, 1. Melanchthon dies, § 141, 10.

1561. Gotthard Kettler, Duke of Courland, § 139, 3. Religious Conference at Poissy, § 139, 14. Mary Stuart in Scotland, § 139, 10. Princes' Diet at Naumburg, § 141, 11.

1562-1563. Resumption and Close of Tridentine Council, § 149, 2.

A.D.

1562. *Confessio Belgica*, § 189, 12. The XXXIX. Articles of the English Church, § 189, 6. Calvinizing of Bremen, § 144, 2. Heidelberg Catechism, § 144, 1. Lælius Socinus dies, § 148, 4.

1564. Calvin dies, § 138, 4. *Professio fidei Tridentinæ*, § 149, 14. Cassander's Union Proposals, § 187, 8. Maulbronn Convention, § 144, 1.

1564–1576. Emperor Maximilian II., § 187, 8.

1566. *Catechasimo Romanus*, § 149, 10. *Confessio Helvetica posterior*, § 138, 7. The League of "the Beggars," § 139, 12

1567. The writings of Michael Baius condemned, § 149, 13.

1570. General Synod at Sendomir, § 189, 13. Peace of St. Germains, § 189, 15.

1572–1585. Pope Gregory XIII., § 149, 8.

1572. John Knox dies, § 139, 11. Bloody Marriage of Paris, August 24th, § 139, 16.

1573. *Pax dissidentium* in Poland, § 189, 18.

1574. Maulbronn Convention, § 141, 12. Restoration of Catholicism in Eichsfelde, § 151, 1.

1575. *Confessio Bohemica*, § 189, 19.

1576. Book of Torgau, § 141, 12. Pacification of Ghent, § 189, 12

1576–1612. Rudolph II., Emperor, § 137, 8.

1577. The Formula of Concord, § 141, 12. Restoration of Catholicism in Fulda, § 151, 1.

1578. The Jesuit Possevin in Sweden, § 151, 8.

1579. The Union of Utrecht, § 189, 12.

1580. Book of Concord, § 141, 12.

1582. Second Attempt at Reformation in Cologne, § 137. 6. Matthew Ricci in China, § 150, 1. Reform of Calendar, § 149, 8.

1585–1590. Pope Sixtus V., § 149, 8.

1587. Mary Stuart on the Scaffold, § 189, 10.

1588. Louis Molina, § 149, 18.

1589–1610. Henry IV. of France, § 189, 17.

1589. Patriarchate at Moscow, § 73, 4.

1592. Saxon Articles of Visitation, § 141, 13.

1593. Assembly of Representatives at Upsala, § 139, 1.

1595. Synod at Thorn, § 139, 18.

1596. Synod at Brest, § 151, 3.

1597. Calvinizing the Principality of Anhalt, § 144, 8. *Congregatio de auxiliis*, § 149. 13.

1598. Edict of Nantes, § 189, 17.

1600. Giordano Bruno at the Stake, § 146, 8.

SEVENTEENTH CENTURY.

A.D.

1645-1742. Accommodation Controversy, § 156, 12.

1647. George Fox appears as Leader of the Quakers, § 163, 4.

1648. Peace of Westphalia, § 153, 2. Close of Westminster Assembly, § 155, 1.

1649. Execution of Charles I. of England, § 155, 1.

1650. Descartes dies, § 164, 1.

1652. Liturgical Reform of the Patriarch Nikon, § 163, 10.

1653. Innocent X. condemns the Five Propositions of Jansen, § 157, 5. Barebones' Parliament, § 155, 2.

1654. Christina of Sweden becomes a Catholic, § 153, 1. John Val. Andreä dies, § 160, 1.

1655. The Bloody Easter in Piedmont, § 153, 5. *Consensus repetitus fidei vere Lutheranæ*, § 159, 2.

1656. George Calixtus dies, § 159, 2. Pascal's *Lettres Provinciales*, § 157, 5.

1658. Outbreak of Cocceian Controversies, § 161, 5.

1660. Vincent de Paul dies, § 156, 8. Restoration of Royalty and Episcopacy in England, § 155, 3.

1661. Religious Conference at Cassel, § 154, 4.

1664. Founding of Order of Trappists, § 156, 8.

1669. Cocceius dies, § 161, 3.

1670. The Labadists in Herford, § 163, 7.

1673. The Test Act, § 153, 6.

1675. *Formula consensus Helvetici*, § 161, 2. Spener's *Pia Desideria*, § 159, 3.

1676. Paul Gerhardt dies, § 154, 4. Voetius dies, § 161, 3.

1677. Spinoza dies, § 164, 1.

1682. *Quatuor propositiones Cleri Gallicani*, § 156, 1. Founding of Pennsylvania, § 163, 4.

1685. Revocation of Edict of Nantes and Expulsion of Waldensians from Piedmont, § 153, 4, 5.

1686. Spener at Dresden and *Collegia philobiblica* in Leipzig, § 159, 3. Abraham Calov dies, § 159, 4.

1687. Michael Molinos forced to Abjure, § 157, 2.

1689. English Act of Toleration, § 155, 3. Return of banished Waldensians, § 153, 5.

1690. The Pietists Expelled from Leipzig, § 159, 3.

1691. Spener in Berlin, § 159, 3.

1694. Founding of University of Halle, § 159, 3.

1697. Frederick Augustus the Strong of Saxony becomes Catholic, § 153, 1.

1699. Propositions of Fénelon Condemned, § 157, 3.

EIGHTEENTH CENTURY.

A.D.

1701. Thomas of Tournon in the East Indies, § 156, 12.

1702. Löscher's "*Unschuldige Nachrichten*," § 167, 1. Buttla. Fanatical Excesses, § 170, 4.

1703. *Collegium caritativum* at Berlin, § 169, 1. Peter Codde deposed, § 165, 8.

1704. Bossuet dies, § 153, 7; § 157, 8.

1705. Spener dies, § 159, 3.

1706. Founding of Lutheran Mission at Tranquebar, § 167, 9.

1707. The Praying Children at Silesia, § 167, 8.

1709. Port Royal suppressed, § 157, 5.

1712. Richard Simon dies, § 158, 1. Mechitarist Congregation, § 165, 2.

1713. The Constitution *Unigenitus*, § 165, 7.

1717–1774. Louis XV. of France, § 165, 5.

1715. Fénelon dies, § 157, 3.

1716. Leibnitz dies, § 164, 2.

1717. French Appellants, § 165, 7. Madame Guyon dies, § 157, 8. Gottfried Arnold dies, § 160, 2. Inspired Communities in the Cevennes, § 170, 2.

1721. Holy Synod of St. Petersburg, § 166. Hans Egede goes as Missionary to Greenland, § 167, 9.

1722. Founding of Herrnhut, § 168, 2.

1727. A. H. Francke dies, § 167, 8. Thomas of Westen dies, § 160, 7. Founding of the Society of United Brethren, § 168, 2.

1728. Callenberg's Institute for Conversion of Jews, § 167, 9.

1729. Buddeus dies, § 168, 2. Methodist Society formed, § 169, 4.

1731. Emigration of Evangelicals of Salzburg, § 165, 4.

1740–1786. Frederick II. of Prussia, § 171, 4.

1741. Moravian Special Covenant with the Lord Jesus, § 168, 4.

1750. Sebastian Bach dies, § 167, 7. End of Jesuit State of Paraguay, § 165, 3.

1751. Semler, Professor in Halle, § 171, 6.

1752. Bengel dies, § 167, 4.

1754. Christ. v. Wolff dies, § 167, 3. Winckelmann becomes a Roman Catholic, § 165, 6.

1755. Mosheim dies, § 167, 3.

1758–1769. Pope Clement XIII., § 165, 9.

1759. Banishment of Jesuits from Portugal, § 165, 9.

1760. Zinzendorf dies, § 168, 3.

1762. Judicial Murder of Jean Calas, § 165, 5.

1765. Universal German Library, § 171, 4.

A.D.

1769–1774. Pope Clement XIV., § 165, 9.

    1772. Swedenborg dies, § 170, 5.

    1773. Suppression of Jesuit Order, § 165, 9.

    1774. Wolfenbüttel Fragments, § 171, 6.

1775–1799. Pius VI., Pope, § 165, 9, 10.

    1775. C. A. Crusius dies, § 167, 3.

    1776. Founding of the Order of the Illuminati, § 165, 13.

    1778. Voltaire and Rousseau die, § 165, 14.

1780–1790. Joseph II., sole ruler, § 165, 10.

    1781. Joseph's Edict of Toleration, § 165, 10.

    1782. Pope Pius VI. in Vienna, § 165, 10.

    1786. Congress at Ems and Synod at Pistoja, § 165, 10.

    1787. Edict of Versailles, § 165, 4.

    1788. The Religious Edict of Wöllner, § 171, 5.

    1789. French Revolution, § 165, 15.

    1791. Wesley dies, § 169, 5. Semler dies, § 171, 6.

    1793. Execution of Louis XVI. and his Queen. Abolition of Christian reckoning of time and of the Christian religion in France. *Temple de la Raison*, § 165, 15.

    1794. *Le peuple français reconnaît l'Etre suprème et l'immortalité de l'âme*, § 165, 15.

    1795. Founding of London Missionary Society, § 172, 5.

    1799. Schleiermacher's " *Reden über die Religion*," § 182, 1.

    1800. Stolberg becomes a Roman Catholic, § 165, 6.

NINETEENTH CENTURY.

1800–1823. Pope Pius VII., § 185, 1.

    1801. French Concordat, § 203, 1.

    1803. Recess of Imperial Deputies, § 192, 1.

    1804. Founding of British and Foreign Bible Society, § 183, 4. Kant dies, § 171, 10.

    1806. End of Catholic German Empire, § 192.

    1809. Napoleon under Ban ; the Pope Imprisoned, § 185, 1.

    1810. Founding of American Missionary Society at Boston, § 184, 1. Schleiermacher professor at Berlin, § 182, 1.

    1811. French National Council, § 185, 1.

    1814. Vienna Congress. Restoration of the Pope, § 185, 1. Restoration of the Jesuits, § 186, 1.

    1815. The Holy Alliance, § 173.

    1816. Mission Seminary at Basel, § 184, 1.

    1817. The Theses of Harms, § 176, 1. Union Interpellation of Frederick William III., § 177, 1.

A.D.

1822. Introduction of the Prussian Service Book, § 176, 1.
Lyons Association for Spreading the Faith, § 186, 7

1823–1829. Pope Leo XII., § 185, 1.

1825. Book of Mormon, § 211, 12.

1827. Hengstenberg's *Evangel. Kirchenzeitung*, § 176, 1.

1829. English Catholic Emancipation Bill, § 202, 9. Founding
of Barmen Missionary Institute, § 184, 1.

1829–1830. Pope Pius VIII., § 185, 1.

1830. July Revolution, § 203, 2. Halle Controversy, § 176, 1.
Abbé Chatel in Paris, § 187, 6.

1831–1846. Gregory XVI., Pope, § 185, 1.

1831. Hegel dies, § 174, 1.

1833. Beginning of Puseyite Agitation, § 203, 2.

1834. Conflict at Hönigern, § 177, 2. Schleiermacher dies,
§ 182, 1.

1835. Strauss' first Life of Jesus, § 182, 6. Condemnation of
Hermesianism, § 193, 1. Edward Irving dies, § 211, 10.
Persecution of Christians in Madagascar, § 184, 3.

1836. Founding of Dresden Missionary Institute, § 184, 1.

1837. Emigrants of Zillerthal, § 198, 1. Beginning of Troubles
at Cologne, § 193, 1.

1838. Archbishop Dunin of Posen, § 193, 1. Rescript of Alten-
burg, § 194, 2. J. A. Möhler dies, § 191, 4. English
Tithes' Bill, § 202, 9.

1839. Call of Dr. Strauss to Zürich, § 199, 4. Bavarian order to
give Adoration, § 195, 2. Synod at Polozk, § 206, 2.

1840–1861. Frederick William IV. of Prussia, § 193.

1841. Schelling at Berlin, § 174, 1. Constitution of Lutherans
separated from National Church of Prussia, § 177, 2.
Founding of Evangelical Bishopric of Jerusalem, § 184,
8. Founding of Gustavus Adolphus Association.
§ 178, 1.

1843 Disruption and **Founding of** the Free Church of Scotland,
§ 202, 7.

1844. German-Catholic Church, § 187, 1. Wislicenus' "Ob
Schrift, ob Geist?" § 176, 1.

1845 Founding Free Church of Vaud, § 199, 2.

1845–1846. Conversions in Livonia, § 206, 8.

1846–1878. Pope Pius IX., § 185, 2–4.

1846. Founding of Evangelical Alliance in London, § 178, 8.
Fruitless Prussian General Synod in Berlin, § 193, 8.

1847. Prussian Patent of Toleration, § 193, 3. War of Swiss
Sonderbund, § 199, 1.

A.D.

1848. Revolution of February and March, § 192, **4.** Founding of *Evangel. Kirchentag*, § 178, 4. Founding of Catholic "Pius Association," § 186, **3.** Bishops' Congress of Würzburg, § 192, 4.

1849. Roman Republic, § 185, **2.** First Congress for Home Missions, § 183.

1850. Institution of Berlin "Oberkirchenrat," § 193, 4. Return of Pope to Rome, § 185, 2. English Ecclesiastical Titles Bill, § 202, 11.

1851. Memorial of Upper Rhine Bishops, § 196, **1.** Taeping Rebellion in China, § 211, 15.

1852. Conference at Eisenach, § 178, 2.

1852–1870. Napoleon III., Emperor of the French, § 203, 3, 5.

1853. The *Kirchentag* at Berlin acknowledges the *Augustana*, § 178, 4. Missionary Institute at Hermannsburg, § 185, **1.** New Organization of the Catholic Hierarchy in Holland, § 200, 4.

1855. Sardinian Law about Monasteries, § 204, **1.** Austrian Concordat, § 198, 2.

1857. The Evangelical Alliance in Berlin, § 178, 3.

1858. Disturbances in Baden about Service Book, § 196, 3. The Mother of God at Lourdes, § 188, 7.

1859. Franco-Austrian War in Italy, 204, 2.

1860. Persecution of Syrian Christians, § 207, 2. Abrogation of Baden Concordat, § 196, 2.

1861. The Austrian Patent, § 198, 3. Introduction of a Constitutional Church Order into Baden, § 196, 3. Radama II in Madagascar, § 184, 3. Schism among Separatist Lutherans in Prussia, § 177, 3.

1862. Hanoverian Catechism Scandal, § 194, 3. Renan's Life of Jesus, 182, 8. Württemberg Ecclesiastical Law § 196, 6.

1863. Congress of Catholic Scholars at Munich, § 190, 10.

1864. Encyclical and Syllabus, § 185, 2. Strauss' and Schenkel's Life of Jesus, 182, 8, 17.

1865. The first *Protestantentag* at Eisenach, § 180, **1.**

1866. Founding of the North German League.

1867. St. Peter's Centenary Festival at Rome, § 185, 2.

1869. Irish Church Bill, 202, 10. Opening of Vatican Council, § 189, 2.

1870. Proclamation of Doctrine of Infallibility, July 18th, § 189 **3.** Revocation of the Austrian Concordat, § 198, 2. Overthrow of the Church States, § 185, 3.

A.D.

1871. Founding of the new German Empire, January 18th, § 197. The first Old Catholic Congress at Munich, § 190, 1. " The Kanzelparagraph," § 197, 4. First Lutheran National Synod in the kingdom of Saxony, § 194, 1.

1872. Dr. Falk, Prussian Minister of Worship, § 193, 5. The Prussian School Inspection Law, § 199, 3. The Roman Disputation, § 175, 3. The German Jesuit Law, § 197, 4. Epidemic of Manifestations of the Mother of God in Alsace-Lorraine, § 188, 6.

1873. The four Prussian Ecclesiastical Laws, § 197, 5. Mermillod and Lachat Deposed from office, § 199, 2, 3. Constitution of Old Catholic Church in German Empire, § 190, 1.

1874. The Austrian Ecclesiastical Laws, § 198, 6. Union Conference at Bonn, § 175, 6.

1875. The Encyclical *Quod numquam* and the Embargo Act, § 197, 8. Berlin Extraordinary General Synod, § 193, 5. Pearsall Smith, § 211, 1.

1876. Marpinger Mother-of-God trick, § 188, 7. The Dutch University Law, § 202, 2.

1878. Leo XIII. ascends the Papal chair, § 185, 5. Organization of a Catholic Hierarchy in Scotland, § 202, 11. Congress of Berlin, § 207, 5. Amnesty to the recalcitrant Clergy of the Jura, § 199, 3. First appearance of the Salvation Army, § 205, 2.

1879. The Belgian Liberal Education Act, § 200, 6.

1880. Abolition of the " *Kulturexamen*" in Baden, § 197, 14. French Decree of March, § 203, 6.

1881. Robertson Smith's Heresy Case, § 202, 8.

1882. The Confessional Lutheran Conflict with the Ritschlian School, § 182, 21.

1883. The Luther Jubilee, § 175, 10.

1884. The Belgian Clerical Education Act, § 200, 6. Conclusion of the " Kulturkampf " in Switzerland, § 199, 2, 3.

1887. Prussian and Hessian Governments conclude Peace with Papal Curia, § 197, 13, 15. Founding of Evangelical *Bund*, § 178, 5.

INDEX.

Aachen, Council of, § 91, 1, 2.
Aargau, § 199, 1.
Abælard, § 102, 1, 2; 104, 10.
Abbacomites, § 85, 5.
Abbadie, § 161, 7.
Abbate, Abbé, § 111, 2.
Abbo of Fleury, § 100, 2.
Abbot, § 44, 3.
Abbuna, § 52, 7.
Abdas of Susa, § 64, 2.
Abdelmoumen, § 95, 2.
Abderrhamann, § 81; 95, 2.
Abdias, § 32, 5.
Abel, von, § 195, 2.
Abelites, § 44, 7.
Abgar Bar Maanu, § 21.
  „   of Edessa, § 13, 2.
About, E., § 185, 3.
Abraham a St. Clara, § 158, 2.
Abrahamites, § 165, 16.
Abrasax, § 27, 3.
Abrenunciatio diaboli, § 35; 58, 1.
Absolution, Formula of, § 89, 5.
Abstinence, Days of, § 56, 2.
Abulfarajus, § 72, 2.
Abyssinian Church, § 64, 1; 72, 2;
  150, 4; 152, 1; 160, 7; 166, 3;
  187, 19.
Acacius of Amida, § 64, 2.
  „   of Constantinople, § 52, 5.
Acceptants, § 165, 7.
Accommodation   Controversy,
  § 155, 12.

d'Achery, § 158, 2.
Achterfeld, § 191, 1.
Acindynos, § 69, 2.
Acoimetæ, § 44, 3; 52, 5, 6.
Acolytes, § 34, 3.
Acominatus, § 68, 5.
Acosta, Uriel, § 155, 14
Acta facientes, § 22, 5.
Acta Pilati, § 22, 7; 32, 4.
Acta Sanctorum, § 158, 2.
Acton, Lord, § 189, 2.
Acts of Apostles, Apocryphal
  § 32, 5, 6.
Acts of Martyrs, § 32, 8.
Adalbert of Bremen, § 96, 6; 97, 2.
  „   the Heretic, § 78, 6.
  „   of Prague, § 93, 13.
  „   of Tuscany, § 96, 1.
Adam, Book of, § 32, 3.
Adam, St. Victor, § 104, 10.
Adamantius (Origen), § 31, 5
Adamites, § 27, 8.
  „   Bohemian, § 116, 5;
  210, 2.
Adamnan, § 77, 8.
Addai, § 32, 6.
Adeodatus, § 47, 18.
Adiaphorist Controversy, § 141. 5.
Adoptionists, § 91, 1; 102, 6.
Adrianus, § 48, 1.
Adrumetum, § 53, 5.
Advent, § 56, 5.
Adventists, § 211, 11.

485

Bobbio, § 78, 1 ; 85, 4.
Boccaccio, § 115, 10.
Bochart, § 161, 6.
Bodelschwingh, § 183, 1.
Bodin, § 117, 4; 148, 3.
Boeckh, § 181, 3.
Boethius, § 47, 23.
Bogatzky, § 167, 6, 8.
Bogomili, § 71, 4.
Bogoris, § 72, 3.
Böhl v. Faber, § 174, 7.
Böhme, Jacob, § 160, 2.
   „ Mart., § 142, 4.
Bohemia, § 79, 3; 93, 6; 139, 19; 153, 2.
Bohemian Brethren, § 119, 8; 139, 19.
Böhmer, § 167, 5.
Böhringer, § 5, 4.
Bois, Professor, § 203, 8.
Bolanden, Cour. v., § 175, 2.
Boleslaw of Poland, § 93, 7.
   „ „ Bohemia, 93, 6.
   „ Chrobry, 93, 7.
Boleyn, Anne, § 139, 4.
Bolingbroke, § 170, 1.
Bolivia, § 209, 2.
Bollandists, § 158, 2.
Bolsec, § 138, 3.
Bolsena, Mass of, § 104, 7.
Bomberg, § 120, 9.
Bomelius, § 125, 2.
Bona, § 158, 2.
Bonald, § 186, 9.
Bonaventura, § 103, 4; 104, 10.
Boniface, Apostle of Germany, § 78, 4–8.
Boniface I., § 46, 6.
   „ II., § 46, 8.
   „ III., IV., § 46, 10.
   „ VI., § 82, 8.
   „ VII., § 96, 2.
   „ VIII., § 110, 1; 99, 4; 117, 1.

Boniface IX., § 110, 6; 117, 2.
Boni homines, § 108, 2.
Bonner, Bp., § 139, 4, 5.
Bonosus, § 62, 2.
Book of Discipline, § 139, 9.
Boos, Mart., § 187, 2.
Booth, General, § 211, 2.
Bordelum, Sectaries at, § 170, 4.
Borgia, § 110, 10, 12.
   „ Francis, § 149, 8.
Borromeo, § 149, 17; 151, 2.
   „ Society, § 186, 4.
Borsenius, § 170, 4.
Boruth, § 79, 1.
Borziwoi, § 79, 3.
Bosio, Ant., § 38, 1.
Boso, § 95, 3.
Bossuet, § 5, 2; 153, 7; 156, 8; 157, 3; 158, 2.
Bost, Pastor, § 156, 1.
Bothwell, § 139, 10.
Bourdaloue, § 159, 2.
Bourges, Pragmatic Sanction of, § 110, 9.
Bourignon, § 157, 4.
Bouthillier de Rancé, § 156, 8.
Boyle, § 164, 3.
Bradacz, M. v., § 119, 8.
Bradwardine, § 113, 2.
Braga, Syn. of, § 76, 4.
Brakel, § 169, 2.
Bramante, § 115, 3; 149, 15.
Brandenburg, § 134, 5; 154, 3.
Brandt, § 181, 4.
Braniss, § 174, 1.
Brant, Seb., § 115, 1.
Braun, Hermesian, § 191, 1.
Brazil, § 150, 3, 209, 3.
Breckling, § 163, 9.
Breithaupt, § 159, 3.
Breitinger, § 162, 6.
Bremen, § 127, 4; 144, 2.
Brendel, § 151, 1.
Brentano, § 188, 3.